Resolving Claims to Self-Determination

Since the end of the Second World War and the formation of the UN, the nature of warfare has undergone changes with many wars being 'intra-State' wars, or wars of secession. Whilst wars of secession do not involve the same number or type of combatants as in the last two World Wars, their potential for destruction and their danger for the international community cannot be underestimated. There are currently many peoples seeking independence from what they perceive as foreign and alien rulers including the Chechens, West Papuans, Achenese, Tibetans and the Kurds. The break-up of Yugoslavia and the former USSR, together with recent conflicts in South Ossetia, reveal that the potential for future wars of secession remains high.

This book explores the relationship between recognition, statehood and self-determination, and shows how self-determination continues to be relevant beyond European decolonisation. The book considers how and why unresolved questions of self-determination have the potential to become violent.

The book goes on to investigate whether the International Court of Justice, as the primary judicial organ of the United Nations, could successfully resolve questions of self-determination through the application of legal analysis and principles of international law. By evaluating the strengths, weaknesses and effectiveness of the Court's advisory jurisdiction, Andrew Coleman asks whether the ICJ is a suitable forum for these questions, and asks what changes would be necessary to provide an effective means for the peaceful 'birth' of States.

Andrew K. Coleman is Senior Lecturer at Monash University, Australia.

'Nothing succeeds like secession, which is why many oppressed peoples resort to force in an attempt to assert what is mockingly termed a "right" of self-determination. This book convincingly establishes that this so-called right has no remedy other than murderous violence and counter-violence, because self-interested states have permitted no means of adjudicating indigenous and ethnic claims that cry out for fair hearing. Andrew Coleman, with this ground-breaking and persuasive argument, shows how international law might develop a solution to its most bloody impasse'.

Geoffrey Robertson QC

Routledge Research in International Law

Available:

International Law and the Third World
Reshaping justice
Richard Falk, Balakrishnan Rajagopal and Jacqueline Stevens (eds)

International Legal Theory
Essays and engagements, 1966–2006
Nicholas Onuf

The Problem of Enforcement in International Law
Countermeasures, the non-injured state and the idea of international community
Elena Katselli Proukaki

International Economic Actors and Human Rights
Adam McBeth

The Law of Consular Access
A documentary guide
John Quigley, William J. Aceves and Adele Shank

State Accountability under International Law
Holding states accountable for a breach of jus cogens norms
Lisa Yarwood

International Organisations and the Idea of Autonomy
Institutional independence in the international legal order
Richard Collins and Nigel D. White (eds)

Self-Determination in the Post-9/11 Era
Elizabeth Chadwick

Participants in the International Legal System
Multiple perspectives on non-state actors in international law
Jean d'Aspremont

Sovereignty and Jurisdiction in the Airspace and Outer Space
Legal criteria for spatial delimitation
Gbenga Oduntan

International Law in a Multipolar World
Matthew Happold (ed.)

The Law on the Use of Force
A feminist analysis
Gina Heathcote

The ICJ and the Development of International Law
The lasting impact of the Corfu Channel case
Karine Bannelier, Théodore Christakis and Sarah Heathcote (eds)

UNHCR and International Refugee Law
From treaties to innovation
Corinne Lewis

Asian Approaches to International Law and the Legacy of Colonialism
The law of the sea, territorial disputes and international dispute settlement
Jin-Hyun Paik, Seok-Woo Lee, Kevin Y.L. Tan (eds)

The Right to Self-Determination Under International Law
"Selfistans," secession, and the rule of the great powers
Milena Sterio

Reforming the UN Security Council Membership
The illusion of representativeness
Sabine Hassler

Threats of Force
International law and strategy
Francis Grimal

The Changing Role of Nationality in International Law
Alessandra Annoni and Serena Forlati

Criminal Responsibility for the Crime of Aggression
Patrycja Grzebyk

Regional Maintenance of Peace and Security Under International Law
The distorted mirrors
Dace Winther

International Law-Making
Essays in honour of Jan Klabbers
Rain Liivoja and Jarna Petman

Resolving Claims to Self-Determination
Is there a role for the International Court of Justice?
Andrew K. Coleman

Forthcoming titles in this series include:

International Law, Regulation and Resistance
Critical spaces
Zoe Pearson

The Cuban Embargo under International Law
El Bloqueo
Nigel D. White

The Changing Nature of Customary International Law
Methods of interpreting the concept of custom in international criminal tribunals
Noora Arajärvi

Technology and the Law on the Use of Force
New security challenges in the twenty first century
Jackson Maogoto

Criminal Diversity in International Law
The effectiveness of the UNESCO Convention on the Protection and Promotion of the Diversity of Cultural Expressions
Lilian Hanania

The United Nations and Collective Security
Gary Wilson

Resolving Claims to Self-Determination

Is there a role for the International Court of Justice?

Andrew K. Coleman

Routledge
Taylor & Francis Group
LONDON AND NEW YORK

First published 2013
by Routledge
2 Park Square, Milton Park, Abingdon, Oxon, OX14 4RN

and by Routledge
711 Third Avenue, New York, NY 10017

Routledge is an imprint of the Taylor & Francis Group, an informa business

British Library Cataloguing in Publication Data
A catalogue record for this book is available from the British Library

Library of Congress Cataloging-in-Publication Data
Coleman, Andrew K. (Law teacher)
Resolving claims to self-determination: is there a role for the International Court of Justice? / Andrew K. Coleman.
pages cm. – (Routledge research in international law)
Includes bibliographical references and index.
ISBN 978-0-415-65958-1 (hardback) – ISBN 978-0-203-07485-5 (ebk)
1. Self determination, National. 2. International Court of Justice.
3. International courts–Political aspects. 4. Political questions and judicial power. I. Title.
KZ1269.C659 2013
341.26–dc23
2013026364

ISBN: 978-0-415-65958-1 (hbk)
ISBN: 978-0-203-07485-5 (ebk)

Typeset in Baskerville
by Cenveo Publisher Services

MIX
Paper from responsible sources
FSC www.fsc.org FSC® C013604

Printed and bound by CPI Group (UK) Ltd, Croydon, CR0 4YY

Contents

Acknowledgements

This monograph grew from an idea I had when completing my minor thesis for my Masters of Laws, *Redefining National Sovereignty*, completed at Monash University in 1997. The idea that the rule of law, rather than violence, could determine the existence of a State and more importantly assist a people to be free from oppression evolved from a quaint notion and curiosity of what appeared to be an odd inconsistency to become at times a passionate and idealistic obsession.

Inspired by Geoffrey Robertson's work, *Crimes Against Humanity* I embarked upon an investigation of the idea of the International Court of Justice resolving claims for self-determination, turning what was a two-page discussion in my Masters thesis into a rather lengthy PhD thesis. I submitted this thesis just as it was announced that the General Assembly at the bequest of Serbia had accepted a Request for an Advisory Opinion regarding Kosovo. And now this project has evolved into a (slighter) shorter monograph.

I am glad the journey is at an end, and many people have assisted me in this long, and at times rather challenging journey. There is no doubt that without their assistance it would have been a much more difficult journey, perhaps an impossible one. So I would like to express my sincere gratitude.

Firstly, I would like to thank my PhD supervisors Professor Timothy McCormack and Associate Professor Tania Voon, both from the Faculty of Law, the University of Melbourne. Their guidance and encouragement throughout my candidature and in the preparation of this monograph was simply fantastic. I am sure that I was, and probably will continue to be, their most nervous and demanding student.

Secondly, many thanks to the administrative staff of the Asia-Pacific Centre for Military Law, the University of Melbourne, Mrs Dianne Costello, with whom I shared many discussions about nutrition and exercise, and Ms Cathy Hutton, who was always very kind, helpful and understanding. I would also like to thank Ms Rebecca Hughes, David George Ireland, and Sophie Rigby for their assistance with the formatting of my footnotes, comments and editing of both my thesis and monograph. And I am most grateful to Katherine Carpenter and Mark Sapwell from Routledge for giving me this opportunity to publish my ideas; you have been fantastic and very patient.

To my former Head of Department (Department of Business Law and Taxation, Monash University) and good friend Professor Richard Cullen, many thanks. Without your encouragement and support the journey would never have begun, let alone been completed.

Most importantly, I would like to thank my parents and friends for putting up with my self-obsessed behaviour for so long, especially my parents, Mr Ken Coleman and Mrs Lorna Coleman, to whom I dedicate this monograph; their love and support, often when faced with their own more important challenges, never waivered for an instant.

Once again, many thanks to you all, this monograph has benefited immeasurably from your assistance, although naturally any errors are mine alone.

Finally, to my good friend Dr Jackson Maogoto, I can say: '*kwisha maneno*'.

Andrew K. Coleman
Melbourne 27 June 2013.

Abbreviations

ECOMOG	Economic Community of West African States Monitoring Group
ECOWAS	Economic Community of West African States
FRG	Federal Republic of Germany (West Germany)
GDR	Democratic Republic of Germany (East Germany)
GNP	Gross National Product
ICCPR	International Covenant on Civil and Political Rights
ICJ	International Court of Justice
ICTY	International Criminal Tribunal for the Former Yugoslavia
OAS	Organisation of American States
PRC	People's Republic of China
PLO	Palestine Liberation Organisation
SWANU	South West Africa National Union
SWAPO	South West Africa People's Organisation
UK	United Kingdom
UN	United Nations
US	United States of America

Introduction[1]

In establishing the International Court of Justice, the United Nations hold before a war-stricken world the beacons of Justice and Law and offer the possibilities of substituting orderly judicial processes for the vicissitudes of war and the reign of brutal force.[2]

A. Background

There are very few concepts or norms of international law that have generated as much controversy as the norm of self-determination. That is the right of *all* peoples to freely determine their political status, and to freely pursue their economic, social and cultural development.[3]

Self-determination is divided into two components: external and internal. External self-determination is a legal right to secession. Secession is defined as: '... the creation of a new [S]tate upon territory previously forming part of, or being a colonial entity of, an existing [S]tate.'[4] Internal self-determination concerns essentially the protection of a variety of human and cultural rights

1. Some of the material included in this chapter will appear in a forthcoming, brief article in the *Irish Law Journal*, see Andrew Coleman, 'The Right to Self-determination: Can it Lapse?', (2013).
2. Nasrat Al-Farsy, *Report of the Rapporteur of the First Committee of the Fourth Commission of the San Francisco Conference*, UNICO Doc No 913 IV/1/74(1), 13 UNICO 393 (12 June 1945). This document was also cited in Helmut Steinberger, 'The International Court of Justice' in Max Planck Institute for Comparative Public Law and International Law, *Judicial Settlement of International Disputes*, New York: Springer Verlag, 1974, p. 195.
3. This description or 'formulation' of self-determination is used in almost all of the various international instruments (as well as by commentators) articulating self-determination, and will, be the basis for discussion throughout this work. See Chapter 1 and, for example, James Summers *Peoples and International Law, How Nationalism and Self-Determination Shape a Contemporary Law of Nations*, Leiden: Martinus-Nijhoff, 2007, p. xxxiii; Marc Weller, *Escaping the Self-Determination Trap*, Leiden: Martinus Nijhoff, 2008, p. 23.
4. Peter Radan, 'Secession: A Word in Search of a Meaning' in Aleksandar Pakovic and Peter Radan (eds), *On the Way to Statehood: Secession and Globalisation*, Aldershot: Ashgate 2008, p. 18.

such as the protection of an ethnic group's language and religion, as well as a right to autonomy, and, according to some commentators, a right to democracy. By ascribing such a right to *peoples*, self-determination has been described as one of the most important norms of international law, a source of human rights,[5] a source of legitimacy for the State and the international system,[6] revolutionary,[7] a 'game-changer',[8] responsible for the maintenance of friendly relations and peace.[9] However, since this right is in opposition to States' authority and power self-determination has been described as subversive, destructive, the bringer of chaos,[10] a threat to the concept of the 'State', and responsible for much of the violence in the later twentieth century: a threat to international peace and security.[11] Marc Weller, one of the leading authors in the field of self-determination,[12] opens his text *Escaping the Self-Determination Trap* in a chilling fashion: 'Self-determination kills. Self-determination conflicts are among the most persistent and destructive forms of warfare.'[13] Robert Lansing, Woodrow Wilson's Secretary of State, was horrified with Wilson's ideas of self-determination: 'The phrase [self-determination] is simply loaded with dynamite. It will raise hopes which can never be realized. It will, I fear, cost thousands of lives. … What misery it will

5. Summers *Peoples*, p. xxxiii.
6. Marc Weller 'Why the Rules on Self-Determination Do Not Resolve Self-Determination Disputes' in Marc Weller and Barbara Metzger, (eds), *Settling Self-Determination Disputes, Complex Power-Sharing in Theory and Practice*, The Hague: Martinus Nijhoff, 2008, p. 17.
7. Karen Knop, *Diversity and Self-Determination in International Law*, Cambridge: Cambridge University Press 2002, p. 13.
8. Antonio Cassese, *Self-Determination of Peoples: a Legal Reappraisal*, Cambridge: Cambidge University Press, 1995, p. 1.
9. Frank Przetacznik, 'The Basic Collective Human Right to Self-Determination of Peoples and Nations as a Prerequisite for Peace' 8 *NYL Sch J Hum Rts*, (1990–1991), at pp. 49–50.
10. 'The wave of ethnic claims to self-determination challenges the very foundations of the international order and the security of the international system … The existing international order based on state sovereignty, territorial integrity, the inviolability of international borders and non-intervention in the internal affairs of another state is giving way to international disorder': K. S. Shehadi, *Ethnic Self-Determination and the Break-Up of States*, (Adelphi Paper 283), London: International Institute for Strategic Studies, 1993, p. 8.
11. R. S. Saini, 'Is the Right to Self-Determination Relevant to Jammu and Kashmir?', (1998) 38(2) *Indian Journal of International Law*, p. 157; W. Raymond Duncan and G. Paul Holman Jr (eds) *Ethnic Nationalism and Regional Conflict, the Former Soviet Union and Yugoslavia*, Boulder: Westview Press, 1994, p. 185.
12. Marc Weller has been prolific. Here is just a sample of his recent works on self-determination: Marc Weller, *Escaping*; Marc Weller and Barbara Metzger, (eds), *Settling Self-Determination Disputes, Complex Power-Sharing in Theory and Practice*, The Hague: Martinus Nijhoff Publishers, 2008; Marc Weller, *Contested Statehood*, Oxford: Oxford University Press, 2009; Marc Weller, 'Modesty Can Be a Virtue: Judicial Economy in the ICJ *Kosovo* Opinion?' (2011) 24 (1) *Leiden Journal of International Law*, p. 127.
13. Weller, *Escaping*, p. 13.

cause!'[14] Sadly, both Lansing and Weller are not exaggerating about self-determination's 'dark side' and its potential to cause harm.

Conflicts caused by claims by groups seeking self-determination have been long and bloody, often accompanied by large-scale abuses of human rights. Gurr, examining the period of 1945–1992, noted that on average it took 14 years of serious conflict for a people claiming self-determination to achieve their goals of either autonomy or independence. He also noted that in the seven instances where the Central government had defeated the group claiming self-determination, the conflicts lasted on average *twenty-five years.*[15] Some conflicts have lasted for *sixty-three years.*[16] Currently there are at least 30 on-going self-determination conflicts,[17] and there are many more unresolved issues of self-determination that could erupt into violence.[18]

Conflicts for self-determination also impose a terrible financial burden on the State involved, often diverting crucial finances needed for the development of the State. These disastrous financial effects do not end with the conflict but continue as the State seeks to recover.[19] One example is Indonesia and its conflicts with the East Timorese, West Papuans and Achenese. East

14. Robert Lansing, Woodrow Wilson's Secretary of State is cited often, this time in Tal Becker, 'Self-Determination in Perspective: Palestinian Claims to Statehood and the Relativity of the Right to Self-Determination' (1998) 32 *Israel Law Review*, p. 301.
15. There were 12 such groups: see Ted Robert Gurr, *Minorities at Risk A Global View of Ethnopolitical Conflicts*, Washington DC: United States Institute of Peace Press Washington, 1993, Table 10.1 pp. 296–7.
16. The conflict between the Karen people and the national government in Myanmar (Burma). Although at the time of writing this monograph a ceasefire entered into in Jan 2012 remained in place and peace talks were continuing. Whether this will result in a permanent solution time will tell: see Andrew Buncome 'End in Sight for Burma's 63-year Old Insurgency' *The Independent*, Friday 13 January 2013, available at: www:independent.couk/news/world/asia/end-in-sight-for-burmas-63year-old-insurgency-6288893.html, (accessed 26 December 2012); and Saw Yan Naing, 'KNU Elects Pragmatic Military Chief' *The Irrawaddy*, 25 December 2012, available at: www:Irrawaddy.org/archives/22150 (accessed 26 Dec 2012); Weller, *Escaping*, p. 13.
17. Including: Balochistan, Pakistan; Jammu and Kashmir, India; Somaliland, Somalia; Palestine, Israel; Western Sahara, Morocco; Ogaden, Ethiopia; Cabinda, Angola; Kurds, Turkey; Jola people in Casamance, Senegal; Darfur, Sudan; Kachin Independence Army and Burma/Myanmar; West Papua, Indonesia; Abu Sayyaf (Islamic Separatist group) the Philipines; Patani-malay National Revolutionary Front–Coordinate (Islamic separatists) Thailand; various Chechen Islamic militias, Russia; Kurds, Iran: Southern Yemen Movement Yemen; and a new conflict began in Jan 2012, between the National Movement for the Liberation of Azawad in Mali. Weller, 'Settling Self-Determination Claims: An Introduction' in Marc Weller & Barbara Metzger, (eds), *Settling Self-Determination Disputes, Complex Power-Sharing in Theory and Practice*, The Hague: Martinus Nijhoff Publishers. 2008, pp. xi–xvii, xi.
18. At least 50 potential conflicts in 2008: Ibid.
19. Saman Kelegama, 'Economic Costs of Conflict in Sri Lanka' in Robert Rotberg (ed), *Creating Peace in Sri Lanka: Civil War and Reconciliation*, Washington DC: The World Peace Foundation and the Belfer Centre for Science and International Affairs, Harvard University Brookings Institution Press, 1999, pp. 78–9.

Timor took 24 years to achieve independence, at the cost of an estimated 100,000 East Timorese lives.[20] A similar number of people have been killed in West Papua, occupied by Indonesia since 1963.[21] The tragic and horrific abuses of human rights of the East Timorese, West Papuans and Acehnese by Indonesian military and police have been well recorded.[22] Indonesia's campaign against *only* the Acehnese – not including Indonesia's conflict with East Timor or West Papua – has cost Indonesia at least US $229.8 million dollars.[23] There are many other examples including Sri Lanka, where the cumulative cost of the conflict between the Sinhaelse and the Tamils was estimated in *1995* to be US$ 16 billion, or *131%* of Sri Lanka's GDP.[24] This cost denied Sri Lanka realizing its huge economic potential at the time of independence.[25] Similarly the First Chechen War brought the fragile Russian economy to the brink of collapse,[26] and Turkey's war against the Kurds has had a significant impact on Turkey's economy, hindering Turkey's efforts to join the European Union.[27] So too has Turkey's human rights record, again due at least in part to abuses against the Kurds.[28]

20. Amnesty International places the figure closer to 250,000, almost half of East Timor's estimated population of 600,000 at the time of occupation. Most were killed immediately. The author does not have reliable information concerning the casualty figures of the Indonesian security forces killed fighting in East Timor. Ted Robert Gurr and Monty Marshall, *Peace and Conflict 2003: A Global Survey of Armed Conflicts, Self-Determination Movements, and Democracy*, College Park, Integrated Network for Societal Conflict Research, (2003) p. 26; Roger Clark, 'The "Decolonisation" of East Timor and the United Nations' Norms of Self-Determination and Aggression' in Catholic Institute for International Relations (CIIR) and International Platform of Jurists for East Timor (IJPET), *International Law and the Question of East Timor, (Catholic Institute for International Relations & International Platform for Jurists for East Timor*, London: Catholic Institute for International Relations & International Platform for Jurists for East Timor, 1995, p. 65, pp. 66–8.
21. Peter King, *West Papua and Indonesia since Suharto: Independence, Autonomy or Chaos?* Sydney: UNSW Press, 2004, p. 127; *Land of the Morning Star*, film released in 2003, Film Australia, National Interests Group, Australia; *World Press Review* (New York), March 2004, p. 25.
22. As have those in other conflicts like in Chechnya.
23. John Martinkus, *Indonesia's Secret War in Aceh*, Milsons Point: Random House Australia 2004, pp. 322–3.
24. Kelegama, *Economic Costs*, p. 79.
25. In 1960, Sri Lanka's per capita income was US$141, comparable to South Korea, (US$156) and higher than Indonesia (US$96). In 1995, after 12 years of fighting, Sri Lanka's per capita income of US$700 was below Indonesia US$ 980: Kelegama, *Economic Costs*, pp. 71–2, p. 85.
26. Pontus Siren, 'The Battle for Grozny' in Ben Fowkes (ed), *Russia and Chechnia: The Permanent Crisis, Essays on Russo-Chechen Relations*, London: Macmillan Press Ltd, 1998, p. 87, pp. 130–1.
27. Resat Kasaba, 'Kurds in Turkey: a Nationalist Movement in the Making' in Daniel Chirot and Martin Seligman (eds), *Ethnopolitical Warfare: Causes, Consequences and Possible Solutions*, Washington DC: American Psychological Association, 2001, p. 164.
28. Munir Morad, 'The Situation of Kurds in Iraq and Turkey' in Philip Kreyenbroek and Stefan Sperl (eds), *The Kurds: A Contemporary Overview*, London: Routledge, 1992, pp. 126–7.

Conflicts for self-determination almost invariably have a significant effect beyond national borders: they become 'internationalized'.[29] There are immense problems caused by refugees fleeing the conflict,[30] which may prompt the receiving State to intervene in the affairs of the source State,[31] or even to go to war.[32] States may intervene on the grounds of humanitarian intervention; to protect the group claiming self-determination from human rights abuses,[33] or even as a means of placating groups within their own population that share the same ethnicity as one of the protagonists.[34] There is also a threat not only from States, but also from non-state actors, which many commentators argue is a greater and more likely threat to be faced in the future.[35] For example, the plight of the Palestinians or indeed Muslim communities in the former Republic of Yugoslavia, provide a rallying cry for extremists that threaten the entire international community.[36] And it should be remembered that the First World War began with the

29. Jacob Bercovitch, 'Managing Internationalised Ethnic Conflict: Evaluating the Role and Relevance of Mediation' in (2003) 166 *World Affairs* p. 3.
30. Ted Robert Gurr, 'Minorities, Nationalists, and Ethnopolitical Conflict' in Chester Crocker, Fen Osler Hampson and Pamela Aall, *Managing Global Chaos: Sources of and Response to International Conflict* (Washington DC: United States Institute for Peace, 1996) p. 54; Alan Dowty and Gil Loescher, 'Refugee Flows as Grounds for International Action' in Michael Brown et al. (eds), *Nationalism and Ethnic Conflict, Cambridge:* MIT Press, 1997, p. 305; Barry Posen, 'Military Responses to Refugee Disasters' in Brown et al., *Nationalism and Ethnic Conflict*, p. 334.
31. Such as the US intervention in Haiti, or the forceful expulsion of Palestinian refugees from Jordan, and later from Lebanon.
32. One of the reasons given by the Arab States for their attack on Israel in the Arab-Israeli War of 1948 was the plight of Palestinian refugees: Dowty and Loescher, *Refugee Flows*, p. 325.
33. India intervened unilaterally to assist the Bengali people of East Pakistan after they claimed independence from Pakistan, and NATO's intervention in Kosovo to protect the Kosovar Albanians from Serbian aggression, and the reaction of the international community to protect the Kurds and Shiites in Iran.
34. India's intervention in the Tamil conflict in Sri Lanka was motivated in part by internecine fighting between factions of India's Tamils in its Tamil Nadu province, caused by the conflict in Sri Lanka: Edgar O'Ballance, *The Cyanide War: Tamil Insurgency in Sri Lanka 1973–1988* (London: Brassey's Ltd, 1989, p. 124. See also Neil De Votta, *Blowback: Linguistic Nationalism, Institutional Decay, and Ethnic Conflict in Sri Lanka*, Stanford: Stanford University Press, 2004, p. 6; Hurst Hannum, *Autonomy, Sovereignty, and Self-determination: The Accommodation of Conflicting Rights*, Philadelphia: The University of Pennsylvania Press, 1990, p. 290; Michael Brown, 'Preface' in Brown et al, *Nationalism and Ethnic Conflict*, p. xi.
35. See generally Philip Bobbitt, *The Shield of Achilles: War, Peace and the Course of History*, London: Penguin Books, 2002; Paul Kennedy and William Hitchcock (eds), *From War to Peace: Altered Strategic Landscapes in the Twentieth Century*, New Haven: Yale University Press (2000), pp. 231–46; Mark Duffield, *Global Governance and the New Wars: The Merging of Development and Security*, New York: Zed Books, 2001.
36. Payam Akhavan, 'Self-determination and the Disintegration of Yugoslavia: What Lessons for the International Community?' in Donald Clark and Robert Williamson (eds), *Self-determination: International Perspectives*, New York, Macmillan Press Ltd 1996, p. 239.

assassination of Archduke Franz Ferdinand one morning in June 1914 by a young Gavrilo Princip, a Serb nationalist, whose actions led to the deaths of millions.[37]

It is clear that conflicts for self-determination are a cause of concern for the entire international community. And the great irony is that self-determination, both as a *process* and as a *goal*, has at its heart peace, and peaceful change. In fact for many commentators peace can *only* be achieved if peoples' right to self-determination is respected and *implemented*.[38] One commentator, Przetacznik, goes further and argues that previous international organisations from the *Pax Romana* to the League of Nations all failed to keep the peace because they did not guarantee the right to self-determination.[39] Even religious leaders such as Pope Paul VI stated that: '... as long as the rights of all the peoples among them the right to self-determination and independence, are not duly recognised and honoured, there cannot be true and everlasting peace, ...'[40] Certainly Woodrow Wilson, one of the most famous proponents of self-determination believed that peace would be obtained through freeing 'trapped nationalities'.[41]

Self-determination has a strong moral foundation, a moral *legitimacy* with close links to liberalism[42] and the protection of human rights.[43] As Anne F Bayefsky states: 'self-determination is an idea rooted in human dignity.'[44] It is a norm intended to free peoples from the evils of colonialism, from repression by a foreign entity. Furthermore, research by Peck and Gurr revealed that the overwhelming majority of claims for self-determination actually begin peacefully,[45] but on average it took 13 years before violence

37. Although some argue Princip's actions may not have been motivated by desires for independence, see: David James Smith, *One Morning in Sarajevo*, London: Phoenix 2008, pp. 232–234; p. 237, p. 292.
38. Przetacznik, *Collective Human Right*, pp. 49–50.
39. Ibid.
40. Address of His Holiness Pope Paul VI to the United Nations Special Committee on Apartheid, 22 May 1974, as cited in Ibid, p. 59, author's note 69.
41. Wentworth B Ofuatey-Kodjoe, *Self-Determination in International Law: Towards a Definition of the Principle*, Ann Arbor: University Microfilms International, 1985, p. 325; Summers, *Peoples*, pp. 127–129; Margaret MacMillan *Peacemakers: Six Months that Changed the World*, London, John Murray Publishers, 2001, pp. 9–24.
42. In particular the concept of remedial self-determination (see the discussion in Chapter 1): Andrew Altman and Christopher Heath Wellman, *A Liberal Theory of International Justice*, Oxford: Oxford University Press, 2009, pp. 44–67; Summers, *Peoples* p. 43, & pp. 343–348; Allen Buchanan, *Justice, Legitimacy and Self-Determination, Moral Foundations for International Law*, Oxford: Oxford University Press, 2004, p. 343, pp. 350–353.
43. Buchanan, *Justice*, p. 343, pp. 350–353.
44. Anne Bayefsky, *Self-Determination in International Law: Quebec and Lessons Learned*, The Hague: Kluwer Law International, 2000, p. 1.
45. Ted Robert Gurr, 'Peoples Against States: Ethnopolitical Conflict and the Changing World System' in (1994) 38(3) *International Studies Quarterly*, p. 365. Peck's research involved a detailed examination of the UN dispute resolution system and of 79 groups involved in intra-State conflicts, including claims for self-determination. Forty-three of these conflicts

occurred: that is 13 years from the formation of political movements and the first occurrence of violence.[46] The conflict in Sri Lanka is one example.[47] So how is it that a philosophy, principle or norm with such benevolent, *noble* intentions, one that Wilson enunciated with such high hopes, has become the source of so much misery and conflict?[48]

A priori the answer is simple and obvious: the divergent and perceived irreconcilable nature of the respective aspirations of the two opposing sides – namely the desire for independence, and the goal of the central government to retain their political authority, and to protect the integrity of their territory. Weller argues that the 'classical' perception of the right to self-determination-statehood and sovereignty or not-is too rigid, an all or nothing choice,[49] and thus only serves to as a source of conflict rather than peace.[50]

There is no doubting that much is at stake for both parties. The loss of a territory rich with natural resources may cause severe financial problems,[51] or a vitally strategic territory may provide a belligerent neighbour with a military advantage.[52] Then there is the loss of face. And for the claimants, there is the lure offered by sovereignty and self-governance, but more importantly all the benefits that statehood entails in international law: full membership of the UN, the protection offered by the *UN Charter*, standing before the contentious jurisdiction of the ICJ: a voice in the international community. More importantly their very survival may be at stake.

However, divergent views can be accommodated, an agreement can be reached to enable an 'amicable divorce' so to speak,[53] or an alternative can

began as peaceful protests and 28 escalated from lower to higher forms of rebellion: Connie Peck, *The United Nations as a Dispute Settlement System, Improving Mechanisms for the Prevention and Resolution of Conflict*, The Hague: Kluwer Law International, 1996, pp. 58–68. Gurr's research identified that, whilst there were twenty-two armed conflicts in 2003, there were also 76 groups using peaceful means to claim self-determination (internal and external): Gurr and Marshall, *Peace and Conflict 2003*, p. 26.

46. Gurr, *Peoples Against States*, p. 365.
47. S. J. Tambiah, *Sri Lanka, Ethnic Fratricide and the Dismantling of Democracy* (London, IB Tauris & Co Ltd, 1986) p. 7, p. 13; Elizabeth Nissan and R. L. Stirrat, 'The Generation of Communal Identities' in Jonathon Spencer (ed.), *Sri Lanka, History and the Roots of Conflict* (London Routledge, 1990) 19, 28; Kelegama, *Economic Costs*, pp. 71–2, p. 85.
48. As Weller remarks: 'Rather than preventing conflict, however, the rule of self-determination has generated a *dynamic* that sustains conflict.' (emphasis added): Weller, *Why Rules*, p. 18.
49. Ibid, at p. 19 and Marc Weller, 'Addressing the Self-Determination Dispute' in Weller and Barbara Metzger, *Settling Self-Determination Disputes*, pp. 387–406; Weller, *Escaping*, p. 14.
50. Cassese agrees: 'As long as self-determination is perceived as primarily as a right to independent statehood it will remain more a source of conflict than a substantive component in the settlement of disputes.' Cassese, *Self-Determination of Peoples*, p. 350.
51. West Papua for example, or arguably Western Australia.
52. The Golan Heights for example.
53. The voluntary separation – the 'velvet divorce' – of the Czech Republic and Slovakia, (Czechoslovakia), is one example: Aleksander Pavkovic and Peter Radan, *Creating New States, Theory and Practice*, Aldershot: Ashgate, 2007, pp. 72–79.

be reached.[54] Furthermore, Quebec's claim for self-determination demonstrates that violence is not necessarily inevitable.[55] As one commentator asked: 'What explains why strong group identity precipitates violent conflict only in *some* situations?'[56] And another commentator noted: 'Why is it that the Sinhalese, the "lion race," find themselves confronted, till death do them part, by "the [Tamil] tigers"?'[57] There must be something more than divergence to explain such violence.

One suggestion is nationalist fervour,[58] perhaps an opportunistic nationalist leader – an ethnic 'entrepreneur' – taking advantage of convenient myths and legends,[59] or historical grievances that 'must be' avenged. However, research has indicated that rather than the claimants' actions causing violence it is the manner of the national government's response to the people's claim.[60] One commentator Peck considered that increasing repression or continued ignorance by the central government was the real cause of the escalation into violence.[61] In particular the probability of violence increased as the level of repression, especially violent repression, increased.[62] Government responses also affected the intensity of violence, which varied in proportion to the degree the people's hopes for relief from oppression were frustrated.[63]

Another reason for violence is international 'inattentiveness'.[64] Gurr's well-acclaimed 'Minorities at Risk' project indicated that without international intervention claims for self-determination were less likely to be resolved peacefully.[65] Sadly, due to the norm of non-intervention, the international

54. Such as the 2001 settlement of the Bouganville dispute: see Anthony J Regan, 'Resolving the Bougainville Self-Determination Dispute: Autonomy or Complex Power-Sharing?' in Weller and Metzger, *Settling Self-Determination Disputes*, pp. 135–137.
55. There was a brief moment of violence, when the Front de Liberation du Quebec formed during the 1960s believed that violence to achieve self-determination was a legitimate use of force. Montserrat Guibernau, *Nations without States: Political Communities in a Global Age*, Oxford: Polity Press, 1999, p. 136.
56. (Emphasis added) Janice Gross Stein, 'Image, Identity and Conflict Resolution' in Crocker, Chester A., Hampson, Fen Osler and Aall Pamela (eds), *Managing Global Chaos*, Washington DC: United States Institute for Peace, 1996, p. 95.
57. Tambiah *Sri Lanka*, p. 3.
58. Thomas Hylland Eriksen, *Ethnicity and Nationalism*, Boulder: Pluto Press, 1993, p. 112.
59. Marc Weller, 'Settling Self-Determination Conflicts: an Introduction' in Marc Weller and Barbara Metzger, (eds), *Settling Self-Determination Disputes*, pp. xi-xvii; Alison Des Forges 'Silencing the Voices of Hate in Rwanda' in Monroe E. Price, (eds) *Forging Peace*, Edinburgh: Edinburgh University Press, 2002, pp. 237–258, at p. 239.
60. Gurr, *Why Men Rebel*, p. 14, p. 60, p. 72; Gurr and Marshall, *Peace and Conflict 2003*, p. 38; Gurr, *Peoples Against States*, p. 365.
61. Peck, *United Nations*, p. 70.
62. Ibid, p. 24 and p. 70.
63. Gurr, *Why Men Rebel*, p. 60 and p. 72.
64. Gurr, *Peoples Against States*, p. 365.
65. The 'Minorities at Risk' project was begun in 1986.

community is reluctant to intervene,[66] and when States act unilaterally on the basis of self-interest, rather than intervening for altruistic purposes, they often *interfere*: supporting the group claiming self-determination simply as a means to obtain some military or political advantage over their neighbour. Such interference actually increases the probability of violence occurring.[67]

There are examples of 'benevolent' international attention: for example the referendum that resolved the tragedy that was the Ethiopian-Eritrean War.[68] Other examples of benevolent intervention in claims for self-determination include India's intervention in the former East Pakistan, which assisted the Bengali people achieve independence, and the creation of Bangladesh.[69] A more recent example is the military intervention in East Timor.[70] However, such intervention does not occur very often and invariably follows an extraordinary event to prompt the attention of the international community.

International support for the Kurds' plight only really became pronounced in the public domain (and perhaps into existence at all) simply because of the Iraqi invasion of Kuwait.[71] It may be only conjecture but one wonders what would have happened to the East Timorese claim for self-determination if

66. The international community considered the Eritrean conflict an internal matter and only intervened when famine threatened the area. Even then humanitarian aid did not mean the end to the fighting. Gurr and Harff argue that meaningful international intervention may have occurred if there had been an effective media campaign: Gurr and Harff, *Ethnic Conflict in World Politics*, Boulder: Westview Press, 1994, pp. 12–13.
67. Seyom Brown, *The Causes and Prevention of War*, (2nd ed), New York: St. Martin's Press, 1994, p. 36. There are many examples. During the First World War both the Allies and the Central Powers sought to weaken their opponents by sowing internal discord through appealing to the nationalist aspirations of repressed minority groups within each other's political domain. Both the Iraqi and Iranian governments actively sponsored Kurdish groups seeking self-determination in the other's territory during and after the Iran-Iraq War. Ethiopia supported and provided sanctuary to Anya-Nya guerrillas fighting in Sudan in 1965, which was a reprisal for Sudanese support for Eritrean guerrillas fighting the Ethiopian government. A Rigo Sureda, *The Evolution of the Right of Self-Determination: A Study of United Nations Practice*, Leiden, A. W. Sijthoff, 1973) p. 20; Thomas Musgrave, *Self-determination and National Minorities* (1997) 16; David McDowall, 'The Kurdish Question; a Historical Review' in Philip Kreyenbroek and Stefan Sperl (eds), *The Kurds: A Contemporary Overview* (1992) 10, 23; Christopher Hewitt and Tom Cheetham, *Encyclopedia of Modern Separatist Movements* (2000) 281.
68. The referendum was held in April 1993 where a vote of 99.8% favoured independence for Eritrea: Gurr and Harff, *Ethnic Conflict*, pp. 12–13, p. 24.
69. Although, even then, India's animosity towards Pakistan, which has resulted in three serious conflicts, raises the question of whether India was motivated out of self-interest.
70. There is no doubt that without international assistance East Timor would still form part of Indonesia today. Again it is open to speculation whether it was in Australia's perceived national interest to assist East Timor, given that Indonesia is often perceived as Australia's greatest rival, and threat in the region.
71. Arguably even then the best the Kurds can hope for is an autonomous state for Iraqi Kurds only, within the 'new' Iraq, whilst Iranian, and Turkish Kurds will continue to suffer.

there had not been a Western journalist who witnessed the infamous massacre of 271 people by Indonesian security forces in the Santa Cruz cemetery in 1991.[72] Again it may be conjecture, but in the case of Aceh it could be argued that if it were not for the tsunami in December 2004, *and the international attention it attracted*, the subsequent peace deal between GAM and the TNI would not have occurred.[73]

International inattentiveness also results in national governments believing that they can act with impunity. This perception combined with the military inequality between the protagonists (usually in favour of the central national government) results in large-scale human rights abuses, ethnic cleansing, and potentially genocide.[74] Human rights abuses also occur for the simple pragmatic reason that both sides recognise that by attacking their opponent's civilian population, this will deny each side's source of potential recruits, in other words a strategy of 'genocidal' attrition.

These reasons are all very important, but the major explanation why claims for self-determination become violent is *structural*.[75] The UN was formed to prevent conflicts between States, not conflicts for self-determination: 'intra-state' conflicts.[76] However, there is more to it than

72. This was British filmmaker Max Stahl. The significance of a Western journalist as opposed to a non-Western one is simply the probability of greater access to Western media, and hence the international community beyond Indonesia, and also the ability to avoid possible censorship by Indonesian authorities. See below n 73 regarding the imprisonment of Western journalists.
73. The day before the tsunami struck, apart from some aid workers, Aceh was closed to foreigners. In fact, journalists investigating the conflict had been imprisoned. (For example, John Martinkus, *Secret War*, p. 44; Lesley McCulloch, *Aceh: Then and Now* (Minority Rights Group International Report, 2005) 6–26. Within days of the tsunami striking thousands of international aid workers descended upon Aceh. The vast financial support from foreign sources, urgently needed by Indonesia, would not come without supervision. Therefore, Indonesia's involvement in Aceh, especially the actions of Indonesian security forces, would be exposed to the international community. Not surprisingly a Memorandum of Understanding was signed in Helsinki, on 15 August 2005, between the Indonesian government and the rebels: 'Indonesian Government, Aceh Rebels Sign Peace Deal', *Japan Economic Newswire* (Japan) 15 August 2005 <http://web.lexis-nexis.com.mate.lib.unimelb.edu.au/universe/document?> at 6 December 2007. For details of the memorandum see the news bulletin: 'Key Passages from Aceh Peace Agreeement', *Agence France Presse* (France) 15 August 2005 <http://web.lexis-nexis.com.mate.lib.unimelb.edu.au/universe/document> (accessed 6 December 2007).
74. Weller, *Settling Self-Determination Conflicts*, pp. xi–xvii.
75. Ibid.
76. *UN Charter*, arts 1, 33(1). See also the quote from Al-Farsy, above n 1. It is debatable whether the UN has achieved this aim, or is totally responsible, but it is clear that without the UN the Cold War would have been more violent or more serious inter-state conflicts would have occurred, thus supporting the argument that a normative approach as opposed to a realist one has the potential to minimise conflict. Stephen C Schlesinger, *Act of Creation, the Founding of the United Nations*, Cambridge: Westview Press 2003, 286–7; Chadwick Alger (ed), *The Future of the United Nations System: Potential for the Twenty-First Century*. New York:

that: the international system provides minimal opportunities for a people to make their claim peacefully.[77] In fact even people's ability to participate in the formulation of the rule is minimized.[78] Arguably their ability to participate at a broader level in international relations, in the UN,[79] is also minimized. So lacking is the international system, and to an extent the UN, UNPO – the Unrepresented Nations and Peoples Organisation – was created to 'fill the gap', to represent those peoples *seeking to resolve their questions of self-determination in a peaceful manner.*[80]

Such a structural deficiency should not be surprising. Despite all the assaults on State sovereignty and the concept of a State, the international system remains a system of States for States. Accordingly it should not be surprising that the very norms of international law, such as territorial integrity, *uti possidetis juris*, and non-intervention, intended to protect States from other States, do not protect people from their central government. *In fact*, they enable governments to use violence and reinforce their perception that they can act with impunity when dealing with claimants within their territory. Claimants can be labelled as 'illegal' secessionists, terrorists, and consequently: '... they can be engaged with minimum international legal restraint, under the very legal order of the state from which they seek to escape.'[81]

As a result peoples seeking self-determination are often left with the perception they have no choice but to resort to violence.[82] This problem has been recognised by many commentators. For example, Lord Avebury argues that the absence of any forum in which peoples seeking self-determination would be able to have their claim heard is a crucial reason why claims for self-determination *become* violent:

The United Nations University Press, 1998; Paul Kennedy, *The Parliament of Man, the United Nations and the Quest for a World Government*, London: Allen Books, 2006, pp. 286–94.

77. Gurr, *Why Men Rebel*, p. 90. Gurr stated: 'Considerable societal evidence suggests that narrow ranges of opportunities increase the impetus to collective violence': at 74. Brown, *Causes*, p. 18, pp. 63–65.
78. Knop, *Diversity*, p. 8.
79. It is possible for a people and other non-State entities to be granted Observer Status. See Chapter 1.
80. See AC Zoller, 'International Representation of Peoples and Minorities' and MC van Walt van Praag, 'The Position of UNPO in the International Legal Order' both in Catherine Broelmann, Rene Lefeber & Marjoleine Zieck (eds), *Peoples and Minorities in International Law* Dordrecht: Martinus Nijhoff Publishers, 1993, pp. 303–305, and pp. 323–324 respectively. See also the original version of the *Covenant of the Unrepresented Nations and Peoples Organization*, as cited in Christopher A Mullen and J Atticus Ryan (eds), *Unrepresented Nations and People Organization Yearbook 1996* The Hague: Kluwer Law International, 1997, p. 8. UNPO's Preamble was updated on 17 May 2008, to reflect changes in the global community: www.unpo.org/article/8196 (accessed 27 December 2012).
81. Weller and Metzger, *Settling Self-Determination Disputes*, xi–xvii, xii.
82. Ibid, pp. xi–xvii, xii.

> The lack of any mechanism for assertion of the right means that large and powerful states can flout it with relative impunity.... Small oppressed peoples, knowing that there is no authoritative tribunal within the UN system to which they can appeal for help in upholding their right to self-determination, have no alternative but to resort to armed struggle, however unequal the odds may be.[83]

Sureda supports Lord Avebury:

> It is a common feature of criticisms about the workability of the right of peoples to self-determination to stress the lack of a competent organ in the international community to determine which peoples are entitled to such a right.[84]

And Marc Weller:

> A vicious cycle ensues. Given the absence of any sort of international remedy-[S]tates having protected their freedom to engage 'rebellions' of this kind in an undisturbed manner through the doctrine of non-intervention-the opposition movements will often see an armed struggle as the only way of furthering their aims.[85]

Also Antonio Cassese wrote:

> Although, as has repeatedly been pointed out, international rules clearly lay down an obligation on States to enable the peoples concerned to make a free choice about their destiny, it remains true that those peoples have no effective means available (except for resort to armed violence, a highly regrettable and dangerous option) to impel States to implement self-determination.[86]

So how can self-determination claims be resolved peacefully? Negotiation is perhaps still the most common method by which international disputes are settled.[87] Marc Weller, one of the most authoritative commentators in this field, noted that since 1988 at least 32 self-determination claims have

83. Lord Eric Avebury, 'A Positive Legal Duty: The Liberation of the People of East Timor' in Donald Clark and Robert Williamson (eds), *Self-determination: International Perspectives*, New York: Macmillan Press, 1996, pp. 221–2.
84. Sureda, *Evolution of Self-Determination*, p. 28.
85. Weller, *Why Rules* in Weller and Metzger, *Settling Self-Determination Disputes*, p. 18.
86. Cassese, *Self-Determination of Peoples*, p. 385.
87. JG Merrills, *International Dispute Settlement*, Cambridge: Cambridge University Press, 2011, p. 284.

been settled.[88] Weller proposes that flexibility and innovation are the keys to resolving self-determination claims peacefully, as well as tackling the underlying grievances in a timely fashion, and a re-conceputalization of sovereignty.[89] Indeed the idea of an agreement concerning 'power-sharing' as a means to resolve self-determination is a powerful and a prominent one mooted by commentators such as Weller.[90] There are a host of potential innovative solutions from autonomy,[91] and enhanced self-governance, to agreements that defer sovereignty after a period of autonomy,[92] to supervised independence and statehood created by an international process.[93] The last two include references to the concept of earned sovereignty.[94]

Earned sovereignty is a recent phenomenon that has been used most noticeably and recently by the Independent Commission on Kosovo.[95] It is a term that: '…describes an entity that is something less than a fully sovereign state, but more than a sub-state entity.'[96] Thus it is intended to apply to a people claiming statehood. The title 'earned sovereignty' suggests that it is a process where the people have in some way proved their right to exercise sovereignty, or that their claim for self-determination, and statehood, is 'approved' by a third party, such as the UN or European Union.[97]

88. Weller, *Escaping*, p. 148.
89. Weller, *Modesty a Virtue*, p. 147; Weller, *Escaping*, p. 157.
90. Weller and Metzger, *Settling Self-Determination Disputes.*
91. There are numerous examples, such as the Kurds in Iraq and the Omoros in Ethiopia, see the list in Weller, *Escaping*, p. 81.
92. Montenegro is one example, Eritrea another: Weller, *Escaping*, pp. 132–133.
93. Kosovo with the assistance of UNMIK-United Nations Mission in Kosovo. Weller, *Escaping*, pp. 136–149; and generally Weller, *Contested Statehood.*
94. Also known as 'intermediate sovereignty' or 'conditional independence': Paul R Williams, 'Earned Sovereignty: The Road to Resolving the Conflict Over Kosovo's Final Status' (2002–03) 31 *Denver Journal of International Law and Policy* 387, p. 391; Weller, *Escaping*, pp. 139–144.
95. Catriona Drew, 'The Meaning of Self-Determination: "The Stealing of the Sahara" Redux?' in Karin Arts and Pedro Pinto Leite (eds), *International Law and the Question of Western Sahara*, Leiden: International Platform of Jurists for East Timor 'IPJET', 2007, pp. 95–6. It has also been used in the Good Friday Accord for Northern Ireland; the Machakos Protocol for Sudan, the Baker Peace Plan for the Western Sahara; the Dayton Accords for Bosnia, the Comprehensive Agreement for Bougnaville, in East Timor and in the Roadmap for Middle East Peace in Palestine/Israel. See James R Hooper, 'Earned Sovereignty: The Political Dimension' in (2002–03) 31 *Denver Journal of International Law and Policy* 355, p. 357.
96. Michael P. Scharf, 'Earned Sovereignty: Juridical Underpinnings' 31 (2002–2003) *Denver Journal of International Law and Policy*, 373, p. 374.
97. See Public International Law and Policy Group for the International Crisis Group, *Intermediate Sovereignty As a Basis for Resolving the Kosovo Crisis* (1998); Williams, *Resolving the Conflict*, p. 400.

However, it is more than an approval process, earned sovereignty entails:

> ... the conditional and progressive devolution of sovereign powers and authority from a state to a substate entity under international supervision. Earned sovereignty most naturally develops within a peace process as a multistage approach to address the issue of the final political status of the substate entity. [98]

In other words it is a managed or supervised exercise of self-determination, and the 'supervision' by the international community extends into the post-independence period.[99] Furthermore, the primary purpose of earned sovereignty is not to promote self-determination but to provide a peaceful resolution to what proponents call 'sovereignty-based conflicts'.[100]

In order to promote peaceful coexistence the theory attempts to fill the gap or lacuna between sovereignty and self-determination,[101] and to reconcile self-determination and humanitarian intervention with the principles of sovereignty and territorial integrity.[102] In order to achieve this the proponents argue that traditional notions of sovereignty – 'possessed in full or not at all' – should be revised, and replaced, with an acceptance that there exists a vast range of intermediate sovereign statuses; heightened autonomy, deferred sovereignty, provisional statehood, conditional sovereignty, and even 'constrained sovereignty'.[103] Thus, proponents argue that in order to promote peaceful coexistence the exercise of self-determination should include a variety of outcomes: autonomy, free association, self-government as well as independent statehood.[104]

However, for the reasons mentioned above, if neither party is willing or even able to negotiate a settlement, or more likely are not willing to deal with the other, then what? Both protagonists in the Bouganville dispute recognized that a peaceful settlement required the intervention of a third party, an

98. Paul R Williams and Francesca Jannotti Pecci, 'Earned Sovereignty: Bridging the Gap Between Sovereignty and Self-Determination' (2004) 40 *Stanford Journal of International Law* 347, p. 350.
99. Drew, *Meaning of Self-Determination*, pp. 95–6.
100. Williams and Pecci, *Bridging the Gap*, p. 355.
101. Ibid, p. 349; Scharf, *Earned Sovereignty*, p. 374; Hooper, *The Political Dimension*, p. 355; Paul A Williams, Michael P Scharf and James A Hooper, 'Resolving Sovereignty-Based Conflicts: The Emerging Approach of Earned Sovereignty' (2002–03) 31 *Denver Journal of International Law and Policy*, p. 349; Williams, *Resolving the Conflict*, p. 388; Weller, *Escaping*, 157.
102. Scharf, *Earned Sovereignty*, p. 374.
103. Ibid.
104. Ibid, p. 379. As Williams and Pecci state the determination of final status is 'generally made through either some sort of referendum or in structured negotiations, but invariably involves the political consent of the international community'. Williams and Pecci, *Bridging the Gap*, p. 365.

'external actor', simply because the divide between them was so great.[105] One key factor is international intervention. As noted above by Gurr without such attention conflicts drag on, causing more and more unnecessary deaths. The concept of intervention by a third external party is nothing new in resolving international disputes.[106]

The question is how to attract international attention rather than interference. Interference results when the intervening party lacks impartiality. Russia, together with the Ukraine and the OCSE acted as mediators to resolve the dispute between Moldova and Transdniestra. Did any of these parties have a vested interest in the outcome of this dispute? If so, did that influence the final result? Certainly Russia at one point formally expressed that it was prepared to intervene unilaterally to protect Transdniestra's claim to self-determination.[107] Russian's proposals in this dispute have been heavily criticised, and further negotiations have been unfruitful, but were they motivated by self-interest? If so was that self-interest the cause of the deadlock, and the final outcome?

Impartiality is touted as being crucial for a successful adjudication of a dispute. So rephrasing the above question: is there a forum where peoples can initiate an action to attract *impartial* international attention? Geoffrey Robertson in his book *Crimes Against Humanity* argues that the ICJ is an appropriate choice:

> The ICJ and a host of *ad hoc* arbitral tribunals have developed principles and precedents for dealing with land ownership disputes between states: it is not an impossible step to adjudicate claims by ethnic minorities to statehood or to increased political recognition. Teams of lawyers are less expensive than armies, and do not slaughter each other. Millions of lives have been lost through secessionist movements, and while it may be idealistic to hope that both sides will respect an international court decision, at least that reasoned adjudication would provide some guide as to whether and on what side other states or the Security Council should intervene to stop the conflict. Imbroglios in places like former Yugoslavia and Somalia, where politicians and diplomats could not agree on which ethnic claims were justified, might well have been better handled had

105. Regan, *Resolving Bougainville*, p. 132.
106. There are many different methods of dispute resolution that use a third party such as mediation, conciliation or arbitration, in addition to adjudication by a legal tribunal. The main characteristic that distinguishes these methods is the role and the 'power' of the third party: can they make binding pronouncements? Do they resolve facts or apply legal principles?
107. Russian peacekeepers had been stationed in the disputed area: Weller, *Escaping*, p. 100 and p. 105.

UN action been preceded and guided by an international court decision as to the sovereign rights of competing groups.[108]

Other commentators like David Copp also believe that the ICJ could play a role in the resolution of self-determination claims.[109] Copp argues that the ICJ could provide a mechanism whereby inappropriate claims ('...where secessionist claims are not well-grounded in social and geographic reality.'[110]) are discouraged, but legitimate claims are able to be 'processed' peacefully. Copp envisages the UN acting upon the ICJ's judgment so that a new State can be formed without interference, and that: '... the resulting state [would] be recognized and treated as a state by other states.'[111]

However, the problem with both Robertson and Copp's models is that currently only States have standing to make a claim before the Court's contentious jurisdiction.[112] Accordingly for their argument to succeed standing must be granted to peoples.[113] Whilst many other commentators also agree that peoples seeking self-determination are 'emerging international legal persons',[114] and many other commentators strongly support the idea that art 34 (1) be amended,[115] such a proposal is unlikely to succeed. In order to amend art 34 of the *ICJ Statute* the same procedure used to amend the *UN Charter* is followed.[116] Amendments to the *UN Charter* require a two-thirds

108. Geoffrey Robertson, *Crimes Against Humanity: The Struggle for Global Justice*, London: Penguin Press, 1999, p. 144.
109. David Copp, 'International Law and Morality in the Theory of Secession' 2(3) *The Journal of Ethics*, (1998) 219–245.
110. Ibid, pp. 244–245.
111. Ibid, p. 245.
112. Article 34 (1) the *ICJ Statute* simply states: 'Only states may be parties in cases before the Court.'
113. Copp, *International Law*, p. 232. A point Robertson acknowledges. See n 108 above.
114. Colonies, colonial peoples seeking self-determination, and so-called 'national liberation movements' have always been considered to have a type of international legal personality: Philip C Jessup, *A Modern Law of Nations: An Introduction*, New York: The Macmillian Company, 1968, p. 23; Weller, *Escaping*, p. 17, the author's note 15; Malcolm N Shaw, *International Law* (5th ed) Cambridge: Cambridge University Press, 2003) 221–223; K Reece Thomas, 'Non-Recognition, Personality and Capacity: The Palestine Liberation Organisation and the Palestinian Authority in English Law' (2000) 29 *Anglo-American Law Review* 228; C Wasserstien Fassberg, 'Israel and the Palestinian Authority' (1994) 28 *Israel Law Review* 319; Anna Meijknecht, *Towards International Personality: the Position of Minorities and Indigenous Peoples in International Law*, Oxford: Intersentia, 2001) p. 107, p. 116, p. 120, pp. 226–228.
115. See the series of articles in A S Muller, D Raič and J M Thuránszky (eds), *The International Court of Justice: Its Future Role after Fifty Years*, The Hague: Kluwer Law International incorporating Martinus-Nijhoff Publishers, 1997; *Review of the Role of the International Court of Justice*, GA Res 2723 (XXV), 25th sess, 1931st plen mtg, [1] (15 December 1970) & *United Nations Decade of International Law*, GA Res 45/50, UN GAOR, 45th sess, 48th plen mtg, UN Doc A/Res/45/40 (28 November 1990).
116. *ICJ Statute*, art 69.

majority of the General Assembly, as well as *all* the permanent members of the Security Council.[117] Amending art 34 (1) of the *ICJ Statute* therefore depends upon the will of States, and it is unclear whether an amendment to art 34 (1) would receive sufficient support in the General Assembly. Even if it did, it is unlikely that it would survive the veto power of the permanent members of the Security Council.[118] So the probability that the States will amend art 34(1) is remote at best.[119]

There is a second problem: the contentious jurisdiction of the ICJ is *consensual* in nature.[120] Although consensual jurisdiction has created a great deal of controversy, it has been affirmed numerous times by the ICJ, and is unlikely ever to change.[121] The ICJ's decision in the *East Timor Case* makes this very clear.[122] States will be reluctant to provide consent, either through a *compromis* and/or allow an action to be initiated through a compromissory clause in a treaty, and even consent granted through an art 36(2) declaration

117. *UN Charter*, art 108, chapter XVIII.
118. The permanent members of the Security Council include Russia and the PRC, both of whom have violently repressed peoples claiming self-determination.
119. Jessup, *Law of Nations*, pp. 16–17; Her Excellency Judge Rosalyn Higgins, 'The Role of the International Court of Justice at the Turn of the Century' (Presidential Address to the Holdsworth Club of the University of Birmingham, UK, 1999), 8.
120. *ICJ Statute*, art 36. Consent can be granted in three different manners: (1) a *compromis*; (2) a *compromissory* clause; (3) a declaration made in advance in accordance with art 36(2) *ICJ Statute*.
121. Renata Szafraz, *The Compulsory Jurisdiction of the International Court of Justice*, The Hague: Kluwer Law International incorporating Martinus-Nijhoff Publishers, 1993, p. 3. See *Monetary Gold Removed from Rome in 1943* [1954] ICJ Rep 32; *Continental Shelf (Libyan Arab Jamahiriya v Malta) (Application for Permission to Intervene)* [1984] ICJ Rep 25; *Military and Paramilitary Activities in and against Nicaragua (Nicaragua v United States of America) (Jurisdiction and Admissibility)* [1984] ICJ Rep 431 ('*Nicaragua Case*'); *Frontier Dispute Case (Burkina Faso v Republic of Mali)* [1986] ICJ Rep 554; *Land, Island and Maritime Frontier Dispute (El Salvador v Hondouras) (Application to Intervene)* [1990] ICJ Rep 114; *Certain Phosphate Lands in Nauru (Narau v Australia) (Preliminary Objections)* [1992] ICJ Rep 259.
122. *East Timor (Portugal v Australia)* [1995] ICJ Rep 90 ('*East Timor Case*') The *East Timor Case* concerned an application brought by Portugal against Australia. Australia had entered into an agreement dated 11 December 1989 with Indonesia that involved rights to explore and exploit mineral resources to be found in the continental shelf in the area known as the East Timor Gap. Portugal claimed that Australia's action had failed to observe and respect certain obligations owed to Portugal, which still claimed to be the administering power of East Timor, a non-self-governing territory, and secondly that Australia should have concluded the treaty with Portugal rather than with Indonesia. Australia argued that the ICJ lacked jurisdiction to determine this matter since it involved the determination of the international legal obligations of Indonesia, which had not consented to the matter being heard. The Court affirmed the consensual nature of the ICJ's jurisdiction, and consequently concluded that it lacked jurisdiction under art 36 (2) of the *ICJ Statute*. Since Indonesia had not given their consent to the Court's determination of the dispute the ICJ was not willing to rule on the merits of Portugal's claims regardless of the importance of the questions of international law raised. At pp. 102–105 [31]–[36].

can be made subject to a reservation that includes self-determination.[123] Such limitations place the contentious jurisdiction firmly out of the reach of peoples, since few if any States will be willing to allow a constituent province to secede.

However, there are alternatives to using the Court's contentious jurisdiction. There are many different methods of dispute resolution that use a third party such as mediation, conciliation or arbitration. And another option is to use the ICJ's advisory jurisdiction.

B. Purpose

Accordingly, it is the purpose of this monograph to examine whether the orderly processes of the legal tribunals of the ICJ can be (to paraphrase Nasrat Al-Farsy above) substituted for the '...vicissitudes of war and the reign of brutal force...'.[124] In other words to what extent can and should legal tribunals by applying legal analysis, and principles of international law, assist with the resolution of claims for self-determination? There are two major roles envisaged for the ICJ in particular: firstly to provide guidance to the UN on the legitimacy of the peoples' claim, and thus whether the international community should support or assist with their progression to statehood *before they become 'imbroglios'*;[125] and secondly, the ICJ could as a 'court of recognition' determining statehood. A request for an Advisory Opinion could be made by the Special Committee of 24 on Decolonisation, part of the UN General Assembly, to assist the committee, or the UN General Assembly. The ICJ was chosen in preference to other legal tribunals, such as the Permanent Court of Arbitration, because it is the principal judicial organ of the UN, and secondly, because through its advisory jurisdiction the Court appears well placed to discuss any principle of international law.[126]

123. With few exceptions (for example the declarations made by Costa Rica and Haiti) all declarations to art 36(2) are subject to a reservation of some form. In the reservations to art 36(2) declarations currently deposited with the UN Secretary-General none specifically mention self-determination, although many may be interpreted to indirectly refer to self-determination, such as reservations regarding 'political matters'. The most common reservation, and potentially the one most applicable to self-determination, is the reservation concerning domestic matters.
124. Nasrat Al-Farsy, *Report of the Rapporteur.*
125. This is paraphrasing Robertson, *Crimes*, p. 53.
126. In 1991 then President of the ICJ, Nagendra Singh in a speech to the General Assembly stated that the Court should be used as 'an arm of preventative diplomacy'. Then Secretary-General Javier Perez de Cuellar responded enthusiastically: 'The relevance of international law, would thus be brought home to a people generally. Such as development must be good not only for the Court but also for the United Nations and for the authority and awareness of international law itself.' Robert Y Jennings, 'The Role of the

The monograph will focus on claims to self-determination that turn or threaten to turn violent, and those claims for independence-external self-determination. Unless noted specifically, all references to self-determination will mean external self-determination. Similarly the term 'peoples' will refer to those groups claiming independence, those 'nations without States'[127] – and not those groups identified as minorities by commentators – seeking protection of their human rights, or increased participation in their adopted State.[128] There are several reasons for this choice.

Firstly, much has been written about the internal element of self-determination.[129] Commentators such as Cassese have argued that scholarly attention should be redirected towards examining internal self-determination.[130] This current trend amongst commentators to focus on internal self-determination has meant that many issues regarding external self-determination remain unresolved.[131] Little has been done, in the words of Cassese himself, to resolve those: '... exceptional circumstances where factual conditions render internal self-determination impossible.'[132] For example, where either due to an existing armed conflict it is too late to resolve the dispute through enhancing a people's autonomy, or where a recalcitrant parent State may continue to refuse to respect a people's internal self-determination, and thus a people remain subject to horrific human rights abuses.[133] Thus, I hope the monograph may prompt discussion that will address these thorny issues.

international Court of justice' in *British Yearbook of International Law* downloaded from their website: http://byil.oxfordjournals.org/ p. 3 (accessed 23 October 2012).

127. 'The Kurds consider themselves to be a nation without a State.': Asbjorn Eide, 'In Search of Constructive Alternatives to Secession' in Christian Tomuschat (ed), *Modern Law of Self-Determination*, The Hague: Kluwer Academic Publishers incorporating Martinus Nijhoff Publishers, 1993, p. 141.
128. See, Meijknecht, *Towards International Personality* & *Draft Declaration on the Right of Indigenous Peoples* in Caroline Foster, 'Articulating Self-Determination in the Draft Declaration to the Rights of Indigenous Peoples' (2001) 12 *European Journal of International Law* 141, pp. 141–57.
129. Some commentators argue that internal self-determination is simply just a creation of 'political talking and scholarly writing': Gudmundur Alfredsson, 'The Right of Self-Determination and Indigenous Peoples' in Tomuschat *Modern Law of Self-Determination*, p. 5; Sureda, *Evolution of Self-Determination*, p. 226; Hurst Hannum, 'Self-Determination in the Post-Colonial Era', in Clark and Williamson (eds), *Self-determination: International Perspectives*, p. 25. For a discussion of the right to democracy, see Thomas Franck, 'The Emerging Right to Democratic Governance' (1992) 86 *American Journal of International Law* 46, 50 & also the outstanding collection of articles in Gregory Fox and Brad Roth (eds), *Democratic Governance and International Law*, Cambridge: Cambridge University Press 2000.
130. Cassese, *Self-Determination of Peoples*, p. 350.
131. For example, the relationship between self-determination and other norms of international law such as *uti possidetis*. See Chapters 1 and 3.
132. Cassese, *Self-Determination of Peoples*, p. 359.
133. Ibid.

C. Structure

Chapter 1 will discuss the definition of self-determination, and when it is legitimate for a people to make a claim. This discussion will begin with determining how to identify a 'people' and will consider the concept of identity and how it is affected by factors such as nationalism. Then it will be argued that the basis for a legitimate claim to self-determination is whether a people are suffering from alien and foreign subjugation. Adopting such an approach is important as a means to counter the floodgate argument, namely self-determination if left unchecked could create instability within the international community. This discussion will then lead to the development of pre-conditions, which the ICJ could examine as part of its deliberations. Finally, the chapter will consider self-determination's relationship with other norms of international law such as *uti possidetis*,[134] territorial integrity, and non-intervention.[135]

Chapter 2 will examine whether there exists legal principles that will allow the ICJ to determine statehood. It will be argued that recognition of statehood is an issue regulated by international law, and that statehood is such an important question that it should be decided by an impartial expert body: one that is free from political considerations, and is an integral part of the UN. As such the ICJ, rather than States, or even the UN, should determine statehood. Furthermore, it will be argued that it is not necessary to create new rules of international law to do so.

The viability of an Advisory Opinion is pursued in Chapter 3, which will argue that there are in fact important advantages when using the advisory jurisdiction. Firstly, it can avoid the consent of the territorial State concerned. Secondly, it provides a voice for peoples barred from appearing in the Court's contentious jurisdiction, and this avoids the problem of standing for non-State entities, and may also be also be more expedient in developing guidelines for future claims. Chapter 3 also examines any potential limitations or disadvantages of the advisory jurisdiction. Advisory Opinions are non-binding, for example, and there have been issues about the endangering of ICJ credibility in the providing of Advisory Opinions in the past. It will also consider ICJ Opinions that have considered self-determination such as the *Western Sahara, the Namibia and Kosovo Opinions.*

The theme of the Court's credibility is continued in Chapter 4, where it is accepted that claims of self-determination take place within a highly charged political background. It is the purpose of this chapter to examine and determine whether the Court is able to make a contribution to the resolution of highly political disputes, and what form that contribution would be. It will be argued that criticisms of the ICJ's role are really criticisms of the nature of the

134. 'As you possess shall you continue to possess.'
135. *UN Charter*, arts 2(4), 2 (7).

international legal system, rather than the Court, and that as shown by a number of crucial and important decisions, such as the *Nicaragua Case, the Nuclear Weapons Opinion, the Wall in Palestine Advisory Opinion* and *the Lockerbie Decision*, in reality the Court can and does make a significant contribution to the peaceful resolution of highly political disputes, and thus can assist to an extent greater than imagined by realists in the resolution of claims for self-determination.

D. Why an international court?

Arguing that the ICJ and legal process can assist in the resolution of claims for self-determination is, to paraphrase one commentator, a rather 'heady' proposition.[136] This assertion exists for at least four reasons: firstly, because a claim for self-determination, and statehood, is essentially a political matter, and well outside the scope of the ICJ, or indeed any legal tribunal; secondly, because there is a false perception of self-determination as a threat to the State, and the stability of the international community; thirdly, because of perceived 'weaknesses' of the international legal system; and finally, because questions persist as to how States involved would actually benefit from intervention by the ICJ and the international community. Whilst these potential criticisms and others will be discussed in more detail throughout relevant chapters of the monograph, I would like to make the following initial responses to such arguments, in particular the four potential criticisms raised above.

Resolving claims for self-determination essentially involves a determination of statehood, and as one commentator noted:

> To break up a [S]tate and create a new one is a serious matter. It raises questions about the political authority, about historic identities, about economic justice, and about the rights of minorities.[137]

Secondly, States will go to great lengths to defend their homeland. Such an emotive desire will not be overcome by a judgment of a court. In fact the territorial State may well be provoked if they 'lose' a court case on a self-determination claim within their own borders.[138] Similarly, the desire for

136. Fredrich Kratochwil, 'How do Norms Matter?' in Michael Byers (ed), *The Role of International Law in International Politics: Essays in International Relations and International Law*, Oxford: Oxford University Press, 2000, 35, p. 36.

137. David Miller, 'Secession and the Principle of Nationality' in Margaret Moore (ed), *National Self-Determination and Secession*, New York, Oxford University Press, 1998, p. 65.

138. Sir Robert Jennings has made this point several times. For example in Sir Robert Jennings, 'Presentation by Sir Robert Jennings' in Connie Peck and Roy Lee (eds), *Increasing the Effectiveness of the International Court of Justice: Proceedings of the ICJ/UNITAR Colloquium to Celebrate the 50th Anniversary of the Court*, The Hague: Kluwer Law International, 1997, p. 78.

freedom from repression by a *foreign and alien presence* is also a passionate one. If a people facing repression were to 'lose' a legal hearing would they stop fighting, particularly if their very existence were threatened?

It is not my intention to argue that the ICJ, or indeed any Court, can stop any protagonist from fighting once it is so determined to do so, but what can?[139] Despite the divergent and perceived irreconcilable nature of the respective aspirations of the two opposing sides – namely the desire for independence, and the goal of the central government to retain their political authority, and to protect the integrity of their territory – Quebec's claim for self-determination demonstrates that violence is not necessarily inevitable.[140] Furthermore, the overwhelming majority of claims for self-determination *begin peacefully*,[141] and are often made peacefully until government response or repression causes a violent reaction. What this monograph will argue is that the Court can play a preventative role, intervening *before the dispute has reached the stage of open conflict*. The Court's intervention, and a timely provision of an Advisory Opinion of the respective rights of the protagonists may enable them to negotiate in a manner that will ensure that they feel secure that their respective legal rights have been respected and will continue to be protected in the future. Alternatively an Advisory Opinion could resolve or clarify legal norms that could be used in a subsequent arbitration agreement.[142]

Using an independent, impartial body or legal tribunal to resolve international disputes peacefully is not a novel one: there are precedents.[143] For example, the Hague Peace Conferences in 1899 led to the development of the Permanent Court of Arbitration, sitting in The Hague in 1900 and, as a result of the Paris Peace Conferences after World War One the Permanent

139. For example, the US Supreme Court decision in *Dred Scott v Sandford*, 60 US (19 Howard) 393 (1857) failed to prevent the American Civil War. See Sir Robert Jennings, 'The Proper Work and Purposes of the International Court of Justice' in Muller et al, *The International Court of Justice*, 35, p. 45; Chapter 4.
140. See n 55 above.
141. Another commentator Brown argues that communities have to be *persuaded* to go to war. Thus he believes that *few if any* wars are inevitable: Brown, *Causes*, pp. 29–30, p. 49.
142. This idea will not be pursued in detail in this monograph. Instead it is planned to explore this in a future separate monograph. An example is the agreement between Sudan and South Sudan: 'The Government of Sudan/The Sudan People's Liberation Movement/Army (Abyei Arbitration)' available at the Permanent Court of Arbitration's website: www.pca-cpa.org/showpasge.asp?pag_id=1306 (accessed 23 June 2013); Markus Bockenforde, 'The Abyei Award: Fitting a Diplomatic Square Peg into a Legal Round Hole' (2010) 23 *Leiden Journal of International Law*, 555; Elizabeth Ward, 'Abyei: an Examination of the effectiveness of Arbitration for African Land Disputes' available at moritzlaw.osuedu/epub/mayhew-hite/wp-content/uploads/012/03/student-spotlight-march-2012.pdf, (accessed 25 June 2013).
143. The idea can be traced as far back as Grotius: Shabtai Rosenne, *The World Court: What It Is and How It Works* (5th ed Revised) The Hague: Kluwer Academic Publishers, 1995, p. 3.

Court of International Justice was created.[144] The extension of the ICJ's jurisdiction to cover internal conflicts including claims for self-determination is not such a radical departure from the existing role of the principal judicial organ of the UN.

It is self-evident that self-determination is a norm of international law. In fact many commentators consider self-determination to be *jus cogens*.[145] In the *East Timor Case* the ICJ held that self-determination was an *erga omnes* obligation,[146] and further, in *Leal Consequences for States of the Continued Presence of South Africa in Namibia (South West Africa) Notwithstanding Security Council Resolution 276* self-determination was described as an 'imperative right of peoples.'[147] In essence when a people claim self-determination they are seeking to change their legal status.[148] The best-placed entity to understand and apply legal principles is a court, and thus the most desirable entity to resolve questions of international law including self-determination claims, is the ICJ.

Finally, involving the ICJ to resolve self-determination claims is consistent with what Woodrow Wilson envisaged when he outlined his doctrine of self-determination. He actually envisaged a global organization

144. Thomas D Musgrave, *Self-determination and National Minorities*, Oxford: Oxford University Press, 1997, p. 46.
145. In accordance with art. 53 of the *Vienna Convention on the Law of Treaties*, opened for signature 23 May 1969, 1155 UNTS 331 (entered into force 27 January 1980). The Special Rapporteur of the UN Sub-Commission on Prevention of Discrimination and Protection of Minorities, Hector Gros-Espiell, stated in his report, that the right to self-determination was *jus cogens*. See Hector Gros Espiell, *The Right to Self Determination: Implementation of United Nations Resolutions*, UN Doc E/CN.4/Sub.2/405/Rev.1 (1980); Cassese, *Self-Determination of Peoples*, pp. 133–40; Lauri Hanniainen, 'The Case of Western Sahara from the Perspective of *Jus Cogens*' in Arts and Leite, *The Question of Western Sahara*, p. 60; Ian Brownlie, *Principles of Public International Law* (6th ed) Oxford: Oxford University Press Oxford 2003, p. 489; *Barcelona Traction, Light and Power Co Ltd (Belgium v Spain) (New Application: 1962)* [1970] ICJ Rep 3, 304 (Second Phase) (Separate Opinion of Judge Ammoun) ('*Barcelona Traction Case*'). Others such as Pomerance oppose this view. In fact Pomerance even doubts self-determination's status as a legal right. See Michla Pomerance, *Self-Determination in Law and Practice*, Baltimore: Johns Hopkins University Press, 1982, p. 71.
146. *East Timor (Portugal v Australia)* [1995] ICJ Rep 90, 28–9. *Erga omnes* obligations are: 'obligations of a State towards the international community as a whole', and so it is important that all States have interests in their protection: see *Barcelona Traction Case* [1970] ICJ Rep 3, 32.
147. *Legal Consequences for States of the Continued Presence of South Africa in Namibia (South West Africa) Notwithstanding Security Council Resolution 276* [1971] ICJ Rep 16, 75 (Judge Ammoun).
148. James Crawford, *The Creation of States in International Law* (2nd ed) Oxford: Clarendon Press, 2006, p. 5. This is consistent with the approach taken to interpret colonialism's effect on the colonial territory and by His Excellency Judge Castro in the *Western Sahara Opinion*. See *Western Sahara (Advisory Opinion)* [1975] ICJ Rep 12, 169–72; and also Blay's interpretation of this approach: Sam Blay, 'Self-Determination *Versus* Territorial Integrity in Decolonization' (1985–86) 18 *New York Journal of International Law and Policy* 441, p. 462.

that would be capable of deciding when and to whom self-determination would apply.[149]

Many commentators have raised the argument that self-determination claims threaten the international community through endangering the State as a concept.[150] Peoples claiming self-determination do not necessarily wish to change the nature of a community comprised of States. In fact quite the opposite: what they want is membership in this 'exclusive club'.[151]

> In fact self-determination does not challenge sovereign statehood as the basic constitutive principle of international relations, for it does not propose an alternative political entity to the State. It is a State that seceding people aspires to be ... Indeed the self-determination of colonial peoples has globalized, not diminished, sovereign statehood.[152]

A variant of the 'fear argument' is what is described here as the 'floodgate argument' brilliantly summarised by Jarat Chopra.[153]

> Decolonisation has itself shown the weight of this problem, where literally no state has been too small to contain a secessionist movement ... Not only has every African state its Katanga, but even Katanga has one ...[154]

Even the former UN Secretary-General Boutros-Boutros Ghali expressed this concern in his Agenda for Peace:

149. Sureda, *Evolution of Self-Determination*, p. 28.
150. The author refers to these as the 'fear arguments'. For example, Asbjorn Eide, 'In Search of Constructive Alternatives to Secession' in Tomuschat, *Law of Self-Determination*, pp. 147–8; Stephen Van Evera, 'Hypotheses on Nationalism and War' in Brown et al, *Nationalism and Ethnic Conflict*, p. 32; Sureda, *Evolution of Self-Determination*, p. 274; S M Makinda, 'Sovereignty and International Security: Challenges for the United Nations' (1996) 2 *Global Governance* 159; and Shehadi, *Ethnic Self-Determination*, p. 8.
151. Christophe W Morris, *An Essay on the Modern State*, Cambridge: Cambridge University Press, 1998, p. 54. This description of an international community as a 'club' for States was made to the author by a political officer of the UN Department of Political Affairs when he visited the UN in 1999.
152. Daniel Philpott 'Self-Determination in Practice' in Moore (ed), *National Self-Determination and Secession*, p. 89.
153. Other commentators include; Otto Kimminich, 'A "Federal" Right of Self-Determination?', in Tomuschat, *Law of Self-Determination*, p. 95; Van Evera, *Principles* p. 32; Hill, *Principles of Self-Determination* p. 123.
154. Jarat Chopra, 'The Obsolescence of Intervention under International Law' in Marianne Heiberg (ed), *Subduing Sovereignty: Sovereignty and the Right to Intervene* (1994) pp. 33, 37.

> … if every ethnic, religious or linguistic group claimed statehood, there would be no limit to fragmentation, and peace, security and economic well-being for all would become ever more difficult to achieve.[155]

What terrifies the international community is the perceived lack of a limit to the application of self-determination.[156] In their eyes self-determination is capable of *infinite* application.[157] It is understandable that self-determination can be perceived in this way. Certainly the number of States has increased due to the successful decolonisation program by the UN in the 1950s and 1960s.[158]

However, the actual number of peoples claiming both internal and external self-determination fluctuates for obvious reasons.[159] In Gurr's 'Minorities at Risk' project he identified that in 1993, of the 233 minority groups that were at risk, 120 were seeking self-determination.[160] Gurr noted in 1993 that 30 peoples had fought 'protracted' wars for either independence or unification with their ethnic brethren in neighbouring states. Subsequently he noted that nearly 100 national and minority peoples took part in serious conflicts between 1945 and 1990: 60 of these conflicts were fought over issues of group autonomy or internal self-determination.[161] The number of groups dropped in 2003 to 98: 22 through armed conflict,[162] and 76 through

155. Boutros Boutros Ghali, *An Agenda for Peace: Preventative Diplomacy, Peacemaking and Peace-Keeping* (Report of the Secretary-General pursuant to the statement adopted by the Summit Meeting of the Security Council on 31 January 1992) UN Doc A/47/277 (June 1992) [17].
156. 'But this leads to a question which has often been asked in discussions in the mass media and the lesser informed public: where is the limit?' Kimminich, *A 'Federal' Right of Self-Determination?*, p. 95.
157. As Jarat Chopra said: 'Decolonisation has itself shown the weight of this problem, where literally no state has been too small to contain a secessionist movement … Not only has every African state its Katanga, but even Katanga has one': Chopra, *The Obsolescence of Intervention* p. 37. See also Kimminich, *A 'Federal' Right of Self-Determination?*, p. 95. A good example is the process that has lead to the conflict of the Chittagong Hill Tracts, in Bangladesh, where the indigenous peoples are seeking self-determination. Bangladesh exercised its right to self-determination when it seceded from Pakistan in violent circumstances in 1971. Pakistan, was once a former British colony and so it too has exercised its right to self-determination through Partition from India after the Second World War. Pakistan now faces other secessionist movements in Sind and Baluchista. Anjoo Upadhyaya, 'Quest for Self-Determination in the Indian Subcontinent: The Recent Phase' in Clark and Williamson, *Self-Determination: International Perspectives*, p. 158.
158. Fifty States signed the *UN Charter*, today there are approximately 200 States, and in 2011 193 were members of the UN.
159. The most useful resources for this topic are: Guibernau, *Nations Without States*; Hewitt and Cheetham, *Encyclopedia of Modern Separatist Movements*; Gurr and Harff, *Ethnic Conflict*; Gurr, *Minorities at Risk*. See also the series by Gurr and Marshall, entitled '*Peace and Conflict*'.
160. Ted Robert Gurr, 'Forward' in Ted Robert Gurr, *Minorities at Risk*, p. ix.
161. See Gurr, *Minorities at Risk*, p. 294.
162. Gurr and Marshall, *Peace and Conflict 2003*; Table 2, Appendix, pp. 57–62.

non-violent or political means.[163] In 2005 Gurr concluded that there were 25 armed conflicts for self-determination,[164] 54 peoples seeking self-determination through peaceful means, and a further 23 groups using predominantly peaceful methods but also employing militant tactics just short of armed force, a total of 102 groups.[165] In 2010 Gurr noted that of the 136 civil wars fought since 1940, 62 involved groups seeking 'separation' – independence.[166]

Clearly there are thousands of ethnic groups, but Gurr's research includes peoples claiming *both internal and external self-determination.* Many indigenous peoples, like the Cree in Canada, do not wish independence; they merely wish to protect their language, culture, and their way of life.

> The Crees believe that self-determination need not be absolute; it need not imply formal statehood, flags, seats on the United Nations. In any event, the Crees are quick to point out, these are white men's inventions. Self-determination means an end to permanent dependency on Government handouts and an end to being the passive spectators to the destruction of their lands. ...[167]

Accordingly not all ethnic groups seek statehood as the above commentators imply.[168] For the vast majority there are good reasons to stay with their current government, and State.[169] Or more importantly, there are good reasons not to form their own State. Given the resources and effort required to

163. The conflicts were: the Corsicans in France; the Basques in Spain; the Chechens in Russia; the Uighers in China; the Kashmiris in India; 'scheduled tribes' and Assamese in India; the Tripuras in India; the Papuans in Indonesia; the Hmong in Laos; the Chin/Zomis in Myanmar; the Kareeni in Myanmar; the Karens in Myanmar; the Shan in Myanmar; the Irogots in the Philippines; the Moros in the Philippine; the Palestinians in Israel; the Kurds in Turkey; the Cabindans in Angola; the Ormos in Ethiopia; the Somalis in Ethiopia; and the Ijaw in Nigeria: Gurr and Marshall, *Peace and Conflict 2003*, p. 29, Table 5.1 at p. 30; Appendix 2, pp. 57–62.
164. The conflicts, in addition to those listed in note 163, included: the Baluchis in Pakistan; the Black Africans in Darfur, Sudan; and the Malay-Muslims in Thailand. Ibid 26; see also Table 11.2 and 11.3 at 84–92.
165. Ted Gurr and Monty Marshall, *Peace and Conflict 2005*, College Park: Center for International Development and Conflict Management, 2005, p. 21; see also Table 11.2 and 11.3 at 84–92.
166. J. Joseph Hewitt, Jonathon Wilkenfeld, and Ted Robert Gurr, *Peace and Conflict 2010 Executive Summary*, p. 1–2, available at economics.ouls.ox.ac.uk/14451/1/exec_sum_2010.pdf (accessed at 25 June 2013).
167. Michael Igantieff, *Blood and Belonging*, London: Vintage, Random House, London 1994, p. 125.
168. Although Van Evera disagrees and argues that: 'the world has some odd 6,000 language groups, many of which have dormant or manifest aspirations for statehood': Stephen Van Evera, 'Hypotheses on Nationalism and War' in Michael Brown et al (eds), *Nationalism and Ethnic Conflict*, p. 32.
169. A group may not be able to survive financially.

successfully create a State arguably for many peoples the circumstances are balanced in favour of remaining part of an existing State. There needs to be a very good reason for any people to seek to break away from the existing State.[170]

In my opinion States perceive and argue that self-determination is a threat to the international community, for the simple reason of the effect that new States have on the equilibrium currently established within the international community.[171] In other words: States fear the creation of new States, simply because with each new addition to this 'club of States' the influence of existing members decreases.

> The states already members of the UN fear a further weakening of this organization should all mini-territories now in colonial status become members on achieving independence: it is felt that voting power and actual strength would be too far apart. Thus it is not surprising that most of the solutions proposed to solve the problems of mini-territories when faced with the issue of self-determination are geared more towards defending the UN against a tide of mini-states membership than towards solving the actual problems of mini-territories in search of an international status in the post-colonial era.[172]

UN membership altered as result of the introduction of new members, who were '... directly or indirectly the "children" of the operation of the Charter Principle of self-determination of colonial peoples and were anxious to seek the membership as an ostentatious badge of sovereignty.'[173] Many of these children formed the non-aligned movement, or component of the UN, and international community, and brought with them a different perspective on international events and relations: one which could be interpreted as a threat to the interests of existing members: 'Thus, the present nonaligned majority provides a new value system, a frame of reference, more in tune with the Purposes/Principles than the earlier majority ever did.'[174]

States protecting their vested interests or influence in the UN should not be used to deny a people's claim to self-determination. Such a position is especially heinous when States know claims are being violently repressed and that large-scale human rights abuses, perpetuated in the name of

170. Clark McCauley, 'The Psychology of Group Identification and the Power of Ethnic Nationalism' in Daniel Chirot and Martin Seligman (eds), *Ethnopolitical Warfare: Causes, Consequences and Possible Solutions* (Washington DC: American Psychological Association, 2001) p. 3.
171. Van Evera, *Hypotheses*, p. 31.
172. Sureda, *Evolution of Self-Determination*, p. 274.
173. Peter Radan, *The Break-up of Yugoslavia* (2002) p. 297.
174. Ibid, p. 299.

protecting the rights of States, are occurring.[175] In fact what proponents of these 'fear' arguments fail to address is the threat to international peace and security that *the denial* of self-determination poses. As shown by the above examples (Sri Lanka, the Kurds, and East Timor) misery is caused not by the creation or even in the recognition of the right to self-determination. Instead misery is caused by its denial. The floodgate argument should not be allowed to restrict *all* future applications of self-determination, or to provide a justification for the policy of non-intervention particularly in the light of massive human rights abuses

The third reason for concluding that the involvement of the Court in determining claims for self-determination is a 'heady proposition' is because of the nature of the international legal system. International law, unlike any other legal system, is *entirely* dependent upon the will of its members.[176] Realists would argue that the potential of international law to *influence* the affairs of States is limited by the political will, and power, of States.[177] Western Sahara, and the unrealised claim of the Saharawi people for self-determination is cited as a good example. Despite an Advisory Opinion and numerous UN resolutions the claim of the Saharawi people for self-determination still remains unresolved.[178]

The failure of the Saharawi people is not due to any failing by the Court, or can be seen as a criticism of the involvement of the ICJ, but rather as a failure of the UN system itself, and the Saharawi people were simply another victim of the Cold War.[179] Sadly the Cold War had a seriously inhibitive effect on the ability of the UN to achieve its goals and purposes.[180] In the absence

175. Such as territorial integrity.
176. Mark W Janis, 'The International Court' in Mark Janis (ed), *International Courts for the Twenty-First Century*, Dordrecht: Martinus Nijhoff Dordrecht (Distributed by Kluwer Academic Publishers, The Hague, 1992) p. 13.
177. This monograph will not engage fully in the debate between realism and constructivism. A brief overview of the respective theories can be found in Christian Reus-Smit (ed), *The Politics of International Law*, Cambridge: Cambridge University Press, 2004, especially the second chapter: Christian Reus-Smit, 'The Politics of International Law' at 14. See also Christian Reus-Smit, 'Constructivism' in Scott Burchill et al (eds), *Theories of International Relations* (2nd ed), New York: Palgrave Publishers, 2001) p. 209.
178. See the series of excellent articles in: Arts and Leite, *The Question of Western Sahara*, a publication of a series of papers presented at the IPJET/ISS Conference. 'International Law and the Question of Western Sahara' held by the International Platform of Jurists for East Timor at The Hague, 27 and 28 October 2006.
179. Yahia H Zoubir, 'Geopolitics and *Realpolitik* as Impediments to the Resolution of Conflict and Violations of International Law: The Case of Western Sahara' in Arts and Leite, *The Question of Western Sahara*, p. 276. In fact the author states that the US played a pivotal role in allowing Morocco to seize Western Sahara, as a reward for Morocco's 'services' in the war against communism. See also Toby Heeley, *Endgame on the Western Sahara, What Future for Africa's Last Colony?*, London: Zed Books, 2004, pp. 8–23.
180. Elisabeth Zoller, 'Contributions of the Court to the Resolution of International Tensions' in Peck and Lee, *Increasing the Effectiveness of the International Court of Justice*, 87; Kennedy, *The Parliament of Man*, pp. 63–7.

of the Cold War influences the plight of the Saharawi people is now being addressed, perhaps not in a manner approved of by commentators, but finally there is some hope that their long held dreams will be realised.[181]

An example that is more encouraging is Serbia's recent reaction to Kosovo's Unilateral Declaration of Independence. Serbia sponsored a draft resolution presented to the General Assembly seeking to request an Advisory Opinion from the ICJ on the following question: 'Is the unilateral declaration of independence by the Provisional Institutions of Self-Government in accordance with international law?'[182] The example of Serbia securing a requisite majority of United Nations General Assembly reflects a growing recognition in the international community that claims to self-determination are capable of adjudication. It may appear unusual that it is Serbia, the actual State that seeks to deny the Kosovars' claim to self-determination, which has sought the General Assembly to request the Advisory Opinion rather than the claimants themselves. After all what benefits do States receive, what is 'in it for them' if the ICJ resolves claims for self-determination? In what possible way could Serbia benefit?

At first glance, it would appear there is very little benefit, and arguably, given the loss of territory, one that may contain large sources of natural resources, there is only a cost incurred by States. Perhaps the cost of losing such territory should be compared to the cost of keeping it. As mentioned above, at the time of achieving independence in 1948 Sri Lanka was touted as *the* post-colonial State that would prove the most successful: 'the best bet in Asia' according to the first Governor-General of Sri Lanka Oliver Goonetilleke.[183] Sadly it could hardly be described in such a manner now.

So how can States benefit? By not having to fight a costly war, which could last decades, and the cost of recovering from a war when it finally ends.[184] Perhaps the cost argument can be more easily understood by referring to the absurdity of the two examples of the former republics of Eritrea and East Timor.[185] Eritrea achieved its independence from Ethiopia after a referendum was held in April 1993, where a vote of 99.8 % favoured independence

181. Refer to the excellent series of articles in Arts and Leite, *The Question of Western Sahara.*
182. 'The General Assembly of the United Nations Requests an Advisory Opinion from the Court on the Unilateral Declaration of Independence of Kosovo' *International Court of Justice Press Release* 10 October 2008, available at www.icj-cij.org (accessed 11 October 2008). 'Serbia to Seek UN Court Ruling on Separatists in Kosovo', Serbianna <http://www.serbianna.com/news/2007/03050.shtml> (accessed 13 December 2007).
183. Kelegama, *Economic Costs*, pp. 71–2, p. 85.
184. Such as the costs of the rehabilitation for those permanently incapacitated and the rebuilding of infrastructure, as well as healing fractures between ethnic groups. Ibid, pp. 71, 78–79.
185. The former Republic of Yugoslavia and how its former constituent units achieved independence is another example.

for Eritrea, thus ending 30 years of conflict, and misery.[186] A similar tragedy occurred in East Timor. The East Timorese claim to self-determination was also successfully concluded through a referendum, but only after a protracted armed conflict that culminated in an estimated 100,000 East Timorese deaths. Was it really necessary for such bloodshed to occur when ultimately the matter was not resolved through military force, but through a referendum that could have been held long before hostilities began?

186. Although there have been subsequent disputes over unresolved border delimination: Gurr and Harff, *Ethnic Conflict*, p. 4.

1 Determining the legitimacy of claims for self-determination[1]

The phrase [self-determination] is simply loaded with dynamite. It will raise hopes which can never be realized. It will, I fear, cost thousands of lives. In the end it is bound to be discredited, to be called the dream of an idealist who failed to realize its danger until too late to check those who attempt to oust the principle in force. What a calamity that the phrase was ever uttered. What misery it will cause![2]

A. Introduction

Robert Lansing's above denunciation of self-determination is quoted often. It provides a chilling warning about the dangers of self-determination, or perhaps more accurately, the dangers of an unqualified right to self-determination. In addition to the very obvious political and economic consequences for the State involved, even a peaceful claim for self-determination raises serious questions of international law.[3] Thus States would prefer if self-determination simply did not exist as a legal norm of international law.

However, States like India have themselves benefited from self-determination, so States cannot deny its existence – the die is cast so to speak. There must be some way, as Umozurike argues, to 'protect the justifiable exercise of the right [to self-determination], while preventing its abuse.'[4] In other

1. Some of the material included in this chapter will appear in a forthcoming issue of the *Irish Law Journal*: Andrew Coleman, 'The Right to Self-determination: Can it Lapse?".
2. Robert Lansing, cited in Tal Becker, 'Self-Determination in Perspective: Palestinian Claims to Statehood and the Relatively of the Right to Self-Determination', (1988) 32 *Israel Law Review*, p. 301.
3. 'The wave of ethnic claims to self-determination challenges the very foundations of the international order and the security of the international system…The existing international order based on state sovereignty, territorial integrity, the inviolability of international borders and non-intervention in the internal affairs of another state is giving way to international disorder': K S Shehadi, *Ethnic Self-Determination and the Break-Up of States*, London: Brassey's for the International Institute for Strategic Studies, 1993, p. 8.
4. U O Umozurike, *Self-Determination in International Law*, Connecticut: Shoe String Press, published as an Archon Book, 1972, p. 200.

words, there must be a way to distinguish a *legitimate* claim from an illegitimate one, and that is the purpose of this chapter.[5]

Such a process is a daunting and controversial one because it will involve *qualifying* the right to self-determination, and or, *qualifying* who are the beneficiaries of this right. Some commentators may question whether self-determination should be qualified since the manner in which the right is expressed in relevant international instruments – the use of the expression 'all peoples', for example – conveys an impression of universalism, and that self-determination is unfettered and unqualified.[6] However, there are some simple but powerful arguments in favour of qualification.

Firstly, a suitable process may encourage States to resolve claims in a more positive and peaceful manner. As mentioned in the introduction to this monograph, what terrifies the international community is the perceived lack of a limit to the application of self-determination. In their eyes self-determination is capable of *infinite* application – the so-called 'floodgate argument' – or, alternatively that it would lead to the total dismemberment of a State. Secondly, whilst States cannot deny self-determination's existence, they can seek to minimise its impact on themselves by arguing that self-determination 'applies to others but not us'. States argue that the content of the right does not include independence, and furthermore, that resolution of the claim is a purely domestic matter, and thus protected by the norm of non-interference in the domestic affairs of a State.[7] Thirdly, States argue that norms of international law, such as territorial integrity, *uti possidetis juris*, and non-intervention enable governments to effectively contain self-determination's application until it is essentially rendered non-existent.[8] As Weller notes: '... governments have taken comfort in the fact that they have constructed the self-determination rule in a way that does not affect their ability to *quash* separatist groups.'[9]

All of the above means that any unresolved and repressed claims to self-determination are likely to erupt into a lengthy conflict that has serious repercussions for the claimants, the State involved and the international community.

It will be argued here that the first step in identifying a legitimate claim is identifying the beneficiaries of the right to self-determination and the

5. As mentioned in the Introduction this monograph will focus on external self-determination, that is the creation of a new independent State, rather than internal self-determination.
6. Catronia Drew, 'The Meaning of Self-Determination: "The Stealing of the Sahara" Redux?' in Karin Arts and Pedro Pinto Leite (eds.), *International Law and the Question of Western Sahara*, Leiden: International Platform of Jurists for East Timor 'IPJET' 2007, p. 90.
7. *UN Charter* art 2(7).
8. Marc Weller 'Why the Rules on Self-Determination Do Not Resolve Self-Determination Disputes' in Marc Weller & Barbara Metzger, (eds), *Settling Self-Determination Disputes, Complex Power-Sharing in Theory and Practice*, The Hague: Martinus Nijhoff Publishers, 2008, pp. 44–45.
9. Ibid, p. 18. (Emphasis added)

second is whether there exist any pre-conditions, such as the application of *uti posseditis juris.* This argument will be made in the following manner. Part B of the chapter will provide the contextual backdrop for the remainder of the chapter, defining and discussing important concepts such as legitimacy and common identity, and identifying the key issues in self-determination. This will be followed in Part C with a discussion of the historical evolution of the legal right to self-determination, which will focus on determining who the beneficiaries of the right are, but will also include a discussion of the impact of territorial integrity. It will be argued that a definition based upon alien and foreign subjugation, which is consistent with the so-called 'just cause' theories, can and should be used by the Court as the basis for determining who are the legitimate claimants.[10] Finally, Part D will consider what pre-conditions should exist such as the norm of *uti possidetis*,[11] as well the important issue of the consent of the parent State, and the applicability of the norm of non-intervention in the domestic affairs of a State.

B. Setting the scene

Identifying which 'self' has the right to exercise self-determination is more than just one key issue: it is *the* key issue. As noted by one commentator: 'On the surface it seem[s] quite reasonable: let the people decide. It [is] in fact ridiculous because the people cannot decide until somebody decides who the people are.'[12]

Self-determination has been mentioned in many international documents, as well as in decisions of the ICJ.[13] For example, it is mentioned twice in the

10. For a discussion of just-cause theories see Wayne Norman, 'The Ethics of Secession as the Regulation of Secessionist Politics' in Margaret Moore (ed), *National Self-Determination and Secession*, New York: Oxford University Press, 1998, pp. 34–44.
11. 'As you possess shall you continue to possess'.
12. Ivor Jennings in *The Approach to Self-Government* (1956), as cited in James Crawford, *The Creation of States in International Law* (2nd ed), Oxford: Clarendon Press, 2006, p. 124.
13. It has been mentioned in *UN Charter*, arts 1(2), 55 and commonly in article 1 of the Covenants on Human Rights. See, eg, *International Covenant on Economic, Social and Cultural Rights*, opened for signature 16 December 1966, 933 UNTS 3 (entered into force 3 January 1976) ('*ICESCR*'); *Declaration on Principles of International Law Concerning Friendly Relations and Co-operation Among States in Accordance with the UN Charter*, GA Res 2625, UN GAOR, 25th sess, 1883rd plen mtg, Agenda Item 85, UN Doc A/RES/2625(XXV) (1970) ('*Declaration on Friendly Relations*'); *Declaration on the Granting of Independence to Colonial Countries and People*, GA Res 1514, UN GAOR, 15th sess, 947th plen mtg, UN Doc A/RES/1514 (XV) (14 December 1960) art 2 ('*Declaration on Colonial Peoples*'); *African Charter of Human Rights*, opened for signature 26 June 1981, 21 ILM 58 (1982), art 20 (entered into force 21 October 1986). Self-determination also has been considered in cases before the International Court of Justice such as *Western Sahara (Advisory Opinion)* [1975] ICJ Rep 23 ('*Western Sahara Opinion*'); *East Timor (Portugal v Australia)* [1995] ICJ Rep 90; *Legal Consequences of the Construction of a Wall in the Occupied Palestinian Territory (Advisory Opinion)* [2004] ICJ Rep

UN Charter, in art 1(2), and art 55.[14] The *UN Charter* does not provide any definition of the term 'people', nor does it clarify what the right actually means or entails.[15]

1. Legitimacy

The purpose of this chapter is to propose a means of how to determine the *legitimacy* of claims to self-determination. Legitimacy, in all its forms – *legitimate, legitimately* – is used frequently in many different contexts. For example, it is often said that self-determination *legitimizes* political authority, even the State itself,[16] and that there is a normative practice of 'recognitional legitimacy' in the recognition of statehood.[17] Thus, it would be helpful if a few words were said regarding the concept of 'legitimacy'.

The Penguin Macquarie dictionary defines *legitimate* as:

> (1) according to law; lawful.
> (2) in accordance with established rules, principles or standards.[18]

Legitimacy's etymology can be traced to the determination of an individual's status, upon which specific rights of inheritance depended; 'legitimate' meant 'born within wedlock'.[19] Accordingly, Summers notes that the concept of legitimacy has four characteristics as follows: (1) a presumption of the existence of certain normative standards; (2) these standards are held or internalised

136; *Legal Consequences for States of the Continued Presence of South Africa in Namibia (South West Africa) Notwithstanding Security Council Resolution 276 (1970) (Advisory Opinion)* [1971] ICJ Rep 16 ('*Namibia Opinion*').

14. *UN Charter*, art 55.
15. See Gerry Simpson's criticism of this point: Gerry Simpson, 'The Diffusion of Sovereignty: Self-Determination in the Post-Colonial Age' 32 (1996) *Stanford Journal of International Law*, pp. 259–74.
16. Aureliu Cristescu, Special Rapporteur of the Sub-Commission on Prevention of Discrimination and Proctection of Minorities in a report authorised by the Economic and Social Council in 1974, *The Right to Self-Determination, Historical and Current Developments on the Basis of United Nations Instruments*', UN Doc. E/CN.4/Sub.2/404/Rev.1,282: James Summers, *Peoples and International Law, How Nationalism and Self-Determination Shape a Contemporary Law of Nations*, Leiden: Martinus Nijhoff Publishers, 2007, p. 33, pp. 44–45 & 400; *In the Matter of Section 53 of the Supreme Court Act, R.S.C. 1985, and in the Matter of a Reference by the Governor in Council Concerning Certain Questions Relating to the Secession of Quebec from Canada as Set Out in Order in Council P.C. 1996–1997* [1998] 2 SCR 217, 287 ('*Reference re Secession of Quebec*').
17. Allan Buchanan, 'Recognitional Legitimacy', 28(1) (1991) *Philosophy and Public Affairs*, pp. 46–78 & 50; Allen Buchanan, *Justice, Legitimacy, and Self-Determination, Moral Foundations for International Law*, Oxford: Oxford University Press, 2004, pp. 262–265; Paul Groarke, *Dividing the State, Legitimacy, Secession and the Doctrine of Oppression*, Aldershot: Ashgate, 2004, 78.
18. *The Penguin Macquarie Dictionary*, Macquarie: Penguin Books, 1986, p. 352.
19. Groarke, *Dividing the State*, p. 11; *Penguin Macquarie Dictionary*, p. 352.

by individuals effecting their perception of those rules; (3) whilst these standards are subjectively held they exist within a context such as others' views; and, (4) these standards effect the behaviour of individual actors.[20]

Franck argues that legitimacy creates what he defines as 'compliance-pull', and 'voluntary obedience'.[21] Accordingly, for him legitimacy contains the following common and critical characteristics, which are similar to Summers' four mentioned above: (1) determinacy; (2) symbolic validation; (3) coherence; and (4) adherence.[22]

In sum, legitimacy, as shall be used throughout this work, is a process of validation that uses recognizable regulatory principles.[23] It also retains a strong moral dimension,[24] as well as notions of justice.[25]

2. Determining the 'self' and the concept of 'identity'

There is an assumption that humanity can be organized conveniently into groups.[26] And there are many different terms used to describe these groups: tribes,[27] clans, communities, indigenous peoples,[28] nations,[29]

20. Summers, *Peoples*, pp. 26–8.
21. TM Franck, 'Legitimacy in the International System' 82 (1988) *American Journal of International Law*, pp. 711–756; TM Franck, *The Power of Legitimacy Among Nations*, Oxford: Oxford University Press, pp. 112–117.
22. Franck, *Legitimacy in the International System*, pp. 711–756.
23. Self-determination has also been described as a process: Summers, *Peoples*, p. 44.
24. Groarke divides *legitimacy* into three dimensions: (1) political; (2) legal, and (3) moral: Groarke, *Dividing the State*, pp. 11–42.
25. Ibid 23; Obiora Chinedu Okafor, 'The Concept of Legitimate Governance in the Contemporary International Legal System', 44 (2009) *Netherlands International Law Review*, pp. 39–40; Buchanan, *Justice*, pp. 71–118. See also the Canadian Supreme Court in the *Reference re Secession of Quebec* where the Court stated: 'Our law's claim to legitimacy also rests on an appeal to moral values..' *Reference re Secession of Quebec* [1998] 2 SCR 217, at [67].
26. Bruno Simma (ed), *The UN Charter, a Commentary*, Oxford: Oxford: Oxford University Press, 1994, p. 59; Ernest Gellner, *Nations and Nationalism*, New York: Cornell University Press New York, 1983, p. 137; Summers, *Peoples*, p. 20; Thomas M Franck, 'Tribe, Nation, World: Self-Identification in the Evolving International System' 11(1) (1997) *Ethics and International Affairs*, pp. 151–3.
27. For example, 'tribes' still exist and continue to maintain their relevancy within many States in Africa, such as the Kikuyu in Kenya. According to Western media reports the conflict between tribal groupings was the central issue in the political crisis in Kenya in 2007–8: Nick Wadhams, 'Will Kenya's Vote Lead to Tribal War', *Time World*, (Monday 31 December 2007, available at www.time.com/world/article/0,8599,1699123,00.html) (accessed 18 March 2013).
28. *United Nations Declaration on the Right of Indigenous Peoples*, UN GAOR, 61st sess, 107th plen mtg, UN Doc A/Res/61/295, (13 September 2007) art 9, available at <www.un.org/esa/socdev/unpfii/documents/DRIPS_en.pdf> (accessed 30 March 2013) ['*Declaration on Indigenous Peoples*'].
29. The term 'nation' is derived from the Latin *natio*, and it is perhaps the most common method of *identifying* or delineating groups of humans. Simma, *UN Charter*, p. 6, p. 59; Paul

minorities, *ethnie*,[30] inhabitants,[31] population, *peoples.*[32] Some of these terms, *nation* and *peoples* in particular, are used synonymously both colloquially and in international instruments.[33] Others, such as *peoples* and *minorities*, are considered to be separate and distinct, and thus result in different legal rights.[34] Thus there is a genuine imperative to be able to discern or distinguish who are a 'people' as opposed to a 'minority'.

So how do we define 'people'– the term used in the international instruments to define the beneficiaries of the right to self-determination? Commentators have different opinions, and their divergent views have given rise to a wealth of material on the topic. However, there is one commonality in commentators' approaches. They use the expression 'identity' or 'identify',[35] and seek to uncover the groups' 'markers'[36] that distinguish them from other groups and tie them together – territory, language, or a shared consciousness.[37] Another way of expressing this idea is to ask what

James, *Nation Foundation, Towards a Theory of Abstract Community*, London: Sage Publications, 1996, 9.

30. *Ethnie* refers to a group that share objective characteristics, cultural awareness or uniqueness, with a '... sense of historical community': Anthony D Smith, *The Ethnic Origins of Nations*, Oxford: Basil Blackwell, 1986, pp. 22–24; John Armstrong, *Nations before Nationalism*, Chapel Hill: University of North Carolina Press, 1982, p. 9.
31. *UN Charter*, art 73.
32. For a discussion of different terms see: Summers, *Peoples*, pp. 1–6; Smith, *Ethnic Origins*, pp. 22–24.
33. For example, 'population' is similar to 'inhabitants' although population is perhaps considered to be larger in scale. '*People*' and '*nation*' have been used synonymously by commentators and also in many UN resolutions when referring to the beneficiaries of the right to self-determination, for example '*Whereas* the right of peoples and nations to self-determination is a pre-requisite to the full enjoyment of all fundamental human rights.' '*The Right of Peoples and Nations to Self-Determination*' in UN GA-GR, A/Res/637(VII) 7th sess, 403rd plen mtg, UN Doc A/PV.403 A/2309 and Corr. 1 (16 December 1952). See also Aureliu Cristescu. UN Doc. E/CN.4/Sub.2/404/Rev.1, p. 280; Summers, *Peoples*, p. 2; Franck, *Tribe, Nation, World*, pp. 155–161.
34. Minorities and indigenous peoples are not entitled to independent statehood. Essentially the two groups are entitled to internal self-determination, whereas a people are entitled to independence. See *International Covenant on Civil and Political Rights*, opened for signature 16 December 1966, 999 UNTS 171, art 1(1) (entered into force 23 May 1976) ('*ICCPR*') art 27; United Nations, *Declaration on Indigenous Peoples*, adopted by the *General Assembly* 2 October 2007, A/Res/61/295, art 4, available at <www.un.org/esa/socdev/unpfii/documents/DRIPS_en.pdf> (accessed 30 December 2013).
35. See, eg, Karen Knop, *Diversity and Self-Determination in International Law*, Cambridge: Cambridge University Press, 2002; Summers, *Peoples;* Robert Williamson, 'In the Search for "A People": The Inuit, Their Habitat, and Economic Politics' in Donald Clark and Robert Williamson (eds), *Self-Determination: International Perspectives*, New York: Macmillan Press Ltd, 1996, pp. 324–5.
36. Summers, *Peoples*, p. 67.
37. Ibid, p. 49.

characteristics does an individual *accept or identify* with. A people exist when the individuals share or retain a common identity.[38]

So what characteristics are used to shape this common identity? Again commentators' theories appear to boil down to a few common ideas.[39]

Do we identify the 'self' through objective characteristics such as shared language, religion, culture and ethnicity?[40] In other words, do we adopt an anthropological or sociological – a nationalist – approach?[41] This method is perhaps the most common, and arguably the most accepted amongst commentators. For example, Summers notes: 'Humans do have a strong tendency to associate in groups, and, although nationality is not inevitable, it is extremely important for how people define themselves.'[42] This approach is essentially a process of simplification,[43] and involves creating an 'imagined community'.[44] The problem with a nationalist approach is that it doesn't always coincide with political organisation of humanity into *States*.[45] This was adequately summarised by an ethnic German Sudenten senator, who described the Germans of Czechoslovakia as 'not an ethnological minority in the territory occupied by the Czechs but a part of the totality of the German people, thrust beyond the present State frontiers'.[46] It also tends to raise a perception or *policy* of 'one nation, one State', which could be misused and

38. Some commentators use the expression 'national' identity, or even 'national consciousness': Ibid, p. 49.
39. However, Brilmayer argues that these approaches are not necessarily competing and in fact work 'in tandem': Lea Brilmayer, 'Secession and Self-Determination: A Territorial Interpretation' 16 (1991) *Yale Journal of International Law*, p. 178.
40. This list is not exhaustive. Other characteristics include shared physical attributes, ancestry, language, history and myths, religion, and a political consciousness or desire for statehood: Wentworth B Ofuatey-Kodjoe, *Self-Determination in International Law: Towards a Definition of the Principle*, Ann Arbor Michigan: University Microfilms, 1995, pp. 53–9.
41. Rodolfo Stavenhagen, 'Self-Determination: Right or Demon?' in Donald Clark and Robert Williamson (eds), *Self-Determination: International Perspectives*, New York: Macmillan Press, 1996, p. 7; Buchanan, *Toward a Theory of Secession*, p. 323. Authors such as Norman have described this approach as the 'nationalist' or 'nationalism' theory, whilst Radan describes this as the 'romantic theory': Norman, *Ethics of Secession*, p. 35; Peter Radan, *The Break-up of Yugoslavia*, New York: Routledge, 2002.
42. Summers, *Peoples*, p. 20.
43. Ibid, pp. 18–19.
44. 'You never know the strangers who make up a nation with you. So you imagine what it is that you have in common… a nation is therefore an imagined community': Michael Ignatieff *Blood and Belonging*, London: Vintage, Random House, 1994, p. 109. A similar quote can be found in Benedict Anderson, *Imagined Communities*, (revised ed.), London: Verso, 1983, pp. 5–6. Social scientists describe nations as an abstract: James, *Nation Foundation*, pp. 1–5.
45. For an example of an anthropological approach see Thomas Hylland Eriksen, *Ethnicity and Nationalism* (2nd ed), London: Pluto Press, 2002.
46. As cited in Thomas Musgrave, *Self-Determination and National Minorities*, Oxford: Oxford University Press, 1997, pp. 58–9.

result in human rights abuses and horrendous violence; it can divide and exclude rather than create a common identity.[47]

So should we instead identify a people simply by what territory they occupy, in other words, a 'territorial' approach?[48] The concept of a 'homeland' is recognised as an important factor in the human psyche,[49] even if it is a powerful memory rather than a place of residence,[50] or even as a desire or hope,[51] because it provides a focus point for a common identity.[52] A third option is to simply identify a people as a 'colonial' people. Arguably this is a variation of the territorial approach, and thus a rejection of a nationalist approach,[53] since the boundaries of the colony are determinative, and the identity as a colony is superimposed over any nationalist identities.[54] It is the act of colonisation rather than any other characteristic of the people, such as language, that both unites and identifies a people.[55] More than 100 new states were formed as a result of decolonisation after WWII.[56] Arguably, decolonisation achieved through the application of self-determination was a successful policy. Accordingly 'peoples' meant colonial peoples.[57]

47. For example one of the major aims of the National Socialist Party in Germany, led by Adolf Hitler, was the reunification of the German 'peoples' in Austria, and Sudetenland in Czechoslovakia. This was noted on the very first page of Hitler's infamous manifesto *Mein Kampf.* Another was the ethnic cleansing in the former Yugoslavia. See Abjorn Eide, 'In Search of Constructive Alternatives to Secession' in Christian Tomuschat (ed), *Modern Law of Self-Determination*, The Hague: Kluwer Academic Publishers incorporating Martinus Nijhoff Publishers, 1993, p. 150.
48. Brilmayer, *Secession*, p. 178; Christopher H Wellman, 'A Defense of Secession and Political Self-Determination' 24 (1995) *Philosophy and Public Affairs*, pp. 142–144; Rosalyn Higgins, *Problems and Process: International Law and How We Use It*, Oxford: Clarendon Press, 1994, p. 124. Radan describes this as the 'classical theory' of self-determination (which he adopted from Martti Koskenniemi): Radan, *The Break-up of Yugoslavia*, p. 8.
49. Ignatieff, *Blood and Belonging*, p. 93.
50. Ibid, pp. 100–1; Smith, *Ethnic Origins*, pp. 28–9.
51. Such as the development of the 'Jewish National Home' in Palestine. See the report and recommendations submitted by the United Nations Special Committee on Palestine (UNSCOP): *Report to the General Assembly, Official Records of the General Assembly. United Nations Special Committee on Palestine, Supplement 11, Volume 1*, UN Doc A/364, (3rd September 1947) [141] [143] [153].
52. 'Central to every nationalism is the nationalist's country, ideally conceived.' Brian E Porter 'Concepts of Nationalism in History' in Winston A van Horne, *Global Convulsions, Race Ethnicity and Nationalism in the Twentieth Century*, New York: State of New York University Press, 1997, p. 94, p. 107.
53. Thus colonial peoples may not share a common language, or religion. As noted by Knop: 'Colonies were often patchwork quilts of different tribes': Knop, *Diversity*, p. 55.
54. Knop, *Diversity*, p. 55.
55. Ibid, pp. 53–60.
56. Michael P Scharf, 'Earned Sovereignty: Juridical Underpinnings' 31 (2002) *Denver Journal of International Law and Policy*, p. 377.
57. However, as will be shown, due to the self-interest of States their attitude was that a colonial people was: 'Someone else's colony, or a people located in another State, but not mine'.

Alternatively, the term 'peoples' may be a subjective concept? One writer noted that what lies at the very heart of the application of self-determination is that it involves a *choice of identity* – 'I am a Kurd: *not a Turk*', for example – which is very much a subjective choice.[58] The adoption or acceptance of a common identity or by accepting that 'you belong' is a powerful process that cuts through barriers of wealth, prestige, social status, and other forms of identity.[59] This process involves transferring allegiance or loyalty from one's family and local community to a newly recognised greater collective persona.[60] Cristescu describes this process as 'national awareness': 'National awareness represents the quintessence of the nation, being a result of the reflection of every characteristic of the nation.'[61] This process is thus an expression of intent, and an epiphany of sorts: '... a people begin to exist only when it becomes conscious of its own identity and asserts its will to exist.'[62]

Finally, the determination of a people could involve a hybrid approach, involving an objective determination along the lines of a nationalist approach, and a subjective element that involves their self-perception as a distinct group.[63] Such approaches often adopt a broad-brush definition of a 'people',[64] and do not depend upon a single criterion, but on a 'cluster' of criteria, which may include territory, language and a subjective choice.[65] All that matters is that the specific set, or combination of characteristics, overall creates 'distinctiveness' – a common identity.[66] For example, Williamson notes:

> A 'people' emerges, then, as a culturally and sometimes politically identifiable societal network of relating institutions and communities unified by functional association with a traditional habitat, a language..., a cosmology, and world view, a shared belief and value system, a shared

58. See the discussion Williamson, *In the Search for 'A People'*, p. 324; Philip Allott, 'Self-determination: Absolute Right or Social Poetry?' in Tomuschat, *Modern Law of Self-Determination*, pp. 177–178.
59. Such as rural or urban, or upper and lower social classes: Summers, *Peoples*, p. 49; Ignatieff, *Blood and Belonging*.
60. Brendan O' Leary, 'Nationalism and Ethnicity: Research Agendas on Theories of Their Sources and Their Regulation' in Daniel Chirot & Martin E P Seligman (eds), *Ethnopolitical Warfare, Causes, Consequences, and Possible* Solutions, Washington DC: American Psychological Association, 1992, 37–49, Porter, *Concepts*, p. 95; Smith, *Ethnic Origins*, p. 151.
61. Aureliu Cristescu, UN Doc. E/CN.4/Sub.2/404/Rev.1, pp. 280–283.
62. *Events in Pakistan*, International Commission of Jurists Secretariat, 1972, p. 49.
63. Scharf's 'two prongs': Scharf, *Earned Sovereignty*, p. 379. See also *Final Report and Recommendations of an International Meeting of Experts on the Further Study of the Concept of the Rights of People for UNESCO*, SNS 89/Conf 602/7.
64. For example Brownlie describes self-determination as 'the right of a community which has a distinct character': Ian Brownlie, 'The Rights of Peoples in Modern International Law' in James Crawford, *The Rights of Peoples*, Oxford: Clarendon Press, 1988, p. 5.
65. This is how Knop describes Ian Brownlie's approach: Knop, *Diversity*, p. 61.
66. Brownlie, *The Rights of Peoples*.

symbology and sense of common identity, and the social, structural and organizational means for the maintenance of these factors.[67]

An important point about the formation of a common identity is that it takes time,[68] and is shaped by events, and therefore can change.[69] In fact some argue that identities are actually manufactured, or at the very least susceptible to manipulation by elites, and charismatic leaders like Slobodan Milosevic.[70] The events most likely to create a change are tumultuous in nature, such as a period of modernisation and urbanisation[71] or an alien threat,[72] which cause people to need a sense of purpose and identity.[73] A more recent example is the development of a Palestinian identity. In a report prepared by *UNSCOP* in 1947 reference is made to the 'Jewish Community' and the 'Arab community in Palestine', or 'Arab population'. There is no mention of Palestinians as a separate identity, distinct from the Arab communities found elsewhere in the Middle East at that time. However, the report does acknowledge the gradual awakening of a Palestinian identity, distinct from an *Arab* identity, in response to perceived threats caused by increasing Jewish immigration and the resulting tense competition for territory within the mandated territory of Palestine.[74]

A final factor that could be relevant in the shaping of a common identity, and thus the definition of a 'people', is the whether there exists a desire for

67. Williamson, *In the Search for 'A People'*, p. 325. See also the criteria listed by UNESCO: (1) a common historical tradition; (2) national or ethnic identity; (3) cultural homogeneity; (4) linguistic unity; (5) religious or ideological affinity; (6) territorial connection & (7) common economic life: UNESCO. International Meeting of Experts on Further Study of the Concept of the Rights of Peoples, Final Report and Recommendations, SHS-89/CONF.602/7 (22nd February 1990), [22]. The Experts were at pains to emphasize these criteria did not constitute a definition but were a *description* only.
68. The length of time is determined by events, and could take centuries: Porter, *Concepts*, pp. 94–95.
69. There are many examples throughout history. Summers, *Peoples*, pp. 67–68.
70. Janince Gross Stein, 'Image, Identity and Conflict Resolution' in *Managing Global Chaos, Sources of and Response to International Conflict*, Washington: United States Institute of Peace Press, pp. 95–96. Serbian nationalists also used folk costumes, and banners rich with Serb national and Orthodox religious symbols: Anthony Oberschall, 'Violence and War in Yugoslavia' in Daniel Chirot & Martin Seligman, *Ethnopolitical Warfare, Causes, Consequences, and Possible Solutions*, Washington DC: American Psychological Association, 2001, p. 131.
71. Particularly a historical myth of shared suffering, conquered by acting cohesively as a group: Summers, *Peoples*, p. 20; Ignatieff, *Blood and Belonging*, p. 149.
72. Industrialisation enabled groups with different identities, such as *rural peasants*, and the *urban working and middle classes*, to share a common identity, since it introduced a greater perspective to the lives of people rather than an introspective 'village perspective': Porter, *Concepts*, p. 100.
73. Ibid, pp. 94–95.
74. See the report and recommendations submitted by the United Nations Special Committee on Palestine (UNSCOP): *Report to the General Assembly*, [120]–[121], referring to the reaction to Zionism, and [166] for emerging Palestinian nationalism.

independent statehood. This is the concept of nationalism. Nationalism involves the recognition of a common identity, or of a loyalty to a group (normally with shared language, religion, customs, culture, history, and traditions), but is consistent with a hybrid approach since it involves both subjective and objective elements. However, nationalism is more than just a process of identification: 'Nationalism is primarily a political principle, which holds that the political and the national unit are congruent.'[75] Thus, there are two core ideas at the centre of nationalism: (1) individual members giving their loyalty to their own 'nation', which supersedes other, say, religious or political, loyalties; and (2) a desire for an independent state.[76] Accordingly, there is a strong link between nationalism and self-determination.[77] Chamberlain argues that it was nationalism that was the major ideological motivator behind the liberation struggles in the decolonisation era, and he argued it was the most important reason for the end of the empires.[78] Another commentator argued that nationalism was significant because it replaced religion as a legitimising process for state political authority.[79]

These alternative approaches have provided the challenge to those drafting the relevant international instruments containing the right to self-determination. Each approach has additional disadvantages that may affect the 'legitimacy' of a group's claim, all relating to the fact that the qualification used could accentuate the risk to international peace and security. Firstly, the nationalist approach raises the floodgate argument.[80] It also could conceivably provide nationalist leaders within a relatively stable state the means to cause disruption and instabiliy.[81] Furthermore, as noted by Franck, there has been a 'great obfuscation', namely the 'inexact and erroneous' link between nation and state,[82] which sadly has led to such horrors as WWII, and ethnic cleansing in the former Yugoslavia. On the other hand, a purely territorial approach can result in a people in a newly independent State continuing to

75. Gellner, *Nations*, p. 1; Summers, *Peoples*, pp. 8–9; John Breuilly, *Nationalism and the State* (2nd ed), Chicago: The University of Chicago Press, 1993, pp. 2–6.
76. Stephen Van Evera, 'Hypotheses on Nationalism and War', in Michael Brown et al (eds), *Nationalism and Ethnic Conflict*, Cambridge: MIT Press, 1997, p. 27; Summers, *Peoples*, p. 9.
77. Summers, *Peoples*, pp. 8–9; Groarke, *Dividing the State*, p. 102.
78. M.E Chamberlain, *Decolonization* (2nd ed.), Oxford: Blackwell Publishers 1999, pp. 18 and 126–127.
79. Groarke, *Dividing the State*, pp. 78, Samuel J Barkin, 'The Evolution of the Constitution of Soveriegnty and the Emergence of Human Rights Norms', 27(2) *Millenium: Journal of International* Studies, pp. 229–252.
80. See Introduction to this monograph.
81. Norman, *Ethics of Secesion*, p. 36.
82. This linkage has given rise to the term 'nation-state', which implies that one *nation*, one 'group' inhabits one State. Self-determination is proof that this implication is simply wrong. Franck, *Power*, pp. 154–158.

suffer repression from what they perceive as an 'alien' or 'foreign' oppressor.[83] A similar criticism can be applied to the definition of peoples as colonial peoples.

We shall now turn to examine the historical evolution of a legal right to self-determination. Examining the historical development of the norm of self-determination will provide a better understanding of the difficulties associated with defining self-determination, and will reveal the interference to this created by States, who have often attempted to obfuscate the criteria for self-determination to suit their own interests.[84] A historical examination will help explain how the Court should identify a people entitled to exercise the right to self-determination. This will help shape a later argument that one of the pre-conditions for determining the legitimacy of a peoples' claim is the existence of repression or subjugation of an alien or foreign oppressor.

C. The evolution of a legal right to self-determination

Many authors trace the origins of political self-determination (as opposed to the legal right of self-determination) to developments in Europe and the United States during the eighteenth and nineteenth centuries,[85] specifically the American and French Revolutions.[86] However, both Revolutions, and the French in particular, were more concerned with establishing a political and constitutional order that respected the consent of the governed as a means to legitimise governance than with statehood.[87] Identifying the origins of these revolutions helps indicate that democracy is the cornerstone to self-determination.[88] However, nothing from the revolutions can help identify the origins of the desire for statehood, or the desire for freedom from domination from a foreign government. This can, rather, be traced to

83. Scharf, *Earned Sovereignty*, p. 80. This is what Philpott describes as 'unionist evils': Daniel Philpott, 'Self-Determination in Practice' in Margaret Moore (ed), *National Self-Determination and Secession*, New York: Oxford University Press, 1998, p. 92.
84. Accordingly care should be exercised when considering the importance of State practice.
85. Hurst Hannum, 'Self-Determination in the Post-Colonial Era' in Clark and Williamson (eds), *Self-Determination: International Perspectives*, p. 12; Musgrave, *National Minorities*, pp. 2–3.
86. Antonio Cassese, *Self-Determination of Peoples: A Legal Reappraisal*, Cambridge: Cambridge University Press, 1995 p. 11; A. Rigo Sureda, *The Evolution of the Right of Self-Determination, A Study of United Nations Practice*, Leiden, A. W. Sijthoff, 1973, p. 17; Joshua Castellino, *International Law and Self-Determination*, The Hague: Kluwer Law International incorporating Martinus Nijhoff Publishers, 2000, p. 11.
87. Castellino, *International Law*, p. 11.
88. Ibid, pp. 11–12.

the era of national consciousness and the development of the modern State in Europe.[89]

1. Concert of Vienna

Political self-determination was also applied in the Concert of Europe, with the reorganisation of sovereignties in Europe after the fall of Napoleon.[90] However, the change of sovereigns was dictated by the victors' ambitions and perceived needs, rather than by the relevant 'selves' – the people or groups supposedly freely determining their own political objectives. As one commentator noted, the Concert of Vienna was one example.[91] Self-determination was used in a manner of speaking as part of the 'victors' justice'.[92] The same could be said for the period following the end of the First World War.

2. The First World War and the League of Nations

The Allies stated that self-determination would guide the redrafting of European borders at the Paris Peace Conference, and Wilson stated that various peoples or 'nations' were entitled to self-determination in his famous 'Fourteen Points', delivered in a speech to the US Congress. These 'nations' were determined by their common identity, language, culture and history, rather than by the territory they inhabited.[93] Even the Bolsheviks, who had promoted and even publicly affirmed a right to self-determination from the Russian Revolution in 1917, maintained a policy of national self-determination.[94]

89. Musgrave, *National Minorities*, p. 2; J G Starke, *Introduction to International Law*, (9th ed), London: Butterworths, 1984, p. 11; Paul Kennedy, *The Rise and Fall of the Great Powers: Economic Change and Military Conflict from 1500–2000*, London: Fontana Press, 1989, p. 55, 89–90; Hannum, *Post-Colonial Era*, p. 12.
90. M Batistich, 'The Right to Self-Determination and International Law', 7 (1992–5) *Auckland University Law Review*, p. 1015.
91. Sureda, *Evolution*, p. 18.
92. Batistich, *Right to Self-Determination*, p. 1015; Sureda, *Evolution*, p. 18.
93. Both Wilson and Lloyd George outlined specific peoples that should be allowed to exercise the right to self-determination. Wilson mentioned the following peoples in his Fourteen Points: the peoples of Austria-Hungry, the nationalities under Turkish rule, and the Poles. Lloyd George referred to the peoples in the German colonies in Africa. See Mitchell A Hill, 'What the Principle of Self-Determination Means Today', 1 (1995) *ILSA Journal of International and Comparative Law*, p. 122; Musgrave, *National Minorities*, p. 26; Hannum, *Post-Colonial Era*, pp. 13–14; Radan, *The Break-up of Yugloslavia*, p. 24.
94. In its declaration of peace with Germany of 1917 the Bolshevik government stated the declaration was based on self-determination, and stated its desire for an immediate peace on the principle of self-determination of all peoples. The Bolshevik action strengthened national liberation movements in Europe, fighting against the Central powers, and also in

However, not all 'nations' achieved self-determination.[95] In reality 'peoples' really meant those groups who occupied a strategically insignificant piece of territory in a former colony of the defeated powers..[96] The actions of the Allies were, in effect, a mere continuation of their campaign against competing empires, since both the Allies and the Central Powers sought to weaken their opponents by sowing internal discord – encouraging them fall from within. They did this predominantly by appealing to the nationalist aspirations of repressed minority groups within each other's political domain.[97] The Allies simply took advantage of their victor status to dismantle their opponents' empires, and self-determination provided a convenient tool. In fact, many of the eventual transfers were actually based on agreements conducted in secret between the Allies *during* the War.[98] The closest that the international community came to acknowledging the existence of a legal right to self-determination was the establishment of the Mandate System by Art 22 of the Covenant, the creation of the Minorities Treaties Regime, and the determination of the Aaland Islands Question.

The purpose of the Mandate system was to enable the mandated territories and their politically undeveloped and inexperienced peoples to be guided to independence by the State appointed as the Mandatory.[99] As such it was the first real acknowledgement of the right to self-determination and also of the international community's legal competence to administer the right to self-determination.[100] Only one community, Iraq, achieved

the Baltic States. Sureda, *Evolution*, p. 20; Cassese, *A Legal Reappraisal*, pp. 14–18; Ofuatey-Kodjoe, *Self-Determination*, p. 137.

95. For example, whilst the Poles and the Czechs gained their independence, the Kurds and the Irish did not: Margaret MacMillan *Peacemakers: Six Months that Changed the World*, London: John Murray Publishers, 2001 p. 19.
96. Point twelve of Wilson's Fourteen Points specifically mentioned that the 'non-Turkish minorities' of the Ottoman Empire should be allowed to develop political autonomy. Indeed the 1920 *Treaty of Sèvres* (*The Treaty of Peace Between the Allied and Associated Powers and Turkey*, opened for signature 10 August 1920, 113 BFSP 652) would have created an autonomous Kurdish region within twelve months of signing. It was never implemented, and instead the Allies signed the Treaty of Lausanne in July 1923, which re-established Turkish sovereignty over areas claimed by the Kurds, and divided the remaining territory between Iran and Iraq. Hannum believes the reason for this was that the Allies' main concern was oil, not the national aspirations of the Kurds. See Hannum, *Post-Colonial Era*, pp. 183–4; fn 588.
97. Sureda, *Evolution*, p. 20. The Germans assisted Sinn Fein, and 'encouraged' the Finns, the Lithuanians and other nationalist groups in the Baltic States to seek independence from Russia: Musgrave, *National Minorities*, p. 15.
98. Such as the Treaty of London 1915, negotiated in secret between Britain, France, Russia and Italy. It gave many territories to Italy, and thus raised Italy to the status of an imperial power. Hill, *Principle of Self-Determination*, p. 122; Musgrave, *National Minorities*, p. 26; Hannum, *Post-Colonial Era*, pp. 13–14; *Summers, Peoples,* p. 132–133.
99. Sureda, *Evolution*, pp. 24–35. Such an appointment was described as the 'sacred trust of civilisation'.
100. Ibid, p. 35.

independence whilst the League existed.[101] Others, such as South-West Africa, remained under the control of their administering authority well after the demise of the League, whilst others, such as Palestine, are still awaiting independence.[102]

The Minorities Treaties Regime failed. Rather than protecting minorities, it actually ensured the continued dominance by the ethnic majority, and in fact worsened their situation.[103] Further, some of the new minorities (encouraged by foreign governments that shared a similar ethnicity) refused to see themselves as belonging to their new sovereign, and actively sought to be reunited with the 'motherland'.[104] Their existence provided the excuse for Hitler's 'reunification' of German peoples throughout Europe, which ultimately led to another 'Great War', the Second World War.[105]

3. The Aaland Islands Question

The Aaland Islands Dispute concerned the formation of the new Finnish State that had recently sought independence as a result of the collapse of the Russian Empire in 1917.[106] The islands were culturally as well as linguistically Swedish in origin and there was overwhelming evidence that the majority of the island population wished to integrate with Sweden, rather than Finland, or alternatively form their own State.[107] During discussions in the Council of the League of Nations, Finland argued that the islanders' right to self-determination was no greater than the right of all Finnish citizens of Swedish origin (thus if a plebiscite were to be held, it must be made available to the broader Finnish population). The Council agreed and concluded that the disposal of the territory was to be determined in accordance with the wishes of all Finnish people, those on the island and the mainland.[108]

To assist in the resolution of the dispute the Council initially appointed an International Commission of Jurists, and subsequently a Commission of Rapporteurs. The Commission of Jurists held that whilst there was no general right to self-determination available in international law, self-determination could apply to either a State that was in transformation due to

101. Ibid.
102. Ibid, pp. 35–48.
103. Ibid, p. 24; Hill, *Principle of Self-Determination*, p. 122; Musgrave, *National Minorities*, p. 41, 55.
104. Musgrave, *National Minorities*, pp. 58–9.
105. For example, one of the major aims of the National Socialist Party in Germany, led by Adolf Hitler was the reunification with German Austria. Eide, *Constructive Alternatives*, p. 150; Musgrave, *National Minorities*, p. 58.
106. Finland was previously known as the Grand Duchy of Finland.
107. Hannum, *Post-Colonial Era*, p. 15.
108. This was the same argument used later when considering the situation of Gibraltar: Sureda, *Evolution*, pp. 116–17; Radan, *The Break-up of Yugoslavia*, p. 30.

a war or revolution, or where a State was *not definitively constituted*.[109] The Commission then concluded that since Finland was a revolutionary entity, self-determination could apply.[110]

The Commission of Rapporteurs disagreed with the findings of the Commission of Jurists, and held that Finland was a definitively constituted State. Furthermore, whilst it acknowledged that if a plebiscite were held, the islanders would choose integration with Sweden, the islanders had no right to self-determination.

Resolving the Aaland Islands dispute was the first serious attempt at quantifying a legal right to self-determination, and thus determining the legitimacy of a claim to self-determination. The findings of the two Commissions, however, do not provide a definitive answer, since the two bodies were almost completely contradictory in their perception of the identity of the Aaland islanders.

The Commission of Jurists noted that the Aaland islanders were ethnically distinct from the Finns – 'the population is united by ties of race, language, and traditions to the Swedish race'[111] – and that the islanders' own perception of identity had been repressed during the Russian Empire.[112] The League Council supported their approach by determining that the Aaland Islanders had no greater right than the rest of the Finnish population. This, in effect, acted to state that the right was available to all of Finnish nationality in some capacity.[113]

The Commission of Rapporteurs took a more territorial-based approach, emphasising the 'geographical link' between the islands and Finland, with the Aaland Sea providing a natural boundary separating the islands from Sweden.[114] Furthermore, whilst the Commission of Jurists downplayed the significance of the historical political ties between the islands and Finnish administration of the Duchy within the Russian Empire, the Commission of Rapporteurs *emphasised* the administrative link.[115] Radan argues that the Commission of Rapporteurs, by acknowledging that a section of

109. 'Report of the International Commission of Jurists' [1920] *League of Nations Official Journal* (Special Supp) 3, 5–6.
110. Ibid; Radan, *The Break-up of Yugoslavia*, pp. 29–31.
111. 'Report of the International Commission of Jurists' [1920] *League of Nations Official Journal* (Special Supp) 3, 12.
112. Ibid.
113. Sureda, *Evolution*, pp. 116–17; Radan, *The Break-up of Yugoslavia*, p. 30.
114. 'Report of the International Commission of Jurists' [1920] *League of Nations Official Journal* (Special Supp) 3, 12; *The Aaland Islands Question: Report Submitted to the Council of the League of Nations by the Commission of Rapporteurs*, League of Nations Doc. B7 [C] 21/68/106 (April 1921), 29.
115. *The Aaland Islands Question: Report Submitted to the Council of the League of Nations by the Commission of Rapporteurs*, League of Nations Doc. B7 [C] 21/68/106 (April 1921) 29.

the population could secede in times of abuse, effectively adopted a territorial definition of a people.[116]

Such contrary positions do not support claims that self-determination could and should be determined through the use of a third party, such as a legal tribunal.[117] One of the few points that the two bodies agreed upon was that self-determination was not a norm of international law, and that self-determination threatened the stability of a State-centric international community. Both bodies also agreed, however, that a right to self-determination *could* arise in situations of abuse and suppression of a 'minority'.[118] The Committee of the Rapporteurs stated:

> The separation of a minority from the State of which it forms a part and its incorporation in another State can only be considered an exceptional solution, a last resort when the State lacks either the will or the power to enact and apply just and effective guarantees.[119]

Importantly, both bodies felt that the solution of the Aaland Islands Question turned on the same critical issue – the correct balance between stability of the international community and protection of minorities.[120] Focusing on this point was the correct approach. It is very pragmatic, but also emphasises the significance of justice and liberty within the determination of the legitimacy of a claim to self-determination.[121]

In conclusion, self-determination at the end of the First World War was nothing more than a political tool. However, the efforts of the Allies did not totally derail the evolution of self-determination into a legal right. Instead, they forced it to the forefront of international politics.[122] Previously the nationalist aspirations of respective peoples within European Empires (Austria-Hungary) lay outside the international regulation agenda. The War, followed by the Aaland Islands Question, rephrased such questions into

116. Sureda, *Evolution*, pp. 116–17; Radan, *The Break-up of Yugoslavia*, p. 30.
117. It then becomes an increasingly political question: *which* 'third party' should be chosen? One that leans towards a pre-conceived or desirable outcome? If so, desirable to whom?
118. The Commission of Jurists raised the idea of 'remedial self-determination' as a possibility, but argued that it was not necessary to resolve this definitively since the issue did not apply to the matter at hand, whilst the Rapporteurs were much more forthright in confirming the right to self-determination did exist in the face of abuse. See 'Report of the International Commission of Jurists' [1920] *League of Nations Official Journal* (Special Supp) 3, 5; *The Aaland Islands Question: Report Submitted to the Council of the League of Nations by the Commission of Rapporteurs*, League of Nations Doc. B7 [C] 21/68/106 (April 1921), 28.
119. *The Aaland Islands Question: Report Submitted to the Council of the League of Nations by the Commission of Rapporteurs*, League of Nations Doc. B7 [C] 21/68/106 (April 1921), 28.
120. Summers, *Peoples*, pp. 278–292, especially p. 288.
121. Ibid, p. 288.
122. Hill, *Principle of Self-Determination*, pp. 122–23.

matters of international concern.[123] Furthermore, Europe had seen several political struggles during the 19th century caused by nationalist movements rebelling against the imperial authority of other ethnic national groups. The common cause was the desire for freedom from alien oppression, and equality of rights. As a result the principle of national self-determination came to be regarded as the theoretical formulation of the demand for national liberation.[124]

Despite these events, self-determination's journey from a political concept into a legal right could not be completed without the period of decolonisation in the aftermath of the Second World War, and the inclusion of the right to self-determination in the *UN Charter*.

4. World War II and the UN Charter

Self-determination was again stated to be one of the objectives of the Allies during the Second World War.[125] The Atlantic Charter affirmed the right of 'national' groups to have self-government restored.[126] The total defeat of Germany and Japan provided a golden opportunity for self-determination's application, particularly due to their extensive occupation of other territories.[127] The right to self-determination was included in the *UN Charter*, in art 1(2) and art 55. Article 1(2) states that one of the purposes of the UN is:

> To develop friendly relations among nations based upon respect for the principle of equal rights and self-determination of peoples, and to take other appropriate measures to strengthen universal peace.[128]

The *UN Charter* was the first international document that contained self-determination, and was the first acknowledgement of self-determination as a legal right.[129] It was also the first time that 'peoples' was articulated as the beneficiary of self-determination.[130] However, the right to self-determination is not explained in any detail,[131] and the term 'people' is not defined. The

123. Ofuatey-Kodjoe, *Self-Determination*, pp. 132–33.
124. Ibid, pp. 141–43.
125. Summers, *Peoples*, p. 145.
126. United Nations, *The Atlantic Charter*, History of the United Nations, <www.un.org/en/aboutun/history/atlantic_charter.shtml> (accessed 14 March 2013).
127. Cassese, *A Legal Reappraisal*, p. 37. Arguably the Allies wished to focus on the territories captured by Germany and Japan. James Summers, *Peoples*, pp. 145–6.
128. *UN Charter* art 1(2). Article 55 states '[w]ith a view to the creation of conditions of stability and well-being which are necessary for peaceful and friendly relations among nations based on respect for the principle of equal rights and self-determination of peoples'.
129. Hannum, *Post-Colonial Era*, p. 17.
130. Radan, *The Break-up of Yugoslavia*, p. 30.
131. See Simpson's criticism of this point: Simpson, *Diffusion*, pp. 259–74.

position is further complicated by the use of three different terms: States, nations and peoples.

According to the provisions of the *Vienna Convention* the term 'peoples' should be interpreted within the context of Chapter I and the Preamble to the *UN Charter.*[132] The preparatory work, the *travaux preparatoires*, can also be used, as outlined in art 32 of the *Vienna Convention.* The first reference to self-determination is in art 1 (2) of the *UN Charter.* Article 1(2) is part of Chapter I, which is concerned with the objectives and purposes of the UN. These include maintaining international peace and security, and developing friendly relations between nations.[133] The Preamble to the *UN Charter* also includes a reference to maintaining international peace and security, developing friendly relations between nations,[134] and promoting and protecting human rights.[135] The first of these objectives – maintaining international peace and security – is the most significant.[136] Self-determination provides a vital means to achieving it. Comments made during the drafting process of the *UN Charter* indicate that self-determination is not to be interpreted in isolation, and that that it must be consider within the context of other provisions of the *UN Charter*, notably art 2(7) relating to non-interference in domestic affairs.[137]

Daes argues that the wording of the *UN Charter* and the context surrounding self-determination indicates that self-determination was not intended to be an '*operative principle*' of the *UN Charter*, that is, a legal right, but rather a *desiderata*, an aspirational goal.[138] This is evident in the *UN Charter*'s non-inclusion of a general right to self-determination. It instead demonstrates an intention that a Trustee System would administer non self-governing

132. Articles 31 and 32 of the *1967 Vienna Convention on the Law of Treaties* contain guidelines for interpreting terms within treaties: *Vienna Convention on the Law of Treaties*, opened for signature 23 May 1969, 1155 UNTS 331, arts 31–33 (entered into force 27 January 1980) ('*Vienna Convention*'). Article 31(1) states that 'a treaty shall be interpreted in good faith in accordance with the ordinary meaning to be given to the terms of the treaty in their context and in the light of their object and purpose.' Article 31(2) states that the 'context' can be determined by any extrinsic materials 'in connexion with the conclusion of the treaty and accepted by the other parties as an instrument related to the treaty.' These guidelines are treated by the ICJ as customary norms of international law: *Maritime Delimination and Territorial Questions (Qatar v Bahrain)* [1995] ICJ Rep 6, 18.
133. *UN Charter* art1 (1).
134. The Preamble to the *UN Charter* begins with the following statement: 'We the peoples of the United Nations determined to save succeeding generations from the scourge of war'.
135. *UN Charter* art 1(3); Summers, *Peoples*, p. 149.
136. Such an interpretation is supported by comments made by State delegates and representatives during the drafting process. See Summers, *Peoples*, pp. 148–150.
137. Ibid, pp. 150–151.
138. Erica-Irene A Daes, 'The Right of Peoples to "Self-Determination" in the Contemporary World Order' in Donald Clark and Robert Williamson (eds), *Self-Determination: International Perspectives* 1996, p. 48; Allan Rosas, 'Internal Self-Determination' in Tomuschat, *Modern Law of Self-Determination*, p. 225.

territories.[139] Articles 73 and 76 deal with non self-governing or trust territories respectively, and both use the expression 'peoples' (plural) and also 'inhabitants'. Article 73 of the *UN Charter* defines non-self-governing territories as those: 'peoples [who] have not yet attained a full measure of self-government.'[140] Therefore it could be argued that the definition of peoples could simply be calculated as being peoples of non-self-governing territories, in essence a territorial definition rather than a nationality approach. However, this is far from clear, and the term 'peoples' as used in the *UN Charter* is ambiguous. The *travaux preparatoires* of the *UN Charter* sadly also do not define a 'people',[141] although some commentators argue that an analysis of the *UN Charter*'s *travaux preparatoires* supports the argument that self-determination would only be applied to non self-governing or trust territories,[142] and thus 'peoples' were defined as being those in the non-self-governing or trust territories.

Daes' argument must be viewed with a degree of care, since the UN, when determining what territories fell within the ambit of art 73 of the *UN Charter*, asked its member States, *including* the very States themselves that controlled these regions, what areas were 'non-self-governing'. States had a vested interest in providing a very restricted definition of non-self-governing.[143] The Western Powers, such as Great Britain and France, supported such an interpretation since they initially feared decolonisation would mean an end to their respective empires.[144] Even the US, although it *appeared to* support decolonisation was determined that it, and not the Micronesians, would determine the future of Micronesia.[145] The Western Powers instead attempted to rely upon Chapters XI and XII of the *UN Charter*, which enabled them, rather than the colonies themselves, to control the pace with which independence was achieved in their colonies.[146]

There is some validity in Daes' argument regarding the inclusion of self-determination in the *UN Charter*. No reference to self-determination was

139. *UN Charter*, Chapters XI, XII. The system was similar to the Mandate System established under the League of Nations.
140. *UN Charter*, art 73. Article 76 offers no definition of what is non-self-governing.
141. Radan, *The Break-up of Yugoslavia*, p. 32.
142. Ibid, p. 38; Helen Quane, 'The United Nations and the Evolving Right to Self-Determination' 47 (1998) *International and Comparative Law Quarterly*, pp. 541–8; Simpson, *Diffusion*, p. 269.
143. For example, Great Britain ensured that the territories subject to the Trustee System were those voluntarily included, those that were previously part of the Mandate system, and those territories controlled by Germany and Japan during World War II. Sureda, *Evolution*, p. 102; Radan, *The Break-up of Yugoslavia*, p. 32; Summers, *Peoples*, p. 151.
144. Simpson, *Diffusion*, p. 265.
145. For strategic reasons: Noam Chomsky, *Deferring Democracy*, London: Vintage 1992, p. 48; Howard P Willens and Deanne C Siemer, *National Security and Self-Determination: United States Policy in Micronesia (1961–1972)*, London: Praeger, 2000, p. 3, 19.
146. Simpson, *Diffusion*, pp. 266–7.

made in the original draft of the *UN Charter*, and it was only included later as an amendment by the Four Sponsoring Governments at Dumbarton Oaks.[147] Initially art 1 (2) was worded as follows: 'to develop friendly relations among nations and to take other appropriate measures to strengthen universal peace'.[148] Similarly the draft for art 55 did not mention self-determination.[149] Articles 1 (2) and 55 were amended to include a reference at the insistence of the USSR delegation so as to hasten the realisation of nations' claims to self-determination.[150] The amendment was received with concern by the Belgian delegate who felt it dangerous to base the pursuit of peaceful relations between States on 'peoples' rights (as opposed to the rights of States) to self-determination since it could lead to intervention. Furthermore, the Belgian delegate also took the view that peoples meant 'national groups which do not identify with the state',[151] and thus felt that a peoples-based approach could give rise to a right of secession.[152]

During further discussion at the later Coordination Committee, French and Colombian delegates also expressed concerns that the terms 'peoples' and 'nations' used in juxtaposition would create a right to secession.[153] These concerns prompted a request by the Committee for clarification, which was provided by the UN Secretariat in a memorandum that defined the three terms – peoples, nations and States – in the draft *UN Charter* as follows:

> 1. The word 'state' is used...to indicate a definite political entity...[it] occurs in both security and non-security fields...[as well as] when a distinction is being made between a member and a non-member...
> 2. The word 'nation' is broad and general enough to include colonies, mandates, protectorates, and quasi-states as well as states...the word 'nation' [as used in art's 1(2), 55 & 14] seem[s] preferable in order to

147. The amendment that the Big Four proposed was that peaceful relations should be 'based on respect for the principle of equal rights and self-determination of peoples': Sureda, *Evolution*, p. 97.
148. Ibid; Hannum, *Post-Colonial Era*, pp. 16–17.
149. The reason for self-determination's absence was due in part to: (1) the inconsistent and self-serving manner which the Allies had applied after the First World War; (2) the perceived association self-determination had with Hitler's justifications at reuniting the German 'nation'; and (3) the concern over the wording proposed in art 1(2), in particular the use of the terms 'peoples 'and 'nations' in the same sentence: Hannum, *Post-Colonial Era*, pp. 16–17.
150. Radan, *The Break-up of Yugoslavia*, p. 32.
151. *United Nations Documents of the Conference on International Organisation* (1945–52) vol VI, 300 ('*UNCIO*').
152. Sureda, *Evolution*, p. 98.
153. Even the use of 'nations' was criticised, since the French delegate argued that international relations was conducted between States: Radan, *The Break-up of Yugoslavia*, p. 33; Cassese, *A Legal Reappraisal*, pp. 39–40.

emphasise the idea of friendly relations among all types of political entities.
3. The word 'peoples' [is] used in connection with the phrase 'self-determination of peoples' – this phrase is in such common usage that no other word seems appropriate.[154]

Secondly, the memorandum justified the use of 'nations' and 'peoples' in art 1(2) and art 55 in juxtaposition because:

> there appears to be no difficulty in this juxtaposition since 'nations' is used in the sense of all political entities, states and non-states, whereas 'peoples' refers to groups of human beings who may, or may not, comprise states or nations.[155]

Consequently, Committee I/I unanimously accepted the original amendment as proposed by the Four Sponsoring Governments.[156]

Sureda argues that the Secretariat's memorandum gives the term 'peoples' as wide a meaning as possible.[157] This interpretation is supported by the fact that the discussion by Committee I/I of the Belgian delegate's proposed amendment regarding art 1 (2) of the *UN Charter* confirmed that the right of self-determination would be available to 'peoples everywhere'.[158] Furthermore, the Chairman, Rapporteur and Secretary of the Technical Committee I/1, when asked whether self-determination in the *UN Charter* did include a right to secession, stated that 'the right of self-determination meant a people may establish any regime which they favour.'[159]

Radan interprets this statement as proof that art 1(2) and art 55 introduce a right of secession simply since it fails to *exclude* a right to secession.[160] Radan argues that, as a matter of logic, secession cannot occur if a people referred to *all* the inhabitants of a State. In other words, in order to secede from a State, a people can only be one component of the 'inhabitants' of that State. Therefore, 'peoples' must mean 'nations'.[161] Such an interpretation is supported by the use of the term 'inhabitants' in arts 73 and 76 of the *UN Charter.* To Radan, the term 'inhabitants' was clearly intended to refer (and logically it must do so) to the entire population of a given non-self-governing territory,

154. *UNCIO*, Vol XVIII, p. 657: Sureda, *Evolution*, p. 100.
155. Aureliu Cristescu, UN Doc. E/CN.4/Sub.2/404/Rev.1, 260–263; Sureda, *Evolution*, p. 100.
156. Sureda, *Evolution*, pp. 97–100.
157. Regarding the right of self-determination, the *UN Charter* recognised the existence of the concept of self-determination of peoples, this concept being given an all-embracing meaning'. Ibid, p. 101.
158. Ibid, pp. 97–99.
159. *UNCIO*, vol VI, p. 298.
160. Radan, *The Break-up of Yugoslavia*, p. 33.
161. Ibid, pp. 32–33.

and accordingly cannot be equated with a single people, since several peoples can inhabit one non-self-governing territory.[162] Furthermore, Radan concludes that whilst the *travaux preparatoires* of the *UN Charter* may not directly define a 'people' as a 'nation' there is nothing in them to contradict such an interpretation.[163]

I do not agree entirely with Radan's argument. Secession was something that the drafters of the *UN Charter*,[164] and subsequent UN policy,[165] wanted to avoid. However, I do agree with Riga's thesis that the word 'peoples' was intended to have a broader meaning than those within non-self-governing territories or trust territories. Certainly the expression, 'groups of human beings who may, or may not, comprise states or nations',[166] used above, provides a very broad definition of people. The UN Secretariat's memorandum provided evidence that there was a reason for making a distinction between the three terms: nations, peoples and States. Thus, at the bare minimum, a 'people' is not synonymous with a 'State', and logically that means a territorial approach was not intended to define a people. This interpretation is supported by the fact that the discussion by Committee I/I of the Belgian delegate's proposed amendment regarding art 1 (2) of the *UN Charter* confirmed that the right of self-determination would be available to 'peoples everywhere'.[167]

However, accepting that the definition of peoples was not intended to be synonymous with States, and was instead intended to have a broader application than non-Self-Governing Territories, still does not clarify what the actual definition is, and does not offer any conclusive solution as to how peoples should be identified by the Court. On the question of whether a people should be defined purely by the territory they occupy *or* through

162. Ibid, pp. 31–32. His argument is supported by His Excellency Judge van Wyck in *South West Africa Cases (Ethiopia v South Africa; Liberia v South Africa) (Second Phase)* [1966] ICJ Rep 6, 166.
163. Radan, *The Break-up of Yugoslavia*, p. 32: Franck, *Legitimacy in the International System*, p. 745; W Ofuatey-Kodjoe, 'Self-Determination' in Oscar Schater and Christopher C Joyner (eds), *United Nations Legal Order*, Volume 1, Cambridge: Cambridge University Press, 1995, p. 354.
164. The Committee at San Francisco agreed that self-determination did not give rise to secession. *UNCIO*, vol VI, 296 (UNICO Doc 343); Aureliu Cristescu, Un Doc. E/CN.4/Sub.2/404/Rev.1, p. 274.
165. UN policy regarding secession was stated clearly by the then UN Secretary-General U Thant when Biafra attempted to claim independence. He stated at a Press Conference: 'As far as the question of secession of a particular section of a State is concerned, the United Nations attitude is unequivocable [*sic*]. As an international organization, the United Nations has never accepted and does not accept and I do not believe it will ever accept the principle of secession of a part of its Member States': 'Secretary-General's Press Conferences' *UN Monthly Chronicle* 7, 1970, p. 36.
166. Ibid.
167. Sureda, *Evolution*, pp. 97–9.

non-territorial characteristics such as culture and shared language (as a non-State entity), the *UN Charter* offers little assistance.[168]

Perhaps this was a reflection of divided opinions within the international community at the time of drafting the *UN Charter*, or perhaps it was a reflection of the inherent challenges of drafting a new and highly controversial norm of international law, one that carried a baggage of self-interest. Nonetheless the inclusion of self-determination as a legal right was a massive step forward in the quest for world peace, and recognised international law's role as a peacemaker. Whatever the true reason for the lack of clarification, the definition of a people has been clarified by post-charter documents, in particular the 1960 and 1970 Declarations.

5. The 1960 Declaration on Colonial Peoples

The 1960 *Declaration on Colonial Peoples* reaffirmed the *right* of self-determination and also announced that self-determination was the underlying concept, as well as the mechanism, behind the UN's official decolonisation policy. The 1960 Declaration supplemented the basic nature of the relevant provisions of the Charter and began a revolutionary process within the UN.[169] The preamble to the 1960 Declaration proclaimed the necessity to bring colonialism to a 'speedy end', that the process of liberation was 'irresistible and *irreversible*' (emphasis added),[170] and finally, that self-determination was the means by which this should be done.[171]

More than 100 new States were formed as a result of decolonisation after WWII,[172] and many commentators argue that it was the UN policy of decolonisation after WWII that was instrumental in the transition of self-determination from a political right to a legal norm.[173] For the first time the creation of States was not purely a political matter, but was subject to a principle of international law.[174] Furthermore, the 1960 Declaration, together with the 1970 Declaration below, formed the basis for later opinions of the ICJ on Namibia[175] and Western Sahara,[176] where the Court confirmed that self-determination was not merely a guide or political policy promoted by

168. Simma, *UN Charter*, p. 58.
169. Hill, *Principle of Self-Determination*, p. 125; Daes, *Right of Peoples*, p. 48.
170. *Declaration on Colonial Peoples*, UN Doc A/RES/1514 (XV) Preamble (emphasis added); Castellino, *International Law*, p. 24.
171. The preamble to the *Declaration on Colonial Peoples*, UN Doc A/RES/1514 (XV), describes in detail the evils of colonialism, and more importantly affirms very stridently that international peace and security is dependent upon bringing colonialism to an end.
172. Scharf, *Earned Sovereignty*, p. 377.
173. Simpson, *Diffusion*, p. 264; Quane, *Evolving Right to Self-Determination*, p. 548; Cassese, *A Legal Reappraisal*; Hannum, *Post-Colonial Era*, p. 17.
174. Scharf, *Earned Sovereignty*, p. 377.
175. *Namibia Opinion* [1971] ICJ Rep 16.
176. *Western Sahara Opinion* [1975] ICJ Rep 23.

the UN, but a genuine legal right that, once validly invoked, entitled peoples to claim independent statehood.[177]

The 1960 Declaration, and the subsequent successful decolonisation policy, states that self-determination applies to colonial peoples.[178] Thus, arguably, the *Declaration on Colonial Peoples* would support a territorial approach, since a colony is essentially defined in this way. This conclusion is supported by the fact that the *Declaration on Colonial Peoples* confirmed the territorial integrity of colonial territories, and affirmed the right of States to non-intervention.[179] However, this interpretation is clouded by the reference in the *Declaration on Colonial Peoples* to the right to self-determination being available to 'all people'.[180] Radan also argues that there is nothing in the actual wording of the *Declaration on Colonial Peoples* that is inconsistent with the idea that a specific colonial territory could contain multiple peoples.[181]

There is some merit in Radan's argument, since the interpretation that the 1960 Declaration is espousing a territorial approach is based on an assumption that only one colonial people exists in a given territory. The argument, that a colonial people could be identified through other means, such as ethnicity, raises the general issue of how a colonial people should be identified. This problem was evidenced by Portugal's refusal to classify its overseas territories as 'colonies'. Instead Portugal argued that they were simply an overseas part of the sovereign territory of Portugal, and therefore not non-self-governing territories. Portugal used this to justify its failure to provide reports to the UN in accordance with Chapter XI of the *UN Charter*.[182]

Essentially Portugal was arguing that a colonial people were 'someone else's colony, or a people located in another State, but not mine'. This attitude was typical of States seeking to protect their self-interest during the decolonisation period, even of the former USSR, the so-called 'advocate' of self-determination, who provided the momentum and support for the UN's decolonisation programme. Other examples included Israel responding to

177. Christian Tomuschat, 'Self-Determination in a Post-Colonial World' in Tomuschat, *Modern Law of Self-Determination*, p. 2. These two legal opinions will be discussed in subsequent chapters.
178. Certainly the title of the 1960 Declaration, 'The Granting of Independence to Colonial Countries and Peoples', lends weight to such an interpretation: Simpson, *Diffusion*, pp. 269–72. However, Brownlie argues that the reference to peoples is in fact 'not confined to colonial situations and applies to all dependent peoples': Ian Brownlie, *The Rule of Law in International Affairs*, The Hague: Kluwer Law International, 1998, p. 40.
179. See *Declaration on Colonial Peoples*, UN Doc A/RES/1514 (XV) [6]–[7]. Daes, *Right of Peoples*, p. 48; Radan *The Break-up of Yugoslavia*, p. 39.
180. *Declaration on Colonial Peoples*, UN Doc A/RES/1514 (XV) 2].
181. Instead the Declaration appears to be more concerned with territorial integrity than with clarifying any definition of a people. Radan, *The Break-up of Yugoslavia*, p. 39.
182. *UN Charter* art 73 (e). See also *Right of Passage Over Indian Territory (Portugal v India)* [1960] ICJ Rep 6.

allegations made by Arab States that it was an imperialist State.[183] In response to Portugal's recalcitrance, the General Assembly passed *Resolution 1541 (XV)*.

6. General Assembly Resolution 1541(XV): Principles Guiding Members in regard to Article 73e of the Charter[184]

General Assembly Resolution 1541 (XV) clearly reaffirms a State's obligation to provide reports in relation to 'territories whose peoples have not yet obtained a full measure of self-government.'[185] *Resolution 1541 (XV)* is a series of principles or guidelines intended to make States aware of their responsibilities towards non-self-governing territories. However, its significance extends beyond that purpose for two reasons. Firstly, it clarifies what is meant by the term 'people', and secondly, it clarifies the *process* of attaining self-government.[186]

The language used in *Principle I*, 'peoples have not yet obtained a full measure of self-government', was an obvious attempt to circumvent Portugal's definition of sovereign Portuguese territory mentioned above. It should also be read in the context of *Principle IV*, which stated that the obligation to provide information exists in relation to 'territory which is geographically separate and is distinct ethnically and/or culturally from the country administering it.'[187]

These two *Principles*, when read together with the *1960 Declaration of Colonial Peoples*, appear to place an emphasis on territory, or geography as the decisive factor identifying a people. As one commentator, Castellino, questioned 'why geography should be given a preference over any one of many other factors that could be of equal if not greater importance'?[188] The answer to this question is obvious – a territorial approach supposedly disallows States from controlling the application of self-determination in a manner designed to prevent any of their citizens claiming self-determination.[189] It is

183. Summers, *Peoples*, pp. 198–200.
184. *Principles Which Should Guide Members in Determining Whether an Obligation Exists to Transmit the Information Called Under Article 73e*, GA Res 1541(XV), UN GAOR, 15th sess, 948th plen mtg, annex, UN Doc (15 December 1960) ('*Resolution 1541 (XV)*').
185. Ibid, *Principle I*.
186. As noted by Summers, self-government is a goal, and self-determination a process to achieve that goal. Hence *Resolution 1541 (XV)* actually defines the process of self-determination: Summers, *Peoples*, p. 295. For example, Principle VI outlines a what is required to achieve a 'full measure of self-government'. It essentially involves a choice between: (1) independent statehood; (2) free association with another State; and (3) integration with another State.
187. *Resolution 1541 (XV)*, Principle IV.
188. Castellino, *International Law*, p. 28.
189. Summers, *Peoples*, p. 210. See the discussion regarding territorial integrity and *uti possidetis* below.

clear that the choice of language was a deliberate attempt to circumvent Portugal's lack of cooperation with the *UN Charter*. The actions of States in this regard are assisted by the reference to territory that is 'geographically separate' in *Principle VI* – the so-called 'salt water' test. Sadly, the terms actually enabled other States to avoid self-determination by claiming that if the territory was not geographically distinct it could not be considered 'non-self-governing' and therefore not a colony.[190] This enabled the development of the argument that for a territory to be identified as a colony it must be 'overseas' in order to be geographically separate.[191]

This is one example of States' interference that has clouded the development of self-determination, and in particular the definition of 'people'. Its effect is still felt today, with commentators like Radan arguing that Serbia was not a coloniser of Croatia and the other former republics of the Socialist Republic of Yugoslavia because each of the republics was not geographically separate.[192] A second example is that during the drafting of *Resolution 1541 (XV)*, Portugal sought to exclude Goa, Macau and East Timor, despite all three being geographically distinct.[193]

As will be seen below, States continued to interfere and obfuscate the meaning of peoples in the 1966 covenants.

7. The Human Rights Covenants

The *ICCPR* was one of two international covenants adopted by the UN General Assembly to protect human rights.[194] The second was the *ICESCR*.[195] Self-determination is mentioned in common article 1 of the two covenants as follows:

> All people have the right of self-determination. By virtue of that right they freely determine their political status and freely pursue their economic, social and cultural development.[196]

190. See the example of West Papua and Indonesia below.
191. Summers, *Peoples*, p. 208. See the discussion regarding the definition of colonial peoples, and also West Papua below.
192. See note 323 below.
193. Summers, *Peoples*, p. 209.
194. The *ICCPR* (see n 34) was adopted by GA Res 2200 (XXI) 16 December 1966, and entered into force 23 March 1976. At the date of publication 167 States were parties, and 74 were signatories. See United Nations, *ICCPR*, UN Treaty Collection, <http://treaties.un.org/Pages/ViewDetails.aspx?mtdsg_no=IV-4&lang=eng> (last accessed 29 Mar 2013).
195. *ICESCR* opened for signature 16 December 1966, 933 UNTS 3 (entered into force 3 January 1976).
196. *ICCPR*, (see n 34) art 1(1). Self-determination is also mentioned in art 1(3) of the *ICCPR*, which states that States shall 'promote the realisation of the right of self-determination'.

Of all the post Charter documents, the 1966 *ICCPR* is perhaps the least helpful. Referring to 'all people' causes problems, since it raises the floodgate argument.[197] Even the *travaux preparatoires* of the *ICCPR* provides little assistance regarding the definition of 'peoples' because of the diversity of views and proposals put forward.[198]

There was much opposition to the adoption of art 1 due to concerns expressed about the uncertainty of the meaning and scope of self-determination, and of the inclusion of what was essentially a 'group' right in covenants that were almost entirely concerned with individual rights. The major concern, however, was that it could be interpreted broadly enough to permit secession.[199] Most Western States concerned with decolonisation, in the vote for its acceptance, either abstained or voted against it.[200] Once again the inclusion of self-determination's inclusion was predominantly a result of the Soviets championing the cause for what they referred to as 'national self-determination' – a right to an independent State. It was a right available to 'every people and every nation.'[201]

However, it was not just colonial powers that were apprehensive. India, a former colony, argued that the term peoples referred to in art 1 of the 1966 *ICCPR*, were those that were subject to 'alien rule', by which the Indian government meant a *foreign* oppressive power.[202] The *ICCPR* states:

> [that the right of self-determination as stated in Article 1 will] apply only to the peoples under foreign domination and that these words do not apply to sovereign independent States or to a section of a people or nation – which is the essence of national integrity.[203]

India's position on this interpretation had been made earlier at the Cairo Conference of the Non-Aligned States in 1964 when the then Indian Prime Minister Shatri stated that '[self-determination] was the right of any country

197. See Introduction.
198. During the period 1949 and 1955.
199. Radan, *The Break-up of Yugoslavia*, pp. 44–45; Cassese, *A Legal Reappraisal*, p. 47.
200. Article 1 was adopted by the Commission on Human Rights by 3 votes to 4 (1 abstention) and by the Third Committee of the General Assembly by 33 votes to 12 with 13 abstentions. The strongest opponents to inclusion of self-determination were the UK, France and Belgium – States with extensive colonies: Rosas, *Internal Self-Determination*, p. 243; Cassese, *A Legal Reappraisal*, p. 49.
201. Cassese, *A Legal Reappraisal*, p. 48.
202. For an excellent discussion of these matters see Antonio Cassese, *A Legal Reappraisal*, p. 47; Duursma, *Fragmentation and the International Relations of Micro-States: Self-Determination and Statehood*, Cambridge: Cambridge University Press, 1996, pp. 17–35. Interestingly India's position drew protest from the Netherlands, France and the Federal Republic of Germany, all arguing that Article 1 should apply to 'all peoples': Rosas, *Internal Self-Determination*, p. 178, 242.
203. As cited in Rosas, *Internal Self-Determination*, p. 242.

[not peoples] dominated by another, but could not be claimed by different areas and regions within a sovereign and independent country.'[204] The Indian Representative to the Security Council made a similar statement that the right of self-determination was available to 'nations and States and cannot be used for the breaking up of a state or fragmentation of peoples.'[205] In essence India was using the norm of territorial integrity to maintain that a territorial approach should be taken to define a people.[206]

As a former colony India's position may at first glance appear surprising, but its policy was such for a very obvious reason. Since partition India had been faced with numerous violent secessionist movements – the Assamese, the Sikhs, and the Muslims in Kashmir. By using the terms 'alien' or 'foreign', the Indian government was attempting to ensure that their government would not be considered a colonial power, and thus attention would be shifted to those peoples directly under the control of *traditional* colonial powers such as France or Great Britain.

Commentators are divided in their interpretation of Common Article 1. For example, Gerry Simpson argues that the failure of the 1966 Covenants to define the term 'peoples' merely continues the uncertainty found within the *UN Charter*, and thus, the Covenants do not alter the perception that the peoples entitled to self-determination were only those within art 73 of the *UN Charter*.[207] Radan argues that the reference to 'all people' can refer to a single group within a territory, and is not restricted to colonial peoples.[208] Other commentators also argue that Common Article 1 was a universal right and not restricted to colonial peoples.[209]

The UN's Human Rights Committee, the UN body responsible for applying the 1966 Covenants, has confirmed the latter interpretation, stating that the *ICCPR* intended to adopt a more expansive definition of people – it could apply to *any* people.[210] This finding may assist in defining a people, but

204. Anjoo Upadhyaya, 'Quest for Self-Determination in the Indian Subcontinent: The Recent Phase' in Donald Clark and Robert Williamson (eds), *Self-Determination: International* Perspectives (1996), p. 169.
205. Ibid.
206. Other States such as Sri Lanka, the Democratic Republic of Korea and the German Democratic Republic subsequently supported India's position and interpretation: Rosas, *Internal Self-Determination*, p. 244.
207. Simpson, *Diffusion*, p. 268.
208. Radan, *The Break-up of Yugoslavia*, p. 50.
209. Ibid, p. 45; Cassese, *A Legal Reappraisal*, pp. 48–52; James Crawford, 'Outside the Colonial Context' in W J A Macartney (ed), *Self-Determination in the Commonwealth*, 1988, 5–6: Duursma, *Fragmentation*, p. 26; Human Rights Committee, *General Comment 12*, 516th mtg, UN Doc CCPR/C/21/Add.3 (12 April 1984) [6].
210. Human Rights Committee, UN Doc CCPR/C/21/Add.3, 2. However, the Committee still did not clarify whether self-determination applied to those peoples that were part of former colonies, such as the Kashmiris in India or the West Papuans in Indonesia: Allen Rosas, *Internal Self-Determination*, p. 244.

does reject a territorial approach. In doing so, the UN's Human Rights Committee has provided an opportunity to argue that the term 'peoples' can be determined by non-territorial criteria. However, such an interpretation is jeopardised when read with the previous *Declaration on Colonial Peoples* and the subsequent *Declaration on Friendly Relations.*

8. The 1970 Declaration on Friendly Relations[211]

The 1970 *Declaration on Friendly Relations* clearly identifies and reaffirms the existence of a right to self-determination. It also expresses how the right is exercised – through the freely expressed will of the peoples concerned – and also contains much more detail than the 1960 *Declaration on Colonial Peoples* in relation to States' obligations towards the claimants. It states:

> Every State has a duty to promote...the realisation of the principle of equal rights and self-determination of peoples, in accordance with the provisions of the Charter, and to render assistance to the United Nations in carrying out the responsibilities entrusted to it by the Charter'.[212]

However, it also does not directly define the term 'peoples', in fact making its definition more difficult by mixing expressions such as 'all peoples', 'the whole people belonging to the territory' and 'race, creed or colour'.[213] Nonetheless, the 1970 Declaration is clear in its position in regard to bringing colonialism to a 'speedy end'.[214]

In relation to the definition of 'all people' the 1970 Declaration gives rise to the same issues of interpretation as the Declaration of ten years earlier – whether it is intended to apply only to colonial peoples, and how colonial peoples are defined, remains up in the air.[215]

Radan rejects such an interpretation, arguing that it implies that the population of that territory must mean the population as a whole. He again argues that the *Declaration on Friendly Relations* clearly enunciates a right to secession and that logically, if a right to secede exists, 'people' must refer to a smaller group within a larger whole State population.[216]

211. *Declaration on Friendly Relations*, UN Doc A/RES/2625(XXV).
212. Ibid.
213. Although the *Declaration on Friendly Relations* clearly includes non-self-governing territories as outlined in the *UN Charter* within the definition of a colony. Ibid.
214. Ibid (b). Earlier in 1970 the General Assembly declared colonialism to be a crime. See *Programme for Action for the Full Implementation of the Declaration on the Granting of Independence to Colonial Countries and Peoples*, GA Res 2621 (XXV), UN GAOR, 25th sess, 1862nd plen mtg, Supp 16, UN Doc A/RES/2621 (12 October 1970).
215. Radan, *The Break-up of Yugoslavia*, pp. 66–7.
216. Ibid, p. 55. If, as Radan notes, secession is equated with self-determination.

As mentioned above, secession was something that the drafters of the *UN Charter* and subsequent UN policy were at pains to avoid. However, Radan's argument is persuasive. It is based upon interpreting the references to self-determination within the context of the 1970 Declaration[217] and the 1960 Declaration, which clearly explain that a valid exercise of self-determination includes the formation of an independent State, which arguably can mean secession.[218] As noted by Radan, 'a people cannot at the same time be the entire population of a State as well as the group that secedes from that State.'[219]

Other commentators argue that the 1970 Declaration was intended to apply beyond a decolonisation context.[220] This is based on the inclusion of the following reference to alien and foreign subjugation:

> Subjugation of peoples to alien subjugation, domination and exploitation constitutes a violation of the principle, as well as a denial of fundamental human rights and is contrary to the Charter of the United Nations.[221]

This reference raises some important questions. Does it broaden the category of claimants to include a people who are subject to alien domination, regardless of whether they are a colonial people? Or alternatively, as argued here, does it create a counter-argument to any attempt by States to obfuscate self-determination? The answer to these questions depends on how a colonial people are defined. We shall consider the definition of a colonial people in the next part.

D. Definition of a colonial people: decolonisation and the attitude of states

As mentioned above, the Western Powers were initially opposed to decolonisation, and it was really due to support from the former USSR that the UN

217. The *Declaration on Friendly Relations*, UN Doc A/RES/2625(XXV) states quite clearly at [2], that the interpretation and application of the principles contained therein 'should be construed in the context of other principles.' See also *Vienna Convention*, opened for signature 23 May 1969, 1155 UNTS 331, arts 31–33 (entered into force 27 January 1980), art 31(1).
218. The *Declaration on Friendly Relations* states that: 'The establishment of a sovereign and independent State, the free association or integration with an independent State or the emergence into any other political status freely determined by a people constitute modes of implementing the right of self-determination by that people': UN Doc A/RES/2625(XXV) (1970).
219. Radan, *The Break-up of Yugoslavia*, p. 55.
220. Cassese, *A Legal Reappraisal*, pp. 38–9, 90. However, Castellino qualifies this by raising the potential limitation to an application of self-determination by the principle of territorial integrity and *uti possidetis*: Castellino, *International Law* p. 24.
221. *Declaration on Friendly Relations*, Doc A/RES/2625(XXV).

was able to pursue its decolonisation policy. However, the Soviets' support was not out of altruism or concern for colonial peoples, but was a reflection of their conflict with the West during the Cold War.[222] In other words, it was in their national interest to support colonial peoples.[223] The lack of altruism, or perhaps the hypocrisy of the USSR, is clearly shown by the fact that it would champion the causes of African and Asian colonies, under Western rule, but would not do so with regard to its own colonies – the Baltic States, Latvia, Lithuania and Estonia – that it had integrated in 1940.[224] In other words, the attitude of the former USSR was consistent with that of other States – colonial peoples meant 'other States' colonies'.

1. The definition of colonies

During the decolonisation era, the colonies that gained independence were those located *offshore*, or in a geographically distant and separate territory – in 'saltwater colonies'.[225] This conclusion was based on the idea of protecting territorial integrity, and by *Resolution 1541 (XV)*.[226] The independence of an island or a territory located on the other side of an ocean does not have the same impact on the territorial integrity of the 'motherland' or colonial power that the independence of a neighbouring province, or internal province, would have.[227] Arguably there would be little if no threat to the territorial integrity of the colonial power.[228] Newly independent former colonial States like India used the concept of 'saltwater colonies' to restrict the definition of

222. Hannum, *Post-Colonial Era*, p. 33; Simpson, *Diffusion*, p. 266.
223. For example, the Soviets were very supportive of indigenous peoples' rights, because it was possible to broadcast to the international community multiple examples of Western mistreatment of indigenous peoples, in particular the US (and their Allies) in Central and South America: Douglas Sanders, 'Self-Determination and Indigenous Peoples' in Tomuschat (ed), *Modern Law of Self-Determination*, p. 69.
224. The former USSR's stance could be justified due to the concept of 'saltwater colonialism': their colonies were not located overseas. However, the USSR also refused to allow the States in its sphere of influence in Eastern Europe any real sovereignty. Simpson, *Diffusion*, p. 267; Quane, *Evolving Right*, p. 567.
225. Another way of expressing this is to say that the inhabitants of areas that are not geographically distinct are more likely to be classified as a minority, as per the Turkish in Cyprus, since it is difficult to draw a border to assist in the definition of a 'people'. Hannum, *Post-Colonial Era*, p. 31.
226. *Principles Which Should Guide Members in Determining Whether an Obligation Exists to Transmit the Information Called Under Article 73e*, GA Res 1541(XV), UN GAOR, 15th sess, 948th plen mtg, annex, (15 December 1960) Principle I.
227. This argument has been referred to as the 'metropolitan territory' argument. West Papua would be another example of a 'metropolitan territory': Sureda, *Evolution*.
228. This argument is supported by the fear that any disruption to an existing State could constitute a threat to international security, thus raising an inference that any people seeking self-determination will be 'inconsistent' or 'incompatible' with the purposes of the *UN Charter*.

colonial powers to mean European powers like Great Britain, France, Portugal and the Netherlands, which would restrict self-determination to situations of independence from European colonial rule.[229] Such an interpretation finds support with for example former Special Rapporteur Asbjorn Eide, who remarked that:

> Colonial territories are those beyond Europe brought under colonial or similar control by European States or by States subsequently populated by people of European stock. Efforts to utilize the concept of colonialism to other situations confuse the problem, and should not be included under the concept of de-colonization.[230]

Clearly such an approach ignores the possibility of non-European empires, and is thus flawed.[231] This flaw can be seen from examining Indonesia, a beneficiary of the successful decolonisation process, and the subsequent denial of the West Papuans' claim to self-determination.

2. Indonesia and West Papua

Indonesia was a former Dutch colony known as Netherlands East Indies. Indonesia exercised its right of self-determination essentially through an agreement to transfer sovereignty from the Dutch government.[232] The borders of the new State, Indonesia, coincided almost exactly with the former colony, and as such included Netherlands New Guinea, which became the province of West Irian (referred to as West Papua).[233]

In 1961 the Dutch government placed before the General Assembly a draft resolution seeking the establishment of a UN Commission to examine the possibility of holding a UN-supervised plebiscite in West Papua to determine the question of self-determination for the former province. The Dutch argued that the inhabitants of West Papua were distinctly different ethnically from the rest of the inhabitants of Indonesia and also were politically unprepared for independence.[234] It is not clear whether the Dutch were motivated

229. Sureda, *Evolution*, p. 237.
230. Eide, *Constructive Alternatives*, p. 153.
231. The approach taken by the UN also ignored those European powers, such as Russia, that did not indulge in 'saltwater colonization'. Hence Chechnya was not classified as a colony during the decolonisation period.
232. The *Charter of Transfer of Sovereignty*, signed in 1949, as cited in Adam Schwarz, *A Nation in Waiting: Indonesia's Search for Stability*, (2nd ed) Boulder: Westview Press, 2000, p. 5; Sureda, *Evolution*, pp. 325–29, 77.
233. However, it did not include East Timor, which was then a Portuguese colony.
234. Sureda, *Evolution*, p. 70, p. 77 & pp. 143–51 & 237. The Dutch proposal was an attempt to apply *Declaration on Colonial Peoples*, UN Doc A/RES/1514 (XV) (14 December 1960): Keith Suter, *East Timor, West Papua/Irian and Indonesia*, Minority Rights Group International, 1997, p. 21.

by the desire to retain control over West Papua for their own benefit, or were simply determined to ensure that West Papua remained out of Indonesia's clutches.

Indonesia's response was to confirm that West Papua was, and historically always had been, part of the territory of Indonesia. So when Indonesia had, by its declaration of independence on 17 August 1945, exercised its right to self-determination, so too had the people of West Papua. Furthermore, the Indonesian government argued that a colony was a territory administered by a power that had no geographical link with the territory.[235] Thus, *the people* of West Papua were not distinct from Indonesians. They were merely one of the many different ethnic groups that comprised the 'people' of Indonesia. Accordingly, Indonesia argued, the Dutch proposal constituted interference in the territorial integrity of Indonesia.[236]

The Indonesian position was reinforced by the lack of international support for the Netherlands, from both the West, particularly the US and Australia, and from the non-aligned movement.[237] The US had applied substantial pressure on the Dutch to surrender West Papua to Indonesia because of their fear that Indonesia was becoming too close to the former USSR.[238] The approach taken by the General Assembly was essentially to do nothing. By implication, this supported the Indonesian argument that West Papua was (and had always been) part of the territory that now formed Indonesia.[239]

However, the Indonesian government later agreed to hold a referendum, where 1,025 tribal leaders chose integration with Indonesia, and subsequently, through the so-called *Act of Free Choice*, of 1969, West Papua was

235. Indonesia also used political control, both existing and historical, as a defining characteristic for the identification of a people. Indonesia's argument was no doubt influenced by the desire to keep its territory united (and perhaps by the wealth of West Papua's natural resources). Sureda, *Evolution*, p. 149.
236. The Indonesian reply was made in an explanatory memorandum to the General Assembly (UN Doc A/ 2694): Ibid, pp. 143–51.
237. Most of the Netherlands' European allies were themselves facing decolonisation issues, and other Asian States in the non-aligned movement naturally favoured Indonesia, which was one of their leaders: Gregory Pemberton, *All the Way: Australia's Road to Vietnam*, Sydney: Allen and Unwin, 1987, p. 103; Suter, *East Timor*, p. 21; Peter King, *West Papua and Indonesia since Suharto: Independence, Autonomy or Chaos?*, Sydney: UNSW Press, 2004, pp. 19–22.
238. At the time the Dutch administration handed over control to the United Nations Temporary Executive Authority, the USSR had brokered a huge arms deal with Indonesia, prompting the US to make a similar deal. In fact Komer, the then senior member of the US Security Council, described West Papua as the 'price' for ensuring Indonesia did not become communist. West Papua was a 'cold war sacrifice': K Peart, '*A Brief History of West Papua*', West Papua Association 4 <http://www.converge.org.nz/wpapua/history.html> (accessed at 18 October 2008).
239. Sureda, *Evolution*, pp. 150–1.

renamed as Irian Jaya, and became a province of Indonesia.[240] Although the General Assembly approved the referendum, many commentators consider it a 'farce',[241] and the so-called *Act of Free Choice* as illegal[242] and a denial of West Papua's right to self-determination.[243] However, it is not likely that *Act of Free Choice* will ever be repealed, since to do so would require an examination of the UN's actions, and such a review is likely to be politically unpalatable.[244]

It is quite clear that the Dutch and the Indonesian governments had different interpretations about what constituted a colony and what, therefore, was the definition of a people able to exercise their right to self-determination. The Dutch proposal involved identifying a 'people' by their ethnic/racial characteristics – their language, religion, and social structure. In other words, the Dutch adopted a 'nationalist approach'.[245] Indonesia, on the other hand, argued that West Papua was part of the territory of Indonesia. By insisting on the protection of a colony's territorial integrity when it becomes independent, the reference to the population of that territory must mean the population as a whole.[246] As noted by Radan: 'The preservation of the territorial integrity of [S]tates can be enhanced by confining the meaning of a people to the population of a [S]tate as a whole'.[247]

240. Suter, *East Timor*, pp. 21–2. King, *West Papua*, pp. 19–20.
241. This was because the Indonesians did not allow all 700,000 West Papuans to vote in the referendum. Instead only 1,025 tribal elders were eligible to vote as representatives of the West Papuan people. In fact UN officials only observed 200 of the these leaders cast their vote, which was apparently made by simply walking over a line drawn on the ground after TNI and Indonesian officials had 'lectured' them. Indonesia was able to determine the process of the 'referendum' since it had gained control over the United Nations Temporary Executive Authority, the UN administrative body supervising the political development of the West Papuans people since May 1963. Also by this stage the anti-communist Suharto had won lot of support from the US: Suter, *East Timor*, p. 21; King, *West Papua*, pp. 19–22; Peart, *A Brief History*, p. 5.
242. Peart, *A Brief History*, p. 5.
243. For example Michela Noonan, Peter King and John Wing, *Peace Building and Development in West Papua – Dialogue versus Violence: Hearing Other Voices: A Report of Workshop IV, August 16–17, 2004*, Position Paper No 5, November 2004, p. 8. See also Stuart Rees, John O Ondawame and Peter King, *Reconciliation and Consolidation Among Papuans: Report on Workshop III*, Centre for Peace and Conflict Studies, The West Papua Project, Position Paper No 4, January 2003, p. 9, 12 <http://www.arts.usyd.edu.au/cpacs>; K Peart, above n 245, 5.
244. Rees, Ondawame and King, *Reconciliation*, p. 11.
245. They also included the West Papuans' lack of political sophistication.
246. Cassese, *A Legal Reappraisal*, pp. 72–3. Radan, *The Break-up of Yugoslavia*, p. 33, 39.
247. Radan, *The Break-up of Yugoslavia*, p. 33.

3. Territorial integrity

The principle of territorial integrity is stated in art 2(4) of the *UN Charter*:

> All Members shall refrain in their international relations from the threat or use of force against the territorial integrity or political independence of any [S]tate, or in any other manner inconsistent with the Purposes of the United Nations.[248]

Territorial integrity is also mentioned in both the 1960 *Declaration on Colonial Peoples* and the 1970 *Declaration on Friendly Relations*.[249] The *Declaration on Friendly Relations* is more expansive and provides an illustration of what the concept seeks to prevent:

> Nothing in the foregoing paragraphs shall be construed as authorizing or encouraging any action that would dismember or impair, totally or in part, the territorial integrity or political unity of sovereign and independent States conducting themselves in compliance with the principles of equal rights and self-determination of peoples as described above and thus possessed of a government representing the whole people belonging to the territory without distinction as to race, creed, or colour.[250]

There is nothing stated specifically in art 2 (4) or 2 (7) of the *UN Charter* that clearly identifies the pre-eminence of territorial integrity over self-determination. However, the wording used in the *Declaration on Friendly Relations* combined with the placement of territorial integrity *after* the right to self-determination in both Declarations raises what Blay describes as one of the persistent controversies associated with self-determination – does self-determination or territorial integrity take precedence?[251]

Certainly both States, and at times the UN, have used the territorial integrity argument when it suited them.[252] The UN, when faced with

248. *UN Charter* art 2(7).

249. Both Declarations state that any attempt to disrupt the territorial integrity of States is 'incompatible with the purposes and principles of the Charter': *Declaration on Colonial Peoples*, UN Doc A/RES/1514 (XV) *Declaration on Friendly Relations*, UN Doc A/RES/2625(XXV).

250. *Declaration on Friendly Relations*, UN Doc A/RES/2625(XXV).

251. Sam K N Blay, 'Self-Determination Versus Territorial Integrity in Decolonization', 18 (1985–1986) *New York Journal of International Law and Politics*, p. 441; Hill, *Principle of Self-Determination*, p. 128.

252. For example, the Indian Representative to the Security Council made a similar statement that the right of self-determination was available to 'nations and States and cannot be used for the breaking up of a state or fragmentation of peoples': Upadhyaya, *Quest*, p. 169. The Indonesians raised a similar argument in relation to claims made by West Papuans and the

self-determination claims in both Cyprus and the Congo, supported the territorial integrity of the State over claims for self-determination.[253]

Recently, the Supreme Court of Canada, when considering the question of Quebec's secession, accepted that territorial integrity overrode the principle of self-determination because 'self-determination has evolved within a framework of respect of the territorial integrity of existing [S]tates.'[254] Secondly, the court's interpretation was based on the fact that the right to self-determination, as contained in international documents, was *immediately and subsequently followed* by a reference to the right of territorial integrity.[255]

Authors such as Asbjorn Eide, who justifies this position on the basis that the overriding concern for the international community was stability of *States*, would agree.[256] Blay also argues that territorial integrity pre-empts self-determination in claims made by people living in an already-established sovereign State, or when an administering authority attempts to 'dismember' a colonial territory prior to independence.[257] However, he qualifies his findings, arguing that self-determination takes precedence over a sovereign State's *claim to a unified colonial territory*,[258] that is, self-determination takes precedence over territorial integrity in cases of decolonisation.[259] Others, such as Radan, also qualify the right to territorial integrity.

According to Radan, the context of art 2(4) of the *UN Charter* would suggest that the principle is directed at members of the UN – States – and therefore logically not intended to apply to a challenge to territorial integrity from *within a Member State*. This interpretation is supported by art 2(7) of the *UN Charter*, which prohibits intervention by one State in the domestic affairs of another – that is, when the State is facing an internal challenge.[260]

Despite its prevalence, the argument that territorial integrity takes precedence over self-determination, and thus determines whether a people are

Dutch. See the explanatory memorandum to the General Asssembly (UN Doc A/ 2694) cited in Sureda, *Evolution*, pp. 143–51.

253. Respectively: *Resolution 1600 (XV)*, UN Doc A/RES/1600 (XV); *Resolution 3212*, UN Doc A/RES/3212 (XXXIX).
254. *Reference re Secession of Quebec* [1998] 2 SCR 217, 287.
255. The Canadian Supreme Court examined the *Declaration on Friendly Relations*, the *Vienna Declaration*, the *Declaration on the Occasion of the Fiftieth Anniversary of the United Nations*, and the *Helsinki Final Act*. The court also relied on expert opinions from the court's *amicus curiae*: Ibid, p. 217, 289.
256. Eide, *Constructive Alternatives*, p. 147.
257. Blay, *Self-Determination Versus Territorial Integrity in Decolonization*, p. 472.
258. Ibid.
259. Ibid.
260. With the exception of when the challenge poses a threat to international security, and attracts intervention according to Chapter VII of the *UN Charter*: art 2(7); Radan, *The Break-up of Yugoslavia*, pp. 36–37.

legitimately entitled to claim self-determination, should be rejected for several reasons.

Firstly, the *Declaration of Colonial Peoples*, which articulates the need to protect territorial integrity, does so *only if* the concept of self-determination has been complied with.[261] In the *Declaration on Friendly Relations* the right to territorial integrity is also conditional on the State complying with the principle of equal rights, and with the right to self-determination.[262]

Secondly, if self-determination is a principle of *jus cogens*, as some commentators claim,[263] then self-determination should override the principle of territorial integrity. In the *Application of the Convention on the Prevention and Punishment of the Crime of Genocide*, His Excellency Judge Lauterpacht discussed whether Security Council Resolution (713 of 1991), implementing the arms embargo in the conflict in Bosnia-Herzegovina, contradicted a principle of *jus cogens*.[264] His Honour made it clear that a right or principle of international law that is *jus cogens* is: 'superior to both customary international law and treaty.'[265]

Thirdly, if international stability and security is a relevant factor,[266] then regard should be had for the amount of violence and international instability caused when self-determination is denied.[267] Whilst the norm of territorial integrity, like the norm of non-intervention, does play an important role in the maintenance of peace and security, it should not be abused, or used to perpetuate gross violations of human rights. As Wayne Norman stated:

> The famous principle of territorial integrity is morally progressive in so far as it forbids aggressive interstate wars; but it cannot be treated as

261. Simpson, *Diffusion*, p. 283.
262. Radan, *The Break-up of Yugoslavia*, p. 39.
263. In accordance with *Vienna Convention*, opened for signature 23 May 1969, 1155 UNTS 331, arts 31–33 (entered into force 27 January 1980) art 53. Hector Gros-Espiell, stated in his report that the right to self-determination was *jus cogens*: Hector Gros-Espiell, *The Right to Self-Determination of United Nations Resolutions*, New York: UN, 1980; Cassese, *A Legal Reappraisal*, pp. 133–40; Lauri Hanniainen, 'The Case of Western Sahara from the Perspective of *Jus Cogens*' in Arts and Leite, *The Question of Western Sahara*, p. 60; Ian Brownlie, *Principles of Public International Law*, (6th ed) Oxford: Oxford University Press, 2003, p. 489; *Barcelona Traction, Light and Power Company Limited (Belgium v Spain) (Second Phase)* [1970] ICJ Rep 3, 304 (Separate Opinion of Judge Ammoun). Others such as Pomerance oppose this view: Michla Pomerance, *Self-Determination in Law and Practice*, Baltimore: Johns Hopkins University Press, 1982, p. 71.
264. His Honour's finding was that art 103 of the *UN Charter* will not allow the UN Security Council relief and that the resolution would be of no legal effect. Effectively such a finding would be *ultra vires*, and should be brought to the attention of the Security Council when reconsidering the arms embargo: *Application of the Convention on the Prevention and Punishment of the Crime of Genocide (Bosnia Herzegovina v Yugoslavia) (Provisional Measures) (Orders)* [1993] ICJ Rep 325, 440.
265. Ibid.
266. Radan, *The Break-up of Yugoslavia*, p. 35.
267. See the Introduction.

legitimating *any* possible action of a government within its internationally secured frontiers.[268]

Fourthly, as a consequence of Blay's conclusion above (territorial integrity pre-empts self-determination claims by people living in an already established sovereign State), once a former colony achieves independence, and becomes a sovereign State, any further claims are nullified.[269] It is submitted that this is logically an inconsistent application of the principle of self-determination.[270] If the Croatian people in the former republic of Croatia of the Former Socialist Republic of Yugoslavia were entitled to self-determination then all other groups within Croatia, such as the Serbs in Krajina, should be as well.[271] Perhaps the denial of self-determination in these situations can be justified on the basis of minimising the 'domino effect' – the apparently unending claims leading to the continual dismemberment of a State. If so, then it allows non-European States such as Indonesia to argue that they cannot be defined as colonial masters.[272] This enables a continuation of an unjust government. This result is not consistent with the purpose of self-determination.

Finally, the ICJ, in the recent *Kosovo Opinion*, after referring to the *Declaration on Friendly Relations* and the *Vienna Convention*, stated that 'the scope of the principle of territorial integrity is confined to the sphere of relations between States.'[273] The Court's conclusion, although somewhat controversial, *is consistent* with the wording used in international instruments to refer to the principle of territorial integrity.[274]

268. Norman, *Ethics of Secession*, p. 34, 43.
269. Radan, *The Break-up of Yugoslavia*, p. 22. The attempted secession of Katanga from the Congo in 1960 and Biafra from Nigeria in 1967 are two other examples.
270. See Ian Brownlie's criticism of limiting self-determination in this manner: Brownlie, *The Rule of Law*, p. 44; Michla Pomerance, 'The Badinter Commission: The Use and Misuse of the International Court of Justice's Jurisprudence', 20 (1998–99) *Michigan Journal of International Law*, p. 56.
271. Radan, *The Break-up of Yugoslavia*, p. 177, 218; Hurst Hannum, 'The Specter of Secession: Responding to Claims for Ethnic Self-Determination' *Foreign Affairs* 77(2), 1998, 17; Thomas Franck, *Fairness in International Law and Institutions*, Oxford: Clarendon Press, 1995, p. 167; D Kofman, 'Secession, Law, and Rights: The Case of Former Yugoslavia', 1(2) (2000) *Human Rights Review*, p. 13.
272. India is another example, and the US also was faced with this question over its dealings with the Trust Territory of Pacific Islands or Micronesia. The US was revealed to be a colonial power: Willens and Siemer, *National Security*, p. 3.
273. *Accordance with International Law of the Unilateral Declaration of Independence by the Provisional Institutions of Self-Government of Kosovo (Request for Advisory Opinion)* [2010] ICJ Rep 403, 437 [80] ('*Kosovo Opinion*'). See also Vidmar's criticism of this part of the Court's Opinion: Jure Vidmar, 'The *Kosovo* Opinion Scrutinized', 24 (2011) *Leiden Journal of International Law*, pp. 368–371.
274. For example, the *Declaration on Friendly Relations*,states: 'Every State has the duty to refrain in its international relations from the threat or use of force against the territorial integrity or political independence of any State': *Annex to The Declaration on Friendly Relations*,

4. Conclusion

Not only would it be racist, and incredibly naïve, to argue that only European peoples are capable of being colonizers but it would but also ignorant of reality, a 'misperception'.[275] Tony Smith neatly sums this up:

> Like a chameleon changing colors, imperialism may be expected to appear in a different form but with similar consequences. We would be naïve indeed not to anticipate that among its chief practitioners may well be some of its former victims and most outspoken critics.[276]

Gerry Simpson remarked 'The end of Empire has merely revealed most states to be imperial.'[277] History is full of non-European empires, but most of these developed before the industrial revolution enabled European States to dominate the globe.[278] Hasan Di Tiro, the founder of the Free Aceh Movement, or GAM,[279] wrote in his *Unfinished Diaries*:

> Decolonisation requires liquidation of all colonial empires with specific steps and procedures, but Indonesia exists on the principle of total territorial integrity of the colonial empire; and an empire is not liquidated if its territorial integrity is preserved, Thus Indonesia is still un-liquidated and un-decolonised colonial empire with Java-men replacing Dutchmen as colonialists.[280]

Other commentators have also described Indonesia as a Javanese empire.[281] It is my opinion that, whilst Indonesia may not have created an empire, it

Principle 1. Vidmar argues that the Court's conclusion is questionable due to the unnecessary restatement of the principle in consecutive paragraphs. I disagree with Vidmar's interpretation. The later paragraphs are merely an elaboration. Furthermore, the *Declaration* consistently repeats the term 'State' whenever stating or describing an obligation, or a variation of a previously mentioned obligation contained therein. For example, 'Every State has the duty to refrain from organizing or encouraging the organization of irregular forces' and 'Every State has the duty to refrain from organizing…or participating in acts of civil strife'. See Vidmar, *Kosovo Opinion Scrutinized*, pp. 368, 71.

275. Connie Peck, *The United Nations As a Dispute Settlement System: Improving Mechanisms for the Prevention and Resolution of Conflict*, The Hague: Kluwer Law International, 1996, pp. 46–47.
276. Tony Smith, 'Introduction' in Tony Smith (ed), *The End of the European Empire: Decolonisation after World War II*, Lexington: DC Heath and Company, 1975, i, xvi.
277. Simpson, *Diffusion*, p. 255.
278. Such as the Mongol, Arabic, Ottoman, and Chinese empires: Marc Ferro, *Colonization: A Global History*, New York: Routledge, 1997, viii; Summers, *Peoples*, p. 208.
279. Gerakan Aceh Merdeka (Bahasa: Indonesia).
280. As cited in John Martinkus, *Indonesia's Secret War in Aceh*, Milson's Point: Random House Australia, 2004, p. 57.
281. See, eg, David Harris, *Let Aceh Hold an Independence Referendum*, 18 January 2000, *Wall Street Journal*, <http://acehnet.tripod.com/referendum.html> Adam Schwarz, *A Nation in*

certainly inherited, and now maintains, one. Indonesian government policies, such as *pancacila*,[282] and *transmigrasi*,[283] reveal the imperialistic nature of the Indonesian government.[284]

To restrict decolonisation to European decolonisation would ignore the issue of whether the people seeking self-determination were oppressed by a colonial overlord.[285] This contradicts the very premise upon which self-determination was based – to remove oppression by a foreign or alien power.[286] It is nonsense to think that *only* Europeans can use armed force to *subjugate populations inhabiting a territory or oppress peoples.* Furthermore, peoples do not *only* identify themselves by the fact that they were colonised by a European power or not, but they do identify themselves as being colonised or oppressed generally. There are many non-European colonies in existence today where peoples are still being oppressed by an administering power that, to the peoples involved, constitute a *foreign and alien power.*[287]

Oppression can lead to serious repercussions. The denial of independence to West Papua has resulted in a conflict that has cost 100,000 West Papuan lives, and, although one of the wealthiest in terms of natural resources, West Papua is currently one of Indonesia's poorest provinces.[288] West Papuans still

Waiting, p. 3; Mieke Kooistra, *Indonesia: Regional Conflicts and State Terror*, Report of the Minority Rights Group International, June 2001, 13; King, *West Papua*, p. 76.

282. *Pancacila* includes five principles as follows: one supreme God; justice and civility among peoples; *the unity of Indonesia*; democracy through deliberation and consensus among representatives; and social justice for all: Kooistra, *Indonesia: Regional Conflicts*, pp. 13–15; Schwarz, *A Nation in Waiting*, p. 10, 24.
283. Aimed at relieving population pressure on Java, this policy has caused huge problems within West Papua. For example, in West Papua, 750,000 mainly Javanese migrants have arrived, forcing an estimated 30,000 West Papuan refugees to flee to Papua New Guinea. West Papuans are fast becoming a minority in West Papua: Dr Jim Elmslie, Centre for Peace and Conflict Studies, *West Papua: Genocide, Demographic Change, the Issue of 'Intent', and the Australia-Indonesia Security Treaty*, The West Papua Project http://www.arts.usyd.edu.au/centres/cpacs/docs/Indo%20Solidarity%20paper.pdf (accessed 26 June 2012).
284. Schwarz, *A Nation in Waiting*, p. 10; King, *West Papua*, p. 77.
285. Simpson, *Diffusion*, p. 273.
286. Anne Orford, *Reading Humanitarian Intervention: Human Rights and the Use of Force in International Law*, Cambridge: Cambridge University Press, 2003, p. 145; Sureda, *Evolution*, pp. 260–62. It is here where the example of Oman becomes important.
287. West Papua is one example. The Palestinians are another, so too East Timor before its successful independence, and the Tibetans.
288. It has the poorest health standards of Indonesia, with the highest infant and maternal mortality rate, the highest HIV-infection rate, and the lowest 'quality of life' in Indonesia, which in 1995 was, in fact, the lowest worldwide: Suter, *East Timor*, p. 20; John Wing and Peter King, *Genocide in West Papua? The Role of the Indonesian State Apparatus and a Current Needs Assessment of the Papuan People*, Centre for Peace and Conflict Studies, West Papua Project, August 2005, pp. 8–11, 29. See also Noonan, (et al) *Peace Building*, p. 12.

claim they were denied self-determination.[289] This has had consequences for its people.

After the end of the Cold War the issue of alien subjugation arose again in relation to the Canadian province of and the break-up of the Former Socialist Republic of Yugoslavia.

E. End of the Cold War

The end of the Cold War saw a proliferation of documents containing a reference to self-determination, and also a right to a democratic government, beginning with the Final Act of the Conference on Security and Cooperation in Europe (referred to as the CSCE), adopted on 1 August 1975, and its *Declaration on the Principles Concerning Mutual Relations.*[290] Other documents include the *African Charter on Human and People's Rights* ('Banjul Charter'),[291] the *Vienna Declaration,*[292] and the 2006 *Declaration on the Rights of Indigenous Peoples.*[293]

1. The Banjul Charter

In 1979 the Heads of State and government representatives of the member States of the Organisation of African Unity (now African Union) sought to emulate the example set in Europe and the Americas, and passed a resolution seeking to create a regional charter on human rights.[294] This led to the

289. Currently West Papua has 'special autonomy' implemented as part of the *reformasi* on 1 January 2003. Whilst some authors have argued that autonomy has benefits, as many as two-thirds of West Papuans have rejected autonomy, and see autonomy as merely a necessary incremental step towards achieving independence: King, *West Papua*, pp. 52–67, 81–94; Rees, Ondawame and King, *Reconciliation.*
290. The Final Act was reaffirmed on 29 June 1990, at a meeting in Copenhagen of the CSCE's Conference on Human Dimension, when the adoption of specific references to free and fair elections were seen as the means by which the will of the people should be expressed. The Chiefs of State of 34 CSCE members also adopted the *Charter of Paris for a New Europe* and the *Moscow Declaration* on 3 October 1991, both of which supported the CSCE's earlier pronouncements on a valid exercise of the right to self-determination: Jean Salmon, 'Internal Aspects of the Right to Self-Determination' in Tomuschat, *Modern Law,* pp. 268–72.
291. Organization of African Unity, *African Charter on Human and People's Rights,* 27 June 1981, CAB/LEG/67/3 rev. 5, 21 I.L.M. 58 (1982) ('*Banjul Charter*').
292. *Vienna Declaration and Programme for Action,* A/CONF.157/23 12 July 1993 ('Vienna Declaration').
293. United Nations, *Declaration on Indigenous Peoples,* adopted by the *General Assembly* 2 October 2007, A/Res/61/295, available at <www.un.org/esa/socdev/unpfii/documents/DRIPS_en.pdf> (accessed 30 Mar 2013).
294. In contrast with other international instruments the *Banjul Charter* only took 30 days to draft: F Ouguergouz, *The African Charter of Human and People's Rights: A Comprehensive*

adoption of the Banjul Charter in Nairobi, Kenya, on 27 June 1981.[295] By 1999, all member-States of the OAU had ratified the Banjul Charter.[296]

Article 20 of the Charter provides a right to self-determination of peoples. In particular, it provides that:

1. All peoples shall have the right to existence. They shall have the unquestionable and inalienable right to self-determination. They shall freely determine their political status and shall pursue their economic and social development according to the policy they have freely chosen.
2. Colonized or oppressed peoples shall have the right to free themselves from the bonds of domination by resorting to any means recognized by the international community.
3. All peoples shall have the right to the assistance of the State Parties to the present Charter in their liberation struggle against foreign domination, be it political, economic or cultural.

Another relevant article of the Charter is Article 19, which proclaims that 'all peoples shall be equal; they shall enjoy the same respect and shall have the same rights' and 'nothing shall justify the domination of a people by another.'

2. Vienna Declaration 1993[297]

The *Vienna Declaration and Programme for Action* arose from the World Conference on Human Rights held in Vienna on the 14–25 June 1993.[298] It was endorsed by the UN General Assembly on 20 December 1993.[299] Essentially the *Vienna* Declaration re-affirmed human rights instruments such as the *Universal Declaration of Human Rights* and proposals on how to implement human rights. The *Vienna Declaration* refers to self-determination in the preamble, and in greater detail in paragraph 2 where it states:

> All peoples have the right of self-determination. By virtue of that right they freely determine their political status, and freely pursue their economic, social and cultural development.

Agenda, for Human Dignity And Sustainable Democracy in Africa, The Hague: Martinus Nihoff Publishers, 2003, p. 48.

295. *Banjul Charter*, 27 June 1981, CAB/LEG/67/3 rev. 5, 21 I.L.M. 58 (1982), art 45.
296. *History of the African Charter*, African Commission on Human and Peoples' Rights, <www.achpr.org/instruments/achpr/history/> (accessed 30 Mar 2013).
297. *Vienna Declaration*, A/CONF.157/23 12 July 1993.
298. Ibid.
299. Ibid.

> Taking into account the particular situation of peoples under colonial *or other alien domination or foreign occupation*, the World Conference on Human Rights recognizes the right of peoples to take any legitimate action, in accordance with the Charter of the United Nations, to realize their inalienable right of self-determination. The World Conference on Human Rights and underlines the importance of the effective realization of this right.[300]

Paragraph 2 then goes on to state that:

> this shall not be construed as authorizing or encouraging any action which would dismember or impair, totally or in part, the territorial integrity or political unity of sovereign and independent States conducting themselves in compliance with the principle of equal rights and self-determination of peoples and thus possessed of a Government representing the whole people belonging to the territory without any distinction of any kind.[301]

3. Declaration on the Rights of Indigenous Peoples

For better or worse, it is generally accepted that indigenous peoples are not entitled to external self-determination, and are restricted to internal self-determination.[302] The 2006 *Indigenous Peoples Declaration* is proof of this. Whilst art 3 of the *Declaration* does recognize the right of indigenous peoples to self-determination, art 4 restricts the scope of that right to 'autonomy or self-government in matters relating to their internal or local affairs, as well as ways and means for financing their autonomous functions.' Furthermore, art 46(1) refers to territorial integrity, and clarifies that:

> Nothing in this declaration may be interpreted as...authorizing or encouraging any action which would dismember or impair, totally or in part, the territorial integrity or political unity of sovereign and independent States.'

300. Ibid, p. 2.
301. Ibid.
302. Some commentators argue that if a State abuses the human rights of their indigenous peoples, then those peoples are entitled to independence or *external self-determination.* Sanders, *Self-Determination and Indigenous Peoples*, p. 78; Daniel Philpott, 'In Defense of Self-Determination', 105 (1995) *Ethics*, p. 382.

Although this monograph focuses on the external right to self-determination, it is appropriate to mention the above instrument because it too provides some guidance on legitimacy, and also on how States sought to reduce the operation of self-determination.

The drafting of the *2006 Declaration* began in 1982 and after a long and difficult journey was concluded in 2006, with the UN Human Rights Council recommending adoption by the UN General Assembly.[303] The General Assembly did so approximately 18 months later.[304] The *2006 Declaration* was adopted by a recorded vote with 143 in favour, 11 abstaining, and 4 'nos'– Canada, Australia, New Zealand, and the US. Notably all four States have substantial populations of communities that would fall within the definition of 'indigenous peoples',[305] although Australia and New Zealand quickly changed their stance with formal statements released by their respective governments.[306]

The drafting process revealed how concerned States were with the potential consequences of a broad definition of indigenous peoples, specifically peoples.[307] Canada in particular wanted to it make clear that whatever term was used, it would not result in a right to secession.[308] However, the result was that the term peoples remained undefined and ambiguous, just as in other international instruments. States preferred this uncertainty. Summers argues that this uncertainty benefits States since it enabled them to define who were the beneficiaries.[309] China, whilst expressing concern for the definition, stated they had no indigenous peoples – a neat solution.[310] Australia and Russia proposed that the solution lay in allowing States the ability to

303. UN Human Rights Council Resolution 1/2, 29 June 2006, *Official Records of the General Assembly, Sixty-First Session, Supplement No 53* (A/61/53), Part One, chap. II, sect. A. p. 76.
304. United Nations, *Declaration on Indigenous Peoples*, adopted by the *General Assembly* 2 October 2007, A/Res/61/295, available at <www.un.org/esa/socdev/unpfii/documents/DRIPS_en.pdf> (accessed 30 Mar 2013).
305. See *Official Records of the General Assembly* 61st sess, 107th plenary mtg, 13th Sept 2007, UN Doc A/61/PV.107.
306. See for example, Australia's statement made by the Hon Jenny Macklin, then Federal Minister for Families, Community Service and Indigenous Affairs, *United Nations Declaration on the Rights of Indigenous Peoples*, 3 April 2009. The change in the Australian government's position was due to a change of government by general election. See jennymacklin.fahcsia.gov.au/node/1711, (accessed 26 June 2013).
307. The term 'population' was suggested instead of 'peoples'. See Summers' excellent discussion of this point at Summers, *Peoples*, pp. 244–5.
308. Secession and 'to secede' were used by Canada, rather than external self-determination. Thus, I make my opinion conjuring an image of 'illegality': 'Report on the Working Group on Indigenous Populations on its Eleventh Session, Addendum, Comments made by Canada', UN Doc E/CN.4/Sub.2/1993/29/Add.1 (27th August 1993).
309. Summers, *Peoples*, pp. 246–254.
310. As noted by Summers, this was a deliberate attempt to ensure the inapplicability of the Declaration to any of China's 'minorities': Summers, *Peoples*, p. 245.

define indigenous peoples themselves through domestic legislation.[311] Summers' argument is persuasive since a broad, potentially unlimited definition of peoples enabled States to successfully argue that the self-determination needed to be 'balanced' by norms such as territorial integrity, and also by restricting self-determination to its internal aspect.[312]

Representatives of indigenous communities and NGOs argued that self-determination in international law *was unrestricted, and universal*.[313] However, even they accepted the argument that self-determination must be balanced.[314] Thus, despite the attempts by indigenous peoples to reassure States that independent statehood was not on their agenda, States were successful in ensuring the right of self-determination was restricted to its internal dimension.[315] And States ensured that the draft *Declaration* was amended to include a further limitation of respecting territorial integrity.[316] In sum, States sought to qualify the right to self-determination, in order to minimise its potential effect on them.[317]

The end of the Cold War was interpreted by some as more than just a sign of the victory of democracy over Soviet-style socialism and communism. Some authors presumed that it signalled 'an end to history' and an end to the redrawing of political boundaries.[318] This assumption was rudely shattered by the spectacular collapse of the former USSR,[319] and by the violent end to the former Socialist Republic of Yugoslavia ('SFRY').[320] The subsequent recognition of the independent statehood of former republics from SFRY

311. 'Indigenous Issues', *Report of the Working Group Established in Accordance with Commission on Human Rights Resolution 1995/32'* UN Doc E/CN.4/1997/102, (10th Dec 1996), 46–7, [238] (Russia) [240] (Australia).
312. Even autonomy was going 'too far' and thus interfering in the domestic affairs of the State, according to Brazil: Ibid 64, [334]. Interestingly the Brazilian representative noted that whilst the constitution of Brazil 'guaranteed' self-determination, their government had problems with listing what the right entailed in the draft declaration; a double standard indeed.
313. Groups such as Aboriginal Land Council argued that the qualifications espoused by States were 'racist' and would breach international human rights norms of non-discrimination and equality. See Ibid [342], noting the submission by the Aboriginal and Torres Strait Islander Social Justice Commissioner.
314. Summers, *Peoples*, p. 251; Ibid, p. 62 [328].
315. See the statement made by the Cree in the Introduction to the monograph, explaining their perspective of self-determination: as cited Michael Igantieff, *Blood and Belonging*, London: Vintage, Random House, London 1994, pp. 125.
316. *Declaration on the Rights of Indigenous Peoples:* art 46(1).
317. This is despite the acceptance that the *Declaration on the Rights of Indigenous Peoples* was not legally binding.
318. See Francis Fukuyama, *The End of History and the Last Man*, New York: Free Press, 1992.
319. Tomuschat describes it in this way: 'History knows of no definitive halting point': Tomuschat, *Self-Determination in a Post-Colonial World*, pp. 6–7.
320. The author adopts Radan's use of the former Socialist Republic of Yugoslavia to describe Yugoslavia prior to 1991: Radan, *The Break-up of Yugoslavia*, pp. 134–53, 160–204. See also Payam Akhavan, 'Self-Determination and the Disintegration of Yugoslavia: What

brought awareness that the redrawing of political borders was not over, but more importantly raised questions of whether self-determination applied in 'non-colonial' situations.[321]

4. Yugoslavia

Yugoslavia was originally formed in 1918 by unifying three distinct ethnic groups; Serbs, Croats, and Slovenians. Whilst the names of the former republics generally reflected a dominant ethnic group,[322] this ethnic division by no means indicated that the republic itself was a result of colonialism by any of the ethnic groups.[323] This division was influential, but hardly the sole reason for the successful exercise of self-determination by four former republics; Slovenia,[324] Croatia,[325] Bosnia-Herzegovina,[326] and Macedonia.[327] Subsequently, Kosovo, formerly an autonomous province of Serbia, has also claimed independence.[328]

Lessons for the International Community?' in Clark and Williamson, *Self-Determination: International Perspectives*, p. 228; Hill, *Principle of Self-Determination*, pp. 130–2.

321. Akhavan, *Disintegration of Yugoslavia*, p. 239.
322. The SFRY comprised six republics; Serbia, Croatia, Slovenia, Bosnia-Herzegovina, Montenegro, and Macedonia. It also had two autonomous regions, Kosovo and Vojvodina: Hill, *Principle of Self-Determination*, pp. 130–32; Radan, *The Break-up of Yugoslavia*, pp. 135–59, 149–53; Ibid, p. 228.
323. Radan, *The Break-up of Yugoslavia*, pp. 229–30. I agree with Radan's conclusion, but not his reasoning.
324. Slovenia declared independence on 25 June 1991. The European Community recognised Slovenia in January 1992, the US on 7 April 1992, and the UN granted membership on 22 May 1992: Ibid pp. 167–74.
325. Independence was declared on 25th June 1991. However, due to fighting in the Serb dominated region of Krajina, Croatia's formal secession from the SFRY did not take place until 8 October 1991, and it was not recognised by the European Community until 15 January 1992, by the US until 7 April 1992, and was admitted as a member of the UN on 2 May 1992: Ibid, pp. 174–82.
326. The Republic of Bosnia-Herzegovina declared independence on 3 March 1992. Somewhat controversially the European Community granted recognition to the Republic of Bosnia-Herzegovina on 6 April 1992, followed by the US on 7 April 1992, and Bosnia-Herzegovina became a member of the UN on 22 May 1992: Ibid, pp. 183–93.
327. Despite an initial reluctance by the international community to grant recognition, all European Union member States except Greece granted recognition throughout 1993, and the UN admitted Macedonia on 8 April 1993: Ibid, pp. 193–6.
328. Kosovo declared independence on 17 February 2008. Since then 100 US states have recognised Kosovo's statehood, although the issue of Kosovo's UN membership is still undecided due to the fear that Russia may exercise its veto power. There is mounting pressure by the European Union and the US on Serbia to grant recognition. See *Who Recognized Kosova as an Independent State? The Kosovar People Thank You*, <www.kosovothanksyou.com/>; (accessed at 26 June 2013). Cedomir Antic, Senior Researcher at the Institute of Balkan Studies in Belgrade speaks on the US and German push for Serbia to regcognise Kosovo, *Serbia Squeezed Over Kosovo*, 5 March 2013, <english.ruvr.ru/2013_03_05/Serbia-squeezed-over-Kosovo-recognition/> (accessed 26 June 2013).

The break-up of the SFRY has important consequences for self-determination. Firstly, that self-determination can apply to 'non-colonial' peoples.[329] A second important point is that the European Community played an important role in the recognition of the new States.[330] The European Community based its policy on a number of opinions handed down by an Arbitration Commission formed as part of the European Community's Conference on Yugoslavia (the 'Badinter Commission').[331] The Commission, headed by Robert Badinter, made a number of legal 'rulings' in its opinions,[332] and these formed the basis of the European Community's policy towards the events in Yugoslavia. The Badinter Commission emphasized the use of a plebiscite as the means to determine the will of the inhabitants, especially when determining Bosnia-Herzegovina's claim for independence.[333]

Thirdly, whilst it would appear that the Badinter Commission used a territorial approach (since all the new States were former republics, and because constituent entities within each republic, such as Serb Krajina, were denied statehood), a more nationalist approach was, in fact, used.[334] Radan argues that that if a territorial approach was used, it must refer to all the inhabitants

329. Radan, *The Break-up of Yugoslavia*, p., 202 This interpretation should be viewed with care since the very first opinion supplied by the Badinter Commission suggested that the SFRY was in a 'process of dissolution': *Opinion No 1 of the Arbitration Commission of the Peace Conference on Yugoslavia* 31 ILM 1494 (1992); *Opinion No 8 of the Arbitration Commission of the Peace Conference on Yugoslavia* (1992) 31 ILM 1521.
330. The European Community announced its policy of recognition in its *Declaration on Yugoslavia*, and its *Declaration on the Guidelines on the Recognition of New States in Eastern Europe and in the Soviet Union*, *Guidelines on the Recognition of New States in Eastern Europe and the Soviet Union* (16 December 1991), as reproduced in David Harris, *Cases and Materials in International Law* (5th ed), London: Sweet & Maxwell, 1998, pp. 147–9; *EC Guidelines on the Recognition of New States in Eastern Europe and in the Soviet Union* 31 ILM 1485, (1992), pp. 1486–7 ('*EC Guidelines*').
331. Formed on 27 August 1991. See Peter Radan, 'Post-Secession International Borders: A Critical Analysis of the Opinions of the Badinter Commission' 24 (2000) *Melbourne University Law Review*, p. 52.
332. The Badinter Commission released a total of 16 opinions, 15 numbered and one unnumbered. For a discussion of the relative merits and criticisms of the Badinter Commission see Ibid 50; Thomas D Grant, *The Recognition of States: Law and Practice in Debate and Evolution*, Westport: Praeger 1999, pp. 153–68; Pomerance, *The Badinter Commission*.
333. Initially the Commission advised against recognising the region as a State until *three separate plebiscites be held for each of the three national groups* to determine the inhabitants' desire for independence. Sadly this was ignored by the European Union, which accepted the results of a single plebiscite despite a Serb boycott of that plebiscite: *Opinion No 4 on the International Recognition of the Socialist Republic of Bosnia-Herzegovina by the European Community and Its Members* 31 ILM 501 (1992) ('*Opinion No 4*'); Radan, *The Break-Up of Yugoslavia*, pp. 186–7.
334. However, he noted that the Badinter Commission did not adopt a purely nationalist approach, merely that a people in a sub-state unit could be considered to be a people: Peter Radan, *The Break-up of Yugoslavia*, pp. 220–21.

of the SFRY, and not to a portion of its inhabitants, who due to historical factors were organised in republics with a dominant ethnic group.[335] Radan's argument is further based upon the insistence of the Badinter Commission that three plebiscites be sued to determine the will of the inhabitants of Bosnia-Herzegovina,[336] and by the fact that a 'minority' could be classified as a people but were not entitled to independence.[337]

Certainly, each new State or former republic based their claim for independence upon their identification with an ethnic group, and did not define themselves by the territory they inhabited.[338] Other authors adopt a similar conclusion to Radan. As noted by Musgrave, the US and Western Europe's response to the Yugoslavia break-up indicated that they too supported the idea that a portion of the inhabitants of a territory can claim self-determination.[339] The fourth important point was the use of *uti possidetis* by the commission as the legal basis for the determination of the borders of the newly formed States.[340]

5. The secession of Quebec from Canada

The Canadian Supreme Court, when considering the issue of Quebec's independence, is perhaps the source of the most recent development in the self-determination discourse. On 30 October 1995 a referendum was held in Canada regarding Quebec's right to self-determination, and by the slimmest of margins the Canadian people decided Quebec remain part of Canada.[341] After the referendum was held the Canadian government asked the Supreme

335. Radan, *The Break-up of Yugoslavia*, pp. 220–21, 246.
336. *Opinion No 4*,31 ILM 501 (1992); Ibid p. 220.
337. Radan, *The Break-up of Yugoslavia*, p. 220.
338. This was evidenced by the wording used in numerous declarations regarding their claims for independence, and the new constitutions they created for their emerging State. For example, the Slovenian parliament used the expression 'the Slovene nation's right to self-determination' in its Declaration on the Sovereignty of the Republic of Slovenia: Ibid, p. 170. The 1990 Croatian Constitution proclaimed by the Croatian parliament on the 22 December 1990, stated: '[T]he Republic of Croatia is hereby established as the national state of the Croat nation, and a state of members of other nations and minorities who are its citizens': Ibid, p. 175.
339. Musgrave, *National Minorities*, pp. 123–4; Duursma, *Fragmentation*, p. 72; Ibid, p. 221.
340. *Opinion No 2 of the Arbitration Commission of the Peace Conference on Yugoslavia* 31 ILM 1497 (1992) ('*Opinion No 2*'); *Opinion No 3 of the Arbitration Commission of the Peace Conference on Yugoslavia* 31 ILM 1499,(1992) ('*Opinion No 3*').
341. By only 54 288 votes, or a 1.16 per cent majority: Montserrat Guibernau, *Nations Without States: Political Communities in a Global Age*, Oxford: Polity Press, 1999 p. 59. Alain-G Gagnon, 'Rethinking Multinational Space: The Quebec Referendum and Beyond' in Shlomo Ben-Ami, Yoav Pled and Alberto Spektorowski (eds), *Ethnic Challenges to the Modern Nation State*, 2000, 198. See also Shlomo Ben-Ami, Yoav Pled and Alberto Spektorowski (eds), *Ethnic Challenges to the Modern Nation State*, 2000, p. 206.

Court of Canada for an Advisory Opinion concerning the proposed *unilateral* secession of Quebec, and specifically to answer these three questions:[342]

(1) Under the Constitution of Canada can the National Assembly, legislature or government of Quebec effect the secession of Quebec from Canada unilaterally?
(2) Does international law give the National Assembly, legislature or government of Quebec the right to effect the secession of Quebec from Canada unilaterally? In this regard, is there a right to self-determination under international law that would give the National Assembly, legislature or government of Quebec the right to effect the secession of Quebec from Canada unilaterally?
(3) In the event of a conflict between domestic and international law on the right of the National Assembly, legislature or government of Quebec to effect the secession of Quebec from Canada unilaterally, which would take precedence in Canada?[343]

The Court, after confirming its jurisdiction to hear these questions provided the following responses.[344] With regard to the first question, the Court said that Quebec could only secede from Canada in accordance with the Constitution of Canada, or through 'principled negotiations' with the Canadian government that would reconcile the various rights and obligations of the Quebec and the remainder of Canada.[345] In essence Quebec could not 'dictate' a proposed secession on the other parties to the federation.[346] However, in spite of this, the other provinces, and the Canadian federal government, could not deny the people of Quebec's right to independence if a majority of Quebecois so choose, as long as they respected the rights of others.[347] The Court said:

> A clear majority in Quebec on a clear question in favour of secession would confer democratic legitimacy on the secession initiative, which all participants in Confederation would have to recognize.[348]

In relation to the second question the Court held that the right to self-determination in international law was only available to a people that were either: (1) part of a colonial empire; or (2) were subject to alien subjugation, domination or exploitation; or (3) 'were denied any meaningful

342. *Reference re Secession of Quebec* [1998] 2 SCR 217.
343. Ibid, p. 218.
344. Guibernau, *Nations Without States*, pp. 28–9.
345. *Reference re Secession of Quebec* [1998] 2 SCR 217, 223.
346. Essentially the other provinces of Canada: Ibid.
347. Ibid.
348. Ibid, pp. 222–3. Guibernau, *Nations Without States*, p. 28.

exercise of its right to self-determination within the state of which it forms a part.'.[349] The Court concluded that the people of Quebec did not satisfy any of these threshold questions,[350] and so were not entitled under international law to the right of self-determination, and thus secession from Canada.[351] Finally, the Court held that due to the answers to the preceding two questions, there was no conflict between international and domestic Canadian law.[352]

The Canadian Supreme Court's decision raised some important points. Firstly, although the Court rejected the idea that international law allows a component part of a State to secede unilaterally,[353] the term people was not defined by territory. Therefore, a people may include a portion of the entire population of a State.[354] The Court noted:

> The right to self-determination has developed largely as a human right, and is generally used in documents that simultaneously contain references to 'nation' and '[S]tate'. The juxtaposition of these terms is indicative that the reference to 'people' does not necessarily mean the entirety of a [S]tate's population. To restrict the definition of the term to the population of existing [S]tates would render emphasis within the majority of the source documents on the need to protect the territorial integrity of existing states, and would frustrate its remedial purpose.[355]

The Court also recognised that if Quebec did secede unilaterally, and in contradiction to domestic constitutional Canadian law, recognition by the international community could still be granted or conferred on Quebec. The court went on to say that whilst recognition was not necessary to prove statehood in international law, the viability of the newly emerged State was, in practical terms, dependent upon international recognition.[356] Although there

349. *Reference re Secession of Quebec* [1998] 2 SCR 217, 224–5. This third point refers to the internal component of self-determination: Radan, *The Break-up of Yugoslavia*, p. 68.
350. In relation to the third threshold the Canadian Supreme Court relied heavily on the advice provided by the court's *amicus curiae*, who noted in their factum that there was no evidence that the people of Quebec were an oppressed people, and had actively participated in the government of Canada: *Reference re Secession of Quebec* [1998] 2 SCR 217, 292.
351. Ibid, p. 225.
352. Ibid, p. 226.
353. Ibid, p. 282.
354. Ibid, p. 287; Radan, *The Break-up of Yugoslavia*, p. 50. Interestingly the Court did refer to colonial peoples in its first threshold, but the choice of words used to identify colonial peoples, 'part of a colonial empire', does not specify whether ethnic or territorial criteria were used.
355. *Reference re Secession of Quebec* [1998] 2 SCR 217, 287.
356. In effect the Canadian Supreme Court rejected the constitutive theory of recognition. The court also noted that whilst the act of recognition may be a political matter it was guided by legal norms: Ibid, p. 295. However, see criticism of this part of the court's decision

was no discussion of the future borders of Quebec, it would appear from the court's discussion of territorial integrity that the Court, in the absence of a negotiated settlement between Quebec and the federal government of Canada, would support an application of *uti possidetis juris.*[357]

6. Conclusion

From the above analysis of the historical evolution of the legal right to self-determination some conclusions can be drawn regarding how a Court can determine the legitimacy of a self-determination claim.

Firstly, self-determination was intended to apply to those peoples that were non-self-governing, and this included colonial peoples. This conclusion is uncontroversial. What has proven controversial, however, is the attempt of States to restrict the meaning of colonial peoples to those situated in 'traditional', that is, European, colonies.

Secondly, it is clear that States have actively avoided encouraging claims to independence. They used every trick in the book to limit or constrain the application of self-determination, for example, by adopting a territorial approach to define people or identifying a people as a colonial people. A territorial approach can be manipulated by running an argument supporting territorial integrity of the parent State. Restricting self-determination to colonial peoples has an obvious limiting effect. States have also argued that a claim to self-determination is subject to the application of *uti possidetis juris*, which would effectively render many claims to independence an illegal secession rather than an act of self-determination.

These arguments, if successful, have the effect of disenabling people within their territory from legally claiming self-determination. As Weller notes: 'governments have taken comfort in the fact that they have constructed the self-determination rule in a way that does not affect their ability to quash separatist groups.'[358] States, in general, would prefer self-determination to simply not exist as a legal norm of international law. While States do have the capacity to benefit from self-determination, for example India, they may seek to minimise the reciprocal impact by arguing that self-determination 'applies to others but not us'. In so doing they have almost constrained self-determination to such an extent that it cannot be exercised.[359]

Freedom from oppression and alien subjugation appears to be the golden thread that runs from the Aaland Islands Dispute through to the issue of

in Daniel Turp and Ginram van Ert, 'International Recognition in the Supreme Court of Canada's 36 (1998) *Quebec Reference*', *Canadian Yearbook of International Law*, pp. 342–45.

357. Radan, *The Break-up of Yugoslavia*, p. 226.

358. Marc Weller, *Escaping the Self-Determination Trap*, Leiden: Martinus Nijhoff Publishers, 2008, p. 35; Weller, *Why Rules*, p. 18.

359. Weller *Why Rules*, p. 23, 44–45.

Quebecois independence. It has been expressed in international instruments and Opinions of the ICJ, the most recent being the *Kosovo Opinion.* States, in constraining self-determination, are in effect putting their own interests added of peoples' freedom.

Clearly the example of Indonesia's treatment of West Papua showed that colonialism is not a purely European trait. Furthermore, the idea that colonial powers are only European contradicts the purpose of all the relevant international documents – to enable any people to remove themselves from foreign and alien power. Applying norms such as *uti possidetis juris* and territorial integrity can result in an injustice. They are both a 'means to an end'; their existence and intended application is to assist with the maintenance of international peace and security, and is not intended to enable human rights abuse, or importantly the continued alien and foreign subjugation of an oppressed people. This conclusion was reinforced by the recent *Kosovo Opinion,* which held that the norm of territorial integrity did not apply to peoples, rejecting one of the strongest arguments States put forward to restrict self-determination's operation.

Freedom from alien and foreign subjugation, then, could now potentially be seen as a defining characteristic of a colonial people – regardless of whether the colonial power is European or not – and therefore a fundamental requirement for claiming statehood.

F. Identifying the 'self' revisited: alien and foreign subjugation

In Part B it was argued that although different approaches could be used to identify the 'self', each of these approaches were similar since they sought to uncover a common identity. Aureliu Cristescu, after examining the international instruments above, as well as discussions regarding self-determination in the United Nations, is emphatic that the definition of a people should be as follows:[360]

> (a) The term 'people' denotes a social entity possessing a clear identity and its own characteristics;
> (b) It implies a relationship with a territory, even if the people in question has been wrongfully expelled from it and artificially replaced by another population;
> (c) A people should not be confused with ethnic, religious or linguistic minorities, whose existence and rights are recognised in art 27 of the International Covenant on Civil and Political Rights.[361]

360. Aureliu Cristescu, UN Doc. E/CN.4/Sub.2/404/Rev.1, 279.
361. Ibid.

His approach is essentially a hybrid approach and, as discussed in Part B, focuses on the establishment of a 'common identity'. No mention is made of alien subjugation, so it could be argued that it is not *necessary* to suffer subjugation in order to create a common identity, or consciousness.[362] In fact, it could be said that a group with a common identity are the ones subjugating others, since that is implied when speaking of colonies, colonial peoples, and colonizers. However, one of the factors that shaped a common identity mentioned in Part B was whether a group had been subject to alien or foreign subjugation. As noted by Knop, it is the act of colonisation that shapes the identity of a colonial people.[363] Other commentators analysing why States embark upon colonisation have concluded that the desire to dominate soon replaces all other motivating factors.[364] Some have taken this even further, and actually define imperialism in terms of domination.[365] For example, Summers noted:

> Independence has a value in itself. It means freedom and dignity. The drafting of UN instruments on decolonisation…are full of painful references to the basic *indignity* of foreign rule.'[366]

Thus, it is the desire to dominate over others that the legal right to self-determination seeks to overcome and prevent.[367] Accordingly, one way of identifying a colonial people is to identify those peoples that are subject to alien and foreign subjugation.

A number of international instruments refer to 'alien subjugation'. The *Declaration on Friendly Relations* states very specifically that alien subjugation was a violation of the principle of self-determination and also of fundamental human rights,[368] and the *Declaration on Colonial Peoples* states that the General

362. Although as also mentioned above, subjugation or a threat from a common enemy is a strong creative factor in the formation of a common identity – an epiphany of sorts.
363. Knop, *Diversity*, pp. 53–60.
364. Geoffrey Parker, *The Geopolitics of Domination*, New York: Routledge, 1988, Preface; Ferro, *Colonization*, p. 13.
365. A J P Taylor, 'The Meanings of Imperialism' in W M Roger Louis (ed), *Imperialism: The Robinson and Gallagher Controversy*, New York: New Viewpoints [A Division of Franklin Watts], 1976, p. 197. John A Hobson defined imperialism as the imposition of one State's will on another: John A Hobson, *Imperialism* 3rd ed, 1938, pp. 8–11.
366. Summers, *Peoples*, p. 20.
367. Orford, *Humanitarian Intervention*, p. 145.
368. Paragraph 1 of the *Declaration on Colonial Peoples* states: 'The subjection of peoples to alien subjugation, domination and exploitation constitutes a denial of fundamental human rights, is contrary to the *UN Charter* and is an impediment to the promotion of world peace and co-operation': UN Doc A/RES/1514 (XV). The *Declaration on Friendly Relations* states: 'subjection of peoples to alien subjugation, domination and exploitation constitutes a violation of the principle, as well as denial of fundamental human rights, and is contrary to the Charter': UN Doc A/RES/2625(XXV) [1].

Assembly was '*convinced* that the subjection of peoples to alien subjugation, domination and exploitation constitutes a major obstacle to the promotion of international relations.'[369] Protocol 1 of 1997 to the *Geneva Conventions* uses a similar expression, 'alien occupation', in its definition of international armed conflict.[370] The Banjul Charter goes further, stating in art 20(2) that 'colonized or oppressed peoples shall have the right to free themselves from the bonds of domination by resorting to any means recognized by the international community.' In paragraph 3 it states:

> All peoples shall have the right to the assistance of the State Parties to the present Charter in their liberation struggle against foreign domination, be it political, economic or cultural.

It continues in art 19, saying that 'nothing shall justify the domination of a people by another.' The *Vienna Declaration* also refers to 'peoples under colonial *or other forms of alien or foreign occupation*' (emphasis added)[371] as does the General Assembly's *Definition of Aggression*: 'peoples under colonial and racist regimes *or other forms of alien domination*' (emphasis added).[372]

The origins of the importance of alien and foreign subjugation can be traced to the *Aaland Islands Dispute*.[373] The Commission of Rapporteurs acknowledged that if Finland could not grant cultural autonomy to the people of the Aaland Islands then secession from Finland would be justified.[374] This qualification of their ultimate decision to disallow self-determination is consistent with the earlier decision of the Commission of Jurists, which also noted that that their opinion (that self-determination did not apply to a definitively constituted State) did not include situations where there was a 'manifest and continued abuse of sovereign power, to the detriment of a section of the population of a State' (emphasis added).[375]

Furthermore, the Canadian Supreme Court also noted that, as a general principle, alien and foreign subjugation would justify a unilateral claim for

369. *Declaration on Friendly Relations*, UN Doc A/RES/2625(XXV).
370. The definition also includes those conflicts where people are fighting against racist regimes in the exercise of the people's right to self-determination: *Protocol Additional to the Geneva Conventions of 12 August 1949, and relating to the Protection of Victims in International Armed Conflicts*, opened for signature 8 June 1977, 1125 UNTS 3 (entered into force 7 December 1978) art 4. Rosas, *Internal Self-Determination*, p. 226.
371. *Vienna Declaration*, A/CONF.157/23 12 July 1993, 2 (emphasis added).
372. *Definition of Aggression*, UN GA Res 3314 (XXIX), 2319th plenary meeting (14th December 1974) art 7 (emphasis added).
373. See the discussion at note 105.
374. 'Report of the International Commission of Jurists' [1920] *League of Nations Official Journal* (Special Supp) 5; Radan, *The Break-up of Yugoslavia*, p. 54.
375. 'Report of the International Commission of Jurists' [1920] *League of Nations Official Journal* (Special Supp) 5; Peter Radan, *The Break-up of Yugoslavia*, pp. 29–31, 54.

self-determination,[376] as did the ICJ in the *Kosovo Opinion.* The Court stated:

> During the second half of the twentieth century, the international law of self-determination developed in such a way as to create a right to independence for the peoples of non-self-governing territories *and peoples subject to alien subjugation, domination and exploration…A great many new States have come into existence as a result of the exercise of this right* (emphasis added).[377]

The term 'and' is inclusive, and implies that peoples that are non-self-governing and peoples subject to 'alien and foreign subjugation' are similar. Such descriptions indicate that 'alien and foreign subjugation' is a means by which a people entitled to self-determination is defined. Thus, it could be argued that the reference to 'all peoples' in international instruments, such as the *Declaration on Colonial Peoples*, is simply an acknowledgement that all groups are created equal – the doctrine of sovereign equality – before the norms of international law, and thus are entitled to be free from domination by other groups.[378]

The reference to alien subjugation as the means of identifying the definition of a people has been taken up by commentators and States alike.[379] For example, Eide argues that a claim for self-determination can only be legitimate, and thus receive the support of the international community, if a group is either a colonial people, or if they are *subject to 'recent alien occupation'* (emphasis added).[380] Ofuatey-Kodjoe states:

> [It is] the right of any politically coherent community to attain full self-government. The right is designed to remedy a deprivation of self-government. Therefore, the right may be validly claimed, only if the international community recognizes that the claiming community is

376. *Reference re Secession of Quebec* [1998] 2 SCR 217, pp. 222–223.
377. *Kosovo Opinion* [2010] ICJ Rep 403, 436 [79] (emphasis added).
378. See *UN Charter*, art 2(4) 2(7); *Banjul Charter.* 27 June 1981, CAB/LEG/67/3 rev. 5, 21 I.L.M. 58 (1982), art 20(3).
379. Daes, *A Right of Peoples*, p. 50; H. Gros Espiell, *The Right to Self-Determination: Implementation of United Nations Resolutions*, UN Doc E/CN.4/Sub.2/404/Rev.1, p. 6; E. Gayim, *The Principle of Self-Determination: A Study of its Contemporary Legal Evolution*, Oslo: Norwegian Institution of Human Rights, 1990, p. 57; Higgins, *Problems and Process*, pp. 115–6; Knop, *Diversity*, pp. 64–5; Anna Michalska, 'Rights of People to Self-Determination in International Law in W Twining (ed) *Issues of Self-Determination*, Aberdeen: Aberdeen University Press, 1991, pp. 78–73; F Prazetacznik, 'The Basic Collective Human Right to Self-Determination of Peoples and Nations as a Prerequisite to Peace', 8 (1990) *New York Law School Journal of Human Rights*, p. 52; K Doehring, 'Self-Determination' in Simma (ed), *UN Charter*, pp. 63–66.
380. Eide, *Constructive Alternatives*, p. 147 (emphasis added).

> under subjugation to another political unit. On the basis of such a recognition, the claimant group then becomes entitled to attain self-government without hindrance. Such hindrance then becomes an international delict.[381]

Commentators have accordingly argued that alien domination forms the criterion of a legitimate claim, and is thus a defining characteristic of legitimate claimants. For example, Ofuatey-Kodjoe notes that 'the beneficiary of the right of self-determination is a self-conscious *politically coherent* community which is under the political subjugation of another community'.[382] Ofuatey-Kodjoe considers that State practice itself proves that subjugation is the most important 'characteristic' of self-determination.[383] Orentlichter expresses it in this manner: 'Alien states may not lawfully impose their rule upon non-consenting peoples. Put differently, international law no longer abides colonization of forcible annexation.'[384] However, other commentators like Summers argue that, whilst alien and foreign subjugation adds a moral and political legitimacy, it is an extremely 'slippery' legal concept.[385]

Summers' comment raises an interesting and important question. If 'alien' and 'foreign' subjugation is to be used to identify a colonial people, or as a means to identify a non-colonial people as a legitimate claimant for self-determination, then how does the Court actually determine: (1) subjugation, and (2) what constitutes 'alien' or 'foreign'? These questions raise another question: who should make this judgment? What constitutes 'foreign' or 'alien' domination is, no doubt, a matter of perception and perspective.[386] For example, it is plausible that many, if not all, Tibetans consider the Chinese military and the government in Beijing as 'foreign', a conclusion supported by their different histories, culture, customs, religion, and language, as well as the armed invasion in October 1950 and the current existence of Chinese troops in Tibet. Despite this, there is little doubt that the government of the PRC would argue that: (1) their actions are but a legitimate attempt to assert their sovereignty, and or to prevent unlawful activity or conflict; and (2) they are not 'foreigners' – the PRC is a multi-ethnic State, as evidenced by the existence of other minority groups throughout

381. Ofuatey-Kodjoe, *Self-Determination*, p. 3 (abstract).
382. Ibid, p. 288.
383. Other important characteristics were political coherence and subject status: Ibid, p. 289.
384. Diane F Orentlichter, 'The Imprint of Kosovo on International Law', 6 (1999–2000) *Journal of International & Comparative Law*, p. 543.
385. Summers, *Peoples*, p. 366. Summers reaches this conclusion despite acknowledging that 'people under foreign or alien domination go to the heart of the conflict of nationalism and international law that defines the law of self-determination': at p. 348.
386. The question of national identity, is very much a subjective action. Accordingly, the identification of an entity as a foreign or alien entity is to a degree subjective.

the country.[387] Similarly, India would not consider itself to be 'foreign' or 'alien' to the Kashmiris, or the Assamese.

Subjugation is perhaps easier to prove. The example of Oman is relevant here. The UN appointed an *Ad Hoc Committee* to determine if Oman was a British colony. The Committee held that the territory was a British colony because: (1) there existed a feudal regime contrary to the concept of self-determination; (2) the British had a presence in the territory to protect such a regime from internal political pressure; and (3) military force had been used in the initial creation and continued administration of the territory, and to deny the inhabitants to freely decide their political status.[388] As one commentator stated:

> Thus 'colonial occupation' is put on the same level as occupation resulting from the use of armed force. In both cases the determining factor is that the present status of the territories is being maintained against the will of the inhabitants.[389]

The use of armed force to deny the free will of the inhabitants is clear enough to see, and could be used even to assist the classification of a dominating power as 'foreign' or 'alien', particularly in internal, rather than international, conflicts.

Whether the conflict in Bosnia-Herzegovina in 1992 was internal or international was considered in the decision of the Appeals Chamber of the ICTY in the *Tadić Case*.[390] The accused, Duško Tadić, had been indicted for a series of crimes that had allegedly been committed in the Prijedor region of Bosnia-Herzegovina between 25 May 1992 and August 1992. As part of its determination of whether Tadić had breached art 2 of the Statute of the ICTY,[391] the Appeals Chamber had to determine whether the conflict was international or internal in character.[392] The Appeals Chamber, after considering the nature and degree of control that Serbia had over the Bosnian Serb forces concluded

387. In fact the Chinese government has claimed that on the basis of 400 blood tests carried out in September 1992 Tibetans were of the same ethnicity as the Chinese, and were not Nepalese or Indian: Author unknown, *SBS World Guide, the Complete Fact File on Every Country*, (13th ed.) Prahran: Hardie Grant Books, p. 157.
388. Sureda, *Evolution*, p. 259.
389. Ibid, p. 261.
390. *Prosecutor v Tadić (Appeals Chamber)* Case No IT-94–1-AR72 (2 October 1995) [24] ('*Tadić*').
391. Article 2 of the ICTY's Statute refers to grave breaches of the Geneva Convention 1949: *Statute of the International Tribunal for the Prosecution of Persons Responsible for Serious Violations of International Humanitarian Law Committed in the Territory of the Former Yugoslavia since 1991*, UN Doc S/25704, annex (1993); adopted by *Resolution 827*, SC Res, 48th sess, 3217th mtg, UN Doc S/RES/827 (25 May 1993).
392. The Appeals Chamber had already approved the Trial Chamber's findings, that prior to 19 May 1992 the conflict was international in character: *Tadić* Case No IT-94–1-AR72 (2 October 1995) pp. 83–87.

that it was an international armed conflict after 19 May 1992.[393] However, as Greenwood notes, clearly the conflict became international in character once Bosnia-Herzegovina became a State, which the Badinter Commission had determined occurred on the 6 March 1992, the day the independence referendum was held.[394]

According to the above analysis, clearly, once a people become a State, any continued attempt by their parent government to used armed force in an on-going conflict would be considered 'alien' or 'foreign' subjugation. However, this does little to assist the Court whilst the people's claim to statehood has yet to be decided. A referendum can only be held with the cooperation of the parent government, and thus can be easily denied by a recalcitrant parent government (arguably this denial could be seen as evidence of a people's subjugation). So could a simple unilateral declaration of independence be evidence that a parent government is 'alien' or 'foreign'?[395] Assuming the declaration is a valid expression of the people's will, it is argued at first glance that the answer would be 'yes'.

This answer, however, raises the question of perception. A unilateral declaration of independence is merely proof of a subjective perception by the people concerned. Given that there will be a competing perception, the Court potentially faces a difficult decision. However, it is submitted here that the subjective nature of these perceptions are unavoidable, and, as such, the will of the oppressed should generally prevail, unless objective evidence suggests otherwise.[396] Monserrat Guibernau stated in his work 'Nations without States' the following:[397]

> Nations which, in spite of having their territories included within the boundaries of one or more [S]tates, by and large do not identify with them. The members of a nation lacking a state of their own regard

393. Ibid, p. 162.
394. Alternative dates for Bosnia-Herzegovina's statehood could be when it was recognised by the EC on 6 April 1992, or even when it was admitted as a member of the UN on 22 May 1992: Christopher Greenwood, 'International Humanitarian Law and the *Tadić* Case', 7 (1996) *European Journal of International Law*, p. 272.
395. If the Court were to use a declaration of independence as a means of identifying whether an entity is foreign or alien it would have to ensure that such a unilateral declaration was not a sham, and indeed represented the free will of the people concerned rather than a dissident minority or sub-group.
396. As mentioned above, the question of national identity is very much a subjective action. Accordingly, the identification of an entity as a foreign or alien entity is to a degree subjective.
397. He defines 'nations without States as follows: 'A nation without [S]tate, as the term indicates, is based upon the existence of a nation, that is, a community endowed with a stable but dynamic core containing a set of factors which have generated the emergence of a specific national identity. The State, that is, the political institution with which the nation should ideally identify, is missing': Guibernau, *Nations Without States*, p. 17.

> the [S]tate containing them as alien, and maintain a separate sense of national identity generally based upon a common culture, history, attachment to a particular territory and the explicit wish to rule themselves.[398]

The mere existence of competing perceptions or claims should not deter or pose a problem for the Court, and in fact *has not posed a problem.* The Court was faced with such a situation when requested to provide the General Assembly with its Advisory Opinion regarding the Western Sahara, and was able to deal with it without great issue.[399]

1. Western Sahara[400]

Spain treated the Western Sahara as an overseas portion of Spain itself. In addition to Spain's perception, the Court was faced with the competing claims of sovereignty over the territory by Morocco and Mauritania. Accordingly, the Court was asked by the General Assembly to provide an Advisory Opinion from the Court on the following questions:[401]

> (i) Was Western Sahara (Rio de Oro and Sakiet El Hamra) at the time of colonization by Spain a territory belonging to no one (terra nullius)?[402]
> (ii) What were the legal ties between this territory and the Kingdom of Morocco and the Mauritanian entity?[403]

The Court was able, through the analysis of historical records and correspondence, to determine that: (1) that there existed a Western Saharan 'people' despite their nomadic existence and despite their political diversity of tribes, confederations and emirates, and that there could conceivably exist a State complete with international legal personality;[404] (2) that Spain had colonised the territory, and therefore despite Spain treating the territory as part of Spain, Spain was in essence a foreign or alien entity; and (3) that at

398. Ibid.
399. *Western Sahara Opinion* [1975] ICJ Rep 12.
400. See Chapter 4.
401. *Question of Spanish Sahara*, GA Res 3292 (XXIX), UN GAOR, 29th sess, 2318th plen mtg, UN Doc A/Res/3292 (13 December 1974).
402. *Western Sahara Opinion* [1975] ICJ Rep 12, 12.
403. The Court concluded by 14 votes to 2 that there were legal ties between this territory and the Kingdom of Morocco, and by 15 votes to 1 that there were links with the Mauritanian entity: Ibid.
404. Ibid, 52. For an excellent discussion of the identity of the Western Saharan people, the Saharawi, see Toby Shelley, 'Resistance and Colonialism: Building the Saharawi Identity' in Arts and Leite, *International Law and the Question of Western Sahara*, p. 31.

the time of colonisation by Spain the territory was not a territory belonging to either Morocco or Mauritania.[405] For example, when considering the respective claims of sovereignty by Morocco and Mauritania the ICJ examined domestic as well as international actions;[406] diplomatic documents and letters between other ruling sovereigns; treaties signed by colonising powers;[407] and other evidence, such as the recovery of sailors from the vessel Esmeralda.[408]

The above discussion shows that the Court was able to determine the status of the respective claimants – Spain, Morocco and Mauritania – and the nature of their relationship with the people inhabiting the Western Sahara. In other words, the Court was able to determine, through placing the subjective perceptions and claims made within the historical context, that Spain, Morocco and Mauritania were all foreign and alien entities.

Accordingly, courts should take the subjective perceptions of the people into account, as well as the perception of the parent government. The Court should take into account the historical context of these perceptions. A unilateral declaration of independence may reflect a culmination of a history of perception that the parent State is 'foreign' and or 'alien'. The accuracy of these perceptions will be reinforced objective criteria such as language, customs, and religion.

Some commentators, such as Eide, argue that domination by an alien and foreign entity should be classified as a 'pre-condition' or threshold question that must be satisfied in order to legitimately claim self-determination, rather than a defining characteristic of a people.[409] This interpretation is often

405. *Western Sahara Opinion* [1975] ICJ Rep 12, 32–33.

406. This was to determine whether other countries had granted recognition of the sovereignty of Morocco or Mauritania.

407. For example, the *Treaty of Marrakesh of 1767* (the ICJ accepted the Spanish version as the most reliable since it was supported by letters written by the Sultan of Morocco to King Carlos III of Spain regarding the same topic), the *Hispano-Moroccan Treaty of 1799*, and a document citing return of shipwrecked sailors in accordance with art 38 of the *Hispano-Moroccan Treaty of Commerce and Navigation of 1861*. The ICJ summarised the relevant documents at *Western Sahara Opinion* [1975] ICJ Rep 12, 42. However, note that in his judgment Ammoun J stated that the ICJ had either left out or misinterpreted certain relevant documents: at 79–84.

408. The recovery indicated that it was the intervention of the Beyrouk clan and other local leaders rather than an order from the Sultan of Morocco that enabled the sailors to be recovered. Thus the ICJ rejected Morocco's claim that art 38 of the *Hispano-Moroccan Treaty of Commerce and Navigation of 1861* proved Moroccan sovereignty. Instead the ICJ accepted Spain's argument that art 38 showed a limited form of authority, and was more accurately described as 'mere influence' as opposed to a sovereign command to arrange ransom of Moroccan crews: Ibid, 44.

409. Eide, in addition to requiring that a people be either a colonial people or subject to foreign or alien subjugation before they can claim self-determination, also says that a group cannot make a claim unless they have been denied a right to a democratic government, *and all other options have been exhausted by the group*: Eide, *Constructive Alternatives*, p. 147.

referred to as 'remedial self-determination', and advocates for the legitimacy of the claim to be determined by the actions of a central government.[410] Eide's approach is supported by the ICJ in the *Kosovo Opinion* where it stated:

> Whether, outside the context of non-self-governing territories and peoples subject to alien subjugation, domination and exploitation, the international law of self-determination confers upon part of the population of an existing State a right to separate from that State is, however, a subject on which radically different views were expressed by those taking part in the proceedings and expressing a position on the question. Similar differences existed regarding whether international law provides for a right of 'remedial secession' and, if so, in what circumstances. There was also a sharp difference of views as to whether the circumstances which some participants maintained would give rise to a right of 'remedial secession' were actually present in Kosovo.[411]

The Court concluded that there was no need to resolve the debate surrounding remedial self-determination since such resolution was unnecessary to decide the matter at hand – whether Kosovo's unilateral declaration breached international law.[412] However, it is interesting to note that the Court appears to be drawing a distinction between remedial and 'traditional' claims to self-determination, the latter including 'non-self-governing territories *and peoples subject to alien subjugation, domination and exploitation*', (emphasis added). The Court's wording strongly implies that a separate category of self-determination exists. The pre-conditions for this approach are discussed below.

G. Pre-conditions

Many commentators argue that there is no automatic right to independence for a people.[413] For example, Philpott argues that there should be a 'presumption against self-determination', and that independence and statehood is a 'last resort' and only justified when a people would otherwise remain exposed to grievous human rights abuses or acts of cruelty.[414] In essence, these commentators argue that the right to self-determination is subject to 'pre-conditions'. Pre-conditions have been used in the UN's attempt to

410. Weller, *Escaping*, p. 59.
411. *Kosovo Opinion* [2010] ICJ Rep 403, 438 [82].
412. Ibid, p. 83.
413. Brownlie, *The Rule of Law*, pp. 46–47.
414. Daniel Philpott, 'In Defense of Self-Determination' (1995) 105 *Ethics* p. 382. This is a return to the opinion provided by the Commission of the Rapporteurs in the 'Report of the International Commission of Jurists' [1920] *League of Nations Official Journal* (Special Supp) 3.

resolve the Israeli-Palestinian conflict,[415] and in the independence claim of Kosovo.[416] Their use appears to mark a return to a management-style approach to resolving self-determination claims, as once used by the UN in its Trustee system and, earlier, by the League of Nations in its Mandate and Minorities systems.[417] The suggestion that a legitimate claim for self-determination requires satisfying pre-conditions suggests that there is no primary or inalienable right to self-determination, but rather that it is a remedial right.[418] Such an interpretation contradicts the traditional interpretation of the right to self-determination contained in the *Western Sahara Advisory Opinion* and international documents, especially the *Declaration on Colonial Peoples.*[419] However, there are some very strong arguments in favour of the concept of pre-conditions.

1. The case in favour of pre-conditions

Commentators have argued that the absence of pre-conditions would open the 'floodgates'.[420] Establishing a set of pre-conditions *could* reduce the number of claims, but would no doubt ameliorate the concerns that an unfettered right and unstructured approach to self-determination will lead to anarchy. It can also minimise the use of spurious arguments used by States seeking to deny all claims to self-determination.

The Canadian Supreme Court provided some insight into how to detect a claim that does not meet the necessary pre-conditions when it provided an Advisory Opinion to the Canadian national government regarding the proposed

415. *A Performance-Based Roadmap to a Permanent Two-State Solution to the Israeli-Palestinian Conflict*, 30 April 2003, US State Department Press Release <http://www.state.gov/r/pa/prs/ps/2003/20062.htm> ('*Roadmap*'). The pre-conditions include constitutional reform, election and an end to violence and terrorism: at Phase I (Ending Terror And Violence, Normalizing Palestinian Life, and Building Palestinian Institutions – Present to May 2003).
416. *Comprehensive Proposal for the Kosovo Status Settlement*, 2 February 2007, Nationbuilding in the Balkans, <http://pbosnia.kentlaw.edu>.
417. Drew, *Meaning*, p. 97.
418. Norman, *Ethics of Secesion*, p. 41; Scharf, *Earned Sovereignty*, p. 381.
419. As discussed above the expression 'all peoples' used in the UN Charter creates the impression that the right is not dependent upon any pre-condition at all. See the discussion in Catriona Drew, *Meaning*, p. 87, 99. Although Catriona Drew's work is more concerned with a critique of 'earned sovereignty', her arguments can also be applied to the use of pre-conditions they have a similar effect.
420. Norman, like Buchanan, defines 'choice theories' as simply requiring a majority in a region *choosing* independence, and not requiring the group to be culturally distinct, the victims of any repression, or having a 'special claim' to the territory in question. Their right to self-determination is both based on and expressed through the simple statement of their will. He argues that 'choice theorists end up merely multiplying well beyond 5000 the number of potential groups with the right to secede': Norman, *Ethics of Secession*, p. 37. See also Allen Buchanan, *Justice*, pp. 327–29; Philpott, *In Defense* p. 371; Brilmayer, *Secession*, p. 177; Wellman, *A Defence of Secession*, p. 142.

unilateral secession of Quebec.[421] The Court concluded that the right to remedial self-determination could include an effective denial of the ability to meaningful participation in the government of Canada. However, they noted that there was no evidence that the people of Quebec were an oppressed people.[422] The Quebecois people had actively participated in the government of Canada – on numerous occasions the Prime Minister of Canada was in fact from Quebec – and many held important and high level positions within the federal government, including the Chief Justice of the Canadian Supreme Court, and Chief of Staff of the Canadian Armed Forces.[423]

Establishing pre-conditions may be of further benefit in protecting peoples since they have the potential to shape State behaviour and treatment of potential claimants. For example, pre-conditions could prevent a people from making a spurious claim to self-determination in order to receive unfair advantages – a form of blackmail.[424] State behaviour may be influenced in a positive way too. For example, if there were pre-conditions that a group must be suffering from severe or violent repression, cultural genocide, or a lack of participation in the governing process, then a State opposed to a people's claim has to actively avoid letting these things occur.[425] As a consequence a State may be more likely to negotiate with the group, grant it more political autonomy or provide guarantees to protect the group's characteristics – for example language and religious freedom.[426] Shaping State behaviour in this manner benefits the whole international community, since it reduces the possibility of threats to international peace and security.[427]

However, care must be taken so that the right balance is found. On one hand they should not encourage frivolous or spurious claims,[428] or provide incentives to opportunistic nationalist leaders to mobilise their discontent

421. On 30 October 1995 a referendum was held in Canada regarding Quebec's right to self-determination, and by the slimmest of margins the Canadian people decided Quebec should stay with Canada. After the referendum was held the Canadian government asked the Supreme Court of Canada for an Advisory Opinion: *Reference re Secession of Quebec* [1998] 2 SCR 217.
422. However, no mention was made of whether they were oppressed by an *alien* or *foreign* entity.
423. *Reference re Secession of Quebec* [1998] 2 SCR 217, 292; *Vienna Declaration*, A/CONF.157/23 12 July 1993. See Crawford, *Creation of States*, pp. 118–122.
424. Norman, *Ethics of Secession*, pp. 41–2; Buchanan, *Toward a Theory of Secession*, p. 337; Philpott, *In Defense*, p. 383.
425. Norman, *Ethics of Secession*, p. 42.
426. Norman argues that currently States have to be pressured into negotiating with claimants: Ibid, p. 46.
427. Norman also believes that just-cause theories, by reinforcing the legitimacy of States when they treat their citizens justly, reinforce an international community based upon States, and thus counter the argument that self-determination poses a threat to the international community: Ibid pp. 42–44.
428. Ibid, p. 53; Buchanan, *Toward a Theory of Secession*, p. 337.

into a claim for independence when none may exist.[429] On the other hand pre-conditions should not make self-determination impossible.[430] A balancing act, as with many legal tests, is necessary.[431]

2. Suggested pre-conditions

Commentators,[432] courts,[433] *ad hoc* commissions[434] and international organisations[435] have all put forward suggested pre-conditions. For example, the Canadian Supreme Court outlined three situations that gave rise to a legitimate claim to self-determination:

> A right to secession only arises under the principle of self-determination of peoples at international law where 'a people' is governed as part of a colonial empire; where 'a people' is subject to alien subjugation, domination or exploitation, and *possibly* where a people is denied any meaningful exercise of its right to self-determination within the state of which it forms a part.[436]

Other suggestions include: (1) an end to hostilities, violence and or terrorism;[437] (2) protection of minorities;[438] (3) a supervised or monitored plebiscite is held to determine the will of the people;[439] (4) constitutional reform or the adoption of a democratic style government;[440] and (5) the new State accept the inviolability of international borders.[441]

429. Norman, *Ethics of Secession*, p. 36.
430. Buchanan, *Toward a Theory of Secession*, p. 337.
431. David Miller, 'Secession and the Principle of Nationality' in Moore, *National Self-Determination and Secession*, p. 65; Brilmayer, *Secession*, p. 199.
432. See eg, Buchanan, *Toward a Theory of Secession*; Philpott, *In Defense*, p. 382.
433. The Canadian Supreme Court, *Reference re Secession of Quebec* [1998] 2 SCR 217.
434. Such as the *Badinter Commission*.
435. For example by the European Community, see *EC Guidelines*, pp. 1486–87.
436. *Reference re Secession of Quebec* [1998] 2 SCR 217, [154]; *Vienna Declaration* A/CONF.157/23 12 July 1993; Scharf, *Earned Sovereignty*, p. 382, (emphasis added).
437. See *Roadmap*, Phase 1.
438. For example, Slovenia's specific guarantees to its Hungarian and Italian minorities. See *Opinion No 7 On the Recognition of the Republic of Slovenia by the European Community and its Member States* (11 January 1992) 31 ILM 1512 (1992) ('*Opinion No 7*').
439. This was an issue for Bosnia-Herzegovina because their Serb minority had boycotted previous referendums: *Opinion No 4*, 31 ILM 501 (1992), Annex 3 76; Crawford, *Creation of States*, p. 398, & pp. 406–9; Roland Rich, 'Recognition of States: The Collapse of Yugoslavia and the Soviet Union', 4 (1993) *European Journal of International Law*, p. 49.
440. See *Roadmap*, Phase 1. A democratic government was a common requirement for all the former republics of the SFRY. See, eg, *Opinion No 7*, 31 ILM 1512 (1992); *EC Guidelines*, 31 ILM 1485 (1992).
441. This was especially important with Macedonia's claim to statehood due to concerns that success may encourage secession or integration with the Greek province of the same

The purpose of establishing pre-conditions is to assist in determining the legitimacy of individual claims for self-determination. They can be used in two ways; to justify the grounds for when a unilateral claim can be made, and to provide transparent criteria which, when met, will ensure the international community regards the determination as valid. The former will be discussed here.[442]

I agree with the underlying sentiment of suggested pre-conditions. The right to self-determination is not an absolute or an unfettered one.[443] It is assumed that a people's claim to self-determination must be made in accordance with the norms of international law.

Accordingly, the following pre-conditions will be examined: (1) the claimants respect international law, such as the rights of minorities; (2) the claimants accept the inviolability of international borders; (3) the free will of the people has been examined through a supervised or monitored plebiscite; (4) there was a denial of a democratic government; (5) the people claiming self-determination are the subject of alien and foreign subjugation, or are the victims of gross abuses of human rights.

a. Respecting the norms of international law

A people's pursuit of its claim for self-determination must comply with the norms that regulate armed conflict and international humanitarian law.[444] This suggestion is justified by the acknowledgment that a legal right is always coupled with an appropriate legal responsibility, and by the belief that all interaction of members of the international community is subject to the norms of international law. In summary, peoples, like States, are bound by the rule of law.[445] Accordingly, I believe that the legitimacy of a people's claim to self-determination is dependent upon whether their claim is made in accordance with international law.[446]

name. Thus Macedonia had a unique pre-condition – it could not indulge in 'hostile propaganda' that would encourage secession by the Greek province: *Opinion No 6 On the Recognition of the Republic of Macedonia by the European Community and its Member States* (11 January 1992) 31 ILM 1507 (1992); Grant, *Recognition of States*, p. 162.

442. See Chapter 2 for further details.
443. Other authors do too. See, eg, Radan, *The Break-up of Yugoslavia*, p. 245.
444. In other words a people's action must be consistent with the norms of customary international law and with the *UN Charter*. This compliance is necessary if a State seeks membership of the UN: *UN Charter* arts 4–6.
445. In essence, I reject realism's thesis that power, rather than law, determines international relations. See also Fergus Green, 'Fragmentation in Two Dimensions: the ICJ's Flawed Approach to Non-State Actors and International Legal Personality', 9 (2008) *Melbourne Journal of International Law*, pp. 70–71.
446. Such a pre-condition, along with others, was included in the UN's Roadmap to create a Palestinian State in the Middle East: *Roadmap*. This is also similar to what the *Final Act of the CSCE* states: 'The participating states will respect the equal rights of peoples and their right to self-determination, acting at all times in conformity with the purposes and the

Consider the example of the Cree in the province of Quebec, Canada. The Cree are not necessarily interested in statehood, but rather value the protection of their way of life, culture, language, and traditional lands.[447] What would happen to the Cree's claims if the Quebecois were successful in their claims for independence from Canada? Would the Quebecois government ignore the Cree's demands, or accede to them? Any claim the Quebecois made to self-determination would have to be based upon their willingness to accept the legal obligation to protect the human rights of the Cree in accordance with international law.

Whilst the author recognises that requiring the makers of a legitimate claim for self-determination to then respect another internal people's claim for statehood raises the so-called domino theory, and there may be strong political reasons to prevent the potential dismemberment of a State, denying a people the right to self-determination because of an earlier successful claim by their new State government is not sufficiently consistent for a legal application of the principle of self-determination. The possible negative consequences of the domino theory can be minimised with some initiative. Ascertaining whether the 'new minorities' wish to be part of the new State or to remain with the parent State (perhaps with increased autonomy), and respecting their choice, can avoid any potential tension.[448] Given the experience during the Partition of India and Pakistan this may not be palatable, however, if monitored by the UN it could be done with less bloodshed, and with greater benefits for long-term stability and security.[449]

b. Respecting the inviolability of borders

Another potential pre-condition is that the new State accepts the inviolability of borders. Such a pre-condition raises the issue of whether the borders of the new State are determined by the norm of *uti possidetis juris*. It could be argued that by subjecting claims for self-determination to the norm of *uti possidetis* a balance between territorial integrity and self-determination will be ensured.

principles of the UN Charter and with the relevant norms of international law, including those relating to territorial integrity of States.'

447. 'The Crees believe that self-determination need not be absolute; it need not imply formal statehood, flags, seats on the United Nations. In any event, the Crees are quick to point out, these are white men's inventions. Self-determination means an end to permanent dependency on Government handouts and an end to being the passive spectators to the destruction of their lands.' Michael Igantieff, *Blood and Belonging*, London: Vintage, Random House, 1994, p. 125.
448. This raises the issue of the inviolability of borders and *uti possidetis*.
449. Radan, *Post-Secession Borders*, p. 75; Miller, *Principle of Nationality*, p. 72.

I. UTI POSSIDETIS JURIS[450]

Originally a principle of Roman law that determined borders after territorial conquest,[451] *uti possidetis juris* was applied in both Latin America and Africa to allow former colonies to retain their existing colonial boundaries upon gaining independence.[452] It was subsequently adopted by a resolution of the Organisation of African Unity, whose members pledged to accept their borders as being those at the time of their independence.[453] In the *Case Concerning the Frontier Dispute* the chamber of the ICJ held that the principle would apply even if a treaty was silent as to how a border dispute was to be decided.[454] As a consequence of this practice, and the Court's decision in the *Frontier Dispute*, it has been argued that self-determination is subordinate to *uti possidetis.*[455] Thus the Badinter Arbitration Commission, in *Opinion No. 3*, a response to a question put by Lord Owen,[456] held that *uti possedetis* was was a general principle of international law, and not confined to a decolonisation context.[457] It therefore applied to the break-up of the SFRY, and borders could not be changed at the time of independence unless by peaceful negotiation.[458] Consequently, the former internal, provincial borders became the international borders of the new States.[459]

The Canadian Supreme Court also discussed *uti possidetis* in its consideration of the secession of Quebec. Although there was no discussion of the

450. 'As you possess shall you continue to possess'.
451. Radan, *Post-Secession Borders*, p. 59.
452. Ibid; Cassese, *A Legal Reappraisal*, p. 69, 192–93; Jochen A Frowein, 'Self-Determination as a Limit to Obligations under International Law' in Tomuschat, *Modern Law of Self-Determination*, p. 216; Radan, *The Break-Up of Yugoslavia*, p. 69; Steven Ratner, 'Drawing a Better Line: *Uti Possidetis* and the Borders of New States', 90 *American Journal of International Law 590*, (1996); Sam K N Blay, 'Self-Determination: A Reassessment in the Post-Communist Era', 22 *Denver Journal of International Law and Policy* 280, (1994).
453. Radan, *Post-Secession Borders*, p. 59.
454. *Frontier Dispute (Burkina Faso v Republic of Mali Case)* [1986] ICJ Rep 554,557 ('*Frontier Dispute Case*'). The case concerned a border dispute between Burkino Faso and the Republic of Mali after the parties had entered into an agreement whereby the ICJ would determine a border according to the frontiers at the time of independence.
455. *Frontier Dispute Case* [1986] ICJ Rep 554, 565; Cassese, *A Legal Reappraisal*, p. 69, & 192; Blay, '*Self-Determination: A Reassessment* p. 280.
456. Lord Owen was the Chairperson of the European Community's Conference on Yugoslavia, and he put the question to the Badinter Commission: 'Can the internal boundaries between Croatia and Serbia and between Bosnia and Hercegovina and Serbia be regarded as frontiers in terms of public international law?': *Opinion No 3*, 31 ILM 1499 (1992).
457. Ibid, p. 1500.
458. Ibid. As noted by Radan, this appears to raise an inconsistency since it treats the borders of the newly emerged States as being 'sacrosanct' when the borders of the former Federal Republic of Yugoslavia were not: Radan, *The Break-up of Yugoslavia*, pp. 217–19 & 228.
459. *Opinion No 3*, 31 ILM 1499 (1992). The principle was also mentioned in *Opinion No 2*, 31 ILM 1497 (1992).

future borders of Quebec, it would appear from the Court's discussion of territorial integrity that the Court, relying heavily on *Opinion No. 3* of the Badinter Commission, would have held that, in the absence of a negotiated settlement between Quebec and the federal government of Canada, it would support an application of *uti possidetis juris.*[460]

The Badinter Commission's interpretation of *uti possidetis* has been heavily criticised by commentators.[461] Both Radan and Pomerance effectively accuse the Badinter Commission of selective quoting, and leaving out the very specific references to decolonisation made by the ICJ in *Frontier Dispute* when discussing the applicability of the *uti possidetis.*[462] Radan convincingly argues that the ICJ intended that the norm would only apply to external borders of a former colonial State, and not to the internal borders of a State, like Yugoslavia that was in the process of dissolution, or where a former constituent entity seceded from the parent State.[463]

As persuasive as their arguments may be – after all, the parties in *Frontier Dispute* did actually make an express request to the Chamber that the dispute be settled on the basis of *uti possidetis*[464] – I am not as convinced as Radan and Pomerance that *uti possidetis* should be confined to a purely decolonisation context. There is some merit in using *uti possidetis* as a starting point in negotiating international borders where a new State emerges through a successful, and legitimate claim to self-determination. The norm can provide stability in an uncertain time.[465]

However, care should be taken with a blind application of *uti possidetis.*[466] Applying *uti possidetis* results in the confirmation of pre-existing borders,

460. The Canadian government disputed the Court's findings on this point, and believed that the borders of the new State would not be 'fixed', and in fact could be 'called into question': Radan, *The Break-up of Yugoslavia*, pp. 224, 226.
461. Radan, *Post-Secession Borders;* Pomerance, 'The Badinter Commission', above p. 31; Frowein, *Self-Determination as a Limit*, p. 216.
462. Radan, *Post-Secession Borders*, pp. 61–63, 66; Pomerance, *The Badinter Commission*, pp. 54–55. However, some authors agree with the Badinter Commission's interpretation: Cassese, *A Legal Reappraisal*, p. 192; Malcolm Shaw, 'Peoples, Territorialism and Boundaries', p. 8 (1997) *European Journal of International Law*, pp. 496–98. See also Radan's rebuttal of Shaw's thesis: Radan, *The Break-up of Yugoslavia*, pp. 62–66.
463. Radan, *The Break-up of Yugoslavia*, pp. 229–30.
464. George N Barrie, '*Uti Possidetis* Versus Self-Determination and Modern International Law: In Africa the Chickens are Coming Home to Roost', (1988) *Journal of South African Law*, p. 452.
465. This is what Radan describes as the doctrine of the stability of borders as espoused in *Temple of Preah Vihear (Cambodia v Thailand)* [1962] ICJ Rep 17: Radan, *Post-Secession Borders*, p. 58.
466. Even the Secretary-General of the OAU stated in 1977 that *uti possedits* is not 'sacrosanct' and, furthermore, could be overruled on the basis of self-determination. The OAU's policy of relying on *uti possidetis* has come under increasing criticism: Radan, *Post-Secession Borders*, p. 70.

which raises the question 'should pre-colonial states or empires be rebuilt?'[467] Some would argue not, since there is a need to overturn 'the results of an illegal occupation and annexation'.[468] It should be remembered that the peoples within these borders did not have an opportunity to participate in the establishment of them.[469] Furthermore, internal borders are established by a government's desire and need to govern, and their objectives do not reflect the wishes of the inhabitants, and are in fact more than likely to be inconsistent with the needs of an *international border.*[470] More importantly, a blind application of *uti possidetis* may create sizeable minorities that may not wish to become part of the new State. Ignoring their wishes merely creates the potential for future problems or conflict.[471] As such, maintaining existing borders may inflame old frustrations. Leaving such issues unresolved could seriously jeopardise the stability of the international community.[472]

The purpose of an application of *uti possidetis*, as explained by the chamber of the ICJ in the *Frontier Dispute*, is to prevent further conflict and to restore a measure of stability in difficult and potentially volatile situations. The Court described the purpose of the concept in these terms:

> It is a general principle, which is logically connected with the phenomenon of the obtaining of independence, wherever it occurs. Its obvious purpose is to prevent the independence and stability of new states being endangered by fratricidal struggles provoked by the challenging of frontiers following the withdrawal of the administering power.[473]

It could be argued that the application of *uti possidetis* in the dissolution of the SFRY did not aid in the stability of borders, and rather than prevent 'fratricidal struggles', it encouraged conflict over borders,[474] and inhibited

467. Sureda, *Evolution*, p. 218.
468. Batistich, *Right to Self-Determination*, pp. 1029–30.
469. Willens and Siemer, *National Security*, p. 2. Zejnullah Gruda claimed that the borders of Kosovo and Albania were drawn by the Great Powers and not in accordance with the right to self-determination, and certainly not in accordance with the wishes of the population: Zejnullah Gruda, 'Some Key Principles for a Lasting Solution of the Status of Kosova: *Uti Possidetis*, the Ethnic Principle, and Self-Determination', *Chicago Kent Law Review* 80, 2005, 388–91. This was also the problem with Nigeria and Biafra. The British arbitrarily created Nigeria to serve their own strategic and economic interests. See M G Kaladharan Nayar, 'Self-Determination Beyond the Colonial Context: Biafra in Retrospect', 10 *Texas International Law Journal* 324, (1975).
470. Radan, *Post-Secession Borders*, p. 71.
471. Ratner, *Drawing a Better Line*, p. 617.
472. Examples would include the conflicts areas of the former USSR, such as in Georgia and Armenia, and Kosovo and the SFRY: Zejnullah Gruda, *Key Principles*, pp. 388–91.
473. *Frontier Dispute Case* [1986] ICJ Rep 554, 551.
474. Radan, *Post-Secession Borders*, p. 51. Radan also questions whether *uti possidetis* actually minimised border conflict in Africa. He cites the examples of Katanga from the Congo in 1960–63, Biafra and Nigeria in 1967–70 and Eritrea and Ethiopia in 1974–93: at 68.

the ability of the European Community to respond to the challenges of peacefully resolving the break-up of SFRY.[475]

A better and much simpler pre-condition would be a general requirement of the people to form a viable State according to the criteria for statehood defined by the Montevideo Criteria.[476] This suggestion is much more practical in nature, and since a State can still satisfy the Montevideo Criteria when its borders are subject to a degree of uncertainty, this would not deny a new State from being recognised, and also allow borders to be changed to reflect the will of the people, including newly formed minorities.[477]

c. Internationally monitored plebiscite

Paragraph 2 of the *Declaration on Colonial Peoples* states:

> All peoples have the right to self-determination; by virtue of that right they freely determine their political status and freely pursue their economic, social and cultural development.

All international instruments referring to self-determination use similar wording, although the statement in the 1970 *Declaration on Friendly Relations* elaborates by clarifying that this choice is 'without external influence'.[478] The *Western Sahara Opinion* emphasised that the freely expressed will of the peoples was the 'very *sine qua non* of all decolonisation'.[479] After the Badinter Commission it is now accepted that a plebiscite is the means through which this 'free choice' is made. Consequently, a plebiscite is often argued to be a

Others agree. The African Union (replacing the OAU) is revising the strict application of *uti possidetis*, and prefers the protection of human rights over stability of borders: Kathryn Sturman, 'New Norms, Old Boundaries: The African Union's Approach to Secession and State Sovereignty' in Aleksandar Pavkovic and Peter Radan (eds), *On the Way to Statehood: Secession and Globalisation*, 2008, p. 66.

475. According to Lord Owen, former Co-Chairman of the Steering Committee of the International Conference on Yugoslavia noted that: 'The refusal to make these borders negotiable greatly hampered the EC's attempt at crisis management': as cited in Radan, *Post-Secession Borders*, p. 67.
476. Radan, *The Break-up of Yugoslavia*, p. 245. The Montevideo criteria are discussed in Chapter 2.
477. Brilmayer, *Secession*, p. 187; Buchanan, *Toward a Theory of Secession*, p. 327.
478. *Declaration on Friendly Relations*, UN Doc A/RES/2625(XXV).
479. 'Again resolution 2625 (XXV) concerning friendly relations goes a long way to further emphasize the point that on decolonization the "emergence into any political status" has to be "freely determined by a people". Thus even if integration of territory was demanded by an interested State, as in this case, it could not be had without ascertaining the freely expressed will of the people – the very *sine qua non* of all decolonisation': Ibid, p. 73. See Summers' discussion of this point: Summers, *Peoples*, pp. 306–307.

pre-condition for a legitimate claim for self-determination.[480] A plebiscite must make the choices to the people very clear. What these choices are – independence, autonomy, or a democratic government, for example – is not as obvious, and depends on the circumstances.[481]

This question is answered by *The Annex to the Declaration of Colonial Peoples*, which in Principle VI states that a non-self-governing territory reaches a full measure of self-government by its:

(a) Emergence as a sovereign independent State;
(b) Free association with an independent State; or
(c) Integration with an independent State.[482]

These choices were confirmed by the *Western Sahara Opinion* as being the essence of the free and genuine expression of the will of a relevant people.[483]

The above suggests that self-determination involves more than one choice. It includes a right for a colonial people to form their own State, and all the legal rights and responsibilities that flow from statehood, but also includes a right to integrate.[484] There is no option, however, of autonomy, or a right to a democracy. So there is some merit in the argument that the internal element of self-determination is simply a creation of scholarly writings and opinions. However, these options may be available as part of a negotiated settlement in cases where a people are not subject to alien and or foreign subjugation, or cannot satisfy the Montevideo criteria.[485]

480. Cassese, *A Legal Reappraisal*, p. 272; Radan, *The Break-up of Yugoslavia*, p. 202.
481. The question of what options should be available and how they should be worded in the proposed referendum on Scottish independence has been a matter of some debate: Ian Jack, 'Scotland's Independence referendum question is Set, but Who Does it Favour?', *The Guardian*, United Kingdom, 8 Feb 2013; Severein Carrell, 'Scottish Government Changes Wording of Independence Referendum Question', *The Guardian*, United Kingdom, 30 Jan 2013.
482. *Declaration on Colonial Peoples*, UN Doc A/4684 annex ('*Principles Which Should Guide Members in Determining Whether or Not an Obligation Exists to Transmit Called For in Article 73 (e) of the Charter of the United Nations*') 29.
483. *Western Sahara Opinion*, [1975] ICJ Rep 12, 32–4 [56]–[60]. Although, somewhat puzzlingly, the Court then stated that the validity of a claim would not be affected if the General Assembly in 'special circumstances' had 'dispensed' with consulting with the relevant people: at 59.
484. Malcolm Shaw, *International Law*, 5th ed, 2003, p. 231; Drew, *Meaning*; Ian Brownlie, *Principles of Public International Law*, p. 553. Perhaps another way of expressing this is: 'It follows from this practice that the exercise of self-determination is equivalent to losing colonial status': Sureda, *Evolution*, p. 226.
485. This is Radan's argument: Radan, *The Break-up of Yugoslavia*, p. 245.

In practice, the three choices should be listed clearly in a plebiscite when determining the free will of a people claiming self-determination.[486] Particularly, the option to integration should not be ignored.

d. Denial of a democratic government

Commentators have argued that when a democratic government does not exist, there is a legitimate right to exercise self-determination.[487] Expressions of the right to political participation, through the electoral process, have been stated in a number of international treaties and agreements: art 21 of the *Universal Declaration on Human Rights of 1948*;[488] art 25(b) of *the ICCPR* (1966); art 23 of the *American Convention on Human Rights*;[489] art 13 of the *African Charter on Human and Peoples' Rights* and art 3 of the *First Protocol to the Convention on Human Rights.*[490]

The expression contained in these documents – 'by virtue of that right they freely determine their political status and freely pursue their economic, social and cultural development' – does imply a *free choice*, and that freedom could extend to the political system of their country. However, it is unclear whether it means an *ongoing choice.*[491] It is clear that States wished to limit self-determination to colonial peoples seeking independence. Thus it could be argued that at the time these documents were prepared and adopted, the object of this free choice included the right of a colonial people to choose whether to remain subject to the sovereignty of the colonial power or their own sovereignty. Such a conclusion is supported by

486. Cassese, *A Legal Reappraisal*, p. 272; Ibid, p. 202.
487. Daes, *A Right of Peoples*, p. 52; Thomas M Franck, 'The Emerging Right to Democratic Governance' *American Journal of International Law* 86, 1992, 47; Gregory H Fox, 'The Right to Political Participation in International Law', *Yale Journal of International Law* 17, 1992, p. 540. See generally Gregory H Fox and Brad R Roth (eds), *Democratic Governance and International Law*, 2000.
488. Article 21 *Universal Declaration on Human Rights of 1948* UN GAOR, 3rd sess 1083rd plen mtg, UN Doc A/Res/217(III) A (10 December 1948) art 21 states that:

    (1) Everyone has the right to take part in the government of his country, directly or through freely chosen representatives.
    (2) Everyone has the right of equal access to public service in his country.
    (3) The will of the people shall be the basis of the authority of government: this will shall be expressed in periodic and genuine elections which shall be by universal and equal suffrage and shall be held by secret vote or by equivalent free voting procedures.

489. International Convenant on Civil and Political Rights, opened for signature 16 December 1966, 999 UNTS 171, art 6 (entered into force 23 March 1976) (ICCPR) art 25.
490. For a detailed discussion of these treaty regimes see Fox, *The Right to Political Participation in International Law*, p. 539.
491. See the discussion by Cassese regarding this point: Cassese, *A Legal Reappraisal*, pp. 52–55.

Principle VI of the *Annex to the Declaration of Colonial Peoples*, which lists the alternative choices available as the expression of free will of a people claiming self-determination.[492] These choices do not explain how self-determination can include what is a purely political concept, such as Western Liberalism.

The decision by the Canadian Supreme Court, and other documents such as the *Vienna Declaration*, make clear that it is not a 'right to democracy', but a fair and equitable participation and representation in government, without discrimination, that triggers a right to claim self-determination. There is a vast difference between participation in government and a specific political system.[493] In considering whether the Quebecois people had a right to self-determination the Canadian Supreme Court considered whether the Canadian government had subjugated the Quebecois by preventing the Quebecois from fair and equitable participation and representation in the government of Canada. To answer this question the Court did not simply consider the nature of Canada's political system. Instead the Court noted that on numerous occasions the Prime Minister of Canada was in fact from Quebec, and many Quebecois held important and high level positions within the federal government, as mentioned earlier in the chapter.[494] Thus, the people of Quebec had not actually been denied any meaningful participation or access to government, and were accordingly not entitled to secede without the consent of the Canadian government.[495] The Court did not address the issue as one of a lack of democracy, but of a lack of governmental representation.

Thus, the failure to have a democratic government in the Western liberal tradition does not provide a legal basis to claim self-determination and definitely does not entitle the people to seek the assistance of the international community.[496] What is more important is whether the people have been subject to alien or foreign subjugation.

492. As mentioned above the three choices are emergence as a sovereign independent state, free association with an independent State; or integration with an independent state.

493. The Canadian Supreme Court merely said *possibly*; their answer was not definitive: *Reference re Secession of Quebec* [1998] 2 SCR 217, 222. See also the *Vienna Declaration*, A/CONF.157/23 12 July 1993.

494. *Reference re Secession of Quebec* [1998] 2 SCR 217, 292; *Vienna Declaration*, A/CONF.157/23 12 July 1993. See the discussion in Crawford, *Creation of States*, pp. 118–22.

495. *Re Secession of Quebec* [1996] 2 SCR 217, 222.

496. Perhaps with the exceptions of the situations where a democratic government is ousted by military force, such as in Haiti in 1994, and where intervention is based on human rights violations. The US's action was also authorised by the UN Security Council. See Andrew Field, 'The Legality of Humanitarian Intervention and the Use of Force in the Absence of United Nations Authority', 26 *Monash University Law Review* 354, (2000); Malcolm Shaw, *International Law*, p. 1048.

e. Alien and foreign subjugation

As noted above, the Canadian Supreme Court recognised that if a people were subject to alien and foreign subjugation this would provide a legal basis for their claim to self-determination. Many authors also accept this reason,[497] and make similar suggestions for situations that give rise to a legal right, including a historical grievance, such as the invasion and subsequent occupation of a people's territory,[498] or a threat of extinction.[499] Norman categorises these suggestions as 'just-cause theories',[500] and they form the basis for the concept of remedial self-determination.

Despite the existence of a remedial right being raised by at least two judicial decisions – firstly, by the European Court of Human Rights in *Loizidou v Turkey*,[501] and secondly, by the Canadian Supreme Court when tackling Quebec[502] – and several entities, such as the African Commission on Human and Peoples Rights[503] and UN Working Groups,[504] commentators and States have recently begun to question the existence of a remedial right to self-determination,[505] or at best expressed tentative support.[506] For example Vidmar, who has written extensively in this area, stated that 'the foundations of the doctrine [remedial right to self-determination] remain controversial both in theory and practice'.[507] He further noted that 'the international

497. Eide, *Constructive Alternatives*; Norman, *Ethics of Secession*, p. 41; Buchanan, *Toward a Theory of Secession*, p. 331; Brilmayer, *Secession*, p. 189; Daniel Philpott, *In Defense*, p. 382. This is a return to the opinion provided by the Commission of the Rapporteurs in the *Aaland Islands Case*: *The Aaland Islands Question: Report Submitted to the Council of the League of Nations by the Commission of Rapporteurs*, League of Nations Doc. B7 [C] 21/68/106 (April 1921), 29.
498. An example of historical grievances would be the Baltic States, which were independent States in 1939 before being annexed by the former USSR in 1939, and again in 1944: Norman, *Ethics of Secession*, p. 41; Brilmayer, *Secession*, p. 189. Another example is East Timor, which was annexed by Indonesia in 1975. Buchanan states that this situation is analogous to legitimate owners reclaiming their stolen property: Buchanan, *Toward a Theory of Secession*, p. 330.
499. The Quebecois claim that statehood is the only sure way to ensure the survival of their culture: Buchanan, *Toward a Theory of Secession*, p. 325; Norman, *Ethics of Secession*, p. 41.
500. Norman, *Ethics of Secession*, p. 41.
501. *Loizidou v Turkey* (1997) 23 EHRR 244, 535 (Wildhaber and Ryssdal JJ).
502. *Reference re Secession of Quebec* [1998] 2 SCR 217, 224–5.
503. In relation to the claim for independence by the Katangese from Zaire: *African Commission on Human and Peoples Rights*, Comm. No 75/92, 1995, [6].
504. *UN Working Group on Minorities*, Asbjorn Eide, 'Possible Ways and Means of Facilitating the Peaceful and Constructive Solution of Problems Involving Minorities', UN Doc, E/CN.4/Sub.2/1993/34, (10 August 1993), [55].
505. Argentina, *Written Submission*, 17 April 2009, p. 34 [85] *Kosovo Opinion*, [2010] ICJ Rep 403; Malcolm Shaw, *Peoples, Territorialism and Boundaries*, pp. 478–507.
506. Summers, *Peoples*, p. 349.
507. Jure Vidmar, 'Remedial Secession in International Law: Theory and (Lack of) Practice', 6 (1) (2010) *St Anthony's International Review*, pp. 50–1; Summers, *Peoples*, pp. 347–348; Weller, *Escaping*, p. 65.

community of states has never accepted either the right of oppressed peoples to secession or the duty to grant recognition when oppressed peoples are trying to create their own state'.[508]

The issue of remedial self-determination was discussed in the *Kosovo Opinion.*[509] Serbia did challenge the existence of the remedial right to self-determination, and they also argued that if a remedial right did exist, it did not apply to Kosovo. They also took pains to argue that these occurred over two decades ago, and the Kosovo Liberation Army also committed numerous violations of Human Rights.[510] In a nutshell, Serbia was arguing that the Kosovar Albanians' right to remedial self-determination had 'lapsed'.[511]

Sadly the Court did not consider this matter as a whole, but His Excellency Judge Trindade did so in his Separate Opinion, where he stated:

> The argument that, since the utmost violence of 1998–1999 one decade has passed and the 'conflict is over', somehow 'buried' into oblivion, and that there is peace today in Kosovo and the aforementioned repression belongs to the past, is in my view superficial, if not unsustainable.... One cannot erase the massive violations of human rights and of International Humanitarian Law of the recent past, by invoking the passing of time.[512]

Despite their doubts, even commentators like Vidmar agree that the idea of a remedial right has some merit, and indeed it does.[513] The concept of a remedial right provides a response to the floodgate argument,[514] and ameliorates the concerns that an unfettered right and unstructured approach to the right of self-determination will lead to anarchy. It can also minimise the use of spurious arguments such as saltwater colonialism, as outlined above, by States seeking to deny *all claims to* self-determination.[515] In other words, the theory provides a convincing method to contain self-determination that is

508. Vidmar, *Remedial Secession*, pp. 50–1.
509. *Kosovo Opinion*, [2001] ICJ Rep 403.
510. Serbia, *Written Submission*, 17 April 2009, pp. 230–233 [626]–[633] & [646] *Kosovo Opinion* [2010] ICJ Rep 403.
511. See for example Cyprus *Written Submission*: 17 April 2009, pp. 36–38 [140]–[148] esp [146]. Note, however, that Argentina argued that human rights abuses were in fact continuing: Argentina *Written Submission*, 17 April 2009, p. 33 [83] & Serbia, *Written Submission,* 17 April 2009, p. 233 [646] & [649] *Kosovo Opinion* [2010] ICJ Rep 403.
512. And: 'The scars of the bloodshed will take a long time to heal, they will take generations to heal': Trindade, Separate Opinion. *Kosovo Opinion* [2010] ICJ Rep 403, 587 [163].
513. Vidmar, *Remedial Secession*, p. 50. Vidmar has written extensively on this topic.
514. Ibid.
515. Ibid *Kosovo Opinion* [2010] ICJ Rep 403, 587, [163].

not inconsistent with decolonisation but prevents spurious claims, such as, for example, the use of the threat of independence as a means to extract an unfair and disproportionate amount of national resources, as was accused of the Quebecois.[516]

The remedial right also promotes the protection of human rights. The remedial theory can protect peoples since it may encourage or shape State behaviour that protects the claimants. For example, a State seeking to deny a people's claim to the remedial rights to self-determination has to prove that they are in fact not being repressed, or alternatively are in some way involved in the political or governing process.[517] As a consequence a State may be more likely to negotiate with the group, grant it more political autonomy, or a greater share in the distribution of resources, or to provide guarantees to protect language, religious freedom, indeed the whole range of political, social and cultural rights as detailed in the *ICCPR*, rather than violently repress a people's claims through military force.[518] Shaping State behaviour in this manner also benefits the international community too, since it reduces the possibility of threats to international peace and security.[519] Thus remedial theories, as well as providing a means to determine the 'legitimacy' of a claim to self-determination, also provide the means to determine the 'legitimacy' of denying a claim.

Whilst the existence of the remedial theories has been challenged, there are very sound reasons for arguing there *should be* a remedial right to self-determination.[520] If the right to self-determination is to be qualified, then the remedial theories provide the right balance between protecting the claimants, the parent government, and also the international community. More importantly, the remedial theory ensures the continued relevance of the norm to self-determination.

516. Philpott, *In Defense*, p. 383; Norman *Ethics of Secession*, pp. 41–42; Buchanan, *Toward a Theory of Secession*, p. 337.
517. Norman, *Ethics of Secession*, p. 42.
518. Norman argues that currently States have to be pressured into negotiating with claimants: Ibid 46. A sample of the rights protected by the *ICCPR* include: the right to life (art 6(1)); the right to freedom from torture (art 7); freedom from slavery (art 8(1)); the right to liberty and security of person (art 9(1)), the right to hold opinions without interference, right to freedom of expression (art 19), and the right of peaceful assembly (art 21).
519. Norman also believes that remedial theories, by reinforcing the legitimacy of States when they treat their citizens justly, reinforce an international community based upon States, and thus counter the argument that self-determination poses a threat to the international community: Norman, *Ethics of Secession*, p. 42.
520. *De lege frenda* (what the law ought to be) as opposed to *lex lata*.

Finally, who would state that a people, when faced with attempted genocide, are not entitled to claim statehood?[521] One only has to remember Halabja.[522] As noted by Igantieff:

> But after seeing Halabja, you realize one thing very clearly: autonomy will never do. It is a stopping point on a destination. But it cannot ever be the end of the road. For Halabja happened, and for a people who have known genocide, there is only one thing that will do: a [S]tate of their own.[523]

However, what happens once a people make their choice clear? If they demand independence, is the parent State obliged to accept this? Are the people entitled to support from the international community? Does a legitimate claim for self-determination require the 'consent' of the parent State? These questions raise the issue of the norm of non-interference in the domestic affairs of a State, which will be discussed below.[524]

f. Is the consent of the parent state required?

The final suggested pre-condition is whether a legitimate claim requires the consent of the State involved. What happens if a people seek to exercise self-determination? Are they entitled to seek the assistance of the international community, and would the consent of the parent State be required before the international community can intervene? After all, the norm of non-intervention is one of the most important aspects of sovereignty, and international law.[525] This discussion will involve a brief discussion of the concept of humanitarian intervention the concept of 'earned sovereignty'. These are radical concepts indeed.

Interestingly, the Canadian Supreme Court held that because Quebec did not satisfy the Court's three pre-conditions, it did not have a right under international law to claim self-determination, and furthermore, it did not have a right under the Canadian Constitution. However, the Court held that

521. Raič argues that an almost fundamental belief held from the very beginnings of mankind's attempts at social and political organisation is that *only* a separate and independent political existence within a defined territory can achieve the effective protection of a community: David Raič, *Statehood and the Law of Self-Determination*, The Hague: Kluwer Law International [Incorporating Martinus Nijhoff Publishers], 2002, p. 9.
522. On the 16th March 1988 the Iraqi air force dropped canisters of mustard gas, nerve gas and cyanide on the town of Halabja. Approximately 5,000 people – men, women, and children – died. The Iraqi army later dynamited the town, and Halabja ceased to exist: Ignatieff, *Blood and Belonging*, pp. 149–50.
523. Ibid, p. 151.
524. *UN Charter*, arts 2(4) 2(7).
525. Brownlie, *Principles of Public International Law*, pp. 292–94.

if Quebec still claimed self-determination, and was recognised by the international community as being an independent State, Canada would have to accept the actions of the international community.[526] This suggests that the consent of the parent State is to an extent irrelevant, outside of it embarking on a ruthless violent armed campaign to repress the self-determination claim. Traditionally, unless it is in a State's vested interests, peoples seeking to claim self-determination are left to fend for themselves, which, given the often one-sided nature of the balance of armed forces, tends to result in disastrous consequences for the claimants.[527]

Circumstances where the State conducts a ruthless armed attack on a people claiming self-determination may justify the direct, and even armed, intervention by the international community to assist the people achieve statehood – an act of humanitarian intervention.[528]

I. HUMANITARIAN INTERVENTION

Humanitarian intervention is the use of armed force which interferes in the affairs of a State 'whose immediate goal is to alleviate or prevent humanitarian suffering'.[529] There are many issues raised by humanitarian intervention, perhaps the most important being whether it is ever legitimate.[530] Humanitarian intervention appears to contradict a number of important norms of international law, such as the norm of non-intervention, the right to territorial integrity and the use of armed force.[531] These norms are important

526. Brownlie, *Rule of Law*, p. 45.
527. Aris Gounaris, 'Self-Determination and Secession: A Moral Theory Perspective' in Aleksandar Pavkovic and Peter Radan (eds), *On the Way to Statehood: Secession and Globalisation*, Aldershot; Ashgate, 2008, p. 129.
528. An in-depth discussion of humanitarian intervention cannot be made. Here is a brief list of selected works on the topic: Nancy D Arnison, 'International Law and Non-Intervention: When Do Humanitarian Concerns Supersede Sovereignty?', 17 (1993) *Fletcher Forum of World Affairs,* p. 199; Susan Brean, *Humanitarian Intervention: The United Nations and Collective Responsibility*, London: Cameron May, 2005; John Currie, 'NATO's Humanitarian Intervention in Kosovo: Making or Breaking International Law?', 36 (1998) *Canadian Yearbook of International Law*, p. 303; Field, *Legality of Intervention*; Orford, *Humanitarian Intervention*; Touko Piiparinen, 'The Lessons of Darfur for the Future on Humanitarian Intervention', 13 (2007) *Global Governance* p. 365; Jianming Shen, 'The Non-Intervention Principle and Humanitarian Interventions Under International Law', 7 (2001) *International Legal Theory*, p. 1; Tania Voon, 'Closing the Gap Between Legitimacy and Legality of Humanitarian Intervention: Lessons from East Timor and Kosovo', 7 (2002–2003) *UCLA Journal of International Law and Foreign Affairs*, p. 31.
529. Voon, *Closing the Gap*, p. 36; Field, *Legality of Intervention*, p. 340.
530. See, eg, John Currie, *NATO's Humanitarian Intervention*, p. 303; Field, *Legality of Intervention*, pp. 344–8; Tania Voon, C*losing the Gap*, p. 33.
531. *UN Charter*, art 2(7), 2(4); Shen, *Non-Intervention*, p. 7.

in the maintenance of international peace and security, so great care must be taken in allowing it to become a norm.[532]

Furthermore, as noted by many commentators, humanitarian intervention can provide a 'smokescreen' for hiding a State's ulterior motives, enabling them to use military force to promote their own self-interest.[533] Balance is also required – the 'cure' cannot be more lethal than the illness it seeks to destroy,[534] and the intervention should not be allowed to escalate into or cause a major multi-State conflict.[535] It is a highly complex topic, and there is a real dilemma between the consequences of non-intervention and intervention.[536] Certainly the examples of Rwanda and Darfur show what can happen if the international community chooses not too intervene, or if it intervenes too late.[537]

However, despite all the controversy surrounding humanitarian intervention, there appears to be a growing acceptance that protection of human rights abuses should supersede sovereignty and the norm of non-intervention, although there may not be a consensus on when and how.[538] Certainly there have been past examples of humanitarian intervention, both unilateral[539] and with the consent of the UN,[540] in situations involving self-determination, with the most recent being the interventions in East Timor and Kosovo.[541]

The issue of legality appears to centre on firstly, whether the UN Security Council has authorised the intervention,[542] and secondly, whether, in the absence of such authorisation, a unilateral action by a State satisfies suggested guidelines.[543] When discussing pre-conditions, if a people are subject to

532. Voon argues that this would have been the situation if Australia had unilaterally intervened into East Timor without Indonesia's consent: Voon, *Closing the Gap*, p. 83.
533. Such as NATO's intervention into Kosovo. This situation is worsened by apparent inconsistencies of States' actions, for example, the US intervening to protect human rights in Kosovo, but then refusing to intervene in East Timor due to the US's relationship with mineral-rich Indonesia: Ibid p. 51, 73, 85; Field, *Legality of Intervention*, p. 343; Shen, *Non-Intervention*, pp. 10–16.
534. Shen argues that NATO's intervention into Kosovo was responsible for many civilian deaths and consequently created additional human rights disasters: Shen, *Legality of Intervention*, pp. 10–16.
535. Voon, *Closing the Gap*, p. 84.
536. Orford, *Humanitarian Intervention*, pp. 1–37.
537. See *Roadmap*, Phase 1.
538. Voon, *Closing the Gap*; Arnison, *International Law and Non-Intervention.*
539. India's intervention into East Pakistan in 1971 that led to the formation of Bangladesh, and arguably NATO's intervention into Kosovo.
540. Australia's intervention into East Timor.
541. Eg. Voon, *Closing the Gap.*
542. Field *Legality of Intervention*, pp. 344–48; Ibid, pp. 37–43.
543. Commentators naturally suggest a diverse range of guidelines. Field examines five suggested guidelines: (1) large-scale human rights abuses or atrocities must have occurred; (2) there must be an overriding humanitarian motive; (3) a preference for joint action

attempted genocide and large-scale human rights abuses by a parent State then the people have a right under international law to unilaterally claim statehood. It is argued here that the people should seek the international community's assistance, including humanitarian intervention.

In conclusion, I believe that only four pre-conditions are required for a legitimate claim to self-determination:

(1) The claimants are a distinct people; either a colonial people, or a non-colonial people subject to alien and foreign subjugation.
(2) The claimants have expressed their free will in an internationally monitored plebiscite to achieve statehood.
(3) The people accept and agree to be bound by the terms of the *UN Charter* and the norms of international law.
(4) The people are capable of forming a State as defined in international law.[544]

Radan argues that if a people 'fail' to meet a recognised set of pre-conditions then 'its right to self-determination would need to be expressed in other ways.'[545] Those 'other ways' would appear to be what many commentators, particularly those writing after the end of the Cold War, describe as 'internal' self-determination.[546] Although some commentators argue that internal self-determination is simply just a creation of 'political talking and scholarly writing',[547] the concept plays an important role in regard to indigenous peoples or minorities, with some commentators believing that for minorities self-determination does not *mean* (or perhaps include) a right to independence,[548] but a protection of their human rights, in particular their ability to participate in their central government.[549]

where possible; (4) the intervention must be proportionate to the threat; (5) all other options or alternatives have been exhausted. Field, *Legality of Intervention*, pp. 339–434. Voon examines the same concept but under different headings: Voon *Closing the Gap* pp. 58–94.

544. See Chapter 2.
545. Radan, *The Break-up of Yugoslavia*, p. 245. Radan does not explain his position clearly, but I assume he is referring to the internal element of self-determination.
546. Such as autonomy, protection of human rights, and, controversially, a right to a democracy: Sureda, *Evolution*, p. 226; Patrick Thornberry, 'The Democratic or Internal Aspect of Self-Determination' in Tomuschat, *Modern Law of Self-Determination*, p. 101.
547. Gudmundur Alfredsson, 'The Right of Self-Determination and Indigenous Peoples' in Tomuschat, *Modern Law of Self-Determination*, 1993, p. 50.
548. Some commentators argue that if the State abuses the human rights of their indigenous peoples, then the indigenous peoples are entitled to independence: Sanders, *Self-Dtermination and Indigenous Peoples*, p. 78.
549. Gudmundur Alfredsson, *Indigenous Peoples*, p. 50; Daes, *A Right of Peoples*, p. 53.

H. Conclusion

The purpose of this chapter was to examine when a claim for self-determination is legitimate according to international law. The examination raised the issues of identifying the legitimate beneficiaries, the existence of pre-conditions, and the interaction of self-determination with other important rules of international law, such as territorial integrity, and the norm of non-intervention into the domestic affairs of a State.

Establishing the means to determine the legitimacy of self-determination and the legitimate claimants is important since it may encourage States to resolve claims in a more positive and peaceful manner. The best approach should provide the correct balance between denying spurious claims and preventing 'unionist evils',[550] and thus counter the floodgate argument that has been used to effectively neuter self-determination. As mentioned in the introduction to this monograph, what *terrifies* the international community is the perceived lack of a limit to the application of self-determination. In their eyes self-determination is capable of *infinite* application, or that it could lead to the total dismemberment of a State. This is not true, and a proper interpretation of the legal right would render these concerns moot.

There are other issues with self-determination, however. Firstly, there is a risk that unresolved claims to self-determination could erupt into a lengthy conflict that has serious repercussions for the claimants, the State involved and the international community. Secondly, currently States have sought to neutralize self-determination through the use of norms such as territorial integrity, but also through manipulation of what was meant by the term 'people'. By proper application of the findings of this chapter, these concerns are ameliorated. Like the maxim *ut res magis valeat quam pereat* – 'the thing may rather have effect than be destroyed'.[551]

Examining the discussions and the drafting of relevant international documents, such as the *UN Charter*, the ICCPR, *the Declaration on Friendly Relations* and *the Declaration on Colonial Peoples*, revealed that States desired to limit who could legitimately claim self-determination. The easiest means to do so was to restrict its application to colonial peoples, which were defined using a territorial approach, but more importantly by defining colonialism as meaning 'saltwater colonialism', and alien as European. However, to restrict decolonisation to European colonies would ignore the issue of whether the people seeking self-determination were oppressed by a colonial overlord, and this contradicted the very premise upon which self-determination was

550. 'The absence of institutions of self-determination may allow unionist evils, just as the presence of such institutions might admittedly promote the ill effects of self-determination': Philpott, *Self Determination in Practice*, p. 79.
551. Dr Frank Przetacznik, 'The Basic Collective Human Right to Self-Determination of Peoples and Nations as a Prerequisite for Peace', p. 8 (1990–91) *New York Law School Journal of Human Rights*, pp. 101–102.

based, and contradicted what was intended in all international documents – to free people from oppression by a foreign or alien power. It was thus concluded that a territorial approach could not be applied to assist in the definition of a legitimate claimant. Instead, the definition should cover a 'people' suffering from alien or foreign subjugation.

The characteristic of foreign and alien domination provided the basis for the discussion of what pre-conditions should be satisfied before a claim could be said to be legitimate. Ultimately only four pre-conditions are required for a legitimate claim to self-determination, and statehood: (1) the claimants are a distinct people subject to alien and foreign subjugation; (2) the claimants have expressed their free will in an internationally monitored plebiscite to achieve statehood; (3) the people accept and agree to be bound by the terms of the *UN Charter* and the norms of international law; and (4) the people are capable of forming a State in accordance with international law.

Analysing the scope of what self-determination involves, it was concluded that self-determination simply implies that a people have more than one choice. They can choose to form their own State, and all the legal rights and responsibilities that flow from statehood, but also choose a right to integrate, or to have a free association with another State.

The chapter's later findings came from a consideration of the findings of the Canadian Supreme Court. At one point, the Court held that if Quebec claimed self-determination, and was recognised by the international community as being an independent State, Canada would have to accept the actions of the international community. Thus, the consent of the parent State appeared to be irrelevant and furthermore, in circumstances where the State conducts a ruthless armed attack on a people claiming self-determination direct, and even armed, intervention by the international community may be justified to assist the people achieve statehood – an act of humanitarian intervention.

In the next chapter the author will consider the second suggested role of the ICJ – playing a role in the recognition of statehood.

2 The determination of statehood

I should regard it as highly improper of me to admit that any country on earth can question the sovereignty of the United States of America in the existence of the highly political act of recognition. ... Moreover, I would not admit ... that there exists a tribunal of justice or any other kind. Anywhere, that can pass judgment upon the legality or the validity of that act of my country...[1]

A. Introduction

In the first chapter the first role proposed for the ICJ was examined, namely determining the legitimacy of a claim to self-determination. It is the purpose of this chapter to now examine what the role of the Court would be in this process of the 'birth of a State'.

Currently there is no accepted mechanism of how States are born other than through 'natural selection'.[2] If an entity that claims statehood can survive then it is worth welcoming into the 'club' by its peers.[3] In international law this 'welcome' is known as recognition whereby States recognise a particular political community as a State.[4] Thus, there is an important link

1. Letter Dated 8 March 1950 from the Secretary-General to the President of the Security Council Transmitting a Memorandum on the Legal Aspects of the Problem of Representation in the United Nations, UN SCOR, 3rd sess, UN Doc S/1466 (9 March 1950) 2–3.
2. Which normally means that a group uses warfare and military success to emerge as a State: Thomas D Grant, *The Recognition of States, Law and Practice in Debate and Evolution*, Westport: Praeger Westport 1999, p. 92; Bruce D Porter, *War and the Rise of the State, the Military Foundations of Modern Politics*, New York: The Free Press, 1994.
3. A Rigo Sureda, *The Evolution of the Right of Self-Determination: A Study of United Nations Practice* Leiden: A. W. Sijthoff, 1973, p. 274; Hilary Charlesworth and Christine Chinkin, *The Boundaries of International Law: A Feminist Analysis* United Kingdom: Manchester University Press, 2000, p. 142.
4. See the Oral Statement of Professor James Crawford acting on behalf of the United Kingdom, *Accordance with International Law of the Unilateral Declaration of Independence by the Provisional Institutions of Self-Government of Kosovo*, CR 2009/32, (Thursday 10 December 2009) at pp. 48–49, para. 7. Available form the ICJ website: www.icj-cij.org/docket/files/141/15734.pdf [accessed 3 May 2013] A form of 'peer review'. Gerad Kreijen,

between self-determination, statehood and recognition.[5] Kreijen describes the relationship between these concepts in the following manner: 'Whereas statehood is the gateway to international legal personality, recognition may be seen as the key to statehood.'[6]

The idea of recognition is problematic on several grounds. Firstly, the recognition of statehood must be distinguished from recognition of governments. Although this issue will not be the focus of this chapter, it is submitted here that often the nature and type of government has affected the recognition of statehood. Secondly, there are competing theories of what recognition of statehood means, and what it actually achieves, the so-called 'Great Debate' between the declaratory and constitutive theories. Thirdly, recognition is considered to be a universal act, so how many acts of recognition constitute the critical threshold? Finally, the nature of recognition is arbitrary, inconsistent, and so plagued by political expediency, that it is more often used as a tool of statecraft, than a genuine attempt to identify a State.[7]

These problems have prompted commentators to seek not just alternative theories of recognition,[8] but alternative mechanisms to determine statehood. One suggestion is that guidelines should be established to assist States when considering recognition,[9] and another suggestion is Dugard's theory of collective recognition by the UN.[10] One commentator, Raič, argues that statehood is determined through a two-step process: resolving the traditional criteria, the Montevideo criteria, before applying the modern criteria or whether the creation of the entity's statehood breached international law.[11] In other words what Raič is arguing is that determining statehood involves firstly determining whether an entity in fact is a State, and then whether in law it is a State.[12]

State Failure, Sovereignty, and Effectiveness, The Hague: Martinus Nijohoff Publishers, 2004, p. 13; Obiora Chinedu Okafor, *Redefining Legitimate Statehood: International Law and State Fragmentation in Africa*, The Hague: Martinus Nijhoff, 2000, pp. 54–65.

5. James Crawford, *The Creation of States in International Law* (2nd ed.) Oxford: Clarendon Press, 2006, p. 107, 376.
6. Kreijen, *State Failure*, p. 13; see also P.K. Menon, *The Law of Recognition in International Law, Basic Principles*. Lampter: The Edwin Mellen Press Ltd., 1994, p. 27.
7. Joseph Starke, *Introduction to International Law* (9th ed) London: Butterworths 1984, pp. 21–33.
8. For example, Kelsen's theories or categories of recognition: political and legal: Kelsen, *Principles of International Law*, (2nd ed., revised edition by Robert W Tucker), New York: Holt, Rinehart, and Winston Inc, 1966 pp. 222–225.
9. Crawford, *Creation of States in International Law*, p. 540; Grant, *Recognition of States*, p. 2.
10. Eg. collective recognition by the UN: John Dugard, *Recognition and the United Nations*, Cambridge: Grotius Publications, 1987.
11. David Raič, *Statehood and the Law of Self-Determination*, The Hague: Kluwer Law International [Incorporating Martinus Nijhoff Publishers] 2002, p. 154.
12. In essence he is rejecting the argument that the formation of a new States is a question of fact only, which is contrary to what early commentators like Oppenheim argued. Raič's

However, Raič remains silent on who or what should determine these questions.[13] Some commentators have expressed the belief that there is no 'competent body' to resolve questions of recognition.[14] Crawford, however, when discussing his own criteria for statehood, suggests that any problems should be subject to settlement by the ICJ.[15]

It is the purpose of this paper to examine whether the ICJ, is able through the use of its advisory jurisdiction to play a role in the determination of a particular international legal person, a State.[16] It will be argued here that the fulfilment of statehood is an issue regulated by international law, thus a better approach is for the ICJ to act as the 'recognising body', and so determine statehood using Raič's two-step process, that involves determination: (1) of a State's factual existence, and (2) that its creation did not breach international law.[17] It will also be argued that the Court could play a more extensive role, something akin to the role played by the Badniter Commission (formed on 27 August 1991 to provide legal advice to the EC's Conference on Yugoslavia).

The chapter will be divided as follows. Firstly, the discussion will begin by examining the Montevideo criteria. The second part will explore recognition and the role States play in determining statehood, in particular how States' interests influence the recognition process. Thus, laying the foundation for the final part, examining what role the ICJ would play.

B. The definition of a state in international law

Whilst it is an easy task to find an example of a State identifying a definition is more difficult, these examples are very diverse, and also do change.[18] Thus,

theory is also in a way similar to the concepts of *de facto* and *de jure* recognition. See Lassa Oppenheim, *International Law: A Treatise* (Sir Hersch Lauterpacht ed, 8th ed, 1955) vol. 1, pp. 544, 209, and Crawford's discussion of Oppenheim's work: Crawford, *Creation of States*, p. 4.

13. Raič, *Statehood*, p 154.
14. Dugard, *Recognition*, p. 41.
15. Crawford, *Creation of States*, pp. 40–41.
16. International legal personality was discussed and defined by the ICJ in the *Reparations Opinion*. See the discussion below, and generally, Roland Portmann, *Legal Personality in International Law*, Cambridge: Cambridge University Press 2010, pp. 248–254.
17. This is Raič's theory: Raič, *Statehood*; John Dugard and David Raič, 'The Role of Recognition in the Law and Practice of Secession' in Marcelo G Kohen, *Secession, International Law Perspectives*, Cambridge: Cambridge University Press, 2006, p. 98.
18. Starke, *International Law*, p. 125; Christian Tomuschat, 'Self-Determination in a Post-Colonial World' in Christian Tomuschat (ed), *Modern Law of Self-Determination*, The Hague: Kluwer Academic Publishers incorporating Martinus Nijhoff Publishers, 1993, p. 5. An example is the dissolution of the former USSR and the numerous new States formed in its wake.

identifying a definition of States is more difficult. During the drafting of the *Declaration of Rights and Duties of States* by the International Law Commission it was noted that whilst the term 'State' was in common usage in international documents, and treaties, speeches, and its meaning was understood, it had no accepted definition. This rather ironic situation prompted Crawford to ask how it was possible that a concept as central to international law as statehood could remain undefined for so long. His answer was that the question of defining a State only arose in borderline cases, and due to political reasons.[19] Furthermore, actually confirming a definition would be highly controversial, and 'immensely' difficult.[20]

This difficulty is due in part to the fact that a 'State' is an artificially created entity,[21] a 'legal fiction':[22] a legal expediency.[23] The difficulty also could be explained by the fact that it may be advantageous to States if a definition remained *elusive*.[24] For example, the failure to acknowledge or create objective standards of statehood prior to 1933 protected and ensured the ability of European States to deny the international legal personality of non-European peoples, and thus justify European imperialism, and dominance.[25] Whilst it is difficult to identify a definition, one point is clear: a State is an international legal person.[26] Accordingly the determination of statehood is a determination of an entity's international legal personality.[27]

If as posited in this monograph that the ICJ is to play a role in the determination of international legal personality and statehood specifically, then a *legal* definition of statehood, or at least legal criteria for statehood must be found.[28] It would appear by consensus amongst commentators that such criteria can be found in art 1 of the *Montevideo Convention of 1933 on the Rights and*

19. Crawford, *Creation of States*, p. 40.
20. Ibid, 38.
21. Analogous in this way to that of a modern-day corporation: Martin van Creveld, *The Rise and Decline of the State* Cambridge: Cambridge University Press, 1999, p. 1.
22. Hans Kelsen, *General Theory of Law and State*, New York: Russell and Russell, 1961, pp. 181–88. See Starke's criticism of Kelsen: Starke, *International Law*, pp. 57, 92; and also Raič, *Statehood*, pp. 21–23.
23. Raič, *Statehood*, p. 1; Hans Kelsen, 'The Pure Theory of Law and Analytical Jurisprudence' 55 (1941–42) *Harvard Law Review*, pp. 64–65.
24. Thomas D Grant, 'Defining Statehood: the Montevideo Convention and its Discontents' (1998–99) 37 *Columbia Journal of Transnational Law*, p. 447.
25. Ibid, p. 449.
26. This was made clear by the ICJ in the Reparations Opinion: *Reparation for Injuries Suffered in the Service of the United Nations (Advisory Opinion)* [1949] ICJ Rep 174 ('*Reparations Opinion*') at 175.
27. Crawford, *Creation of States*, pp. 28–30, & pp. 40–2; Kelsen, *Principles*, p. 183: *Opinion No 8 of the Arbitration Commission of the Peace Conference on Yugoslavia* (1992) 31 ILM 1521 ('Opinion No 8'), where the Badinter Commission stated that the dissolution of a State meant that it no longer had legal personality.
28. Raič, *Statehood*, p. 19.

Duties of States.[29] Examining these criteria is important since it was argued in chapter I of the monograph that one pre-condition of a legitimate claim for self-determination would include satisfying this criteria.

1. The Montevideo criteria

The purpose of the *Montevideo Convention* was to introduce objective 'empirical' criteria that could be assessed without involving the political desires of States.[30] Although only adopted by 16 States, the criteria of the *Montevideo Convention* have been widely accepted by the international community as reflecting the requirements of statehood in customary international law.[31] As noted by Grant, even commentators who are critical of the Montevideo criteria acknowledge their importance in the discourse on statehood.[32] Thus very few commentators suggest alternative criteria,[33] whilst others merely modify them, or suggest additional criteria such as sovereignty or independence.[34]

Article 1 contains four characteristics of a State as follows:

1. a permanent population;
2. a defined territory;
3. a government;
4. a capacity to enter into relations with other States.

a. A permanent population

Permanent population 'refers to the presence of a group of persons in respect of whom government authority is exercised in a certain territory.'[35] There

29. *The Montevideo Convention of 1933 on the Rights and Duties of States*, signed 26 December 1933, 135 LNTS 19 (entered into force 26 December 1934) adopted at a meeting of the 7th International Convention of American States held in Montevideo.
30. This goal is stated very clearly in art 3, which states *inter alia*: 'the political existence of a State is independent of recognition by other States.' Raič, *Statehood*, p. 36; Oyvind Osterud, 'Sovereign Statehood and National Self-Determination: A World Order Dilemma' in Marianne Heiberg (ed.), *Subduing Sovereignty and the Right to Intervene*, London: Pinter Publishers, 1984, pp. 21–22.
31. David Harris, *Cases and Materials in International Law*, (5th ed), London: Sweet & Maxwell, 1988, p. 102; Crawford, *Creation of States, p.* 45, (who describes the criteria as the 'best known formulation'); Grant, *Recognition of States*, p. 6; Dugard, *Recognition*, p. 7; Starke, *International Law*, p. 91; Marius Olivier, 'Aspects of the Establishment of Sovereignty and the Transfer of Government Authority' (1988–89), 14 *South African Yearbook of International Law* pp. 85, 102.
32. Grant, *Defining Statehood*, p. 414, and his list of refines in his note 51 at p. 425.
33. See for example Crawford's list, Crawford, *Creation of States* pp. 40–41.
34. For example, Devine's suggestion of 'good government': Dermott J Devine, 'The Requirements of Statehood Re-Examined' (1971) 34 *Modern Law Review* 410, 410.
35. Olivier, *Establishment of Sovereignty*, p. 102.

does not appear to be a minimum size.[36] The definition of 'permanent' refers to the intention to inhabit a habitable territory permanently,[37] and includes nomadic tribes, provided a definitive area in which they move can be determined.[38] Population on its own cannot prove statehood, since many areas contain a population with a degree of permanence but are not regarded as States.[39]

b. Territory

As a matter of logic a State cannot exist without territory, so it can be described as an essential element.[40] However, as the examples of Poland, pre-1939 Yugoslavia, pre-1939 Czechoslovakia, and Baltic States suggest, a State can still exist where its territory has been lost through invasion, and the State as a consequence has lost effective control over its territory.[41] As succinctly stated by Grant: whilst a State can still exist if it loses territory: it cannot be 'born' without it.[42] There does not appear to be a 'minimum size'.[43] Furthermore, the territory's borders do not need to be defined precisely for this element to be fulfilled,[44] and all parts of a State's territory do

36. The Vatican City had a population of only 921 in 2004–05: *SBS World Guide: The Complete Fact File on Every Country* (2005) 792. Harris, *Cases and Materials*, p. 103; P K Menon, 'The Subjects of Modern International Law' (1990) 3 *Hague Yearbook of International Law*, pp. 36–7; Raič, *Statehood*, p. 58; Crawford, *Creation of States*, p. 52.
37. Raič, *Statehood*, p. 58.
38. Ingrid Delupis, *The International Legal Order*, Aldershot: Dartmouth, 1994, p. 38; *Western Sahara (Advisory Opinion)* [1975] ICJ Rep 12 ('*Western Sahara*').
39. For example, Antarctica.
40. Crawford, *Creation of States*, p. 36; Sir Arthur Watts, 'The Importance of International Law' in Michael Byers (ed), *The Importance of Law in International Politics*, Oxford: Oxford University Press, 2001, p. 10; Raič, *Statehood*, p. 95.
41. Poland, pre-1939, Yugoslavia and pre-1939 Czechoslovakia lost control to the belligerent actions of Nazi Germany and the Baltic States through the actions of the former USSR. In all cases the territory was illegally annexed by the belligerent power. Grant, *Defining Statehood*, p. 435.
42. Ibid.
43. Crawford, *Creation of States*, pp. 221–33 (see especially 226). Monaco and Nauru are respectively 1.5 and 21 square kilometres in size and their statehood is not questioned.
44. *North Sea Continental Shelf (Federal Republic of Germany v Denmark; Federal Republic of Germany v The Netherlands)* [1969] ICJ Rep 3, 32; and the decision of the German-Polish Mixed Arbitral Tribunal in *Deutsche Continental Gas-Gesellschaft v Polish State* (1929) 5 ILR 11, 14–5 ('*Deutsche Continental*'). Israel was recognised as a State in 1948 despite her borders being uncertain, and even now there is no negotiated agreement on the border between Israel proper and the occupied West Bank of the Jordan River. Another example is the border between India and Pakistan in Kashmir, and also their conflict over the Siachen glacier. Eric Margolis, *War at the Top of the World*, London: Routledge, 2001, p. 120, pp. 133–6; Delupis, *International Legal Order*, p. 37.

not need to be adjacent or be joined to one another.[45] All that is required is that the boundaries are sufficient to clarify to the international community what territory is being claimed by the State.[46] Territory and the exercise of government are closely linked.[47]

c. Government

Government is considered by some to be an essential criterion for statehood for the simple reason that it is necessary to conduct international relations, and because it indicates '... a certain legal status'.[48] Although the Montevideo criterion does not state what form the government should be, increasingly writers consider the requirement for government to mean '*democratic*' government.[49] So would a non-democratic government be 'unacceptable' enough to deny an entity's statehood?[50] This statement implies that States with non-democratic governments are in breach of international law. This position is supported by the signatories of the *Charter of Paris for a New Europe* (essentially members of the European Community) which have stated that they will not accept new members to their community unless, in addition to guaranteeing human rights and protection of minorities, the aspirant States have a democratic government.[51]

45. Delupis, *International Legal Order*, p. 37. Delupis supplies the example of Pakistan before Bangladesh secured its independence.
46. Raič, *Statehood*, p. 61.
47. Hillgruber, *The Admission of New States*, p. 492.
48. Crawford, *Creation of States*, p. 60; Raič, *Statehood*, p. 62. This is based on the *Deutsche Continental* decision, (1929) 5 ILR 11, p. 11, & pp. 14–15, which found that a State *must* consist of a territory governed by an independent authority. Independence is also considered to be indicative of the final criterion capacity to enter foreign relations. See below.
49. Delupis, *International Legal Order*, p. 41. Other authors have argued that there is a right to democracy. Thomas M Franck, 'The Emerging Right to Democratic Governance' (1992) 86 *American Journal of International Law* 46. Whilst this right may be debatable, there does appear to be a right to have a democratic government restored to power after being overthrown by a coup. One obvious example is the Haitian crisis, where the democratically elected government of President Jean-Bertrand Aristide was overthrown by a coup by the Haitian military in 1991. Despite the fact that the coup leaders had effective control over Haiti, the international community refused to recognise the new government and deal with representatives from the new government. They continued to recognise the government of President Aristide as the 'rightful' and the 'legitimate' government of Haiti: Sean Murphy, 'Democratic Legitimacy and the Recognition of States and Governments' (1999) 48 *International and Comparative Law Quarterly*, 545: Lois Fielding, 'Taking the Next Step in the Development of New Human Rights: The Emerging Right of Humanitarian Assistance to Restore Democracy' (1995) 5 *Duke Journal of Comparative and International Law* p. 329; Brad Roth, *Governmental Illegitimacy in International Law*, Oxford: Clarendon Press, 1999.
50. Roth, *Governmental Illegitimacy*, p. 137; Murphy, *Democratic Legitimacy*, p. 546.
51. Christian Hillgruber, 'The Admission of New States to the International Community' (1998) 9 *European Journal of International Law*, p. 492.

Perhaps future political communities must have a democratic government in order to claim statehood,[52] however, whilst democracy may be a characteristic of a type of political system there are several States who do not have this particular characteristic and whose statehood would never be in doubt. Furthermore, such a requirement would appear to be inconsistent with the reasoning in the *Admissions Opinion*, where the Court advised that Member States were not entitled to require additional criteria for membership applications other than those contained in art 4 (1) of the *UN Charter*.[53] Therefore, it is debatable that the type of political system, or government, is an essential part of the definition of government.[54] Instead what is fundamentally more important is that the government respects the rule of law, particularly in the protection of human rights, and minorities, and is representative of the whole of its population.[55]

One suggested definition for government is a 'stable political organization' in control of territory.[56] Raič argues that government is comprised of the executive administrative machinery that regulates the community, and this executive is effective.[57] So what appears to be a more important question is whether the government is in effective control over its territory. Many commentators,[58] and State officials,[59] regard the government's effectiveness as essential, even as a pre-condition of statehood. The existence and extent of the government's effectiveness has been considered to be pivotal in some cases. One example is example is the *Republika Srpska*, because its government was not in effective control of the claimed territory: the government of the SFRY was.[60] Another example is the Turkish

52. Delupis, *The International Legal Order*, p. 41.
53. *Conditions of Admission of a State to Membership in the United Nations (Article 4 of the Charter) (Advisory Opinion)* [1948] ICJ Rep 57, 64, 65 ('*Admissions Opinion*').
54. This issue is linked to the problem of confusing recognition of statehood with the recognition of a government. See the discussion below.
55. This is what the Canadian Supreme Court also held in relation to the secession of Quebec. See the discussion in Chapter 1 above.
56. Harris, *Cases and Materials*, p. 104. Crawford adopts a similar definition: Crawford, *Creation of States*, p. 59.
57. Raič, *Statehood*, p. 62.
58. Kreijen, *State Failure*, pp. 25–26; Robert J Delahunty and John Woo, 'Statehood and the Third Geneva Convention' (2005–06) 46 *Virginia Journal of International Law*, pp. 131–34; Crawford, *Creation of States*, p. 59; Raič, *Statehood*, pp. 52–57; Delupis, *International Legal Order*, p. 40.
59. For example, Sir Roger Makins, the British Ambassador to PRC in 1954, Thomas M Frank, *The Power of Legitimacy Among Nations*, New York: Oxford University Press, 1990, p. 125. Senator Evans, Australia's then Minister of Foreign Affairs in 1991: see Commonwealth of Australia, *Parliamentary Debates*, 22 August 1991, p. 975 (Senator Gareth Evans); Roland Rich, 'Recognition of States: The Collapse of Yugoslavia and the Soviet Union' (1993) 4 *European Journal of International Law*, p. 40.
60. *Prosecutor v Tadić (Appeals Chamber)* Case No IT-94-I-A (15 July 1999) (Judgment) [145]–[154].

Republic of North Cyprus,[61] where the European Court of Human Rights held in *Loizidou v Turkey* that:

> ... it is not necessary to determine whether ... Turkey exercises detailed control over the policies and actions of the authorities of the 'TRNC'. It is obvious from the large number of [Turkish] troops ... that [Turkey's] army exercises effective overall control over that part of the island.[62]

Raič defines effective as being: 'an entity or organ capable of establishing and maintaining a legal order throughout the territory.'[63] However, what is meant by 'effective' is not clear, since like independence, is very relative.[64] Furthermore, there are examples of a State coming into existence when there is a substantial if not a total absence of effectiveness, for example: Guinea-Bisseau;[65] Angola;[66] the Congo;[67] and Bosnia-Herzegovina.[68] Existing governments can lose their effectiveness, as with Somalia in 1991,[69] and Albania in March 1997, and still be considered States,[70] although, ultimately the

61. Crawford, *Creation of States*, p. 81; generally Metin Tamkoc, *The Turkish Cypriot State: The Embodiment of the Right of Self-Determination*, London: K Rustem & Brother, 1988.
62. *Loizidou v Turkey (Merits)* (1996) VI Eur Court HR (ser A) 466–7. This case concerned a claim for compensation by a Cypriot citizen whose property had been forcefully seized by the local TRNC authorities.
63. Raič, *Statehood*, pp. 62–63; Crawford, *Creation of States*, p. 59.
64. Raič, *Statehood*, pp. 53–8; Crawford, *Creation of States*, p. 59.
65. Guinea-Bisseau, when it declared its independence, was recognised as a State by many other States before being recognised by Portugal on 26 August 1974. This was followed by the UN Security Council also granting recognition on 12 August 1974, despite the government not having effect authority over its territory at the time of its declaration of independence: Raič, *Statehood*, pp. 98–99.
66. In Angola, the Portuguese government did 'transfer' authority to the newly independent State in November 1975. However, there was no effective government at that time due to the conflict between three rival factions (National Union for the Total Independence of Angola, the National Front for the Liberation of Angola, and Popular Movement for the Liberation of Angola) competing for control over the new State: Ibid, pp. 99–100.
67. At the time of independence, 30 June 1960, the new Congolese government was unable to exert control due to rioting and a mutiny by the armed forces, and the attempted secession of Katanga: Ibid, pp. 64–67.
68. See the discussion of this point and the *Genocide Case* in Thomas D Grant, 'Territorial Status: Recognition, and Statehood: Some Aspects of the *Genocide* Case (*Bosnia-Herzegovina v Yugoslavia*)' (1997) 33 *Stanford Journal of International Law*, pp. 330–41.
69. Somalia was (and is still) recognised as a State, and still participated as a member of the UN, despite the collapse of its central government in 1991, and the incessant fighting between rival clans, which lead to a UN-led intervention between 1992–95. Given these circumstances Somalia's government could hardly be described as 'effective' government. Harris, *Cases and Materials p.* 104; Raič, *Statehood*, pp. 52–57, pp. 65–67, 70.
70. As noted by Raič, despite the Albanian government's complete lack of effectiveness, at no time was Albania's statehood questioned by the UN. See the preambles to *Resolution 1114*, SC Res 1114 (1997), UN SCOR, 52nd sess, 3791st mtg, UN Doc S/Res/1114 (19 June

persistent absence of an effective government could lead to the extinction of statehood.[71]

Consequently some commentators prefer to describe the criterion of government as being the potential for effective government, where the government has been denied effectiveness due to external political circumstances.[72] Where effective government is denied due to civil war, or the belligerent occupation by another State, the statehood of the occupied territory remains intact.[73] However, care must be taken if using potential as opposed to actual effectiveness since its relative nature adds even further vagueness to the definition which then becomes heavily dependent upon considerations of relativity.[74]

d. Capacity to enter into foreign relations

Starke believes that, of the four criteria of the *Montevideo Convention*, the capacity to enter foreign relations is the only one that needs to be proven and therefore is deemed by him to be a necessity.[75] Starke's reason is simple; the capacity to enter into foreign relations distinguishes between a part of a State and the State itself.[76] A State can delegate this capacity to another and still retain statehood as evidenced by Liechtenstein who did so to save the expense of maintaining foreign embassies.[77]

Detter, however, assumes that it is an incidence of statehood rather than a defining characteristic, and describes this characteristic as 'viability' since it may be denied to a State through the realistic economic and military inequality of States.[78] For example, if States are denied the ability to enter foreign relations due to embargoes and other sanctions by the UN (such as Iraq during the Gulf War) do they cease to be States? Or is it more accurate to say that their capability is merely suspended and dependent on satisfying the relevant demands of the UN, or complying with international law? Secondly, there are examples of constituent units of federal States that have

1997); *Resolution 1101*, SC Res 1101 (1997), UN SCOR, 3758th mtg, UN Doc S/Res/1101 (28 March 1997). Raič, *Statehood* pp. 69–70.

71. Raič, *Statehood*, pp. 72–73. Although this has never happened.
72. Delupis refers to Croatia when it first claimed independence in 1991 and, as a result, was invaded, casting doubt as to the effectiveness of its government: Delupis, *International Legal Order*, p. 40.
73. There are many examples such as those States (Poland) occupied by the Nazi's during WWII: Raič, *Statehood*, p. 67.
74. Harris, *Cases and Materials*, p. 104; Raič, *Statehood*, pp. 52–57.
75. However, as discussed above, logically a State must have territory.
76. Starke, *International Law*, p. 91, 127.
77. Ibid; Harris, *Cases and Materials*, p. 108.
78. Delupis, *International Legal Order*, pp. 42–43. Crawford also assumes that it is a consequence of statehood rather than a criterion: Crawford, *Creation of States*, p. 61; Starke, *International Law*, p. 127.

had the ability to enter into foreign relations, but which neither claim statehood nor are considered States.[79] International organisations can also enter into treaties.[80]

Capacity to enter into foreign relations has been described as 'independence' which means the State is not subordinate to another State.[81] Independence is often touted as an additional criterion for statehood, as not all commentators accept the Montevideo criteria as identifying all the characteristics of statehood.[82] The suggestion of the use of additional criteria will be considered next.

2. Additional criteria

The Montevideo criteria do distinguish a State from other international legal persons such as an international organisation like the World Health Organisation, but constituent units of a State such as a province will share the same factual elements as a State: a people, a defined territory, an effective government, and even foreign relations with States.[83] This similarity doesn't render the Montevideo criteria unsuitable, if other criteria are used. For example a provincial government despite its degree of autonomy or any constitutional allocation of legislative responsibilities may not be the final political authority over their territory. It will be subordinate to a higher, national government, like the federal parliament in Australia. Thus the provincial government is neither sovereign nor independent,[84] and, accordingly, commentators argue these additional elements, sovereignty and independence, together with effectiveness are additional if not the criteria for statehood.[85]

79. Such as Belarus – formerly Byelorussia – and the Ukraine of the former USSR. Harris, *Cases and Materials*, p. 107.
80. Grant, *Defining Statehood*, p. 435.
81. Crawford, *Creation of States*, p. 61: Raič, *Statehood*, pp. 74–82; Harris, *Cases and Materials*, pp. 106–108.
82. See especially Grant, *Defining Statehood*, pp. 434–57; Osterud, *Sovereign Statehood*, pp. 21–22; Crawford, *Creation of States*, pp. 31–33; Raič, *Statehood*, p. 24; Verzijl, *International Law*, pp. 266–69; Brownlie *Principles*, p. 70.
83. The Rhone-Alpes region in France maintains trade 'embassies' in other States. German Laender and British local governments also have something similar in the EU headquarters in Brussels. JT Matthews, 'Power Shift', (1997) Jan\Feb. *Foreign Affairs*, p. 62. Secondly, there are examples of constituent units of federal States that have had the ability to enter into foreign relations, but which neither claim statehood nor are considered States such as Belarus – formerly Byelorussia – and the Ukraine of the former USSR: Harris, *Cases and Materials*, p. 107.
84. Bodin defined sovereignty as: '... the absolute and perpetual power of a Commonwealth': Julian H Franklin, 'Book I Chapter 8', in Julian H Franklin (ed), *On Sovereignty: Four Chapters from the Six Books of the Commonwealth* Cambridge: Cambridge University Press, 1992, p. 4.
85. Grant, *Defining Statehood*, pp. 434–57; Osterud, *Sovereign Statehood*, pp. 21–22; Crawford, *Creation of States*, pp. 31–3; Raič, *Statehood*, p. 24; generally JHW, Verzijl, *International*

Effectiveness relates to the ability of the government to retain control over the territory of the claimed State. Thus, it is linked to the Montevideo criteria of government as discussed. In view of this overlap with government in the Montevideo criteria it is questionable whether it should be considered as a separate criterion of statehood. Sovereignty's usefulness as a criterion also has to be doubted since it is unclear whether it defines statehood, or is a mere consequence of statehood. And the question of whether a State is exercising sovereignty or not, would appear to be determined by considering the extent of its ability to exercise their authority free from the interference from other sources, in particular other States. Thus some commentators like Crawford reject sovereignty as a criterion of statehood,[86] and instead consider independence to be the key criterion of statehood.[87]

Independence features strongly in other commentators' definition of a State,[88] and is closely linked to effectiveness.[89] Lack of independence has been important in the international community denying previous claims to statehood. For example, Manchukuo was denied recognition by the League of Nations because it was clearly a puppet State of Japan created through the illegal actions of Japan.[90] A more recent example was the *Republika Srpska's* lack of independence due to the Serbia's control over the claimed republic's capacity to enter into foreign relations.[91] Finally, South Ossetia's claim to statehood was challenged because of its dependence on Russia.[92]

However, independence's relative character and paucity in the 'two Germanies',[93] the 'two Koreas',[94] and the 'two Vietnams',[95] did not prevent their ultimate recognition as a State, or acceptance as a member State of the UN. So care should be taken with using independence as a criterion. If an absolute definition were required then no State would be considered to be independent, since many States depend upon others for their existence.[96]

Law in Historical Perspective, Volume 1, Leydon, AW Sijthoff-Leydon, 1968, pp. 266–9; Ian Brownlie, *Principles of Public International Law*, (6th ed) Oxford: Oxford University Press 2003, p. 70.

86. Crawford, *Creation of States*, p. 89.
87. Ibid, p. 40, 62: Crawford's conclusions regarding independence are based upon Judge Huber's definition of independence in the Island of Palmas Arbitration Case (1928) 2 *Reports of International Arbitral Awards* 829, 838.
88. Grant, *Defining Statehood*, p. 409.
89. Crawford, *Creation of States*, p. 54, 59.
90. The Lytton Commission: Grant, *Recognition of States*, p. 131; Crawford, *Creation of States*, p. 75, 78–79, pp. 130–131.
91. This was made clear in *Prosecutor v Tadić (Appeals Chamber)* Case No IT-94-I-A (15 July 1999) (Judgment) [145]–[160]; Crawford, *Creation of States*, p. 82.
92. International Crisis Group, 'South Ossetia: the Burden of Recognition', *Europe Report No 205–7 June 2010*, 23.
93. Crawford, *Creation of States*, pp. 452–66.
94. Ibid, 466–72.
95. Ibid, 472–77.
96. Ibid, 88; Raič, *Statehood*, pp. 76–78, 82.

These examples do not prevent independence's suitability as a criterion, because few States are totally free from influence of other States, and as noted by Raič, if such an absolute definition of independence was adopted, there would be very few entities that would be considered States.[97]

Independence can be clearly determined by answering a simple question: is the State subject to the authority of another State? His Excellency Judge Anzilotti in the *Austro-German Customs Union Case* suggested such an approach.[98] His approach could be described as referring to the ability to enter into foreign relations,[99] but it is something additional to the Montevideo Criteria.[100] Provided a State does not place itself under the legal authority of another State, it will be independent.[101] Or as Oliver states: '... a [S]tate is juridically independent from any other legal subject, irrespective of any factual independence.'[102] Thus in theory a State could surrender its ability to enter into foreign relations subsequently, which implies it must have had that capacity initially. If an entity never had such a capacity, it cannot be said to be independent.

3. Conclusions

The *Montevideo criteria* provide a convenient basis for the definition of statehood, but on their own are insufficient, and they only partially succeed in achieving their goal as stated in article 3 of the Convention (namely to enable the identification of a State without involving the political desires of States,) because capacity to enter foreign relations and effective government can be controlled by the acts of States.[103] Accordingly independence, despite its vagueness and relativity,[104] should be combined with the Montevideo criteria to better determine the factual existence of a State. Independence is especially crucial in situations of doubt.[105] Once so combined the Montevideo

97. Raič, *Statehood*, pp. 74–82. See the Opinion of the PCIJ, in particular the Separate Opinion of Judge Anzilotti, in *Austro-German Customs Union Case (Advisory Opinion)* [1931] PCIJ (ser A/B) No 1; Harris, *Cases and Materials*, pp. 106–108.
98. *Austro-German Customs Union Case* [1931] PCIJ (ser A/B) No 41, 57–8. Crawford's concept of independence is based upon His Excellency's Opinion: Crawford, *Creation of States*, p. 65.
99. The third and fourth elements of the Montevideo criteria.
100. Crawford, *Creation of States*, p. 66.
101. His Excellency Judge Anzilotti in his Separate Opinion in *Austro-German Customs Case*, pp. 57–8. A similar definition was applied in *Gur Corporation v Trust Bank of Africa Ltd* [1987] QB 599 where the Court held that Ciskei, one of the Bantustans, was merely a subordinate government of South Africa, and also in *Carl Zeiss Stiftung v Rayner & Keeler Ltd* [1967] 1 AC 853, where the Court held that the DGR was also a subordinate government of the former USSR.
102. Olivier, *Establishment of Sovereignty*, p. 91.
103. Crawford, *Creation of States*, Chapter 2.
104. Somalia for example: Harris, *Cases and Materials*, p. 104; Raič, *Statehood*, pp. 52–57.
105. The former republics of the SFRY are a good example of this problem.

criteria do serve admirably as a means of achieving Raič's initial objective: namely identifying that the factual elements of a State exist, and thus are adequate as being the first of his two-steps.

However, what about his second step? Her Excellency Judge Higgins, arguing that proving the Montevideo criteria is merely the 'starting point' in determining statehood noted:

> ... while the concept of what constitutes a state has a certain undeniable core, the application of the component elements [the Montevideo Criteria] will also depend upon the purpose for which the entity concerned is claiming to be a state, and the circumstances in which the claim is made.[106]

By mentioning '... the circumstances in which the claim is made. ...' and '... the purpose for which the entity concerned is claiming ...' could Her Excellency be referring to whether the examination of the circumstances involve applying international law?[107] And thus support Raič's notion that the second step requires a determination or application of legal norms? Other commentators such as Osterud agree with Her Excellency and argue that proving the Montevideo criteria is merely the 'starting point', but Osterud argues that the determination of statehood still requires an act of recognition by States.[108]

So is recognition the 'second step'? If so then that raises the issue of States, with all their vested national interests, acting as the recognizing body, which suggests that international norms do not play a role in determining statehood. What will be argued is that whilst recognition does play a role when determining statehood the real issue is whether States, due to their vested interests plaguing recognition, should be the 'recognising body'.

C. Recognition and the role of states in determining statehood

Determining the extent of the role played by recognition in determining statehood is an important question for a people claiming self-determination against the wishes of the central government, or parent State because it is likely that that State would withhold recognition.[109]

International treaties as well as academic commentators have long acknowledged the importance of the link between recognition, and

106. Rosalyn Higgins, *The Development of International Law through the Political Organs of the United Nations*, Oxford: Oxford University Press 1963, p. 42.
107. Crawford, *Creation of States*, p. 107.
108. Osterud, *Sovereign Statehood*, pp. 21–22.
109. Raič, *Statehood*, p. 29.

statehood.[110] Whilst commentators acknowledge this link they are divided as to what is the effect of recognition. For example, Kreijen states that: 'Recognition constitutes the acknowledgement of statehood. ...',[111] whilst Oppenheim, in contrast, argues that: 'A [S]tate is, and becomes, an International Person through recognition only and exclusively.'[112] This divergence is at the heart of the 'Great Debate',[113] which has dominated the academic discourse on recognition,[114] and can be summarised as follows: does an entity that meets the factual criteria of a State (essentially the Montevideo criteria) automatically become one, or does it require in addition the acts of recognition of other States?

1. Theories of recognition and the 'Great Debate'

Traditionally, there have been two theories of the effect of recognition: the declaratory and the constitutive. Other theories of recognition include *recognition de jure* and *recognition de facto*.[115] These concepts refer to recognition of governments rather than States, a practice that most States have discontinued.[116] There is also Kelsen's idea of political and legal recognition, which were created in an attempt to resolve the Great Debate between the declaratory and the constitutive theories. However, it is the latter theories

110. Sir Hersch Lauterpacht, *Recognition in International Law*: Cambridge: Cambridge University Press, 1947, p. 1, & 90 & 'Recognition of States in International Law', (1944) 53 (1) *The Yale Law Journal*, p. 385; Franck, *Legitimacy*, p. 112; Menon, *Law of Recognition*, p. 27; Hillgruber, *The Admission of New States*, p. 492; art 10 *Bogota Charter of the Organisation of American States*, open for signature 30 April 1948, 119 UNTS 48 (entered into force 13 December 1951) ('Bogota Charter').
111. Kreijen, *State Failure*, p. 13.
112. Lassa Oppenheim, *International Law: A Treatise* (Sir Hersch Lauterpacht ed, 8th ed) McKay, 1955, vol. 1, p. 125.
113. Many authors use this expression to describe the tensions between these two theories. For example, Crawford, *Creation of States*, p. 19; Grant, *Recognition of States*, p. 1.
114. Dugard, *Recognition*, p. 10; Lauterpacht, *Recognition of States*, p. 419. The debate is perhaps a reflection of the greater debate between advocates of realism, liberalism and constructivism. See generally Byers *Importance of Law*; Scott Burchill, Scott, (et al) (ed) *Theories of International Relations*, (2nd ed) New York: Palgrave 2001, p. 28.
115. *Recognition de jure* is where the recognising State acknowledges that the new government or State has '...*formally* fulfil[ed] the requirements laid down by international law for the effective participation in the international community'. *Recognition de facto* on the other hand is where the new State or government has only 'provisionally' or 'temporarily' fulfilled the requirements for *effective participation* in the international community, and thus the recognition granted by the recognising government is subject to '... all due reservations for the future, ...'. Starke, *International Law*, p. 137.
116. Colin Warbrick, 'Recognition of Governments' (1993) 56 *Modern Law Review*, p. 92; Starke, *International Law*, p. 133. Essentially, the UK's policy was that it would consider relations with new governments based on that government's present and future effective control of its territory. The US and also Australia have also adopted this policy in 1988: Ivan Anthony Shearer, *Starke's International Law* (11th ed), London: Butterworths 1994, p. 127.

that have dominated discussion in the academic discourse on determining statehood.

Crawford defines the declaratory theory as: '... the theory that statehood is a legal status independent of recognition ...'.[117] In other words recognition is merely a formal acknowledgment of established facts, and thus is evidentiary in nature.[118] And the constitutive theory as: '... the theory that the rights and duties pertaining to statehood derive from recognition only...'.[119] In other words: '... it is the act of recognition alone which creates statehood...'[120]

Initially the declaratory theory predominated, however, by the nineteenth century the constitutive theory replaced the declaratory theory.[121] Commentators today believe that the Great Debate has been decided in favour of the declaratory theory,[122] but there is no denying that States have played a role in determining statehood, and the Opinions of the Badinter Commission in relation to the dissolution of the SFRY have breathed new life into the Great Debate. Although the Badinter Commission stated explicitly also that recognition was declaratory in nature, and that the existence of a State was a question of fact, only the actions of the EC in recognising Bosnia-Herzegovina could be argued did have a creative effect.[123]

Thus, an examination of State practice may assist in resolving the Great Debate, and also whether Raič's second step of applying legal norms is involved in determining statehood. It also raises in the author's opinion, a more pertinent question: whether States should be the recognising body. It will also be shown that State practice proves that determining statehood does involve determination and application of legal norms.

117. Crawford, *Creation of States*, p. 4; Lauterpacht, *Recognition of States*, pp. 425–33.
118. Starke, *International Law*, p. 128.
119. Crawford, *Creation of States*, p. 4; Lauterpacht, *Recognition of States*, pp. 425–33.
120. Shearer, *Starke's International Law*, p. 120; Starke, *International Law*, p. 128; Grant, *Recognition of States*, pp. 2–4; Crawford, *Creation of States*, pp. 19–28.
121. Crawford, *Creation of States*, pp. 11–15; Dugard, *Recognition*, p. 10; Starke, *International Law*, p. 24.
122. Grant, *Recognition of States*, p. 4; Jure Vidmar, 'International Legal Responses to Kosovo's Declaration of Independence' in 42 *Vand. J. Transnat'l L.* 2009, pp. 779, 828; Crawford, *Creation of States*, pp. 25–27. Their views are supported by the Badinter Commission, and the Canadian Supreme Court in *Reference re Secession of Quebec* [1998] 2 SCR 217, 295 ('Quebec Secession'); *Opinion No 1 of the Arbitration Commission of the Peace Conference on Yugoslavia* 31 ILM 1494 (1992) ('*Opinion No 1*'); (29 Nov 1991), [1(a)]; Alain Pellet, 'The Opinions of the Badinter Arbitration Committee: A Second Breath for the Self-Determination of Peoples' (1995) 3 *European Journal of International Law* 178.
123. *Opinion No 1*, [1(a)], as cited in the Appendix to Alain Pellet, 'The Opinions of the Badinter Arbitration Committee: A Second Breath for the Self-Determination of Peoples' (1995) 3 *European Journal of International Law*, p. 178. This position was restated in [2] of *Opinion No 8, Badinter Commission* (4 July 1992) 92 ILR 199, 201.

2. State practice

Initially the State practice of recognition resulting in a State will be considered, followed by examples where States have refused recognition, which has resulted in a denial of statehood.

a. Creation of statehood

There are many examples where the acts of States have had a constitutive effect. For example, the early support of the US certainly helped consolidate Israel's independence.[124] Another example is the former USSR's recognition of the Baltic States prior to their acceptance as members of the UN,[125] and arguably Pakistan's recognition of Bangladesh also paved the way for its successful claim for UN membership.[126] This recognition paved the way for their acceptance as members of the UN, and accordingly due to art 4(1) of the *UN Charter*, their statehood.[127] Other examples include the Republic of Korea, which did not have effective control over its territory, and the Democratic People's Republic of Korea, which did not appear to be independent given it was established by the former USSR and, yet they were both recognised as States, and consequently granted UN membership.[128]

A similar situation occurred with the subsequent division of post-war Germany into two States (the 'two Germanies'), the Federal Republic of Germany, and the German Democratic Republic. Concern was raised whether the two States were actually independent, particularly given the foreign nature of the Quadripartite Allied Government (and the immense amount of military forces in occupation).[129] Eventually the statehood of the two Germanies was accepted through a series of agreements signed between

124. Franck, *Legitimacy*, p. 126.
125. Lithuania, Latvia, and Estonia.
126. India was the first State to recognise Bangladesh, in December 1971, and by end of February 1972 a total of 31 States had also granted recognition. However, as noted by Crawford these further acts of recognition only occurred *after* the surrender of Pakistan military forces in east Bengal (Bangladesh) in December 1971. Thus suggesting that no State (other than India) wished to do so prior to the capitulation of Pakistani forces, and arguably that if Pakistan had won a military victory no recognition may have been forthcoming. Pakistan recognised Bangladesh's statehood on 2 February 1974, and Bangladesh was admitted to UN membership on 17 September 1974. See Joshua Castellino, *International law and Self-Determination: The Interplay of the Politics of Territorial Possession with Formulations of post-Colonial National Identity*, The Hague: Martinus Nijhoff Publishers, 2000, p. 167; Crawford, *Creation of States*, p. 393.
127. Crawford, *Creation of States*, p. 394.
128. Ibid, p. 471.
129. The Federal Republic of Germany (referred to as 'FRG') created by the Western powers, and the German Democratic Republic (referred to as 'GDR') was created by the former USSR. The two Germanies and the issues surrounding them were clearly a result of the Cold War. The two Germanies were created as a result of the collapse of the Allied Control

the two Germanies,[130] as well as between the FGR and the former USSR,[131] and a formal declaration by all four controlling powers, and they were both admitted to the UN as members on 18 September 1973.[132] Ultimately the two Germanies reunited after a plebiscite was held, and became one State again in 1990.[133]

Perhaps the best example is Bosnia-Herzegovina, whose claim to statehood had serious flaws.[134] Firstly, at no stage was Bosnia-Herzegovina in effective control of the entirety of its territory.[135] Furthermore, Bosnia's dependence on international assistance raised serious issues regarding its independence.[136] Finally, concerns were raised regarding the 'free will' of its inhabitants since the Serb minority had boycotted both the declaration of independence and the referendum.[137]

The EC recognised Bosnia-Herzegovina on 6 April 1992,[138] and many States soon followed the EC's example.[139] Did the actions of the EC, through the Opinions provided by the Badinter Commission create new States, or merely declare an existing fact? When Croatia and Slovenia, the first two of the former republics to unilaterally declare independence, first announced

Council, itself a result of the breakdown of relations between the former USSR and the Western powers: Crawford, *Creation of States*, p. 454.

130. *Treaty on the Basis of Intra-German Relations*, signed 21 December 1973, Federal Republic of Germany–German Democratic Republic, 12 ILM 16 (1973).
131. Crawford, *Creation of States*, p. 458.
132. *Admission of the Federal Republic of Germany and the German Democratic Republic to Membership in the United Nations*, GA Res 3050 (XXVIII), UN GAOR, 28th sess, 2117th plen mtg, UN Doc A/RES/3050 (18 September 1973); Crawford, *Creation of States*, p. 458.
133. Two treaties between the two Germanies were entered into: *Treaty Establishing a Monetary, Economic and Social Union*, signed 18 May 1990, Federal Republic of Germany–German Democratic Republic, 29 ILM 1108 (1990) (entered into force 30 June 1990); *Treaty on the Establishment of German Unity*, signed 31 August 1990, Federal Republic of Germany–German Democratic Republic, 30 ILM 457 (1991), and a *Unification Treaty*, signed 31 August 1990, Federal Republic of Germany–German Democratic Republic (entered into force 3 October 1990), available from <http://www.ena.lu/unification-treaty-frg-gdr-berlin-31-august-1990-020300527.html> at 17 October 2008. Also the four governing powers entered into a treaty with the two Germanies: *Treaty on the Final Settlement with Respect to Germany*, signed 12 September 1990, 29 ILM 1187 (1990) (entered into force 15 March 1991).
134. See *Opinion No 1 of the Arbitration Commission of the Peace Conference on Yugoslavia* 31 ILM 1494 (1992) ('*Opinion No 1*'); *Opinion No 8*; Grant, *Recognition of States*, p. 163; Crawford, *Creation of States*, p. 399.
135. Rich, *Collapse of Yugoslavia*, p. 49; Grant, *Recognition of States*, pp. 164–65.
136. Rich, *Collapse of Yugoslavia*, p. 49, 51.
137. *Opinion No 4 on the International Recognition of the Socialist Republic of Bosnia-Herzegovina by the European Community and Its Members* 31 ILM 501 (1992) ('*Opinion No 4*'), see Annex 3, 76; Crawford, *Creation of States*, p. 398, 406–409; Rich, *Collapse of Yugoslavia*, p. 49.
138. Crawford, *Creation of States*, p. 400; Rich, *Collapse of Yugoslavia*, pp. 49–50.
139. The US on 7 April 1992; Croatia on 7 April 1992; Canada on 8 April 1992; New Zealand on 8 April 1992; Czechoslovakia on 9 April 1992; Hungary on 9 April 1992; Poland on 9 April 1992; Egypt on 16 April 1992; Saudi Arabia on 17 April 1992: Rich, *Collapse of Yugoslavia*, pp. 50–51.

their declarations of independence, the international community, with the exception of Germany, refused to grant recognition.[140] Consequently, after the creation of the Badinter Commission, all the former republics seeking statehood were recognised and admitted to the UN, even Bosina-Herzegovina. Thus it must be concluded that the process of the Badinter Commission was constitutive in character.

The above examples show that the actions of States, through recognition, and admission to the UN can have a constitutive effect. Any defects in the respective claims to statehood were cured by time, through the agreement between the parties involved, and the acquiescence of the international community.

b. Denial of statehood

There have been many examples of unsuccessful claims for statehood.[141] By far the reason why these claims fail is due to the lack of international support, and recognition of their claims. As the following examples show, the international community is not reluctant to refuse recognition: Rhodesia, the 'Bantustans', Katanga, Biafra, and Northern Cyprus. Rhodesia unilaterally declared its independence on 11 November 1965.[142] Both the Security Council and the General Assembly passed resolutions requesting States not to recognise Rhodesia,[143] despite the fact that Rhodesia would have satisfied the four criteria of the *Montevideo Convention*.[144] Therefore factually it was a State, however, it was not considered to be a State legally since its

140. The US, the former USSR, and most Western European States. In fact it could be argued that Germany's actions, and stated intention to grant recognition was instrumental in prompting the EC to take the action it did, and convene the Conference on Yugoslavia. Grant, *Recognition of States*, p. 153; Rich, *Collapse of Yugoslavia*, p. 39; Crawford, *Creation of States*, p. 396.
141. See the list in Crawford, *Creation of States*, p. 403. Although the list needs to be updated since Kosovo's claim for independence, and the recent conflict in South Ossetia and Abkhazia, and their subsequent claims for independence and recognition.
142. It was formerly part of the British Empire: Dugard, *Recognition*, pp. 90, 96.
143. Ibid: 94. See *Question of Southern Rhodesia*, GA Res 2022 (XX), UN GAOR, 20th sess, 1368th plen mtg, UN Doc A/RES/2022 (XX) (5 November 1965); *Resolution 216*, SC Res 216, UN SCOR, 20th sess, 1258th mtg, [8] UN Doc S/ResRES/216 (12 November 1965) [8]; *Resolution 217*, SC Res 217, UN SCOR, 20th sess, 1265th mtg, UN Doc S/RES/217 (20 November 1965) [8]–[9]; *Resolution 277*, SC Res 277, UN SCOR, 25th sess, 1535th mtg, UN Doc S/RES/277 (18 March 1970); *Resolution 288*, SC Res 288, UN SCOR, 25th sess, 1557th mtg, UN Doc S/RES/288 (17 November 1970) [7].
144. Dugard, *Recognition*, p. 91. However, the call for economic sanctions imposed by Security Council Resolutions: *Resolution 232*, SC Res 232, UN SCOR, 21st sess, 1340th mtg, UN Doc S/RES/232 (16 December 1966) [7] (imposing sanctions against Southern Rhodesia); *Resolution 253*, SC Res 253, UN SCOR, 23rd sess, 1428th mtg, UN Doc S/RES/253 (29 May 1968) [5]–[6] (establishing a committee to monitor sanctions), limited their ability to enter into foreign relations.

government like South Africa continually breached human rights,[145] in particular due to the racist policies of its government.[146]

The 'Bantustans' were a series of 10 homelands, one each for a single Black ethnic group, created by South Africa.[147] Four were initially granted independence.[148] Both the General Assembly,[149] and the Security Council appealed to States to not grant recognition to the Bantustans,[150] further describing the creation of these homelands as an international 'crime'.[151] The UN's refusal was undoubtedly motivated by political considerations, but was based upon breaches of international law,[152] most notably the South African government's policy of apartheid. Essentially the South African Government gave the relative ethnic groups a simple choice; stay as part of South Africa and have no political or social rights or move to the new homelands and receive full rights otherwise denied to them in South Africa.[153]

There were similar reasons in the refusal to recognise the Turkish Republic of Cyprus. The Security Council condemned the attempted secession as

145. Dugard, *Recognition*, p. 91.
146. Ibid, p. 96.
147. Ibid, p. 107.
148. Transkei, Bophuthatswana, Venda, and Ciskei.
149. The General Assembly had provided warnings about the impending claims of independence in *Policies of Apartheid of the Government of South Africa*, GA Res 2775 (XXVI), UN GAOR, 26th sess, 1997th mtg, Supp 29, UN Doc A/RES/2775 (29 November 1971) Part E; *Policies of Apartheid of the Government of South Africa*, GA Res 3411, UN GAOR, 30th sess, 2421st plen mtg, UN Doc A/RES/3411 (XXX) (28 November 1975) Part D. The General Assembly resolution rejecting the claim for independence for Transkei was adopted by an overwhelming vote 130 to none: *Policies of Apartheid of the Government of South Africa*, UN GAOR, 42nd mtg, UN Doc A/RES/31/6 (26 October 1976) [A].
150. The Security Council subsequently endorsed the General Assembly's position. *Security Council 401 (1976) on South Africa's Closure of Border Posts between Lesotho and South Africa*, UN SCOR, 31st sess, 1982nd mtg, UN Doc S/RES/402 (22 December 1976) [13]; *Security Council Resolution 407 on Assistance to Lesotho*, UN SCOR 2009th mtg, Un Doc S/Res/407 (25 May 1977) [7]. Similar rejections were made with the granting of independence of the other homelands, eg. for Bophuthatswana: Policies of Apartheid of the Government of South Africa, (Bantustans) UN GAOR, 32nd sess, 102nd plen mtg, UN Doc A/Res/32/105 (14 December 1977) [N], the resolution was passed 140 votes to none.
151. *Policies of Apartheid of the Government of South Africa*, UN GAOR, 37th sess, 97th plen mtg, UN Doc A/Res37/69, (9 December 1982) [A] and then *Importance of the Universal Realization of the Right of Peoples to Self-Determination and of the Speedy Granting of Independence to Colonial Countries and Peoples for the Effective Guarantee and Observance of Human Rights*, GA Res 37/43, UN GAOR, 37th sess, 90th plen mtg, UN Doc A/Res/37/43 (3 December 1982). Then in 1993 the GA called upon South Africa to dismantle the Bantustans: *Elimination of Apartheid and Establishment of a United, Democratic and Non-Racial South Africa*, GA Res 48/159, 48th sess, 85th plen mtg, UN Doc A/RES/48/159A (20 December 1993) [2].
152. It was an attack on the territorial integrity of South Africa (Art 2(4) *UN Charter*), and the people of South Africa had not exercised their right to freely determine their political status, since the people of South Africa were not consulted in the formation of these homelands: Dugard, *Recognition*, pp. 104–106.
153. Ibid, pp. 104–106.

'illegal' on the following grounds:[154] (1) Turkey's use of force breached art 2 (4) of the *UN Charter* and the 1960 *Treaty of Guarantee* signed by Greece, Turkey and Cyprus; (2) it was not a genuine act of self-determination since the Turkish community was not a valid 'unit of self-determination';[155] and (3) the act of the secessionist entity was an 'impermissible fragmentation' of the territorial integrity of Cyprus.[156] Only Turkey recognised the entity as an independent State.[157]

Another example is Katanga. The UN opposed the claim of Katanga's independence on the basis of: (1) protecting the territorial integrity of the Congo;[158] (2) that this was an internal affair of the Congo;[159] and (3) because Katanga's claim breached the principle of *uti possidetis*, which was UN and OAS policy.[160] This conclusion was reached in spite of the fact that Katanga was more stable than the central Congolese Government.[161] Further, the UN labelled the activities of Katanga as illegal secessionism and condemned the alleged use of foreign mercenaries.[162]

The issue of Katanga's statehood arose indirectly in the *Certain Expenses Opinion*.[163] The General Assembly requested the ICJ to provide an Advisory Opinion to assist the General Assembly deal with some members of the UN who had fallen behind in their financial contributions to the UN. These members had refused to pay because their contributions included a proportion that represented the cost of the UN Force in the Congo (UNOC) sent in response to the request of the Congolese government to combat the Katanganese claim for independence. The Court was asked whether

154. *Resolution 514*, SC Res 514, UN SCOR, 38th sess, 2500th mtg, UN Doc S/RES/514 (19 November 1983) [15] (on declaration by the Turkish Cypriot community of its secession from Cyprus); *Resolution 550*, SC Res 550, 39th sess, 2539th mtg, UN Doc S/RES/550 (11 May 1984) [13] (on secessionist actions in Cyprus).
155. Dugard, *Recognition*, p. 111.
156. Ibid.
157. Grant, *Recognition of States*, p. 12.
158. *Question Considered by the Security Council at Its 906th Meeting on 16 September 1960*, GA Res 1474 (ES-IV), UN GAOR, 15th sess, 863rd plen mtg, UN Doc A/RES/1474 (ES-IV); below n 292; Raič, *Statehood*, pp. 64–67.
159. *Resolution 261*, SC Res 261, UN SCOR, 16th sess, 982nd mtg, UN Doc S/RES/169 (24 November 1961) [4] (on an arms embargo against the Congo). See also UN Doc S/4405, UN SCOR (22 July 1960).
160. Antonio Cassese, *Self-Determination of Peoples*, Cambridge: Cambridge University Press Cambridge 1995, p. 192; Harris, *Cases and Materials*, pp. 120–1, p. 126; *Opinion No 2 and No 3 of the Arbitration Commission, EC Conference on Yugoslavia, January 11 1992*, 92 ILR 167 ('*Opinions No's 2 and 3*'); *Burkina Faso and Mali (Frontier Dispute)* [1986] ICJ Rep 554, p. 565.
161. Crawford, *Creation of States*, p. 404.
162. *Resolution 241*, SC Res 241, UN SCOR, 22nd sess, 1378th mtg, UN Doc S/RES/241 (15 November 1967) [14] (on the question concerning the Democratic Republic of the Congo (Zaire).
163. *Certain Expenses of the United Nations (Advisory Opinion)* [1962] ICJ Rep 151.

the costs of ONUC were expenses of the UN in accordance with art 17(2) of the *UN Charter*. As part of their deliberations the Court noted that:

> The armed forces which were utlilized in the Congo were not authorized to take military action against *any State*. The operation did not involve 'preventive or enforcement measures' against any State under Chapter VII...[164]

In other words, in the Court's Opinion, Katanga was not considered to be an independent State. Katanga's claim for statehood could be interpreted as a claim for self-determination. However, the Court's decision, combined with the refusal of the international community to recognise Katanga's statehood, ensured that there was little hope that their right would be achieved.

The Republic of Biafra shared a similar fate to Katanga. Led primarily by the Igbo people Biafra declared its independence from Nigeria on 30 May 1967, but its claim to statehood was brief, ending with a ceasefire on 12 January 1970, whereupon it was reabsorbed into Nigeria. Only five States recognized Biafra's claim to statehood, which prompts many commentators to conclude that Biafra was not (and arguably never was) a State.[165]

3. Observations

What observations can be drawn from the above discussion of State practice? Firstly, that determination of statehood is more than a mere question of fact, and the Montevideo criteria on their own are insufficient to prove statehood, especially in situations of doubt. The examples of the two Germanies, the two Koreas, and Bosnia-Herzegovina show that in situations of doubt, even where a claimant may lack a criterion to statehood, such as effectiveness or independence, a claim to statehood can be assisted by recognition: 'Thus recognition can create elements of statehood lacking in the objective situation of the putative state.'[166] Or in other words: 'Recognition perfects statehood.'[167] Therefore, at first glance it appears that recognition is

164. Ibid, 177. However, His Excellency Judge Moreno Quintana held that the Katangan entity, was a belligerent community, and as such should be recognised by the international community as having some form of international legal personality: at 246.
165. Crawford, *Creation of States*, p. 406. There is still support for a Biafran State amongst many of the Igbo Diaspora: Will Ross, 'The Biafrans Who Still Dream of Leaving Nigeria' 21 December 2012, available at the BBC News Africa website: www.bbc.uk/news/world-africa-20801091 [last accessed 18 April 2013].
166. Grant, *Recognition of States*, p. 90. See also Jorri C Duursma, *Fragmentation and the International Relations of Micro-States: Self-Determination and Statehood* (1996) 92; Crawford, *Creation of States*, pp. 387–89.
167. Grant, *The Recognition of States*, p. 2.

predominantly constitutive in nature, with States acting as the recognizing body.[168]

Despite, or rather in spite of, these examples commentators today believe that the Great Debate has been decided in favour of the declaratory theory.[169] There is some logic to this position since the act of recognition on its own does not create borders, towns, and peoples with all their culture: in other words the physical attributes of a State.[170] Furthermore, there are some serious objections with adopting a strict constitutive position. What is the position where recognition is not universal? State practice has proven this to be common,[171] because States believe that they are under no obligation in international law to acknowledge the existence of a State, nor to withhold recognition from any entity they wish to extend it to.[172] Thus, one State will not grant recognition simply because another State has done so, and the act of recognition by one State does not bind other States.[173]

State practice would also suggest that unilateral recognition is insufficient. For example, only Turkey recognised the Turkish Republic of Northern Cyprus,[174] and only South Africa recognised the statehood of the Bantustans.[175] None of these entities were considered States by the international community as a whole, or by the majority of commentators. That does not mean that unilateral actions are insignificant. As noted, US support helped consolidate Israel's statehood,[176] and the EC's support of Bosnia-Herzegovina was crucial in the latter's ultimate recognition and membership in the UN.[177] However, State practice does not indicate how many acts of recognition will be sufficient? Approximately 88 States have recognized Kosovo's statehood,[178] and Kosovo's status remains unclear.

Thirdly, the examples of Rhodesia, the Bantustans, and the failed *Republika Srpska* showed that even where an entity satisfies the Montevideo criteria if

168. Osterud's theory that recognition is a two-step process that requires the consent of States: Osterud, *Sovereign Statehood*, p. 21.
169. Their views are supported by the Badinter Commission, and the Canadian Supreme Court: Grant, *Recognition of States*, p. 4; Vidmar, *International Legal Persons*, p. 828; Crawford, *Creation of States*, pp. 25–27.; *Opinion No 1 Badinter Commission*, [1(a)]; Pellet, *Opinions*, p. 178; Quebec Secession.
170. Whilst the constitutive theory cannot create the physical attributes of the State, it can affect its abilities to enter into foreign relations with States, the final criterion of the Montevideo criteria.
171. Refer to the example of Biafra above.
172. Grant, *Recognition of States*, pp. 2–3.
173. Shearer, *Starke's international Law*, pp. 30–1; Grant, *Recognition of States*, pp. 2–3.
174. Grant, *Recognition of States*, p. 12.
175. Crawford, *Creation of States*, p. 342.
176. Franck, *Legitimacy*, p. 126.
177. The actions of the EC were criticized: Crawford, *Creation of States*, p. 400; Grant, *Recognition of States*, p. 164.
178. Vidmar, *International Legal Persons*, p. 779.

its creation is due to breaches of international law, especially those of *jus cogens*, then statehood will be denied.[179] Alternatively, as the example of Turkish Republic of Northern Cyprus shows, if force is used illegally to support a claim to statehood, or alternatively a claim to statehood is made for ulterior purposes, then recognition is more likely to be denied.[180] Thus exposing the flaw inherent within the declaratory theory. It confuses questions of fact with questions of law and thus obscures the possibility that the birth or creation of States could be regulated by other means.[181] In other words the declaratory theory cannot assess the legality of the formation of the State under international law.[182]

State practice does not resolve the Great Debate in favour of either the declaratory or constitutive theory of recognition. Perhaps this is to be expected given what one commentator, Dugard, in his examination of recognition has stated: 'No theoretical exposition of the law of recognition can account for all the factual anomalies and logical inconsistencies in this branch of the law. …'[183] Both theories of recognition have flaws: the constitutive theory on its own cannot create the physical attributes of a State, and on the other hand the declaratory theory cannot adequately explain why the combination of physical characteristics creates a State, or why a certain combination does not.

Thus, State practice strongly supports Raič's assertion that statehood is determined through a two-step process: resolving the traditional criteria; or the Montevideo criteria, and secondly, determining whether the creation of the entity's statehood has breached international law.[184] However, it is States themselves, either unilaterally or collectively through the political organs of the UN, that are in effect acting as a judicial body.[185] Can States be trusted to act impartially when applying norms of international law, and should they remain the recognising body?

179. Grant, *Territorial Status*, p. 323.
180. Evriviades argued that the Turkish invasion and subsequent claim for statehood by Northern Cyrus was merely to divide Cyprus into two halves and so provide an opportunity for Turkey to annex it in the future. The invasion also breached international law since it violated the independence and territorial integrity of Cyprus: Marios L Evriviades, 'The Legal Dimension of the Cyprus Conflict' (1975) 10 *Texas International Law Journal* 227, 264.
181. Crawford, *Creation of States*, p. 5. He cites the example that a State is not a fact in the same manner that a chair is a fact.
182. For an excellent discussion of when statehood has been denied due to its creation has violated international law, please refer to Raič, *Statehood*, ch. 4, 8.
183. Dugard, *Recognition*, p. 164. Other commentators express a similar line of reasoning arguing that the debate has achieved little in determining what is the nature of recognition: see, Grant, *Recognition of States*, p. 73, pp. 214–17.
184. Raič, *Statehood*, p. 154.
185. Kelsen argues that States through the practice of recognition perform the function of a court determining statehood: Hans Kelsen, 'Recognition in International Law: Theoretical Observations' (1941) 35 *American Journal of International Law* 605, 606.

D. States acting as the recognising body

In this next part how States became the recognising body will be considered, and then it attempts to answer the following question: should States remain the recognising body? This question will be answered by examining how their national interests have influenced acts of recognition followed by determining whether alternative theories such as Dugard's concept of collective recognition and or Lauterpacht's concept of political and legal recognition can counter the issue of national interests, and thus allow States to remain as the recognising body.

1. Why are states the recognising body?

States are the recognising entity only for historical reasons, and not because of the nature or effect of recognition. As States emerged from the Thirty Years War and the signing of the *Treaties of Westphalia in 1648* they were the pre-eminent political entity.[186] International relations and international law recognised no entity other than States as subjects of international law. And States, flush with their recent victory over Empire and Church, would not have accepted the authority of any entity that would challenge their newly cemented authority or independence, least of all one that determined their existence as a State.

So how did one determine a State in such circumstances? The answer was by recognition by those of 'equal status', in other words by other States.[187] Emerging States sought the approval of their peers since it established the validation of their political community and confirmation of the legality of their political entity,[188] thus rendering this highly important act of recognition to be a form of peer review,[189] as States welcomed a new member into their exclusive club.[190] Thus, it was this desire, this craving for peer recognition that enabled States to develop their role as the 'recognising body'.[191]

186. Generally, F.H Hinsley, *Sovereignty*, (2nd ed) Cambridge: Cambridge University Press, 1986; Ingrid Delupis, *International Law and the Independent State*, Essex: Gower Press Limited, 1974.
187. Franck, *Legitimacy*, p. 114.
188. Ibid, p. 117.
189. Kreijen, *State Failure*, p. 13; Okafor, *Redefining Statehood*, pp. 54–65.
190. Other commentators use similar language, see: Sureda, *Evolution of Self-Determination*, p. 274; Charlesworth and Chinkin, *Boundaries*, p. 142.
191. Franck, *Legitimacy*, pp. 112–17.

2. National interests and recognition

Throughout history there are many examples of national self-interests resulting in non-recognition. One example is that the European States' refusal to recognise the emergence of Southern American States was '... not on account of the violation of any principle of law, but on the ground that the creation of such States ran counter to European public policy of resisting the establishment of non-monarchical institutions.'[192] Then there was the famous Hallstein Doctrine where the FRG threatened termination of economic and diplomatic ties with any State that recognised DRG.[193] Another example was the refusal of the US to grant recognition to the People's Republic of China (PRC). In an extremely blunt statement in regard to the non-recognition of the PRC, the US State Department stated that granting recognition would not be in the national interests of the US and, further, that it would only serve the interests of the PRC, in particular their interests abroad, because it could encourage the spread of communism throughout Asia.[194] The PRC did not sit in the UN as the official and accepted representative of 'China' until 1972: despite gaining control in 1949. It is obvious that the decision of the US, made in the background of the Cold War and the West's struggle against communism, was based entirely on national self-interest. Franck argues that this attitude was rare and that the US was in the minority,[195] however, other members of the minority club include African and Arabic States opposed to South Africa and Israel.[196]

The decision of the US not to grant recognition to the PRC reveals another major criticism of allowing States to act as the recognising body. Recognition by States allows recognition of a State to be confused with diplomatic recognition, and recognition of governments.[197] In theory there is a distinction between recognising a State and recognising its government, since many argue that the failure to recognise a change of government should not affect

192. Dugard, *Recognition*, p. 25.
193. Finally, in 1972, there was mutual recognition and they were admitted to the UN in 1973, Admission of New Members to the United Nations, UN SCOR 28th sess, 1730 mtg, UN Doc S/Res/335 (22 June 1973) [17]; Dugard, *Recognition*, p. 83.
194. 'US Policy on Non-Recognition of Communist China' (State Department Memorandum) 39 Department of State Bulletin 385 (September 1958), as cited in Franck, *Legitimacy*, p. 125.
195. In other words a rejection of the declaratory theory: Ibid. 126.
196. Ibid. For example see 'Credentials Committee Reports Adopted' (1987) 24 *UN Chronicle*, 16, where Oman on behalf of 20 Arabic States proposed an amendment to exclude Israel from General Assembly approval.
197. This occurred in the situation of the PRC and Taiwan, although the problem was exacerbated by both entities claiming to be the legitimate representative of Mainland China: Crawford, *Creation of States*, pp. 200–201. Diplomatic recognition relates to recognition of a State's government only, not the existence of the State itself.

the recognition of the State.[198] However, there is a well-established practice of States adopting a policy of non-recognition because a government was unacceptable to the recognising State. For example, Dugard argued that the Congress of Vienna and Congress of Troppau were 'directed' against the emergence of revolutionary/representative, non-monarchical governments in Europe.[199] Another example was the threat made by the US to not recognise any Latin American government that threatened revolution to replace a constitutional government.[200] Also that the US did not grant recognition to the USSR until 1933, even though it had effective control since the end of the war of 1919, was because of the nature of its government.[201]

More recent examples of national interests influencing recognition include Greece's refusal to recognise Macedonia, formerly part of the SFRY, which claimed self-determination after a majority of its people had chosen independence in a referendum.[202] Macedonia was in effective control of its territory, and would have satisfied the factual criteria of statehood. Furthermore, in order to appease the concerns of Greece regarding alleged Macedonian expansionism, Macedonia amended its constitution to declare clearly that it had no territorial claim against another State.[203] Despite such efforts Greece refused to recognise the new State.[204]

National interests have also played a role in granting recognition. The Allied Powers (France, Great Britain, and the US) granted recognition to Poland and Czechoslovakia before they actually existed independently as States simply as part of their grand strategy to defeat Germany and her allies

198. Starke, *International Law*, p. 133. For example, Kelsen concluded that whilst a State may wish to deny political recognition, it cannot deny legal recognition. This would appear to suggest that Kelsen, despite other statements, was leaning towards adopting a legal duty of recognition, as per Lauterpacht: Kelsen, *Principles*, p. 228.
199. Dugard, *Recognition*, p. 25.
200. This was another of Woodrow Wilson's policies. Wilson believed that representative government was a pre-condition for recognition. This policy is also described as the Tobar Doctrine. Tobar was the Ecuadorian Minister of Foreign Affairs in 1907 who stated that intervention into the internal affairs of American States was justified for reasons of humanity and altruism. The intervention was really just non-*de facto* recognition. The policy was also contained in Latin American Conventions of 1907 and 1923. See Dugard, *Recognition*, p. 26, especially his note 59.
201. Starke offers another reason, namely that the Soviet government had refused to honour obligations created by the Tsarist Government: Starke, *International Law*, p. 128.
202. Grant, *The Recognition of States*, pp. 161–162.
203. This intention was reinforced in a letter to the Badinter Commission from the Minister of Foreign Affairs that stated that Macedonia would also not engage in the dissemination of any hostile propaganda against any neighbouring State, that is Greece. Ibid.
204. However, the EC did grant recognition on 16 December 1993, after Macedonia had been admitted as a member of the UN as 'The Former Yugoslav Republic of Macedonia' on 8 April 1993: *Admission of the State whose Application is Contained in Document A/47/876-S/25147 to Membership in the United Nations*, GA Res 47/225, UN GAOR, 47th sess, 98th plen mtg, UN Doc A/RES/47/225 (8 April 1993).

during the First World War. They adopted a similar policy during the Second World War.[205] Finally, Russia justified its support for the breakaway regions of South Ossetia and Abkhazia by using Kosovo as a precedent for granting recognition to both regions, after it had condemned the West's support for Kosovo's independence. As questioned by commentators, was Russia really acting out of humanitarian concerns?[206] Their record in Chechnya mitigates such altruistic claims, and a more likely conclusion is that the claims by South Ossetia and Abkhazia provided an opportunity for Russia to exert its influence over Georgia, itself a former constituent republic of the former USSR. Or more simply it may be due to Russia's desire for 'territorial aggrandizement'.[207] As mentioned above Russia cited Kosovo as precedent for their actions. The former Russian President Dmitri Medvedev stated:

> ... ignoring Russia's warnings, Western Countries rushed to recognize Kosovo's illegal declaration of independence of Serbia. We argued consistently that it would be impossible, after that, to tell the Abkhazians and Ossetians (And dozens of other groups around the world) that what was good for the Kosovo Albanians was not good for them. In international relations, you cannot have one rule for some and another rule for others.[208]

He is correct, there are little advantages for inconsistent application of norms,[209] but what the then Russian President forgot to add, perhaps deliberately, is that the reasons for this inconsistency is because States with all their vested interests are acting as the recognising body.

3. Alternative theories: collective recognition

This lack of consistency together with the uncertainty regarding the critical threshold has prompted commentators to describe recognition as: '...the weakest link in international law.'.[210] Thus, they have sought to develop more coherent theories. One suggestion made by Lauterpacht was to compel States to grant recognition when an entity satisfied the definition of a State in international law.[211] However, this is unsupported by State practice.[212] Kelsen

205. Starke, *International Law*, p. 126.
206. Sebastian C St J Anstis and Mark w Zacher, 'The Normative Bases of the Global Territorial Order', (2010) 21 *Diplomacy and Statecraft*, p. 317.
207. Ibid.
208. As cited in Anstis and Zacher, *Normative Bases*, p. 317.
209. In fact inconsistent application leads to the weakening of the norm's acceptance by States: the norm loses its 'authority' so to speak.
210. Dugard, *Recognition*, p. 1; Starke, *International Law*, pp. 21–23.
211. Lauterpacht's theory is based on acceptance of the Montevideo criteria, and is an attempt to reconcile the declaratory and constitutive theories by merging them together: Lauterpacht, *Recognition in International Law*, p. 8.
212. Dugard and Raič, *Role of Recognition*, p. 98.

also developed the theories of legal and political recognition. Political recognition is the expression by the recognising State of a '...willingness to enter into political and other relations with the recognised State, relations of a kind which normally exist between members of the Family of Nations.'[213] Kelsen admitted that a willingness to enter into diplomatic relations is declaratory in character since 'Political recognition presupposes the legal existence of the State to be recognized.'[214] Legal recognition is '...the ... procedure [of recognition] provided by international law to ascertain the fact of the State in a concrete case.'[215] In other words, legality is conferred by granting recognition by States, which in turn is based upon satisfying the physical elements of State. Thus Kelsen's legal recognition is constitutive in character,[216] and accordingly suffers from the same flaws as Lauterpacht, namely an assumption that States will act impartially, and not out of self-interest. Kelsen's theories do not resolve the Great Debate.

Another, Dugard has suggested the concept of collective recognition, created by the act of granting UN membership.[217] Dugard's logic is simple: to be admitted to the UN an entity must be a State. If a political entity is admitted as a member, then, *ipso facto*, it must be a State.[218] Other authors such as Franck believe that Dugard's thesis has merit,[219] and Kelsen also agrees that a State can 'transfer' the right of recognition to either: (1) another State, or (2) to a Union of States, or (3) to the representative organs of the Union, such as the League of Nations.[220] Dugard's ideas are supported by the decision of the ICJ in the *Genocide Case* where the Court rejected the preliminary objections of the SFRY on the basis that Bosnia's membership of the UN was sufficient to prove the standing to bring an action pursuant to the provisions of the Genocide Convention.[221]

213. This is done by treaty. Kelsen, *Principles*, p. 222.
214. Ibid, p. 223.
215. Ibid.
216. Dugard, *Recognition*, p. 165.
217. Ibid.
218. There are non-State entities such as Palestine participating as observers in the UN General Assembly. Dugard's theory also does not explain Byelorussia and the Ukraine: both original members of the UN, but for many years merely part of the former USSR, and not independent States.
219. Franck, *Legitimacy*, p. 113. Thus UN membership would satisfy Franck's concept of 'symbolic validation'. Crawford notes that collective recognition has 'substantial probative value'. Crawford, *Creation of States*, p. 540.
220. Thus membership of the League would satisfy both Kelsen's political and legal recognition of statehood, and is based upon the author's interpretation of art 1(2) of the *Covenant of the League of Nations*. However, Kelsen's conclusion is similar to Dugard's analysis simply because art 1(2) of the Covenant only allows entry to States regardless of whether they have been granted recognition by other States, or who may have voted against the admission within the League's Assembly: Kelsen, *Principles*, p. 227.
221. *Application of the Convention on the Prevention and Punishment of the Crime of Genocide (Bosnia and Herzegovina v Yugoslavia) (Judgment)* [1996] ICJ Rep 595, 611 [18] ('*Genocide Case*'). See

The UN political organs have acted as a 'recognising body' in three different ways. Firstly, by calling for the collective non-recognition of specific entities, such as Rhodesia;[222] the Bantustans;[223] the Turkish Republic of Northern Cyprus;[224] and Katanga.[225] Secondly, through determination of the credentials of Member State's representatives, as it did when examining whether Portugal represented the territory of Guinea-Bissau which had declared its independence in 1973.[226] Portugal refused to accept its independence despite 40 States recognising Guinea-Bissau's statehood,[227] as well as the General Assembly.[228] So in another resolution the General Assembly approved the representatives of Portugal's credentials, but excluded their credentials in relation to Guinea-Bissau, because it was now an independent State.[229] Guinea-Bissau was admitted as a member of the UN on 12 August 1974.[230] Finally, it could be argued that the UN through the granting of Observer Status to unrecognised non-State entities that subsequently became accepted as member States of the UN has prompted recognition, or perhaps even acted in a constitutive manner.[231] Examples include: South West Africa

Grant's criticism of this point: Grant, *Territorial Status*, p. 306, 310, 324–5, 339. See also *Application of the Convention on the Prevention and Punishment of the Crime of Genocide (Bosnia and Herzegovina v Yugoslavia)* (*Preliminary Objections)* [1993] ICJ Rep 325 ('*Genocide Case Provisional Measures*').

222. See the references at nn 143–151 above.
223. See the references at nn 147–150 above. *Bantustans*, GA Res 32/105N, UN GAOR, 32nd sess, 102nd plen mtg, UN Doc A/RES/32/105N (14 December 1977).
224. See the references listed above nn 154–157.
225. See the references listed above nn 163–164.
226. The African Party of Guinea and the Cape Verde Islands was formed in September 1956, and had been fighting for the colony's independence since 1963, gaining control over substantial areas of the former colony's territory by 1970: Crawford, *Creation of States*, p. 386.
227. In fact Portugal did not extend *de jure* recognition until 26 August 1974: Crawford, *Creation of States*, p. 386.
228. *Illegal Occupation by Portuguese Military Forces of Certain Sectors of the Republic of Guinea-Bissau and Acts of Agression Committed by Them against the People of the Republic*, GA Res 3061 (XXVIII), UN GAOR, 28th sess, 2163rd plen mtg, UN Doc A/RES/3061 (XXVIII) (2 November 1973) [1] (emphasis added).
229. *Credentials of Representatives to the Twenty-Eighth Session of the General Assembly*, GA Res 3181 (XXVIII), UN GAOR, 28th sess, 2204th plen mtg, UN Doc A/RES/3181 (XXVIII) (17 December 1973).
230. *Resolution 356*, SC Res 356, 29th sess, 1791st mtg, UN Doc S/RES/356 (12 August 1974). Commentators argue that the actions of the UN by not acknowledging that the credentials of Portugal's representatives extended to its former colonies, was constitutive in nature, because it was made in defiance of the former colonial power's claim to sovereignty over the territory. Crawford, *Creation of States*, p. 386; Dugard, *Recognition*, p. 74.
231. For example the FDG was awarded Observer Status in 1952, and was admitted as a member of the UN in 1973. The DRG was granted Observer Status in 1972, and as a member of the UN in 1973. The RVN was granted Observer Status in 1952, and the DRVN was granted Observer Status in 1975, and the (unified) Socialist Republic of Vietnam was admitted as a member of the UN in 1977: Crawford, *Creation of States*, p. 194.

People's Organisation (SWAPO), which was actively seeking the independence of Namibia,[232] the ROK,[233] and the DPRK.[234]

Dugard's idea is dependent upon a very high level of acceptance of the value of UN membership. However, this is not a serious flaw. For example, although the League did not achieve universal membership, the practice of admission to the League seriously undermined the absolute nature of States' discretion, and the impact of their acts of unilateral recognition they had exercised prior to the formation of the League.[235] Furthermore, collective recognition through UN membership will succeed in replacing unilateral recognition when universal membership is achieved.[236] Accordingly there is some merit in Dugard's thesis. However, there are flaws with his theory.

Another flaw with Dugard's thesis is revealed by the Cold War, which was a dark time for impartial recognition.[237] The admission procedure for membership of the UN requires a recommendation of the Security Council to the General Assembly. As a substantive matter it requires the consent of the Permanent members of the Security Council, so the procedure raises the spectre of their dreaded veto power.[238]

As mentioned above, the former USSR declared that they would use their veto power to defeat any Western-sponsored proposal for admission of client States to the UN unless the West with its majority of votes would agree in advance to support Soviet-sponsored socialist candidates.[239] Patil in his examination of the use of the Veto Power between 1946–1990 provides many examples of Cold War politics preventing and influencing the admission process. Initially the applications of many States were rejected because of their role in the Second World War.[240] For example, applicants such as Austria were rejected multiple times because they had been 'the enemy' during the

232. Namibia was admitted as a member of the UN on 23 April 1990.
233. Crawford, *Creation of States*, p. 471.
234. Ibid.
235. Dugard, *Recognition*, p. 23.
236. Interestingly Dugard quotes from another author, Chen, who stated that when UN membership has obtained 'complete universality, the notion of 'recognition' will wither away': Dugard, *Recognition*, p. 167.
237. Ibid, p. 58.
238. Anjiali Patil, *The UN Veto in World Affairs 1946–1990* (1992) p. 56.
239. This then prompted a request for an advisory opinion from the ICJ on whether member-States could impose conditions. Instead the ICJ found that essentially the applicant must comply with art 4(1) of the *UN Charter* which states that an applicant must be: (1) a State; (2) peace-loving; (3) willing to accept the obligations of the *UN Charter*; (4) able to carry out the obligations of the *UN Charter*; and (5) be willing to carry out the obligations of the *UN Charter*. Further that Member States could not provide additional conditions: *Admissions Opinion* [1948] ICJ Rep 57, pp. 62–63.
240. Rejecting an applicant is essentially based on their failure to meet the criteria in art 4(1) of the *UN Charter*. Thus the failure to be considered a peace-loving nation-state was often used to disqualify an applicant.

Second World War.[241] Others like Ireland [on four separate occasions] were rejected on the grounds that they had been friendly towards the Axis Powers.[242] However, many applicants were denied membership simply as a result of Cold War politics.

For example Mauritania's application was vetoed by the USSR simply because the Western Powers had for 15 years rejected the application of the Mongolian People's Republic as part of their 'discriminatory policy' towards States that had a socialist government.[243] Then there are more obvious examples such as the applications of the two Vietnams, and the two Koreas.

The USSR's objection to the application of RVN (South Vietnam) was based on its belief that the only true government was the Democratic Republic of Vietnam (North Vietnam) and therefore it was the only true State to be admitted. Further, when both Vietnams were sponsored for admission in 1975, the US vetoed the application because the application for the ROK had been rejected. Then later after the reunification of Vietnam, the US again rejected the application because of the alleged lack of assistance in regard to US servicemen missing in action.[244]

It could be argued that the Cold War is over, and that there may be a period of cooperation between the Big Five that will enable a more objective assessment of new applications. If so, then consider whether Russia would support an application by Chechnya, or PRC with regard to Tibet?[245] Political self-interest will always be a factor where the interests of the permanent members of the Security Council, are involved, indeed or of any emerging power such as India, that may not be a permanent member, but whose influence in world events increases. So it would appear that collective recognition is not as free of political arbitrariness as Dugard hopes.[246] For example, States have been admitted to UN membership when they have lacked one or more of the Montevideo criteria, or alternatively doubt has been expressed as to their effective control over their territory, or that they were not independent.[247]

241. Patil, *UN Veto*, pp. 21–26.
242. Ibid, p. 28. Ireland's conduct was based on a lack of assistance to the Allied parties.
243. Ibid, p. 35.
244. Ibid, pp. 47–52; Stephen Jacobs and Marc Poirer, 'The Right to Veto United Nations Membership Applications: The United States Veto of the Viet-Nams' (1976) 17 *Harvard International Law Journal*, p. 581.
245. And PRC position on Taiwan is also a pertinent example.
246. This is evident in the Joint Dissenting Opinion of their Excellencies Judges Basdevant, Winiarski, Read and Sir Arnold McNair, in the Admissions Opinion, where they held that: 'The admission of a new Member is pre-eminently a political act, and a political act of he greatest importance': *Conditions of Admission of a State to Membership in the United Nations (Article 4 of the Charter) (Advisory Opinion)* [1948] ICJ Rep 57, 62 ('*Admissions Opinion*').
247. For example, the Congo, Israel and Bosnia-Herzegovina. See the discussion at above nn 124–138; Crawford, *Creation of States*, p. 180, pp. 432–34 (regarding the formation of Israel).

Another criticism of Dugard's thesis, one that he acknowledges, is that admission to the UN does not confer legitimacy upon a State.[248]

> It is readily conceded that admission to the United Nations does not confer political legitimacy on the State of Israel *or remove the defects* in the original title of Israel.[249]

Henry Cattan, a spokesperson on behalf of the Palestinian people, commented on the role of the UN's political organs in recognition:

> The UN is not vested under the Charter with any power to legitimate a State which is illegitimate. The admission of a State does not depend upon the legitimacy or otherwise of the State applying for membership. Nor does the procedure of admission involve any inquiry into the constitutional legitimacy or the manner of creation of the applicant State. All that is required under the Charter is evidence of its ability and willingness to accept and carry out the obligations contained in the Charter. The admission of Israel to UN membership therefore cannot be construed to involve a legitimation of her creation.[250]

Israel has been accepted into the international community despite the above concerns, and yet in other situations, such as Rhodesia, the UN has justified its call for the collective non-recognition on the basis of a breach of international law. Thus it could be argued that using collective recognition doesn't address the problem of political arbitrariness, or political self-interest as well as Dugard hopes. After all States dominate the political organs of the UN. The effectiveness of the Security Council during the Cold War for example was questionable. One author has described it as being paralysed during this period.[251] The problem for the Security Council is that political considerations are more important than the application of justice and fairness.

Some telling examples illustrate this point. The UN Security Council did not consider the crisis in Liberia in 1990 or even make a public comment on it until Jan 1991, 13 months after the establishment of Economic Community of West African States Monitoring Group (ECOMOG), despite Liberia's ambassador to the UN attempting to have the Security Council do so. Why?

248. Dugard defines legitimacy as referring to the claim 'that a state and its institutions are worthy of respect on the ground that they are democratic and reflect the will of the people of the territory': Dugard, *Recognition*, p. 61.
249. Ibid, p. 62 (emphasis added).
250. Ibid.
251. Elisabeth Zoller, 'Contributions of the Court to the Resolution of International tensions' in Connie Peck and Roy Lee (eds), *Increasing the Effectiveness of the International Court of Justice: Proceedings of the ICJ/UNITAR Colloquium to Celebrate the 50th Anniversary of the Court* (1997) 77, p. 87.

Several States already did not desire UN consideration of the situation. Cote d' Ivoire supported Taylor's National Patriotic Front of Liberia (NPFL). Others, including two members of the Security Council Ethiopia and Zaire, also opposed intervention in Liberia, because they feared that intervention would create a precedent that could in the future mean intervention into their own affairs.[252] This fear of intervention was also recognised by the President of Burkina Faso who warned that ECOMOG would receive a hostile reception from African States. Also amongst many African States there were divisions based upon whether they were Francophone or Anglophone, while smaller States feared Nigeria.[253]

There is the additional complication of the veto power of the permanent members, which often renders political solutions unobtainable.[254] For example, would the PRC agree to self-determination for Tibet, or for some of its western provinces where there is a high percentage of ethnic Turkic people? In fact the only permanent members of the Security Council that have allowed territories independence, the UK, France and Russia, did so after violent wars of independence had occurred, and arguably perhaps they did so out of economic necessity rather than through altruism.[255]

Such an attitude is not unique, but is shared by non-permanent members of the Security Council and indeed any other State. For States such as Indonesia that comprise many ethnic groups that desire self-determination there is perception of a domino effect. The fear that the entire State could splinter into competing, warring entities is a very real one.[256] So if self-determination is left to States to decide as if it were an internal domestic matter then it is hard if not impossible for the matter to be decided in any objective, impartial, independent manner.[257] Today one of the States where the Kurds

252. Herbert Howe, 'Lessons of Liberia: ECOMOG and Regional Peacekeeping' in Michael Brown et al (eds), *Nationalism and Ethnic Conflict*, Cambridge: MIT Press, 1997, p, 399, 405 (n 12).
253. Its GNP and population equalled 15 other Economic Community of West African States (ECOWAS) members: Ibid, p. 406.
254. Russia, France, Great Britain, the United States of America and the PRC.
255. The former British colony of India was divided into the States of India and Pakistan. These States did not use violence to gain their independence, although violence did occur afterwards during what was called 'Partition'. However, Vietnam, Cambodia, Laos, Algeria, Malaysia, Singapore, Aden, and others had their share of violence. For a discussion of the economic considerations and advantages of decolonisation to the imperials powers see, eg, the introduction to Tony Smith (ed), *The End of the European Empire: Decolonisation after World War II*, Lexington: DC Heath and Company, 1975; xi; Bernard Waites, *Europe and the Third World: From Colonisation to Decolonisation, c 1500–1998*, New York: St. Martin's Press Inc, 1999, p. 279, pp. 280–90 (see especially at 285).
256. What has happened to the SFRY.
257. This reason is similar to that expressed by supporters of an international criminal tribunal. 'For however objective and impartial national courts may in fact be, because they are the courts of particular states there will inevitably be a suspicion of bias when a national court tries an international criminal': J Bridge, 'The Case for an International Court of Criminal

are located, Turkey, is an important partner in NATO.[258] Another State, Iran was an important tool to counter Iraq in the muddled geopolitics of the Middle East. Many in the international community consider the plight of the Kurds secondary to the strategic importance of both Turkey and Iran particularly now with the rise of fundamentalist terrorist movements from the Middle East.

In the search for a political solution, the lack of 'equality of bargaining power' places the weaker party, the people seeking self-determination and recognition, at an immense disadvantage. At present when States introduce their own political solution, regardless of the real situation, doubts will be raised over truly free expressions of the people's will. That is why the UN demands to monitor plebiscites. Neutrality, impartiality and objectivity are all necessary pre-requisites for a credible expression of the people's will. They are also necessary to achieve a more just result, which is another reason why the ICJ is more qualified than States to determine statehood.

Finally, the national interests of States' should be placed in context of the consequences of non-recognition. Firstly, an unrecognised State lacks standing before the ICJ, and domestic courts.[259] There are more important consequences of non-recognition. Slovenia and Croatia were considered constituent units of Yugoslavia until they had been recognised. As such they were denied the protection of non-intervention and the use of force available to Member States under the *UN Charter*. Furthermore, the Serb government arguably would be justified in using military force to attempt to prevent the dissolution, and thus maintain the territorial integrity of the former Socialist Federal Republic of Yugoslavia. Furthermore, this would mean that the Slovene and Croatian nationals would not be protected by international law until those entities were recognised as sovereign independent States in their own right.

The same problem faced Bosnia-Herzegovina and in order to prevent continual conflict the German government sought to use the act of recognition, to convert an intra-State conflict into an international one. This had some success since what followed were resolutions by the Security Council confirming the status of Bosnia-Herzegovina as a State entitled to territorial integrity, independence and freedom from interference in its domestic affairs from other States.[260] As a State it could enter into international agreements,

Justice and the Formulation of International Criminal Law' in Mark Janis (ed), *International Courts for the Twenty-First Century*, The Hague: Martinus Nijhoff Dordrecht [Distributed by Kluwer Academic Publishers,1992, p. 223. The important point is that it needs to be seen that the process as impartial as much as it actually is impartial. One exception is Canada and its handling of Quebec's claim to independence.

258. North Atlantic Treaty Organization.
259. Starke, *International Law*, p. 142.
260. Germany recognised Croatia and Slovenia on 23 December 1991, and the EU followed on 15 January 1992. Other members of the European Union were not happy with this

and lawfully seek military assistance.[261] It is these rights that peoples seeking self-determination desire.[262]

Fifteen years ago Abkhazia, together with South Ossetia, broke away from Georgia in a bloody war of secession. Since then Abkhazia has remained in political limbo:[263] is it an independent State, is it part of Georgia, or Russia?[264] The fifteen years of uncertainty have not been kind to Abkhazia, despite receiving large quantities of aid from Russia.[265] Many within Abkhazia lay the blame squarely at Georgia's feet, and its failure to recognize Abkhazia's statehood.[266] So far only six States have recognized Abkhazia as an independent State.[267] Abkhazia's plight represents all that is wrong with the current process of the birth of States: States acting as the recognising body.

4. Conclusion

As the above discussion has shown, States' desire for legitimacy through a process of peer review has become twisted, providing States with an increased potential to play the 'Great Game' instead.[268] Consequently their national interests plague recognition to the point that in Franck's words they have 'squandered their magic'.[269] Franck describes recognition (whether individually or collectively through membership of the UN) as 'symbolic validation'

pre-emptive recognition by Germany, alleging that Germany's act had precipitated the civil war in Bosnia-Herzegovina: Grant, *Recognition of States*, p. 153; Hillgruber, *The Admission of New States*, pp. 493–94.

261. Murphy, *Democratic Legitimacy*, p. 545.
262. Morris, Christopher W, *An Essay on the Modern State*, Cambridge: Cambridge University Press, 1998, p. 54.
263. There are many other examples including Nagorno-Karabakh: Sebastian C St J Anstis & Mark W Zachter, 'The Normative Bases of the Global Territorial Order', 21 (2010) *Diplomacy & Statecraft*, p. 310.
264. It could be argued that since Russia provides as much as 70% of Abkhazia's budget that this is evidence that the region is a constituent unit, and part of Russia.
265. Neal Ascherson, 'A Chance to Join the World' available on the London Review of Books website: http://www.lrb.co.uk/v30/n23/neal-ascherson/a-chance-to-join-the-world (accessed 15 March 2012).
266. According to the Abkhaz foreign minister: 'unless the Georgian leadership reverses its policy of not Recognizing Abkhazia, we will have conflict forever between Abkhazia and Georgia': Damien Mcguinness 'Abkhazia Election: Breakaway Georgia Region Votes' http://www.bbc.co.uk/news/world-europe-17313353 (accessed 15 March 2012) and Neal Ascherson, 'A Chance to Join the World' available on the London Review of Books website: http://www.lrb.co.uk/v30/n23/neal-ascherson/a-chance-to-join-the-world (accessed 15 March 2012).
267. Russia, Nauru, Nicaragua, Tuvalu, Venezuela, and Vanuatu. Non-state entities that have recognized Abkhazia include; Nagorno-Karabakh, South Ossetia, and Transnistria. All of these are claiming statehood also.
268. The reference is to Kipling's great work 'Kim', set in India as the empires of Russia and England played the 'Great Game' of geopolitics: Rudyard Kipling, *Kim* (1901).
269. Franck *Legitimacy*, p. 112, 134.

by one's peers.[270] He acknowledges that '...symbolic validation sometimes is used fraudulently...'[271] and that it was crucial in the maintenance of the credibility of this validation process that it be exercised legitimately.[272]

Thus, in conclusion States should not remain as the recognising body. Instead it should be the ICJ that determines statehood. The Court's impartiality is a very important advantage the ICJ has over a political institution such as the UN General Assembly, where political or economic influences are crucial in determining the outcome of a dispute.[273] The ICJ provides greater protection to the weak from the strong.[274] The Court should consider the merits of both parties' claims, and not be swayed by their relative political power and influence.[275] The role of the ICJ will be considered in the final part of this chapter.

E. Determining statehood: the ICJ as the 'recognising body'

Raič's theory that statehood is determined through a two-step process is as follows:[276]

> Once an entity meets the traditional criteria for statehood ..., it exists as an effective territorial entity. In order to become a State in the sense of international law, the entity should be created lawfully, that is to say, its creation should not be accompanied by, or be the result of, a violation of certain fundamental rules of international law... The breach of international law forms a bar to the attribution of full international legal personality to the entity concerned. Therefore, while existing in fact, the entity does not come into existence as a Sate under international law.[277]

270. Ibid, pp. 112–17. Franck argues that recognition was 'symbolic validation' of an emerging or aspirant State's *political community*. It is this desire for sovereign equality, a craving for 'peer recognition' that is in the opinion of some authors enabled States to develop their role as the 'recognizing body'.
271. Ibid, p. 112.
272. Ibid, p. 133.
273. Patil, *UN Veto*, p. 56. As noted by their Excellencies Judges Basdevant, Winiarski, Read and Sir Arnold McNair in their Joint Dissenting Opinion in the *Admissions Opinion*, the General Assembly, and the Security Council are *political organs*. As such they are expected to take into account *political considerations*, provided they still comply with art 4(1) of the *UN Charter*. *Admissions Opinion*, [1948] ICJ Rep 57, 85, [9].
274. Mohamed Shahabuddeen, 'The World Court at the Turn of the Century' in AS Muller, D Raič & JM Thuránszky (eds), *The International Court of Justice: Its Future Role after Fifty Years*, The Hague: Kluwer Law International incorporating Martinus-Nijhoff Publishers, 1997, p. 7. For example when the ICJ discussing the intervention by Great Britain into Albanian sovereign waters, in the *Corfu Channel* case: *Corfu Channel (United Kingdom v Albania) (Merits)* [1949] ICJ Rep 4, 35.
275. Either supporting a powerful party or being more sympathetic for a 'weaker' party.
276. Raič, *Statehood*, p. 154.
277. Ibid.

In essence what Raič's process aims to do is to firstly determine whether an entity in fact is a State, and then whether in law it is a State. This process is perfectly consistent with what was argued above that the determination of statehood is a question of fact and law, and as revealed by State practice. Resolving issues that involve questions of fact and law is a task that any domestic court or legal tribunal does every day of its working life. In fact domestic courts have actually considered questions of recognition.[278]

After examining the Montevideo criteria we concluded that with the addition of the element of independence they do provide adequate means to determine the factual elements of a State. Accordingly we will consider his second question: whether the claimant to statehood has been created 'lawfully' before discussing the Court's role.

1. A question of international law

Commentators, for example Lauterpacht, Kelsen, Kreijen, Raič, Menon, and Crawford, regard the determination of statehood as a legal question.[279] Kelsen and Oppenheim argued that an incorrect recognition of State was a breach of international law.[280] This is because illegal, or premature recognition breaches the rule of non-intervention and threatens a State's territorial integrity.[281] Hillgruber also described the effect of recognition as conferring a legal status,[282] although he argues that non-recognition does not affect the entity's legal status as a State.[283] As mentioned above State practice makes it clear that States also consider recognition to be a legal question, or at the very least involves norms of international law.

278. For example, *Morgan Guaranty Trust Co v Republic of Palau*, 639 *Federal Supplement* 706, 713 (SD NY 1986). In this case five banks brought an action to reclaim a US$35 million loan from the Republic of Palau. In order to determine this matter the US District Court had to decide that the Palau was a foreign State within the meaning of the (US) Foreign Sovereign Immunities Act. The District Court decided that Palau had exercised self-determination, and had reactivated its dormant sovereignty. Accordingly Palau was a foreign State; *Upright v Mercury Business Machine Co*, 13 AD 2d 36, 213 NYS 2d 417 (1961). In this case an American company Mercury imported typewriters from an East German manufacturer but refused to pay the manufacturer, who then assigned the debt to Upright who then sought to enforce the debt. Mercury refused on the basis that the claim was unenforceable because the East German government had not been recognised by the US government. Other examples include the *Gur Corporation v Trust Bank of Africa Ltd* [1987] QB 599; *Carl Zeiss Stiftung v Rayner & Keeler Ltd* [1967] 1 AC 853. Franck, *Legitimacy*, p. 132.
279. Lauterpacht, *Recognition of States*, p. 428; Menon, *Law of Recognition*, p. 24; Raič, *Statehood*, p. 48; Crawford, *Creation of States*, p. 61; Kreijen, *State Failure*, p. 13.
280. Raič, *Statehood*, p. 95; Kelsen, *Pure Theory*, pp. 224–25. Raič, *Statehood*, p. 92; Kreijen, *State Failure*, p. 13.
281. It is called 'premature' recognition because the entity doesn't satisfy the Montevideo criteria. Raič, *Statehood*, p. 95.
282. Hillgruber, *The Admission of New States*, p. 492.
283. Ibid.

With perhaps the sole exception of Antarctica the entirety of the Earth's land surface has been claimed, or controlled, by an existing State. Accordingly the most common reason for the emergence of a new State is because of a claim to (external) self-determination. Self-determination is a norm of international law, and claims for self-determination involve other fundamental international legal concepts such as sovereignty,[284] territorial integrity,[285] *uti possidetis*,[286] and also examine the very conceptual foundation of the State, its right or legitimacy to exercise sovereignty over a specific group in a specific territory.[287] These matters may have political implications, but all involve questions of international law. How they affect the lawfulness of a self-determination claim, and hence a claim to statehood, has been discussed in Chapter 1.

What other norms relate to the lawfulness of State creation? Dugard suggest that only those norms that have acquired the status of *jus cogens*.[288] Dugard justifies his conclusion by arguing that (1) firstly these are rules that are the concern of all States; and (2) secondly, the underlying basis of the concept of *jus cogens* is the overriding imperative that the international community must exercise constant vigilance to ensure that an illegal act does not create a source of legal rights. This is particularly evident in the creation of States:[289]

> An act in violation of a norm having the character of *jus cogens* is illegal and is therefore null and void. This applies to the creation of States, the acquisition of territory and other situations, such as the case of Namibia.[290]

Dugard cites the following principles of *jus cogens* applicable in the practice of recognition:

1. The prohibition of the use of force;
2. The prohibition of territorial acquisition by means of force;

284. Hinsley, *Sovereignty*, p. 17.
285. See generally Crawford, *Creation of States*; Dugard, *Recognition*, p. 7; Starke, *International Law*, p. 91; Olivier, *Establishment of Sovereignty*, p. 102.
286. 'As you possess shall you continue to possess.'
287. Ronald Cohen, as cited in Morris, *On the Modern State*, p. 16; Hinsley, *Sovereignty*, p. 17.
288. Dugard, *Recognition*, p. 16. See also where Dugard stated: 'If the practice of non-recognition is to be kept within reasonable bounds, it must be confined to those cases which most seriously offend international law and public policy. This can best be achieved by limiting non-recognition to cases involving the violation of a peremptory norm': at p. 149.
289. An example of Dugard's fears can be seen in the acceptance of India's forceful occupation of Goa, then a Portuguese protectorate, which was an illegal act, yet accepted nevertheless because it was seen as furtherance of decolonisation. Ibid, p. 116.
290. Ibid, p. 135.

3. The prohibition against racial discrimination and other human rights apartheid;
4. *The prohibition of the denial of self-determination.*[291]

Grant also makes suggestions that include external legality (ie complying with *jus cogens* norms) and internal legality (ie protection of human rights and maybe a right to democracy).[292] In particular Dugard emphasises that a denial of self-determination should automatically result in non-recognition.[293]

> ...the collective action taken by the United Nations in this case [Rhodesia] serves to confirm the principal thesis of this Chapter that a number of basic norms, founded in the principles of non-aggression, self-determination and respect for human rights, are in the main responsible for the resort to non-recognition by the international community.[294]

Crawford agrees with Dugard, arguing that: '... norms that are non-derogable and peremptory cannot be violated by state-creation any more than by treaty-making.'[295] Crawford also went on to argue that even where formal independence is not an issue, if it can be proven where an entity's creation has violated international law then a presumption should be made against statehood.[296] Crawford also recognises that self-determination plays an important role in the determination of statehood.[297] Raič, takes their arguments further, boldly asserting that self-determination plays a crucial role in the process of legitimising the creation of a State:

> Whether a new State is created as a result of devolution, integration, dissolution, or secession, it is submitted that, in principle, in all of these cases, self-determination forms the legitimising principle for the creation of a new State.[298]

291. Ibid, p. 154 (emphasis added). He then goes on to examine each and conclude that each are norms of *jus cogens*: at pp. 154–60.
292. Grant, *Defining Statehood*, p. 45.
293. Dugard, *Recognition*, p. 98. This is shown by the example of Rhodesia. Dugard's argument is partly based on Crawford's examination of the events in Rhodesia: Ibid, p. 98, 116.
294. Ibid, p. 122.
295. However, he argues that arts 53 and 64 of the *Vienna Convention* that define *jus cogens* were not intended to directly affect statehood: Crawford, *Creation of States*, p. 107.
296. Crawford, *The Creation of States*, p. 89.
297. As cited in Dugard, *Recognition*, p. 116.
298. Raič, *Statehood*, p. 29, pp. 167–68, 418–38.

This position is reinforced by articles 40 and 41 of the International Law Commission Articles of State Responsibility,[299] and also by the recent *Kosovo Advisory Opinion.*[300] The Court considered submission that the Security Council's actions in condemning the declarations of independence by Rhodesia, Cyprus and Republika Srpska meant that this was evidence of a general proposition that any unilateral declaration of independence was illegal. The Court noted that:

> ...the illegality attached to the declarations of independence [by Rhodesia, Cyprus and Republika Srpska] thus stemmed not from the unilateral character of these declarations as such, but from the fact that they were, or would have been, connected with the unlawful use of force or other egregious violations of norms of general international law, in particular those of a peremptory character *(jus cogens).*'[301]

Thus, in sum there is much support for Raič's proposition. So what role the Court could play? If legal norms, particularly those of *jus cogens* are being applied in the determination of a State, shouldn't the Court be the most appropriate body to determine whether they have been breached? Thus, one obvious role would be for the Court to determine whether any such norms have been breached, but it is suggested here that the Court could in fact adopt a more ambitious role.

2. The court's role

It is suggested here that the ICJ could provide guidance to the UN in a role similar to that exercised by the Badinter Commission. The violence associated with the break-up of the SFRY, and the subsequent claims for independence by Slovenia, Croatia, Bosnia-Herzegovina, and Macedonia (and subsequently Kosovo), created a great deal of concern in Western Europe, and led to the appointment by the EC of the Badinter Commission to provide legal advice to the EC's Conference on Yugoslavia.

The Badinter Commission laid down a variety of pre-conditions for the republics seeking to secede from the SFRY.[302] The Badinter Commission's

299. *Responsibility of States for Internationally Wrongful Acts 2001*, available at untreaty.un.org/ilc/texts/instruments/English/draft%20articles/9_6_2001.pdf (accessed 25 June 2013)
300. *Accordance with International Law of the Unilateral Declaration of Independence in Respect of Kosovo, (Advisory Opinion)*, [2010] ICJ Rep 403 ['*Kosovo Opinion*'].
301. *Kosovo Opinion*, [2010] ICJ Rep 403, 437 [81].
302. For example in regard to Bosnia-Herzegovina's claim the new 'State' must hold a referendum to ensure all its inhabitants had expressed their free will. There was some concern that the ethnic Serbs' wishes, that is to secede if Bosnia became independent, had not been

work led to the adoption of the EC of guidelines for recognition that established a procedure of recognition for the emerging States in both the SFRY and the former USSR.[303] The EC Guidelines incorporated the following requirements: (1) respect for the *UN Charter* as well as the *Final Act of Helsinki* and the *Charter of Paris*; (2) respect for human rights, including the protection of minorities, as well as a requirement for democratic government;[304] (3) as well as the protection of territorial integrity; and (4) commitment to disarmament, and nuclear non-proliferation, as well as regional security.[305]

In addition the EC Guidelines were accompanied by a *Declaration on Yugoslavia*, which included a number of threshold criteria,[306] and outlined an 'application' procedure for recognition, whereby the applicants would apply through the chair of the Conference on Yugoslavia, and the Badinter Commission would determine the application's merits.[307] Furthermore, the Declaration extended the commitment to territorial integrity to include a commitment to adopt 'constitutional guarantees' not to make territorial claims to neighbouring territories.[308]

The Guidelines concluded with the following statement: 'The commitment to these principles opens the way to recognition by the Community and its member States and to the establishment of diplomatic relations.'[309] This conclusion made it clear that these 'guidelines' were in effect pre-conditions. This paragraph also suggests that, despite statements to the

adequately addressed by the declaration of Bosnia' independence. *Opinion No 4*; Grant, *Recognition of States*, pp. 160–61. Other requirements included protection of minorities, arms agreements.

303. *Guidelines on the Recognition of New States in Eastern Europe and the Soviet Union* (16 December 1991) ('*EC Guidelines*'), as reproduced in Harris, *Cases and Materials*, pp. 147–49. Harris also notes Dec 16 1991 UKMIL 1991. The *EC Guidelines* were accompanied by a *Declaration on Yugoslavia* that 'invited' the new States in Yugoslavia to seek recognition in accordance with the EC Guidelines: in other words to satisfy the pre-conditions laid down there. See the discussion in Crawford, *Creation of States*, pp. 397–402; Grant, *Recognition of States*, pp. 157–9; Rich, *Collapse of Yugoslavia*, p. 43.
304. As such the guidelines reflected many of the political thoughts and philosophies of the EC, namely democracy as the preferred form of governance: Crawford, *Creation of States*, pp. 397–402. See the discussion above regarding a requirement for a democratic government, and the discussion in Chapter 1.
305. *EC Guidelines*; See the discussion in Grant, *Recognition of States*, p. 158.
306. These included: (1) acceptance of provisions regarding human rights and ethnic minorities as contained in the Draft Convention on Yugoslavia (then being reviewed by the Conference on Yugoslavia); (2) cooperation with the efforts of the UN (Secretary-General and Security Council) to create peace; (3) to continue to participate in the Conference on Yugoslavia; (4) to accept the *EC Guidelines*: Grant, *The Recognition of States*, p. 157.
307. Ibid.
308. This last requirement was constructed to address Greek concerns about Macedonian expansionism. Greece was concerned that the new State of Macedonia would join with the similarly named Greek province in a free association to form a larger Macedonian State: Ibid, p. 159.
309. *EC Guidelines*; See the discussion in Grant, *The Recognition of States*, p. 158.

opposite by the Badinter Commission, recognition is constitutive in nature, and that statehood is dependent upon the approval by other States, in this instance collective recognition by the EC.

The Badinter Commission has received criticism for the quality of this legal advice for a variety reasons: (1) that its conclusion the SFRY was in a state of dissolution was incorrect and not in accordance with international legal principles;[310] (2) their application of territorial integrity, and *uti possidetis* to internal borders was not only incorrect, but may have worsened the existing violence;[311] and (3) because not all of its Opinions were followed by the EC.[312]

However, whilst the first two criticisms are justified as part of the continual evolution of norms of international law regulation the determination of statehood, and recognition, the third is a rather unfair criticism, since the Badinter Commission was the first time that an entity had been created to deal with recognition claims, and little if any guidelines were provided to assist the Commission. Perhaps because of this inexperience the Commission's mandate was very vague, as was its procedure, and no enforcement mechanisms were stated in any detail.[313] Consequently, the Commission was not equipped with any real authority to make a binding decision. Instead its purpose was to provide advice. In spite of these problems the Commission made a valuable contribution regarding the role that international law can play in the determination of statehood.[314] In fact it could be said that the Badinter Commission did introduce a 'new legality' into the process of recognition.[315]

The Badinter Commission laid down a variety of pre-conditions for the republics seeking to secede from the SFRY.[316] Its Opinions led to the

310. *Opinion No 1;* Peter Radan, 'Post-Secession International Borders: A Critical Analysis of the Opinions of the Badinter Commission', 24 (2000) *Melbourne University Law Review*, pp. 66–67.
311. *Opinion No 2 of the Arbitration Commission of the Peace Conference on Yugoslavia* 31 ILM 1497 (1992) *('Opinion No 2'); Opinion No 3 of the Arbitration Commission of the Peace Conference on Yugoslavia* 31 ILM 1499 (1992) *('Opinion No 3')*; Radan, *Post-Secession*, pp. 59–65; Michla Pomerance, 'The Badinter Commission: the Use and Misuse of the International Court of Justice's Jurisprudence', (1998) 20 (1) *Michigan Journal of International Law*, pp. 56–57, 68–74.
312. Grant, *Recognition of States*, p. 166.
313. A part from stating that the '[t]he relevant authorities will submit their differences to an Arbitration Commission of five members', little else was stated. Grant, in a very strong understatement, describes the mandate as 'loosely worded'. See the discussion in Grant, *Recognition of States*, pp. 154–55.
314. It must be remembered that the Badinter Commission's work took place in a difficult political background: the disintegration of the former USSR, the impending formation of the European Union, and the worst outbreak of violence in Europe in fifty years.
315. Although its extent is debatable and somewhat controversial. See Grant, *Recognition of States*, p. 168.
316. For example in regard to Bosnia-Herzegovina's claim the new 'State' must hold a referendum to ensure all its inhabitants had expressed their free will. There was some concern that the ethnic Serbs' wishes, that is to secede if Bosnia became independent, had not be

adoption of the EC of guidelines for recognition that established a procedure of recognition for the emerging States in both the SFRY and the former USSR,[317] (although it could be argued that the EC's guidelines (democracy, protection of human rights and minorities for example) go beyond the current requirement of international law[318]) and provided: '… a reference point for future attempts at governing recognition through international institutions.'[319] For example, its work was considered by a panel of experts formed by the Canadian federal government to advise them regarding the question of Quebec's right to secession.[320]

Thus, the role envisaged for the ICJ is to provide guidance to the UN political bodies. This guidance could focus on a range of matters.

Firstly, the Court could clarify the facts surrounding the claim for statehood. In essence acting as a court of inquiry.[321] Parties to a dispute will always have different or conflicting perceptions of events, or even may seek to deliberately distort facts for their own advantage. One example concerns the disputed territory of Nagorno-Karabakh in Azerbaijan. Armenia's interpretation of history that proved that the territory had been part of their respective territory for thousands of years contrasted starkly with Azberbaijan's interpretation of history.[322] This is a role envisaged by commentators such as Crawford, who whilst listing his alternative criteria for statehood noted that any 'problems' with them or uncertainty should be subject to settlement by the ICJ.[323] Kelsen too stated that: 'In the realm of law there is no immediately evident fact, there are only facts ascertained by

adequately addressed by the declaration of Bosnia' independence. *Opinion No 4*; Grant, *Recognition of States*, pp. 160–1. Other requirements included protection of minorities, arms agreements.

317. *EC Guidelines.* See the discussion in Crawford, *Creation of States*, p. 397; Grant, *Recognition of States*, pp. 157–9; Rich, *Collapse of Yugoslavia*, p. 43.
318. The ICJ held in the *Admissions Opinion* that Member States are not entitled to require additional criteria for membership beyond the requirements contained in *UN Charter* art 4(1). See *Admissions Opinion* [1948] ICJ Rep 57, 64, 65.
319. Grant, *Recognition of States*, pp. 163.
320. Mainly in relation to the application of *uti possidetis* so that the internal borders of the province could become the external borders if Quebec became independent. This reliance prompted further criticism by commentators: Peter Radan, 'The Supreme Court of Canada and the Borders of Quebec', (1998) *Australian International Law Journal*, p. 175.
321. For a discussion of the effectiveness and general nature of 'inquiry' as a dispute resolution method, please refer to: JG Merrills, *International Dispute Settlement*, (5th ed), Camridge: Cambridge University Press, 2011, p. 41 onwards. Examples of successful inquiries include: the *Dogger Bank Inquiry of* 1905, and the *Red Crusader Inquiry of* 1962.
322. See James Summers, *Peoples and International Law, How Nationalism and Self-Determination Shape a Contemporary Law of Nations*, Leiden: Martinus-Nijhoff, 2007, pp. 73–74. Armenia, CCPR/C/92/Add.2, (1998) 6, [21] & *Letter dated 5 March 1999 from the Permanent Representative of Azerbaijan to the United Nations Office in Geneva addressed to the Secretariat of the Fifty-Fifth Session of the Commission on Human Rights* E/CN.4/1999/123/, 2.
323. Crawford, *Creation of States*, pp. 40–41.

the competent authorities in a procedure determined by law.'[324] Furthermore that recognition required proof of facts by a 'competent authority.'[325]

Alternatively, the ICJ could be asked to determine whether the existing State government actually represents a people who have formally declared independence, or whether another State has denied a people their right to exercise self-determination, or whether the State government's credentials extend to include representation of a people that are subject to alien and foreign subjugation. For example the UN General Assembly refused to accept that Portugal represented the territory of Guinea-Bissau, which had declared its independence in 1973.[326]

The major role envisaged here is for the Court to provide guidance regarding an entity's claim to statehood, so that they could be admitted as a member-State of the UN. Essentially this determination would be done through the application of Raič's two steps; (1) the factual existence according to the Montevideo criteria as well as considering the claimant's level of independence from other States, including specifically a former parent or colonial State, and (2) the legality of the creation of the entity's statehood. In essence the Court's role would be to determine statehood prior to collective recognition by the UN.[327] It is important that this process takes place before the entity applies for admission in the UN because as noted by the ICJ in the *Admissions Opinion* that additional political considerations cannot be imposed in addition to the conditions in art 4(1) of the *UN Charter.*[328] Sadly the ICJ appears to have missed an opportunity to do exactly what is proposed here when deliberating in the *Genocide Case (Preliminary Objections).*[329]

It could be argued that those same national interests that it was argued should prevent States from acting as the recognising body will prevent a claimant from achieving UN membership due to the veto power of the permanent five of the Security Council. Kosovo is facing such a situation, as either Russia or PRC could veto a resolution proposing Kosovo's

324. Kelsen, *Principles*, p. 221.
325. Ibid.
326. *Credentials of Representatives to the Twenty-Eighth Session of the General Assembly*, GA Res 3181 (XXVIII), UN GAOR, 28th sess, 2204th plen mtg, UN Doc A/RES/3181 (XXVIII) (17 December 1973).
327. Thus the argument used here dovetails neatly with Dugard's theory of collective recognition.
328. Art 4(2) of the *UN Charter; Admissions Opinion*, [1948] ICJ Rep 57, 62.
329. However, the Dissenting Opinion of Judge Kreca did examine this in substantial detail: see Grant's criticism of the Court's failure in: Grant, *Territorial Status*, p. 324. It is important that this two-step process takes place before the entity applies for admission in the UN because as noted by the ICJ in the *Conditions of Admission of a State to Membership in the United Nations (Article 4 of Charter) (Advisory Opinion)* [1948] ICJ Rep 57, 62 '*Admissions Opinion*' that no additional political considerations can be imposed in addition to the requisite conditions in art 4(1) of the *UN Charter*. Such an imposition of additional criteria would breach art 4(2) of the *UN Charter*. See *Admissions Opinion*, [1948] ICJ Rep 57, 62.

membership.[330] This may be true, but as noted by D'Aspremont, an entity can still be a State in spite of being denied UN membership.[331]

As mentioned above, recognition is a question of law because it involves the determination of an entity's international legal personality. Commentators such as Hillgruber, Menon and Raič argue, recognition concerns determination of an entity's international legal status as a State.[332] For example, Menon believes:

> Recognition of a new State is the acknowledgement by another State of the legal personality of a community whose international status had been previously indeterminate.[333]

Thus, rather than just focus on determining whether an entity is a State or not, what the Court could do is to determine the extent of an entity's international legal personality. If the entity has full international legal personality, it can be welcomed into the community of States, and be admitted as a member of the UN, as a State.

If not considered to be a State, then could the Court recognise the entity as being another type of international legal person: perhaps a State *in statu nascendi?*[334] What would be needed to qualify as a State *in statu nascendi?*[335] Firstly, as a discussed in Chapter 1 the people would have to satisfy the preconditions to self-determination, which would include satisfying the Montevideo criteria, except perhaps they lacked substantial effective control over their territory, and, or were not able to act independently through the actions of the parent State to deny or challenge their right to self-determination. In addition, these people would have, as Brownlie suggests, statehood as their goal.

The rights and obligations that such a legal person might have would need further examination beyond this monograph (perhaps they could be determined by the Court on a case by case basis) but given the *erga omnes* character of self-determination one right that should be available is the ability to exercise the right to self-determination free from interference from States, including the State the people are attempting to secede from.[336] This right would be similar in nature to a State's right to territorial integrity or

330. Time will tell how the UN will ultimately use the guidance of the *Kosovo Opinion.*
331. Jean D'Aspremont, 'Regulating Statehood: the Kosovo Status Settlement', (2007) 10 *Leiden Journal of International Law*, p. 657.
332. Raič, *Statehood*, p. 48.
333. Menon, *Law of Recognition*, p. 27.
334. As mentioned above Brownlie already considers a State *in statu nascendi* to be a category of international legal person: Brownlie, *Principles of Public International Law*, pp. 77–8; Crawford, *Creation of States*, pp. 193–94. See Chapter 3.
335. See Brownlie's definition: *Principles of Public International Law*, pp. 77–8.
336. *East Timor Case* [1995] ICJ Rep 90, 102.

non-interferences as contained in the *UN Charter*,[337] and would be consistent with the ICJ's call for collective non-recognition in the *Namibia Opinion*.[338] It would also be consistent with the International Law Commission's *Articles on State Responsibility*, which states in art 41(1) that:[339] 'States shall cooperate to bring to an end through lawful means any serious breach within the meaning of article 40'.[340] And also with article 41(2): 'No State shall recognize as lawful a situation created by a serious breach within the meaning of article 40, nor render aid or assistance in maintaining that situation.'[341]

Furthermore, the UN could on the basis of the Court's findings that a people constituted a State *in statu nascendi* grant them Observer Status, which could lead eventually to formal acceptance as a State once the flaws within its statehood were cured or rectified as part of a process similar to the concept of earned sovereignty.[342] Thus these would continue the example set by the UN when granting Observer Status to SWAPO, and Palestine.

F. Conclusion

This chapter began with the proposal that the ICJ that should act as the recognising body, determining statehood by using a two-step process based on Raic's theory. This idea may be a bold statement. To some it may be too bold since they would consider recognition to be a purely political act. However, as the examination of the concept of recognition and State practice has shown it is not too bold and more importantly it is desirable.

The examination of recognition has shown that whilst recognition concerns the determination of the existence of statehood, it is really concerned with the determination of an entity's international legal personality, and a change in an entity's legal status. More importantly, that determination of statehood involves answering questions of fact and questions of law. And this explains why neither the declaratory and constitutive theories resolve the Great Debate. Whilst it is tempting to conclude that State practice supports a constitutive approach, the constitutive theory simply does not explain the

337. *UN Charter* arts 2(4), 2(7). See Chapter 1.
338. *Legal Consequences for States of the Continued Presence of South Africa in Namibia (South West Africa) notwithstanding Security Council Resolution 276 (1970) (Advisory Opinion)* [1971] ICJ Rep 16, 56 ('*Namibia Opinion*'). See also at 31, where the Court stated that self-determination applied to all territories.
339. *Draft Articles on Responsibility of States for Internationally Wrongful Acts* were adopted after 40 years of work on 9 August 2001. See James Crawford, *The International Law Commission's Articles on State Responsibility*, Cambridge: Cambridge University Press, 2007, pp. 249–51.
340. Ibid, p. 249.
341. This request for collective non-recognition of a State's action is consistent with the UN calling for non-recognition of the statehood of Rhodesia, and the Bantustans (see the discussion above) and also with the *Namibia Opinion* [1971] ICJ Rep 16, 31.
342. As discussed in Chapter 1.

factual existence of a State: the act of recognition on its own does not create borders, towns, and peoples with all their culture, language and the government that administers all of this. The constitutive theory does not consider the possibility that the relevant legal principles are based on facts and similarly the declaratory theory does not recognise the effect of international law on facts. Expressed in a different manner: neither theory can adequately explain how an entity has acquired the international legal personality of a State.[343] Or as Crawford notes neither can explain why the entity has the right to exercise authority in a defined territory.[344]

Examining State practice reveals that States, acting as either members of the UN or independently, allow their national self-interests to interfere when considering recognition, and by allowing their self-interests to influence their decision have reduced the validity of their role as the recognising body. Therefore recognition *by* States should not be a requirement for a State's existence, and should not be a reason to deny a people their right to self-determination.[345]

Furthermore, as shown by the examples discussed above (the Bantustan homelands, Northern Cypurs, or Rhodesia, etc.) it is significant that States, and the political organs of the UN, have consistently referred to grounds of illegality to deny recognition, and statehood. This leads to the conclusion that international law plays an important role in the process of recognition, either as a means of camouflaging national self-interests or simply because it is crucial for the entire process. In any event both conclusions emphasise the necessity to have the ICJ as the recognising body since it is best placed to apply the rules of international law. Courts recognise and apply inescapable conclusions of logic whereas States will seek to deny or avoid such conclusions where it is politically expedient to do so.

The examination of the grounds of illegality raised in cases of denial indicate that it is not so much that the political community fails to meet the criteria of the *Montevideo Convention*, i.e. that it does not have an effective government to administer it, but rather the illegality refers to the means of the creation of the new State. Transkei was a good example of this. There are wider questions of international law that need to be considered, and again the ICJ with its wealth of experience is the best suited body to consider and apply any of the relevant rules of international law to complex factual situations.

If recognition were a purely political act, and widely acknowledged as such, why do States even need to legitimise their decisions, unless their decisions were based on such norms? If norms of international law are

343. Raič, *Statehood*, p. 28.
344. Crawford, *Creation of States*, p. 44. Crawford's interpretation is based on recognition of the Congo. See also Raič, *Statehood*, p. 65.
345. Crawford, *Creation of States*, pp. 16–25.

already being used and are going to be used in this manner, then it makes sense that the very body created as the UN's 'legal advisor' apply those norms, since it can be trusted to do this impartially, and won't be influenced by self-interest which could cause real problems for the implementation of any UN policy.

Resolving questions of fact and law is a task that the ICJ is well equipped to deal with, and should deal with.[346] This may appear to be applying a constitutive approach, but this is not necessarily in contradiction with State practice, or with the role played by the Badinter Commission. Furthermore, by using the ICJ to replace States as a constitutive body this will remove the major (and perhaps only) flaw with the constitutive theory: namely the political arbitrariness of States. Ultimately if the ICJ rather than States was to determine statehood political arbitrariness would evaporate, and this would assist in the maintenance of international stability and security.[347]

The entire concept of recognition is such an important question of international law that it should not, in fact it cannot, be left to other mechanisms to resolve.[348] Certainly not to the whims and agendas of States seeking an advantage regardless of the cost to the claimant or indeed even to the international community. Given the significance of the consequences if recognition is denied, and that recognition is a question of international law, it is staggering that the very entity created to resolve questions of international law is denied this role:

> ... there is a fundamental contradiction between any profession of attachment of the rule of law among nations and the denial of jurisdiction of the highest international judicial organ to adjudicate upon disputes involving legal rights and obligations.[349]

Finally it is not being argued here, as suggested by the US spokesperson above, that the ICJ pass judgment on a State's act of recognition, but rather that the ICJ can advise the UN whether an entity should be denied statehood due to breaches of international law. This is an entirely different question, and one that may be more palatable for States. Furthermore,

346. Kelsen too stated that: 'In the realm of law there is no immediately evident fact, there are only facts ascertained by the competent authorities in a procedure determined by law': Kelsen, *Principles*, p. 221.
347. Dugard, *Recognition*, p. 41.
348. 'The Court [ICJ] would be better paced to provide judicial authority on those peremptory norms of international law where violation impacts either upon non-state actors or is of genuine transboundary concern, for example, environmental damage': Shahabuddeen, *The World Court*, p. 52.
349. Sir Hersch Lauterpacht, as quoted in Shahabuddeen, *The World Court*, p. 9.

States may find a UN decision or action more acceptable if it is consistent with the norms of international law and supported by a relevant Advisory Opinion of the ICJ.

Whether the ICJ is able to consider applications for self-determination, and thus determine statehood as suggested here, will be considered in the following chapter.

3 The International Court of Justice and claims to self-determination

'Imbroglios in places like former Yugoslavia and Somalia, where politicians and diplomats could not agree on which ethnic claims were justified, might well have been better handled had UN action been preceded and guided by an international court decision as to the sovereign rights of competing groups.'[1]

'[E]ven those disputes which seem political ... have a clearly legal component. If, for any reason, the parties fail to refer the matter to the Court, the process of achieving a fair and objectively commendable settlement and thus defusing an international crises situation would be facilitated by obtaining the Court's advisory opinion.'[2]

A. Introduction

The sentiments expressed above by Geoffrey Robertson and the former Secretary-General Javier Perez de Cuellar, are noble sentiments indeed, but how would a question of a people's statehood (or a question of recognition) be brought before the ICJ? The ICJ's jurisdiction is divided into two major components, contentious and advisory, which are contained respectively in Chapters II, and IV of the *ICJ Statute*.[3] The Court's contentious jurisdiction involves resolving disputes between States,[4] and the advisory jurisdiction,

1. Geoffrey Robertson, *Crimes Against Humanity, the Struggle for Global Justice*, London: Penguin Press, 1999, p. 144.
2. Former Secretary-General of the United Nations Javier Perez de Cuellar: UN Doc A/41/1, (1991) 14.
3. Reference to the Court's jurisdiction is also made in Chapter VI (Pacific Settlement of Disputes) of the *UN Charter*, which concerns disputes that, as defined in art 33(1), by their nature threaten international peace and security. Article 36 of the *UN Charter* empowers the Security Council when attempting to resolve a dispute as defined by art 33, to make any recommendation, including under art 36(3), to refer 'legal' disputes to the ICJ. However, see Brownlie's criticism of art 36(3) in Ian Brownlie, *Principles of Public International Law* (5th ed) Oxford: Oxford University Press, 1998, p. 716.
4. See the Court's description of its contentious jurisdiction in *Northern Cameroons (Cameroon v United Kingdom)* [1963] ICJ Rep 15, 38 ('*Northern Cameroons Case*').

involves the provision of an Advisory Opinion at the request of an authorised organ or specialised agency of the UN.[5]

As highlighted by the *East Timor Case*,[6] the Court's contentious jurisdiction has important limitations that effectively place the use of the Court's contentious jurisdiction outside the reach of peoples claiming self-determination. Firstly, due to article 34 (1) of the *ICJ Statute* only States have standing to make a claim before the Court.[7] Secondly, States, intent on protecting their national interests, ensured during the drafting of the *ICJ Statute* and the *UN Charter* that the Court's contentious jurisdiction was based upon the consent of the parties.[8] The advisory jurisdiction avoids these limitations, and according to Pomerance:

> There is in existence a perfected advisory procedure. If, and when, there is a need of the assistance of the Court, and there is willingness to submit the legal issues involved in a difference to the Court's wisdom, the procedure will be readily available.[9]

Whilst perfected is an overstatement, the Court's advisory jurisdiction has a number of advantages for peoples seeking self-determination. The procedure is very flexible in scope because it involves the provision of a legal opinion to a Requesting body, but there are also some disadvantages. The nature of advice or an opinion implies that the decision is not binding, and in fact States are not bound to comply with an Advisory Opinion. Consequently some commentators argue that the advisory jurisdiction has been under utilized,[10] and others argue that the advisory jurisdiction should not be used where the matter is an actual dispute, or one that is highly political or controversial in nature.[11] However, even critics like Falk acknowledge the ability of

5. Kenneth James Keith, *The Extent of the Advisory Jurisdiction of the International Court of Justice* (1971) 18: *ICJ Statute* art 65(1); *UN Charter* art 96 (1), (2) & 7(1).
6. *East Timor (Portugal v Australia)* [1995] ICJ Rep 90 ('*East Timor Case*').
7. Article 34 (1) the *ICJ Statute* simply states: 'Only states may be parties in cases before the Court.' Refer to the Introduction of the monograph above.
8. Shabtai Rosenne, *The World Court: What it is and How it Works* (5th rev ed, 1995) The Hague: Kluwer Academic Publishers, incorporating Maartinus Nijhoff Publishers, p. 85.
9. Dharma Pratap, *The Advisory Jurisdiction of the International Court*, Oxford: Oxford University Press, 1972, p. 270.
10. Michla Pomerance, *The Advisory Function of the International Court in the League and UN Eras*, Baltimore: Johns Hopkins University Press, 1973, p. 44; Terry Gill, *Rosenne's The World Court, What it is and How it Works*, (6th ed, revised by Terry Gill), Leiden: Martinus Nijhoff, 2003, p. 89 ('*Rosenne's World Court*').
11. Anthony Aust, 'Advisory Opinions', (2010) 1(1) *Journal of International Dispute Settlements*, (2010), 123; Richard Falk, 'The *Kosovo* Advisory Opinion: Conflict Resolution and Precedent' (2011)105(1) *American Journal of International Law*, pp. 50, 52–53. Falk even argues that attempts to implement controversial Opinions have resulted in bitter confrontations, pp. 52–53.

the advisory jurisdiction to influence outcomes, and thus contribute to the resolution of disputes.[12]

Accordingly this chapter will focus on the feasibility of using the ICJ's advisory jurisdiction to either determine the legitimacy of a claim to self-determination, as raised in Chapter 1, or alternatively to act as a court of recognition as discussed in Chapter 2. In order to do this the chapter will determine what is the purpose of the advisory jurisdiction, and then any potential limitations it may have, and finally a detailed examination of existing Advisory Opinions concerning self-determination: (1) the *Namibia Opinion*;[13] and secondly (2) the *Western Sahara Opinion*;[14] the *Wall in Palestine Opinion*;[15] and more recently the *Kosovo Opinion*.[16]

B. The advisory jurisdiction

1. Background

The advisory jurisdiction appears to be contrary to the traditional dispute-resolving role of a court, but other tribunals have an advisory jurisdiction. For example, the Indian Supreme Court, the European Court of Human Rights, the Court of Justice of the European Communities, Inter-American Court of Human Right, and the Canadian Supreme Court can provide an advisory opinion.[17] In fact advisory opinions have been used in Western legal jurisdictions as early as the twelfth century where the King of England sought legal advice from his judges on questions of law.[18] The PCIJ also had an advisory jurisdiction.[19] Although there was much controversy and scepticism regarding the wisdom of allowing the PCIJ to provide Advisory Opinions, the PCIJ delivered a total of 27 Advisory Opinions and its advisory jurisdiction was considered to be such a success that it provided the model for the ICJ's jurisdiction.[20] So successful in fact, those former opponents of the

12. Falk, *The Kosovo Advisory Opinion* p. 55.
13. *Legal Consequences for States of the Continued Presence of South Africa in Namibia (South West Africa) Notwithstanding Security Council Resolution 276 (1970) (Advisory Opinion)* [1971] ICJ Rep 16 ('*Namibia Opinion*').
14. *Western Sahara (Advisory Opinion)* [1975] ICJ Rep 12 ('*Western Sahara Opinion*').
15. *Legal Consequences of the Construction of a Wall in the Occupied Palestinian Territory (Advisory Opinion)* [2004] ICJ Rep 136 ('*Wall in Palestine Opinion*').
16. *Accordance with International Law of the Unilateral Declaration of Independence in Respect of Kosovo* (Advisory Opinion) [2010] ICJ Rep 403 ('*Kosovo Opinion*').
17. Pratap, *The Advisory Jurisdiction*, p. 264; Keith, *Extent of the Advisory Opinion* pp. 16–17; Mahasen M Aljaghoub, *The Advisory Function of the International Court of Justice 1946–2005*, New York: Springer, 2006, p. 13; Aust, *Advisory Opinions*, pp. 126–130.
18. Aljaghoub, *The Advisory Function of the International Court*, p. 14.
19. *Covenant of the League of Nations*: art 14. Article 14 differs from art 65(1) of the *ICJ Statute* by specifically including actual disputes as a ground for requesting an Advisory Opinion.
20. Indeed the very first matter to be heard before the PCIJ was in fact a request for an Advisory Opinion: *Designation of the Worker's Delegate for the Netherlands at ILC,*

PCIJ's advisory function become supporters during the drafting stage of the ICJ Statute,[21] and also the new court's advisory jurisdiction was made available to an extended range of requesting bodies.[22]

However, it was the planned 'organic relationship' with the other organs of the UN that subsequently influenced the Court's own perception of the role of its advisory jurisdiction, and the purpose of its Advisory Opinions.[23]

2. The nature and purpose of advisory opinions and the Court's advisory jurisdiction

Broadly speaking an advisory opinion is: '…an authoritative but non-binding explanation of a question or issue.'[24] Such a definition is supported by the Court itself, which stated in the *Peace Treaties Opinion*: 'The object of the Request is … [to obtain] from the Court certain clarifications of a legal nature regarding the applicability of the procedure for the settlement of disputes by the Commissions …'[25] Accordingly there are two possible interpretations of the role of the Court when exercising its advisory jurisdiction: (1) firstly, it is a legal adviser, and thus its relationship with the requesting body is that of a lawyer/client; alternatively (2) it is acting in the traditional role of a Court where a quasi-ruling is provided to parties involved in a dispute.

Many commentators believe that the purpose of an advisory function is to act in the manner of a legal counsel providing advice to assist the UN organs in performance of their duties.[26] This argument is reinforced by art 68 of the *ICJ Statute* which states: 'In the exercise of its advisory functions the Court shall further be guided by the provisions of the present Statute which apply in contentious cases to the extent to which it recognizes them to be applicable.'[27]

PCIJ, Ser. B, No.1, 1922; Aljaghoub, *The Advisory Function of the International Court*, pp. 28–29.

21. For example the US.
22. Thus, art 65(1) *ICJ Statute* and 96 (2) *UN Charter* were expanded, enabling authorised bodies to request an advisory jurisdiction.
23. Aljaghoub, *The Advisory Function of the International Court*, p. 2, pp. 14–22, p. 28.
24. Jo M Pasqualucci, *The Practice and Procedure of the Inter-American Court of Human Rights*, Cambridge: Cambridge University Press, 2003, p. 29; *Interpretation of Peace Treaties with Bulgaria, Hungary and Romania, (Advisory Opinion)* [1950] ICJ Rep 65, 70–71; *Wall in Palestine Opinion*, p. 157 at [47].
25. *Interpretation of Peace Treaties with Bulgaria, Hungary and Romania, (Advisory Opinion)* [1950] ICJ Rep 65, 70. ['*Peace Treaties Opinion*']
26. Mohammed Sameh M Amr, *The Role of the International Court of Justice as the Principal Judicial Organ of the United Nations*, The Hague: Kluwer Law International, 2003, p. 114; Pomerance, *The Advisory Function*, p. 2.
27. See also *ICJ Rules of Court*, art 102(2), (3): *Rules of Court*, opened for signature 14 April 1978, [treaty series], art 105(1) (entered into force I July 1978) (incorporating amendments as of 29 September 2005) ('*ICJ Rules of Court*').

Statements made by the Court also emphasise the client-lawyer perspective.[28] In the *Reservations Opinion* the Court stated that:

> The object of this request for an opinion is to guide the United Nations in respect of its own action. It is indeed beyond any dispute that the General Assembly, who drafted and adopted the Genocide Convention, and the Secretary-General, who is the depositary of the instruments of ratification and accession, have an interest in knowing the legal effects of reservations to that Convention and more particularly the legal effects of objections to such reservations.[29]

And in the *Kosovo Opinion* the Court stated: '... the purpose of the advisory jurisdiction is to enable organs of the United Nations and other authorized bodies to obtain opinions from the Court which will assist them in the future exercise of their functions.'[30]

The perception of the role of the Court as the UN's legal advisor is reinforced by the organic relationship the Court has with the UN.[31] As the principal judicial organ of the UN the ICJ is effectively part of the UN, and therefore arguably the ICJ has a greater obligation than the PCIJ had to act as a legal advisor to the political organs of the UN.[32] This perception has been reinforced by the nature of many of the requests to the ICJ, which concerned 'organizational issues of the UN', rather than dispute-type questions that dominated the PCIJ's era.[33]

However, not all commentators agree with this simplistic perception: that the ICJ's role is to evaluate the lawfulness of the actions of the UN's organs.[34] For example Hudson argues that Advisory Opinions are not: '... legal advice in the ordinary sense, not views expressed by counsel for the guidance of client, but pronouncements as to the law applicable in given

28. *Namibia Opinion* [1971] ICJ Rep 16, 24; *Legality of the Threat or Use of Nuclear Weapons (Advisory Opinion)* [1996] 1 ICJ Rep 226, 236–7 ('*Nuclear Weapons Opinion*'). See also *Peace Treaties Opinion.*
29. *Reservations to the Convention on the Prevention and Punishment of the Crime of Genocide (Advisory Opinion)* [1951] ICJ Rep 19 ('*Reservations Opinion*').
30. *Kosovo Opinion*, [2010] ICJ Rep 403, 421 [44].
31. *Peace Treaties Opinion* [1950] ICJ Rep 65, 71.
32. In accordance with art 92 of the *UN Charter.* The PCIJ may not have had an 'organic relationship' with the League, but its relationship was still very strong and productive. See Amr, *The Role of the International Court of Justice*, p. 47: Aljaghoub, *The Advisory Function of the International Court*, pp. 25–27.
33. Pomerance, *The Advisory Function*, p. 20, 329; Amr, *The Role of the International Court of Justice*, p. 84; Pratap, *The Advisory Jurisdiction*, p. 16. This difference could also be explained by the fact that art 14 of the *Covenant of the League* made specific reference to disputes as well as questions.
34. Aljaghoub, *The Advisory Function of the International Court*, p. 242.

situations formulated after deliberation by the Court.'[35] Falk rejects the use of the expression advisory, or the interpretation that the Opinion is advice to a client. In his words Advisory Opinions are: '… the most authoritative international law assessments available, and deserve respect by affected parties and by the political organs of the United Nations as well as by scholars.'[36] Pomerance describes the relationship between the Court and the UN political organs as more than just a: '… simple lawyer-client affair.'[37] And that the Court's Opinion is more like a quasi-ruling rather than a legal consultation. Her argument is based on her perception that the purpose of the advisory jurisdiction includes assisting the UN political organs in the peaceful settlement of disputes.[38] Brownlie also ascribes a more expansive role of the Court to include assisting the UN to resolve disputes:

> The uses of the advisory jurisdiction are to assist the political organs in settling disputes and to provide authoritative guidance on points of law arising from the functions of organs and specialized agencies.[39]

Commentators' perceptions, like Brownlie's above, that the Court's advisory jurisdiction include dispute resolution, or at the least includes assisting with dispute resolution are based on the judicial character of the advisory jurisdiction, and when providing an Advisory Opinion it is performing a judicial function, not a political one.[40] The Court's judicial character is obvious. As Pratap argues, advisory opinions are judicial pronouncements made by the highest international tribunal.[41] There is much similarity between the procedure used in the advisory jurisdiction and with the contentious jurisdiction.

35. Manley Hudson, 'The Effect of the Advisory Opinions of the World Court' (1948) 42 *American Journal of International Law*, p. 630; Kaikobad would agree: Kaiyn H Kaikobad, *The International Court of Justice and Judicial Review: A Study of the Court's Powers with Respect to Judgments of the ILO and UN Administrative Tribunals,*' The Hague: Kluwer International, 2000, p. 56.
36. Falk, *The Kosovo Advisory Opinion* p. 52.
37. Pomerance, *The Advisory Function*, p. 40, 291.
38. Especially, Pomerance believes, the resolution of disputes between international organisations since it was decided at San Francisco to deny international organisations access to the Court's contentious jurisdiction. And by way of compensation the founding fathers of the UN and the ICJ decided to allow international organisations a pseudo contentious jurisdiction by allowing them through clauses in their treaties access to 'binding' advisory opinions: 'advisory compromissory clauses'. An example includes the 'Headquarters Agreements'. Pomerance, *The Advisory Function*, pp. 30–32, 43, 291; Aljaghoub, *The Advisory Function of the International Court*, p. 33.
39. Brownlie, *Principles of Public International Law*, 5th edn p. 728.
40. Aljaghoub, *The Advisory Function of the International Court*, p. 123. See the discussion below regarding possible limitations of the advisory jurisdiction.
41. Pratap, *The Advisory Jurisdiction*, p. 16, 230–31.

For example, *ad hoc* judges can be appointed in both jurisdictions.[42] And art 68 of the *ICJ Statute* permits the Court to adopt as much of the rules and procedure of the Court's contentious jurisdiction as the Court deems necessary.[43] Finally, the Court's Advisory Opinions are based upon the same norms and sources of international law as outlined in art 38 (1) *ICJ Statute* and used in the Court's rulings in its contentious jurisdiction.[44]

The role of the ICJ as the principal judicial organ of the UN is to assist the UN achieve its *prima* objective as stated in art 1 of the *UN Charter* namely: 'To maintain international peace and security.' As stated by Lauterpacht: '.. [T]he primary purpose of the International Court lies in its function as one of the instruments for securing peace in so far as this aim can be achieved through law.'[45] The ICJ's role is to consider the legal dimension of the UN's pursuit of this objective, and the manner in which this is done is to ensure the rule of law is not just a theoretical concept in international relations but a pragmatic reality. As such its role is akin to that of a legal guardian, not just for the UN,[46] but also for the wider international community. This is the true purpose of the advisory jurisdiction, and of Advisory Opinions.

Aljahoub concluded her examination of the advisory jurisdiction as follows:

> An advisory opinion, in contrast to a judgment in a contentious case, addresses a wide section of the international community. Therefore the Court in giving an opinion must not only address the advisee directly

42. Article 102 (3) *ICJ Rules of Court* states: 'When an advisory opinion is requested upon a legal question actually pending between two or more States, Article 31 of the Statute shall apply, ...' Article 31 of the *ICJ Statute* refers to the appointment of *ad hoc* judges of the same nationality as the parties involved in a contentious matter. In the *Western Sahara Opinion* [1975] ICJ Rep 12, p. 23, Morocco and Mauritania both requested an *ad hoc* judge. Morocco's request was successful, whilst Mauritania's request was not.
43. Although under art 30 of the *ICJ Statute* the Court is permitted to determine and set its own procedural rules when considering requests for and providing Advisory Opinions.
44. Indeed the authoritativeness and credibility of the Court and individual Advisory Opinions are determined by the soundness of the legal arguments that they are based on: Shabati Rosenne, *The Law and Practice of the International Court*, The Hague: Martinus Nijhoff Publishers, 1997, p. 1070; Edvard Hambro, 'The Authority of Advisory Opinions of the International Court of Justice', (1954) 3 *International Comparative Law Quarterly*, p. 21; Aljaghoub, *The Advisory Function of the International Court*, p. 256.
45. Hersch Lauterpacht, *The Development of International Law by the International Court*, London: first published by Stevens & Sons limited reprinted by Grotius Publications limited, p. 3.
46. This point raises the question of whether the Court has the ability to judicially review the decisions of the political organs of the UN, such as the Security Council, a highly controversial topic: see Aljaghoub, *The Advisory Function of the International Court*, pp. 79–92; generally Kaikobad, *The International Court of Justice and Judicial Review*; Rosenne, *The World Court*, p. 36.

> concerned with the opinion, but also all those parties who may be affected by the Court's clarification of the law.[47]

And as the Court noted in the *Wall in Palestine Opinion*:

> The object of the request before the Court is to obtain from the Court an opinion which the General Assembly deems of assistance to it for the proper exercise of its function. The opinion is requested on a question which is of particularly acute concern to the United Nations, and one which is located in a much broader frame of reference than a bilateral dispute.[48]

The broader application of an Advisory Opinion beyond a bilateral dispute, and thus enable the Court to act as the legal guardian, is achievable because of the nature of the procedure followed by the Court. The procedure enables the Court to examine in full the necessary rules of international law, and to call upon a wide range of resources to answer the question in the Request.

3. Procedure of the Court

The procedure begins with a written request from the authorised body.[49] Upon receipt of the Request the Registry of the Court notifies all parties, including States,[50] non-State actors, such as international organisations,[51] and NGO's, that may be interested in the matter.[52] After receiving the written statements the Court will determine whether Oral proceedings will be needed, and if so then the Registrar will fix a date, and notify the interested parties of the timings of the Oral proceedings.[53] The purpose of the

47. Aljaghoub, *The Advisory Function of the International Court*, p. 256.
48. *Wall in Palestine Opinion*, pp. 158–9, at [49–50].
49. *ICJ Statute*, art 65(2). At the time the Request is made all necessary information is attached to the Request.
50. In addition to notifying the relevant States, the Registry is obliged to 'by means of a special and direct communication, notify any State entitled to appear before the Court' or, if necessary, furnish written or oral statements. See the *Questions Relating to Settlers of German Origin in Poland* [1923] PCIJ (ser C) No 3(3) 1051, p. 1055 where the PCIJ rejected the argument presented by Poland that the Court should not have notified Germany, because such notification was in breach of art 73 of the *Rules of Court* of the PCIJ. The PCIJ held that art 73 did not preclude notifying those States that may be able to furnish information, which may assist the Court.
51. *Reservations to the Convention on Genocide (Advisory Opinion)* [1951] ICJ Rep 15, 17 ('*Reservations Opinion*'); *Competence of the General Assembly for the Admission of a State to the United Nations (Advisory Opinion)* [1950] ICJ Rep 48.
52. *ICJ Statute*, art 66(1), (2). Notification is by forwarding to the relevant parties a copy of the Request.
53. The interested parties are also entitled to receive copies of the written statements: *ICJ Rules of Court*, art 105(1).

hearing is to provide additional information necessary to supplement information from the written statements, and to also eliminate superfluous information.[54] The hearing is normally held in the same manner as in contentious proceedings, particularly if the subject-matter of the Request involves a dispute between States.[55] During the Oral proceedings the Court may question witnesses, including experts in a particular field, representatives of States, and those interested parties such as international organisations, as well as ask for corroborative evidence if necessary.[56] Once all presentations have been made, the hearing is closed, and the Court then prepares its Opinion in secret.[57]

The 'secrecy' of the Court's deliberations does not mean that individual members of the Court prepare in isolation from one another. Members may prepare Dissenting, or Separate Opinions, but still the members engage in robust and thorough discussion,[58] a collegiate approach according to His Honour former member of the ICJ Sir Robert Jennings.[59] Once their deliberations are complete the Court then delivers its Opinion in an open Court.[60] In addition the Secretary-General of the UN and the relevant officer of the requesting body are notified of the date of the Court's delivery of the Opinion, and copies are filed in the archives of the Court and with the administration of the requesting body.[61]

The procedure has been criticised as being slow, with an Advisory Opinion taking on average 254 days to complete.[62] However, this is still faster than contentious matters, which on average take approximately two years to resolve.[63] The relative expediency of the advisory jurisdiction is achieved for a variety of reasons. Advisory proceedings are also given priority over contentious matters, as they take less time than contentious hearings. So the Opinion can be ready before the next session or meeting of the requesting body.[64] Also the Court has discretion to consider whether it needs written and oral statements, enabling it to adjust the proceedings so that time is not

54. Pratap, *The Advisory Jurisdiction*, p. 214.
55. It is normally a public hearing, as per *ICJ Rules of Court*, art 59 amended on 29 September 2005.
56. *ICJ Rules of Court*, art 61.
57. *ICJ Statute*, art 54(1)-(3).
58. Art 85 *ICJ Rues of Court*. See for example the *Kosovo Opinion* where of the total of 15 members sitting, two attached a separate declaration to the Court's Opinion; four attached a Separate Opinion, and three attached Dissenting Opinions: *Kosovo Opinion*, [452].
59. Sir Robert Jennings, 'The Role of the International Court of Justice' (1997) 68 *British Yearbook of International Law*, p. 47.
60. Again this is exactly the same procedure as the Court's contentious jurisdiction: *ICJ Statute*, art 67.
61. *Rules of Court:* art 108–109.
62. Aljaghoub, *The Advisory Function of the International Court*, p. 217.
63. With possible exception of interim measures, from the author's own research.
64. Except perhaps for a request for interim measures: Pratap, *The Advisory Jurisdiction*, p. 179.

wasted.[65] Secondly, whilst, it is true that the Court has to firstly consider whether it is seized of jurisdiction, (that the Request has been made in accordance with the *UN Charter*, and the *Statute of the ICJ*) this determination takes places as part of its overall deliberations, and not a separate hearing as it would in a contentious matter.[66] In fact, advisory proceedings rarely suffer from any delays caused by the parties' actions.[67]

The procedure also ensures that a wealth of information is presented to the Court.[68] Thus, it enables the Court to fulfil its role of legal guardian by considering the broader implications of its Opinion for the international community. There is great potential in such a role, as noted by the former Secretary-General of the United Nations Javier Perez de Cuellar,[69] but there is great danger if the court over-extends itself, in other words it goes beyond its judicial propriety.[70]

4. The receipt of advisory opinions

Once the duly signed, and sealed copies of the Opinion are forwarded to the archives of the Court, to the Secretary-General of the UN, and to the chief administrative officer of the Requesting body this ends the role of the Court.[71] What happens next is totally up to the Requesting organ as noted by Pratap:

> With the delivery and communication of an advisory opinion, the task of the Court is over. Thereafter it rests with the requesting organ and the States to accept it and to implement it in action. The extent of this reception and the effect given to the opinions depends upon their nature, apart from political considerations.[72]

The requesting body of the UN is free to: '... determine the course which they will adopt in respect of the matter to which the opinion relates, and their course may be determined by practical rather than legal considerations.'[73]

65. *Rules of Court*, art 105(2)(b); Pratap, *The Advisory Jurisdiction*, p. 214.
66. *ICJ Statute*, art 65 (1).
67. In contentious proceedings there may be applications to intervene, preliminary objections raised, all of which take time to resolve. Pomerance, *The Advisory Function*, p. 295; Pratap, *The Advisory Jurisdiction*, p. 179.
68. See the discussion below.
69. See the quote at note 2 above.
70. Amr, *The Role of the International Court of Justice*, p. 84.
71. *ICJ Rules of Court*, adopted 14 April 1978, art 109 (entered into force 1 July 1978) (incorporating amendments which entered into force 14 April 2005) available at <http://www.icj-cij.org/documents/index.php?p1=4&p2=3&p3=0> (accessed 16 October 2007) ('*Rules of Court*').
72. Pratap, *The Advisory Jurisdiction*, p. 227; Pomerance, *The Advisory Function*, p. 2.
73. Pratap, *The Advisory Jurisdiction*, pp. 247–48.

Referral of the advice back to the Requesting Organs is a disadvantage when using the advisory jurisdiction to assist in the resolution of claims for self-determination since it exposes the claim to all the political disadvantages of the Requesting Organ, something this monograph argues should be avoided.[74] For example, during the drafting of the questions for the Request for the *Namibia Opinion* in the General Assembly, the South African government expressed concern that whilst South Africa was prepared to accept and abide by the opinion; it was clear that the General Assembly would not abide by the Court's Opinion if it were in favour of South Africa.[75] The South African representative argued that there was a lack of equity within the Assembly, and whilst the South African government would respect the rule of law, it opposed the specific formulation of the General Assembly resolution requesting the opinion; and also the attitude of the General Assembly majority.[76]

Amr argues that the requesting body will more than likely accept the Advisory Opinion, and act upon it, since to do otherwise would jeopardise the Court's credibility.[77] Amr's conclusion is not completely accurate. Pomerance noted that during the period of the League the PCIJ's Advisory Opinions were well received, not just by the League's Council, but also by the States involved.[78] Unfortunately, the same could not be said for the UN period. The Court's opinions have been favourably received by the requesting organs, with the post-opinion recommendations of the Requesting body evidencing more often than not a complete acceptance of the Court's advice. However, the Court's Advisory Opinions have not been well received by

74. Such as the veto power of the permanent members of the UN Security Council.
75. The South African government's apprehension was due to the anti-colonial statements expressed by the Asian and Latin-American representatives to the General Assembly.
76. Pomerance, *The Advisory Function*, p. 115.
77. As Amr notes, if a requesting body were to reject or accept the Court's Opinion, then this may create within the organ a power akin to that of an appellate tribunal: Amr, *The Role of the International Court of Justice*, p. 115. For example, the General Assembly accepted the Opinion of the ICJ in the *South West Africa (Status) Case* and then requested South Africa to abide by the Opinion. This point has been stated openly by the ICJ itself: see *Namibia Preliminary Objections* [1962] ICJ Rep 319. The Council of the League of Nations adopted eight Opinions, noted ten, and transmitted to the ILO eight of the Opinions provided by the PCIJ. Pratap, *The Advisory Jurisdiction*, p. 227, pp. 230–31; & 235–44. See the discussion below.
78. Pomerance, *The Advisory Function*, p. 337; see especially the examples set out at 330–41. For example, both Albania and Yugoslavia accepted the PCIJ's Advisory Opinion in the *Monastery of Saint-Naoum Opinion* and in the *Access to German Minority Schools in Polish Upper Silesia*, Poland accepted and complied with the PCIJ's Opinion, even before the League Council considered by the League Council. For further examples see Pratap, *The Advisory Jurisdiction*, pp. 240–41.

interested States.[79] The UN period is characterised by extensive debate over the '... *authority and effect of* the advisory opinions'. (emphasis added)[80]

Pomerance described the attitude of States towards the Court's Advisory Opinions as follows: '...[the] obdurate attitude adopted by certain states effectively sabotaged attempts to implement the Court's opinions.'[81] Her view is based on the former USSR and the Communist bloc consistently objecting to the requests being made by the General Assembly and or other authorised organs arguing that the Court lacked competency to provide opinions, or worse that the opinions be ignored.[82] The former USSR even went as far as requesting the General Assembly to remove all references to the *Admission Opinion* from the General Assembly resolutions intended to implement the Court's advice.[83] Other States have also criticised opinions where they conflicted with the respective State's view on the question or dispute subject to the request.[84]

The role of the Court in providing an Advisory Opinion is to provide guidance on legal questions to the requesting body. The Opinion is a response to a Request from an authorised UN body. The advice is not directed at a State, but the Requesting Body. The implementation of the Court's Opinion is up to the political organs of the UN.

> The Court's task would be to determine in a comprehensive manner the legal consequences of the construction of the wall, while the General Assembly – and the Security Council – may then draw conclusions from the Court's findings.[85]

Therefore any failure to implement the Advisory Opinion is not a failing of the Court, but of the requesting organ, normally a political body of the UN.[86]

79. The Court's Opinions have been treated with the 'utmost respect by the organs that solicited them': Pomerance, *The Advisory Function*, p. 368.
80. As well as the terminology used when drafting the relevant resolutions by the General Assembly: Ibid.
81. Ibid, p. 341.
82. Pratap, *The Advisory Jurisdiction*, p. 245.
83. Pomerance, *The Advisory Function*, p. 356. Rosenne stated that during the Cold War the communist States led by the former USSR showed an attitude of: '... ill-conceived mistrust towards the Court.' Shabtai Rosenne, 'On the Non-Use of the Advisory Competence of the International Court of Justice' (1963) 39 *British Yearbook of International Law*, p. 24.
84. Or arguably supported them when it suited their national interest. See, eg, the comments made by the French, and Israeli delegates regarding the *Reservations Opinion* in *Reservations Opinion to the Convention on the Prevention and Punishment of the Crime of Genocide: Advisory Opinion of the International Court of Justice*, UN GAOR (VI), 6th Comm, 266th mtg, [80], [81], UN Doc A/C.6/SR2.66. Pratap, *The Advisory Jurisdiction*, p. 246.
85. *Wall in Palestine Opinion* [2004] ICJ Rep 136, [62]; see also *Kosovo Opinion*, [421].
86. It is rather rich to criticise the ineffectual nature of the *Wall in Palestine Opinion* when the UN General Assembly or UN Security Council have not resolved the Palestinian-Israeli conflict, despite many years of dealing with the issue.

However, there have been some clear examples of the effectiveness of an Advisory Opinion. For example, on the basis of the *International Status of South West Africa Opinion*,[87] the UN established the necessary administration to continue the League's Mandate system.[88] Also as discussed above it appears that historically the Requesting Organ will accept the Advisory Opinion.

Whilst the above argument may be perceived as a convenient one, it is nonetheless accurate. Furthermore, any criticism regarding the failure of an entity to act upon Advisory Opinions does not justify the argument that they provide little or no value to resolving claims for self-determination or international relations.

5. Potential limitations to the Court's advisory jurisdiction

Article 65 (1) *ICJ Statute* states:

> The Court may give an advisory opinion on any legal question at the request of whatever body may be authorized by or in accordance with the Charter of the United Nations to make such a request.[89]

And article 96 (1) of the *UN Charter* states: 'The General Assembly or the Security Council may request the International Court of Justice to give an advisory opinion on any *legal question*.'[90]

Accordingly there are two pre-conditions that must be met before the court can exercise its advisory jurisdiction: (1) *ratione materie* and (2) *ratinoe persone*. In other words the request must concern the correct subject matter, and the request must be by the correct 'person', and with the exception of the General Assembly and the Security Council the request must relate to the performance of their requesting organ's duties.[91]

87. *International Status of South West Africa Opinion (Advisory Opinion)* [1950] ICJ Rep 128. (*'International Status of South West Africa Opinion'*)
88. The General Assembly adopted the ICJ's Opinion, in *Question of South West Africa*, GA Res 449(V), UN GAOR, 5th sess, Supp No 20, 322 plen mtg, UN Doc A/Res 449(V) [A] (13 December 1950).
89. *ICJ Statute:* art 65(1).
90. *UN Charter* art 96(2) permits organs, and authorised agencies of the UN other than the Security Council or the General Assembly, also refers to legal questions.
91. *Kosovo Opinion*, at [412]; Aljaghoub, *The Advisory Function of the International Court*, pp. 38–61. The only time the ICJ has refused to supply an Advisory Opinion was when the World Health Organisation [WHO] requested an Advisory Opinion in regard to the use of nuclear weapons by a State. The ICJ refused the request on the grounds that the request did not fall within the scope of WHO's activities, but then the IJC accepted a similar request from the UN General Assembly: *Nuclear Weapons in an Armed Conflict (World Health Organisation) (Advisory Opinion)* [1996] 1 ICJ Rep 66.

In relation to the first condition Amr argues that it is clear that the Request for an Advisory Opinion must at least involve a legal question, but what is actually restricted by article 65 (1) is not so clear.[92] Could it include a legal question that was '*abstract in nature*?'[93] The *UN Charter* is a multi-lateral treaty, and practice of the Court when interpreting treaties is to interpret their terms in accordance with their 'natural and ordinary meaning' in the context of the purpose and object of the respective treaty.[94] The ordinary meaning of 'question' implies that art 65(1) cannot apply to actual disputes.[95] Such an interpretation is strengthened by the existence of a separate contentious jurisdiction, especially one that is consensual in nature. Thus, the ICJ has been asked many times not to provide an Advisory Opinion in matters where there is a lack of a State's consent, as well as when the Request concerns a dispute. Finally, it must be a legal question. It may be argued that self-determination is not a legal matter, but a political one, and thus outside the Court's jurisdiction entirely.[96]

There is also a third pre-condition. The Court retains a discretion: whether or not to respond to a request for an Advisory Opinion even if the above two conditions are satisfied. Article 65(1) uses the verb may and the discretion exists so as to protect the integrity of the Court's judicial function and its

92. Amr, *The Role of the International Court of Justice*, p. 84; Pratap, *The Advisory Jurisdiction*, p. 42.
93. Amr's definition of abstract questions will be used. It is as follows: 'A question that does not fall within the context of a concrete legal or factual situation involving a specific issue, or whether this question should be related to some definite issue or circumstance': Amr, *The Role of the International Court of Justice*, p. 91.
94. *Vienna Convention on the Law of Treaties*, opened for signature 23 May 1969, 1155 UNTS 331, art 31(1) (entered into force 27 January 1980) ('*VCLT*') states *inter alia*: 'A treaty shall be interpreted in good faith in accordance with the ordinary meaning to be given to the terms of the treaty in their context and in the light of its object and purpose.' Article 32 of the *VCLT* states that recourse to supplementary materials, including the *travaux preparatoires*, may be had to assist the Court to identify the meaning of the treaty provisions resulting from the application of art 31 (1), or where the application results in an obscure or manifestly absurd or unreasonable interpretation. See also the comments by Judge Azevedo in *Interpretation of Peace Treaties with Bulgaria, Hungary and Romania (1st Phase) (Advisory Opinion)* [1950] ICJ Rep 65, p. 82 ('*Peace Treaties Opinion*'); and also the discussion in D J Harris, *Cases and Materials on International Law* (3rd ed), London; Sweet & Maxwell, 1983, pp. 813–20.
95. *Competence of the General Assembly for the Admission of a State to the United Nations* [1950] ICJ Rep 48; *Constitution of the Maritime Safety Committee of the Inter-Governmental Maritime Consultative Organization* [1960] ICJ Rep 150, 159–60; *South-West Africa (Ethiopia v South Africa; Liberia v South Africa) (Preliminary Objections)* [1962] ICJ Rep 151, 155.
96. This argument is based on the belief that legal methodology is unable to resolve what are essentially political disputes.

nature as the principal judicial organ of the United Nations: its judicial propriety.[97]

Thus the Court does not have an unfettered advisory jurisdiction. There are potential limitations to the Court's advisory jurisdiction as follows: disputes, abstract questions, and political matters.

a. Actual disputes

Commentators have suggested that disputes cannot be the subject of a Request for an Advisory Opinion. Their suggestion is based on the PCIJ's refusal to provide an Opinion in the *Eastern Carelia Case.*[98] The *Eastern Carelia Case* concerned a dispute between Russia – which was not a member of the League – and Finland over the question of Eastern Carelia's autonomy.[99] The PCIJ did refuse to provide an Opinion, stating that answering the question asked in the Request necessitated the determination of facts, which could not be done.[100]

In the later Advisory Opinion of the ICJ in the *Peace Treaties Case*, Bulgaria, Hungary and Romania, argued that the ICJ must refuse to provide an Opinion on the basis of the PCIJ's decision in the *Eastern Carelia Case*: namely that if the ICJ did provide an Opinion it would amount to deciding the merits of a legal dispute. The ICJ rejected this argument and distinguished the *Eastern Carelia Case* on the grounds that there was an inability to resolve factual questions, which was not so in the *Peace Treaties Case*, and furthermore, that providing the Opinion would in no way jeopardise the legal positions of the respective parties.[101] In the *Western Sahara Opinion* the Court distinguished the *Eastern Carelia Case* on numerous grounds. Firstly, whilst Russia was not a member of the League and the Statute of the PCIJ, Spain was a member of the UN, and thus had consented to the *ICJ Statute.*[102] Secondly, the central issue was the nature of their rights during the period of decolonisation, and not a dispute between Morocco and Mauritania, and providing

97. *Western Sahara (Advisory Opinion)* [1975] ICJ Rep 12, 23 ('*Western Sahara Opinion*') [23]; Legal *Consequences of the Construction of a Wall in the Occupied Palestinian Territory, (Advisory Opinion)*, [2004] ICJ Rep 136, 156, [44]. ('*Wall in Palestine Opinion*').
98. *Eastern Carelia Case* [1923] PCIJ (ser B) No 5, 7, p. 25. This refusal is famous and has even been referred to as the '*Eastern Carelia* principle'. See, eg, Pomerance Pomerance, *The Advisory Function*, p. 20. The *Eastern Carelia Case* was considered by the PCIJ in the *Mosul Case* [1925] (ser B) No 12, 6.
99. The territory of Eastern Carelia lay between Russia and Finland, and had been declared to be an autonomous part of Russia by the Treaty of Dorphat 1920 (signed 14 October 1920). Finland argued that Russia was not respecting Eastern Carelia's autonomy. Russia argued that the question of the autonomy of Eastern Carelia was a domestic matter. *Eastern Carelia Case* [1923] PCIJ (ser B) No 5, 7, pp. 12–16.
100. *Eastern Carelia Case* [1923] PCIJ (ser B) No 5, 7, p. 25.
101. *Peace Treaties Opinion* [1950] ICJ Rep 65, 72.
102. *Western Sahara Opinion* [1975] ICJ Rep 12, 24.

an opinion would assist the General Assembly in the decolonisation of the Western Sahara.[103] Furthermore, an adequate amount of material was made available to the Court, unlike the *Eastern Carelia Case.*[104]

Adopting a literal interpretation of art 65 (1) is not consistent with the *Rules of Court.* Art 102 of the *Rules of the Court* make it clear that the Court is able to hear actual disputes when exercising its advisory jurisdiction.[105] A literal interpretation is also inconsistent with the founding fathers' intentions for the Court's advisory jurisdiction.[106] The discussions of the respective Committees at the San Francisco Conference, (Committee II/2, and Committee IV/2), made it quite clear that the envisaged and arguably the primary purpose of Advisory Opinions was to provide assistance in the peaceful settlement of disputes. Even in the Dumbarton Oaks proposals this purpose was evident, since the Security Council's proposed purpose was to maintain peace and security.[107]

The Court has refused to adopt a literal interpretation of art 65 (1) and has considered, and accepted, requests for Opinions that have related to a dispute between States.[108] For example, in the *Namibia Opinion* South Africa's Counsel argued that the Court should reject the Request on the grounds that it was based on an international dispute. The Court rejected this argument stating that to refuse to provide the opinion would not: 'Remain faithful to the requirements of its judicial character'; and furthermore to listen to the request was appropriate to do so because it would 'discharge its [the Court's] functions as the principal judicial organ of the United Nations.'[109]

> It is not the purpose of the request to obtain the assistance of the Court in the exercise of the Security Council' functions relating to the peaceful

103. Ibid, 25.
104. Ibid, 27.
105. As mentioned above, art 102(2) directs the Court to be guided by the procedures of its contentious jurisdiction as far as necessary. Article 102(2) states: 'for this purpose it shall above all consider whether the request for the advisory opinion relates to a legal question actually pending between two or more states'. Article 102(3) states that if the request involves an actual dispute between States, then art 31 of the *ICJ Statute*, which refers to *ad hoc* judges, applies. Also the Court's opinions in *Peace Treaties Opinion* [1950] ICJ Rep 65 and *Reservations Opinion* [1951] ICJ Rep 15 would tend to support the argument that it was intended that the wording of 'legal question' in art 96 (1) would include legal disputes. See the Dissenting opinion of His Excellency Judge Winiarski in *Peace Treaties Opinion* [1950] ICJ Rep 65; *Reservations Opinion* [1951] ICJ Rep 15, 19.
106. Article 32 of the *VCLT* states that recourse to supplementary materials, including the *travaux preparatoires*, may be had to assist the Court to identify the meaning of the treaty provisions resulting from the application of art 31 (1).
107. This is consistent with the intended purpose of the advisory jurisdiction of the PCIJ: Pomerance, *The Advisory Function*, p. 42.
108. *Peace Treaties Opinion* [1950] ICJ Rep 65, 65; *Reservations Opinion* [1951] ICJ Rep 15; *Western Sahara Opinion* [1975] ICJ Rep 12, 23; *Wall in Palestine Opinion* [2004] ICJ Rep 136, [46].
109. *Namibia Opinion* [1971] ICJ Rep 16, 27.

> settlement of a dispute pending before it between two or more States. The request is put forward by a United Nations organ with reference to its own decisions and it seeks legal advice from the Court on the consequences and implications of these decisions.[110]

Finally, the argument that the Court's Advisory Opinion can be used to resolve disputes was clarified by the *Difference Relating to Immunity from Legal Process Case.*[111] In this matter the Request for an Advisory Opinion was made pursuant to art VIII, section 30 of the *Convention on the Privileges and Immunities of the United Nations.*[112] This provision states that where a difference exists between a member State and the UN an Advisory Opinion can be requested, and more importantly art VIII section 30 states that the Opinion by the Court: '... shall be accepted as decisive by the parties.'[113] In essence this stipulation enables the difference, or dispute, between the UN and the member State to be resolved. Therefore, it is concluded that the fact the Request concerns an actual dispute is not by itself a sufficient ground to reject a Request,[114] and that the Court's advisory jurisdiction can be used to resolve disputes.

Another reason why it is argued that the Court lacks the competence to provide an Advisory Opinion in a dispute is that States may not have granted their consent for the dispute to be decided by the Court exercising its contentious jurisdiction. As discussed above if a State has not granted consent then the Court is prevented from hearing the dispute, so shouldn't the same principle apply to the Court when exercising its advisory jurisdiction?

b. Consent of States in a dispute

Concerns have been raised that the advisory jurisdiction could be abused if contentious matters, where there is doubt that parties may not consent to the Court's exercise of jurisdiction, were the basis for a request for an advisory jurisdiction.[115] Thus commentators have also suggested that the Court is not

110. Ibid, 24
111. *Difference Relating to Immunity from Legal Process Case of Special Rapporteur (Advisory Opinion)* [1999] ICJ Rep 62.
112. *Convention on the Privileges and Immunities of the United Nations* opened for signature 13 February 1946, 1 UNTS 15, art VIII, section 30 (entered into force 17 September 1946): art VIII, section 30.
113. Ibid.
114. Malcolm Shaw, *International Law* (5th ed) Cambridge: Cambridge University Press Cambridge, 2003, pp. 1000–1002.
115. Elisabeth Zoller, 'Commentary' in Connie Peck and Roy Lee (eds), *Increasing the Effectiveness of the International Court of Justice: Proceedings of the ICJ/UNITAR Colloquium to Celebrate the 50th Anniversary of the Court,* The Hague: Kluwer Law International incorporating Martinus-Nijhoff Publishers, 1997, p. 86, 89. See also Her Excellency Judge Rosalyn

permitted to provide an Advisory Opinion in the absence of States' consent. Their suggestion is also based on the PCIJ's refusal to provide an Opinion in the *Eastern Carelia Case*.[116] As mentioned above the PCIJ had refused to provide an Opinion. In relation to the issue of the existence of consent the PCIJ stated:

> There has been some discussion as to whether questions for an advisory opinion, if they relate to matters which form the subject of a pending dispute between nations, should be put to the Court without the consent of the parties. It is unnecessary in the present case to deal with this topic.[117]

The above statement by the PCIJ is ambiguous. It could be interpreted as meaning that the PCIJ had refused to provide an opinion because the matter concerned an existing dispute, or because Russia had not consented to the PCIJ exercising its contentious jurisdiction in the matter.[118] However, as Keith so correctly surmises, the Court was simply acknowledging that it was unnecessary to discuss the issue, because it could not give an opinion for other reasons. Those other reasons were as follows. Russia at the time was not a member of the League. The settlement procedure laid down by arts 12–16 of the *Covenant of the League of Nations* referred to members, and only applied to non-members if the non-member had accepted to be bound by the settlement procedure.[119] Russia had clearly rejected the invitation on 1 February 1923. Thus, the lack of Russia's consent did not affect the PCIJ's competence to provide an Opinion, it affected the competence of the Council of the League, the Requesting organ: an entirely different question.[120] Keith's reasoning is consistent with later Advisory Opinions. In the *Peace Treaties Case* the Court stated:

> … no State, whether a Member of the United Nations or not, can prevent the giving of an Advisory Opinion which the United Nations considers to be desirable in order to obtain enlightenment as the course of action it should take.[121]

Higgins, 'The Role of the International Court of Justice at the Turn of the Century' (Presidential Address to the Holdsworth Club of the University of Birmingham, UK, 1999) p. 7; Michla Pomerance, 'The Badinter Commission: The Use and Misuse of the International Court of Justice's Jurisprudence' (1998) 20(1) *Michigan Journal of International Law* 31, 42.

116. *Eastern Carelia Case* p. 25.
117. *Eastern Carelia Case* p. 27.
118. Keith, *Extent of the Advisory Opinion* p. 93. Harris, *Cases and Materials on International Law* pp. 737–9 & Shaw, *International Law*, pp. 1000–1002.
119. After being invited to do so in accordance with art 17 of the *Covenant of the League of Nations.*
120. Keith, *Extent of the Advisory Opinion* p. 92, 100.
121. *Peace Treaties Opinion* [1950] ICJ Rep 65, 71.

In the *Wall in Palestine* the Court rejected Israel's argument that it lacked jurisdiction because Israel had not granted consent to what was a dispute between Israel and Palestine.[122] In doing so the Court stated: 'The Court observes that the lack of consent to the Court's contentious jurisdiction by interested States has no bearing on the Court's jurisdiction to give an Advisory Opinion.'[123] However, the lack of a State's consent may be relevant to when the Court exercises its discretion under art 65 of the *ICJ Statute* to reject the Request.[124]

c. Abstract questions

The concern raised by abstract questions is that it may encourage the Court to act *ultra vires*, to become involved in a policy-making role rather than a judicial one.[125] States argued in the *Nuclear Weapons Opinion* that the question in the Request, was 'vague and abstract' and that the Court by providing its opinion might make '... hypothetical or speculative declarations outside the scope of its judicial function.'[126] Furthermore, any Opinion provided by the Court would not '... provide [any] practical assistance to the General Assembly in carrying out its functions under the Charter.'[127]

Whilst the Court held in the *Northern Cameroons Case* that is there little point considering a question that is a purely hypothetical, the ICJ firmly rejected concerns about the nature of abstract questions, stating quite clearly

122. *Wall in Palestine Opinion* [2004] ICJ Rep 136 [46]. The fact that Israel refers to Palestine when raising this argument prompts the consideration whether this implies recognition of Palestine as a State.
123. Ibid. The Court cited with approval *Peace Treaties Opinion* [1950] ICJ Rep 65; *Reservations Opinion* [1951] ICJ Rep 15; and *Western Sahara Opinion* [1975] ICJ Rep 12, 23–5 as supporting this conclusion. Interestingly in the *Nuclear Weapons Opinion* some States argued that the Court did not have jurisdiction to provide an advisory opinion *because there was no underlying dispute!*: *Nuclear Weapons Opinion* [1996] 1 ICJ Rep 226, 236–37.
124. Keith raises this question, and then discards it since there is little evidene that the Court would do so. Keith, *Extent of the Advisory Opinion* p. 124, 230.
125. Pomerance, *The Advisory Function*, p 308. During the League period concerns were expressed about abstract questions. Also the Informal Inter-Allied Committee argued against abstract questions being allowed as the basis for a Request. Pratap, *The Advisory Jurisdiction*, p. 92.
126. *Nuclear Weapons Opinion* [1996] 1 ICJ Rep 226, 236–7. In other words encroaching on areas that lay within the political organs of the UN, the Security Council and the General Assembly. See also His Excellency Judge Zoricic in *Conditions of Admission of a State to Membership in the United Nations (Article 4 of the Charter) (Advisory Opinion)* [1948] ICJ Rep 57, 96 ('*Admissions Opinion*') where he stated: 'In human life all activity is based on concrete considerations of fact. To attempt to judge ... acts in the abstract would be ... to work in a vacuum, and to misunderstand the meaning of real life.'
127. As contained in the written statements of the following States: US; UK; France; Finland; The Netherlands; Germany: *Nuclear Weapons Opinion* [1996] 1 ICJ Rep 226, 236–7.

that the expression legal question in art 96 (1) of the *UN Charter* and art 65(1) of the *ICJ Statute* includes abstract questions.[128] For example, in the *Admissions Opinion*, the Court stated:

> It has also been contended that the Court should not deal with a question couched in abstract terms. That is a mere affirmation devoid of any justification. According to Article 96 of the Charter and Article 65 of the Statute, the Court may give an advisory on any legal question abstract or otherwise.[129]

If the purpose of the Court's advisory function were to provide advice then arguably it would be entirely consistent with this purpose to ask a question that is abstract in nature. As noted by the PCIJ in the *German Interests in Polish Upper Silesia*:

> There seems to be no reason why States should not be able to ask the Court to give abstract interpretation of a treaty; rather would it appear that this is one of the *most important functions* which it can fulfil.[130]

Secondly, abstract questions may offer an advantage over more specific ones. For example, if a question regarding self-determination did not refer to a specific territory, arguably it stands less chance of raising a protest from an interested State, since there is no apparent threat to their national interests. In fact as noted by Pratap it may actually be advantageous for the requesting body to pose an abstract question because it may '...play down the political element in the dispute'.[131]

For example, a Request may ask whether self-determination was a principle of *jus cogens*, or alternatively how the principle of self-determination related to other rules of international law such as *uti possidetis*, and whether these rules should override self-determination. Such questions could be justified on the grounds that it would assist the Decolonisation Committee, or even the UN General Assembly, to resolve current issues of colonialism.[132]

128. Such a question enters an area that the Court considered not only pointless, but one that jeopardised the Court's judicial propriety. *Northern Cameroons Case* [1963] ICJ Rep 15, 34–8.
129. *Admissions Opinion* [1948] ICJ Rep 57, 61. This was cited with approval by the Court in *Wall in Palestine Opinion* [2004] ICJ Rep 136, [41].
130. *German Interests in Polish Upper Silesia* [1926] PCIJ (ser A) No 7, 4, 18–19 (emphasis added).
131. Pratap, *The Advisory Jurisdiction*, p. 92. Thus enabling the Court to provide an alternative method of dispute resolution when the political organs of the UN have reached an impasse. This raises the argument that advisory opinions can be used to resolve actual disputes.
132. This would be consistent with the purpose of the Court's advisory jurisdiction, namely to provide advice to assist the UN organs with the performance of their tasks, by resolving

d. Legal versus political matters

According to Pomerance the only apparent reason why the word 'legal' was added to qualify the nature of questions was perhaps to promote the ICJ's role as legal advisor to the UN's organs.[133] Alternatively it may have been added to prevent a repeat of the *Customs Union Opinion*,[134] which discussed the issue of political questions as opposed to legal questions.[135]

Careful distinction must be drawn between a political dispute, and a legal dispute that takes place in a political background (which is the context in which all international legal disputes occur) or that are politically motivated.[136] The Court has mentioned numerous times that a legal question has a 'political aspect' or background, does not deprive the question of its legal character and does not therefore, deprive the Court of jurisdiction.[137] In the *Wall in Palestine Opinion* the Court stated:

> ... the Court cannot accept the view, which has also been advanced in the present proceedings, that it has no jurisdiction because of the 'political' character of the question posed.[138]

e. Factual matters

The Court in the Namibia Opinion stated that answering a legal question may require determinations of facts, and furthermore art 96 (1) of the *UN Charter*, and art 65(1) of the *ICJ Statute* did not place such a limitation on the

legal questions. In the *Western Sahara Opinion* the Court stated that it would 'furnish the General Assembly with elements of a legal character relevant to its further treatment of the decolonisation of Western Sahara.' In the *Western Sahara Opinion* the Court stated that it would 'furnish the General Assembly with elements of a legal character relevant to its further treatment of the decolonisation of Western Sahara.' *Western Sahara Opinion* [1975] ICJ Rep 12, 37.

133. The term 'legal' was actually *removed* from the draft of art 14 of the *Statute of the PCIJ*. Furthermore, the term 'legal' has not in the subsequent practise of the ICJ acted as a 'real' limitation. Pomerance, *The Advisory Function*, p 34.
134. *Austro-German Customs Regime (Customs Unions Case)* [1931] PCIJ (ser A/B) No 41, 37. Pomerance, *The Advisory Function*, p. 34.
135. This would be consistent with the Court's contentious jurisdiction. Article 36(2) of the *ICJ Statute* states *inter alia*: 'the jurisdiction of the Court in all *legal* disputes' (emphasis added).
136. See Chapter 4 below.
137. If that were the case would the Court ever be able to consider a dispute? For a list of decisions where the Court has stated this see the *Wall in Palestine Opinion* [2004] ICJ Rep 136, [41], and also the discussion in Amr, *The Role of the International Court of Justice*, p. 88. For further detail regarding the role of the ICJ in highly political matters see Chapter 4 below.
138. *Wall in Palestine Opinion* [2004] ICJ Rep 136, [41].

Court, thus the simple requirement that facts must be determined did not provide a ground to reject the Request.[139]

It would appear that there are very few limitations to the type of questions that could be contained in a Request for an Advisory Opinion. Indeed abstract questions appear to be eminently suited to Requests. This conclusion is due to the very purpose of the advisory jurisdiction, namely assisting a UN organ to fulfil its duties and obligations in accordance with the *UN Charter*. In fact the only real limitation imposed by the wording in article 65 (1) is whether the background to the Request involves the activities of the requesting organ, and the legal question occurred within the activities of the requesting body.

> It is a ... precondition of the Court's competence that the advisory opinion be requested by an organ duly authorised to seek it under the Charter, that it be requested on a legal question, and that except in the case of the General Assembly or the Security Council, that the question be one arising within the scope of the activities of the requesting organ.[140]

Thus, it would be appropriate to consider which organs and agencies of the UN are authorised to make a Request that could refer to matters of unresolved self-determination, and furthermore, which one would be more suitable.

6. Agencies authorised to request an opinion

Article 96 of the *UN Charter* outlines which entities are authorised to make a request. Article 96 (1) of the *UN Charter* grants the General Assembly and the Security Council authority to make a Request, and art 96 (2) states that: 'other organs and specialised agencies, ... authorized by the General Assembly ...' are permitted to make a Request on legal questions associated with the performance of their activities.[141] The General Assembly rather than the Security Council was chosen as the body to empower other UN organs, for a variety of reasons, but mainly because it is the only organ within the

139. This was the argument presented by Spain. *Namibia Opinion* [1971] ICJ Rep 16, 27. This decision is consistent with what the PCIJ stated in the *Eastern Carelia Case* [1923] PCIJ (ser B) No 5, 7.

140. *Application for Review of Judgement No. 273 of the United Nations Administrative Tribunal (Advisory Opinion)* [1982] ICJ Rep 325, 333–4, as cited by the Court in *Wall in Palestine Opinion* [2004] ICJ Rep 136, [14].

141. The parameters of their activities, and therefore any Requests made are defined by their respective constitutions. See *Peace Treaties Opinion* [1950] ICJ Rep 65, 70. The General Assembly can also impose a limit on what is contained within the Request made by the authorised agencies. See Pratap, *The Advisory Jurisdiction*, p. 61.

UN that has the right to receive and consider reports from other UN organs.[142] Its ability to authorise other organs is a general one and once an organ has been authorised, that authority is permanent, unless revoked.[143]

Article 96 (2) does not define organs, but it has been interpreted as including all principal organs as defined by article 7 (1) of the *UN Charter*,[144] and all subsidiary organs as defined in article 7 (2) *UN Charter*, including those created under art 22 and 29 of the *UN Charter*.[145] The expression specialized agencies within article 96 (2) has been interpreted as referring to agencies of the UN organisations.[146]

a. Which agency should make a request?

There are quite a number of authorised bodies that could make a Request concerning self-determination.[147] However, some entities that are authorised

142. Other reasons cited include: (1) Its role as the plenary organ of the UN it has a broad authority to discuss any matter within the scope of the Charter; (2) it plays an important part in electing the officials of other UN organs, (3) it is closely linked to the other organs of the UN, and most importantly (4) it is the only organ within the UN that has the right to receive and consider reports from other UN organs: Amr, *The Role of the International Court of Justice*, p. 53. Article 10 of the *UN Charter* authorises the General Assembly to make recommendations to the members of the UN on: 'any questions or any matters within the scope of the present charter or relating the powers and functions of any organs provided for in the present charter, except in accordance with Article12'.
143. See Amr's criticism of the General Assembly's ability to unilaterally revoke an organ's authority: Amr, *The Role of the International Court of Justice*, pp. 54–65.
144. However, commentators have argued that art 96(2) does not include the Secretariat, in particular the Secretary-General, despite the recommendation made by the former Secretary-General Boutros Boutros Ghali in his famous *An Agenda for Peace: Preventative Diplomacy, Peacemaking and Peace-keeping* (Report of the Secretary-General pursuant to the statement adopted by the Summit Meeting of the Security Council on 31 January 1992) UN Doc A/47/277 (June 1992) [18]. Amr, *The Role of the International Court of Justice*, pp. 57–61; Rosalyn Higgins, 'The Current Health of Advisory Opinions' in Vaughan Lowe and Malgosia Fitzmaurice (eds), *Fifty Years of the International Court of Justice: Essays in Honour of Sir Robert Jennings*, Cambridge University Press: Cambridge 1996, 567, pp. 567–86.
145. Article 96(2) has been interpreted strictly. For example, when it was proposed in 1950 that a proposed Human Rights Committee of the Human Rights Commission of ECOSOC be able to make requests for an Advisory Opinion, the Secretary-General held that the proposed committee was not an organ or a specialized agency of the UN: Amr, *The Role of the International Court of Justice*, pp. 62–3; Pratap, *The Advisory Jurisdiction*, pp. 64–5. Article 7(2) states: 'Such subsidiary organs as may be found necessary may be established in accordance with the present Charter.' Article 22 simply empowers the General Assembly to create subsidiary organs as necessary, and art 29 empowers the SC to do the same.
146. See art 57(1), (2) and art 63(1) of the *UN Charter*, which the *Convention on the Privileges and Immunities of the Specialized Agencies*, opened for signature, 21 November 1947, 33 UNTS 261, (entered into force 2 December 1948) refers to as being the defining articles of specialized agencies. Amr, *The Role of the International Court of Justice*, p. 64.
147. This is advantageous since a Request for an advisory opinion on self-determination could arise in a variety of ways. For example, through the risk posed to international peace and

to make a request are also unlikely to do so. For example due to the problem of the veto power available to the permanent members of the Security Council, a request may be more successfully obtained from the General Assembly.[148]

Perhaps the most obvious choice for a request concerning self-determination would be the Trusteeship Council. However, this is not possible because the Trusteeship Council's role has effectively come to an end with Palau achieving statehood.[149] In any event using the Trustee Council may not have been the most advisable because the Trusteeship Council consisted of the five permanent members of the Security Council, and therefore would not be free from political influence.

In order to avoid political influences then the Special Committee of 24 on Decolonisation may be a more appropriate choice.

b. The Special Committee of 24 on Decolonisation[150]

The UN General Assembly established the Decolonisation Committee in 1961 as part of the General Assembly's implementation of its *Declaration on Colonial Peoples.*[151] The Decolonisation Committee meets annually and its official role is to assist non-self-governing territories *and '...all other territories which have not yet attained independence ...'* to make a smooth transition to independence.[152] Currently there are 23 members, and apart from PRC, and the Russian Federation, the five Permanent Members of the Security Council do not dominate its membership.[153]

security, in which both the General Assembly, in accordance with arts 11(2) and 12(1), and the Security Council as per art 96(1) of the *Charter of the UN* would be able to request an advisory opinion.

148. This is indeed what happened in the lead-up to the General Assembly making a Request for an advisory opinion from the ICJ in the matter of *Wall in Palestine Opinion* [2004] ICJ Rep 136.
149. As from October 1994; *Security Council Resolution 956 (1994) [On Termination of the Status of Palau as a Trust Territory]* UN SCOR 3455th mtg, [UN Doc S/Res/956 (1994) (10 November 1994). All eleven Trust territories have either achieved statehood or chosen association with other States. (However, there does exist some 17 non-self-governing territories.)
150. Referred to as the Decolonisation Committee.
151. The original number of members was 17 but was increased to 24 in 1962: see <http://www.un.org/Depts/dpi/decolonization/special_committee-main.html> at 10 December 2007; and also *The Situation with Regard to the Implementation of the Declaration on the Granting of Independence to Colonial Countries and Peoples*, UN GAOR, 17th sess, 1195th plen mtg, UN Doc A/Res/ 1810 (VXII) [72–73] (17 December 1962).
152. The Decolonisation Committee was created by a resolution of the General Assembly; *The Situation with Regard to the Implementation of the Declaration on the Granting of independence to Colonial Countries and Peoples*, UN GAOR 16th sess, 1066th plen mtg, UN Doc A/Res/1654 (XVI), (27 November 1961) (emphasis added).
153. The current non-permanent members as at 13 June 2013 are: Argentina, Australia, Azerbaijan, Guatemala, Luxembourg, Morocco, Pakistan, Republic of Korea, Rwanda,

The Decolonisation Committee sends missions to identified territories to obtain information about their progress towards statehood, which is then disseminated via seminars to the general public as well as to the UN.[154] The Decolonisation Committee also receives reports from appointed and elected representatives from Non-self-governing Territories, as well as other 'petitioners', on the implementation of the *Declaration on Colonial Peoples*.[155] It also receives petitions from peoples seeking statehood.[156] As such it has a vast amount of experience in monitoring and assisting the emergence of a new State.

Given this experience it would be advantageous for the Decolonisation Committee to make a Request concerning self-determination. Certainly such a Request would fit within the scope of their activities as required by article 96(2) of the *UN Charter*, and the only apparent limitation to the type of Requests that can be made to the Court.[157] It would be advantageous for the obvious reason that the Opinion will be provided to an organization that was created to assist colonial peoples achieve independence, and that has the necessary administration, experience and expertise. Furthermore, the Decolonisation Committee is less likely to experience the same degree of political interference that influences the political organs of the UN, such as the Security Council, which is dominated by the veto power of the permanent members. History has shown how detrimental political machinations have been in self-determination's development.[158]

Currently, the Decolonisation Committee does not have authority to request an advisory opinion. This state of affairs could be changed if the General Assembly granted the committee such authority.[159] However, in order to avoid the possibility of the ICJ refusing a request for an Advisory Opinion, on the grounds that the request is outside the scope of the authorised agencies' activities, it may be preferable if a request concerning self-determination came from the General Assembly rather than the Decolonisation Committee.[160]

and Togo. UN Security Council website: <http://www.un.org/sc/members.asp> at 13 June 2013).

154. Special Committee of 24 on Decolonization web page as noted above in n 151.
155. Ibid.
156. For example, the General Assembly, 'Questions of Gibraltar, Guam, Western Sahara Discussed in Special Political and Decolonization Committee', Press Release GA/SPD/184 (27 September 2000); UN General Assembly, 'Fourth Committee, Concluding General Debate on Decolonization Issues, Hears Petitioners from Western Sahara and New Caledonia', Press Release GA/SPD/186 (29 September 2000).
157. See the discussion of the *Western Sahara Opinion* [1975] ICJ Rep 12, below.
158. One example is the pressure brought to bear by the Indonesian government on the Australian government over West Papuans seeking refugee status within Australia.
159. *UN Charter*, art 10(1).
160. This is what happened when the World Health Organisation [WHO] requested an advisory opinion in regard to the use of nuclear weapons by a State. The ICJ refused the

C. Existing advisory opinions and self-determination

In addition to highlighting the suitability of the Court's advisory jurisdiction, each of the following Opinions raised important questions for the determination of claims for self-determination. For example, in the *Namibia Opinion* the Court had to consider a claim for self-determination that was more than just a 'straight forward' application of European decolonisation. Furthermore, the Court was faced with South Africa's reluctance to surrender their control over the territory in question. In the *Western Sahara Opinion* the Court was faced with the competing claims of two States, Mauritania and Morocco, who both considered themselves as the 'rightful' sovereign over the Western Saharan region. Although the *Wall in Palestine Opinion* related to Israel's construction of a security fence in occupied Palestinian territory, the Court had to consider whether the construction of the wall violated international law, and how the construction affected the Palestinian people's claim for self-determination.[161] Finally, despite its factual background – the Kosovars seeking independence from Serbia – strictly speaking the *Kosovo Opinion* did not concern self-determination, or statehood. (In fact the Court made it explicitly clear that it didn't need to discuss these matters.)[162] Instead the Request for the Advisory Opinion concerned whether the unilateral declaration of independence was illegal. However, as will be seen the *Kosovo Opinion* did make an important contribution to the scholarship on self-determination.

Each of these Opinions will be considered in turn, with special attention being applied to the *Kosovo Opinion* for two important reasons. Firstly, because it is an example of the approach suggested in Chapters 1 and 2, particularly Chapter 2 and how the ICJ could assist with the determination of statehood. And secondly, because the Opinion received a lot of criticism, much of

request on the grounds that the request did not fall within the scope of WHO's activities, but then the ICJ accepted a similar request from the UN General Assembly. See the *Nuclear Weapons in an Armed Conflict (World Health Organisation) (Advisory Opinion)* [1996] 1 ICJ Rep 66. See also *Nuclear Weapons Opinion* [1996] 1 ICJ Rep 226.

161. *Wall in Palestine Opinion* [2004] ICJ Rep 136, 151, 153. See Adam M Smith, 'Good Fences Make Good Neighbours?: The "Wall Decision" and the Troubling Rise of the ICJ as a Human Rights Court', (2005) 18 *Harvard Human Rights Journal* 251 (available at <http://www.law.harvard.edu/students/orgs/hrj/iss18/smith.pdf> at 27 August 2007).
162. *Accordance with International Law of the Unilateral Declaration of Independence in Respect of Kosovo* [2010] ICJ Rep 403, 423 [51]: 'The question is narrow and specific; it asks for the Court's opinion on whether or not the declaration of independence is in accordance with international law. It does not ask about the legal consequences of that declaration. In particular, it does not ask whether or not Kosovo has achieved statehood. Nor does it ask about the validity or legal effects of the recognition of Kosovo by those States which have recognized it as an independent State.'

which raises the question of whether as argued here the ICJ is indeed capable of assisting with the resolution of claims to self-determination.

1. The Namibia Advisory Opinion [1950–1971][163]

a. Background

Namibia was a former German colony, known as German South West Africa.[164] After the First World War Germany renounced all her rights and titles in the territory in favour of the Allies. Namibia was then placed under a Mandate conferred upon the Union of South Africa.[165] After the end of WWII and the decline of the Mandate System caused by the dissolution of the League of Nations, South Africa sought permission from the General Assembly to incorporate Namibia into South Africa.[166]

After being refused by the General Assembly South Africa's response was a mixture of defiance, and obedience. It did give up its plans to incorporate Namibia, and furnished a report in 1947 regarding its administration of its territory, even supplying additional or supplementary information at the request of the Trustee Council in 1948.[167] However, South Africa also stated it would

163. Of the series of decisions and advisory opinions of the ICJ regarding Namibia, two will be considered in passing only: *Voting Procedures on Questions Relating to Reports and Petitions Concerning the Territory of South West Africa Case* [1955] ICJ Rep 67 ('*Namibia Voting Procedures Opinion*') and *Admissibility of Hearings of Petitioners by the Committee on South West Africa Case* [1956] ICJ Rep 23 ('*Admissibility of Hearings Opinion*').
164. In accordance with the wishes of the local population the General Assembly by resolution in 1968 changed the name of the territory from South West Africa to Namibia. See *Question of South West Africa*, GA Res 2372 (XXII), UN GAOR, 22nd sess, supp 16A, 1671st plen mtg, UN Doc A/Res/3314 (21 June 1968) as noted in D J Harris, *Cases and Materials on International Law*, p. 106.
165. In accordance with art 119 of the *Treaty of Versailles*, protocol to *Treaty Between the Allied and Associated Powers and Germany*, open for signature 29 June 1919, TREATY SERIES (entry into force 10 January 1920).
166. The General Assembly refused and urged that South Africa conclude the trust agreement Mandate on three separate occasions. See *Future Status of South West Africa*, GA Res 65 (I), UN GAOR, 64th plen mtg, UN Doc A/Res/65(1) (14 December 1946); *Consideration of Proposed New Trusteeship Agreements, if Any: Question of South West Africa*, GA Res 141 (II), UN GAOR, 105th plen mtg, UN Doc A/Res/141 (II) (1 November 1947); *Question of South West Africa*, GA Res 227 (III), UN GAOR, 164th plen mtg, UN Doc A/Res/ 227 (III) (26 November 1948); Pomerance *The Advisory Function*, p. 107. The desire for integration is not as strange as it may appear, since under the Mandate, South Africa 'was to have full power of administration and legislation over the Territory as an integral portion of the Union. The Union Government was to exercise [the] administration on behalf of the League, with the object of promoting the well-being and development of the inhabitants.' *International Status of South West Africa Case (Advisory Opinion)* [1950] ICJ Rep 128 ('*International Status of South West Africa Opinion*').
167. In a letter dated 23 July 1947 South Africa expressed their intention to not incorporate Namibia. *Question of South West Africa*, GA Res 227 (III), UN GAOR, 164th plen mtg, UN Doc A/Res/ 227 (III) (26 November 1948). Pomerance, *The Advisory Function*, p. 108.

not furnish any more reports.[168] Furthermore, South Africa stated that it aimed to bring about a closer relationship between Namibia and South Africa, through a Union statute.[169] The language used in the statute and the letter, in reference to Namibia, made no mention of the term mandate. The UN considered this denial of the territory's official international status as a deliberate challenge, evidence of South Africa's intention to totally deny the UN's role,[170] and a confirmation of South Africa's claim of total authority for Namibia.[171]

South Africa's actions prompted a series of resolutions by the General Assembly as well as actions brought before the ICJ. The first was a request to the ICJ by the General Assembly, on 6 December 6 1949, for an Advisory Opinion regarding the status of the territory and the international obligations of South Africa, given the collapse of the League of Nations.[172]

b. The International Status of South West Africa Opinion[173]

The *International Status of South West Africa Opinion* involved the ICJ considering three precise questions:

> What is the international status of the Territory of South-West Africa and what are the international obligations of the Union of South Africa arising there from, in particular:
> (a) Does the Union of South Africa continue to have international obligations under the Mandate for South-West Africa and, if so, what are those obligations?
> (b) Are the provisions of Chapter XII of the Charter applicable and, if so, in what manner, to the Territory of South-West Africa?
> (c) Has the Union of South Africa the competence to modify the international status of the Territory of South West Africa, or, in the event of a negative reply, where does competence rest to determine and modify the international status of the Territory?[174]

168. In a letter dated 11 July 1949: UN Doc A/239. See Pomerance, *The Advisory Function*, p. 108.
169. South Africa justified their planned actions on the basis that it was within the 'spirit' of the Mandate.
170. South Africa had previously refused to place Namibia under the UN Trusteeship System, intended to replace the Mandate System. For an excellent discussion of the historical background regarding Namibia, see John Dugard (ed), *The South West Africa/Namibia Dispute*, Berkeley: University of California Press, 1973. See also John Dugard 'Namibia–South Africa's Presence Found to be Illegal–United Nations' Measures Declared Valid' (1972) 5 *New York University Journal of International Law and Politics* 117, 118–121.
171. Pomerance, *The Advisory Function*, p. 109.
172. *Question of South West Africa: Request for an Advisory Opinion of the International Court of Justice*, GA Res 338(IV) UN GAOR, 4th sess, 269th plen mtg, UN Doc A/ Res/ 338(IV) (1949). See the extract in Dugard, *The South West Africa/Namibia Dispute*, pp. 128–29.
173. *International Status of South West Africa Opinion* [1950] ICJ Rep 128.
174. Ibid, p. 129.

The first question involved an examination of art 22 of the *Covenant of the League of Nations*; the second required an examination of articles 75 and 77 of the *UN Charter*, and the third, who or what organization, had the authority to alter the international status of Namibia.

The ICJ advised the General Assembly that South Africa continued to have international obligations in administering Namibia.[175] Namely, South Africa's obligation to forward reports to the General Assembly and also to acknowledge the right for the local population to lodge petitions with the General Assembly. Also the ICJ advised that Chapter XII did apply to Namibia, although Chapter XII did not impose a legal obligation upon South Africa to place Namibia under the trusteeship system of the *UN Charter*. Finally, only with the agreement of the General Assembly could South Africa change the international status of Namibia.[176]

South Africa's continuing international obligations were based on the 'sacred trust of civilization' and the practical machinery to implement this.[177] The Court advised that the first concept was not dependent upon the existence of the League of Nations, and South Africa's obligations could not be brought to an end because this supervisory organ had ceased to exist. Furthermore, South Africa had recognised and accepted their obligations, as evidenced by declarations made both to the League and the UN.[178] Secondly, the resolution of the League of Nations of April 18 1946 stated that the League's functions with respect to mandated territories would come to an end, but did not state that the Mandates themselves had come to an end.[179] Furthermore, this resolution indicated that the Mandates would continue until arrangements were put into place to replace the Mandate system, and that the UN would assume the supervisory obligations of the League.[180]

Acting on this Opinion the UN began establishing the necessary administration to continue the previous supervisory role of the League under the Mandate system.[181] South Africa refused to cooperate.[182] The UN responded

175. As detailed in the *Covenant of the League of Nations*, art 22.
176. *International Status of South West Africa Opinion* [1950] ICJ Rep 128, 131–44.
177. The 'securities for the performance of this trust': see *Covenant of the League of Nations* art 22.
178. This was confirmed by art 80 (1) of the *UN Charter*, which maintains the rights of States, and peoples, and the terms of existing international instruments *until* the territories in question were placed under the trusteeship system in accordance with the *UN Charter*.
179. *International Status of South West Africa Opinion* [1950] ICJ Rep 128, 137.
180. Ibid.
181. This is despite the ICJ advising that South Africa was under no *legal* obligation to place Namibia under the UN Trustee system. The General Assembly adopted the ICJ's Opinion, in *Question of South West Africa*, GA Res 449(V), UN GAOR, 5th sess, Supp No 20, 322 plen mtg, UN Doc A/Res 449(V) [A] (13 December 1950).
182. Harris, *Cases and Materials on International Law*, p. 103. This was on the basis that important information had not been presented as evidence before the ICJ. Dugard, *The South West Africa/Namibia Dispute*, p. 164.

by forming an *ad hoc* committee, and later a permanent committee.[183] South Africa continued to refuse to cooperate and its actions, particularly the failure to provide reports regarding their administration of Namibia, resulted in two further Advisory Opinions being sought from the ICJ:[184] (1) *the Voting Procedures on Questions Relating to Reports and Petitions Concerning the Territory of South West Africa Advisory Opinions;*[185] and (2) the *Admissibility of Hearings of Petitioners by the Committee on South West Africa Opinion.*[186]

In the *Namibia Voting Procedures Opinion* the ICJ was asked whether the General Assembly required a two-thirds majority when considering resolutions regarding Namibia.[187] Under the Mandate System of the League, a unanimous vote was required and therefore this included the Mandatory.[188] This was consistent with the finding in the first Advisory Opinion that the extent of the UN's supervision, and South Africa's obligations, were no greater than when under the League. The ICJ held that the UN General Assembly only required a two-thirds majority.[189] The UN General Assembly sought approval of the use of oral hearings, which had been disallowed under the Mandate System, in the *Admissibility of Hearings Opinion.* Again the ICJ found in favour of the General Assembly.[190]

The stalemate worsened, with numerous resolutions passed by the General Assembly,[191] and the publication by South Africa of the Odendaal

183. Both were established by the General Assembly, by *Question of South West Africa*, GA Res 449(B), UN GAOR, 5th sess, 322 plen mtg, (13 December 1950). Dugard, *The South West Africa/Namibia Dispute*, pp. 162–63.
184. Dugard, *The South West Africa/Namibia Dispute*, pp. 166–73. The *Ad Hoc* Committee was replaced with a permanent one in 1953, by *Question of South Africa*, GA Res 749(A), UN GAOR, 8th sess, 460th plen mtg, UN Doc A/Res 749(A) (28 November 1953).
185. *Namibia Voting Procedures Opinion* [1955] ICJ Rep 67.
186. *Admissibility of Hearings Opinion* [1956] ICJ Rep 23.
187. The UN itself without any assistance by South Africa prepared these reports. Dugard, *The South West Africa/Namibia Dispute*, pp. 176–77.
188. Given South Africa's lack of cooperation, this was a natural concern.
189. Dugard, *The South West Africa/Namibia Dispute* pp. 176–84.
190. Oral hearings were necessary because South Africa refused to release petitions from the local population: Dugard, *The South West Africa/Namibia Dispute*, p. 192.
191. The GA passed numerous resolutions often in response to actions or inaction by South Africa. For example, creating the 'Good Offices Committee', *Establishment of a Good Offices Committee on South West Africa*, GA Res 1143 (XII), UN GAOR, 12th sess, Supp No 18, 709th plen mtg, UN Doc A/Res/1143 (XII) (25 October 1957); and requesting the Permanent Committee to consider what legal action could be taken against South Africa, *Study of Legal Action to Ensure the Fulfilment of the Obligations Assumed by the Mandatory Power under the Mandate for South West Africa*, GA Res 1060 (XI), UN GAOR, 11th sess, Supp No 17, 661st plen mtg, UN Doc A/Res/1060 (XI) (26 February 1957). This was followed by another resolution, *Legal Action to Ensure the Fulfilment of the Obligations Assumed by the Union of South Africa in Respect of the Territory of South West Africa*, GA Res 1142 (XII) (A), UN GAOR, 12th sess, Supp No 18, 709th plen mtg, [A], (25 October 1957), that drew the attention of member States to the repeated breaches of by South Africa and that under art 7 of the Mandate and art 37 of the *ICJ Statute*, *any* member of the former League of Nations that

Report,[192] the creation of such political organisations as SWAPO and SWANU,[193] and finally, the declared intention by two African States to bring an action against South Africa, claiming that it had failed in its obligations under the Mandate.[194]

c. South Africa's failure to comply with its mandate

The action brought by these two parties was conducted in two stages: (1) an examination by the ICJ of the parties' standing in the *Namibia Preliminary Objections*;[195] and then (2) the merits of the claims were considered in 1966, in the *South West Africa Cases, 2nd Phase.*[196] In *Namibia Preliminary Objections*, the ICJ held that the ICJ had jurisdiction and therefore that both Ethiopia and Liberia had *locus standi.*[197] Then in what has been described as a reversal of the earlier *Namibia Preliminary Objections*, the ICJ in the *South West Africa Cases, 2nd Phase*, rather than concentrating on the merits of the claim, *returned* to the issues in the *Namibia Preliminary Objections*, and found that both Ethiopia and Liberia had failed to establish any legal interest or right in the matter.[198]

The majority of the ICJ held the following. Firstly, that Applicants by acting as custodians of the Mandate System did not possess a self-contained right as individual members of the League to enforce the Mandate, this right was available only to the 'League organs'.[199] Secondly, that the principle of

was then a member of the UN had standing to refer matters to the ICJ. In other words, encouraging states to bring South Africa before the ICJ. Dugard, *The South West Africa/Namibia Dispute* pp. 185–238.

192. The Odendaal Report was named after the chairman of the South African Commission of Inquiry into South West Africa, and was a statement of the government's policy that created separate homelands for each of the peoples of Namibia, who would retain possession of only 40% of Namibia. Another 48 % of Namibia, the so-called 'White Area' would become part of South Africa. Dugard, *The South West Africa/Namibia Dispute* pp. 185–238.
193. South West African Peoples' Organisation and South West Africa National Union respectively.
194. Earlier Opinions of the ICJ were not binding upon South Africa. This prompted Ethiopia and Liberia, as former members of the League, to declare at the Second Conference of Independent African States held in Addis Abba in 1960, their intentions to institute action against South Africa. The UN General Assembly then passed another resolution approving of this intention: *Legal Actions to Ensure the Fulfilment of the Obligations Assumed by the Union of South Africa in Respect of the Territory of South West Africa*, GA Res 1565 (XV), 15th sess, Supp No 16, 954th plen mtg, UN Doc A/1565 (XV)(18 December 1960). Dugard, *The South West Africa/Namibia Dispute*, pp. 185–238.
195. *Legal Consequences for States of the Continued Presence of South Africa in Namibia (South-West Africa)* [1962] ICJ Rep 319 ('*Namibia Preliminary Objections*').
196. *South West Africa Cases (2nd Phase)* [1966] ICJ Rep 6 ('*South West Africa Cases (2nd Phase)*').
197. By the narrowest of margins, 8 votes to 7.
198. *South West Africa Cases (2nd Phase)* [1966] ICJ Rep 6, 17–51, see especially [33], [99]. Dugard, *The South West Africa/Namibia Dispute* p. 292.
199. Ibid, pp. 17–51, 33. The Majority then went on to justify their decision at [34]–[40].

the 'sacred trust of civilisation…' which formed the basis of the obligations of the Mandatory under art 22 of the *League's Covenant* was only moral in character and not juridical in nature.[200] As such, it remained a humanitarian ideal and each member of the League's right to enforce this principle, could only be through the organs of the League, since only legal rights and interests could be enforced in the ICJ.[201] Thirdly, the rights of the organs of the League to enforce such principles did not, as a rule of international law, pass automatically to former members with the dissolution of the League.[202] Finally, that the Mandate system did allow for juridical protection for the 'special interests' of States, but not peoples.[203]

The Court's findings received severe criticism by academics, political leaders and diplomats alike.[204] Local black African political leaders in Namibia had expected the ICJ to condemn South Africa's administration, thus paving the way for independence. The Court's decision now created a perception that their independence must come through revolution, and in the wake of the Court's Opinion violence broke out in Namibia.[205] Geoffrey Robertson summarised the decision as follows:

> In 1966, the ICJ …. By ruling the very subject non-justiciable, they withheld from the world the one tried and tested means of resolving grievances short of conflict and strife, namely the submission of the question to impartial arbitration.[206]

The General Assembly matched commentators' outrage, since the UN had expected to obtain a decision to allow them to pursue enforcement action against South Africa.[207] Denied this, the General Assembly renounced South

200. Ibid, [51]–[55], in particular at [54].
201. Ibid.
202. Ibid, [55].
203. Ibid. His Excellency Honour Judge Jessup in his Separate Opinion rejected the majority's view whole-heartedly at 352.
204. Dugard, *The South West Africa/Namibia Dispute* p. 292.
205. Jariretundu Kozonguizi, then president of SWANU, and many of the black leaders publicly proclaimed their intention to move in the direction of armed struggle, ultimately leading to the 'terrorism trial' of Tuhaddeleni by South Africa: as cited in Dugard, *The South West Africa/Namibia Dispute* p. 377, 413.
206. Robertson, *Crimes Against Humanity*, pp. 143–4. Whilst the Court did not treat this matter as 'non-justiciable', but rather held that the applicants had not proven their legal interests in the claims made, the author agrees with the sentiments expressed by Robertson. *South West Africa Cases (2nd Phase)* [1966] ICJ Rep 6, 51 [99].
207. In accordance with art 94 of the *UN Charter*. Dugard writes that the UN General Assembly regarded the ICJ as the 'enemy' and immediately refused to pass an application for additional funding and also at the next triennial election of judges, *ensured that no white Commonwealth judges were elected to the bench:* Dugard, *The South West Africa/Namibia Dispute*, pp. 376–378.

Africa's Mandate.[208] The resolution went on to state that the General Assembly was mindful of the obligations of the UN to the people of Namibia; and that they had an inalienable right to self-determination.[209] The UN then formed another *ad hoc* Committee, to enable them to exercise that right.[210] South Africa responded by implementing its Odendaal Report, which created legislative and executive bodies for respective tribal groupings of the local populations in Namibia. The effect of these initiatives was to integrate the area with South Africa in an administrative sense, but also to grant 'homelands' to certain ethnic groups.[211] This action led to the involvement of the Security Council.[212]

d. The Namibia Opinion[213]

The *Namibia Opinion* came about as a result of the Security Council 'despairing' of the large number of their resolutions that South Africa refused to implement requesting the ICJ for an Opinion.[214] The Request concerned an investigation of the legality of the continued presence of South Africa in Namibia.

The ICJ advised the Security Council that: (1) the continued presence of South Africa was illegal; (2) that South Africa's policy of apartheid, was a breach of the *UN Charter*, and in particular a denial of internal self-determination;[215] (3) South Africa must withdraw immediately; (4), members

208. *Question of South West Africa*, GA Res 2145 (XXV), UN GAOR, 21st sess, Supp No 16, 1454th plen mtg UN Doc A/Res/ 2145 (XXV) (27 October 1966). The language was harsh, with a statement that the situation in Namibia had *deteriorated*, caused by the 1966 decision of the ICJ. Dugard, *The South West Africa/Namibia Dispute* p. 379. Dugard neatly summarises the legal issues with the resolution: at pp. 381–408.
209. *Question of South West Africa*, GA Res 2145 (XXV), UN GAOR, 21st sess, Supp No 16, 1454th plen mtg [1], [3], [6] UN Doc A/Res/ 2145 (XXV), (27 October 1966).
210. Dugard, *The South West Africa/Namibia Dispute* p. 380. The committee comprised fourteen representatives from; Canada, Chile, Czechoslovakia, Ethiopia, Finland, Italy, Japan, Mexico, Nigeria, Pakistan, Senegal, the former USSR, and the UAR.
211. Dugard, *The South West Africa/Namibia Dispute*, p. 434.
212. The Security Council's resolutions basically asked for the withdrawal from Namibia by South Africa. See Security Council Resolutions: *The Situation in Namibia*, SC Res 264, UN SCOR, 1465th mtg, UN Doc S/Res/264 (20 March 1969); *The Situation in Namibia*, SC Res 269, UN SCOR, 1497th mtg, UN Doc S/Res/ 269 (12 August 1969); *The Situation in Namibia*, SC Res 276, UN SCOR, 1529th mtg, UN Doc S/Res/276 (30 January 1970).
213. *Legal Consequences for States of the Continued Presence of South Africa in Namibia (South West Africa) Notwithstanding Security Council Resolution 276 (1970) (Advisory Opinion)* [1971] ICJ Rep 16; ('*Namibia Opinion*').
214. Under *ICJ Statute*, art 96(1). *The Situation in Namibia*, SC Res 284, UN SCOR, 1550th mtg, 4, UN Doc S/INF/25 (29 July 1970).
215. Antonio Cassese, 'The International Court of Justice and the Right of Peoples to Self-Determination', in Vaughan Lowe and Malgosia Fitzmaurice (eds), *Fifty Years of the*

of the UN were obliged to recognise this, and members were to refrain from any action that would imply recognition or validate South Africa's presence; and (5) finally non-members should assist the UN and its members in their actions against South Africa.[216] The Security Council accepted the Opinion on 20 October 1971.[217] This was followed by two more resolutions as a result of a special meeting held in Addis Ababa.[218] The local population of Namibia welcomed the ICJ's findings.[219] Not surprisingly South Africa did not, and it was not until 1978 that negotiations for such an event began.[220]

Commentators have approved of the *Namibia Opinion*, and believe it is important for the following reasons.[221] Firstly, it appeared to offset the damage done by its previous decision in *South West Africa Cases, 2nd Phase.*[222] Secondly, the Court confirmed that self-determination also applied to present and more importantly *future* behaviour, and that whilst initially the UN may have only intended to apply self-determination to those territories within the international trustee system, the practice of the international community had developed so that the concept now applied to 'all dependent territories'.[223] This reasoning was applied in the *Western Sahara Opinion*, where the Court emphasised that the free will of the people played a prominent role when exercising their right to self-determination.

International Court of Justice: Essays in Honour of Sir Robert Jennings, Cambridge: Cambridge University Press, 1996, pp. 357–58.

216. *Namibia Opinion* [[1971] ICJ Rep 16, 58 [133].
217. *The Situation in Namibia*, SC Res 301, UN SCOR, 1598th mtg, UN Doc S/Res/ 301(20 October 1971). Dugard, *The South West Africa/Namibia Dispute*, pp. 502–504.
218. *The Situation in Namibia*, SC Res 309, & SC Res 310, UN SCOR, 1638th mtg, UN Doc S/Res/309& UN Doc S/Res/ 310 (4 February 1972); which basically reaffirmed the position of the Security Council and condemned the continued presence of South Africa in Namibia. Resolution 309 mentioned the 'inalienable and imprescriptible right of the people of Namibia to self-determination and independence.' Dugard, *The South West Africa/Namibia Dispute.*
219. Dugard notes the respective groups' responses. He also noted that the South African Government was confident that if a plebiscite were held, that the respective groups would vote for continued South African administration. The response of the local groups showed that they had misjudged the situation badly. Dugard, *The South West Africa/Namibia Dispute*, pp. 517–18.
220. See the statement made by the Minister of Foreign Affairs of South Africa Hilgard Muller, who condemned the ICJ's opinion as evasive and that: 'The purpose of the Court's censure [of South Africa's policy] was clearly political rather than legal, and emphasized the basically political nature of the Opinion': as cited in Dugard, *The South West Africa/ Namibia Dispute*, pp. 502–503.
221. Cassese, *The International Court of Justice and the Right of Peoples*, p. 354.
222. *South West Africa Cases (2nd Phase)* [1966] ICJ Rep 6.
223. This last phrase is Cassese's own words, but the emphasis is mine: Cassese, *The International Court of Justice and the Right of Peoples*, pp. 354–55. This conclusion was evident in the interpretation of art 80 (1) of the *UN Charter* which the ICJ emphasised showed self-determination was a right available to 'peoples'.

2. The Western Sahara Opinion

a. Background

Western Sahara is located between Morocco and Mauritania. It is mostly desert, sparsely populated by nomadic tribes, and was colonised when Spain declared a protectorate over the region's southern portion in 1884. Spain treated the Western Sahara as an overseas portion of Spain itself until, under pressure from the decolonisation policy of the UN, Spain began to provide the General Assembly with relevant information as if it were a colony.[224]

In the interim, both Morocco and Mauritania had exercised their right to self-determination and became independent.[225] Both immediately claimed the entire Western Sahara as belonging to their respective pre-colonial territories and both argued that Western Sahara's act of self-determination should mean integration of the territory within their borders. Spain's declaration of its intention to allow the people of Western Sahara to exercise their right to self-determination by referendum was opposed by Morocco, who argued that the matter should be presented to the Court in order to determine whether the territory was *res nullius* before being colonised by Spain, or whether the Western Sahara had been allied with the Sultan of Morocco. Spain refused to consent to the Court's jurisdiction, however, the UN General Assembly decided to request an Advisory Opinion from the Court on the following questions:[226]

> (i) Was Western Sahara (Rio de Oro and Sakiet El Hamra) at the time of colonization by Spain a territory belonging to no one (terra nullius)?[227]
> (ii) What were the legal ties between this territory and the Kingdom of Morocco and the Mauritanian entity?[228]

Spain lodged a number of objections to the Court arguing that the Court should exercise its discretion and refuse the Request:[229] (1) that the questions

224. This occurred as a result of the Declaration of Colonial Peoples being passed by the UN General Assembly. Pressure to decolonise increased after 1966: Gill, *Rosenne's The World Court*, p. 173.
225. Both were former French colonies, or protectorates: Morocco achieved independence in 1956 and Mauritania in 1960.
226. Gill, *Rosenne's The World Court*, p. 173. *Question of Spanish Sahara*, GA Res 3292 (XXIX), UN GAOR, 29th sess, 2318th plen mtg, UN Doc A/Res/ 3292, (13 December 1974).
227. *Western Sahara Opinion* [1975] ICJ Rep 12, 14.
228. The Court concluded by 14 votes to 2 that there were legal ties between this territory and the Kingdom of Morocco, and by 15 votes to 1 that there were links with the Mauritanian entity: Ibid.
229. As summarised by Gill, *Rosenne's The World Court*, p. 174.

were historical or purely academic, rather than legal questions: (2) the request concerned a dispute between Spain and Morocco, and Spain had not consented to any contentious proceedings; (3) the Court lacked competence to provide an Advisory Opinion in a contentious matter.

b. The Court's opinion

The ICJ rejected all of Spain's objections, confirming that a contentious matter did not deprive the Court of its ability to provide an Opinion.[230] Secondly, that Spain's lack of consent was no obstacle for the ICJ rendering their Opinion.[231] The Court concluded unanimously that at the time of colonization by Spain the territory was not a territory belonging to either Morocco or Mauritania. It then went on to mention the 'freely expressed will' of the relevant people as the means by which they exercised their self-determination.[232]

> Thus the Court has not found legal ties of such a nature as might affect the application of resolution 1514 (XV) in the decolonization of Western Sahara and, in particular, of the principle of self-determination through the free and genuine expression of the will of the peoples of the Territory.[233]

Furthermore, the Court noted that the nomadic tribes of Western Sahara, rich in their political diversity, still constituted a people and a nation. Therefore there could conceivably exist a Western Saharan State, complete

230. *Western Sahara Opinion* [1975] ICJ Rep 12, [18]. The Court referred to the *Application for Review of Judgement No. 158 of the United Nations Administrative Tribunal (Advisory Opinion)* [1973] ICJ Rep 166, where it held: 'The mere fact that it is not the rights of States which are in issue in the proceedings cannot suffice to deprive the Court of a competence expressly conferred on it by its Statute': Ibid.
231. The Court concluded that Spain was a member of the United Nations and had accepted the provisions of the *UN Charter* and the *ICJ Statute*, and accordingly had consented to the exercise of the ICJ's advisory jurisdiction: ibid 24, see esp [29], [30]. Excellency Judge Singh's judgment: Ibid, p. 78.
232. Ibid, pp. 12, 32–33.
233. Ibid, p. 60. The freely expressed will of the peoples was a consistent theme throughout the Opinion, and described as the '… very *sine qua non* of all decolonization.' For example, His Excellency Judge Nagendra Singh: 'The Court has recognized the validity of the principle of self-determination, "defined as the need to pay regard to the freely expressed will of the peoples."' Furthermore, that even if there was evidence that could justify the reintegration of the territory into one State, it could not be done without first determining the freely expressed will of the people. He went on to say the only time that this requirement could be dispensed with is when the 'will' of the peoples is a foregone conclusion. Ibid, pp. 72–73.

with international personality.[234] His Excellency Judge Nagendra Singh in his declaration summarised the ICJ's decision as follows:

> The main reason for this conclusion is simply that, at the time of Spanish colonization, there was no evidence of the existence of one single State comprising the territory of Western Sahara and Morocco, or Western Sahara and Mauritania, which would have been dismembered by the colonizer and thus justify reunion on decolonization at the present time. Accordingly, the facts and circumstances of this case would not attract the provisions of paragraph 6 of resolution 1514 (XV) which holds disruption of national unity or territorial integrity of a country as incompatible with the Charter of the United Nations and thus points to reintegration of territory.[235]

The Court's decision involved a determination of whether Morocco or Mauritania had exercised sovereignty over Western Sahara. This examination would involve the following principles of international law: whether the territory was *terra nullius* at the time of colonisation, recognition, and self-determination. Diplomatic documents, letters from other ruling sovereigns, and treaties signed by colonising powers, were used to determine the parties' claims.[236] One particularly telling piece of evidence was art 38 of the *Hispano-Moroccan Treaty of Commerce and Navigation of 1861*, which was crucial in the ICJ's rejection of Morocco's claim to sovereignty.[237]

The Court also considered the claims made that Spain and Great Britain had extended recognition of Moroccan sovereignty of Western Sahara.[238] The ICJ rejected this argument since documents proved that Great Britain had not granted recognition of Moroccan sovereignty, but merely acknowledged a Moroccan interest.[239] The ICJ also rejected Morocco's claims of

234. Ibid, p. 52.
235. Ibid, p. 72.
236. The ICJ summarised the relevant documents at Ibid, p. 42. The Court also had to contend with different versions of the same documents presented by the parties. For example, there was a dispute over the wording of the *Treaty of Marrakesh* of 1767 with different versions presented as 'authentic' texts by both Spain and Morocco. The ICJ felt that the Spanish version was the most reliable since it was supported by letters written by the Sultan of Morocco to King Carlos III of Spain regarding the same topic, and later by the *Hispano-Moroccan Treaty* of 1799: Ibid, at p. 42.
237. Article 38 of the treaty showed a limited form of authority, 'mere influence', as opposed to a sovereign command. Other evidence supported this finding. *Western Sahara Opinion* [1975] ICJ Rep 12, pp. 44–45.
238. The claim that Great Britain had granted such recognition was because of the *Anglo-American Agreement* of 13th March 1895, which concerned the purchase by the Sultan of Morocco of a trading station from the North-West African Company. *Western Sahara Opinion* [1975] ICJ Rep 12, p. 45.
239. *Western Sahara Opinion* [1975] ICJ Rep 12, [46].

recognition by Great Britain because there was no first-hand evidence of an agreement to transfer territory, either in Spanish or Moroccan archives.[240] This ability to determine the veracity of competing claims, and to sift through inconsistent information supplied by interested parties, supports the argument made in Chapter 2 above that the Court is able to resolve issues that involve questions of fact and law. The level of historical detail that the Court is able to access, and then analyse is further proof of the Court's ability to consolidate a factual background in order to apply the relevant legal norms. Thus, for example the Court would be, and is, able to determine whether there has been a history of foreign and alien subjugation, or alternatively to apply the pre-conditions listed in Chapter 1 of this monograph.

The *Western Sahara Opinion* is also important due to its emphasis on the freely expressed will of the peoples, as the '... very *sine qua non* of all decolonisation ...'.[241] Some commentators have suggested that the *Western Sahara Opinion*'s statement of the right of the Western Saharan people to self-determination was made in the context of decolonisation, and this indicates that the ICJ believes that the right of self-determination applies to decolonisation only.[242] This is incorrect. After referring to art's 1 (2), 55 & 56 of the *UN Charter*, the Court stated:

> The principle of self-determination as a right of peoples, and its application for the purpose of bringing all colonial situations to a speedy end, were enunciated in the Declaration on the Granting of independence to Colonial Countries and peoples, General Assembly resolution 1514 (XV). In this resolution the general assembly proclaims 'the necessity of bringing to a speedy end and unconditional end colonialism in all its forms and manifestations'.[243]

This conclusion is consistent with the *Namibia* Opinion, and was confirmed in the *Wall in Palestine Opinion.*[244]

240. Ibid, pp. 46–47.
241. 'Again resolution 2625 (XXV) concerning friendly relations goes a long way to further emphasize the point that on decolonization the 'emergence into any political status' has to be 'freely determined by a people'. Thus even if integration of territory was demanded by an interested State, as in this case, it could not be had without ascertaining the freely expressed will of the people-the very *sine qua non* of all decolonisation': Ibid, p. 73.
242. Ibid [36]. Gerry Simpson refers to the statement made by Judge Petren stating that the law of decolonisation is derived from self-determination. Gerry Simpson, 'The Diffusion of Sovereignty: Self-Determination in the Post-Colonial Age' (1996) 32(2) *Stanford Journal of International Law*, p. 272.
243. *Western Sahara Opinion* [1975] ICJ Rep 12, [31].
244. The amount of material available on the Israeli-Palestinian conflict is extensive and diverse. The account here is obviously brief and is only intended to place the advisory opinion into context.

3. The Wall in Palestine Opinion

a. Background

In 1967 as part of the on-going conflict between Israel and the Arab States, Israel occupied the former Mandated territory of Palestine including the West Bank, and declared Jerusalem as the capital of Israel. This prompted numerous UN Security Council resolutions that stated in very clear terms that this occupation by Israel was illegal, and Israel an occupying power.[245] Due to continued attacks by militant Palestinian groups, in particular the repeated use of suicide attacks, the Israeli cabinet on 23 June 2003 authorised the construction of what it described as a security fence, a continuous barrier along the West Bank.[246]

In a letter addressed to the Security Council the Chairman of the Arab Group requested the Security Council to convene an urgent meeting to consider a draft resolution stating the construction of the security fence was illegal.[247] The Security Council met, but did not adopt either of the proposed resolutions.[248] So the Chairman of the Arab Group then requested the Tenth Emergency Special Session of the UN General Assembly on 5 October 2003 to resume its examination of Israel's allegedly illegal actions in the Occupied Palestinian Territory.[249] The General Assembly then on 27 October 2003

245. *The Situation in The Middle East*, SC Res 242, UN SCOR, 1382nd mtg, UN Doc S/Res/ 242 (22 November 1967); SC Res 298, *The Situation in The Middle East*, UN SCOR, 1582nd mtg, UN Doc S/Res/ 298 (25 September 1971); *Wall in Palestine Opinion* [2004] ICJ Rep 136, [72]–[75]. Israel's status was determined in accordance with Art 42 of the *Regulations Respecting the Laws and Customs of War on Land Annexed to the Fourth Hague Convention of 18 October 1907.*
246. *Wall in Palestine Opinion* [2004] ICJ Rep 136, [71]–[81].
247. This was made on behalf of the member States of the League of Arab States.
248. A second draft resolution was submitted by Guinea, Malaysia, Pakistan and the Syrian Arab Republic.
249. The Tenth Emergency Special Session of the UN General Assembly was convened at the request of the Chairman of the Arab Group in a letter addressed to the UN Secretary-General dated 31 March 1997. The first meeting of the Tenth Emergency Special Session of the UN General Assembly took place on the 25th of April 1997, and adopted resolution ES-10/2, which stated, inter alia, that 'the repeated violation by Israel, the occupying Power, of international law and its failure to comply with relevant Security Council and General Assembly resolutions and the arguments reached between the parties undermine the Middle East peace process and constitute a threat to international peace and security': *Illegal Israeli Actions in Occupied East Jerusalem and the Rest of the Occupied Palestinian Territory*, UN GAOR, 10th Emergency Special Session, 3rd plen mtg, UN Doc A/Res/ES-10/2 (25th April 1997). The Chairman made the request in response to the UN Security Council rejecting draft resolutions; (1) *Draft Resolution on the Israeli Decision to Initiate New Settlement Activities in East Jerusalem*, UN SCOR, 52nd sess, UN Doc S/1997/199, (7th March 1997) please refer to the record of the meeting held to discuss the situation and the Draft Res S/1997/199: *The Situation in the Occupied Arab Territories*, 52nd sess, 3747th mtg, UN Doc S/PV.3747 (7th March 1997); (2) *Draft Resolution on the Construction by Israel of the Jabal abu Ghneim Housing Settlement in East Jerusalem*, UN SCOR,

adopted a resolution demanding that Israel stop the construction of the security wall in the occupied Palestinian Territory.[250] Following the temporary adjournment of the Tenth Emergency Special Session of the General Assembly the Security Council endorsed the 'Quartet Performance-based Roadmap to a Permanent Two-State Solution to the Israeli-Palestinian Conflict'.[251] Then again at the request of the Chairman of the Arab Group the Tenth Emergency Special Session reconvened, and requested an Advisory Opinion.[252]

b. The question asked of the Court

The question asked of the Court was as follows:

> What are the legal consequences arising from the construction of the wall being built by Israel, the occupying power, in the Occupied Palestinian territory, including in and around East Jerusalem, as described in the Report of the Secretary-General, considering the rules and principles of international law, including the Fourth Geneva Convention of 1949, and relevant Security Council and General Assembly resolutions?[253]

Israel argued that the Court should exercise its discretion and refuse the Request because the Court lacked jurisdiction on numerous grounds: (1) firstly, that the General Assembly had acted *ultra vires* when making the Request: (2) that the question within the Request was not a legal question; (3) that the question lacked clarity; (4) that the question was too abstract in its nature; (5) due to the political nature of the matter at the heart of the Request; (6) it was a contentious matter between Israel and Palestine: and (7) finally, that if the Advisory Opinion were provided it would interfere in the Roadmap and the solution to the on-going Israeli-Palestinian conflict.[254]

52nd sess, UN Doc S/1997/241, (21st March 1997) discussed at UN SC meetng to discuss *The Situation in the Occupied Arab Territories*, 52nd sess, 3756th mtg, UN Doc S/PV.3756, (21st March 1997). Both resolutions were rejected by one vote, the US, which, as a permanent member, has a veto power.

250. *Illegal Israeli Actions in Occupied East Jerusalem and the Rest of the Occupied Palestinian Territory*, UN GAOR, 10th Emergency Special Session, 22nd plen mtg, UN Doc A/Res/ES-10/13 (27th October 2003).
251. *The Situation in the Middle East, Including the Palestinian Question*, UN SC Res 1515, UN SCOR, 4862nd mtg, UN Doc S/Res/1515 (19th November 2003) ('*Roadmap*').
252. *Illegal Israeli Actions in Occupied East Jerusalem and the Rest of the Occupied Palestinian Territory*, UN GAOR, 10th Emergency Special Session, 23rd plen mtg, UN Doc A/Res/ ES-10/14 (8th December 2003).
253. *Wall in Palestine Opinion* [2004] ICJ Rep 136, [1].
254. Ibid, [24]–[51].

c. The Opinion of the Court

The Court dealt with Israel's arguments as part of its obligation to determine that it is seised of jurisdiction.[255] The Court concluded that there were no compelling reasons to reject the Request,[256] and advised the General Assembly that:

> ... the construction of the wall by Israel in the Occupied Palestinian Territory is contrary to international law and has stated the legal consequences that are to be drawn from that illegality.[257]

Furthermore, the Court advised that: (1) Israel should terminate construction, and dismantle existing portions of the wall; (2) Israel was under an obligation to make reparation for all damage caused by the construction of wall; (3) all States were under an obligation to not recognise the illegal 'situation', and to not render assistance in maintaining the situation; (4) States were obliged to take action to ensure Israeli compliance with international humanitarian law; (5) and, finally that both the UN General Assembly and Security Council should consider what actions should be taken to '... end the illegal situation resulting from the construction of the wall.'[258]

The Court considered whether construction of the Wall breached art's 6, 7, 10, 11, 12, 13, and 14 of the *International Covenant on Economic, Social and Cultural Rights*;[259] art's 16, 24, 27, and 28 of the *United Nations Convention on the Rights of the Child*;[260] arts 46 and 52 of the *Hague Regulations of 1907*; art 53 of the *Fourth Geneva Convention*;[261] *Common Article 1 of the ICCPR*; and the *Declaration Concerning Friendly Relations*.[262]

255. The Court reviews this issue for every Request. Although Israel made written submissions arguing that the ICJ should reject the request, Israel did not participate in the oral proceedings. For a discussion of Israel's arguments regarding jurisdicition see the series of articles in vol 99 (2005) *American Journal of International Law* including Geoffrey R Watson, 'The "Wall" Decisions in Legal and Political Context' (2005) 99 *American Journal of International Law*, pp. 8–11.
256. *Wall in Palestine Opinion* [2004] ICJ Rep 136, [53]. The Court was unanimous in its decision that it had jurisdiction, at [163], although His Excellency Judge Buergenthal opposed the Court's decision to comply with the Request; see His Excellency 's Declaration in *Wall in Palestine Opinion* [2004] ICJ Rep 136, [240].
257. Ibid, [162].
258. With the exception of the obligation of States to not render assistance to Israel maintaining the illegal situation, all of these conclusions were decided by 14 votes to 1. His Excellency Judge Buergenthal voting against each point, except for the rendering of assistance where the vote was 13 to 2, where His Excellency Judge Kooijmans joined His Excellency Judge Buergenthal, and dissented. *Wall in Palestine Opinion* [2004] ICJ Rep 136, [163].
259. Ibid, [130].
260. *Convention on the Rights of the Child*, opened for signature 20 November 1989, 1577 UNTS 3 (entered into force 2 September 1990). *Wall in Palestine Opinion* [2004] ICJ Rep 136, [131].
261. *Wall in Palestine Opinion* [2004] ICJ Rep 136, [132].
262. *Declaration on Principles of International Law Concerning Friendly Relations and Co-operation Among States in Accordance with the UN Charter*, GA Res 2625, UN GAOR, 25th sess, 1883 plen mtg, item 85, UN Doc A/RES/2625(XXV) (1970).

The Court also concluded that the construction of the wall clearly breached customary international humanitarian law. The wall would enclose numerous Palestinians separating them into enclaves.[263] It would also separate Palestinians from their agricultural lands, their wells, and their means to survive.[264] The Court also carefully considered Israel's right to self-defence under art 51 of the *UN Charter*, as well as art 53 of the *Fourth Geneva Convention*.[265] The Court concluded that art 51 of the *UN Charter* had '... no relevance in this case. ...';[266] that Israel had acted contrary to the provisions of the *Fourth Geneva Convention*;[267] that the route chosen by Israel was not necessary to '... attain its [Israel's] security objectives.';[268] and:

> In conclusion, the Court considers that Israel cannot rely on a right of self-defence or on a state of necessity in order to preclude the wrongfulness of the construction of the wall. ... The Court accordingly finds that the construction of the wall, and its associated regime, are contrary to international law.[269]

The Court also felt it important to remind the General Assembly that its Opinion should be placed in the context of the on-going conflict between Israel and Palestine, that both sides had current obligations in international law to resolve their conflict peacefully, and in accordance with international humanitarian law. These obligations included *respect for the right of the Palestinian people to self-determination*.[270]

> The Court considers that it has a duty to draw [the] attention of the General Assembly, to which the present opinion is addressed, to the need for these efforts to be encouraged with a view to achieving as soon as possible, on the basis of international law, a negotiated solution to the

263. For example, Phase A would entrap 56,000 Palestinians in numerous enclaves, and if the full wall were completed some 160,000 Palestinians would be cut off in communities completely encircled by the wall: *Wall in Palestine Opinion* [2004] ICJ Rep 136, [81]–[84].
264. In addition 30 Palestinian communities would be separated from health services, 22 from schools, 8 from primary water sources and 3 from electricity sources. Also the Special Rapporteur on the Right to Food of the United Nations Commission on Human Rights noted that the 'security' wall would enable Israel to annex 51 per cent of the West Bank's water resources: ibid [83]–[84], [133].
265. Considering Israel's stated purpose for construction: ibid [88], [116], [118], [135]. *Convention (IV) Relative to the Protection of Civilian Persons in Time of War*, opened for signature 12 August 1949, 75 UNTS 287, art 53 (entered into force 21 October 1950).
266. *Wall in Palestine Opinion* [2004] ICJ Rep 136, [139].
267. Ibid, [135].
268. Ibid, [136], [140].
269. Ibid, [142].
270. Ibid, [115] and [162] (emphasis added.) This issue was decided 14 votes to one, with His Excellency Judge Buergenthal dissenting.

outstanding problems and the establishment of a Palestinian State, existing side by side with Israel and its other neighbours, with peace and security for all in the region.[271]

4. *Kosovo Opinion*[272]

a. Background

The terrible events surrounding Kosovo's passage from being part of the former Yugoslavia to claiming independent statehood, has been discussed exhaustively elsewhere, and by and large do not need repeating here.[273] However, to understand the significance of the *Kosovo Opinion*, its merits and criticisms, some events need highlighting.

Faced with a serious humanitarian tragedy in Kosovo the UN Security Council acting in accordance with Chapter VII of the *UN Charter* adopted Resolution 1244 in June of 1999.[274] The purpose of Resolution 1244 was to firstly put an end to the conflict, and secondly, to authorise the UN Secretary-General to establish 'an international civilian presence' in Kosovo, whose purpose was to create an interim administration/government pending a final political solution.[275] Consequently in June 1999 the United Nations Interim Administration Kosovo (UNMIK) was created and headed by a Special Representative of the Secretary-General but was to work closely with the Security Council. The Special Representative then enacted UNMIK resolution 2001/9 of 15 May 2001, which established a constitutional framework, which in turn outlined the responsibilities of the Provisional Institutions of Self-Government (PISG).[276] The PISG were to act as interim administration, but were in no way to diminish or act contrary to the authority of the Special Representative of the UN Secretary-General. The PSIG were to act in accordance with the terms of Resolution 1244, and furthermore, the Special Representative was empowered to 'correct' any actions taken by the PISG if they were inconsistent with the terms of Resolution 1244.[277]

In November 2005 acting with the approval of the Security Council the UN Secretary-General in response to a report prepared by Special Envoy

271. Ibid [162]. This was decided 14 votes to 1 with His Excellency Judge Buergenthal dissenting.
272. *Accordance with International Law of the Unilateral Declaration of Independence in Respect of Kosovo, (Advisory Opinion)*, [2010] ICJ Rep 403 ('*Kosovo Opinion*').
273. See for example Marc Weller, *Contested Statehood, Kosovo's Struggle for Independence*, Oxford University Press: Oxford 2009.
274. *Kosovo Opinion* [2010] ICJ Rep 403, 426 [58]: 'The Situation in Kosovo' UN Doc S/Res/1244 (10 June 1999) adopted at its 4011th mtg, p 2 [3]–[5] &[10]; Annex 2 to the resolution at 5.
275. *Kosovo Opinion* [2010] ICJ Rep 403, 426 [58].
276. Ibid, 426–430 [59]–[63]. See http://www.unmikonline.org/regulations/2001/reg09-01.html (accessed 5 November 2013).
277. Ibid, 426–430 [59]–[63].

Kai Eide appointed Martti Ahtisaari, former President of Finland, as his Special Envoy for determining the future status process for Kosovo. Some time after a series of unsuccessful negotiations between representatives of Serbia and Kosovo Special Envoy Ahtisaari prepared the Comprehensive Proposal for the Kosovo Status Settlement. This settlement concluded that the only viable alternative for Kosovo was independent statehood.[278] Although the UN Secretary-General, the European Union and the US fully supported these proposals Russia did not, and using its veto power in the Security Council prevented the adoption of the Ahtisaari Report, and instead proposed that the Security Council appoint their own 'mission' to report on the future of Kosovo.[279] However, the Security Council were unable to reach a decision on Kosovo's future. Subsequently, representatives of the European Union, the Russian Federation and the US (the 'Troika') conducted negotiations between 9 August and 3 December 2007, but once again an agreement could not be reached.[280] This deadlock prompted the ethnic Albanian leadership in Kosovo to announce they would take action to seek independence,[281] which in turn prompted Serbian President Boris Tadić to announce at the end of 2007 that if they did Serbia would seek an Advisory Opinion regarding the legality of their actions.[282]

On 17 February 2008, the elected representatives of the Kosovo Assembly, part of the PISG, held an extraordinary meeting and adopted, by 109 out of the 120 members, including the Prime Minister of Kosovo and by the President of Kosovo (who was not a member of the Assembly) a Unilateral Declaration of Independence (UDI), which included *inter alia*:[283]

278. 'The Comprehensive Proposal for Kosovo Status Settlement, Report of the Special Envoy of the Secretary-General on Kosovo's Future Status' ('The Ahtisaari Report') available at he United Nations office of the Special Envoy for Kosovo website: www.unosek.org/unosek/en/statusproposal.html [as at 13 June 2013]; *Kosovo Opinion* [2010] ICJ Rep 403, 426–432, [59]–[69].
279. Russia vetoed the resolution attempting to adopt the Ahtisaari Report. See 'Russia Rejects U.N. Kosovo resolution' 20 June 2007, available from the USA Today Website: http://usatoday/30.usatoday.com/news/world/2007-06-20-kosovo_N.html [accessed 17 June 2013]. The findings of the Security Council mission can be found in: 'Report of the Security Council Mission on the Kosovo Issue' UN Doc S/2007/256, 4 May 2007.
280. 'Report of the European Union/United States/Russian Federation Troika on Kosovo', 4 December 2007, annexed to S/2007/723; *Kosovo Opinion* [2010] ICJ Rep 403, 433, [72].
281. 'Serbia to seek UN Court ruling on separatists in Kosovo', *Serbianna:* <http://www.serbianna.com/news/2007/03050.shtml> at 30 May 2013.
282. 'To ask the Security Council to Request an advisory opinion on the legality or illegality of the possible independence of Kosovo 'Serbia to Seek UN Court Ruling on Separatists in Kosovo', *Serbianna*: <http://www.serbianna.com/news/2007/03050.shtml> at 13 December 2007.
283. Ten members of the Assembly representing the Kosovo Serb community and one member representing the Kosovo Gorani community did not attend the meeting. The declaration was not sent to the Special Representative of the Secretary-General and was not published

> We, the democratically-elected leaders of our people, hereby declare Kosovo to be an independent and sovereign state. This declaration reflects the will of our people and it is in full accordance with the recommendations of UN Special Envoy Martti Ahtisaari and his Comprehensive Proposal for the Kosovo Status Settlement.[284]

Serbia immediately requested an emergency public meeting of the Security Council, which took place on 18 February 2008. Serbian President Boris Tadić participated in the meeting, and denounced the UDI as an unlawful act.[285] And as warned earlier Serbia took action in the General Assembly to request an Advisory Opinion from the ICJ. Serbia drafted the question in the Request,[286] which the General Assembly adopted on 8 October 2008.[287]

b. The question asked of the Court

The Request contained a very simple question: 'Is the unilateral declaration of independence by the Provisional Institutions of Self-Government in accordance with international law?'[288]

The Court unanimously concluded that it had jurisdiction (the Court rejected the argument that the question was not a legal one). However, it was only by nine votes to five that the Court decided to accept the Request, with some judges arguing that the Court should exercise its discretion and not provide the Opinion. Their reasons varied. Their Excellencies Judges Keith and Tomka felt that the General Assembly was not seized of the matter, and only the Security Council could legitimately make a request.[289] Others

in the Official Gazette of the Provisional Institutions of Self-Government of Kosovo: *Kosovo Opinion* [2010] ICJ Rep 403, 434, [75].

284. *Kosovo Opinion* [2010] ICJ Rep 403, 435, [75].
285. Ibid.
286. The draft question to the Court was introduced in the General Assembly by the then Minister of Foreign Affairs of Serbia Vuk Jeremić: 'Request for an Advisory Opinion of the International Court of Justice on Whether the Unilateral Declaration of Independence of Kosovo Is in Accordance with International Law', UN Doc. A/63/L.2 63rd sess, Agenda item 71, (2008) (23 September 2008); '*Backing Request by Serbia, General Assembly Decides to seek International Court of Justice Ruling on Legality of Kosovo's Independence*' *63rd plen session, 22nd meeting,* UN Doc GA/10764, (8 October 2008).
287. *Request for an Advisory Opinion of the International Court of Justice on Whether the Unilateral Declaration of Independence of Kosovo is in Accordance with International Law*, UN GAOR, 63rd sess, 22nd plen mtg, UN Doc A/Res/63/3 (2 October 2008).
288. *Kosovo Opinion* [2010] ICJ Rep 403, [1].
289. Separate Opinion of Judge Keith, *Kosovo Opinion* [2010] ICJ Rep 403, 2 [6]. Declaration of His Excellency Vice-President Tomka, *Kosovo Opinion* [2010] ICJ Rep 403, 456 [9]. There is some logic to their conclusions since as outlined above the Security Council, acting under Chapter 7 of the *UN Charter*, was much more actively involved in resolving the issues in Kosovo than the General Assembly.

however, argued that the Court should refuse on the grounds of protecting the judicial propriety of the Court.[290] For example, His Excellency Judge Bennouna felt that the Request was 'frivolous', and that the Court was exposing itself to an attempt to exploit its Opinion.[291]

After concluding that they would provide an Opinion the Court examined the scope of the question and held that: 'To answer that question, the Court need only determine whether the declaration of independence violated either general international law or the *lex specialis* created by Security Council resolution 1244 (1999).'[292]

c. The Court's decision

A total of nine judges provided Declarations, Dissenting or Separate Opinions.[293] Thus, whilst many concurred with the Court's overall final decision they did so for different reasons, and were often critical of the majority's reasoning. By a vote of 10 to 4 the Court found that the UDI did not breach general international law,[294] nor the *lex specialis* created by Resolution 1244 or the Constitutional Framework:[295]

> The Court has concluded above that the adoption of the declaration of independence of 17 February 2008 did not violate general international law, Security Council resolution 1244 (1999) or the Constitutional Framework. Consequently the adoption of that declaration did not violate any applicable rule of international law.[296]

I. GENERAL INTERNATIONAL LAW

In coming to the conclusion that there was no general prohibition in international law the Court responded to a number of arguments presented during the Written and Oral proceedings: (1) that the Security Council had in the past condemned UDI's, for example in relation to Rhodesia, Northern Cyprus, and *Republika Sprska*; and, (2) that the principle of territorial integrity prohibited UDI's. In relation to the first argument the Court stated:[297]

290. Those voting against providing the Opinion were: Vice-President His Excellency Tomka; Judges Koroma, Keith, Bennouna, Skotnikov. *Kosovo Opinion* [2010] ICJ Rep 403, 452 [123].
291. Dissenting Opinion of His Excellency Judge Bennouna, Ibid, 500 [3].
292. Ibid, 438 [83].
293. Not quite a record but indicative of the divisions within the bench.
294. *Kosovo Opinion* [2010] ICJ Rep 403, 29–32 [79]–[84]. The four dissenting judges were: His Excellency Vice-President Tomka; Judges Koroma, Bennouna, and Skotnikov.
295. Ibid, 452 [119].
296. Ibid, 452 [122].
297. Ibid, 436 [80]–[81].

> The Court notes, however, that in all of those instances the Security Council was making a determination as regards the concrete situation existing at the time that those declarations of independence were made; the illegality attached to the declarations of independence thus stemmed not from the unilateral character of these declarations as such, but from the fact that they were, or would have been, connected with the unlawful use of force or other egregious violations of norms of general international law, in particular those of a peremptory character *(jus cogens)*. In the context of Kosovo, the Security Council has never taken this position.[298]

In response to the issue regarding territorial integrity the Court came to a bold and controversial conclusion: 'the scope of the principle of territorial integrity is confined to the sphere of relations between States.'[299] Some commentators questioned the correctness of the Court's findings,[300] whilst other commentators questioned the wisdom in reaching this conclusion. For example, Kohn and del Mar argued that the Court's findings jeopardised the ability of the UN to resolve future conflicts because the Court's conclusion effectively nullified and rendered meaningless any future Security Council 'guarantees' regarding territorial integrity. Thus, they argued the ICJ's Advisory Opinion had actually made it more difficult for the UN to resolve claims to self-determination in the future.[301]

More alarmingly Christakis argued that breaching the guarantee of Serbia's right to territorial integrity allowed Serbia: 'to defend its territorial integrity against separatism, in exactly the same way as any sovereign country in the world has the right to defend its territory against secession.'[302] This suggestion is alarming when it is remembered how the former Yugoslavia 'defended' its territorial integrity in the past, and in no way should the use of force, in particular the use of ethnic cleansing, and other

298. *Kosovo Opinion* [2010] ICJ Rep 403, 436 [80]–[81].
299. Ibid.
300. Christakis argues that State practice opposes the Court's conclusion, whilst Vidmar argues that there is little proof within international instruments: Theodore Christakis, 'The ICJ Advisory Opinion on Kosovo: Has International Law Something to Say about Secession?' (2011) 24 (1) *Leiden Journal of International Law*, p. 84 & Jure Vidmar, 'Remedial Secession in International Law: Theory and (Lack of) Practice' in (2010) 6(1) *St Anthony's International Review*, pp. 50–51; Jure Vidmar, 'The *Kosovo* Opinion Scrutinized' (2011) 24(1) *Leiden Journal of International Law*, pp. 368–371.
301. Marcelo G Kohen and Katherine del Mar, 'The Kosovo Advisory Opinion and UNSCR 1244 (1999): A Declaration of 'Independence from International Law'? (2011)24 (1) *Leiden Journal of International Law*, p 124.
302. Christakis, *The ICJ Advisory Opinion on Kosovo*, p. 85.

potential breaches of the *Genocide Convention*,[303] be encouraged.[304] Such suggestions do more to jeopardise the ability of the UN to resolve self-determination claims peacefully than the Court's conclusions about territorial integrity.[305]

II. SECURITY COUNCIL RESOLUTION 1244 AND THE CONSTITUTIONAL FRAMEWORK

The Court recognized Resolution 1244 as a *lex specialis* that could prohibit a UDI. After much analysis the Court held that the purpose of Resolution 1244 was to create an interim civil administration, a legal regime, to govern Kosovo,[306] not to settle Kosovo's final status, and accordingly did not prohibit a UDI.[307] Crucial to this finding was the Court's opinion that the authors of the UDI were not acting within their capacity as members of the PISG, although they were still acting as representatives of the Kosovar people.[308] If the authors were not official representatives, or not acting within their capacity as members of the PISG, merely as a group of individuals, then Security Council Resolution 1244 *could not* prohibit them from making a UDI.[309] Consequently, they also could not violate the Constitutional Framework.[310]

Whilst this logic is sound,[311] what mystified commentators is how the Court could possibly identify the authors of the UDI as not acting in their official capacity as the PISG.[312] Arguably the Court did exercise its discretion by concluding that the authors of the UDI were not acting as members of the PISG, but as private individuals who represented the Kosovar people.[313]

303. See *Case Concerning Application of the Convention on the Prevention and Punishment of the Crime of Genocide (Bosnia and Herzegovina v Serbia and Montenegro)* (2007), ICJ Rep 43, p. 238, [471(5)].
304. Leading to in the words of Peters: '... a potential *reconquista* of Kosovo with military means.' Anne Peters, 'Does Kosovo Lie in the *Lotus-Land* of Freedom?', (2011) 24 (1) *Leiden Journal of International Law*, p. 108.
305. Furthermore, the 'deal' was with the Security Council, not the ICJ, and as the Court has said many times the Court should not allow the political factors to interfere with its decisions: *Kosovo Opinion*, p. 15, [35].
306. *Kosovo Opinion*, [2010] ICJ Rep 403, 444 [100].
307. Ibid, 449 [114].
308. Ibid, 445–446 [105]; Vidmar, *The Kosovo Opinion Scrutinized*, p. 377; Kohen and del Mar, *Kosovo A Declaration of Independence*, p. 114.This is based on the argument presented by Prof James Crawford, which as noted above, was influential in the Court's ultimate decision.
309. *Kosovo Opinion*, [2010] ICJ Rep 403, 449–452, [114]–[119].
310. Ibid, 452 [120]–[121].
311. See Vidmar's analysis on this point: Vidmar, *The Kosovo Opinion Scrutinized*, pp. 358–360.
312. For example, Kohen and del Mar, *Kosovo A Declaration of Independence*, p. 114.
313. Ibid, p. 114. According to His Excellency Judge Koroma this essentially reworded the question as: 'Is the unilateral declaration of independence by the authors in accordance with international law?' Dissenting Opinion of His Excellency Judge Koroma, *Kosovo Opinion* [2010] ICJ Rep 403, 467–468 at [3].

The Court justified its conclusions on various grounds. Firstly, that the language of the UDI indicated that the authors of the declaration did not seek to act within the standard framework of the interim self-administration of Kosovo.[314] There was no reference to the PISG, or the Assembly of Kosovo in the original version of the UDI.[315] Thirdly, the UDI was signed not by members of the Assembly of Kosovo, but by the 'democratically-elected leaders of our people' including the President of Kosovo, who was not a member of the Assembly.[316] Finally, that the 'silence' of the Special Representative of the UN Secretary-General was also significant, because previously the Special Representative had qualified or even declared *ultra vires* certain actions by the Kosovo Assembly as being outside the scope of the Constitutional Framework created by the UN.[317] Thus, the Court appeared to interpret this silence as recognition by the Special Representative that the UDI was not made by persons acting within their capacity as the Assembly of Kosovo or as the PISG.

d. Reception of the Court's opinion

The judgment of the Court, described as a traditional approach of legal-neutrality,[318] generated a great deal of commentary.[319] That the Opinion generated so much interest is to be expected given the factual background, and the highly charged nature of the potential legal issues raised. Unfortunately most of the commentary was critical. For example, the Opinion was: 'overly restrictive';[320] 'unsettling';[321] a 'bland assertion'[322]; 'unsatisfactory';[323] of 'minimal significance'.[324] And worse, it exacerbated the violence associated

314. *Kosovo Opinion*, [2010] ICJ Rep 403, 445–446 [105].
315. Ibid, 446 [106].
316. Ibid, 446–447 [107].
317. Ibid, 447 [108].
318. Oliver Corten, 'Territorial Integrity Narrowly Interpreted: Reasserting the Classical Inter-State Paradigm of International Law' (2011) 24 (1) *Leiden Journal of International Law*, p. 90 and see the author's list of refines in his note 19.
319. Some journals ran a series of themed articles in a single issue. For example, volume 11 (2010) of the *German Law Journal*, the 'Agora' in volume 105 (1) *American Journal of International Law*; and the Symposium in (2011) 24 *Leiden Journal of International Law*.
320. Separate Opinion of His Excellency Judge Yusuf, *Kosovo Opinion*, [2010] ICJ Rep 403, 618 [2].
321. Kohen and del Mar, *Kosovo A Declaration of Independence*, p. 109.
322. Falk, *The Kosovo Advisory Opinion* p. 50.
323. See the Declaration of His Excellency Judge Simma, *Kosovo Opinion*, [48] at para 3; the Dissenting Opinion of His Excellency Judge Benouna *Kosovo Opinion*, para 69; Peters, *Lotus-Land of Freedom*, p. 108.
324. Hurst Hannum, 'The Advisory Opinion on Kosovo: an Opportunity Lost, or a Poisoned Chalice Refused?', (2011) 24 (1) *Leiden Journal of International Law*, p. 159.

with self-determination;[325] and was 'outcome-determinative',[326] or a 'political' decision.[327] Perhaps the harshest criticism came from Falk:

> It is unfortunate for international law, international justice, international lawyers and the system of international governance as a whole if the International Court of Justice, the supreme judiciary of the international governing system, acts as a rubber stamp for the dominant power of the Security Council and the judges' national political affiliations by adopting an economy of judicial reasoning in its decisions. The ICJ's recent advisory opinion on Kosovo's unilateral declaration of independence from Serbia seems to fall within this unsatisfactory category.[328]

These are strong criticisms that contradict the arguments raised here regarding the use of the advisory jurisdiction to assist with the resolution of self-determination claims. In particular Falk's because it suggests that the Court had been influenced by political considerations and seemed intent on appeasing the US and other European States, those that had supported Kosovo's claim for statehood.[329] In sum, the three major criticisms raised by commentators were: (1) that the Court by adopting a narrow approach to the interpretation of the question in the Request lost an opportunity to resolve many questions about self-determination; (2) that the Court erred in finding that that the UDI did not breach Security Council Resolution 1244; and (3) that the outcome was influenced by political considerations.[330] These criticisms need to be answered before considering how the advisory jurisdiction can assist with the resolution of claims to self-determination.

In order to consider the merits of these criticisms it is advisable to be reminded of the events that led to the request for the Opinion. Burri provides a neat summary:

> It had involved war. International forces had intervened to stop ethnic cleansing. It has polarized the entire international community. ... [the]

325. 'What the Court has said about 'territorial integrity' could render countries extremely skeptical of international involvement in their separatist conflicts exactly at the point in time that it is needed the most.'; Christakis, *The ICJ Advisory Opinion on Kosovo*, p. 86.
326. Declaration of His Excellency Vice-President Tomka, *Kosovo Opinion*, [2010] ICJ Rep 403, 454 [1].
327. Falk, *The Kosovo Advisory Opinion* p. 50.
328. Ibid.
329. Ibid.
330. For example, Christakis, *The ICJ Advisory Opinion on Kosovo*, p. 74; Hurst Hannum, 'The Advisory Opinion on Kosovo: An Opportunity Lost, or a Poisoned Chalice Refused?' (2011) 24(1) *Leiden Journal of International Law*, p. 157; Kohen and del Mar, *Kosovo A Declaration of Independence*, p. 114.

> legal assessment was *challenging.* ... the stakes were *high.* Nothing less than the foundation of the international order was at issue.[331]

The highly charged political environment placed the Court in a difficult situation. The Court's Opinion was going to receive criticism, either for being too conservative, or for exceeding its mandate.[332] In a manner of speaking damned if it was too conservative and damned if it were too radical:

> The Kosovo opinion would thus ... mirror ... the Court-portraying either an ambitious Court, one that asserts the role of the 'principal judicial organ of the United Nations' ... creatively if necessary, or a less insistent Court, one that sticks to a low-key role.[333]

Furthermore, it was clear that there was an impasse, that years of negotiations had failed, that the UN had been unable to resolve the situation.[334] In view of the deliberate drafting of the question the Court had to tread wearily on a matter that States were unable to, and probably would have received more criticism if it took a more ambitious approach. Thus, it is not surprising if the Court were reluctant to be judicially active or creative when pursuing its role within the UN.[335]

I. NARROW APPROACH TAKEN BY THE COURT REGARDING THE SCOPE OF THE QUESTION

The Court did acknowledge that several participants raised the issue of Kosovo's claim to statehood, the concept of remedial self-determination, and noted that there were many divergent views.[336] Whilst acknowledging these matters the Court simply stated that it was unnecessary to resolve these issues '*in the present case*'.[337]

As noted by Kohen and del Mar, there is a world of difference between rewording a vague or poorly drafted question, and rewording a very precise and carefully considered question.[338] And it is clear that the question presented to the Court was carefully drafted: in other words it was intentionally

331. Thomas Burri, 'The Kosovo Opinion and Secession: the Sounds of Silence and Missing Links' (2010) 11 *German Law Journal*, p. 881.
332. Marc Weller, 'Modesty can be a Virtue: Judicial Economy in the *Kosovo* Opinion?', (2011) 24 *Leiden Journal of International Law*, p. 130.
333. Burri, *Sounds of Silence*, p. 881; Weller, *Modesty can be a Virtue*, pp. 129–131.
334. See the discussion below.
335. Arguably even to accept the Request for an Advisory opinion: see Weller, *Modesty can be a Virtue*, pp. 129–130.
336. *Kosovo Opinion*, [2010] ICJ Rep 403, 438 [82].
337. Ibid. [83] (emphasis added).
338. Their comment was in fact a criticism of the Court's approach regarding the authors of the UDI. Kohen and del Mar, *Kosovo A Declaration of Independence*, p. 118.

narrow. The question could have been phrased differently very easily, as suggested by commentators.[339] Furthermore, previous requests had specifically sought an examination of the 'legal consequences',[340] (a point that featured prominently in the Court's reasoning)[341], all of which begs the question: why was the question framed the way it was?[342]

The General Assembly may have made the Request, but Serbia drafted the question. In fact Serbia was the sole sponsor of the question, and thus arguably was totally responsible for the format of the question.[343] No doubt Serbia chose a specific and narrow question for strategic reasons, namely believing that a narrow question would result in a negative answer, that the UDI would be considered to be illegal. Receiving such a declaration could have enabled Serbia to take action before the UN General Assembly to reassert its authority over Kosovo. With Serbia's ally Russia retaining a veto power in the Security Council this is not far-fetched.[344] Peters goes one step further arguing that: 'a negative answer might have inspired Serbian actors to propagate a *reconquista* of Kosovo with military means.'[345]

Serbia sought to gain a political advantage from the Opinion, because the Opinion would enlighten Member States and thus guide their behaviour, and response to the UDI: for example, it may persuade them to not grant recognition of Kosovo's statehood.[346]

Arguably Peter's comment is slightly far-fetched given the support by the US and the European Union, but at the very least a negative decision by the Court would assist in any negotiations aimed at partitioning

339. For example, Christakis suggests a question similar to that asked of the Canadian Supreme Court, something like: 'Did international law give the Provisional Institutions of Self-Government of Kosovo the right to issue a unilateral declaration of independence of Kosovo from Serbia? In this regard, is there a right to self-determination under international law that would give Kosovo the right to unilateral secession from Serbia?' Another suggestion this time by Hannum: 'Does the recognition by states of the juridical independence of Kosovo violate their obligations under international law not to interfere with the territorial integrity and political independence of Serbia?' Christakis, *The ICJ Advisory Opinion on Kosovo*, p. 76; Hannum, *An Opportunity Lost* pp. 158–159, respectively.
340. Such as: *the Namibia Opinion*, the *Wall in Palestine Opinion* and the *Nuclear Weapons Opinion*: Kohen and del Mar, *Kosovo A Declaration of Independence*, p. 114.
341. *Kosovo Opinion* [2010] ICJ Rep 403, 423 [51].
342. Weller, *Modesty can be a Virtue*, p. 131.
343. Hannum *An Opportunity Lost*, p. 159; Weller, *Modesty can be a Virtue*, p. 130.
344. Weller, *Modesty Can Be a Virtue*, p. 131.
345. Peters, *Lotus-Land of Freedom*, p. 108.
346. The expression enlightenment was part of a quote used by Serbia in its Written Submission from the *Peace Treaties Advisory Opinion*. See Serbia's Written Statement filed by Serbia 17 April 2009, p 46, [91] available at the ICJ's website: http://www.icj-cji.org/docket/index.php?pl=3&p2=4&k21&case=141&code=kos&p3=1 (accessed 25 May 2013).

Kosovo, in particular any proposed settlement of the Serbian north in Kosovo.[347]

A narrow question may have been necessary for the Request's approval by the General Assembly,[348] although Hannum doubts that the General Assembly, (or for that matter members of the Security Council) would have wanted to draft a broader question: 'One should also note that such a [broad] question would have embarrassed Russia, as well, which is one of very few states to have recognized the breakaway regions of Abkhazia and South Ossetia, both of which seek independence …'[349]

Hannum's comments suggest that Russia did not want the Court to consider remedial self-determination on the grounds that such an examination may raise questions about the legality of Russia's support for Abkhazia and South Ossetia. There is little impartial evidence of repression by the Georgian authorities other than that claimed by Russia, as a pretext for its military operations in Georgia.[350] Another reason why various members of both the General Assembly and the Security Council may be unwilling to entice a broader question is the fear that if the Court were to set guidelines, or preconditions that permitted independence or at least legitimised a self-determination claim, then various States, Russia or the PRC, and Israel for example, would be exposed to claims from peoples within their territories. Falk argues that a careful reading of the majority's Opinion supports the idea

347. Falk, *The Kosovo Advisory Opinion*, p. 55.
348. 'The lowest common denominator' was how the US described the question in its Written Statement *Kosovo Opinion* filed by the US on 17 April 2009, available at the ICJ's website: http://www.icj-cji.org/docket/index.php?pl=3&p2=4&k21&case=141&code=kos&p3=1 (accessed 24 May 2013).
349. Hannum *An Opportunity Lost*, pp. 158–159.
350. In a public statement by Russian President Dimtry Mevedev on August 26 2008, then President Medvedev stated that Georgia had attempted to annex South Ossetia through '… the annihilation of a whole people'. And that this was not the first time that Georgia had attempted to do so, alluding to a history of repression, and attempted genocide, or at the very least crimes against humanity. The statement also refers to the use of force by Russia as well as South Ossetians, to protect, and then assist the peoples in South Ossetia to achieve independence was the 'only possibility to save lives', in other words as a 'last resort'. All of these expressions are part of the lexicon used when referring to the remedial right to self-determination. It is clear that the Russian President was attempting to make a 'case' for remedial self-determination to apply to South Ossetia. See 'Statement by President of Russia Dimitry Medvevev' 26 August 2008, available at President of Russia's website: http://archive.kremlin.ru/eng/speeches/2008/08/26/1543_type82912-205752.stml [last accessed 24 May 2013]. In its Written Statement regarding the *Kosovo Opinion*, Russia acknowledged the concept of remedial self-determination, but concluded that the facts did not show it applied to Kosovo: see the Written Comments *Kosovo Opinion* filed by Russia of 16 April 2009 at pp. 31–32, [88]–[90]; available at the ICJ's website: http://www.icj-cji.org/docket/index.php?pl=3&p2=4&k21&case=141&code=kos&p3=1 [last accessed 24 May 2013].

that the majority did not want to open the floodgates.[351] A fear clearly held by some States arguing that the Kosovo situation was unique,[352] an obvious attempt to minimise the precedent value of the Opinion.[353] As noted by Weller these fears are to a degree exaggerated, what motivates a people to claim independence is the level of repression by the parent government or access to resources, rather than the Opinion of the Court.[354]

There is a simpler explanation for the Court's approach. It was argued that Serbia as the sole sponsoring State would take advantage of the Court's neutrality.[355] The Court's response rejecting this argument was as follows:

> The advisory jurisdiction is not a form of judicial recourse for States but the means by which the General Assembly and the Security Council, as well as other organs of the United Nations and bodies specifically empowered to do so by the General Assembly ... may obtain the Court's opinion in order to assist them in their activities. The Court's opinion is given not to States but to the organ which has requested it ...[356]

It is not the role of the Court to cater to the wishful thinking or desires of States, and certainly not commentators, but to advise the Requesting Organ. The Court's decision to adopt a narrow interpretation can be explained simply on the basis that it was doing what was asked of it. It was clear that the General Assembly had chosen a narrow question when they could have chosen a broader question, and this was obvious to the Court. Thus, if the Court had ignored the General Assembly's choice it may have exceeded its mandate, and if the Court had taken a broader approach it would have exposed itself to even worse criticism. Peters makes this point:

> It would have been possible to give a broader answer to [a broader]... question posed, but a broad response, besides being unable to gain consensus in the Court, would have surely provoked criticism of judicial

351. Falk, *The Kosovo Advisory Opinion*, p. 58; Christakis, *The ICJ Advisory Opinion on Kosovo*, p. 80; generally James Summers (ed) *Kosovo: a Precedent?*, The Hague: Martinus Nijhoff Publishers, 2011.
352. See for example the Written Comments *Kosovo Opinion*, filed by the UK of 15 July 2009 at [11]-[14]; available at the ICJ's website: http://www.icj-cji.org/docket/index.php?pl=3&p2=4&k21&case=141&code=kos&p3=1 [accessed 24 May 2013] and the commentary by Hannum, *An Opportunity Lost*, p. 159.
353. This fear refers to the 'floodgate' argument raised in Chapter I above. See as an example the statement by the then President of Serbia, Tadić, in UNSC, sixty-third year, 5839th meeting, 18 February 2008, UN Doc. S/PV.5839 (2008), p. 5.
354. Weller, *Modesty Can Be a Virtue*, p. 147.
355. *Kosovo Opinion*, [2010] ICJ Rep 403, 416, [32].
356. Ibid, 417 [33].

> activism. The Court probably had no choice in letting pass an opportunity to clarify a crucial question of international law.[357]

A broader interpretation (assuming it still resulted in a similar decision that the UDI was not in breach of international law) would have undoubtedly provoked and even enabled Serbia to protest vehemently, and argue successfully in the General Assembly, and through its ally – Russia – in the Security Council that the Opinion was invalid and thus should be ignored by the Requesting Body. And as noted by Falk, who was critical of the Court's Opinion – that due to the nature of the question asked: '… the outcome regarding Kosovo is likely in the future to be read broadly even though the majority view is written narrowly, precisely to discourage such a broad endorsement of unilateral declarations of statehood.'[358]

II. RESOLUTION 1244 AND THE AUTHORS OF THE UDI

The Court's decision that the authors of the UDI were acting not as the Kosovo Assembly, but as the elected representatives of the people of Kosovo has drawn some intense criticism by commentators,[359] and judges alike,[360] who see an inconsistency in the Court's approach, as well as some creative judicial reasoning.[361] Whilst the majority of the Court was unprepared to reword the question in order to extend its scope beyond the literal issue of a UDI's legality, by concluding that the UDI was not made by members of the PISG the Court seemed prepared to reword the question so that it read as follows: 'Is the unilateral declaration of independence by the authors in accordance with international law?'[362]

Secondly, to many commentators the Court's reasoning is flawed. In Kohen and Del Mar's opinion there was an 'abundant' amount of evidence to indicate that other entities such as the General Assembly considered the authors of the UDI were acting in their role as the PISG, and not in some other capacity when they issued the UDI, including the very wording of the question in the Request, which was: 'Is the unilateral declaration of independence by the Provisional Institutions of Self-Government of Kosovo in accordance with international law?'[363] A point that the authors emphasised, but it must be remembered that Serbia was the sole sponsor responsible for drafting the question, and as discussed Serbia did so with important

357. Peters, *Lotus-Land of Freedom*, p. 98.
358. Falk, *The Kosovo Advisory Opinion*, p. 51.
359. For example, Kohen and del Mar, *Kosovo A Declaration of Independence.*
360. Their Excellencies Judges Koroma and Bennona.
361. See for example, Vidmar, *The Kosovo Opinion Scrutinized*, p. 360.
362. Dissenting Opinion of His Excellency Judge Koroma, *Kosovo Opinion*, [2010] ICJ Rep 403, 467–468. Vidmar, *The Kosovo Opinion Scrutinized*, p. 359.
363. Kohen and del Mar, *Kosovo A Declaration of Independence*, p. 116.

political and strategic considerations in mind. Thus, the fact that the Court did not blindly or automatically accept the wording of the question without some judicial examination is reassuring. As Weller points out: 'This finding confirms the independent exercise of the judicial function by the Court. The Court was unwilling to be bound by the General Assembly, or the sponsor of the resolution, to a particular answer.'[364] The Court is entitled to confirm a finding of fact, and even correct a factual error (a point acknowledged by Kohen and Del Mar),[365] the question is whether there was sufficient evidence for the Court to do so.

The Court examined a number of different factors, considering them together as a matrix of facts rather than single out any particular fact.[366] Firstly, it considered that the UDI: 'must be seen in its larger context, taking into account the events preceding its adoption, notably relating to the so-called final status process.[367] Secondly, the UDI reflected: '… the awareness of its authors that the final status negotiations had failed and that a critical moment for the future of Kosovo had been reached.'[368] Thirdly, that the language of the UDI evidenced an intention on behalf of the authors to operate outside the context of the Constitutional Framework.[369] In addition the UDI did not refer to the PISG, nor indicated that the UDI was the 'work' of the Kosovo Assembly, and furthermore, referred to the authors of the UDI as: 'We, the democratically-elected leaders of our people …'[370] And finally, the silence of the Special Representative of the Secretary-General, particularly when the Special Representative had an obligation, and practice showed, that they should take steps to correct an action of the Kosovo Assembly if it had acted *ultra vires*.[371] This silence indicated to the Court that the Special Representative did not consider the authors to be acting within their capacity as the Kosovo Assembly, and thus within the Constitutional Framework.[372] Although the silence of the Secretary-General's

364. Weller, *Modesty can be a Virtue*, p. 143. The Court itself acknowledged this point: *Kosovo Opinion*, p. 54.
365. Kohen and del Mar, *Kosovo A Declaration of Independence*, p. 116. They merely questioned whether there was sufficient evidence available for the Court to arrive at its conclusion.
366. *Kosovo Opinion* [2010] ICJ Rep 403, 447 [109].
367. Ibid, 445 [104].
368. Ibid, 445 [105].
369. Ibid, 445 [105]–[107].
370. Ibid.
371. Ibid, 447 [108].
372. Notwithstanding a report prepared by the Special Representative, the Report of the Secretary-General on the United Nations Interim Administration Mission in Kosovo, submitted to the Security Council on 28 March 2008, which stated that: 'the Assembly of Kosovo held a session during which it adopted a "declaration of independence"'. The Court considered this to be a 'normal periodic report' and not a legal analysis of who were the authors of the UDI: *Kosovo Opinion* [2010] ICJ Rep 403, 447 [109].

representative could be interpreted as an act in furtherance of the neutral-status policy adopted by the UN, there is some merit to the Court's logic.[373]

However, there is a sense that the Court was splitting hairs. In Vidmar's opinion the Court did so simply because without this finding the Court would be forced to conclude that the UDI was illegal (in breach of the *lex specialis*),[374] something which Falk suggests that Court was determined not to do, since he argues the Court was acting as a rubber stamp for the US and other dominant powers of the Security Council. Or alternatively at the very least this aspect of the Court's Opinion was outcome-determinative.

III. THE COURT'S OPINION WAS POLITICALLY MOTIVATED

The Court's analysis of the authors' of the UDI does appear to be influenced by the argument proposed by Professor James Crawford, counsel acting on behalf of the UK:[375]

> Mr President, Members of the Court, I am a devoted but disgruntled South Australian. 'I hereby declare the independence of South Australia.' What has happened? Precisely nothing. Have I committed an internationally wrongful act in your presence?
>
> Of course not. ... The reason is simple, A declaration issued by persons within a State is a collection of words writ in water; it is the sound of one hand clapping.[376]

373. 'It is common knowledge that the silence of the Special Representative was due to the "neutral-status" policy adopted by the Secretary-General with regard to the issuance of the UDI...' Kohen and del Mar, *Kosovo A Declaration of Independence*, p. 122. Interestingly, Mr Lamberto Zannier, the UN Special Representative whilst attending a later meeting of the Security Council noted that: 'The United Nations preliminary legal assessment is that the opinion does not affect the status of UNMIK or a status-neutral policy. Indeed, the judgment confirms the applicability of resolution 1244 (1999).' The Special Representative did not appear to mention that the Court erred at all in relation to identifying the role of the authors of the UDI when given an opportunity to do so. It would appear that there is a difference between maintaining a status neutral policy in the dealings that UNMIK or the Special Representative had with ethnic Serbs or Albanians, and whether the authors were acting as the PISG, and thus acting *ultra vires*: see Security Council Meeting, 6367th meeting, 3 August 2010, UN Doc S/PV.6367, p. 4.
374. Vidmar, *The Kosovo Opinion Scrutinized*, p. 382.
375. Oral Statement of Professor James Crawford, *Accordance with International Law of the Unilateral Declaration of Independence by the Provisional Institutions of Self-Government of Kosovo*, CR 2009/32, (Thursday 10 December 2009) p. 49, [8]. Available from the ICJ website: www.icj-cij.org/docket/files/141/15734.pdf (accessed 3 May 2013).
376. Oral Statement of Professor James Crawford, *Accordance with International Law of the Unilateral Declaration of Independence by the Provisional Institutions of Self-Government of Kosovo*, CR 2009/32, (Thursday 10 December 2009) pp. 48–49, [5]–[6]. Available from the ICJ website: www.icj-cij.org/docket/files/141/15734.pdf (accessed 3 May 2013).

Is this evidence of bias, of acting as a rubber stamp, or at the very least that the Opinion was 'outcome-determined' on this issue?[377]

This question is difficult to answer conclusively, but it would appear that the Court's deliberations took account of key elements of the factual context and background. Specifically that a critical moment for the future of Kosovo had arrived.[378] Negotiations had proved fruitless, so too the efforts of the Troika, and so too, it would appear, any future talks.[379] This was evident in the 2005 Report to the Secretary-General (and which had been forwarded to the Security Council) prepared by Mr. Martti Ahtisaari, the UN Secretary-General's Special Envoy for Kosovo, which concluded that:

> It is my firm view that the negotiations' potential to produce any mutually agreeable outcome on Kosovo's status is exhausted. No amount of additional talks, whatever the format, will overcome this impasse. The time has come to resolve Kosovo's status. Upon careful consideration of Kosovo's recent history, the realities of Kosovo today and taking into account the negotiations with the parties, I have come to the conclusion that the only viable option for Kosovo is independence, to be supervised for an initial period by the international community.[380]

Despite the above conclusion, despite Kosovo's *de facto* independence for nearly a decade, and recognition from approximately 60 States, Serbia's position towards Kosovo at the time of the Opinion remained unchanged.[381] The Court was conscious that the UN's handling of the Kosovo Situation was also at an impasse. The Court noted that the Security Council, rather than act upon the clear findings of Mr. Martti Ahtisaari, simply chose to appoint its own mission to investigate, one which achieved nothing but a recognition that there was a deadlock.[382]

377. Declaration of His Excellency Vice-President Tomka, *Kosovo Opinion*, [2010] ICJ Rep 403, 454 [1].
378. *Kosovo Opinion*, [2010] ICJ Rep 403, 447, [105].
379. For example, the Court noted that the UN Special Envoy had concluded: 'It is my firm view that the negotiations' potential to produce any mutually agreeable outcome on Kosovo's status is exhausted. No amount of additional talks, whatever the format, will overcome this impasse.' *Kosovo Opinion*, [2010] ICJ Rep 403, 432, [69].
380. The Ahtisaari Report, paras 3 & 5 as cited in *Kosovo Opinion*, [2010] ICJ Rep 403, 432, [69].
381. Serbia's position is not surprising, and is reminiscent of South Africa's intransigence over Namibia.
382. The recommendations were contained in the Comprehensive Proposal for the Kosovo Status Settlement, *Kosovo Opinion* [2010] ICJ Rep 403, 433 [71]. The Court also made a reference to the veto power held by Russia, Serbia's ally, where it noted that the whist Security Council Resolutions are binding, the voting procedure of the Council was a 'different process': See *Kosovo Opinion*, [2010] ICJ Rep 403, 442, [94].

Whilst the Court has stated often that it is not concerned with the political implications its Opinion may have when determining jurisdiction,[383] it certainly does not operate in a political vacuum, and is aware of the potential consequences of its Opinion. It is conscious too of its role to assist the UN to achieve its purpose of maintaining international peace and security. Falk who was highly critical of the Court's approach, stated:

> From the standpoint of human rights, as well as political realism, the Kosovo claim is highly reasonable. It would be irresponsible and extremely destabilizing to insist on a legal reversal of the de facto independence that Kosovo has enjoyed, with UN backing and administration, and regional and geopolitical reinforcement ... for more than a decade.[384]

Thus, the Court's findings could be described as outcome-determinative only because it sought to assist the UN move forward towards a solution, one that was painstakingly clear as early as 2005. Peters who was critical of the Court's approach nonetheless acknowledged that the approach: '... was the key to securing a broad acceptance amongst states, even among those who did not (yet) recognize Kosovo, including Serbia.'[385] Did the Court's Opinion do so? The answer is 'yes', and this is not an insignificant contribution by anyone's imagination.

e. Contribution of the Kosovo Opinion

Despite the criticisms many commentators still found the Opinion to be significant,[386] and also to be right. Perhaps not because of what it said, but by its silence,[387] and the consequential implications thus raised.[388]

383. The Court has mentioned this repeatedly, see for example the list of authorities contained in the *Kosovo Opinion*, [2010] ICJ Rep 403, 415, [27].
384. Falk, *The Kosovo Advisory Opinion*, p. 58.
385. Peters, *Lotus-Land of Freedom*, p. 108.
386. For example, Weller, *Modesty Can Be a Virtue*, p. 127; Theodore Christakis and Oliver Corten, 'Symposium: the ICJ Advisory Opinion on the Unilateral Declaration of Independence of Kosovo, Editors' Introduction' (2011) 24 *Leiden Journal of International Law*, p. 71.
387. For example, Weller noted that: 'One may therefore conclude that in confirming that there is no prohibition of a declaration of independence in general international law, the Court has also confirmed that there is no prohibition of unilateral secession.' Weller, *Modesty can be a Virtue*, p. 137. This silence is what His Excellency Judge Simma identified as 'deliberative silence', which Peters explains as: '... the opposite of a legal lacuna. Deliberate silence of the international law-makers means that secession remains prohibited – or allowed, depending on what one take's as the residual rule.' See the Declaration of His Excellency Judge Simma, *Kosovo Opinion* [2010] ICJ Rep 403, 480 [9] & Peters, *Lotus-Land of Freedom*, p. 99.
388. Vidmar, *The Kosovo Advisory Opinion Scriutinized* p. 356 & Peters, *Lotus-Land of Freedom*, p. 108.

Falk's acknowledgment of the value of the Court's opinion is noted above.[389]

Despite his harsh criticism of the Court's decision Hannum stated: 'But, if the Court's task is to interpret the law as it is rather than as it might be, it is very difficult to disagree with the modest conclusion that it reached, by a vote of ten votes to four.'[390] And finally, Tams concluded:

> The problem with the Court's answer is not that it is wrong, but that it is right. In giving the correct answer to the General Assembly's curiously formulated question, the Court has drawn attention to a serious gap in the international legal system: international law's failure to provide meaningful rules that give normative guidance on how the international community should deal with claims to statehood.[391]

This final point is significant. That even when heavily criticised, the Court is able to make a contribution, one that is subtle, but still significant, the least of which as Tams points out is that the Court identifies areas that need addressing by the political organs of the UN. However, does this resolve the dispute or issue at the heart of the Request for an Advisory Opinion? Hannum argues that there is nothing in the *Kosovo Opinion* to either encourage or discourage any further acts of recognition of Kosovo's statehood.[392] One hundred and one States have provided recognition, but most of these acts of recognition were prior to the handing down of the Court's Opinion (approximately 30 were made post the ICJ decision). And it could be argued that many States withholding recognition will probably continue to do so because their decisions are influenced by political and strategic considerations, rather than due to the Court's Opinion.[393] Thus, it could be argued that the Advisory Opinions can do little to assist with resolving self-determination claims.

On a simple numerical analysis it is true that the Opinion did not result in a rush of recognitions. However, the Court's Opinion had an immediate

389. Falk, *The Kosovo Advisory Opinion*, p. 58.
390. Hannum, *An Opportunity Lost*, p. 156.
391. Christian J Tams, 'The Kosovo Opinion', *EJIL Talk!*, www.ejiltalk.org/the-kosovo-opinion/ (accessed 16 March 2012).
392. Hannum, *An Opportunity Lost*, p. 159.
393. For example, Armenia is probably hesitant because firstly it does not want to upset Russia, and secondly, because it wants to placate or convince Azerbaijan to accept the loss of Karabakh in the Nagorno-Karabakh dispute. Argentina does not want to grant recognition because it may affect its position on the return of the Falkland Islands. Similarly Israel is holding back on granting recognition since it may encourage Palestine's claim for statehood: it might be used as an argument of precedent.

impact, it stymied recurrent Serbian attempts to stall and even terminate Kosovo's path to statehood. Within a week of the Court's Opinion being handed down Serbia attempted to re-ignite the debate regarding the UDI by presenting a draft resolution to the General Assembly suggesting how the Assembly should respond to the Opinion. The initial draft contained the statement: 'Taking into account the fact that one-sided secession cannot be an accepted way for resolving territorial issues.'[394] This was clearly rejected by the General Assembly. Turkey for example stated that the Opinion marked an end to the legal discussion on the matter. There was a notable consensus amongst States, even those like India or China that reiterated their support for the paramount nature of territorial integrity, that this question was behind them. Thus, the parties should move forward and resolve the issue through dialogue, on the basis that the UDI *was not* illegal. Weller describes the discussions as reflecting an air of 'enough is enough', that Serbia had had their 'day in court'.[395] Instead as Weller notes the emphasis was on: 'practical issues relating to the co-operative management of relations between the parties are to be addressed.'[396]

It may be far-fetched to make a connection between the Opinion, and recent negotiations between Pristina and Belgrade seeking to normalise relationships, and more importantly not hinder each other's membership of the EU, but it is clear that since the Opinion Serbia has found it increasingly difficult to deny Kosovo's status as an independent entity, and furthermore, Serbia's sovereignty over Kosovo.[397] This agreement to normalise relations is more than just historic; it is extremely significant because self-determination claims are rarely, if ever, resolved without the cooperation of the parent State. What is proposed here is that without the Opinion Serbia's cooperation would not have been forthcoming. Thus, the Court's Opinion proves thc ICJ can make a contribution to resolve claims to self-determination.

394. 'Serbia Submits Kosovo draft to UN GA' B92 News website, 28 July 2010, located at www.b92.net/eng/news/politics.php/yyyy=2010&mm=07=28&nav_id=68748 (accessed 11 June 2013).
395. 'Request for an Advisory Opinion of the International Court of Justice on Whether the Unilateral Declaration of Independence of Kosovo is in Accordance with International Law' Draft Resolution (A/64/L.65/Rev.1) UN Doc A/64/PV.120, 120th plenary sess, GA 64th session, 9th September 2010; Weller, *Modesty can be a Virtue*, p. 145.
396. Weller, *Modesty can be a Virtue*, p. 146.
397. Piotr Smolar, 'Serbia and Kosovo Sign historic Agreement', 30th April 2013, available at the Guardian Website: wwww.guardian.co.uk/world/2013/apr/30/Serbia-kosovo-historic-agreement-brussels (accessed 12 June 2013).

D. Advantages of the Court's advisory jurisdiction

The advisory jurisdiction is more flexible and expeditious than typical contentious hearings. The failure of Israel to act in accordance with the Opinion of the court would appear to minimise these advantages, and raises the question that if the Opinions are ignored, then what value do they have?

Whilst for this reason an Opinion may not appear to offer an immediate resolution of a particular claim for self-determination they play an important role in refining norms of international law, and so an Opinion, by being less confrontational, may be more effective than a contentious matter, by providing a foundation for negotiations to enable future, if not current, claims to be resolved peacefully and in the best interests of both parties.[398]

1. Avoiding the limitations of the consensual jurisdiction

The first advantage is that issues of consent do not necessarily prevent the Court answering the Request. Interested parties have argued that the Court exercise its discretion and refuse to provide an Opinion on the basis that the Request concerned an actual dispute where the parties had not granted their consent for a contentious hearing.[399] The lack of consent was one reason why the PCIJ refused to provide an Opinion in the *Eastern Carelia Case*.[400]

The Court is well aware that the advisory jurisdiction could be abused in order to avoid issues of consent.[401] However, that does not mean that the Court will refuse to provide an opinion every time a State claims it has not provided its consent.[402] For example, in both the *Western Sahara Opinion* and the *Namibia Opinion*[403] the Court held that since both parties were members of the UN, and both were signatories of both the *UN Charter* and the *ICJ Statute*, therefore they had consented to the exercise of the ICJ's advisory

398. Also if an Opinion is followed once, then this could assist in future Requests being made.
399. Eg, *Western Sahara Opinion* [1975] ICJ Rep 12, 23; *Namibia Opinion* [1971] ICJ Rep 16; and, most recently, *Wall in Palestine Opinion* [2004] ICJ Rep 136.
400. *Eastern Carelia Case* [1923] PCIJ (ser B) No. 5, 7, 25. See *Western Sahara Opinion* [1975] ICJ Rep 12, 73, [1]; Pomerance, *The Advisory Function*, p. 20.
401. It is for this reason that Her Excellency Judge Higgins has argued that the UN Secretary-General should not be authorised to make a Request: Higgins, *The Role of the International Court of Justice*, p. 7.
402. *Peace Treaties Opinion*, [1950] ICJ Rep 65, 71; *Interpretation of Peace Treaties with Bulgaria, Hungary and Romania (Pleadings)* [1949] ICJ Rep 196–7; 203–4; *Reservations to the Convention on the Prevention and Punishment of the Crime of Genocide (1950–1951) (Advisory Opinion)* [1951] ICJ Rep, 15, 19 ('*Reservations to Genocide Convention Case*'); *Western Sahara Opinion* [1975] ICJ Rep 12, 23.
403. *Western Sahara Opinion* [1975] ICJ Rep 12, 29; *Namibia Opinion* [1971] ICJ Rep 16 23, [31].

jurisdiction.[404] In the *Peace Treaties Case*, the ICJ rejected the lack of consent argument proposed by Bulgaria, Hungary and Romania, and distinguished the *Eastern Carelia Case* on the grounds that there was an inability to resolve factual questions, which was not so in the *Peace Treaties Opinion*. Furthermore, the Court held that providing the Opinion would in no way jeopardise the legal positions of the respective parties.[405] Furthermore, the lack of consent does not prevent the Court from providing an Opinion on the legal consequences of a UN organ's course of action attempting to resolve a dispute between parties; or provide legal advice on the effect of multilateral conventions.[406]

Secondly, the advisory jurisdiction has the important advantage of providing a voice for those entities that lack standing. Upon receiving the Request the Court notifies all interested parties including non-State entities such as individuals, international organisations and specialised agencies of the UN. This is because if the Request affects those entities, for example, individuals then the Court must allow them to participate if it is to avoid breaching the principle of *audiatur et altera pars*.[407] Non-state entities such as the Palestinian Authority and the UN Secretary-General provided information to assist the Court in *the Wall in Palestine Opinion*.[408] This in effect provided the Palestinian people with a 'voice', an opportunity to appear before the ICJ and avoid the problem of standing in art 34 (1) *ICJ Statute*, and as occurred in the *East Timor Case*.[409]

In the *East Timor Case* the issue of the East Timorese self-determination was only brought before the Court through a convoluted claim made by Portugal, and even then whilst the right of the East Timorese was acknowledged, it could not be heard. In the *Wall in Palestine Opinion*, not only were the Palestinian people given an opportunity to be heard, the issue of Israel's consent did not deny this opportunity.[410] And finally, in the *Kosovo Opinion* the

404. The full quote is as follows: 'Spain is a member of the United Nations and has accepted the provisions of the Charter and the Statute; it has thereby in general given its consent to the exercise by the Court of its advisory jurisdiction. It has not objected, and could not validly object, to the General Assembly's exercise of its powers to deal with the decolonization of a non-self-governing territory and to seek an opinion on questions relevant to the exercise of those powers': *Western Sahara Opinion* [1975] ICJ Rep 12, p. 24, [30].
405. *Peace Treaties Opinion* [1950] ICJ Rep 65, p. 72.
406. *Reservations to the Genocide Convention Case* [1950] ICJ Rep 15, 19; *Western Sahara Opinion* [1975] ICJ Rep 12, 23; *Namibia Opinion* [1971] ICJ Rep 16, 23, [31]; *Wall in Palestine Opinion* [2004] ICJ Rep 136, [14]–[51].
407. Pratap, *The Advisory Jurisdiction*, p. 189. This expression means that both sides affected by the proceedings should be in a position to submit their views to the Court.
408. *Wall in Palestine Opinion* [2004] ICJ Rep 136, [57].
409. *Case Concerning East Timor (Portugal v Australia)* [1995] ICJ Rep 90. See Chapter 4.
410. Hilary Charlesworth summarises the comparison between these two decisions beautifully, by describing the *East Timor Case* as using a Westphalian, bilateral 'lens' which merely promoted State's pursuit of their self-interest. Whilst the Court's multilateral approach in the *Wall in Palestine Opinion* supported the values inherent in the UN Charter: Charlesworth, *Judge ad hoc*, p. 182.

authors of the UDI were permitted to supply written statements to the Court. There may be some criticism of this point, however, on the grounds that the Court as an integral part of the UN, as a legal advisor, must assist the UN achieve its primary purpose – maintaining international peace and security – this controversial position may be justified.

The Court's advisory jurisdiction appears to provide the best opportunity for peoples. It is already part of the ICJ's jurisdiction and to enable people access would not require anything as radical as amending art 34 (1) of the *ICJ Statute*, since the Request comes from an authorised organ of the UN rather than the people themselves. Thus it avoids the issue of standing completely.

2. *The Court's right to reject or reword the request*

a. Rejecting the request

After receiving the Request the Court must firstly satisfy itself that it has jurisdiction to consider the Request.[411] States frequently seek to persuade the Court to exercise its discretion and reject the Request.[412] The practice of the ICJ indicates that it will not do so unless there were compelling reasons to do so.[413]

Two examples of what may fall short of compelling reasons can be found in the *Wall in Palestine Opinion* and the *Western Sahara Opinion*. Firstly, in the *Wall in Palestine Opinion* Israel argued that the Court's consideration of the Request could jeopardise the negotiations or 'Roadmap' for a solution to the Israeli-Palestinian conflict.[414] The Court rejected this argument by

411. Some commentators have argued that as the principal judicial organ of the UN the ICJ has an obligation to cooperate with the other UN organs, which suggests that the Court should consider Requests from the UN organs very carefully, and not reject them without good reasons. See Gill, *Rosenne's The World Court*, p. 86; Amr, *The Role of the International Court of Justice*, pp. 107–109 suggests the following reasons would be valid grounds for rejecting a Request: (1) if providing an opinion complicates the matter or creates difficulties for the requesting body; (2) if it is against the judicial nature of the Court; (3) the Opinion would be ineffective; and (4) it would infringe the Court's judicial character due to the lack of information.
412. For example, Spain in the *Western Sahara Opinion* [1975] ICJ Rep 12; Israel in the *Wall in Palestine Opinion* [2004] ICJ Rep 136.
413. One ground to deny the request is that the request is not a legal question; another is that the agency making the request was not authorised; and a third that it was a matter of domestic concern. See *Peace Treaties Opinion* [1950] ICJ Rep, 65, 71. Perhaps the most important is the need to protect the 'judicial nature' of the Court: see *Eastern Carelia Case* [1950] ICJ Rep 1281, 27–9, where the PCIJ declined the request. In fact the *Eastern Carelia Opinion* is the only time the Court exercised its discretion and refused to provide an opinion: despite numerous attempts by States to do so, for example South Africa in *Namibia Opinion* [1971] ICJ Rep 16, 16. Pomerance, *The Advisory Function*, ch 5.
414. *Wall in Palestine Opinion* [2004] ICJ Rep 136, [51]. As noted by the Court, similar arguments were raised in *Legality of the Threat or Use of Nuclear Weapons (Advisory Opinion)* [1996] 1 ICJ Rep 226 ('*Nuclear Weapons Opinion*') and *Western Sahara Opinion* [1975] ICJ Rep 12.

concluding that there was no evidence that this indeed would be the result.[415] In the *Western Sahara Opinion* the ICJ concluded that answering the Request would assist the GA with decolonisation of the Western Sahara region.[416]

Some commentators have argued that the Court should exercise its discretion and refuse to provide an Opinion in highly political or controversial matters.[417] A variety of reasons are given: namely to protect the Court's reputation; that an Advisory Opinion is not a judgment but just an opinion, and as such can be misunderstood by the general public; and Advisory Opinions are incapable of resolving highly controversial and political matters. In a nutshell an Opinion can cause more problems than it solves.[418] Similar arguments were raised in the more recent *Kosovo Opinion.*[419] It was argued that Serbia would take advantage of the Court's neutrality,[420] (because the Opinion would 'enlighten' Member States and thus guide their behaviour, and response to the UDI: for example, it may persuade them to not grant recognition) and thus, the Court should decline the Request.[421] The Court's response rejecting this argument was as follows:

> The advisory jurisdiction is not a form of judicial recourse for States but the means by which the General Assembly and the Security Council, as well as other organs of the United Nations and bodies specifically empowered to do so by the General Assembly … may obtain the Court's opinion in order to assist them in their activities. The Court's opinion is given not to States but to the organ which has requested it …[422]

And further:

> Nor does the Court consider that it should refuse to respond to the General Assembly's request on the basis of suggestions, advanced by some of those participating in the proceedings, that its opinion might lead to adverse political consequences. Just as the Court cannot substi-

415. *Wall in Palestine Opinion* [2004] ICJ Rep 136, 160, [53].
416. *Western Sahara Opinion* [1975] ICJ Rep 12, 27–9.
417. Aust, *Advisory Opinions*, p. 123.
418. Ibid, pp. 147–151. Aust for example states that: 'Try telling a Palestinian that the *Wall Opinion* is just that, only an Opinion. The Opinion is seen by a large number of Palestinians as confirming their right to use force to make settlers in the occupied territories to leave or even to kill them.' (At 151) Despite the author's efforts the link between the Court's condemnation of the Wall and the promotion of violence is unclear, and puzzling.
419. *Kosovo Opinion*, [2010] Rep 403, 416–417, [32].
420. Ibid.
421. The expression enlightenment was part of a quote used by Serbia in its Written Submission from the *Peace Treaties Advisory Opinion.* See Serbia's Written Statement filed by Serbia 17 April 2009, p. 46, [91] available at the ICJ's website: http://www.icj-cji.org/docket/index.php?pl=3&p2=4&k21&case=141&code=kos&p3=1 (accessed 25 May 2013).
422. *Kosovo Opinion*, [2010] ICJ Rep 403, 417, [33].

> tute its own assessment for that of the requesting organ in respect of whether its opinion will be useful to that organ, it cannot in particular where there is no basis on which to make such an assessment substitute its own view as to whether an opinion would be likely to have an adverse effect.[423]

Put simply, the Court considers a rejection of a Request simply on the basis of political expediency as an abandonment of its role as the principal judicial authority of the UN, and the UN's objectives, namely to maintain international peace and security. And to do so would be an abandonment of the rule of law, something that the UN is eager to implement and reinforce in international relations as a means of achieving that objective.[424]

b. Rewording the request

The ability to clarify, or even reword, the question within the Request (provided the Court's interpretation does not go beyond what is necessary) in order to avoid potential problems is a major advantage. Both the PCIJ and the ICJ have done this on many occasions.[425] In fact as noted by

423. *Kosovo Opinion*, [2010] ICJ Rep 403, 418, [35].
424. Peters, *Lotus-Land of Freedom*, p. 108.
425. Pomerance, *The Advisory Function*, p. 322. The PCIJ redefined the question in the Request for its Opinion in *Competence of the ILO in Regard to International Regulation of the Conditions of the Labour of Persons Employed in Agriculture* [1922] PCIJ (ser B) No 2, 8, 21; *Competence of the ILO to Examine Proposal for the Organization and Development of the Methods of Agricultural Production* [1922] PCIJ (ser B) No 3, 48, 59; *Nationality Decrees Issued in Tunis-Morocco* [1923] PCIJ (ser B) No 4, 7, 21–2; *Eastern Carelia Opinion* [1950] ICJ Rep 1281, 24–7; *Competence of the ILO to Regulate Incidentally the Personal Work of the Employer* [1926] PCIJ (ser B) No 13, 5, 12–14; *Jurisdiction of the Courts of Danzig* [1928] PCIJ (ser B) No 15, 3, 13–15; *Interpretation of the Greco-Turkish Agreement of 1 December 1926 (Final Protocol, Article IV)* [1928] PCIJ (ser B) No 16, 3, 14–16; *Free City of Danzig and ILO* [1930] PCIJ (ser B) No 18, 3, 9–10; *Access to, or Anchorage in, the Port of Danzig, of Polish War Vessels* [1931] PCIJ (ser A/B) No 43, 127, 140; *Treatment of Polish Nationals and Other Persons of Polish Origin or Speech in the Danzig Territory* [1932] PCIJ (ser A/B) No 44, 3, 19–20. The ICJ has redefined questions in the following matters: *Conditions of Admission of a State to Membership in the United Nations (Article 4 of the Charter) (Advisory Opinion)* [1948] ICJ Rep 57, 60–1; *Reparation for Injuries Suffered in the Service of the United Nations (Advisory Opinion)* [1949] ICJ Rep 174, 177 ('*Reparation Opinion*'); *Competence of the General Assembly for the Admission of a State to the United Nations (Advisory Opinion)* [1950] ICJ Rep 4, 7; *Peace Treaties Opinion* [1950] ICJ Rep 65, 75–6; *Effect of Awards of Compensation Made by the United Nations Administrative Tribunal (Advisory Opinion)* [1954] ICJ Rep 47, 156–8; *Namibia Voting Procedures Opinion* [1955] ICJ Rep 67, 72; *Admissibility of Hearings Opinion* [1956] ICJ Rep 23, 25–6; *Constitutive of the Maritime Safety Committee of the Inter-Governmental Maritime Consultative Organization (Advisory Opinion)* [1960] ICJ Rep 150, 152–3 ('*Maritime Safety Committee Opinion*'); *Certain Expenses of the United Nations (Article 17, Paragraph 2, of the Charter) (Advisory Opinion)* [1962] ICJ Rep 151, 156–8; *Interpretation of the Agreement of 25 March 1951 Between the WHO and Egypt (Advisory Opinion)* [1980] ICJ Rep 73,

Pomerance, except in the *Reservations Opinion*, where the Court merely confirmed the wording in the Request, the ICJ has redefined the vast majority of UN Requests, and modified the questions contained therein.[426] For example, in the *Constitution of the Maritime Safety Committee of the Inter-Governmental Maritime Consultative Organization*, the question put to the Court was:

> Is the Maritime Safety Committee of the Inter-Governmental Maritime Consultative Organization, which was elected on 15 January, constituted in accordance with the Convention for the Establishment of the Organization?[427]

The Court interpreted the question as asking them whether in the establishment of the organization the General Assembly:

> ... in not electing Liberia and Panama to the Maritime Safety Committee, exercised its electoral power in a manner in accordance with the provisions of Article 28 (a) of the Convention.[428]

In the *Interpretation of the Agreement of 25 March 1951 Between the WHO and Egypt*, His Excellency Judge El Erian interpreted the 'true legal question' as:

> What are the legal principles and rules applicable to the question, under what condition and in accordance with what modalities, a transfer of the Regional Office from Egypt may be effected?[429]

And in the *Application for Review of Judgment No. 273 of the United Nations Administrative Tribunal* the Question put before the Court was:

> Is the judgement of the United Nations Administrative Tribunal in Judgment No, 273, ... warranted in determining that General Assembly resolution 34/165 of 17 December 1979 could not be given immediate

in particular the Separate Opinion of His Excellency Judge El Erian at 166; *Application for Review of Judgment NO. 273 of the United Nations Administrative Tribunal (Adviosory Opinion)* [1982] ICJ Rp 325; *Applicability of Article VI, Section 22, of the Covention on the Privileges and Immunities of the United Nations (Advisory Opinion)* [1989] ICJ Rep 177, 186–187 at [27]; *Legal Consequences of the Construction of a Wall in the Occupied Palestinian Territory (Advisory Opinion)* [2004] ICJ Rep 136, where the Court held that even if the Request lacks clarity, the Court is able to add clarity through its interpretation of the questions raised; at [13–42].

426. Pomerance, *The Advisory Function*, p. 322.
427. *Maritime Safety Committee Opinion* [1960] ICJ Rep 150, 150–2.
428. Ibid, 153.
429. *Interpretation of the Agreement of 25 March 1951 Between the WHO and Egypt (Advisory Opinion)* [1980] ICJ Rep 73, Separate Opinion of His Excellency Judge El Erian at 166.

> effect in requiring, for the payment of reparation grants, evidence of relocation to a country other than the country of the staff member's last duty station?[430]

The Court interpreted the question as requiring it to determine, in relation to the specific matters mentioned, whether the Administrative Tribunal had 'erred on a question of law relating to the provisions of the Charter of the United Nations' or 'exceeded its jurisdiction or competence.'[431]

The Court's ability to redefine the Request in order to render it workable is an important advantage, one that received support rather than criticism from commentators. In the words of His Excellency Judge Lauterpacht:

> The previous practice of the Court supplies authority for the proposition that the Court enjoys considerable latitude in constructing the question put to it for formulating its answer in such a manner as to make its advisory function effective and useful...[432]

The Court by redefining the question, or by refusing a Request, has the potential to avoid situations where providing an Opinion would discredit the Court. This discretion counters the potential argument raised by the interested parties that the unchanged Request would result in the Court overstepping its judicial boundaries, and obliging the Court to refuse to provide an Opinion.[433] Secondly, it could minimise the possibility that the Requesting organ will refuse to act upon the Request, and furthermore may encourage States to also respect and even act upon the Opinion.

For example, the *Nuclear Weapons Opinion* is an example of the argument that Advisory Opinions are ineffectual.[434] The Court was asked by the General Assembly for an Advisory Opinion on whether 'the threat or use of nuclear weapons in any circumstance [is] permitted under international law.'[435] The Court concluded that: (1) in customary and conventional international law there was no comprehensive and universal prohibition of the threat or use of nuclear weapons; (2) that 'there is in neither customary nor

430. *Application for Review of Judgment No. 273 of the United Nations Administrative Tribunal (Advisory Opinion)* [1982] ICJ Rep 325.
431. Ibid, 350 [48].
432. Separate Opinion of Sir Hersch Lauterpacht *Admissibility of Hearings Opinion* [1956] ICJ Rep 23, 37. Article 96 (1) of the *UN Charter* authorises the General Assembly and the Security Council to request an opinion on *any* legal question.
433. Pomerance noted that the PCIJ was also particularly active in going beyond the question within the Request in order to resolve the issues that lay at the heart of a dispute, whereas the ICJ has been far more 'restrained': Pomerance, *The Advisory Function*, pp. 323–24.
434. *Nuclear Weapons Opinion* [1996] 1 ICJ Rep 226. See Chapter 4 for more detail.
435. *General and Complete Disarmament*, GA Res 49/75, UN GAOR, 49th sess, 90th plen mtg, [75K], UN Doc A/RES/49/75 (9 January 1995).

conventional international law any specific authorization of the threat or use of nuclear weapons'; and (3) a threat or use of nuclear weapons should also be compatible with the requirements of the international law applicable in armed conflict and the *UN Charter*.[436] Despite this opinion, not only have States retained their nuclear weapons, more States like Iran and North Korea wish to obtain them.

However, if the Court had refined the Request it could have perhaps engineered a more effectual response from States that may have led to a reduction in nuclear weapons. For example, if the Request had been reworded in manner similar to this: 'In *what circumstances would* the threat or use of nuclear weapons be permitted under international law…' this may have not have necessarily resulted in a different Opinion being provided by the Court, but the wording may have placed the Court's opinion in a perspective that was less controversial and less challenging of States' perceived right to self-defence. This may have encouraged States to work towards agreeing through treaties not to use nuclear weapons in those illegal circumstances, which could even lead to the withdrawal of the specific type of weapons that could only be used illegally.

However, as the *Kosovo Opinion* revealed the Court will at times adopt a 'literal' or narrow interpretation, an approach that attracted a lot of criticism. For example, Christakis noted that: 'The narrowness of the question submitted by the UN General Assembly permitted the Court to "duck" all the important questions concerning Kosovo'.[437]

3. The nature of giving advice

The ICJ as an integral part of the UN was intended to assist the UN by providing an Advisory Opinion to guide the UN organs regarding '… legal questions arising within the scope of their activities'.[438]

> For example, an authorised organ of the United Nations entrusted with the resolution concerning self-determination, could seek an advisory opinion from the International Court of Justice on a carefully prepared 'legal question'. The question submitted to the Court would not be a 'disguised' contentious proceedings as such, but rather, the basis for establishing an authoritative though reasonably flexible juridical framework for negotiations.[439]

436. *Nuclear Weapons Opinion* [1996] 1 ICJ Rep 226, [105].
437. Christakis, *The ICJ Advisory Opinion on Kosovo*, p. 74; Hannum, *An Opportunity Lost*, p. 157; Kohen and del Mar, *Kosovo A Declaration of Independence*, p. 114.
438. *UN Charter*, art 96 (2).
439. Payam Akhavan, 'Self-determination and the Disintegration of Yugoslavia: What Lessons for the International Community?' in Donald Clark and Robert Williamson (eds), *Self-determination: International Perspectives*, New York: Macmillan Press Ltd, 1996, p. 244.

Thus an Advisory Opinion can overcome political deadlocks, since the Court will ignore political factors when determining their Opinion.[440] For example, the Request for the *Namibia Opinion* came at a time of crisis for the UN's authority:

> At this critical juncture, many Western [S]tates became convinced that their doubts regarding the territory's status and the union government's obligations would have to be clarified by a higher legal authority than the Assembly if any progress was to be made.[441]

As noted by Pomerance during the crisis between South Africa and India created by the South African government introducing in 1946, *the Asiatic Land Tenure and Indian Representative Act*:[442]

> ... a Court opinion might readily have served a dual purpose: clarification of the extent of the Assembly's competence and removal from the Assembly members of some of the onus of decision-making in this highly emotional-charged issue.[443]

The Court when providing an Advisory Opinion is able to avoid political interference to an even great extent than in contentious matters simply because it has greater control over the nature of the proceedings than in a contentious matter where the parties initiate and direct the Court on the matter to be resolved.

440. *Nuclear Weapons Opinion* [1996] 1 ICJ Rep 226, [16]. This stance has been repeated often by the Court both in contentious cases and advisory opinions: see, eg, *Questions of Interpretation and Application of the 1971 Montreal Convention Arising from the Aerial Incident at Lockerbie (Libyan Arab Jamahiriya v United Kingdom) (Order)* [1992] ICJ Rep 3, 56 ('*Lockerbie Case*') (Dissenting Opinion of Judge Weeramantry); *Questions of Interpretation and Application of the 1971 Montreal Convention Arising from the Aerial Incident at Lockerbie (Libyan Arab Jamahiriya v United States of America) (Order)* [1992] ICJ Rep 114, 166 (Dissenting Opinion of Judge Weeramantry) (The *Lockerbie Case* involved a dispute between Libya and both the UK and the US. The judgment relating to the US follows that relating to the UK and is virtually identical. Henceforth, all citations from the *Lockerbie Case* shall refer to the UK dispute); *Certain Expenses of the United Nations (Advisory Opinion)* [1962] ICJ Rep 151, 155 ('*Certain Expenses Opinion*'). It has also been used by other international tribunals such as the International Criminal Tribunal for the former Yugoslavia ('ICTY'): *Prosecutor v Tadić (Defence Motion for Interlocutory Appeal on Jurisdiction)*, Case No IT-94-1-AR72 (2 October 1995) ('*Tadić Case*') [24].
441. Pomerance, *The Advisory Function*, p. 116.
442. This Act resulted in the Indian government withdrawing its High Commissioner and also cancelling trade agreements, leading to a deadlock in the UN General Assembly about how to resolve the matter: Ibid p. 242.
443. Ibid. This was indeed what the UK government argued, that a judicial solution would be more acceptable to both parties, and consequently in the long run more beneficial to the Indians than a majority decision in a purely political forum.

a. Control over proceedings

The Court has greater control over proceedings when exercising its advisory jurisdiction. The Court by requesting States to participate as interested parties is not engaging them as parties appearing before the Court as disputants in contentious matters. Instead the role of States is one of an informant, supplying information to assist the Court. Even where the Request concerns an existing dispute between parties this does not alter the fact that States, or indeed any of the interested parties, are, as Pratap suggests merely helping the Court with information.[444] Thus States do not have the same ability to control the matters being discussed as they would if they were litigants in a contested matter.

b. Access to materials

For example, in the *Wall in Palestine Opinion* the Court received written statements from 44 States, including Palestine, and four international organisations including the UN and the European Union.[445] In addition, the UN Secretary-General supplied written statements and reports.[446] The Court had access to the vast amount of information gathered by the Tenth Emergency Special Session of the General Assembly, and the Security Council concerning the Israeli-Palestinian conflict from its very beginnings.[447] Oral Statements from thirteen States, including Palestine,[448] and two international organisations (other than the UN),[449] were received at the oral hearings held between the 23–25 of February 2003. In the *Kosovo Opinion* 35 States filed written

444. International organisations also fall within the definition of interested parties, and as such will be notified by the Court and asked to supply information when needed. In fact, Pratap likens the role of States to that of an 'amicus curiae': Pratap, *The Advisory Jurisdiction*, pp. 180–82.
445. *Wall in Palestine Opinion* [2004] ICJ Rep 136, p. 142.
446. The information provided by the Secretary-General was contained in a single dossier which in addition to the Report of the Secretary-General prepared in accordance with *Illegal Israeli Actions in Occupied East Jerusalem and the Rest of the Occupied Palestinian Territory*, UN GAOR,10th Emergency Special Session, 22nd plen mtg, UN Doc A/Res/ES-10/13 (27 October 2003), and included an updated Written Statement by the Secretary-General, as well as reports from other UN organs such as the World Health Organisation, the United Nations Commission on Human Rights, Special Rapporteurs, and Palestinian Organisations: see *Wall in Palestine Opinion* [2004] ICJ Rep 136, [57].
447. See *Wall in Palestine Opinion* [2004] ICJ Rep 136, 161–62 [57].
448. The remaining states were the Republic of South Africa; the People's Democratic Republic of Algeria; the Kingdom of Saudi Arabia; the People's Republic of Bangladesh; Belize; the Republic of the Cuba; the Republic of Indonesia; the Hashemite Republic of Jordan; the Republic of Madagascar; Malaysia; the Republic of Senegal; and the Republic of Sudan.
449. The League of Arab States, and the Organization of the Islamic Conference.

statements,[450] so too did the authors of the UDI.[451] In addition 26 States as well as the authors of the UDI participated in oral hearings held from 1 to 11 December 2009.[452] A number of eminent international academics and experts participated in these hearings as representatives for various States.[453]

Access to such a wealth of material breaks the stranglehold States have on the information available to the Court when deliberating on a matter, and provides the Court with an enhanced opportunity to thoroughly examine which rules of international law apply thus providing the Court with a greater opportunity to provide the correct advice to the requesting body, as well as providing the Court with the ability to explore and develop international law for future matters, arguably more so than if confined to the narrow confines of a dispute. For example, in the *Wall in Palestine Opinion* the Court, by being asked to consider the legal consequences of Israel's construction of the security fence, was able to examine what the right to self-determination actually means.[454]

The Court by providing legal advice to the requesting body refines and develops further the rules of international law adding clarity where needed which benefits the entire international community.

E. Contribution of the advisory jurisdiction

Some commentators, such as realists like Morgenthau and Carr, or neo-realists like Waltz, who question the ability of international law to influence States' behaviour, may be even more sceptical of the value of an Advisory Opinion that would appear to be less effective than a confirmed norm in resolving actual disputes, or even influencing States' behaviour at all.[455] However, even critics like Falk acknowledge that:

> In fact, both sides and the large number of participating parties seemed to believe that an advisory opinion in their favour could substantially

450. Czech Republic, France, Cyprus, China, Switzerland, Romania, Albania, Austria, Egypt, Germany, Slovakia, Russian Federation, Finland, Poland, Luxembourg, Libyan Arab Jamahiriya, United Kingdom, United States of America, Serbia, Spain, Islamic Republic of Iran, Estonia, Norway, Netherlands, Slovenia, Latvia, Japan, Brazil, Ireland, Denmark, Argentina, Azerbaijan, Maldives, Sierra Leone, Bolivia, and Venezuela.
451. *Kosovo Opinion* [2010] ICJ Rep 403, 408–09, [6]–[9].
452. Austria, Albania, Argentina, Azerbaijan, Belarus, Brazil, Bulgaria, Burundi, Cyprus, Croatia, Denmark, Finland, Federal Republic of Germany, France, Jordan, Norway, Romania, Russian Federation, Spain, Saudi Arabia, Serbia, the United Kingdom, the Netherlands, US, Venezuela, and Vietnam. *Kosovo Opinion* [2010] ICJ Rep 403, 409, [14].
453. Ibid.
454. Shaw, *International Law*, p. 249.
455. Two sceptics of the viability of the Advisory Jurisdiction's ability to contribute in highly political matters or disputes are: Aust, *Advisory Opinions*, p. 123 and Hambro, *The Authority of Advisory Opinions*, p. 21.

> influence future diplomacy despite the limitations discussed above with respect to authoritativeness and compliance.[456]

As will be seen below, the contribution the advisory jurisdiction makes to the resolution of disputes is in the refinement of norms of international law.[457]

1. Clarifying norms of international law

Previous Advisory Opinions have already clarified many important questions of international law,[458] including self-determination:[459]

> But the work of the Court in the field of self-determination and decolonization has not been merely the occasion for international law on other topics. It has been a positive source of that law itself. One can trace with fair completeness the lineaments of the modern law of external self-determination through decisions and dicta of the Court. And it is interesting to do so, if only as a corrective to the programmatic treatments that characterize much of the literature. Whether one likes the image of the law so presented is another question. But it is worthwhile to suspend belief in one or another set of formulae and to observe what the Court has said and done.[460]

For example, in the *Wall in Palestine Opinion* the Court stated:

> … the Court has already observed … in the *East Timor* case, it described as 'irreproachable' the assertion that 'the right of peoples to self-determination, as it evolved from the Charter and from the United Nations practice, has an *erga omnes* character.'[461]

Judicial statements such as these add more weight to comments made by commentators such as the *Special Rapporteur of the UN Sub-Commission on Prevention of Discrimination and Protection of Minorities*', H. Gros-Espiell, who also argued that self-determination has an *erga omnes* character.[462]

The *Western Sahara Opinion* also clarified that the *1960 Declaration on Granting Independence to Colonial Countries and Peoples* stated that there were

456. Falk, *The Kosovo Advisory Opinion*, p. 55.
457. Note Weller's opposition to this point: Weller, *Modesty can be a Virtue*, p. 132.
458. Gill, *Rosenne's The World Court*, p. 87. See for example: *Reparations Opinion* [1949] ICJ Rep 174; *Certain Expenses Opinion* [1962] ICJ Rep 151.
459. See *Namibia Opinion* [1971] ICJ Rep 16; *Western Sahara Opinion* [1975] ICJ Rep 12.
460. James Crawford, 'The General Assembly, the International Court and Self-Determination', Lowe and Fitzmaurice, *Fifty Years of the International Court of Justice*, p. 586.
461. *Wall in Palestine Opinion* [2004] ICJ Rep 136, [156].
462. See above Chapter 1.

three choices, for the freely exercised will of the people when claiming self-determination:

1. Emergence as a sovereign independent State.
2. Free association with an independent State.
3. Integration with an independent State.[463]

Many commentators, and even members of the Court itself criticised the approach taken by the Court in the *Kosovo Opinion*.[464] For example, His Excellency Judge Yusuf was particularly critical of the Court for missing an opportunity to refine the norms of international law regarding self-determination.[465]

> The Court had a unique opportunity to assess, in a specific and concrete situation, the legal conditions to be met for such a right of self-determination to materialize and give legitimacy to a claim of separation. It has unfortunately failed to seize this opportunity, which would have allowed it to clarify the scope and normative content of the right to external self-determination, in its post-colonial conception, and thus to contribute, *inter alia*, to the prevention of unjustified claims to independence which may lead to instability and conflict in various parts of the world.[466]

Whilst it is disappointing that the Court did not discuss remedial self-determination, with all due respect to His Excellency, the Court did make a number of significant contributions to the right of self-determination, and thus to the resolution of claims. Many commentators also believe so.[467]

463. *Western Sahara Opinion* [1975] ICJ Rep 12, 32.
464. Separate Opinion of His Excellency Judge Yusuf, *Kosovo Opinion* [2010] ICJ Rep 403, 624, [17]; Separate Opinion of His Excellency Judge Sepulveda-Amor, *Kosovo Opinion* [2010] ICJ Rep 403, 498–499, [33]–[35]; Declaration of His Excellency Judge Simma, *Kosovo Opinion*, [2010] ICJ Rep 403, [7]; Guiseppe Bianco 'And Nothing Else Matters. The ICJ's Judicial Restraint in its Opinion on Kosovo's Independence', 2(2) (2010) *Perspectives on Federalism*, p 34; Kohen and del Mar, *Kosovo A Declaration of Independence*, p. 120.
465. See His Excellency Judge Trindade, Separate Opinion, *Kosovo Opinion* [2010] ICJ Rep 403, 585, [162]–[163].
466. Separate Opinion of His Excellency Judge Yusuf, *Kosovo Opinion* [2010] ICJ Rep 403, 624–625, [17]. See also the Separate Opinion of His Excellency Judge Sepúlveda-Amor, *Kosovo Opinion* [2010] ICJ Rep 403, 499, [35].
467. Many commentators agree, for example: Weller, *Modesty can be a Virtue*, p. 127; Theodore Christakis and Oliver Corten, 'Symposium: the ICJ Advisory Opinion on the Unilateral Declaration of Independence of Kosovo, Editors' Introduction' (2011)24(1) *Leiden Journal of International Law*, p. 71; Vidmar, *The Kosovo Advisory Opinion Scriutinized*, p. 356 and Peters, *Lotus-Land of Freedom*, p. 108.

For example, Weller identified the following contribution made by the Court: (1) there is no prohibition of unilateral declaration of independence; (2) a State remains a matter of fact, unless its creation breaches a norm of *jus cogens*; (3) a State can be created through the constitutive will of either the State's individuals or elected representatives; (4) a peoples seeking self-determination must exhaust all alternatives to claiming statehood, and where negotiations with the parent State fail a people should then seek their independence through 'an international framework'.[468]

There are three particular contributions that are worth noting in detail. The first two relate to the normative content of self-determination and third relates to the resolution of claims.

Firstly, the Court in its discussion of the history of self-determination confirmed the use of alien and foreign subjugation as a defining characteristic of claimants:

> During the second half of the 20th century, the international law of self-determination developed in such a way as to create a right to independence for the peoples of non-self-governing territories *and peoples subject to alien subjugation, domination and exploration.* ... A great many new States have come into existence as a result of the exercise of this right (emphasis added).[469]

And later:

> Whether, outside the context of non-self-governing territories and peoples subject to alien subjugation, domination and exploitation, the international law of self-determination confers upon part of the population of an existing State a right to separate from that State is, however, a subject on which radically different views were expressed by those taking part in the proceedings and expressing a position on the question.[470]

The term 'and' is inclusive. Its use directly after reference to non-self-governing clearly identifies that peoples entitled to self-determination include or fall into two categories: (1) those that are non-self-governing; and (2) peoples that are subject to alien and foreign subjugation. This description clearly supports the argument in chapter I of this monograph that alien and foreign subjugation is a means by which either a people entitled to self-determination is defined, or more accurately how a legitimate claimant is described, and thus defined. Thus, the Court by clarifying who were legitimate claimants did make a contribution to assist in preventing 'unjustified claims'.[471]

468. Weller, *Modesty can be a Virtue*, p. 146.
469. *Kosovo Opinion* [2010] ICJ Rep 403, 436, [79].
470. Ibid, 438, [82].
471. Please refer to His Excellency Judge Yusuf's comments, see above n 466.

The second, and perhaps by far most important contribution made by the Court related to the norm of territorial integrity. In the *Western Sahara Opinion* His Excellency Judge Petren mentioned in his Separate Opinion that territorial integrity must be taken into account when considering self-determination in certain circumstances.[472] The certain circumstances needed further clarification because the desire to protect territorial integrity is one of the most powerful counter-arguments to an application for self-determination. Firstly, because the status of territorial integrity within international law and its importance to the maintenance of the security and stability of the international community are both unquestionable and well recognised in treaties,[473] as well as by States.[474] Secondly, a claim to statehood unavoidably threatens a State's territorial integrity simply because it involves a physical change in the State's international borders. This perception/position is clearly evident in the statement of Mr Vuk Jeremić, then Serbian Foreign Minister, introducing to the General Assembly a draft resolution to the General Assembly in the wake of the *Kosovo Advisory Opinion.* The Minister noted that 27 Member States of the European Union had co-sponsored the draft resolution, and stated: 'Some of them continue to respect the territorial integrity of Serbia, while others have recognized Kosovo's unilateral declaration of independence.'[475] Consequently, it could be argued that every claim for external self-determination must be illegal including even those by colonial peoples, because every claim would challenge the territorial integrity of the parent State.

Accordingly, the Court by holding that 'the scope of the principle of territorial integrity is confined to the sphere of relations between States' made a

472. *Western Sahara Opinion* [1975] ICJ Rep 12, 110.
473. See, eg, art 10 of the *Covenant of the League of Nations*; arts 2 (4) and 2 (7) of the *UN Charter.* Interestingly the League of Nations Assembly passed a resolution on 11 March 1932 declaring that it is incumbent on members to not recognize any 'situation etc' that breaches the *Covenant of the League of Nations* and the *Pact of Paris.* The Assembly later on 24 February 1933 subsequently approved a committee report that recommended non-recognition in these circumstances.
474. Dugard, *The South West Africa/Namibia Dispute*, pp. 35–38. Dugard refers to the example of 19 American Republics agreeing that they would not recognise any territorial acquisitions made during the Chaco War of 1932 between Bolivia and Paraguy. Also in 1933 the Saavedra Lamas Anti-War Treaty was signed by Latin American States. Article 2 stated that the signatories would not recognise territorial acquisition or reorganisation brought about by force or non-pacific means. Ultimately the actions of these States became the basis for the *Montevideo Convention on the Rights and Duties of States*, signed 26 December 1993, 135 LNTS 19 (entered into force 26 December 1934). Similarly the US refused to recognise the territorial annexations of Ethiopia, Czechoslovakia, Albania and Austria.
475. *'Request for an Advisory Opinion of the International Court of Justice on Whether the Unilateral Declaration of Independence of Kosovo is in Accordance with International Law'* Draft Resolution (A/64/L.65/Rev.1) UN Doc A/64/PV.120, 120th plenary sess, GA 64th session, (9 September 2010).

very bold and controversial finding.[476] Some commentators questioned the correctness of the Court's findings,[477] whilst other commentators questioned the wisdom in reaching this conclusion. Kohn and del Mar argued that the Court's findings jeopardised the ability of the UN to resolve future conflicts because the Court's conclusion effectively nullified and rendered meaningless any future Security Council 'guarantees' regarding territorial integrity, resulting in a State being less receptive to the UN attempting to resolve a dispute. Thus, they argued the ICJ's Advisory Opinion had actually made it more difficult for the UN to resolve claims to self-determination in the future.[478] More alarmingly Christakis argued that breaching the guarantee of Serbia's right to territorial integrity allowed Serbia: 'to defend its territorial integrity against separatism, in exactly the same way as any sovereign country in the world has the right to defend its territory against secession.'[479] This suggestion is alarming when it is remembered how Serbia and the former Yugoslavia defended its territorial integrity in the past, and in no way should the use of force, in particular the use of ethnic cleansing and other potential breaches of the *Genocide Convention*,[480] be encouraged.[481] Such suggestions do more to jeopardise the ability of the UN to resolve self-determination claims peacefully than the Court's conclusions about territorial integrity.[482] In fact the Court's Opinion ensures that territorial integrity cannot be used to excuse or camouflage a situation of oppression by a foreign and alien government to continue.

The Court has resolved one of the seemingly intractable issues at the heart of self-determination, namely its consistency with the norm of territorial integrity, and puts to rest the conundrum that has consistently plagued claims to self-determination. As noted by Dinah Shelton:

> From the breakup of the Austro-Hungarian and Ottoman Empires after World War I to the struggle of colonial territories for independence following World War II and the later dissolution of the former Yugoslavia, there has been an unavoidable conflict between the efforts of peoples to

476. *Kosovo Opinion* [2010] ICJ Rep 403, 437, [80].
477. Christakis argues that State practice opposes the Court's conclusion, whilst Vidmar argues that there is little proof within international instruments: Christakis, *The ICJ Advisory Opinion on Kosovo*, p. 84 & Vidmar, *Remedial Secession* pp 50–51; Vidmar, *The Kosovo Opinion Scrutinized.* pp. 368–71.
478. Kohen and del Mar, *Kosovo A Declaration of Independence*, p. 124.
479. Christakis, *The ICJ Advisory Opinion on Kosovo*, p. 85.
480. See *Case Concerning Application of the Convention on the Prevention and Punishment of the Crime of Genocide (Bosnia and Herzegovina v Serbia and Montenegro)* ICJ Rep (2007) 43, 237, [471(5)].
481. Leading to in the words of Peters: '... a potential *reconquista* of Kosovo with military means.' Peters, *Lotus-Land of Freedom*, p. 108.
482. Furthermore, the 'deal' was with the Security Council, not the ICJ, and as the Court has said many times the Court should not allow the political factors to interfere with its decisions: *Kosovo Opinion* [2010] ICJ Rep 403, 415, [27].

achieve independence and the demands of exiting states to preserve their territorial integrity.[483]

Thus the Court's findings are truly far-reaching because as Eduard Sharmazanov (spokesperson for the ruling Republican party of Armenia) recognised: 'That for the first time … an international court has stated that: '… a people's right to self-determination is more important than the territorial integrity of States.'[484] Putting Human Rights, specifically peoples' rights before the rights of States, has far-reaching consequences and implications for the international legal system that has been overwhelmingly dominated by States for so long.

In fact the entire *Kosovo Opinion* provides a glimpse of what these implications could be. In coming to the conclusion that there was no general prohibition in international law the Court responded to the argument presented during the Written and Oral proceedings that the Security Council had in the past condemned UDI's, for example in relation to Rhodesia, Northern Cyprus, and *Republika Sprska.*[485] In response the Court stated:

> The Court notes, however, that in all of those instances the Security Council was making a determination as regards the concrete situation existing at the time that those declarations of independence were made; the illegality attached to the declarations of independence thus stemmed not from the unilateral character of these declarations as such, but from the fact that they were, or would have been, connected with the unlawful use of force or other egregious violations of norms of general international law, in particular those of a peremptory character *(jus cogens).* In the context of Kosovo, the Security Council has never taken this position.[486]

The Court's conclusion is exactly the approach suggested in Chapter 2 of this monograph, namely that statehood should be denied when its creation involved a breach of international law, in particular a principle of *jus cogens.*[487] In fact the overall approach of using the Court to determine the legality of the UDI is consistent with the approach suggested by Raič, and also argued in Chapter 2 above: that the process of determining statehood is a two-step

483. Dinah Shelton, 'Self-Determination in Regional Human Rights Law: from Kosovo to Cameroon' (2011) 105 *(1) American Journal of International Law,* p. 61 citing Antonio Cassese, *Self-Determination of Peoples: a Legal Reappraisal* (1995).
484. Author unknown 'Armenia Hails Court Ruling on Kosovo Independence', *Radio Free Europe,* available at website: www.rferl.org/content/Armenia_Hails_Court_Ruling_On_Kosovo_Independence/2109757 26 July 1010 (accessed 28 April 2013).
485. *Kosovo Opinion* [2010] ICJ Rep 403, 437, [80]–[81].
486. Ibid, [81].
487. See Chapter 2 above.

process, which involves determining questions of fact and law. Other commentators acknowledged this approach taken by the Court, and its implications for self-determination.

> We thus consider that the position of the Court confirms that secession is not only a question of 'fact', but also a question of 'law' and that the traditional factual criteria for statehood can be and have been progressively complemented by some legal ones. The maxim ex injuria jus non oritur defines the external limits of acceptance of the principle of effectiveness. It is interesting to observe that the overwhelming majority of [S]tates participating in the proceedings, including many who pleaded in favour of Kosovo, accepted that in some cases, and especially in case of illegal use of force, secession is illegal.[488]

This suggests that recognition, long considered the domain of States, is subject to and can be determined by legal norms, specifically *jus cogens.* In sum the Court's findings are far-reaching,[489] and the Opinion has advanced the cause of self-determination, thereby removing one of the greatest obstacles and arguments used by States to deny self-determination. This is no little thing by any means.

However, future Requests could explore the concept of self-determination, and help refine and clarify its application even further. For example, clarifying what rights flow from a successful claim for self-determination, whether national sovereignty or relative shades of autonomy, or what factors should be considered, all could therefore avoid the zero-sum approach that both States and peoples claiming self-determination adopt-independence or not- and thus the Court may be able to find a solution that is favourable to both parties, such as autonomy, or additional protection of human rights.[490]

A future Advisory Opinion could clarify how the doctrine of *uti possidetis* interacts with the continued application of self-determination.[491] As mentioned in Chapter 1 above originally this was a principle of public international law that allowed belligerent parties to retain territory captured by force of arms, but was applied to the decolonisation process in Africa as a

488. Christakis, *The ICJ Advisory Opinion on Kosovo*, p. 82

489. Jure Vidmar, 'The *Kosovo* Opinion and General International Law: How Far-Reaching and Controversial is the ICJ's Reasoning?' p. 2, available at the Hague Justice Portal: www.haguejusticeportal.net/index.php?id=12110 (accessed 6 June 2013).

490. As outlined by the ICJ *Western Sahara Opinion* [1975] ICJ Rep 12 there are three choices, for the freely exercised will of the people: (1) emergence of as a sovereign independent State; (2) free association with an independent State; or (3) integration with an independent State.

491. 'As you possess shall you continue to possess'.

means to avoid chaos and violence. The ICJ in the *Burkina Faso-Republic of Mali Case* described the purpose of the concept in these terms:

> It is a general principle, which is logically connected with the phenomenon of the obtaining of independence, wherever it occurs. Its obvious purpose is to prevent the independence and stability of new states being endangered by fratricidal struggles provoked by the challenging of frontiers following the withdrawal of the administering power.[492]

The Court's judgement was supported by the Badinter Arbitration Committee, which in answer to the question of whether the Serbian people in Bosnia-Herzegovina had the right to self-determination, stated that:

> ...whatever the circumstances, the right to self-determination must not involve changes to existing frontiers at the time of independence (*uti possidetis juris*) except where the states concerned agree otherwise.[493]

Thus a future Advisory Opinion could clarify whether the rule of *uti possidetis*, as suggested by the Badinter Committee above, must always be applied, even where to do so could endanger international peace and security.[494] The Badinter Committee's findings would appear to contradict the purpose of *uti possidetis* as explained by the ICJ in the *Frontier Dispute*, which is to prevent further conflict and to restore a measure of stability in difficult and potentially volatile situations.[495] Furthermore, applying *uti possidetis* raises the question: '...should pre-colonial states or empires be rebuilt?'[496] Some would argue not since there is a need to restore pre-colonial frontiers in order to overturn '...the results of an illegal occupation and annexation'.[497] It should be remembered that the peoples within these borders did not

492. *Frontier Dispute (Burkina Faso-Republic of Mali)* [1986] ICJ Rep 554, 565.
493. *Opinion No 2 and No 3 of the Arbitration Commission*, EC Conference on Yugoslavia, January 11 1992, 92 ILR 167–70 ('*Badinter Commission*'); Harris, *Cases and Materials on International Law*, pp. 120–1, 126; Jochen A Frowein, 'Self-Determination as a Limit to Obligations under International Law,' in Christian Tomuschat, *Modern Law of Self-Determination*, The Hague: Kluwer Academic Publishers incorporating Martinus Nijhoff Publishers, p. 216. Frowein has criticised the Committee's application of the principle because it lacked 'any underlying justification'.
494. Such as the conflicts involving former republics of the USSR, Armenia, Georgia and Azerbaijan when gained their independence from their 'colonial' masters in Moscow. Brian Taylor Summer, 'Territorial Disputes at the International Court of Justice' [2004] 53 *Duke Law Journal*, p. 1810.
495. *Frontier Dispute Case* [1986] ICJ Rep 554, 551.
496. Rigo Andreas Sureda, *The Evolution of the Right of Self-Determination, A Study of United Nations Practice*, Leiden: A. W. Sijthoff, 1973, p. 218.
497. Marija Batistich, 'The Right to Self-Determination and International Law' (1992–1995), 7 *Auckland University Law Review*, pp. 1029–1030; Summer, *Territorial Disputes*, p. 1810.

have an opportunity to participate in the establishment of such borders.[498] So maintaining existing borders rather than protecting territorial integrity may actually inflame old frustrations. Leaving such issues unresolved could seriously jeopardise the stability of the international community.[499] The ICJ has had much experience handling border or territorial disputes, which included applications of *uti possidetis*, and thus would be well placed to address these concerns, however, it depends on how the Request is worded.[500]

One point the *Kosovo Opinion* confirms that the potential benefit of an Advisory Opinion depends very much on how the Request is actually worded. A Request by the Decolonisation Committee or the General Assembly would not have to be specific to advance the development of self-determination. A specific request such as: 'Are the Chechens entitled to independence?' or 'Are the West Papuans a people entitled to claim self-determination?' may attract the same sort of opposition found in a contentious matter.[501] Alternatively, a Request could also be made to determine whether a people could be awarded Observer Status at the UN, which may not appear as confrontational to a State, as the above questions may be, and may be a way of involving the people in the international community whilst still remaining a non-State entity, and paving the way for an eventual and gradual acceptance of the people's claim to statehood. Whilst general questions or abstract questions may pose difficulties for the Court, given their lack of a factual context, the Court may actually prefer them to a question that derived from a current dispute.

Unlike common law legal systems the ICJ is not bound by its own decisions in either its contentious or its advisory jurisdictions. However, the accumulation of a body of knowledge may make future applications before the ICJ unnecessary. It may also assist other peoples and their central governments to resolve the matter peacefully and in the best interests of both parties.[502]

498. Howard P. Willens & Deanne C. Siemer, *National Security and Self-Determination, United States Policy in Micronesia (1961–1972)*, London: Praeger, 2000, p. 2.
499. Examples would include the conflicts areas of the former USSR, such as in Georgia and Armenia. See Summer, *Territorial Disputes* p. 1791.
500. For example, *Sovereignty over Certain Frontier Land (Belgium v Netherlands)* ICJ Rep [1959] 209; *Minquiers and Ecrehos Case (France v Great Britain)* ICJ Rep [1953] 47; *Land and Maritime Boundary between Cameroon and Nigeria (Cameroon v Nigeria; Equatorial Guinea Intervening)* ICJ Rep [2002] 303; *Frontier Dispute (Burkino Faso v Niger)*(16 April 2013) Available at the ICJ's website: http://www.icj-cij.org/docket/files/149/17306.pdf (accessed 23 June 2013); Summer, *Territorial Disputes*, pp. 1804–1812.
501. Unless a Request focused on a more benign claim for self-determination, such as the Quebecois' claim.
502. Pratap, *The Advisory Jurisdiction*, pp. 256–59.

2. Developing norms of international law

In spite of the arguments raised by these commentators norms of international law do matter, and do influence States' behaviour.[503] As noted by Hurrell the weaknesses of international law do not mean '... that the normative aspirations of international law do not matter.'[504] The fact that murder is committed in a domestic legal system does not render the entire legal system to be unimportant or non-existent, or more importantly support the argument that people are not influenced by the existence of a norm prohibiting murder.[505] For example, Hurrell states: 'It is impossible to think seriously about international relations today without reference to norms prohibiting the aggressive use of force or proscribing genocide, or up-holding self-determination and human rights.'[506]

Norms matter because they create a structure for States' interaction.[507] As noted by Watts the only alternative to the rule of law is anarchy and chaos[508] and, in a world full of supposedly absolute and equal sovereign States – that by the definition of national sovereignty acknowledge no higher authority than their own – chaos is not too far away.[509] Thus States themselves recognise

503. It is the extent of influence that international norms have, rather than whether such influence exists, that is at the core of the debate of how effectual international norms are. This argument is essentially constructivist in nature. Christian Rues-Smit, 'Constructivism' in Scott Burchill et al. (eds), *Theories of International Relations* (2nd ed) New York: Palgrave 2001, p. 209 and Scott Burchill, 'Realism and Neo-Realism' in Burchill et al. *Theories of International Relations*, pp. 92–99.
504. Andrew Hurrell, 'Conclusion, International Law and the Changing Constitution of International Society' in Michael Byers (ed), *The Role of Law in International Politics*, Oxford: Oxford University Press Oxford, p. 335.
505. Sir Arthur Watts, 'The Importance of International Law' in Byers, *The Role of Law in International Politics*, p. 9.
506. Hurrell, *Changing Constitution of International Society*, p. 335; Watts, *The Importance of International Law*, p. 7.
507. Thus norms regulating inter-State commerce appear to be more readily acceptable, and entities such as the WTO more successful in obtaining compliance than other norms of international law, even with States like the US who has been accused of flouting international law when it does not suit their perceived national interests. Philippe Sands, *Lawless World, America and the Making and Breaking of Global Rules* London; Penguin Books, 2005, p. 237; Anthony Anghie, 'International Financial Institutions' in Christian Reus-Smit (ed), *The Politics of International Law*, Cambridge: Cambridge University Press p. 228; Watts, *The Importance of International Law*, p. 7.
508. Watts, *The Importance of International Law*, p. 7.
509. In 1576, Jean Bodin wrote in his famous work, *Six Books of the Commonwealth* that '[s]overeignty is the absolute and perpetual power of a Commonwealth' and, further, that sovereignty meant 'the most high, absolute, and perpetual power over the citizens and subjects in a commonwealth': as contained in Franklin (ed), *On Sovereignty: Four Chapters from the Six Books of the Commonwealth* (Cambridge: Cambridge University Press, 1992, pp. 1–4; Jarat Chopra, 'The Obsolescence of Intervention under International Law' in Marianne Heiberg, (ed.), *Subduing Sovereignty and the Right to Intervene*, London: Pinter Publishers, 1984, p. 41.

that is in the self-interest of all States that a structure imposed by the rule of law, as opposed to the rule of power and might, provides a greater opportunity for States to prosper and grow.[510] By enabling the ICJ to retain both a contentious and an advisory jurisdiction the UN's founding fathers clearly acknowledged the important role played by international law in maintaining international peace and security.[511] Acknowledging the importance of States' behaviour in the development of customary norms of international law is not an acknowledgement that States' behaviour as a superior means of creating international law.

As noted by Roth, what is more important is that the right type of behaviour becomes accepted as customary:

> Yet, as we have seen ... the establishment of a meaningful international law of peace and security requires a collective denial of recognition of the fruits of illegal acts; otherwise, violations of international law are permitted to create rights in international law. If such an eventuality were to be allowed, the resulting loss of integrity of the international system would erode any influence international law may have on the behaviour of international actors, since one finds no benefit in respecting the system's demands when others are rewarded for defying them.[512]

Development of international law by the ICJ has an important advantage over norms created by States: impartiality. Whilst States through their practice, through treaties and arguably through the political organs of the UN, make a significant and large contribution to the development of norms of international law, their contribution is always subject to political influence and the pursuit of national self-interest. States will interpret custom to conveniently suit their own agendas, for example, as the US did in the *Nicaragua Case* arguing that the customary rules of international law relating to self-defence had been 'subsumed' and replaced by art 51 of the *UN Charter*.[513] In relation to treaties, even multi-lateral treaties can reflect the desires of States to protect and maintain their position and influence. One important example is the much criticised veto power of the permanent members of the Security Council.[514] In comparison the ICJ has no interests to protect other than the

510. *The Importance of International Law*, p. 7
511. Pratap, *The Advisory Jurisdiction*, p. 26–39; Pomerance, *The Advisory Function*, p. 26, 43–44. Amr, *The Role of the International Court of Justice*, pp. 50–51, note 14.
512. Brad R. Roth, *Governmental Illegitimacy in International Law*, Oxford: Claredon Press, 1999, p. 125.
513. This argument was rejected by the Court: *Military and Paramilitary Activities in and against Nicaragua (Nicaragua v United States of America) (Merits)* [1986] ICJ Rep 14; 94–95.
514. Paul Kennedy, *The Parliament of Man, the United Nations and the Quest for World Government*, (2006), pp. 51–59.

maintenance of international peace and security, and impartiality is crucial to retain the trust of the international community, so that States will continue to bring their disputes before the Court. As one commentator Otto Kimminich, also noted: 'We cannot leave it to the State concerned to decide whether a group entitled to self-determination may be granted its own sovereign entity or not.'[515] Impartiality is particularly important if norms of international law, like self-determination, will be developed in a manner consistent with the common interest of the entire international community, rather than a single member. This ensures greater acceptance and potential compliance with the norm by all States.[516] It is in the area of redefining international law that the advisory jurisdiction reveals its true potential to resolve disputes peacefully, which is perhaps the purpose of international law,[517] and in the best interests of both parties.[518]

F. Conclusion

The purpose of this chapter was to examine the feasibility of using the ICJ's advisory jurisdiction to resolve self-determination claims or disputes. After an examination of the procedure and purpose of the advisory jurisdiction as well as existing Opinions, *Namibia Opinion*; the *Western Sahara Opinion*; the *Wall in Palestine Opinion*; and the *Kosovo Opinion*, the answer to this question is 'yes'. It could provide an Opinion regarding whether the claimants are legitimate, and thus assist the UN in finding the balance between rightful cases of self-determination and illegal claims. Also what could be more appropriate than to have the ICJ, the UN's principal judicial organ, in its role as a legal advisor, advise the General Assembly whether a new member, that is a colonised people, be recognised as a new State, and admitted to the UN? Any action taken, such as the holding of a referendum or even a retrospective recognition of statehood, would be strengthened immeasurably by a supportive Advisory Opinion.

Abstract questions, political matters, and actual disputes do not prevent the Court from providing an Opinion. In fact there are very few situations that provide sufficiently compelling reasons for the Court to refuse to comply with the Request. And despite the advisory and non-binding nature of

515. Otto Kimminich, 'A "Federal" Right of Self-Determination?' Christian Tomuschat, *Modern Law of Self-Determination*, The Hague: Kluwer Academic Publishers incorporating Martinus Nijhoff Publishers, p. 96.
516. Lung-chu Chen, *An Introduction to Contemporary International Law: A Policy-Orientated Approach*, New Haven: Yale University Press 1989, p. 3.
517. Watts, *The Importance of International Law*, p. 7.
518. Both the PCIJ, and the ICJ have followed previous decisions, including their advisory opinions. The ICJ has even quoted the decisions and the opinions of the PCIJ in matters appearing before it. Thus the concept does apply to a limited extent to international law. Pratap, *The Advisory Jurisdiction*, pp. 256–59.

Advisory Opinions, States they consider advisory proceedings to be of great import, and are not to be 'belittled', this: '... testifies to the importance the leadership of many States attributes to the advisory opinion process.'[519]

However, there is a slight caveat attached to this answer.

The examination of the *Namibia Opinion*; the *Western Sahara Opinion*; the *Wall in Palestine Opinion*; and the *Kosovo Opinion* revealed that the advisory jurisdiction's greatest contribution to the resolution of self-determination claims lay in its ability to refine international legal principles. As noted by commentators the advisory jurisdiction is well suited for this type of task.[520] Falk in particular stated : '... an advisory proceeding enables an international law question on very sensitive issues to be put before the ICJ in face of the strenuous objections of concerned states, even leading states.'[521] And by providing guidance to the relevant requesting body, the Court also provides guidance for the entire international community. This clearly assists in the maintenance of international peace and security and hopefully enables future disputes to be peacefully resolved. The benefit that such clarifications of international law bring to the international community cannot be under estimated, and also for the parties. The recommendations or clarifications could be helpful to assist other forms of dispute resolution, arbitrators in subsequent arbitration proceedings,[522] or mediators, where the parties reach some sort of power-sharing arrangements, or deferred independence, and practical matters such as holding referendums or access to natural resources.[523]

However, and this is the caveat, these benefits are more long-term in nature. Again as noted by Falk:

> ... an advisory opinion can also help shape wider public attitudes that over time may exert pressure on governments to act in accordance with

519. As evidenced by how many States participated in *The Kosovo Opinion*, and secondly as Falk notes because States were represented by some of the world's best and influential jurists (e.g. James Crawford). Falk, *The Kosovo Advisory Opinion*, p. 52.
520. Pratap, *The Advisory Jurisdiction*, p. 270.
521. Falk, *The Kosovo Advisory Opinion*, p. 53.
522. Such as the agreement between Sudan and South Sudan: 'The Government of Sudan/ The Sudan People's Liberation Movement/Army (Abyei Arbitration)' available at the Permanent Court of Arbitration's website: www.pca-cpa.org/showpasge.asp?pag_id=1306 (accessed 23 June 2013); Markus Bockenforde, 'The Abyei Award: Fitting a Diplomatic Square Peg into a Legal Round Hole' (2010) 23 *Leiden Journal of International Law*, 555; Elizabeth Ward, 'Abyei: An Examination of the Effectiveness of Arbitration for African Land Disputes' available at moritzlaw.osuedu/epub/mayhew-hite/wp-content/ uploads/012/03/student-spotlight-march-2012.pdf, (accessed 25 June 2013).
523. There are many detailed and diverse options that are too complex to discuss in detail here. However, please refer to the various options and examples in: Marc Weller & Barbara Metzger, (eds), *Settling Self-Determination Disputes, Complex Power-Sharing in Theory and Practice*, The Hague: Martinus Nijhoff Publishers, 2008 & Marc Weller, *Escaping the Self-Determination Trap*, Leiden: Martinus Nijhoff Publishers, 2008.

a legal mandate contained in its findings, and perhaps eventually generate respect and confidence.[524]

Sadly, whilst Kosovo appears to be moving forward towards independence, aided by the *Kosovo Opinion*, Israel continues with the construction of the wall and its conflict with Palestine also continues, and the peoples of Western Sahara are still waiting to achieve self-determination, prompting some to argue that this renders the advisory jurisdiction to be ineffectual and consequently inappropriate for the resolution of disputes, particularly those of a highly political matter.[525] This rather gloomy caveat suggests that the Court should not deal with a dispute in which highly political issues are predominant.[526] This will be examined in the following chapter.

524. Ibid, p. 54.
525. Howse Robert and Teitel Ruti, 'Delphic Dicum: How has the ICJ Contributed to the Global Rule of Law by its Ruling on Kosovo?' (2010) 11 *German Law Journal*, p. 845.
526. The issue of the wall, as well as the emergence of a new State, is a highly political matter. T Sugihara, 'The Judicial Function of the International Court of Justice with respect to Disputes involving Highly Political Issues', in AS Muller et al (eds), *The International Court of Justice*, The Hague: Kluwer Law International incorporating Martinus-Nijhoff Publishers, the Hague, 1997, p. 118.

4 The International Court of Justice and highly political matters[1]

'...the plain fact [is] that nations no less than men are ruled by law and are so ruled at all times.'[2]

A. Introduction

Whilst the right to self-determination is a fundamental principle of international law, there is no denying that its application takes place within a highly charged political background. After all, the inability to maintain order and control over its territory must be one of the greatest fears for the central government of any State. Allowing a province or area to become independent raises the obvious question of 'who else?' exaggerating fears of widespread fragmentation, with all the inherent violence and suffering such anarchy is associated with.[3] It may also mean the loss of a province that is extremely valuable, in either strategic or economic terms or even the mere loss of sovereign pride.[4] Thus the response of a central government, to deny and repress independence movements is predictable and perhaps understandable.[5] Where political and diplomatic solutions are denied to peoples seeking independence, then often the only option perceived to be available by such peoples is to seek their independence through violence, thus leading to a civil war.[6]

1. A previous version of this chapter was published as 'The International Court of Justice and Highly Political Matters' (2003) 4 *Melbourne Journal of International Law* p. 29.
2. Professor Clive Perry in his criticisms of Sir Edward Grey, the British Foreign Minister between 1905–1916 as cited in Eugene Rostow, 'Disputes Involving the Inherent Right of Self-Defense' in Lori Damrosch (ed), *The International Court of Justice at A Crossroads* New York: Transnational Publishers, Inc, 1987, p. 267.
3. Such a perception is not as exaggerated or unwarranted as it would appear, when the events that occurred in the break-up of the former USSR are considered.
4. For example, West Papua in Indonesia.
5. Even if their actions are not acceptable.
6. It must be remembered that both sides are capable of committing crimes against humanity. For example, Muslim separatists in the Philippines have kidnapped western tourists and then held them for ransom.

Traditionally, domestic or national courts in western legal systems have considered themselves to be inappropriate for resolving highly political issues. This judicial reticence is based on the separation of powers theory advanced by the French political theorist Baron de Montesquieu, but also exists for pragmatic reasons.[7] At the international level, even members of the Court itself have often expressed concerns about the ICJ's ability to participate and to make a valid contribution to the resolution of highly political issues.[8] For example, Helmut Steinberger, the Vice-President of the OSCE Court of Conciliation and Arbitration noted that:

> Experienced observers of international relations are right when they consistently note that the function of international law and of international jurisdiction in the area of the peaceful settlement of highly political disputes, and in particular of disputes containing a threat to peace or international security, is of necessity quite limited.[9]

As Mohamed Shahabuddeen, a former judge of the ICJ, has said, '[t]o be sure, judicial process alone cannot banish war'.[10] This raises the important

7. Takane Sugihara, 'The Judicial Function of the International Court of Justice' in A S Muller, D Rai and J M Thuránszky (eds), *The International Court of Justice: Its Future Role after Fifty Years*, The Hague: Kluwer Law International incorporating Martinus-Nijhoff Publishers, 1997, p. 130 and Edward McWhinney, *Judicial Settlement of International Disputes: Jurisdiction, Justiciability and Judicial Law-Making on the Contemporary International Court* M. Nijhoff Dordrecht: Sold and distributed in the U.S.A. and Canada by Kluwer Academic Publishers, 1991 pp. 40–3. McWhinney rejects the argument that this applies equally to the international legal system by identifying an important distinction between the international community and domestic systems. In domestic systems, the legal source of the power of the respective institutions of governance – the legislature, the judiciary and the executive – are all contained in the one constitution, whereas in the international system, the International Court of Justice has its own 'autonomous constitutional basis'; its own statute distinct from the *UN Charter*.
8. See, eg, *Military and Paramilitary Activities in and against Nicaragua (Nicaragua v United States of America) (Merits)* [1986] ICJ Rep 14, p. 168 (Separate Opinion of Judge Lachs) ('*Nicaragua Case*'), where Judge Lachs stated that not all disputes are suitable for judicial solution.
9. Helmut Steinberger, 'The International Court of Justice' in Max Planck Institute for Comparative Public Law and International Law, *Judicial Settlement of Disputes: International Court of Justice, Other Courts and Tribunals, Arbitration and Conciliation – An International Symposium*, New York: Springer Verlag, 1974. pp. 207, 209.
10. Judge Mohamed Shahabuddeen, 'The World Court at the Turn of the Century', in Muller, Rai and Thuránszky, *Role after Fifty Years*, p. 18. At the ICJ/UNITAR Colloquium to celebrate the 50th anniversary of the ICJ, Professor Weil in reply to a paper given by Sir Robert Jennings, stated that some conflicts could not be resolved by the ICJ: Professor Prosper Weil in 'General Discussion Chaired by Judge Carl Fleischhauer' in Connie Peck and Roy Lee (eds), *Increasing the Effectiveness of the International Court of Justice: Proceedings of*

question of 'whether the Court, as a court of justice, has a limitation on its judicial function, and is legally prevented from dealing with a dispute in which highly political issues are predominant.'[11]

It is the purpose of this chapter to examine this question and determine whether the Court is able to make a contribution to the resolution of highly political disputes – that is, those disputes where the national interests or perceived national interests of States are threatened. It is argued here that criticisms of the ICJ's role are really criticisms of the nature of the international legal system rather than of the Court itself and that, in reality, the Court can and does make a significant contribution to the peaceful resolution of highly political disputes.[12]

B. International disputes

International disputes arise basically from the discordant or competing 'national interests' of States as they play what Kipling termed the 'Great Game'.[13] Whilst debate and controversy continue regarding increasing globalisation and the creation of supra-national entities such as the European Union, the fact remains that the international community is comprised of political communities called 'States' that consider themselves to be independent sovereigns. In accordance with theories of national sovereignty, these independent sovereigns are reluctant to admit, and indeed on occasion even deny, where it suits their interests, the existence of a higher political authority.[14] Thus, in a world of 'competing sovereignties', the protection of real and perceived vital national interests becomes

the ICJ/UNITAR Colloquium to Celebrate the 50th Anniversary of the Court The Hague: Kluwer Law International incorporating Martinus-Nijhoff Publishers, 1997, pp. 93–94. See also Jennings' more detailed discussion in Sir Robert Jennings, 'The Proper Work and Purposes of the International Court of Justice' in Muller, Rai and Thuránszky, *The International Court of Justice: Its Future Role* p. 45, in particular his mention of the US Supreme Court decision in *Dred Scott v Sandford*, 60 US (19 Howard) 393 (1857), and the claim that it failed to prevent the American Civil War.

11. Sugihara, *Judicial Function*, pp. 118–19.
12. An earlier attempt to measure the effectiveness of the ICJ in resolving international disputes was by Susan Tiefenbrun, 'The Role of the World Court in Settling International Disputes: A Recent Assessment' (1997) 20 *Loyola of Los Angeles International and Comparative Law Journal*, p. 1.
13. The reference is to Kipling's great work 'Kim', set in India, with its tale of intrigue and adventure as the empires of Russia and England played the 'Great Game': Rudyard Kipling, *Kim* (1901).
14. In view of the historical development of national sovereignty and the interaction between supposedly absolute sovereigns, it is not surprising that a State's government acts primarily in its own 'self-interest'. However, the pursuit of national interests is one reason given for arguing that the ICJ is prevented from hearing highly political disputes: see, eg, Edward McWhinney, *Judicial Settlement*, p. 39.

a higher priority for national governments than strict adherence to international law.[15]

The desire of States to protect their national interests means that all international disputes will, therefore, be 'political' in nature – what changes is merely the degree of political volatility.[16] Just how 'political' a dispute will be is extremely subjective and is dependent upon a matrix of diverse factors that affect the national interest, such as external economic pressures, domestic needs, and even national pride and prestige.[17] The willingness of the parties to allow a third party to resolve the dispute is also affected by the 'political' nature of the matter. The more vital the outcome of the dispute, the less prepared States will be to devolve control of its resolution to an independent body.[18]

Thus, many authors would question the Court's suitability, and indeed ability, to comprehend and consider highly political matters or 'non-justiciable issues'.[19] For example, Sir Robert Jennings (himself a judge of the ICJ for many years) provides the example of the weapons embargo put in place by the Security Council during the conflict in Bosnia-Herzegovina.[20] He argues that if the Court were faced with the question of whether such an embargo was a denial of the Yugoslavian right to self-defence, a legal right contained in art 51 of the *UN Charter*, then this would involve the Court passing judgment on UN policy.[21] Such a judgment would be inappropriate, he argues,

15. In the words of Anand, the international community is a 'jungle world': R P Anand, 'Role of International Adjudication' in Leo Goss (ed), *The Future of the International Court of Justice*, New York: Oceana Publications, 1976 vol 1, p. 1.
16. Gerry Simpson, 'Judging the East Timor Dispute: Self-Determination at the International Court of Justice' (1994) 17 *Hastings International and Comparative Law Review*, p. 330 uses the expression 'contentious political disputes' to describe clashes between vital national interests that involve deep ideological rifts.
17. A good example of the interplay of these factors is the background surrounding the *Nicaragua Case* [1986] ICJ Rep 14, which is discussed in further detail below.
18. States prefer a 'political' solution, because of their belief that they will be able to influence the outcome in their favour.
19. McWhinney, *Judicial Settlement*, p. 41; Sugihara, *Judicial Function*, pp. 117–18, 137; Simpson, *Judging the East Timor Dispute*, p. 330. See also Sir Robert Jennings who, in a paper presented to the ICJ/UNITAR Colloquium, stated that 'the judgments of the Court are binding in law, but do they, in fact, resolve the matter?': Sir Robert Jennings, 'Presentation by Sir Robert Jennings' in Connie Peck and Roy Lee (eds), *Increasing the Effectiveness of the International Court of Justice: Proceedings of the ICJ/UNITAR Colloquium to Celebrate the 50th Anniversary of the Court* The Hague: Kluwer Law International incorporating Martinus-Nijhoff Publishers, 1997, p. 81.
20. *Socialist Federal Republic of Yugoslavia*, SC Res 713, UN SCOR, 46th sess, 3009th mtg, art 6, UN Doc S/RES/713 (25 September 1991).
21. In Application of the Convention on the Prevention and Punishment of the Crime of Genocide (Bosnia-Herzegovina v Yugoslavia) (Provisional Measures) [1993] ICJ Rep 325, 443 (Separate Opinion of Judge Lauterpacht), Judge Lauterpacht mentioned this very issue. His Honour discussed whether Security Council Resolution 713, which implemented the arms embargo in the conflict in Bosnia-Herzegovina, contradicted a principle of jus cogens.

since the Court, as a court of law, could not understand or attach the same degree of importance to such issues as the overriding need to contain violence and the fear of escalation of violence in the delicate balance of affairs in the Balkans powder keg.[22] He goes further and asserts that in such a situation the Court may actually worsen a highly political dispute.[23]

States have realised that there are advantages to a third party adjudicating their disputes. This recognition led to the adoption of the 1899 and 1907 *Hague Conventions for the Pacific Settlement of International Disputes*[24] and compulsory arbitration as a means of avoiding armed conflict. States, however, still desired to retain as much control as they could, and so developed the concept of 'political disputes' or 'matters' as an exception to compulsory arbitration, and thus also a distinction between legal and political questions.[25] Although arbitration as a means of conflict avoidance has declined since the end of the Second World War, the distinction between political and legal disputes or questions can still be found in the draft *Convention on Conciliation and Arbitration* within the Conference on Security and Cooperation in Europe,[26] and also in the *UN Charter* and the *ICJ Statute*.[27]

Article 36 of the *ICJ Statute* restricts the jurisdiction of the Court to legal questions, thus begging the question: what is a 'legal dispute'? There have been attempts to distinguish a legal or 'justiciable' dispute from a political or 'non-justiciable' one, but it is difficult, if not impossible, to do so.[28] Several

22. Jennings, *The Proper Work*, p. 40.
23. What Jennings believes would be necessary is 'clever "management"' of the situation: Jennings, '*Presentation by Sir Robert Jennings*', p. 78. See also Jerzy Sztucki, 'International Organizations as Parties to Contentious Proceedings before the International Court of Justice?' in Muller, Rai and Thuránszky, *The International Court of Justice: Its Future Role* pp. 155–56.
24. *Hague Convention for the Pacific Settlement of International Disputes*, opened for signature 29 July 1899, [1901] ATS 130 (entered into force 29 July 1899); *Hague Convention for the Pacific Settlement of International Disputes*, opened for signature 18 October 1907, [1997] ATS 6 (entered into force 18 October 1908).
25. See, eg, the *Arbitration Agreement Between Great Britain and France*, opened for signature 14 October 1903, 194 ConTS 194, art 1 (entered into force 14 October 1903) which stated that only matters of a 'legal nature', eg those relating to the interpretation of a treaty, should be referred to arbitration. Those disputes that were vital to the respective parties national interest were exempt. Other examples containing the distinction between legal and political disputes include the *Arbitration Convention*, opened for signature 16 October 1925, 54 LNTS 303 (entered into force 14 September 1926) and the *General Act of Arbitration (Pacific Settlement of International Disputes)*, League of Nations Doc 2123 (1929). See also Vera Gowlland-Debbas, 'The Relationship Between the International Court of Justice and the Security Council in Light of the *Lockerbie Case*' (1994) 88 *American Journal of International Law*, pp. 649–50.
26. Conference for Security and Cooperation in Europe, *Final Act of the Conference on Security and Cooperation in Europe* (1975) <http://www.osce.org/docs/english/1990-1999/summits/helfa75e.htm> at 23 April 2003.
27. Gowlland-Debbas, *The International Court of Justice and the Security Council*, pp. 649–50.
28. Edward McWhinney, *Judicial Settlement*, pp. 40–46.

leading authors reject an absolutist position that basically defines international disputes as either entirely legal or political (that, they are mutually exclusive).[29] As Jennings notes, for all practical purposes all serious international disputes retain both political and legal elements.[30]

So is it possible to reduce, or to refine, a political dispute into questions of facts and law; 'justiciable issues' that courts and judges have been trained to face and resolve?[31] Many authors would agree with Jennings that in an international dispute a mixture of law and politics is unavoidable, and would also be sceptical of any claims to an ability to distinguish between political and legal questions within a dispute.[32]

This argument was used by the US Government to justify its withdrawal from any further involvement in the *Nicaragua Case*.[33] The US Government stated that the conflict was not a 'narrow legal dispute' suitable for resolution by the ICJ and that '[t]he International Court of Justice was never intended to resolve issues of collective security and self-defence and is patently unsuited for such a role.'[34] Further, due to the nature of international disputes, there were certain areas, described as political/legal 'No-Man's Lands' where it was too dangerous for an international institution and the Court to venture.[35] This was so for a number of reasons including that, 'with public passions running too high' there is the danger that the individual judges

29. Such as that adopted by Westlake as cited by Jennings, *The Proper Work*, p. 43.
30. Ibid. See also *Nicaragua Case* [1986] ICJ Rep 14, 168 (Separate Opinion of Judge Lachs) and Shaw where he stated: 'Politics is much closer to the heart of the [international] system than is perceived within national legal orders, and power much more in evidence. The interplay of law and politics in world affairs is much more complex and difficult to unravel ...' Malcom N Shaw, *International Law*, (5th ed) Cambridge: Cambridge University Press, 2003, p. 12.
31. Jennings, *The Proper Work*, p. 33.
32. See McWhinney's discussion of Professor Mosler who, as an ad hoc judge in *North Sea Continental Shelf (Federal Republic of Germany/Denmark; Federal Republic of Germany/Netherlands) (Merits)* [1969] ICJ Rep 3, believed that it was impossible to draw a distinction between legal and political disputes: McWhinney, *Judicial Settlement*, pp. 40–3.
33. McWhinney, *Judicial Settlement*, p. 39. It was also used by critics, mainly from the US, and including Eugene Rostow, of the Court's decision. See also the discussion of the *Nicaragua Case* in 'The World Court' (1986) *American Society of International Law: Proceedings of the 80th Annual Meeting*, pp. 201–21; Ibrahim Wani, 'The Future of Compulsory Jurisdiction: Rethinking the Political Question Doctrine After *Iran* and *Nicaragua*' (1986) *American Society of International Law: Proceedings of the 80th Annual Meeting*, pp. 468–69; and the series of articles in Harold Maier (ed), 'Appraisals of the ICJ's Decision: *Nicaragua v United States (Merits)*' (1987) 81 *American Journal of International Law*, p. 77.
34. The US Government statement attached to their formal withdrawal of January 1985: 'Statement of Department of State on US Withdrawal from Nicaragua Proceedings, 18 January 1985', 24 (1985) *International Legal Materials*, p. 264; McWhinney, *Judicial Settlement*, pp. 38–39.
35. McWhinney, *Judicial Settlement*, p. 39.

would be unable to resist becoming embroiled in the political aspects and controversies of the dispute.[36]

However, the attitude of the Court to this perceived problem was clearly stated in the *Legality of the Threat or Use of Nuclear Weapons (Advisory Opinion)*:[37]

> once the Assembly has asked, by adopting a resolution, for an advisory opinion on a legal question, the Court, in determining whether there are any compelling reasons for it to refuse to give such an opinion, will not have regard to the origins or to the political history of the request, or to the distribution of votes in respect of the adopted resolution.[38]

One very pragmatic attempt taken by Professor Mosler involves clarifying whether the Court is able, through the existing state of the law, to actually resolve the issue.[39] Other commentators, such as Kelsen, would agree with such a definition:

> The legal or political character of the dispute does not depend, as the traditional doctrine seems to assume, on the nature of the dispute, that is to say, on the subject matter to which the dispute refers, but on the nature of the norms to be applied in the settlement of the dispute. A dispute is

36. Ibid, p. 42. This concern is evident in allegations of a lack of impartiality of members of the bench who are nationals of one of the parties to the dispute before the Court and in the procedure of appointing an ad hoc judge when the Court does not have a judge of its nationality sitting on the bench. An example of this can be seen in the series of cases brought by Yugoslavia against the member States of NATO during NATO's bombing campaign in 1999: *Legality of Use of Force (Yugoslavia v Belgium; Yugoslavia v Canada; Yugoslavia v France; Yugoslavia v Germnay; Yugoslavia v Italy; Yugoslavia v Netherlands; Yugoslavia v Portugal; Yugoslavia v Spain; Yugoslavia v US)* <http://www.icj-cij.org> (accessed at 23 October 2007).
37. *Legality of the Threat or Use of Nuclear Weapons (Advisory Opinion)* [1996] 1 ICJ Rep 226 ('*Nuclear Weapons Opinion*').
38. *Nuclear Weapons Opinion* [1996] 1 ICJ Rep 226, [16]. This stance has been repeated often by the Court both in contentious cases and advisory opinions: see, eg, *Questions of Interpretation and Application of the 1971 Montreal Convention Arising from the Aerial Incident at Lockerbie (Libyan Arab Jamahiriya v United Kingdom) (Order)* [1992] ICJ Rep 3, 56 ('*Lockerbie Decision*') (Dissenting Opinion of Judge Weeramantry); *Questions of Interpretation and Application of the 1971 Montreal Convention Arising from the Aerial Incident at Lockerbie (Libyan Arab Jamahiriya v United States of America) (Order)* [1992] ICJ Rep 114, 166 (Dissenting Opinion of Judge Weeramantry) (The *Lockerbie Case* involved a dispute between Libya and both the UK and the US. The judgment relating to the US follows that relating to the UK and is virtually identical. Henceforth, all citations from the *Lockerbie Case* shall refer to the UK dispute.); *Certain Expenses of the United Nations (Advisory Opinion)* [1962] ICJ Rep 151, 155. It has also been used by other international tribunals such as the the International Criminal Tribunal for the former Yugoslavia ('ICTY'): *Prosecutor v Tadić (Defence Motion for Interlocutory Appeal on Jurisdiction)*, Case No IT-94-1-AR72 (2 October 1995) [24] ('*Tadić*').
39. As cited in Gowlland-Debbas, *The International Court of Justice and the Security Council*, pp. 652–53.

> a legal dispute if it is to be settled by the application of legal norms, that is to say, by the application of existing law.[40]

Whilst this may appear to be a tautology a similar approach was taken in the *Tadić Case*, where the ICTY considered the distinction between political matters or 'non-justiciable' questions as simply a residue of antiquated concepts of national sovereignty. The ICTY, following the ICJ's opinion in *Certain Expenses of the United Nations*, considered that the definition of a legal dispute was one that 'turns on a legal question capable of a legal answer.'[41] Can highly political disputes be resolved by a simple legal decision?[42] Some authors, such as Sir Hersch Lauterpacht, think so:

> there is no fixed limit to the possibilities of judicial settlement. All conflicts in the sphere of international politics can be reduced to contests of a legal nature. The only decisive test of the justiciability of the dispute is the willingness of the disputants to submit the conflict to the arbitrament of law.[43]

This willingness of States is indeed crucial, as can be seen by examining the legal system that they have chosen to adopt to resolve their disputes.

40. Ibid. However, it is also possible for the Court to ignore strict legal rules, and to determine the matter on the basis of fairness and justice as the circumstances require, but only if the parties so agree: art 38 (2) *ICJ Statute.* This is the so-called rule of adjudication *ex aequo et bono,* which Lauterpacht describes as a 'species of legislative activity.' Sir Hersch Lauterpacht, *The Development of International Law by the International Court,* (reprinted by Grotius Publications limited) London: Cambridge, 1982 first published by Stevens & Sons limited, London 1958, p. 214. *This* rule could potentially increase the difficulty in separating political questions from legal questions as shown by the *Free Zones Case,* where the PCIJ had to consider the regimes concerning the Free Zones of Upper Savoy and the District of Rex. This involved an interpretation of article 435 paragraph 2 of the *Treaty of Versailles,* and whether it abrogated the regime of the Free Zones, and if the parties failed to reach an agreement to settle all questions raised by art 435. The Court held that art 435 did not abrogate the Free Zones, and also that interpretation of article 435 paragraph 2 of the *Treaty of Versailles* did not empower the PCIJ to make an arrangment that the parties themselves were unable to conclude. Furthermore, it held that making such an arrangement was an economic question rather than a legal one. *Case of Free Zones Of Upper Savoy and the District of Gex (France v Switzerland)* [1932] PCIJ (Ser A/B) No. 46, 158. 162. However, it was a spilt decision and as Lauterpacht stated: 'It would not be accurate to deduce from the reasoning of the majority any general conclusion on the attitude of th Court on the subject.' Ibid, p. 215.
41. *Tadić,* Case No IT-94–1-AR72 (2 October 1995) [24] and *Certain Expenses of the United Nations (Advisory Opinion)* [1962] ICJ Rep 151, 155.
42. Hermann Mosler, 'Problems and Tasks of International Judicial and Arbitral Settlement' in Hermann Mosler and Rudolph Bernhardt (eds), *Judicial Settlement of International Disputes,* Berlin: Springer, 1974, p. 11.
43. Lauterpacht as cited in *Nicaragua Case* [1986] ICJ Rep 14, 169 (Separate Opinion of Judge Lachs).

C. The international legal system

As discussed in Chapter 3 above the legal system that States have chosen to administer and resolve their disputes is a voluntary one and the basis of the contentious jurisdiction of the ICJ is likewise consensual in nature.[44] This phenomenon of consensual jurisdiction is a direct result of national sovereignty.[45] Originally the Committee of Jurists that was tasked with designing the new world court intended to make the jurisdiction of the ICJ completely compulsory. However, according to Steinberger, voluntary jurisdiction was chosen by the 'victors' of the Second World War as part of a deliberate policy to ensure they could retain the ability to protect their national interests in the post-war world.[46]

Voluntary jurisdiction in contentious matters has been described as the ICJ's greatest weakness.[47] In my view this is not an exaggeration since in real terms the Court's ability to function, indeed its very existence, is totally dependent upon the consent of States.[48] If not a single State granted its consent then, with the exception of delivering Advisory Opinions, the Court would not function.[49] Also, not all States have given

44. For a State to consent to the jurisdiction of the ICJ, it first needs to be a party to the *ICJ Statute*: *ICJ Statute*, art 35(1). The *UN Charter* art 93(1) states that any member of the UN is also a party to the *ICJ Statute*. The Court's contentious jurisdiction is still 'open to other States', that is those that are not parties to the ICJ Statute, subject to conditions determined by the Security Council. These conditions must not cause any inequality: article 35 (2) *ICJ Statute*. For an example of the operation of art 35(2) see the series of cases brought by Serbia and Montenegro concerning the use of Force in Kosovo: *Case Concerning the Legality of the Use of Force (Serbia and Montenegro v. Belgium) (Judgment)* [2004] ICJ Rep, 279, [92–114]; *Case Concerning the Legality of the Use of Force (Serbia and Montenegro v. United Kingdom) (Preliminary Objections)* [2004] ICJ Rep 1307, 1346–1351 at 101–113.
45. Renata Szafraz, *The Compulsory Jurisdiction of the International Court of Justice*, the Hague: Kluwer Law International incorporating Martinus-Nijhoff Publishers, 1993, p. 3.
46. In fact the opposition to compulsory jurisdiction came from the 'stronger,' Western powers, in particular those that later became permanent members of the Security Council. It was so intense that it was felt that if compulsory jurisdiction were pursued, it would jeopardise the very existence not just of the ICJ, but also of the UN, and so jurisdiction became optional in the *ICJ Statute*, art 36(2): *Steinberger*, *The International Court of Justice*, p. 196. The First Committee of Commission IV of the San Francisco Conference decided by 31 to 14 votes to retain the optional clause. See also Stanmir Alexandrov, A, *Reservations in Unilateral Declarations Accepting the Compulsory Jurisdiction of the International Court of Justice*, the Hague: Martinus Nijhoff Publishers, Dordrecht [Distributed by Kluwer Academic Publishers], 1995, p. 8.
47. See, eg, Joaquin Tacsan, *The Dynamics of International Law in Conflict Resolution* The Hague: Kluwer Law International incorporating Martinus-Nijhoff Publishers 1992, p. 138.
48. Once again it should be remembered that the so-called 'compulsory jurisdiction' implemented in art 36(2) of the *ICJ Statute* is still dependent upon an initial act of consent, and that this consent can be so watered down as to be no true consent at all.
49. This phenomenon is not as far-fetched as it would appear. For a substantial period the ICJ was virtually at a standstill, which prompted some to declare that the ICJ could not make a contribution to the resolution of disputes: see, eg, Anand, *Role of International Adjudication*', p. 2; Leo Gross, 'The International Court of Justice: Consideration of Requirements for

their consent,[50] and there is nothing preventing a State from withdrawing its consent after making the declaration.[51] When these difficulties are combined with the use of reservations by States when accepting jurisdiction the potential for non-appearance or non-participation by parties when the Court seeks to invoke its jurisdiction in accordance with article 36(2) is high.[52] Indeed as noted by Janis, there were many incidents of non-appearance in cases involving the application of art 36(2) during the 1970s and 1980s,[53] for example, Iceland in the *Fisheries Jurisdiction Case*,[54] France in the *Nuclear Tests Case*,[55] Turkey in the *Aegean Sea Continental Shelf Case*[56] and Iran in the *Diplomatic and Consular Staff in Tehran Case.*[57]

1. Non-appearance by parties

In highly political matters, non-appearance may be a tempting proposition for States that feel that they can achieve more advantageous outcomes

Enhancing its Role in the International Legal Order' (1971) 65 *The American Journal of International Law*, p. 262.

50. The statistics have varied over the years. As of 1988–9, only 49 States had given their consent: see, eg, Mark Janis, 'The International Court' in Mark Janis (ed) *International Courts for the Twenty-First Century* The Hague: Martinus Nijhoff Dordrecht [Distributed by Kluwer Academic Publishers], 1992, p. 22. In 1992, only 29 per cent of the UN members had accepted the ICJ's jurisdiction, a decline from 55 per cent in 1955, and of the 46 who had, 27 reserved the right to modify or terminate their acceptance at any stage: Tacsan, *The Dynamics of International Law*, p. 138. In 1995, however, only 58 of the 186 States who were parties to the *ICJ Statute* – a total of 31 per cent – reserved this right: Philippe Couvreur, 'The Effectiveness of the International Court of Justice' in Muller, Rai and Thuránszky, *The International Court of Justice: Its Future Role* p. 83, n. 30.
51. See, eg, the US withdrawal of its consent after the *Nicaragua Case.* Also Australia recently qualified its consent under art 36(2) in relation to maritime boundary disputes.: Government of Australia, *Declarations Recognizing as Compulsory the Jurisdiction of the Court* (2002) International Court of Justice <http://www.icj-cij.org/jurisdiction/index.php?p1=5&p2=1&p3=3&code=AU&> at 23 October 2007.
52. And the ICJ will honour such reservations: the PCIJ in *Phosphates in Morocco (Italy v France) (Preliminary Objections)* [1938] PCIJ Rep 10, 23 held that the Court's jurisdiction 'existed only within the limits within which it has been accepted.'
53. Mark Janis, 'Somber Reflections on the Compulsory Jurisdiction of the International Court' (1987) 81 *American Journal of International Law* 144, p. 144.
54. *Fisheries Jurisdiction (United Kingdom v Iceland) (Interim Protection)* [1972] ICJ Rep 12; *Fisheries Jurisdiction (Federal Republic of Germany v Iceland) (Interim Protection)* [1972] ICJ Rep 30; *Fisheries Jurisdiction (United Kingdom v Iceland) (Jurisdiction)* [1973] ICJ Rep 3; *Fisheries Jurisdiction (Federal Republic of Germany v Iceland) (Jurisdiction)* [1973] ICJ Rep 49; *Fisheries Jurisdiction (United Kingdom v Iceland) (Merits)* [1974] ICJ Rep 3; *Fisheries Jurisdiction (Federal Republic of Germany v Iceland) (Merits)* [1974] ICJ Rep 175.
55. *Nuclear Tests (Australia v France) (Judgment)* [1974] ICJ Rep 253; *Nuclear Tests (New Zealand v France)(Judgment)* [1974] ICJ Rep 457.
56. *Aegean Sea Continental Shelf (Greece v Turkey) (Jurisdiction)* [1978] ICJ Rep 3.
57. *United States Diplomatic and Consular Staff in Tehran (United States of America v Iran) (Order)* [1979] ICJ Rep 7.

through a purely political solution. The non-appearance of parties in contentious cases other than those in which jurisdiction is granted by a *compromis* or special agreement poses a difficult problem, since regardless of which action the Court takes – to proceed or not proceed – one party will be disadvantaged. This may raise concerns that justice has not been done in two ways. Firstly, when a party fails to appear, it may allow them 'to profit from their absence' since, if the matter were not to proceed to judgment, then the claim of the party who appeared is defeated not because of a deficiency in the merits of their claim but by the recalcitrance of the other party whose own claims may be unsupportable. Parties could easily abuse this as a particularly useful tactic when the legal merits of their claims are dubious, or weak at best, or when their national interest would not be served by having the matter adjudicated by the ICJ.[58] Secondly, if the matter were to proceed to judgment, then the non-appearing party would be unable to counter any of the arguments presented or examine any of the witnesses, and also would be unable to present their claim.[59]

It could be argued that the disadvantages caused by non-appearance are a concern only for the non-appearing party and are entirely self-inflicted. What non-appearance does, however, is raise a perception in the broader international community of the irrelevance of the ICJ in resolving international disputes. If it is perceived that a party is simply the victor by virtue of its appearance in the absence of the other party, rather than by the strength of its claim this then raises serious concerns about the validity of the Court's findings, impacting upon the Court's credibility in the eyes of the international community. Credibility is important to all courts but particularly to the ICJ due to the problems of enforceability it faces.

2. Enforceability

Even if States do consent to the ICJ's jurisdiction, who or what enforces the Court's decision? Whilst provision is made in both the *ICJ Statute* and the *UN Charter* to enforce the Court's judgments and Advisory Opinions through a resolution of the Security Council[60] there is no international 'police force' that will actually ensure compliance with the resolution itself.[61] The lack of an overall sovereign means there is no real means of enforcement other than 'peer group pressure' from other States.[62] Indeed, Ojo writes that

58. *Nicaragua Case* [1986] ICJ Rep 14, [32] (Separate Opinion of Judge Lachs).
59. The Court mentioned this concern specifically in the *Nicaragua Case* [1986] ICJ Rep 14, [67].
60. The *ICJ Statute* art 59 states that the judgment of the ICJ has no binding force except between the parties involved in the dispute. (See also *UN Charter* art 94(1).) *ICJ Statute* art 60 states that the judgment of the ICJ is final and without appeal.
61. Assuming that the self-interests of the respective members of the Security Council, in particular the permanent members, can be put aside to enable such a resolution to be made.
62. Couvreur, *Effectiveness*, p. 111.

'[t]here is no independent international legal system, capable of enforcing agreements and international law. The system is defective because it depend [sic] so much on the behavior and attitude of those it is suppose [sic] to regulate.'[63]

This dependency provides States with the ability, unheard of in domestic legal systems, to avoid the ICJ's authority[64] to a degree that leads some to argue that international adjudication has been unable to realise its expectations as an instrument of dispute resolution.[65] This substantial argument is strengthened as States have a history of non-compliance with the Court's rulings

Charney, in an analysis of States' resistance to the authority of the ICJ, revealed that in contentious cases, excluding those subject to a special agreement, States have refused to participate or even comply in at least ten cases. In fact, during the period 1972–86, the only decisions that met with no resistance were those that were the subject of a special agreement.[66] The record of the ICJ, in this respect, appears to be worse than that of the PCIJ.[67]

63. Bamidele Ojo, *Human Rights and the New World Order: Universality, Acceptability and Human Diversity* (1997) 53. Charney would agree with this summation. See his comparison with domestic courts: Jonathan Charney, 'Disputes Implicating the Institutional Credibility of the Court: Problems of Non-Appearance, Non-Participation, and Non-Performance' in Damrosch *At a Crossroads* pp. 303–4.
64. This ability to resist the authority of the ICJ is due to the concept of national sovereignty. Ojo, *Human Rights*, p. 53. To suggest that the jurisdiction of a domestic court should be dependent on the consent of the parties to the dispute would be regarded by practitioners, judges and citizens as nonsense for many reasons and quite clearly render any domestic legal system unworkable. However, few of the parties would be capable of causing the destruction of the globe.
65. Charney, *Disputes*, p. 299.
66. That is at the date of his publication, which was in 1987: ibid 293–7. The decisions Charney listed were as follows: *Corfu Channel (United Kingdom v Albania) (Merits)* [1949] ICJ Rep 4; *Monetary Gold Removed from Rome in 1943 (Italy v France, United Kingdom and the United States of America) (Merits)* [1954] ICJ Rep 19; *Asylum (Columbia v Peru) (Merits)* [1950] ICJ Rep 266; *Haya de la Torre (Colombia v Peru) (Merits)* [1951] ICJ Rep 71; *Anglo-Iranian Oil Co (United Kingdom v Iran) (Interim Protection)* [1951] ICJ Rep 89; *Nottebohm (Liechtenstein v Guatemala) (Preliminary Objection)* [1953] ICJ Rep 111; *Right of Passage over Indian Territory (Portugal v India) (Merits)* [1960] ICJ Rep 6; *Trial of Pakistani Prisoners of War (Pakistan v India) (Interim Protection)* [1973] ICJ Rep 328; *Fisheries Jurisdiction Case (United Kingdom v Iceland) (Merits)* [1974] ICJ Rep 3; *Nuclear Tests Case (New Zealand v France) (Judgment)* [1974] ICJ Rep 457; *Nuclear Tests Case (Australia v France) (Judgment)* [1974] ICJ Rep 253; *Aegean Sea Continental Shelf (Greece v Turkey) (Jurisdiction)* [1978] ICJ Rep 3; *United States Diplomatic and Consular Staff in Tehran (United States of America v Iran) (Judgment)* [1980] ICJ Rep 3 ('*Hostages Case*'); and *Military and Paramilitary Activities in and against Nicaragua (Nicaragua v United States of America) (Provisional Measures)* [1984] ICJ Rep 392. The *Hostages Case* was particularly difficult given the failed US rescue attempt. As noted by the Court: 'an operation taken in those circumstances, from whatever motive, is of a kind calculated to undermine respect for the judicial process in international relations …'. See *Hostages Case*, 44 [93].
67. Charney notes that of the 49 cases heard by the PCIJ, none of the 'losing' States refused to comply with its decision and there were only three cases in which one of the parties unexpectedly refused to appear: Charney, *Disputes*, p. 299.

Pratap believes that the decline of compliance with the ICJ, when compared with the PCIJ, is due mainly to the attitude of the States, with either an attitude of distrust or indifference towards the ICJ.[68]

The potential for States to resist the authority of the ICJ would appear to be even greater when the ICJ exercises its advisory jurisdiction, since the parties are not bound to comply with the opinion.[69] States can state, in advance, their willingness to accept 'unreservedly' the decision of the Advisory Opinion even if it would contradict their State's position on the matter.[70] But, as Lissitzyn notes, only a low proportion of States do so.[71] This is self-explanatory since the very nature of the advisory jurisdiction implies that the parties will not honour their commitments to accept the Advisory Opinion.[72] Charney's analysis shows that in seven situations parties have refused to act in accordance with the Advisory Opinion when that opinion opposed their positions and national interest.[73] However it must also be remembered that since the advisory jurisdiction is not dependent upon the consent of States, they cannot prevent the Court from considering the legal question that is the subjcct of the request.[74]

States have constructed a system whereby the simple action of non-participation – either through not granting an initial consent, granting consent subject to reservations, or by withdrawing their consent – arms them with an ability to undermine the authority of the Court. Thus, for the Court

68. Dharma Pratap, *The Advisory Jurisdiction of the International Court* (Oxford: University Press 1972 pp. 267–68.
69. *ICJ Statute*, art 65(1).
70. Pratap refers to delegates from the following States: Australia, Argentina, USA, Norway, and Venezuela: Pratap, *The Advisory Jurisdiction*, p. 245.
71. Oliver Lissitzyn, *The International Court of Justice: Its Role in the Maintenance of International Peace and Security* (1978) 84. In fact many States will actually refuse in advance.
72. The very fact that a request for an advisory opinion on a question directly connected with a dispute between States is made by an international political organ is usually an indication that the States concerned have not agreed to settle the dispute by a binding judicial decision within the framework of existing law. Ibid 84.
73. Charney, *Disputes*, p. 298. The decisions he listed were: *Conditions of Admission of a State to Membership in the United Nations (Article 4 of Charter) (Advisory Opinion)* [1947–1948] ICJ Rep 57; *Reparation for Injuries Suffered in the Service of the United Nations (Advisory Opinion)* [1949] ICJ Rep 174; *Interpretation of Peace Treaties with Bulgaria, Hungary and Romania (1st Phase) (Advisory Opinion)* [1950] ICJ Rep 65; *International Status of South West Africa (Advisory Opinion)* [1950] ICJ Rep 128; *Certain Expenses of the United Nations (Advisory Opinion)* [1962] ICJ Rep 151; *Legal Consequences for States of the Continued Presence of South Africa in Namibia (South West Africa) Notwithstanding Security Council Resolution 276 (1970) (Advisory Opinion)* [1971] ICJ Rep 16; *Western Sahara (Advisory Opinion)* [1975] ICJ Rep 12. However since 1947 there has been a total of 26 Advisory Opinions, so the fear of non-compliance is not as great as it would seem. A further 28 were provided by the PCIJ.
74. *Interpretation of Peace Treaties with Bulgaria, Hungary and Romania (1st Phase) (Advisory Opinion)* [1950] ICJ Rep 65, 71, which was affirmed in the *Western Sahara (Advisory Opinion)* [1975] ICJ Rep 12, 19.

to succeed, indeed for the Court to even function, it appears to be dependent upon the attitude and actions of States: almost it would appear, on the whims of an aggrieved party.

The combination of States' belief in the absoluteness of their sovereignty and reluctance to surrender total control over the dispute resolution process has resulted in the traditional distinction between legal and political disputes.[75] The distinction is based on the argument that there are specific types of international disputes, 'highly political matters,' that because of their nature would be inappropriate to resolve before a court or, indeed, any non-political organ. In other words, such disputes require a particular methodology that a Court is unable to provide; a 'political' solution.[76]

Given these problems it is difficult to believe that the Court is able to make a contribution to the resolution of highly political disputes – those disputes where national interests are threatened in such a manner that the respective parties seek to use political methodology simply because they believe they stand a better chance of protecting their interests. Yet the Court firmly does believe that it can contribute in such cases.

D. The Court's attitude and its contribution

To state that the Court is not ignorant of the overall political context of international legal problems brought before it would appear to be obvious and unnecessary. However, the Court has felt that it should, indeed, make such statements. An example can be found in the *Hostages Case*, where the Court stated that 'legal disputes between sovereign States by their very nature are likely to occur in political contexts, and often form only one element in a wider and long-standing political dispute between the States concerned.'[77]

Whilst there have been occasions where individual members of the Court have expressed concern regarding the Court's role in highly political matters,[78] the Court has consistently held, both in deciding contentious cases

75. This can be traced as far back as Vattel's theories in 1758: Gowlland-Debbas, *The International Court of Justice and the Security Council*, p. 649. See also the *Tadić*, Case No IT-94-1-AR72 (2 October 1995) [24].
76. Essentially a political solution is implemented by political organs such as the General Assembly or the Security Council of the UN: see *Lockerbie Decision* [1992] ICJ Rep 3, 57 (Dissenting Opinion of Judge Weeramantry), where he referred to Kelsen's statement that the Security Council was not a judicial body *simply* because its members were not independent and therefore were not impartial. See also the distinction between legal and political solutions made in the *Lockerbie Decision* [1992] ICJ Rep 3, [1] (Separate Opinion of Judge El-Kosheri).
77. *United States Diplomatic and Consular Staff in Tehran (United States of America v Iran) (Judgment)* [1980] ICJ Rep 3, 20.
78. See, eg, *Nicaragua Case* [1986] ICJ Rep 14, [59], [72]. However as noted by Oscar Schachter, Judge Oda's concern did not extend to denying the Court's ability to become involved simply because the dispute involved armed force. Oscar Schachter, 'Disputes Involving the

and when providing Advisory Opinions, that the reality of mixed legal and political aspects to disputes *does not* prevent the Court from deciding upon the legal issues before it.[79] For example, in the *Nuclear Weapons Opinion* the Court was united in their attitude that the political background should not interfere with their decision on whether to provide an Advisory Opinion. Similarly in the *Nicaragua Case*, the Court was adamant that it could enter, the so-called 'No-Man's Lands' where political and legal questions were mixed including, in that particular opinion, on the right of individual or collective self-defence.[80] In the *Lockerbie Decision*, Judge Weeramantry, after emphasising the judicial integrity and independence of the Court, stated that:

> As a judicial organ, it will be the Court's duty from time to time to examine and determine from a strictly legal point of view matters which may at the same time be the subject of determination from an executive or political point of view by another principal organ of the United Nations. ... What pertains to the judicial function is the proper sphere of competence of the Court. The circumstance that political results flow from a judicial decision is not one that takes it out of that sphere of competence.[81]

As mentioned above, Sir Hersch Lauterpacht believed that all political disputes could be rendered down to legal questions, if there was sufficient political will. However, he also conceded that the Court was a better vehicle for developing the rules of international law than maintaining international

Use of Force' in Damrosch *At a Crossroads* p. 229. See also Sugihara, *Judicial Function*, for further discussion of this point.

79. There are many examples. In contentious cases consider *Aegean Sea Continental Shelf Case (Greece v Turkey) (Jurisdiction)* [1978] ICJ Rep 3, 13; *United States Diplomatic and Consular Staff in Tehran (United States of America v Iran) (Provisional Measures)* [1979] ICJ Rep 7, 15; *Military and Paramilitary Activities in and against Nicaragua (Nicaragua v United States of America) (Provisional Merits)* [1984] ICJ Rep 392, 437–8; *East Timor (Portugal v Australia) (Merits)* [1995] ICJ Rep 90, 219 (Dissenting Opinion of Judge Weeramantry). However, see the *Nicaragua Case* [1986] ICJ Rep 14, [55]–[59] (Separate Opinion of Judge Oda), where he suggested that the Court should not be involved in highly political matters. However, his Honour did not believe that the dispute involving armed force was a non-justiciable one beyond the jurisdiction of the Court: at [53]. With regard to providing Advisory Opinions see *Conditions of Admission of a State to Membership in the United Nations (Article 4 of Charter) (Advisory Opinion)* [1948] ICJ Rep 57, 107–9; *Certain Expenses of the United Nations (Advisory Opinion)* [1962] ICJ Rep 151, 155. The PCIJ came to a similar conclusion in *Customs Regime Between Germany and Austria* [1931] PCIJ Rep 41, 68–9. See also *Nuclear Weapons Opinion* [1996] 1 ICJ Rep 226.
80. *Military and Paramilitary Activities in and against Nicaragua (Nicaragua v United States of America) (Merits)* [1986] ICJ Rep 14; Sugihara, *Judicial Function*, p. 121.
81. *Lockerbie Decision* [1992] ICJ Rep 3, 56 (Dissenting Opinion of Judge Weeramantry). Such statements have also been noted and approved by other international tribunals, such as the ICTY. See the *Tadić*, Case No IT-94-1-AR72 (2 October 1995) [24].

peace.[82] Takane Sugihara, in his article on the Court and its role in highly political matters, reminded readers of the old Anglo-Saxon saying that hard cases make bad law, implying that, in the context of international law, highly political cases made 'bad international law'.[83]

As mentioned above, States play the 'Great Game', that is they compete with and against one another in the international community. States use all aspects of their power to protect their perceived national interests in order to maintain their position in this community. However, States through the creation of the ICJ, and through developing the norms of international law, have developed mechanisms to restrain, however imperfectly, the use of power (or at least sought to lay down principles that validate the exercise of power). In a sense they seek to regulate their competitive behaviour. Law constrains the exercise of power by limiting its use according to predetermined categories of validity and invalidity.[84] Whilst law may either validate or invalidate the use of power, determining the existence of constraints on the exercise of power is a legal question. Although legal and political questions are interrelated perhaps some examples may clarify any distinctions.

One method to measure and to protect or maintain a State's position is through military strength, in particular in the possession of weapons whose destructive power is such that other States fear attacking them directly, or even fear being perceived to challenge their national interests in the most minor fashion. Thus, the question of whether States should retain possession of immensely powerful weapons – nuclear weapons for example – may be considered to be a political question outside the competence of the ICJ. However, now through the development of norms of international law the question of whether there exists a constraint on possession of such weapons is a legal question. On this very issue or nuclear weapons and international law, several States argued that the ICJ ought to exercise its discretion not to give an Advisory Opinion on the question of the legality of the threat or use of nuclear weapons. The argument was based on the view by these States that the question was a political one. The ICJ chose to ignore their arguments and proceeded to deliver the Opinion indicating its willingness to decide upon key legal questions despite the existence of complex and sensitive political issues.

Another example is that a State may wish to maintain access to natural resources, particularly those that its economy is heavily dependent upon. This is a political matter. Furthermore, whether a State is sufficiently

82. Lauterpacht, *The Development of International Law* pp. 4–5; Janis, *Somber Reflections*, p. 145.
83. Sugihara, *Judicial Function*, p. 138.
84. Or as Ingram describes the rule of law: '… the rule of law, which works to limit the power of the most powerful.' David Ingram, *Law, Key Concepts in Philosophy*, London: Continuum, 2006, p. 14. See generally Samantha Ashenden 'The Problem of Power in Luhmann's Systems Theory' in Michael King and Chris Thornhill (eds), *Luhmann on Law and Politics Critical Appraisals and Applications*, Oxford: Hart Publishing, 2004, pp. 127–144.

powerful enough to successfully invade and occupy another State that has an abundant supply of natural resources will also involve strategic political calculations. However, the question whether a State is permitted to use military force to invade and occupy is a legal question. If the proposed use of military force to seize and protect those resources cannot be justified as an act of self-defence, or as an act of humanitarian intervention then the proposed use of military force is *prima facie* illegal. The international community has determined that the use of military force without legal justification should be constrained for the mutual benefit and collective security of all States.

Another example is that States would prefer their neighbours to have a government that does not pose a threat to their existence or to their perceived national interests: this is a political matter. Perhaps the easiest way to achieve such security is to ensure that neighbouring States have a political and economic system, or a political ideology, that is either similar to or sympathetic to their own or at least tolerant of difference where there is diversity. The conflict during the Cold War between Western liberal democracies, led by the US, and communism or socialism lead by the former USSR involved an ideological struggle. However, States on both sides of that struggle had committed themselves to constraints on resort to military force and international legal obligations imposed some limitations on the justifiable means for the waging of the struggle. Despite the intense political and ideological rivalry of the Cold War period, there were still some fundamental legal principles that established demarcation lines.

These issues, the possession of powerful weapons, the interference in the domestic affairs of another State and limitations on the right to resort to military force have been considered by the ICJ in decisions such as the *Nicaragua Case*, the *Nuclear Weapons Advisory Opinion* and the *Lockerbie Decisions*, which involved some of the most highly controversial and political matters brought before the Court. An examination, of these decisions reveals that the Court can in fact make a valuable contribution even in such complex cases.

1. The Nicaragua Case

The *Nicaragua Case* unquestionably involved highly political issues dealing with armed intervention by one party into the territory of the other party.[85] Nicaragua claimed: (1) that the US had acted in violation of art 2(4) of the

85. The context in which the dispute took place, in particular the secrecy surrounding the intervention into Nicaragua, the involvement of intelligence organisations such as the Central Intelligence Agency (US) and the political interests of the parties involved, added to the difficulty of resolving the dispute. To make matters worse, the US, perhaps the most powerful in all aspects of the term, withdrew from the dispute after unsuccessfully contesting the original questions of jurisdiction.

UN Charter and customary international law by the use of force against it; (2) that the actions of the US – through supporting the armed opposition to the Nicaraguan government, known as the Contras, mining of Nicaraguan harbours, and other attacks – amounted to intervention in the internal affairs of Nicaragua, in breach of the *Charter of the Organization of American States* and of rules of customary international law; (3) that the US had violated the national sovereignty of Nicaragua; and (4) that the actions of the US also defeated the object and purpose of a *Treaty of Friendship, Commerce and Navigation* concluded between the Parties in 1956,[86] and put it in breach of provisions of that Treaty.

In their counter-memorial on jurisdiction and admissibility, the US asserted that its actions constituted collective self-defence in response to requests from El Salvador, Honduras and Costa Rica, for assistance against armed aggression by Nicaragua. The US alleged that Nicaragua had 'promoted and supported guerrilla violence in neighboring countries' – specifically in El Salvador in early 1981 – and also that Nicaragua had conducted cross-border military attacks on Honduras and Costa Rica.[87] The US argued further that they were entitled and indeed obliged to provide assistance to these countries in accordance with the terms of the *Inter-American Treaty of Reciprocal Assistance*.[88]

The Court rejected this argument of collective self-defence and held that by training, arming and providing overall military support for the Contras, the US had breached its obligation under customary international law not to intervene in the affairs of another State. Further, the Court held that the US had, through certain attacks on Nicaraguan territory in 1983–84, specifically the mining of harbours and attacks on Nicaraguan port facilities, breached its obligations under customary international law not to use force against another State and not to violate the sovereignty of another State.[89] These had also placed the US in violation of its obligations pursuant to the *Treaty of Friendship, Commerce and Navigation* between the Parties.[90] Consequently, the Court ordered the US to make reparations to the Republic of Nicaragua for all injury caused by the said breaches.[91]

86. *Treaty of Friendship, Commerce and Navigation (with Protocol), opened for signature 21 January 1956, US–Nicaragua, 367 UNTS 3 (entered into force 24 May 1958).*
87. *Nicaragua Case* [1986] ICJ Rep 14, [128].
88. *Inter-American Treaty of Reciprocal Assistance*, opened for signature 2 September 1947, 21 UNTS 77 (entered into force 3 December 1948).
89. *Nicaragua Case* [1986] ICJ Rep 14, [292](6) (President Nagendra Singh, Vice-President de Lacharrière, Judges Lachs, Ruda, Elias, Ago, Sette-Camara, Mbaye, Bedjaoui, Ni and Evensen, Judge ad hoc Colliard; Judges Oda, Schwebel and Sir Robert Jennings dissenting).
90. Ibid, [292](7) (President Nagendra Singh, Vice-President de Lacharrière, Judges Lachs, Ruda, Elias, Oda, Ago, Sette-Camara, Sir Robert Jennings, Mbaye, Bedjaoui, Ni and Evensen, Judge ad hoc Colliard; Judge Schwebel dissenting).
91. Wisely choosing the reality of a friendly relationship with the US over the theoretical value of a monetary judgment that was unlikely ever to be satisfied, President Chamorro

In spite of the very difficult circumstances in this dispute, the Court was not only prepared to, but actually did perform its task. The withdrawal of the US from proceedings did not prevent the Court from reaching its findings and, it is argued here, also did not affect the quality of the Court's findings. The Court's decision contributed to the development of international law in a number of areas, such as: the importance of art 36(2) of the *ICJ Statute* and the nature of a party's consent to the ICJ's jurisdiction; the effect of non-appearance on the legal process, in particular the ability to determine evidence and, of course, in relation to substance; and perhaps most importantly, the interpretation of art 2(4) of the *UN Charter* and the use of force.

The significance of the Court's approach to questions of consensual jurisdiction has been raised in other cases.[92] The ICJ applied a ruling from the *Nicaragua Case* in *Oil Platforms (Islamic Republic of Iran v United States of America) (Preliminary Objections)* in considering whether a treaty provision denied it jurisdiction to hear the dispute, thus rejecting the US' preliminary objection and concluding that the Court had jurisdiction to hear the dispute.[93]

Whilst the ICJ expressed regret at the non-appearance of the US in the *Nicaragua Case*, the Court firmly stated that non-appearance should not prevent it from performing its judicial role. What is more important is that the Court also held that the non-appearance of the respondent state does not result in an 'automatic judgment' in accordance with art 53 of the *ICJ Statute*, in favour of the appearing party.[94] Rather, the Court must proceed on the basis of a fundamental commitment to justice for both parties to the dispute before it.[95]

of Nicaragua agreed to withdraw Nicaragua's request for reparations in 1991. On the 26th September the President of the Court Sir Robert Jennings filed on record Nicargua's request for a discontinuance, and ordered that the case be removed from the Court's list. That marked the end of all proceedings.

92. *Legality of Use of Force (Yugoslavia v United States of America) (Provisional Measures)* [1999] ICJ Rep 916.
93. Basically the issue was whether the *Treaty of Amity, Economic Relations and Consular Rights*, opened for signature 15 August 1955, US–Iran, 284 UNTS 93 (entered into force 16 June 1957) removed disputes involving the use of force from the jurisdiction of the Court. The Court rejected the US's submission that it did on the basis of the rules of interpretation as derived from the *Nicaragua Case*. See *Oil Platforms (Iran v United States of America) (Preliminary Objections)* [1996] ICJ Rep 803, p. 811.
94. *Nicaragua Case* [1986] ICJ Rep 14, [28]. *ICJ Statute* art 53(1): 'Whenever one of the parties does not appear before the Court, or fails to defend its case, the other party may call upon the Court to decide in favour of its claim.' In accordance with art 53(2) of the *ICJ Statute*, the Court has to confirm it has jurisdiction, and further that the claim is well-founded in fact and law.
95. *Nicaragua Case* [1986] ICJ Rep 14, [28].

How does the ICJ ensure justice in the face of non-appearance of a party? To what extent must the Court fulfil its judicial obligation, to 'satisfy itself'?[96]

> The use of the term 'satisfy itself' in the English text of the Statute (and in the French text the term 's'assurer') implies that the Court must attain the same degree of certainty as in any other case that the claim of the party appearing is sound in law, and, so far as the nature of the case permits, that the facts on which it is based are supported by convincing evidence.[97]

The Court was to some extent able to lessen the impact of the absence of one party.[98] The Court was supplied with a liberal amount of information, sufficient to 'satisfy itself' of the merits of Nicaragua's claim.[99] Also, a number of witnesses were called and oral testimony was used by the Court to resolve particular issues.[100] The Court then itself took the task of determining the veracity and validity of the evidence presented by the witnesses, in a sense, assuming the role of a cross-examiner.[101]

The judgment of Judge Oda was indicative of the Court's approach. He divided witnesses into two distinct categories that reflected their level of credibility; those who constituted a 'disinterested witness' and those who did not.[102] Accordingly, the evidence and testimony of the latter were treated 'with great reserve.'[103] In spite of the Court's stated attitude and the obvious steps taken to 'satisfy itself' many commentators still felt that the decision could be questioned simply because of the absence of the US.[104] Other commentators noted the opposite, namely that the actions of the

96. In *Nicaragua Case* the Court stated in regard to a party's non-appearance: 'There is however no question of a judgment automatically in favour of the party appearing, since the Court is required, as mentioned above, to 'satisfy itself' that that party's claim is well founded in fact and law': ibid.
97. Ibid, [29].
98. The Court took a more interventionist role in resolving practical questions regarding evidence led in support of either party's claim.
99. *Nicaragua Case* [1986] ICJ Rep 14, [62].
100. See, eg, the issue regarding the ability of the USA to observe and prevent the alleged arms trafficking by Nicaragua into El Salvador. Nicaragua made the most of their witnesses: see Terry Gill's explanation of the relative importance and significance of the witnesses called by Nicaragua in Terry Gill, *Litigation Strategy at the International Court: A Case Study of the Nicaragua v United States Dispute* (1989), pp. 186–200.
101. *Nicaragua Case* [1986] ICJ Rep 14, [67] (Separate Opinion of Judge Oda).
102. Ibid, p. 69 (Separate Opinion of Judge Oda). Those who were not disinterested included representatives of the parties' national governments and had also been actively involved in the preparation of public statements regarding the dispute and the events in Nicaragua.
103. Ibid, p. 70 (Separate Opinion of Judge Oda).
104. See, eg, Thomas Franck, 'Some Observations on the ICJ's Procedural and Substantive Innovations' (1987) 81 *American Journal of International Law* p. 117; Anthony D'Amato,

Court, in giving the US the 'benefit of the doubt' in 'grey areas' and bending over backwards in consideration of the US' non-appearance, gave great weight to the decision.[105]

Much of the controversy surrounding the Court's decision relates to the majority's ruling in regard to the definition of an armed attack, and the interpretation of art 2(4) of the *UN Charter*, which was crucial to the basis of the US' claim of collective self-defence.[106] Whilst the Court rejected many of the allegations made against Nicaragua, they did hold that Nicaragua had supplied arms and provided limited support to rebels in El Salvador. This, however, fell short of an 'armed attack'.[107] What these actions constituted was an 'unlawful use of force' which may or may not justify the use of armed force by the victim State.[108] The importance of the Court's conclusion was that a third party, the US, is not justified under the grounds of collective self-defence to intervene using armed force to counter something less than an armed attack.[109]

That the supply of arms and equipment did not constitute an armed attack, justifying a military response in self-defence, albeit an 'indirect' form of aggression, has puzzled some commentators and raised the ire of others.[110] Some authors point out inherent limitations in the applicability of the Court's

'Trashing Customary International Law' (1987) 81 *American Journal of International Law*, p. 105.

105. Richard Falk, 'The World Court's Achievement' (1987) 81 *American Journal of International Law*, pp 106–7, 110, described the Court's approach as 'exemplary' and argued that the failure of the US to appear did not result in a failure to examine a factual or legal position favourable to the USA. See at 112 where he concluded that anyone with a '25% open mind' would accept the majority's opinion.
106. The majority of the Court firmly stated that the right of self-defence existed only in the event of an 'armed attack': *Nicaragua Case* [1986] ICJ Rep 14, [238].
107. Thus the Court rejected the US's claim of the right to act in collective self-defence: ibid. This prompted some commentators to suggest even where a State provides 'direct' or 'active' support to terrorist groups, it would still not be considered an armed attack under the *UN Charter*, art 51: Gregory Travalio, 'Terrorism, International Law, and the Use of Military Force' (2000) *Wisconsin International Law Journal*, p. 158.
108. *Nicaragua Case* [1986] ICJ Rep 14, [238].
109. For a detailed discussion and analysis of the Court's findings in regard to the definition of armed attack see generally John Hargrove, 'The *Nicaragua* Judgment and the Future of the Law of Force and Self-Defense' (1987) 81 *American Journal of International Law*, pp. 137–8. See also Christopher Greenwood, 'The International Court of Justice and the Use of Force' in Vaughan Lowe and Malgosia Fitzmaurice (eds), *Fifty Years of the International Court of Justice: Essays in Honour of Sir Robert Jennings* Cambridge: Cambridge University Press, 1996, pp. 380–1.
110. In particular, this included Judge Schwebel: *Nicaragua Case* [1986] ICJ Rep 14 (Dissenting Opinion of Judge Schwebel). See also Greenwood, *The International Court of Justice and the Use of Force*, p. 380; John Moore, 'The *Nicaragua* Case and the Deterioration of World Order' (1987) 81 *American Journal of International Law*, pp. 152–3. For a more balanced critique, see Hargrove *The Nicaragua Judgment*, pp. 135–43.

statement.[111] Others criticise the Court's narrow definition of armed attack since it offered protection to those revolutionary groups fostered or sponsored by a State, and also because it would restrict the development of humanitarian intervention.[112] Abraham Sofaer, in his examination of NATO's intervention in Kosovo, believes that the Court's definition of armed attack raised concern about the legality of NATO's actions in preventing genocide and other war crimes committed against the Kosovar Albanians. He also argues that the narrow approach taken by the Court limited the right of regional organisations to act in self-defence, a right envisaged by the drafters of the *UN Charter* and enshrined in art 51.[113]

US criticism of the case verged on hyperbole, containing protestations that '[w]e [the US government] will not risk US national security by presenting such sensitive material in public or *before a Court that includes two judges from* Warsaw Pact *nations*.'[114] One of the grounds of criticism was that the Court had made bad law because of its desire not to be seen to be intimidated by powerful States, making a political statement at the cost of the principles of international law.[115] Others alleged that whilst the Court may have had 'good motives', it had actually worsened human rights, the rule of law and the political chaos in Central America – hardly a ringing endorsement of the potential of the Court in helping to monitor or restore world order.[116]

However, not all commentators disagreed with the Court's decision. Some believe that the Court's decision reflects State practice since 1945 and therefore is a true reflection of customary international law.[117] Some of those commentators who disagree with the Court's decision and interpretation of the relevant legal principles do not doubt the significance of

111. See, eg, Travalio, *Terrorism, International Law*, p. 158, where *inter alia* he asks would it make a difference to the definition of armed attack if the terrorists were operating from a secure base protected by the patron State, or alternatively if the terrorists were armed with nuclear weapons.
112. See, eg, Michael Glennon, 'The New Interventionism (Getting Involved in Other Nations' Conflicts and Affairs)' (1999) 78(3) *Foreign Affairs*, pp. 2–3 and Hargrove, *The Nicaragua Judgment*, p. 139.
113. Abraham Sofaer, 'International Law and Kosovo' (2000) 36 *Stanford Journal of International Law* p. 9. However, the ICJ's approach is justified, since the right of self-defence is indeed tightly controlled under the *Charter of the UN*, through the Security Council. This is an intentional response to the problems experienced by the League of Nations. See *Lockerbie Decision* [1992] ICJ Rep 3, 57–8 (Dissenting Opinion of Judge Weeramantry).
114. *Statement of the US Withdrawal* as cited in Keith Highet, 'Between a Rock and a Hard Place – The United States, the International Court, and the *Nicaragua Case*' (1987) 21 *The International Lawyer*, p. 1086 (emphasis added). As noted by Highet, this statement received a 'stinging rebuke' from Judge Lachs, the member of the bench it was directed at.
115. See, eg, Hargrove, *The Nicaragua Judgment*, p. 143.
116. Moore, *The Nicaragua Case and the Deterioration of World Order*, p. 152. The author acted as Counsel for the US in the *Nicaragua Case*.
117. Greenwood, *The International Court of Justice and the Use of Force*, p. 379.

the Court's contribution.[118] As Richard Falk noted, even the dissenting Judge Schwebel felt that the majority opinion was deserving of respect.[119] The majority's decision did appear to undermine the whole system of covert warfare employed through client States in the broader context of the Cold War.[120]

As the Court stated, to allow the US to intervene in the domestic affairs of Nicaragua simply at the request of the Contras would seriously undermine the principle of non-intervention and would be disastrous for the international community:

> Indeed, it is difficult to see what would remain of the principle of non-intervention in international law if intervention, which is already allowable at the request of the government of a State, were also to be allowed at the request of the opposition. This would permit any State to intervene at any moment in the internal affairs of another State, whether at the request of the government or at the request of its opposition. Such a situation does not in the Court's view correspond to the present state of international law.[121]

Whilst it can be said that this decision reflects the ICJ's desire to protect a small State,[122] no State would, as a general principle, disagree with the right to non-intervention. Even the US would defend its right to non-intervention. Going one step further, which State would disagree that there is no right to intervene at the request of a party opposed to the central government? Would the US countenance intervention by another State simply because that State disagreed with the political philosophy and structure of representative democracy? The answers to these questions are self-evident. There is no reason why any State should feel any differently to the US. In other words, there is a strong element of universalism to the decision.

Richard Falk commented upon this aspect of the majority's decision. He noted that in the majority decision not one legal school or thought, including '[t]he implicit legal hegemony of Western approaches', dominated:[123]

> As such, the majority opinion is of great help to all sectors of world public opinion seeking to comprehend the contours of minimum world

118. See Falk, 'The World Court's Achievement', p. 106; Franck, *Some Observations*, p. 116; Hargrove, *The Nicaragua Judgment*, pp. 135–43 and also Fred Morrison, 'Legal Issues in the *Nicaragua Opinion*' (1987) 81 *American Journal of International Law*, p. 163.
119. Falk, 'The World Court's Achievement', p. 111.
120. This point is made particularly strongly by The *Nicaragua* Case and the Deterioration of World Order, p. 152.
121. *Nicaragua Case* [1986] ICJ Rep 14, [246].
122. Falk, 'The World Court's Achievement', p. 108.
123. Ibid, p. 107.

public order on matters of war and peace. The possibility of legal universalism has been powerfully validated.[124]

Finally, the value of the *Nicaragua Case* can be measured by its recent application in the *Bosnian Genocide Case.* In this recent decision the Court preferred the test of 'effective control' developed in the *Nicaragua Case* to determine State responsibility for the actions of armed persons in Bosnia-Herzegovina, and not the 'overall control' test developed by the International Criminal Tribunal for Yugoslavia.[125]

2. *The Nuclear Weapons Opinion*

Another case that examined and developed the rules relating to the use of force was the *Nuclear Weapons Opinion.* The Court was asked by the UN General Assembly for an Advisory Opinion on whether 'the threat or use of nuclear weapons in any circumstance [is] permitted under international law.'[126] Like the *Nicaragua Case,* discussed above, this Advisory Opinion involved intensely political issues.[127] In fact, many authors believe that the *Nuclear Weapons Opinion* was, and arguably remains, one of the most controversial and highly political matters ever examined by the Court.[128] In the

124. Ibid. The *Nicaragua Case* was applied most recently in the Bosnian Genocide Case: *Case Concerning the Application of the Convention on the Prevention and punishment of the Crime of Genocide (Bosnia-Herzegovina v Serbia and Montenegro)* (Judgment) [2007] ICJ Rep <http://www.icj-cij.org at 25 October 2008>, in relation to jurisdiction, at 48, and matters of proof relating to conduct directed or controlled by a State:[143]. ('*Bosnian Genocide Case*').
125. *Bosnian Genocide Case.)* [2007] ICJ Rep, 143 [399–406].
126. *General and Complete Disarmament,* GA Res 49/75, UN GAOR, 49th sess, 90th plen mtg, [75K], UN Doc A/Res/49/75 (15 December 1994).
127. As an indication of how significant this matter was to the international community, 43 States supplied written statements to the Court; a record. A further 23 provided oral statements. See Manfred Mohr, '*Advisory Opinion of the International Court of Justice on the Legality of the Use of Nuclear Weapons Under International Law* – A Few Thoughts on its Strengths and Weaknesses' (1997) 316 *International Review of the Red Cross,* p. 94.
128. Eric David, 'The Opinion of the International Court of Justice on the Legality of the Use of Nuclear Weapons' (1997) 316 *International Review of the Red Cross* p. 21 described it as a landmark decision in 'the history of the Court, if not in history itself.' See also Luigi Condorelli, 'Nuclear Weapons: A Weighty Matter for the International Court of Justice' (1997) 316 *International Review of the Red Cross* p. 11; Christopher Greenwood, '*Jus ad Bellum* and *Jus in Bello* in the *Nuclear Weapons* Advisory Opinion' in Laurence Boisson de Chazournes and Phillipe Sands (eds), *International Law, the International Court of Justice and Nuclear Weapons* (1999), p. 249; Christopher Greenwood, 'The Advisory Opinion on Nuclear Weapons and the Contribution of the International Court to International Humanitarian Law' (1997) 316 *International Review of the Red Cross* 65, p. 65, where he stated that the request was one 'which the Court might well have preferred to do without.' John McNeill, 'The International Court of Justice Advisory Opinion in the *Nuclear Weapons* Cases – A First Appraisal' (1997) 316 *International Review of the Red Cross,* p. 117 claimed that this was one of the 'hardest cases ever' addressed by any court.

words of Judge Schwebel, the position of nuclear weapons in the international community was a problem of 'titanic tension between State practice and legal principle.'[129] Given the increasing support for nuclear disarmament and also for nuclear armament, within the international community, any decision would have received intense examination and criticism was inevitable.

The Court concluded by eleven votes to three, that in customary and conventional international law there is no comprehensive and universal prohibition of the threat or use of nuclear weapons.[130] It also held (unanimously), however, that 'there is in neither customary nor conventional international law any specific authorization of the threat or use of nuclear weapons'.[131] Similarly (and again unanimously) it held that:

> A threat or use of force by means of nuclear weapons that is contrary to Article 2, paragraph 4, of the *United Nations Charter* and that fails to meet all the requirements of Article 51, is unlawful;[132]

and (again unanimously) that:

> A threat or use of nuclear weapons should also be compatible with the requirements of the international law applicable in armed conflict, particularly those of the principles and rules of international humanitarian law, as well as with specific obligations under treaties and other undertakings which expressly deal with nuclear weapons;[133]

The most controversial part of the Opinion concerned the use of nuclear weapons in situations *in extremis*, where the survival of the State is dependent upon the threat of or the actual use of nuclear weapons, is legal. The Court concluded by the narrowest of majorities, seven to seven – the decision

129. *Nuclear Weapons Opinion* [1996] 1 ICJ Rep 226, 311 (Dissenting Opinion of Judge Schwebel). Part of the reason for such levels of tension is the important role nuclear weapons play in the defence policies of many of the dominant States in the international community, in particular the permanent members of the Security Council of the UN. David, *The Legality of the Use of Nuclear Weapons*, p. 21.
130. *Nuclear Weapons Opinion* [1996] 1 ICJ Rep 226 [105](2) (President Bedjaoui, Vice-President Schwebel, Judges Oda, Guillaume, Ranjeva, Herczegh, Shi, Fleischhauer, Vereshchetin, Ferrari Bravo, Higgins; Judges Shahabuddeen, Weeramantry, and Koroma dissenting).
131. Ibid, p. 105. However as noted by Professor Tim McCormack, 183 States are now party to the *Treaty on the Non-Proliferation of Nuclear Weapons*, opened for signature 1 July 1968, 729 UNTS 169, (entered into force 5 March 1970) and thus there is an effective comprehensive worldwide ban on nuclear weapons: Timothy L H McCormack, 'A *Non Liquet* on Nuclear Weapons – The ICJ avoids the Application of General Principles of International Humanitarian Law' (1997) 316 *International Review of the Red Cross* 76, p. 80.
132. *Nuclear Weapons Opinion* [1996] 1 ICJ Rep 226, [105].
133. Ibid.

determined by the President's casting vote – that the existing state of international law was insufficient to conclude whether the use of nuclear weapons in the situation of the survival of a State was illegal or legal.[134] Given the split decision, it may be argued that the Court in the *Nuclear Weapons Opinion* did not actually achieve clarification of international law on the use of nuclear weapons and may have muddied it even further.[135]

Such criticism is overly harsh. An analysis of the voting patterns reveals that three out of the fourteen refused to vote for the contentious paragraph 2E because it did not definitively hold that the use of threat of use of nuclear weapons was always illegal. Thus, in reality, ten of the fourteen judges supported, at the very least, that generally speaking nuclear weapons were illegal. Also, examining the Separate Opinions reveals that it was really only the use of nuclear weapons in situations of national survival that divided the Court, and that there was no doubt that the use in other circumstances would be illegal.[136] It was also very clear, in spite of the number of dissenting and Separate Opinions, that the Court as a whole believed that the principles and rules of armed conflict, both *jus ad bellum* and *jus in bello* – specifically the concepts of proportionality and necessity in self-defence – as well as the principles of international humanitarian law, applied to the use of nuclear weapons and indeed any weapon.

The *Nuclear Weapons Opinion* provided an exhaustive examination of both customary international law and treaty law, including the *UN Charter* and art 6 of the *International Covenant on Civil and Political Rights.*[137] The Court clarified some important applications of international law, such as that in any armed conflict parties are required by international law to take into account environmental considerations,[138] and that art 6 of the *ICCPR* does not override the law of armed conflict.[139] The Court's examination of humanitarian law has been used in subsequent cases, such as *Legality of Use of Force (Yugoslavia v United Kingdom) (Provisional Measures)*, where the Court examined the definition of genocide.[140]

134. Ibid, [105](2) (President Bedjaoui; Judges Ranjeva, Herczegh, Shi, Fleischhauer, Vereshchetin, Ferrari Bravo; Vice-President Schwebel; Judges Oda, Guillaume, Shahabuddeen, Weeramantry, Koroma, Higgins dissenting).
135. This is the *non liquet* argument raised by commentators and was even addressed by the Court itself. See ibid 584 at [7] (Dissenting Opinion of Judge Higgins); ibid 279 (Declaration of Judge Vereschetin); ibid 389 part 6, (Dissenting Opinion of Judge Shahabuddeen). See also McCormack, *A Non Liquet on Nuclear Weapons*, pp. 76–91.
136. Mohr, *Advisory Opinion*, p. 102.
137. *International Covenant on Civil and Political Rights*, opened for signature 16 December 1966, 999 UNTS 171, art 6 (entered into force 23 March 1976) ('*ICCPR*').
138. *Nuclear Weapons Opinion* [1996] 1 ICJ Rep 226, [30].
139. Greenwood, *The International Court of Justice and the Use of Force*, pp. 68–75.
140. *Legality of Use of Force (Yugoslavia v United Kingdom) (Provisional Measures)* [1999] ICJ Rep 826, 838.

Despite its contribution to the development of the law of armed conflict, the Court's Opinion received much criticism, mainly for not taking the opportunity to finally end one of the greatest threats posed to humanity's existence.[141] There are several arguments that can be raised supporting the notion that the use of nuclear weapons even *in extremis* (where the survival of the State is at stake) will not comply with the laws of armed conflict.

For example, the situation of a State fighting for its survival conjures images of foreign armies invading its territory with an inevitable confusion of both troops and civilians fleeing the invaders. In such a context it is difficult to imagine being able to isolate a military target within a State's own borders. Under the enormous pressure of the need to survive, will States be willing or able to comply with international law? What target would be chosen? Would it choose an isolated military target as a method of sending a clear message to the attackers that if they do not desist, they will be attacked with nuclear weapons?[142] Or will it use the weapons to destroy the attacking forces? Or would it simply decide to obliterate the territory of the attacker together with its civilians?[143]

There is, perhaps, an even more important and fundamental consideration. The consideration of the use of nuclear weapons by States *in extremis* raises a very important question that strikes at the heart of international law. At the core of the *Nuclear Weapons Opinion* is an examination of the relative importance of the State in the context of the international legal system and the international community in general. Another way of expressing this question is: 'Are States more important than the international community or humanity itself?'[144]

141. Some members of the Bench expressed this view. See, eg, Judge Weeramantry who criticised his brethren for failing to seize the day and denounce the use of nuclear weapons as always being illegal. See generally *Nuclear Weapons Opinion* [1996] ICJ Rep 226 (Dissenting Opinion of Judge Weeramantry).
142. This is similar to the so-called 'low-yield warning shot' raised by Malaysia and dismissed comprehensively by Judge Weeramantry: *Nuclear Weapons Opinion* [1996] 1 ICJ Rep 226, 538–42 (Dissenting Opinion of Judge Weeramantry).
143. In discussing the effect of nuclear weapons, Judge Weeramantry wrote that an attacked State would be 'so ravaged that it will not be able to make fine evaluations of the exact amount of retaliatory force required. In such event, the tendency to release as strong a retaliation as is available must enter into any realistic evaluation of the situation': ibid 470 (Dissenting Opinion of Judge Weeramantry).
144. No clearer statement of this principle can be found than in *Nuclear Weapons Opinion* [1996] ICJ Rep 226, [22] of the Court's Opinion:

> A State's right to survival is also a fundamental law, similar in many respects to a 'natural' law. However, self-defence – if exercised in extreme circumstances in which the very survival of a State is in question – cannot produce a situation in which a State would exonerate itself from compliance with the 'intransgressible' norms of international humanitarian law. … It would thus be quite foolhardy unhesitatingly to set the survival of a State above all other considerations, in particular above the survival of mankind itself.

Many of those criticising the opinion feel strongly that no State is more important than any other State, and certainly not more so than 'humanity' itself.[145] Kohen summarises this point very well:

> Even assuming that the existence of [S]tates is considered a basic value, this existence cannot be seen in an isolated way: the existence of one state cannot be considered more important than the existence of any other, and even less can it be considered more important than the existence of the whole international community.[146]

In another brilliant statement, Kohen argues that '[i]nternational law has as its main social function not to ensure the continued existence of single [S]tates, but to guarantee the *coexistence* of [S]tates.'[147] This issue raises the eternal debate of positivism and natural law, and once again Kohen expresses the question very well:

> The assumption that sovereign [S]tates are not subordinated to any higher power does not entail the negation of the simple – but often neglected – idea that they are subordinated to international law. It is important not to lose sight of the fact that the existence of any society implies that its members do not have absolute freedom to act, that their rights must be exercised within the rules they have adopted to regulate their relations. This is the main difference between society and the state of nature.[148]

Many members of the Court, in particular Judges Weeramantry, Koroma and Shahabuddeen would agree with Kohen. They argued that since States were part of a highly interdependent community, no single State has a legal right to possess or use weapons that are able to destroy the entire community.[149]

145. Judith Gardam, 'Necessity and Proportionality in *Jus ad Bellum* and *Jus in Bello*' in Laurence Boisson de Chazournes and Phillipe Sands (eds), *International Law, the International Court of Justice and Nuclear Weapons*, Cambridge: Cambridge University Press 1999, p. 287 states that '[t]he opinion of Judge Fleischhauer [in his Separate Opinion] places considerations of State sovereignty ahead of the interests of humanity, an approach that fails to reflect the developing emphasis of international law.' The choice of expression 'humanity' is deliberate, and is in the sense of the language used in the *UN Charter*: 'We the peoples…'. This involves adopting a non-Statist perspective of international law and this is in contradiction to a purely positivist approach.
146. Marcelo Kohen, 'The Notion of 'State Survival' in International Law' in de Chazournes and Sands, *International Law*, p. 312. Kohen concluded that it is not the survival of States that is at stake but the survival of international law, p. 313.
147. Ibid, p. 312 (emphasis in original).
148. Ibid, p. 311.
149. See, eg, *Nuclear Weapons Opinion* [1996] 1 ICJ Rep 226, 465 (Dissenting Opinion of Judge Weeramantry), where his Honour stated: 'An individual's right to defend his own interests is a right he enjoys against his opponents. In exercising that right, he cannot be considered entitled to destroy the village in which he lives.' See also and especially at 393–4

This constitutes a very clear rejection of a positivist approach and a clear message to States that their sovereignty was far from absolute.[150] Judge Shabuddeen writes:

> Thus however far-reaching may be the rights conferred by sovereignty, those rights cannot extend beyond the framework within which sovereignty itself exists; in particular, they cannot violate the framework. The framework shuts out the right of a State to embark on a course of action which would dismantle the basis of the framework by putting an end to civilisation and annihilating mankind. It is not that a State is prohibited from exercising a right which, but for the prohibition, it would have; a State can have no such right to begin with.[151]

International law has chipped away at the so-called 'absoluteness' of national sovereignty for decades in a variety of areas, however the statements referred to above are unusually frank, and the implications of such judgments for the international community are important. The reference to a 'framework' implies that there exists a higher authority to which States are answerable. In essence Judge Shahabuddeen's statement above rejects the positivist *Lotus* principle, which claims that States have a sovereign right to do whatever is not prohibited under international law.[152] Judge Shahabuddeen further stated that:

> There is not any convincing ground for the view that the '*Lotus*' Court moved off on a supposition that States have an absolute sovereignty which would entitle them to do anything however horrid or repugnant to the sense of the international community, provided that the doing of it could not be shown to be prohibited under international law. ... The existence of a number of sovereignties side by side places limits on the freedom of each State to act as if the others did not exist. These limits define an objective structural framework within which sovereignty must necessarily exist.[153]

(Dissenting Opinion of Judge Shahabuddeen): 'is there anything in the sovereignty of a State which would entitle it to embark on a course of action which could effectively wipe out the existence of all States by ending civilization and annihilating mankind? An affirmative answer is not reasonable'.

150. In fact, Judge Weeramantry went even further and stated in Part IX of his Dissenting Opinion in Ibid, p. 553 (Dissenting Opinion of Judge Weeramantry) that: 'As stated at the outset, my considered opinion on this matter is that the use or threat of use of nuclear weapons is incompatible with international law *and with the very foundations* on which that system rests' (emphasis added).
151. Ibid, p. 393 (Dissenting Opinion of Judge Shahabuddeen).
152. *S S Lotus Case (France v Turkey)* [1927] PCIJ (ser A) No 10 ('*Lotus Case*').
153. *Nuclear Weapons Opinion* [1996] 1 ICJ Rep 226, 393 (Dissenting Opinion of Judge Shahabuddeen). Ibid, 394 (Dissenting Opinion of Judge Shahabuddeen) he states that the

However, the full potential of such findings was not realised as the Court split when deciding the question of whether nuclear weapons were always illegal. This question rested on whether existing principles of international law, both treaty and customary, were sufficient to provide an answer.[154] The Court was not assisted by the wording of the request, described by Greenwood as not an 'easy one', since it forced the court to consider two (in his opinion) ridiculous extremes; that nuclear weapons are always illegal or always legal.[155] Thus, in Greenwood's opinion, it made their conclusion in the controversial paragraph (2E of the *Dispositif*) inevitable.[156] As such the Opinion received admiration as well as criticism.

> The Hague Court probably did its best in this near-impossible task for any judicial body, rather adroitly avoiding potential damage first of all to its own prestige and reliability. At the same time, the Advisory Opinion (which has to be read together with the Separate and Dissenting Opinions of all the judges) reflects existing real world controversies.[157]

Lotus Case should be distinguished on the basis that that decision concerned a case of collision at sea and not the survivability of the human race.

154. This not surprisingly split the Court, due to the differing interpretations of whether existing international law was sufficient to answer this question. In the eyes of the majority and some commentators to proceed further was going beyond the role of the Court as a judicial entity. One member of the bench, Judge Fleischauer, in *Nuclear Weapons Opinion* [1996] 1 ICJ Rep 226, [3] (Separate Opinion of Judge Fleischhauer) felt that even to find that the use of nuclear weapons were illegal even in self-defence would breach the principle of sovereign equality.
155. Greenwood '*Jus ad Bellum* and *Jus in Bello* p. 249. See also Condorelli, *Nuclear Weapons: A Weighty Matter*, 11. Peter Bekker similarly concluded that it was 'unrealistic to expect the International Court of Justice to solve this immense problem by way of an advisory opinion in reply to a vigorously contested request that consisted of a mere fifteen words': Peter Bekker, 'Legality of the Threat or Use of Nuclear Weapons' in Peter Bekker (ed), *Commentaries on World Court Decisions (1987–1996)* (1998) 233, 242.
156. Paragraph 2E stated:

> It follows from the above-mentioned requirements that the threat or use of nuclear weapons would generally be contrary to the rules of international law applicable in armed conflict, and in particular the principles and rules of humanitarian law; However, in view of the current state of international law, and of the elements of fact at its disposal, the Court cannot conclude definitively whether the threat or use of nuclear weapons would be lawful or unlawful in an extreme circumstance of self-defence, in which the very survival of a State would be at stake

Nuclear Weapons Opinion, [1996] ICJ Rep 66, [2E].

157. Rein Mullerson, 'On the Relationship Between *Jus ad Bellum* and *Jus in Bello* in the General Assembly Advisory Opinion' in Laurence Boisson de Chazournes and Phillipe Sands (eds), *International Law, the International Court of Justice and Nuclear Weapons* (1999) p. 274. See also Mohr, *Advisory Opinion*, p. 102.

The questionable existence of sufficient principles of international law to answer the Request caused the split in the Court. In the opinion of the majority they did not exist and, if the Court were to go beyond the existing principles of international law, to 'fill the gap', as it were, the Court would be exposed to the argument that it had overstepped its role as a judicial body and had become a 'legislator'.[158] Simpson discusses the criticism received by the ICJ for overreaching its jurisdiction in, for example, the *Military and Paramilitary Activities In and Against Nicaragua* and the *Nuclear Tests (Australia v France)*.[159] Other similar examples include *Western Sahara (Advisory Opinion)*[160] as mentioned above, and also the *South West Africa (Ethiopia v South Africa; Liberia v South Africa) (Second Phase) (Judgment)*.[161] Despite the difference of opinions of the members of the bench, the Court was united in its belief that it should act as a judicial body only and not as a legislator.[162] Any criticism overlooks this one important fact.

It is not surprising that current treaty law does not state that the use of nuclear weapons would be illegal since, as Greenwood notes, the powers that signed and ratified the treaties were nuclear powers themselves.[163] This raises the argument that the Court should have taken on the role of legislator in this instance, as it was aware of the probability of nuclear powers refusing to adopt a treaty to deprive them of the very weapons that maintain their status and security in the

158. Greenwood agrees with the majority of the Court that finding that nuclear weapons are illegal in all situations would have meant going beyond their judicial function: Greenwood, *The Advisory Opinion on Nuclear Weapons*, p. 74. This issue played a crucial role in the President of the Court Bedjaoui casting his vote with the majority. See His Excellency Bedjaoui's Declaration, where he stated at [9]:

> [a]s its Advisory Opinion shows, at no time did the Court lose sight of the fact that nuclear weapons constitute a potential means of destruction of all mankind. Not for a moment did it fail to take into account this eminently crucial factor for the survival of mankind. ... But the Court could obviously not go beyond what the law says. It could not say what the law does not say.

159. *Military and Paramilitary Activities in and against Nicaragua (Nicaragua v United States of America) (Provisional Measures)* [1984] ICJ Rep 392 and *Nuclear Tests (Australia v France) (Judgment)* [1974] ICJ Rep 253, respectively: Simpson, *Judging the East Timor Dispute*, p. 330. He uses the expression 'contentious political disputes'.
160. [1975] ICJ Rep 12. This decision in particular created a problem of perception, since many former colonies and non-European States, viewed it as another attempt at re-colonisation and the establishment of European dominance in particular. However, this may not be as valid an argument today. Mohamed Shahabuddeen writes that this perception may have been valid two decades ago but today, the ICJ is in 'no danger of developing law from a preponderantly European standpoint': Shahabuddeen, *The World Court*, p. 20.
161. [1966] ICJ Rep 6.
162. Judge Guillaume expressed this succinctly in *Nuclear Weapons Opinion* [1996] 1 ICJ Rep 226, [14] (Separate Opinion of Judge Guillaume). See also *Nuclear Weapons Opinion* [1996] 1 ICJ Rep 226, [9] (Declaration of President Bedjaoui).
163. Greenwood, *The Advisory Opinion on Nuclear Weapons*, pp. 65–75.

international community. The Court, however, refused to do so.[164] If international law is insufficient, then it is imperative that the ICJ reveals such flaws to the international community for it to make the necessary changes.[165]

3. The Lockerbie Decisions

There are two decisions that relate to the tragedy that occurred in the skies above Lockerbie, Scotland.[166] The first decision refers to virtually identical orders of April 1992 made in relation to the request from Libya for provisional measures in accordance with art 41 of the *ICJ Statute* against the UK and the US.[167] The second decision concerns Preliminary Objections and was finally resolved in 1998.[168]

On 21 December 1988 Pan Am Flight 103 exploded in mid-air above Lockerbie, Scotland, killing 270 crew and passengers, mainly American and British citizens, as well as killing Scottish civilians on the ground.[169] As a result of investigations by US and UK police and intelligence organisations, the cause of the explosion was attributed to an act of terrorism by two Libyan nationals, Fhimah and Megrahi, who were then charged with the destruction of Pan Am Flight 103 by the Lord Advocate of Scotland. Further, it was alleged by the US and UK that the two were sponsored by the Libyan Government.[170] The US and the UK then issued a joint request to Libya to surrender the two charged for trial in the US or UK. The Security Council subsequently endorsed this request in Resolution 731 on 21 January 1992.[171] Libya responded by instituting proceedings against both the US and the UK before the ICJ on 3 March 1992.

Libya, in its applications before the ICJ, sought to obtain a declaration: (1) that Libya had complied fully with the 1971 *Convention for the Suppression*

164. Since 1991 the trend has been increased usage of the Court by States and thus the Court has been able to continue the development of international law, to the extent that there is a rich source of knowledge and the idea of 'gaps' within international law is fast becoming an issue of the past.
165. Condorelli, *Nuclear Weapons: A Weighty Matter*, p. 11; Bekker, *Legality of the Use of Nuclear Weapons*, pp. 241–42.
166. For an idea of the impact the tragedy has had upon families of those killed see the article by Aphrodite Tsairis, 'International Terrorism: Prevention and Remedies: Lessons of Lockerbie' (1996) 22 *Syracuse Journal of International Law and Commerce*, pp. 31–40.
167. *Lockerbie Decision* [1992] ICJ Rep 3.
168. *Questions of Interpretation and Application of the 1971 Montreal Convention Arising from the Aerial Incident at Lockerbie (Libyan Arab Jamahiriya v United States of America) (Preliminary Objections)* [1998] ICJ Rep 115 ('*1998 Lockerbie Decision*').
169. In fact, the 270 killed were from a total of 21 different countries: Tsairis, *International Terrorism*, p. 31.
170. Ibid, pp. 31–32.
171. *Libyan Arab Jamahiriya*, SC Res 731, UN SCOR, 47th sess, 3033rd mtg, art 3, UN Doc S/Res/731 (21 January 1992).

of Unlawful Acts against the Safety of Civil Aviation;[172] (2) that the US and the UK had breached, and continued to breach, various articles of the *Montreal Convention*; and (3) that the US and the UK should cease to use or threaten to use force against Libya, as well as to violate Libyan sovereignty and territorial integrity. Finally, Libya also sought provisional measures under art 41 of the *ICJ Statute* seeking to prevent the US and the UK from taking action to force Libya to surrender the two alleged to be responsible for the Lockerbie Incident.[173]

On 31 March 1992, a mere three days after the close of the ICJ's oral hearings of Libya's request for provisional measures, the Security Council adopted Resolution 748, which stated *inter alia* that all States should take action (using economic as well as diplomatic measures) if Libya failed to comply with Security Council Resolution 731. This was clearly designed to coerce Libya to surrender the two nationals charged with the bombing. The Court thus dismissed Libya's request for provisional measures on the basis that the adoption of Resolution 748 effectively destroyed the rights Libya claimed under the *Montreal Convention*, and that there were thus no rights to protect by provisional measures.[174]

The issue before the ICJ was indeed 'highly political,' with the Security Council invoking Chapter VII of the *UN Charter* to adopt Resolution 748. The actions of the Security Council thus appeared in conflict with the Libyan request for provisional measures, and further with the Court's ability to consider the request. This potential conflict between the respective organs of the UN, both in the process of resolving the same dispute, raised the issue of the legal/political dichotomy, and the role of both in the resolution of highly political matters. The matter also provided an opportunity for the ICJ to examine and clarify its relationship with the Security Council.[175]

There were a number of interesting aspects to the judgment. Firstly, the Court confirmed its independence and judicial integrity by once more stating that it would not let 'political considerations' interfere with the performance of its role as the primary judicial body of the UN.[176] Thus, the Court rejected

172. Opened for signature 23 September 1971, 974 UNTS 178 (entered into force 26 January 1973) ('*Montreal Convention*').
173. *Lockerbie Decision* [1992] ICJ Rep 3. For an excellent summary see the article by Gowland-Debbas, *The International Court of Justice and the Security Council*.
174. *Lockerbie Decision* [1992] ICJ Rep 3, pp 14–15.
175. The ICJ needed to examine whether it could function as a constitutional court exercising judicial review of the Security Council. A similar issue arose in the *Tadić Case* where the ICTY, in a manner similar to the ICJ in the *Lockerbie Decision*, confirmed that establishing its jurisdiction was a judicial task, since it involved a task necessary to achieve its purpose as stated in art 1 of its *Statute*, and thus was not a review of the Security Council's resolution establishing the tribunal. The ICTY also rejected the political/legal dichotomy: see *Tadić*, Case No IT-94-1-AR72 (2 October 1995) [15–20], [24].
176. *Lockerbie Decision* [1992] ICJ Rep 3, [18].

the arguments put forward by both the US and UK counsel that the very fact that the Security Council was now involved meant that the Court had no role to play.[177] Secondly, the Court drew attention to the differences between the Security Council and the Court, noting that whilst there was a clear distinction between the two, each played a role in the pacific settlement of disputes; a role that was intended by the *UN Charter*.[178] Thirdly, the Court held that there was no 'exclusivity' in the nature of the power granted to the Security Council under art 24 of the *UN Charter*,[179] and further that the *UN Charter* does not establish a hierarchy between the ICJ and the Security Council.[180] Finally, the Court found that there was no provision in the *ICJ Statute* equivalent to art 12 of the *UN Charter*, forbidding the Court from performing its role once a dispute was before the Security Council.[181]

There were two significant aspects of the Court's decision. Firstly, the Court affirmed that in highly political matters, its role as the principal judicial organ of the UN is to resolve legal questions so as to assist the UN to achieve its prime objective; the maintenance of peace and security.[182] Secondly, the Court completely rejected the 'traditional' dichotomy of legal/political questions.[183] This was particularly evident in the Dissenting Opinions of Judges Weeramantry and El-Kosheri. The former stated that:

> As a judicial organ, it will be the Court's duty from time to time to examine and determine from a strictly legal point of view matters which may at the same time be the subject of determination from an executive or political point of view by another principal organ of the United Nations. The Court by virtue of its nature and constitution applies to the matter before it the concepts, the criteria and the methodology of the judicial

177. The argument put forward by the US and the UK was that Libya's application was intended to interfere with the Security Council's primary responsibility, namely the maintenance of peace and security, a responsibility that was within the *exclusive competence* of the Security Council: Gowlland-Debbas, *the International Court of Justice and the Security Council*, pp. 654–55.
178. *Lockerbie Decision* [1992] ICJ Rep 3, [56] (Dissenting Opinion of Judge Weeramantry); [7] (Dissenting Opinion of Judge El-Kosheri).
179. Thus reaffirming the Court's earlier decision in *Certain Expenses of the United Nations (Advisory Opinion)* [1962] ICJ Rep 151, p. 163.
180. *Lockerbie Decision* [1992] ICJ Rep 3, [36]. This again reaffirmed an earlier decision of *United States Diplomatic and Consular Staff in Tehran (United States of America v Iran) (Judgment)* [1980] ICJ Rep 3.
181. *UN Charter* art 12(1) states: '[w]hile the Security Council is exercising in respect of any dispute or situation the functions assigned to it in the present *Charter*, the General Assembly shall not make any recommendation with regard to that dispute or situation unless the Security Council so requests.'
182. *UN Charter*, art 92.
183. *Lockerbie Decision* [1992] ICJ Rep 3; 22 (Declaration of Judge Ni); 34 (Dissenting Opinion Judge Bedjaoui); Gowlland-Debbas, *the International Court of Justice and the Security Council*, pp. 653–55.

> process which other organs of the United Nations are naturally not obliged to do. The concepts it uses are juridical concepts, its criteria are standards of legality, its method is that of legal proof. Its tests of validity and the bases of its decisions are naturally not the same as they would be before a political executive organ of the United Nations.[184]

His Honour then referred to the *Aegean Sea Case*,[185] where Judge Lachs stated:

> The frequently unorthodox nature of the problems facing States today requires as many tools to be used and as many avenues to be opened as possible, in order to resolve the intricate and frequently multidimensional issues involved.[186]

The Court, as one of the organs of the United Nations, will assist the overall body to resolve international disputes and maintain peace and security, by doing what it is equipped and trained to do – resolve those necessary legal questions so that a final resolution can be achieved by the UN. The Court does not even attempt to claim that it operates on its own, but rather has acknowledged that it works with the Security Council to achieve the maintenance of international peace and security. In other words, the Court's decision is a means to an end – not the end itself.[187]

This analysis was reinforced by the ICJ's determination in 1998 of the Preliminary Objections to its jurisdiction filed by the US. The ICJ concluded that it did indeed have jurisdiction on the basis that there existed a dispute between the parties concerning the interpretation of art 7 of *Montreal Convention*, or any other legal regime applied, and that these were questions that could be decided by legal methodology through a judicial process.[188] The ICJ also confirmed its previous decision in the *Lockerbie Decision*, that for the purposes of establishing its jurisdiction, its decision was unaffected by the Security Council's adoption of Resolution 748 and 883 since they were adopted after the filing of Libya's application.[189]

4. Arrest Warrants Case

The three matters brought before the ICJ and discussed above were all highly political. One significant pattern has emerged from the ICJ's handling

184. *Lockerbie Decision* [1992] ICJ Rep 3, 56 (Dissenting Opinion of Judge Weeramantry).
185. *Aegean Sea Continental Shelf Case (Greece v Turkey)* [1978] ICJ Rep 3.
186. *Lockerbie Decision* [1992] ICJ Rep 3, 69 (Separate Opinion of Judge Lachs); *Aegean Sea Continental Shelf Case (Greece v Turkey) (Jurisdiction)* [1978] ICJ Rep 3, 52.
187. Thus confirming what Kelsen and Mosler had argued. See above nn. 32, 39 and 40 and accompanying text.
188. *1998 Lockerbie Decision* [1998] ICJ Rep 115, [24]–[38].
189. Ibid, [38].

of these matters – that the Court is clearly able to, and does, insulate itself from the political background, thus ensuring that its decision remains judicial in nature. This was also evident in the *Arrest Warrants Case.*[190]

This case arose after the then incumbent Foreign Minister of the Democratic Republic of the Congo (referred to as the Congo), Abdoulaye Yerodia Ndombasi, was accused of breaching humanitarian law, specifically crimes against humanity, by inciting racial hatred during August 1998. Belgium charged Mr Yerodia and issued a warrant for his arrest, even though the accused's alleged offences took place outside Belgium, he was not a Belgian national, and the victims were also not Belgian nationals.[191] In response, the Congo filed an application with the registry of the ICJ requesting that the Court 'declare that the Kingdom of Belgium shall annul the international arrest warrant issued on 11 April 2000'.[192] By thirteen votes to three, the Court held that the issue of the arrest warrant violated Belgium's legal obligations towards the Congo, because it failed to respect the immunity from criminal jurisdiction and the inviolability which the then incumbent Minister for Foreign Affairs of the Congo enjoyed under international law.[193]

Whilst this decision can be criticised in view of the increasing recognition and willingness of the international community to prosecute crimes against humanity, it should be recognised that the Court performed its judicial function admirably. It answered the specific legal question placed before it, rather than merely responding to the political pressure and desire of the international community to bring those accused of crimes against humanity to justice. As Judge Koroma asserted:

> In the light of the foregoing, any attempt to qualify the Judgment as formalistic, or to assert that the Court avoided the real issue of the commission of heinous crimes is without foundation. The Court cannot, and in the present case, has not taken a neutral position on the issue of heinous crimes. Rather, the Court's ruling should be seen as responding to the question asked of it. The ruling ensures that legal concepts are consistent with international law and legal tenets, and accord with legal truth.[194]

In other words the Court will not instigate a witch hunt, and that must be reassuring to the parties involved.

190. *Arrest Warrant of 11 April 2000 (Democratic Republic of Congo v Belgium) (Judgment)* [2002] ICJ Rep 3 ('*Arrest Warrants Case*').
191. The 'local' Belgian Law was the *Loi relative à la répression des violations graves de droit international humanitaire*, enacted on 16 June 1993, as amended by the Law of 10 February 1999. For an English translation see Stefan Smis and Kim van der Borght, 38 ILM 918 (1999).
192. *Arrest Warrants Case* [2002] ICJ Rep 3, 9.
193. Ibid, 32 [78] (2).
194. Separate Opinion of Judge Koroma. *Arrest Warrants Case* [2002] ICJ Rep 3, 62, [11].

5. Bosnian Genocide Case

The *Bosnian Genocide Case* involved the claim by Bosnia-Herzegovina that Serbia had committed acts of genocide by killing 7–8,000 military-aged Bosnian Muslim males in and around Srebrenica, during 1995.[195] The judgment, handed down on 26 February 2007, marked the end of fourteen years of political manoeuvrings, and nationalistic fervour in an area torn apart by bitter conflict. As such the decision took place in the context of one of the most politically and emotionally charged backgrounds in the Court's history.[196] As noted by Dimitrijevic and Milanovic:

> It is certainly true that every case before an international court has a broader context, that many a proceeding is but a facet of a larger dispute, and that politics will always play a part. The *Genocide* case, however, is *special*. There is no other ICJ case which meant so much to so many people, no other case in which internal politics so manifestly prevented an applicant from arguing its best legal position, and no other ICJ judgment which has been so badly misinterpreted, again due to politics.[197]

In a nutshell the ICJ decided that whilst the deaths of the Bosnian Muslims at Srebrenica amounted to genocide, there was insufficient evidence to prove Serbian responsibility. Whilst the Court held that Serbia was neither responsible for the commission of genocide, nor was it complicit in the killings, the ICJ held that Serbia had failed to prevent the massacre, and also had failed to punish those who were responsible for the massacre.[198]

The Court's controversial decision is significant for a variety of reasons: (1) firstly, its determination of jurisdiction, and the identification of the respondent party, no simple task given the problems caused by the continued dissolution of the SFRY with Montenegro's successful claim to independence after proceedings were initiated, and the doubtful status of the UN

195. *Case Concerning the Application of the Convention on the Prevention and Punishment of the Crime of Genocide (Bosnia-Herzegovina v Serbia and Montenegro)* [2007] ICJ Rep 43, 155 ('*Bosnian Genocide Case*'). The allegations extended to killings at a variety of detention camps, for example Susica; Foca Kazneno-Popravni Dom; and Batkovic. Ibid: 146–147 [252]–[255].
196. As noted by Dimitrijevic and Milanovic, the high emotions generated by, and surrounding, the *Bosnian Genocide Case*, were clearly displayed by the actions of a prominent Bosnian intellectual who immediately after the decision was handed down, dramatically tore up the judgment of the Court outside the gates of the Peace Palace. The response in the various national newspapers of the SFRY were also a testament to the emotions of citizens from all sides of the dispute. Vojin Dimitrijevic and Marko Milanovic, 'The Strange Story of the Bosnian *Genocide* Case', (2008) 21 *Leiden Journal of International Law*, pp. 85–86.
197. Dimitrijevic and Milanovic, 'The Strange Story of the Bosnian *Genocide* Case', 21 (2008) *Leiden Journal of International Law*, p. 92.
198. By thirteen votes to two. *Bosnian Genocide Case*, 168, [471].

membership of the Federal Republic of Yugoslavia, the successor State to the SFRY;[199] (2) the discussion of State responsibility under the Geneva Convention, particularly in the absence of a conviction of an individual perpetrator;[200] (3) matters of proof, which was particularly controversial;[201] and (4) finally, holding a State responsible for failing to take the necessary steps to prevent genocide.[202]

However, perhaps the greatest significance of the decision is that the Court actually managed to hand down a judgment at all, given the intensity of the attempts to derail the matter – or in the words of Dimitrijevic and Milanovic – to sabotage the Court's effort to determine the matter – by ethnic Serbs within the government of Bosnia-Herzegovina itself,[203] by the political manoeuvrings of the parties concerned,[204] on-going events in the region,[205] and by the sheer emotion the events in Kosovo created.[206] As noted by Dimitrijevic and Milanovic: '... what makes the *Genocide* Case truly distinctive is that it was, perhaps more than any other ICJ case, from its beginning to its end at the mercy of political considerations outside the courtroom.'[207]

For example, the complex constitutional structure of the government of Bosnia-Herzegovina required a collective head of State that represented the three ethnic groups. So the presidency comprised a Serb, a Croat and a Muslim, and the chairmanship of the presidency rotated periodically. This enabled the Serb member of the presidency, Zivko Radisic, without consulting the other members of the presidency to attempt to discontinue Bosnia-Herzegovina's application, with which Serbia gratefully agreed.[208] The purported discontinuance delayed proceedings for approximately a year, as well as the postponement of oral hearings.[209] Another example of sabotage was the deliberate removal of funding for Bosnia-Herzegovina's management of the matter, again due to actions of the ethnic Serb president,

199. For a discussion of the significance of the Court's decision, please refer to: C.F. Amerasinghe, 'Hague International Tribunals, the *Bosnia Genocide* Case' 21 (2008) *Leiden Journal of International Law*, p. 412; Dimitrijevic and Milanovic, *The Strange Story*, p. 92; Susana Sa Couto, 'Reflections on the Judgment of the International Court of Justice in Bosnia's Genocide Case Against Serbia and Montenegro', 15 *Human Rights Brief*, 2, p. 3.
200. Amerasinghe, *The Bosnia Genocide Case*, p. 412; Sa Couto, *Reflections*, pp. 2–3; Dimitrijevic and Milanovic, *The Strange Story*, p. 81.
201. Amerasinghe, *The Bosnia Genocide Case*, p. 412; Sa Couto, *Reflections*, pp. 2–3.
202. Amerasinghe, *The Bosnia Genocide Case*, p. 412; Sa Couto, *Reflections*, pp. 2–3.
203. Dimitrijevic and Milanovic, *The Strange Story*, pp. 74–76.
204. Ibid, p. 74.
205. Such as the conflict in Kosovo, and the successful claim of Montenegro for independence, as well as domestic issues such as election campaigns within Serbia itself.
206. Dimitrijevic and Milanovic, *The Strange Story*, pp. 86–87.
207. Ibid, p. 66.
208. Ibid, p. 74.
209. Ibid. The Court did determine that the purported discontinuance did not represent the true will of the State of Bosnia-Herzegovina. *Bosnian Genocide Case* [2007] ICJ Rep 43, 54, [24].

acting with the Croat president.[210] Finally, Borislav Paravac, the Serb member of the Bosnia-Herzegovina presidency, lodged a request with the Constitutional Court of Bosnia-Herzegovina to examine the constitutionality of Bosnia-Herzegovina's application to the ICJ.[211]

Secondly, the conflict in Kosovo resulted in Serbia and Montenegro lodging an application to the ICJ regarding the use of force by the ten NATO States on 29 April 1999 involved in air strikes against Serbia.[212] The subsequent dismissal of Serbia and Montenegro's application was because the Court lacked jurisdiction on the basis that Serbia and Montenegro was not a UN member in 1999 (at the time of their application) and therefore, could not access the Court under art 35(1) of the *ICJ Statute*.[213] Such a conclusion then caused difficulties for the Court to determine that it did indeed have jurisdiction to hear the claim made against Serbia and Montenegro in the *Bosnian Genocide Case*.[214] Dimitrijevic and Milanovic, argue that this decision in 2004 was a deliberate attempt by a majority of judges, newly admitted to the bench of the ICJ, to 'sink' the *Bosnian Genocide Case*, which was still pending.[215] This decision prompted Serbia to redouble its efforts to have the *Bosnian Genocide Case* dismissed on jurisdictional grounds.[216]

Thirdly, the application brought by Bosnia-Herzegovina in the *Bosnian Genocide Case* was from the very beginning, constrained to invoking Article

210. For the next four years the matter only proceeded due to funding from private sources. Dimitrijevic and Milanovic, *The Strange Story*, pp. 74–75.
211. Ibid, p. 75. The Bosnian Court managed to avoid a ruling until after the ICJ had handed down its decision in the *Bosnian Genocide Case*, which then enabled them to decide that it was not appropriate for a further ruling to be made in the circumstances.
212. *Legality of the Use of Force (Serbia and Montenegro v Belgium)*; *(Serbia and Montenegro v Canada)*; *(Serbia and Montenegro v France)*; *(Serbia and Montenegro v Germany)*; *(Serbia and Montenegro v Italy)*; *(Serbia and Montenegro v Netherlands)*; *(Serbia and Montenegro v Portugal)*; *(Serbia and Montenegro v Portugal)*; *(Serbia and Montenegro v United Kingdom)*; *(Serbia and Montenegro v United States)*. Serbia and Montenegro also sought an order for provisional measures, which the Court dismissed by twelve votes to four in its order of 2 June 1999. *Case Concerning the Legality of the Use of Force (Serbia and Montenegro v Belgium) (Provisional Measures)* [1999] ICJ Rep 124 140 [51].
213. The ICJ also denied Serbia and Montenegro under art 35(2): *Case Concerning the Legality of the Use of Force (Serbia and Montenegro v Belgium)(Preliminary Objections)* [2004] ICJ Rep 279, 315–324 [92–114].
214. This decision was also a reversal of the Court's position in its decision made a year earlier in the *Application for Revision of the Judgment of 11 July 1996 in the Case Concerning Application of the Convention on the Prevention and punishment of the Crime of Genocide (Bosnia-Herzegovina v Yugoslavia) (Preliminary Objections) (Yugoslavia v Bosnia and Herzegovnia)*, Judgment of 3 February 2003 [2003] ICJ Rep 7.
215. Dimitrijevic and Milanovic, *The Strange Story*, pp. 82. The minority of 7 judges made this point very clear in their Joint Declaration: *Case Concerning the Legality of the Use of Force (Serbia and Montenegro v Belgium) (Preliminary Objections)* [2004] ICJ Rep 279, 330, 334. (Joint declaration of Vice-President Ranjeva, Judges Guillaume, Higgins, Kooijmans, Al-Khasawneh, Buergenthal, and Elaraby.)
216. Dimitrijevic and Milanovic, *The Strange Story*, p. 82.

IX of the *Genocide Convention* as the basis of the ICJ's jurisdiction to hear the application. This restriction was because Serbia and Montenegro had not accepted the ICJ's compulsory jurisdiction under art 36 (2) of the *ICJ Statute*.[217] Secondly, in an attempt to obtain an order for provisional measures from the ICJ to declare the arms embargo created by Security Council Resolution 713 as illegal, the Bosnian government claimed that the arms embargo denied it the means to defend itself from genocide.[218] The constant reference to genocide in these legal proceedings meant that genocide came to be associated in the broader context of public discussion with every action that Serbia undertook in Bosnia-Herzegovina.[219] Thus the perception of the meaning of genocide in the public discourse became distorted, and increasingly distant from the strict legal definition.[220]

Consequently, a finding by the Court that no genocide took place could have been perceived by the Serbian authorities as a validation of their actions, and even of the lawful existence of the *Republika Srpska*, and Bosnian Muslims would consider anything other than a guilty verdict as ignoring the illegality of Serbian aggression.[221] This background must have placed immense pressure on the Court to avoid legal niceties and technical interpretations in favour of a populist definition that would appear to offer a sense of justice to so many people. And yet the Court did not buckle: it applied what it believed to be a legal definition of genocide, and the Court's findings in no way dismissed the events that happened in Kosovo. Furthermore, it was indicated by Her Excellency Judge Higgins that these events may have amounted to war crimes or crimes against humanity.[222] The Court has not in the past

217. Ibid, p. 68.
218. Ibid, p. 69.
219. Ibid.
220. Dimitrijevic and Milanovic call this 'genocide inflation'. Ibid, p. 88.
221. Ibid, p. 88.
222. In a Press Statement delivered in the Small Hall of Justice of the Peace Palace, immediately after the decision was made 26 February 2007, Her Excellency Judge Higgins, the President of the Court, was at pains to make this clear:

> With respect to 'killing members of the protected group' (Article II (a) of the Convention), the Court finds that it is established by overwhelming evidence that massive killings throughout Bosnia and Herzegovina were perpetrated during the conflict. However, the Court is not convinced that those killings were accompanied by the specific intent on the part of the perpetrators to destroy, in whole or in part, the group of Bosnian Muslims. It acknowledges that the killings may amount to war crimes and crimes against humanity, but that it has no jurisdiction to determine whether this is so.

See the Court's website: http://www.icj-cij.org/docket/index.php?pr=1897&code=bhy&p1=3&p2=3&p3=6&case=91&k=f4 (accessed 17 October 2008). However, as noted by Dimintrijevic and Milanovic the Court's subtlety was lost in the sea of emotions surrounding the case. Dimitrijevic and Milanovic, *The Strange Story*, pp. 86–88.

been wary of holding that actions were war crimes, breaches of human rights law, and even crimes against humanity.[223] Unfortunately in the *Bosnian Genocide Case* the Court was, for reasons of jurisdiction, restricted to acts of genocide, and it decided accordingly.

In view of the above factors it is indeed a wonder that the Court was able to come to a decision, at all, and the fact that the Court did not take advantage of the opportunity to avoid all these pressures by simply concluding that it lacked jurisdiction, in other words simply following the previous decision in the *Legality of Force Cases*,[224] an indication of the integrity and as argued here a determination and an ability to perform their task even when faced with an almost impossible task.

> With all the things that stood in the Court's way, it is remarkable that the *Genocide* judgment turned out as well as it did, even if it is far from perfect. This, of course, is a tribute to the Court's integrity and expertise.[225]

Whilst it may be reassuring to the respective parties involved in the immediate dispute that the ICJ is not going to instigate a 'witch hunt', the decision in the *Arrest Warrants Case* raises an important question – is the Court making a 'real contribution'? Such a question is supported by criticisms of the failure of the ICJ to grant the provisional measures in the *Lockerbie Decision* and since despite or perhaps because of, the *Nuclear Weapons Opinion*, nuclear weapons remain. Is the Court in effect a paper tiger? What real contribution can the Court make to a highly political dispute?

E. What 'real' contribution is the ICJ able to make?

The role of the ICJ of clarifying, indeed even developing, the relevant principles of international law, which may then assist the resolution of future

223. See for example *Case Concerning Armed Activities on the Territory of the Congo (Democratic Republic of the Congo v Uganda) (Judgment19 December 2005)* [2005] ICJ Rep 168, 280, [345] (3) where the Court held, by sixteen votes to one:

> that the Republic of Uganda, by the conduct of its armed forces, which committed acts of killing, torture and other forms of inhumane treatment of the Congolese civilian population, destroyed villages and civilian buildings, [failed] to take measures to respect and ensure respect for human rights and international humanitarian law in Ituri district, violated its obligations under international human rights law and international humanitarian law…

224. *Case Concerning the Legality of the Use of Force (Serbia and Montenegro v Belgium) Preliminary Objections)* [2004] ICJ Rep 279, 330, 334.
225. Dimitrijevic and Milanovic, *The Strange Story*, p. 92.

disputes, is of obvious benefit to the international community. However, can the ICJ actually assist in the resolution of an immediate political dispute? The Court recognises the importance of the above question and argues that its decisions must have some 'real effect' upon the parties in the dispute before it.[226] Many members of the Court believe that rather than resolve the dispute entirely the Court's decision will assist in its resolution.[227]

For example, in the *Nicaragua Case* Judge Lachs said that the decision would not just assist in the resolution of the specific conflict between the US and Nicaragua, but would also assist in furthering the whole region's aim of peace and security: 'The Judgment can thus make a constructive contribution to the resolution of a dangerous dispute – paving the way to stability in a region troubled for decades by conflict and confrontation.'[228] Similarly, in the *Hostages Case*, his Excellency stated that: 'now that the Judgment has, with force of law, determined one of the major issues in the question, it should in my opinion be possible for negotiations to be resumed with a view to seeking a peaceful solution to the dispute.'[229] The Court, in the *Nuclear Weapons Opinion*, also stated firmly that it had an important role to play by clarifying the legal principles:

> It has been argued that, whatever may be the law, the question of the use of nuclear weapons is a political question, politically loaded, and politically determined. This may be, but it must be observed that, however political be the question, there is always value in the clarification of the law. It is not ineffective, pointless and inconsequential.[230]

226. See, eg, *Northern Cameroons (Cameroon v United Kingdom) (Judgment)* [1963] ICJ Rep 15, 34 where the Court said 'The Court's judgment must have some practical consequence in the sense that it can affect existing legal rights or obligations of the parties, thus removing uncertainty from their legal relations.'
227. For example, Judge Mohamed Shahabuddeen stated that:

> [t]o be useful, the Court does not have to deal with the entirety of a dispute; it could make a substantial contribution by sorting out any particular legal aspects with a view to promoting or facilitating the final settlement of the remainder of the dispute by other methods

Shahabuddeen, The World Court, p. 23. See also Gross, *Enhancing its Role*, pp. 258–59.
228. *Nicaragua Case* [1986] ICJ Rep 14, 172–3 (Separate Opinion of Judge Lachs).
229. *United States Diplomatic and Consular Staff in Tehran (United States of America v Iran)* (Judgment) [1980] ICJ Rep 3, 49 (Separate Opinion of Judge Lachs).
230. *Nuclear Weapons Opinion*, [1996] 1 ICJ Rep 226, 328 (Dissenting Opinion of Judge Weeramantry). Others too believed that the ICJ had a role to play. Judge Koroma stated that the ICJ's 'decision can contribute to the prevention of war by ensuring respect for the law': at 557 (Dissenting Opinion of Judge Koroma). At [13] the Court noted that:

> Furthermore, as the Court said in the Opinion it gave in 1980 concerning the Interpretation of the *Agreement of 25 March 1951* between the WHO and Egypt: 'Indeed, in situations in which political considerations are prominent it may be

It is not surprising that members of the Court express such a strong sense of self-belief, but such an attitude, by itself, does not necessarily prove the argument raised here. However, the Court's attitude has been supported by commentators such as Steinberger who, in spite of his doubt noted above, stated that the ICJ played a critical role in the maintenance of peaceful relations.[231] In addition, senior members of the UN itself share similar views, including the former Secretary-General of the United Nations, Dag Hammarskjöld, who stated in 1957 that '[e]ven in the present state of international society there are many disputes which would be closer to settlement if the legal issues involved had been the subject of judicial settlement.'[232]

However, are these points of view substantiated by the actions of States? Two cases, both political matters specifically involving armed conflict, would appear to support such a conclusion. They also encourage some confidence that, by resolving legal issues, a resolution of the overall political problem can be achieved. The first is the case of *Burkina Faso/Mali*, involving a boundary dispute that was referred to the Chamber of the Court by a special agreement by the parties who sought to use the Court's directions to support a ceasefire brokered by the Organisation of African Unity.[233] Not only did the ceasefire continue, but both parties then also honoured the Court's determination of the actual border dispute.[234] The second decision is that of *Libyan Arab Jamahiriya/Chad*, which again involved a special agreement between the parties to a territorial dispute. As a consequence of the Court's determination that the territory belonged to the Republic of Chad, a peace agreement was signed and, under the control and supervision of the UN, the Libyan forces withdrew from the disputed territory.[235]

However, it could be argued that in the two examples above, the 'political effectiveness' of the Court's decision was due to the political wills of the respective national governments of the parties involved because both parties

particularly necessary for an international organization to obtain an advisory opinion from the Court as to the legal principles applicable with respect to the matter under debate.'

231. 'In addition, the clarification of a legal issue relevant to a dispute can favourably influence the subsequent political settlement', Steinberger *The International Court of Justice*, p. 210.
232. *Introduction to the Annual Report of the Secretary-General on the Work of the Organization: 16 June 1956 – 15 June 1957*, UN GAOR, 12th sess, Supp No 1A, 4–5, UN Doc A/3594/Add.1 (1957).
233. *Frontier Dispute (Burkina Faso v Republic of Mali) (Provisional Measures)* [1986] ICJ Rep 3.
234. *Frontier Dispute (Burkina Faso v Republic of Mali) (Merits)* [1986] ICJ Rep 554.
235. *Territorial Dispute (Libyan Arab Jamahiriya v Chad) (Judgment)* [1994] ICJ Rep 6. See Sir Robert Jennings discussing 'Contributions of the Court to the Resolution of International Tensions' in Connie Peck and Roy Lee (eds), *Increasing the Effectiveness of the International Court of Justice: Proceedings of the ICJ/UNITAR Colloquium to Celebrate the 50th Anniversary of the Court* (1997), 77, 81–82.

to the dispute had agreed to submit them to the Court for resolution. What would happen in situations of a recalcitrant State?

1. The issue of recalcitrance

A former member of the ICJ, Sir Robert Jennings, whilst acknowledging that it is inevitable the Court has to consider highly political matters, believes that the successful resolution of legal issues does not by itself provide a solution to the overall political problem. In fact, he argues that the legal element of these disputes played a 'minor role' in comparison to the political component in the resolution of these disputes.[236] Others agree, arguing that a legal hearing determines a 'winner' and 'loser' in a particular dispute. The identification of a 'winner' and a 'loser' can exacerbate tensions and ultimately the dispute, since such a finding can cause a substantial loss of face for a State.[237]

An example was the US's reaction in the Security Council to the *Nicaragua Case*. Nicaragua sought Security Council enforcement of the order of the Court after the decision was delivered[238] but the US vetoed this attempt and also a later draft of a similar resolution.[239] After the US vetoed the Security Council draft resolution, Nicaragua then went to the General Assembly, which adopted a resolution on 6 November 1986, urgently calling for compliance with the Court's decision.[240] However, it was not 'peer group pressure' that eventually forced the US to change its position and policies in Nicaragua – it was internal pressure brought about by the Court's decision.[241]

236. Jennings was discussing this in the context of suggestions that the role of the ICJ should be expanded: Jennings, *Presentation by Sir Robert Jennings*, pp. 78–79.
237. Steinberger, *The International Court of Justice*, p. 208. This could result in the 'loser' refusing to comply with the decision and perhaps even going one step further and withdrawing their consent to the ICJ's jurisdiction for future matters. The US' withdrawal of the USA from the compulsory jurisdiction of the ICJ in the wake of the *Nicaragua Case* is a clear example.
238. Highet, *Between a Rock and a Hard Place*, p. 1093.
239. Morrison, *Legal Issues in the Nicaragua Opinion*, p. 160. *Personal Verbatim Record of the 2704th Meeting, … 31 July 1986*, UN Doc S/PV.2704, 54–5, 57–61 (31 July 1986) rejecting the resolution proposed in *Draft Resolution [Calling for the Compliance with the Judgment of the International Court of Justice in the Case of Military and Paramilitary Activities In and Against Nicaragua]*, UN SCOR, 41st sess, 2703rd mtg, UN Doc S/18250 (31 July 1986). The US had also vetoed Nicaragua's initial resolution before the Security Council.
240. UN Doc A/41/PV.53, 92 (6 November 1986). The vote was 93 in favour, 3 against (US, El Salvador and Israel), 43 abstentions: Highet, *Between a Rock and a Hard Place*, 59.
241. The contentious jurisdiction of the ICJ being voluntary in nature has prompted the argument that the enforceability of the court is achieved through pressure by another State.

Falk made an interesting point regarding the disrespect shown by the US towards the Court, arguing that the *Nicaragua Case* forced US citizens to 'question whether we believe that national interest is served by a foreign policy that is not bound by *impartial* interpretations of international law.'[242] He also argued that:

> It was not necessary to change everyone's thinking on US policy toward Nicaragua. All that was required to defeat Contra aid was to change the votes of about fifteen or twenty members of Congress, most of them House Democrats. Public opinion and media attention stirred by Nicaragua's suit was certain to be helpful in facilitating their conversion.[243]

Was such a 'conversion' evident? In fact public opinion had begun to turn against the US Government well before the final decision on the merits due, as Reichler writes, at least in part to the Court's decision regarding interim measures:

> The decision [for interim measures] was published on May 10, 1984. The House of Representatives voted on Contra aid on May 25. The final tally was 177 in favor and 241 against. Contra aid was defeated for the first time. And it was not the last. For the next two years, the House of Representatives consistently opposed the White House's requests for renewed aid to the Contras. While a number of factors contributed to the House's defeat of Contra aid, Nicaragua's suit and its focus on international law, the Reagan Administration's ham-handed attempts to escape

242. Falk, 'The World Court's Achievement', p. 108. Falk also went on to say that all that

> If the effect of the World Court decision is to shift even slightly the internal and international balance of opinion on the wisdom and propriety of further uses of force against the Sandinista Government, it may yet contribute to the political process whereby legal claims are indirectly upheld.

Ibid, p. 112. Francis Boyle also wrote

> In the unfortunate event that the Reagan administration is allowed to escalate its war against Nicaragua any further, the American people will forfeit any right to claim political or moral leadership of the democratic peoples in Europe, the Western Hemisphere and the Pacific

Francis Boyle, 'Determining US Responsibility for Contra Operations Under International Law' (1987) 81 *American Journal of International Law* 86, p. 92.

243. Paul Reichler, 'Holding America to its Own Best Standards: Abe Chayes and Nicaragua in the World Court' (2001) 42(Winter) *Harvard International Law Journal* 15, p. 23.

judgment, and the Court's rulings in Nicaragua's favor on interim measures and (later) jurisdiction indisputably played their part.[244]

The significance that this had for the military aspect of the conflict within Nicaragua cannot be underestimated. Congress, by banning aid to the Contras for a two-year period, enabled Nicaraguan government forces to regain the military initiative that they had previously lost, and the Contras failed to pose a serious threat to Nicaragua thereafter.[245] However, the ban by Congress had an even more significant effect – it forced the Reagan government to use illegal methods to re-continue their assistance to the Contras and inevitably led to the scandal involving Lieutenant Colonel Oliver North and the so-called Irangate affair.[246] This scandal ultimately led to the destruction of the credibility of the Reagan Government's Central American policies within US public opinion.[247] It also led to a number of influential US politicians taking action to end US support to the Contras and to find a peaceful solution in Central America.[248]

In the words of Reichler, which echo the words of Judge Lachs above:[249]

> Thus, the World Court delivered what turned out to be a devastating blow to the Reagan Administration's war on Nicaragua. It set off a chain reaction that helped convince Congress to cut off funding for the Contras, gave Nicaragua the respite it needed to turn the tide of battle, and forced the White House into egregious tactical errors that ultimately undid its entire policy.[250]

244. Ibid, p. 34.
245. Ibid.
246. The Iran-Contra scandal began with the capture of a downed CIA pilot named Hussenfas who had been supplying arms to the Contras and revealed to the media and eventually led to Lieutenant Colonel Oliver North: Ibid, p. 44; Boyle, *Determining US Responsibility*, pp. 87–88.
247. For a discussion of the US domestic response see Boyle, *Determining US Responsibility*, p. 91, where he discusses the acquittal by a US domestic court of protestors who were charged with serious offences such as 'mob action' after demonstrating against the US involvement in Nicaragua. He claims that many of the jurors responsible for the acquittal based their decision on the acceptance of the defence of necessity, based on the 'shocking' evidence of US involvement in Nicaragua.
248. US House of Representatives Speaker Jim Wright appointed Representative David Bonior of Michigan to head a specially created House Task Force on Central America, with these objectives in mind. Also in the Senate, Christopher Dodd of Connecticut, who spoke Spanish fluently and knew Latin America well, became the leading spokesman for a new, peace-oriented policy in Central America: Reichler, *Holding America*, p. 44. This eventually led to the adoption of a peace plan developed by Oscar Arias, the President of Costa Rica, who was awarded the Nobel Peace Prize.
249. See n. 229 *op. cit.* and accompanying text.
250. Reichler, *Holding America*, p. 35.

The Court, through its expertise and objective analysis of the facts presented to it, was able to draw and express publicly, conclusions that a State never could nor would do. For example, in the *Nicaragua Case*, although the US had claimed collective self-defence as its justification for intervention – ie to stop the arms flow into El Salvador – the Court found that the US wished to change the nature and political 'type' of government in Nicaragua.[251] The Court stated that:

> … it strains belief to suppose that a body formed in armed opposition to the Government of Nicaragua, and calling itself the 'Nicaraguan Democratic Force', intended only to check Nicaraguan interference in El Salvador and did not intend to achieve violent change of government in Nicaragua.[252]

That US support for such a body was quite clearly in breach of international law was also evident to the Court:

> The Court considers that in international law, if one State, with a view to the coercion of another State, supports and assists armed bands in that State whose purpose is to overthrow the government of that State, that amounts to an intervention by the one State in the internal affairs of the other, whether or not the political objective of the State giving such support and assistance is equally farreaching.[253]

The exposure the Court's findings regarding the party's/litigant's actions and intentions received, not just amongst elements within the party's/litigant's own government, but also amongst the international community of other States, NGOs and the political organs of the UN, therefore has a significant effect.[254] It enables the international community to discuss and pass judgement upon the relative merits of the parties' actions in the appropriate forum, such as the UN General Assembly. In Reichler's words, it enables the international community to see who has acted in the more appropriate manner and gained the so-called 'moral high ground'. As such the Court appears to have acted as the international community's conscience.

251. This involved the Court concluding that Nicaragua's obligation in the 1979 Resolution of the OAS Meeting of Consultation to install a democratic government was not a *legal obligation but a political one*: see, eg, Falk, *The World Court's Achievement*, p. 110.
252. *Nicaragua Case* [1986] ICJ Rep 14, [243].
253. Ibid.
254. Falk stated that '[w]e must rethink the question of judicial effectiveness in the broader setting of public opinion and political democracy, and not confine our evaluation to conventional concerns about governmental nonresponsiveness': Falk, *The World Court's Achievement*, p. 112.

In 1980, the Carter Administration had gone to the Court to challenge Iran's seizure of the US Embassy in Tehran and scores of diplomatic personnel. The Court responded with a unanimous condemnation of Iran's actions and an order to return the Embassy and free the hostages. The position of the US remained strengthened in spite of its failed rescue attempt, which could have undermined the Court's authority, and potentially aggravated the situation had not the Court remained focused on the actions of Iran. (The fact the Court was able to remain focused in spite of such events is further proof that the Court is able to make a contribution in the most difficult of circumstances.) The moral and legal authority of the Court's order strengthened the US position vis-à-vis Iran and helped persuade the latter to accept a diplomatic settlement. Nicaragua's suit was similarly designed to capture the moral high ground and to use it to win the support of the international community, US public opinion and, ultimately, US Congress. Reichler writes that '[i]n its suit, Nicaragua would carry the same banner that the United States had against Iran – fighting for compliance with international law. Like Iran, the United States would be cast in the role of defending the indefensible.'[255]

The significance of being 'right' in the eyes of the international community cannot be underestimated. Kornbluh, writing in his work on the US Intervention in Nicaragua, noted that:

> Flouting the institutions of international law and order established to promote peace in a dangerous world carried real and potential security repercussions for the United States; The Reagan Doctrine of fostering a militarist counterrevolution in Central America incurred widespread enmity in the Third World. And in Europe, ... US policy contributed to 'strains' in America's number one military alliance, the North Atlantic Treaty Organization[256]

Twice the European Economic Community urged the US to cease their intervention because of its concern that the impression of the US as an 'uncontrolled gunslinger' was particularly hypocritical since the US, which publicly spouted concern for, and a commitment to, democracy and the protection of human rights, now operated in a secret war where human rights abuses were committed by the forces it supported. This caused such a degree of distrust amongst the European members of NATO that it threatened to cause NATO's collapse.[257]

255. Reichler, *Holding America*, p. 23. The author was a member of Nicaragua's legal team in the action against the USA before the Court.
256. Kornbluh, *Nicaragua, the Price of Intervention* (1987), p. 218.
257. Ibid.

So Steinberger's concern about the perception of a 'winner' and a 'loser' exacerbating tensions is unwarranted and also ignores the fact that such a fear may actually prompt settlement of a dispute. A party may be persuaded to compromise or to alter their position simply because they do not wish such exposure to judgment by their peers. For example, the French discontinued atmospheric testing in Polynesia in the early 1970s in part because Australia and New Zealand filed actions with the ICJ.[258] Similarly, in the *Trial of Pakistani Prisoners of War Case*,[259] although Pakistan failed to 'drag' India before the ICJ, the threat of legal proceedings assisted the two entering into a bilateral settlement, the *Simla Agreement* of 1974.[260] Pakistan then withdrew their action.[261]

Another example can be seen in *Border and Transborder Armed Actions (Nicaragua v Honduras)*.[262] Here, Honduras 'attributed significance in the context of political negotiations to the withdrawal by Nicaragua of its parallel application instituting proceedings against Costa Rica'.[263]

Portraying the role of the Court as the international community's conscience is perhaps melodramatic but can be accurate. Judge Weeramantry noted that whilst the Court's decision in *Legal Consequences for States of the Continued Presence of South Africa in Namibia (South West Africa) Notwithstanding Security Council Resolution 276 (1970)* did not immediately cause the end of apartheid, particularly in South Africa, it assisted and indeed paved the way for its end with the increased international public awareness of the illegality of the regime.[264] Judge Weeramantry in the *Nuclear Weapons Opinion* believed that the ICJ, by clarifying the legal position, was able to widen the comprehension and understanding of the general public in the international community:[265]

258. The ICJ took France's actions as a confirmation by France that there existed a binding obligation to discontinue: *Nuclear Tests Case (Australia v France) (Judgment)* [1974] ICJ Rep 253. See also *Nuclear Tests Case (New Zealand v France) (Judgment)* [1975] ICJ Rep 457.
259. *Trial of Pakistani Prisoners of War (Pakistan v India) (Order)* [1973] ICJ Rep 344.
260. *Agreement on Bilateral Relations*, opened for signature 2 July 1972, India–Pakistan, 858 UNTS 71 (entered into force 4 August 1972).
261. *Trial of Pakistani Prisoners of War (Pakistan v India) (Order)* [1973] ICJ Rep 347.
262. *Border and Transborder Armed Actions (Nicaragua v Costa Rica) (Nicaragua v Honduras) (Merits)* [1988] ICJ Rep 69.
263. Hearing of 6 June 1988, CR 88/4, 11, as cited in Nagendra Singh, *The Role and Record of the International Court of Justice*, Dordrecht: Kluwer Academic Publishers incorporating Martinus Nijhoff Publishers, 1989, p. 30.
264. This point was also noted by John Burroughs, *The Legality of Threat or Use of Nuclear Weapons: A Guide to the Historic Opinion of the International Court of Justice* Munster: LIT, 1998, p. 68.
265. The Court itself noted the value of clarification at [15] of its Opinion: 'The purpose of the advisory function is not to settle – at least directly – disputes between States, but to offer legal advice to the organs and institutions requesting the opinion (cf *Interpretation of Peace Treaties with Bulgaria, Hungary and Romania (Advisory Opinion)* [1950] ICJ Rep 64). The fact

> The Court's decision on the illegality of the apartheid régime had little prospect of compliance by the offending Government, but helped to create the climate of opinion which dismantled the structure of apartheid. Had the Court thought in terms of the futility of its decree, the end of apartheid may well have been long delayed, if it could have been achieved at all. The clarification of the law is an end in itself, and not merely a means to an end. When the law is clear, there is a greater chance of compliance than when it is shrouded in obscurity.
>
> The view has indeed been expressed that, in matters involving 'high policy', the influence of international law is minimal. However, as Professor Brownlie has observed in dealing with this argument, it would be 'better to uphold a prohibition which *may* be avoided in a crisis than to do away with standards altogether'.
>
> I would also refer, in this context, to the perceptive observations of Albert Schweitzer, cited at the very commencement of this opinion, on the value of a greater public awareness of the illegality of nuclear weapons.[266]

Others, such as Burroughs, also believe that ICJ decisions, by exposing the limits or flaws within existing international law, may prompt new action that could eventually lead to a treaty signed by members of the UN forever banning nuclear weapons:

> The landmark opinion of the International Court of Justice reflects that our thinking has finally begun to change, and stimulates further change. It marks and reinforces a global shift in attitudes that is making the threat, use, and possession of weapons of mass destruction the object of a planetary taboo, and points the way toward what for half a century has been practically unthinkable – the abolition of nuclear weapons.[267]

There is no doubt that if the Request had been left to the Security Council it would not have been answered in a way that was counter to the interests of the nuclear powers, since all five of the permanent members are 'the' nuclear powers and have been for some time.[268] Even in the General Assembly there

that the question put to the Court does not relate to a specific dispute should consequently not lead the Court to decline to give the opinion requested': *Nuclear Weapons Opinion* [1996] 1 ICJ Rep 226, [15].

266. Ibid, p. 550 (Dissenting Opinion of Judge Weeramantry).
267. Burroughs *A Guide to the Historic Opinion*, p. 69.
268. This is not strictly true since Israel, Pakistan and India are also nuclear powers. However, the statement makes sense when considering that the five permanent members of the Security Council are also the five 'nuclear-weapon States' of the *Treaty on the*

were some concerns raised by the voting process for the Request of the Opinion.[269] As Judge Koroma argued:

> [t]he suggestion that it should be left to individual States to determine whether or not it may be lawful to have recourse to nuclear weapons is not only an option fraught with serious danger, both for the States that may be directly involved in conflict, and for those nations not involved, but may also suggest that such an option is not legally reprehensible. Accordingly, the Court, instead of leaving it to each State to decide whether or not it would be lawful or unlawful to use nuclear weapons in an extreme circumstance of 'State survival', should have determined whether or not it is permissible to use nuclear weapons even in a case involving the survival of the State.[270]

The Court, because of its impartiality, is able to do what the Security Council cannot do.[271] The UN Security Council is a political body. It was established that way and is likely to continue to operate that way.[272] As Judge Lachs noted in the *Nicaragua Case*:

> A member of the government of a State engaged, not merely in international litigation, but in litigation relating to armed conflict, will probably tend to identify himself with the interests of his country, and to be anxious when giving evidence to say nothing which could prove adverse to its cause.[273]

Non-Proliferation of Nuclear Weapons, opened for signature 1 July 1968, 729 UNTS 169, (entered into force 5 March 1970). It is also interesting to note that it is customary practice for judges from the permanent five members to sit on the bench, and still the Court found that generally that the nuclear weapons were illegal, thus confirming that the ICJ bench is impartial whereas the Security Council was not.

269. The vote in the General Assembly was 78 votes for, 43 against and 38 abstentions. In actual fact the affirmative vote was 64% and therefore not the required two-thirds majority required for 'important questions' required by the *Charter of the UN* art 18(2)–(3): Paul Szasz, 'Addendum: The Vote in the General Assembly' in Peter Bekker (ed), *Commentaries on World Court Decisions (1987–1996)* (1998) 243, 243. Contrast this with the voting in the World Health Organisation where there were 73 affirmative votes to 40 opposing with only 10 abstentions: Bekker, *Legality of the Use of Nuclear Weapons*, p. 247.
270. *Nuclear Weapons Opinion* [1996] 1 ICJ Rep 226, p. 552 (Dissenting Opinion of Judge Koroma).
271. 'The task of the International Court of Justice as well as the Permanent Court of Arbitration is to bring an element of impartiality and objectivity to bear on dealings between states': Pope John Paul II in a speech in The Hague as quoted in Szafraz, *The Compulsory Jurisdiction*, vii.
272. The same can be said of the UN General Assembly. Singh, *The Role and Record*, p. 29.
273. *Nicaragua Case* [1984] ICJ Rep 392, [70] (Separate Opinion of Judge Lachs).

2. Impartiality

Academics have attempted to measure the impartiality of the ICJ by examining the voting patterns of individual judges. In an early work completed in 1968, one commentator noted that judges had a tendency to vote more often in favour of their national government as compared to other judges. However, from the evidence obtained, the strategic importance of the matter – that is, the degree of significance to the national policies of their government – did not appear to influence judges voting patterns.[274] Further, ad hoc judges had a tendency to vote in favour of the State that appointed them.[275] However, there have been situations where ad hoc judges have voted against the nominating government.[276] Also, as Hensley noted, other judges may have voted in favour of another member's national government more often than the judges of that particular State did.[277] It was also clear that all judges were willing to vote against their national governments. For example, Judge Schwebel, from the US, has on nine occasions voted against his country.[278]

The conclusion that commentators have drawn from such quantitative research is that it is more likely that judges are influenced by cultural values and other subtle influences that their legal training and experience have given them, rather than actually being guilty of voting in the national interest, and that this in no way 'violates the criterion for impartial adjudication.'[279] This phenomenon was recognised by the drafters of the *ICJ Statute*.[280] Further, the ability of ad hoc or national judges to influence the outcome of the Court's decision is very minor, since they are at best two sitting on the bench from a total of 17.[281] In some ways, the inclusion of a national judge is

274. Thomas Hensley, 'National Bias and the International Court of Justice' (1968) 12 *Midwest Journal of Political Science*, p. 568. This trend was observed both in contentious matters and in advisory opinions: see at 579; at Tables 1, 7.
275. For example, *ad hoc* judge, Judge El-Kosheri in *1998 Lockerbie Decision* [1998] ICJ Rep 115. However as another author has noted this should not be surprising given that national governments prior to making their selection are unlikely to choose a tribunal member that is opposed to their cause: Il Ro Suh, 'Voting Behaviour of National Judges in International Courts' (1969) 63 *American Journal of International Law* 224, 226.
276. Such as for example, Judges Castilla of Colombia and Morelli of Italy. See Table 4 in Hensley, *National Bias*, p. 574 and the discussion at p. 575.
277. For example, Judge Caneiro (Brazil) voted in favour of the US more times than did Judge Hackworth (US). Also whilst no other judge supported the UK more times than did Judge McNair (UK), three other judges, Judge Read (Canada), Judge Fabela (Mexico) and again Judge Caneiro (Brazil) supported the UK at least as many times as Judge McNair: Hensley, *National Bias*, p. 576 and Table 5 at p. 575.
278. Tacsan, *The Dynamics of International Law*, p. 142. The author admits that this alone is not conclusive proof, but it is persuasive. For a detailed study see E B Weiss, 'Judicial Independence and Impartiality' in Damrosch *At a Crossroads*, p. 123.
279. Hensley, *National Bias*, p. 580.
280. *ICJ Statute* art 9 and Hensley, *National Bias*, pp. 581–82.
281. Fifteen judges plus two *ad hoc*.

important since it guards against cultural misunderstandings or problems of language, thus reassuring the litigants, and also assists to ensure that unfavourable decisions will be more 'palatable'.[282] What is significant is that there has never been any indication or evidence of a judge acting in accordance with instructions received from their national government.[283] On the whole, the evidence is inconclusive regarding whether there exists a national bias of some form. Certainly, the ICJ does not share the problems of bias experienced by the political organs of the UN, such as the General Assembly.

An example of the Court's impartiality can be seen in the *Nicaragua Case*, where the Court was considering the liability of the US for the actions of the Contras. The Court held that:

> It is clear that considerable economic loss and damage has been inflicted on Nicaragua by the actions of the *contras*: apart from the economic impact of acts directly attributable to the United States, … the Court has not found the relationship between the *contras* and the United States Government to have been proved to be such that the United States is responsible for all acts of the *contras*.[284]

Many academic writers acknowledged the impartiality of the Court's decision.[285] What is more important is that the impartiality and integrity of the Court remained unscathed by the vigorous attacks (as mentioned above)

282. Suh, above n. 275, pp. 233–4.
283. Hensley, *National Bias*, p. 585.
284. *Nicaragua Case* [1986] ICJ Rep 14, [278]. The Court further held that the arming and the training of the Contras constituted an act of intervention by the USA but not a use of force: at p. 278.
285. For example, Falk, *The World Court's Achievement*, p. 106 stated 'the Judgment is exemplary in striking a balance between fairness to a sovereign states accused of serious violations of international law and a diligent effort to interpret the relevant rules and principles in a constructive manner.' For a discussion of the Court's impartiality, please see Thomas D Hensley, 'National Bias and the international Court of Justice' (1968) 12 (4) *Midwest Journal of Political Science*, p. 568; Adam M Smith, '"Judicial Nationalism" in International Law: National Identity and Judicial Autonomy at the ICJ' (2004–2005) 40 *Texas International Law Journal*, p. 197; Gleider I Hernandez, 'Impartiality and Bias at the International Court of Justice', (2012) 1(3) *Cambridge Journal of International and Comparative Law*, p 183; Eric A Posner, 'Is the International Court of Justice biased?' in *John M Olin Law & Economics Working paper no 234 (2nd Series)*, (December 2004) available at: http://www.law.uchicago.edu/Lawecon/index.html (accessed 18 May 2013). Posner is the only study that concludes that the judges of the ICJ are biased. Judges being able to recuse themselves from hearings further maintain impartiality. There have even been examples where the clerks of ICJ judges have recused themselves in order to avoid any suggestion of partiality. See for example Marko Milanovic, the clerk to His Excellency Judge Thoms Buergenthal, who recused himself from the Bosnian Genocide Case, Vojin Dimitrijevic and Marko Milanovic, 'The Strange Story of the Bosnian Genocide Case' (2008) 21 *Leiden Journal of International Law*, p. 65.

made by the US regarding the integrity of the Court. In fact, as Highet has noted, the attack by the US did not undermine the Court's integrity as many feared, but rather reinforced the Court's position and respect by the 'preponderance of member States', in particular by 'weaker States'. He further noted that at the time there was a noticeable increase in the actions brought by Third World States to the Court.[286] As Kahn writes:

> The Security Council may provide for a great power veto, but there is no similar reflection of political power within the International Court of Justice. Just for this reason, appeals to international law have been one of the tools available to weaker states in their battles with more powerful states.[287]

Impartiality is something few States' involved in disputes can ever claim.[288] States are not impartial when it comes to the development of international norms as well, due to their desire to protect their national self-interests.[289] As noted by several commentators States play a 'double role' within the international system: '...that of the sovereign State who is master in his own realm and that of the member State which subscribes to the lofty goal of the organization.'[290] The significance of States' double role is that they cannot be trusted in certain matters. For example, Meijknecht noted that States could not be trusted to protect the rights of minorities or indigenous peoples, because not only was it not in their interest to do so, but also because States were the major perpetrators of crimes committed against these groups:

> It [the double role of States] could even lead to a paradoxical situation: can a sovereign State, who itself poses the greatest danger to minorities and indigenous peoples, be entrusted with their protection?[291]

286. Highet, *Between a Rock and a Hard Place*, p. 1096.
287. Paul Kahn, 'Speaking Law to Power: Popular Sovereignty, Human Rights, and the New International Order' (2000) 1 *Chicago Journal of International Law*, p. 1.
288. The Court is certainly not fearful of criticising States' actions. See, eg, *Namibia Opinion* [1971] ICJ Rep 16, 18; *Western Sahara Opinion* [1975] ICJ Rep 12; *Wall in Palestine Opinion* [2004] ICJ Rep 136, [163].
289. Eg, Anna Meijknecht, *Towards International Personality: The Position of Minorities and Indigenous Peoples in International Law* (2001), who writes 'States have attempted, in several ways, to control and monopolise international law': at 9.
290. Luncheon Address by Pieter Hendrik Kooijmans, 'Human Rights: the Actors and the Play' in Wybo Heere (ed), *Contemporary International Law Issues: New Forms New Applications (Proceedings of the Fourth Hague Joint Conference held in the Hague, The Netherlands, 2–5 July 1997)* (1997) 110, 112; Meijknecht, *Towards International Personality*, p. 20.
291. Meijknecht, *Towards International Personality*, pp. 20–21.

Impartiality benefits both parties. As stated by the Court in *ILO Administrative Tribunal Opinion*:[292]

> The judicial nature of the Court requires that both sides directly affected by these proceedings should be in a position to submit their views and their arguments to the Court. … The principle of equality of the parties follows from the requirements of good administration of justice.[293]

States also value impartiality highly. For example, at the 1962 Punta del Este meeting of the OAS, many anti-Cuban resolutions were adopted.[294] This led the Cuban representative to the Security Council to ask the Security Council to request an Advisory Opinion. The former USSR supported Cuba's recommendation because they believed the Court was the most competent UN body and the only one that could provide an impartial Opinion on the legal points raised in the shortest time.[295] It could be argued that the former USSR's comments merely reflected their desire to prevail in the Cold War, and their support for a fellow communist State. However, if the USSR wanted a favourable outcome then surely this would have been more likely in the UN General Assembly where the USSR could exert more influence?

Impartiality is important since it lends greater credibility to the final decision. For example, the decision of an impartial ICJ that determined that no human rights abuses have been carried out by the Central Government is arguably more likely to be accepted by the international community than say if a similar statement was released by the Central Government investigating the claims itself.[296]

292. *Judgments of the Administrative Tribunal of the ILO upon Complaints Made Against the UNESCO* [1956] ICJ Rep 77, 86 ('*ILO Administrative Tribunal Opinion*').
293. Ibid, p. 86. How that was achieved was by the Court dispensing with Oral statements and allowing the individuals using an intermediary, UNESCO, to provide their information via a written statement from the legal advisor of the UNESCO staff members. This procedure was expressed by the Court as being adopted purely to ensure fairness in the matter before it, and was not intended to become a rule for future advisory proceedings, and also was not intended as a means to permanently resolve the issue. Ibid; Pratap, *The Advisory Jurisdiction*, p. 192.
294. One of the effects of these resolutions was that Cuba was excluded from participation in the inter-American system, and some trade was suspended.
295. Michla, Pomerance, *The Advisory Function of the International Court in the League and UN Eras*, Baltimore: Johns Hopkins University Press, 1973, p. 260.
296. The Russo-Chechen conflict provides a good example of this. Due to Moscow's inability to provide accurate information concerning Russian casualties concerned mothers formed the 'Committee of Soldiers' Mothers' to investigate and provide information to affected families. Masha Gessen, 'Mothers in Arms: Missing in Action in Chechnya' 215 (12–13) *The New Republic* (US), 16 September 1996, 20(2); Valery Tishkov, 'Ethnic Conflicts in the Former USSR: the Use and Misuse of Typologies and Data' (1999) 36 *Journal of Peace Research* pp. 571–91; 'Bloody Chechen Conflict Spreads to Neighbour', *The Age* (Australia),

What drives this impartiality is respect for the principles of international law and legal reasoning. No clearer statement of this principle can be found than that of Judge Weeramantry in his Dissenting Opinion in the *Nuclear Weapons Opinion*:

> If indeed the principles of international law decree that the use of the nuclear weapon is legal, it must so pronounce. The anti-nuclear forces in the world are immensely influential, but that circumstance does not swerve the Court from its duty of pronouncing the use of the weapons legal if that indeed be the law. A second alternative conclusion is that the law gives no definite indication one way or the other. If so, that neutral fact needs to be declared, and a new stimulus may then emerge for the development of the law. Thirdly, if legal rules or principles dictate that the nuclear weapon is illegal, the Court will so pronounce, undeterred again by the immense forces ranged on the side of the legality of the weapon.[297]

Whilst the ICJ has been criticised for not going 'far enough' in its decision in the *Nuclear Weapons Case*, the Court did strive for a balance between jeopardising its existence and maintaining its purpose, namely resolving legal issues to assist in the maintenance of international peace and security.

There is one other significant and 'real' contribution that the ICJ makes to the UN in its quest to maintain peace and international security, and thus to the international community: its decisions, for example, the *1992* and *1998 Lockerbie Decisions*, have assisted and guided other international courts and tribunals, such as the ICTY, when faced with highly political matters. The Appeal Chamber of the ICTY in the *Tadić Case* was asked to consider its jurisdiction as established by the Security Council and, followed the example by the ICJ in the Lockerbie Decisions (and other decisions such as the *Arrest Warrants Case*) that once a legal question was placed before it, the Tribunal would consider that question free from political influences.[298] The ICTY, in concluding that the tribunal was *intra vires*, also adopted a similar approach and analysis to the ICJ from the *Lockerbie Decision* – that the Security Council is not itself 'above the law'.[299]

26–7 June 2004, 15 ('The World' section); Amnesty International's report for 2003 on their website at: http://web.amnesty.org/library/index/engeur460042002 (accessed 30 October 2007).

297. *Nuclear Weapons Opinion* [1996] 1 ICJ Rep 226, 440 (Dissenting Opinion of Judge Weeramantry).
298. *Tadić*, Case No IT-94–1-AR72 (2 October 1995) [24] and *Certain Expenses of the United Nations (Advisory Opinion)* [1962] ICJ Rep 151, 155.
299. *Tadić*, Case No IT-94–1-AR72 (2 October 1995) [28] and *Lockerbie Decision* [1992] ICJ Rep 3, 56 (Dissenting Opinion of Judge Weeramantry).

There is, however, one area in which the Court could make a further contribution to the resolution of highly political matters that goes beyond the clarification of the legal issues involved in an international dispute – a greater use of provisional measures.[300] Unfortunately, the Court has been reluctant to use the full potential of provisional measures.[301] The problem with the suggestion that provisional measures could be used to protect human rights or rights *erga omnes* like self-determination is that these are rights that belong to individuals or people, not States, and the ICJ is essentially concerned with inter-State disputes.[302] However, the ICJ has considered requests for provisional measures in these circumstances.[303] Furthermore, in response to the request for provisional measures by Bosnia-Herzegovina in the *Genocide Case (Bosnia–Herzegovina v Yugoslavia)* did order the SFRY to 'take all measures within its power to prevent the commission of the crime of genocide.'[304] Thus in situations where a people suffering from alien or foreign repression, or even worse from human rights abuses, or genocide, it is conceivable that an order for provisional measures could be sought to protect their lives whilst their claim to self-determination was resolved.[305] Given the *erga omnes* character of self-determination, any State could request an order for provisional

300. *ICJ Statute* art 41. See *Lockerbie Decision* [1992] ICJ Rep 3, 70 (Dissenting Opinion of Judge Weeramantry). The ICJ also refused to grant provisional measures in the *1998 Lockerbie Decision*: see above.
301. See, the *Arrest Warrants Case*, where the Congo requested that the Court issue provisional measures that ordered Belgium to cancel the warrant on the ground that Belgium had irreparably infringed the Congo's capacity to conduct foreign relations, because the arrest warrant would impede the travel of their former Foreign Minister. The Court rejected the request because at the time of the request, Yerodia was no longer the Congo's Foreign Minister: *Arrest Warrants Case* [2002] ICJ Rep 3. The Court did, however, adopt an Order for provisional measures in *Vienna Convention on Consular Relations (Paraguay v United States of America) (Provisional Measures)* [1998] ICJ Rep 248.
302. See Judge Oda's Separate Opinion in *La Grand, (Federal Republic of Germany v United States of America)* (Provisional Measures) [1999] ICJ Rep 9, 19–20.
303. For example, *La Grand, (Federal Republic of Germany v United States of America)* (Provisional Measures) [1999] ICJ Rep 9; *Case Concerning Application of the Convention on the Prevention and Punishment of the Crime of Genocide (Bosnia–Herzegovina v Yugoslavia (Serbia and Montenegro))* (Interim Protection Order of 8 Apr 1993) [1993] ICJ Rep 325; *United States Diplomatic and Consular Staff in Tehran (United States of America v Iran) (Provisional Measures)* [1979] ICJ Rep 7.
304. *Case Concerning Application of the Convention on the Prevention and Punishment of the Crime of Genocide (Bosnia–Herzegovina v Yugoslavia (Serbia and Montenegro)* (Interim Protection Order of 8 Apr 1993) [1993] ICJ Rep 3, 24.
305. Alison Duxbury, 'Saving Lives in the International Court of Justice: The Use of Provisional Measures to Protect Human Rights' (2000) *California Western International Law Journal*, pp. 157 & 176; Rosalyn Higgins, 'Interim Measures for the Protection of Human Rights in Politics, Values and Functions-International Law in the 21st Century' in Jonathon I. Charney et al (eds) *Essays in Honor of Professor Louis Henkin* the Hague; Martinus Nijhoff, 1977, p. 101.

measures, provided the State involved consented.[306] However, it is conceded that whether such orders would be complied with is doubtful.

F. Recent trends

The ability of the ICJ to develop international law was doubted in the aftermath of the US's withdrawal from both the *Nicaragua Case* and the ICJ's jurisdiction. In the fallout from the *Nicaragua Case*, some commentators, particularly in the US, expressed concern that the Court was in urgent need of reform.[307] However, in a manner that surprised many commentators, the Court was swamped under a deluge of diverse cases, in many instances initiated by States who had previously never used the Court as a means of conflict resolution.[308]

> The Court like a phoenix, appears to have emerged from the ashes of Nicaragua. It has become a hot court – perhaps even a 'hot bench' in the American phrase. It is positioned, for the first time in its collective seventy-year history, to become the great international judicial institution that its friends and supporters always knew it could be.[309]

Even the US, with all its bitterness over the *Nicaragua Case*, evidenced a renewed confidence in the Court[310] and, despite not being a successful litigant since the *Nicaragua Case*, still retains a positive attitude.[311]

306. *East Timor Case* [1995] ICJ Rep 90, 102.
307. Keith Highet, 'The Peace Palace Heats Up: The World Court in Business Again?' (1991) 85 *American Journal of International Law*, pp. 646–47.
308. A total of nine cases were brought in a two-year period following the *Nicaragua Case*, as follows: *Maritime Delimitation in the Area between Greenland and Jan Mayen (Denmark v Norway) (Order)* [1988] ICJ Rep 66; *Aerial Incident of 3 July 1988 (Islamic Republic of Iran v United States of America) (Order)* [1989] ICJ 132; *Certain Phosphate Lands in Nauru (Nauru v Australia) (Order)* [1989] ICJ Rep 12; *Arbitral Award of 31 July 1989 (Guinea-Bissau v Senegal) (Judgment)* [1991] ICJ Rep 53; *Territorial Dispute (Libyan Arab Jamahiriya v Chad) (Judgment)* [1994] ICJ Rep 6; *East Timor (Portugal v Australia) (Judgment)* [1995] ICJ Rep 90; *Maritime Delimitation between Guinea-Bissau and Senegal (Guinea-Bissau v Senegal) (Order)* [1995] ICJ Rep 423; *Passage through the Great Belt (Finland v Denmark) (Provisional Measures)* [1991] ICJ Rep 12; and *Maritime Delimitation and Territorial Questions between Qatar and Bahrain (Qatar v Bahrain) (Order)* [1991] ICJ Rep 50. Eight of these new cases were brought by application, and the Court, not the Chamber, heard all nine cases: Tiefenbrun, *The Role of the World Court*, p. 13.
309. Highet, *The Peace Palace Heats Up*, p. 654.
310. The US at the time was involved in an incident involving the shooting down of Iran Air Flight 655 by the USS Vincennes in the Persian Gulf. The case concerned the use of armed force and self-defence under the *UN Charter*, art 51 and, as noted at the time, the US had not disappeared as it did during the *Nicaragua Case*: Highet, *The Peace Palace Heats Up*, p. 650.
311. See the commentary by Peter Bekker on the 1998 Lockerbie Decision: Peter Bekker, 'Questions of Interpretation and Application of the 1971 Montreal Convention Arising from the Aerial Incident at Lockerbie' (1998) 92 *American Journal of International Law*, p. 508.

The year 1991 marked a turning point for the ICJ, with developing States greatly heartened by the ICJ's decision in the *Nicaragua Case* that proved it was indeed capable of acting impartially and further was capable of making a significant contribution in highly political matters.[312] The trend of increased confidence in the Court thus continued, with 11 cases (at different stages of resolution) before the ICJ in October 1993.[313] In the period 1993–1994, there were twelve contentious cases and one Advisory Opinion before the ICJ, a 'record number', and the Court also delivered two judgments in two cases.[314] The ICJ began 2001 with 24 cases pending and added a further three, delivered three judgments, and finished the year with one case in deliberation.[315] An additional 22 were on the Court's docket.[316]

Although the Court only issued one judgment in 2006 it was still a busy year for the ICJ.[317] In July the ICJ denied an order for provisional measures, and more importantly concluded the oral proceedings stage of the *Application of the Convention on the Prevention and Punishment of the Crime of Genocide (Bosnia-Herzegovina v Serbia and Montenegro)* which had lasted over two and half months, as well as holding public hearings in other matters.[318] In 2007 the Court decided the *Territorial and Maritime Dispute between Nicaragua and Honduras in the Caribbean Sea (Nicaragua v. Honduras)*[319] and the highly political *Application of the Convention on the Prevention and Punishment of the Crime of Genocide (Bosnia-Herzegovina v Serbia and Montenegro).*[320] On 23 May 2008 the Court handed down its judgment in *Sovereignty over Pedra Branca/Pulau Batu Puteh, Middle Rocks and South Ledge (Malaysia/Singapore)*, and on 4 June 2008 it decided *Certain Questions of Mutual Assistance in Criminal Matters (Djibouti v.*

312. Tiefenbrun, *The Role of the World Court*, pp. 13, 26.
313. Ibid, p. 14.
314. Ibid, pp. 15–16.
315. *Arrest Warrants Case* [2002] ICJ Rep 3. This matter was decided in February 2002.
316. The three judgments were *Maritime Delimitation and Territorial Questions between Qatar and Bahrain (Qatar v Bahrain) (Merits)* [2001] ICJ Rep 40; *La Grand (Germany v United States of America) (Judgment)* [2001] ICJ Rep 466; *Sovereignty Over Pulau Ligitan and Pulau Sipadan (Indonesia v Malaysia) (Judgment)* [2001] ICJ Rep 575. See John R Crook, 'The 2001 Judicial Activity of the International Court of Justice' (2002) 96 *American Journal of International Law*, pp. 397–411.
317. *Armed Activities on the Territory of the Congo (New Application 2002) (Democratic Republic of the Congo v Rwanda)* [2006] ICJ Rep 6. In addition the Court elected a new President and Vice-President, and celebrated its sixtieth anniversary: Stephen Mathias, 'Current Developments, the 2006 Judicial Activity of the International Court of Justice' 101 (2007) *American Journal of International Law*, p. 602.
318. Ibid, p. 602. *Case Concerning Pulp 'Mills' on the River Uruguay (Argentina v Uruguay).* [2010] ICJ Rep 14.
319. *Territorial and Maritime Dispute between Nicaragua and Honduras in the Caribbean Sea (Nicaragua v. Honduras)* [2007] ICJ Rep 659.
320. *Bosnian Genocide Case* [2007] ICJ Rep 43.

France).[321] During 2009 – June 2013 the Court decided numerous contentious matters,[322] including successful applications for preliminary objections,[323] and also provided two Advisory Opinions.[324] At the date of publication the Court is seized of thirteen cases.[325] As one commentator noted:

> Until recently, an applicant State would select the World Court to adjudicate its dispute only if it believed that it would win. Or, if the applicant State wanted to make a statement or teach a lesson without using force, it also might bring its dispute before the World Court ... Until recently a State generally appealed to the World Court to settle or solve the dispute only if it were absolutely desperate.[326]

321. *Sovereignty over Pedra Branca/Pulau Batu Puteh, Middle Rocks and South Ledge (Malaysia/Singapore)* [2008] ICJ Rep 12; and *Certain Questions of Mutual Assistance in Criminal Matters (Djibouti v France)* [2008] ICJ Rep 177.
322. *Dispute Regarding Navigational and Related Rights (Costa Rica v Nicaragua)* [2009] ICJ Rep 214;*Maritime Delimination in the Black Sea (Romania v Ukraine)* [2009] ICJ Rep 62;*Request for the Interpretation of the Judgment of 31 March 2004 in the Case Concerning Avena and Other Mexican Nationals (Mexico v US)* [2009] ICJ Rep 3; *Pulp Mills on the River Uruguay (Argentina v. Uruguay*) [2010] ICJ Rep 14; *Application of the Interim Accord of 13 September 1995 (the former Yugoslav Republic of Macedonia v. Greece); Jurisdictional Immunities of the State (Germany v. Italy: Greece Intervening*); *Ahmadou Sadio Diallo (Compensation Owed by the Democratic Republic of the Congo to the Republic of Guinea) (Republic of Guinea v. Democratic Republic of the Congo); Questions Relating to the Obligation to Prosecute or Extradite (Belgium v. Senegal); Territorial and Maritime Dispute (Nicaragua v Colombia; Honduras Intervening); Frontier Dispute (Burkino Faso v Niger).* All available at the ICJ's Website: http://www.icj-cij.org/docket/index.php?p1=3&p2=2 (accessed 23 June 2013).
323. *Application of the International Convention on the Elimination of All Forms of Racial Discrimination (Georgia v. Russian Federation*) available at the ICJ's Website: http://www.icj-cij.org/docket/index.php?p1=3&p2=3&k=4d&case=140&code=GR&p3=6 (accessed 23 June 2013).
324. *Accordance with International Law of the Unilateral Declaration of Independence in respect of Kosovo (Advisory Opinion)* [2010] ICJ Rep 403;*Judgment No 2867 of the Administrative Tribunal of the International Labour Organization Upon a Complaint Filed Against the international Fund for Agricultural Development (Advisory Opinion)* [2012] ICJ Rep 1.
325. *Certain Activities carried out by Nicaragua in the Border Area (Costa Rica v. Nicaragua) these proceedings joined with Construction of a Road in Costa Rica along the San Juan River (Nicaragua v. Costa Rica); Whaling in the Antarctic (Australia v. Japan: New Zealand intervening); Armed Activities on the Territory of the Congo (Democratic Republic of the Congo v. Uganda)Gabcikovo-Nagymaros Project (Hungary v Slovakia); Application of the Convention on the Prevention and Punishment of the Crime of Genocide (Croatia v. Serbia); Maritime Dispute (Peru v. Chile); Aerial Herbicide Spraying (Ecuador v. Colombia); Proceedings instituted by Bolivia against Chile; Request for interpretation of the Judgment of 15 June 1962 in the case concerning the Temple of Preah Vihear (Cambodia v. Thailand) (Cambodia v. Thailand).* All available at the ICJ's website http://www.icj-cij.org/docket/index.php?p1=3&p2=1 (accessed 23 June 2013).
326. Tiefenbrun, *The Role of the World Court*, p. 22.

That, however, has changed. The Court now 'plays the role of a teacher, an advisor, a source of developing international law, and the hope of a world built on law and justice.'[327]

G. Conclusion

Many commentators have questioned the Court's ability to resolve highly political matters, even including former members such as Sir Robert Jennings. In every international dispute there will be political issues that loom threateningly over the legal questions. The *Nicaragua Case* and the *Nuclear Weapons Opinion*, for example, both raised a number of issues that lie at the heart of the structure and organisation of the international community, namely the right to self-defence and the right to non-intervention. Both rules flow from the concept of national sovereignty and are concepts that most, if not all, States would consider essential for the maintenance of international peace and security. Further, the nature of the environment in which the ICJ operates is one that could be described as being in the very least disadvantageous and, at times, hostile to the ICJ. Nevertheless, the ICJ has made, and continues to make, a valuable contribution to the peaceful resolution of highly charged political disputes.

The doubts and criticisms must be viewed from a correct perspective. Jennings' criticism of the ICJ is simply that the successful resolution of legal issues within a political dispute between States does not of itself automatically resolve or provide a solution to the overall political problem. Despite his strong criticism, Jennings did not deny that the ICJ had a role to play. He believed that political and legal decision-making processes both were and are complementary and if used together can be effective.[328] It must be emphasised that the ICJ should not be expected to find a political solution. No domestic court is expected do so. Instead, the role of the Court is to resolve legal questions so that a political solution can be found either by the parties themselves or by the appropriate organ of the UN. The Court's expertise in clarifying the legal principles and applying them to the facts and its ability to sift through dubious and biased statements made by national representatives in the guise of evidence are crucial in assisting political organs to then take the appropriate political steps as part of the resolution process. If this then reduces the likelihood of even one dispute escalating into an armed conflict, then this is a significant achievement.

It is self-evident that if the international community wishes to resolve and prevent conflicts in a peaceful manner, it needs an impartial third party trained to deal with legal questions. By 'ignoring' the political issues and

327. Ibid, p. 24.
328. Jennings, *Presentation by Sir Robert Jennings*, p. 79.

ensuring that the Court restricts itself to the legal issues involved in the dispute or request, as it did in the *Lockerbie Decision* and the *Arrest Warrants Case*, the Court has ensured its on-going ability to make a contribution and fulfil its role as the chosen judicial instrument of the UN.[329] The Court, by avoiding unnecessary political entanglements, maintains its effectiveness as an independent judicial body.[330]

One of the crucial aspects of any legal hearing – and one which is touted here as an important advantage of a legal tribunal over political entities such as the General Assembly when resolving highly political international disputes – is the fact that both parties are guaranteed a fair and impartial hearing, regardless of their status in the world community, and regardless of their relative strengths and weaknesses.[331] Recognition by States that this is indeed the role that the Court plays – that of an impartial arbitrator and not a legislator – maintains their confidence in the Court's determinations and resolutions and thus encourages States to bring matters before the Court.[332] The increased usage of the Court since 1991 is strong evidence that the level of confidence in the Court is extremely high, for the very reason that it can be trusted to be impartial and effective. As events unfolded in the aftermath of the *Nicaragua Case*, the Court, as the chosen judicial organ of the UN, was able to demonstrate through its use of legal methodology that it could make a valuable contribution to the resolution of highly political matters.[333]

The Court has described its role not as the international community's conscience but as (stated in the *Lockerbie Case*) the '...guardian of legality for the international community as a whole, both within and without the United Nations.'[334] Determining whether a people are entitled to national sovereignty, to self-determination, falls within this role. As discussed in the

329. Sugihara noted that the Court has to date managed not to concern itself with the political aspects of the matters brought before it: Sugihara, *Judicial Function*, p. 134 and Jennings, *Presentation by Sir Robert Jennings*, p. 88.
330. At the Colloquium celebrating the 50th anniversary of the Court, Professor Zoller stated that the ICJ is 'very good' at avoiding the political entanglements in cases brought before it and mentioned the *Hostages Case* as an example. Zoller argued that if the ICJ did not step too far out of itself by focusing on resolving questions of law, albeit in an abstract manner, it could continue to avoid these political entanglements and also do something constructive by making a contribution to the resolution of international disputes: Professor Elizabeth Zoller, 'Commentary by Elizabeth Zoller' in Connie Peck and Roy Lee (eds), *Increasing the Effectiveness of the International Court of Justice: Proceedings of the ICJ/UNITAR Colloquium to Celebrate the 50th Anniversary of the Court* (1997), p. 88.
331. This is the principle of equality between States. J G Starke, *Introduction to International Law* (9th ed), London: Butterworths, 1984, p. 103.
332. Steinberger believes that 'a party could be more willing to compromise if it had to fear the consequences of submitting the matter to the Court': Steinberger, *The International Court of Justice*, p. 210.
333. Jennings discusses this in the context of suggestions that the role of the ICJ should be expanded: Jennings, *Presentation by Sir Robert Jennings*, p. 79.
334. *Lockerbie Decision* 1992 ICJ Rep 3, 26 (Separate Opinion of Judge Lachs).

previous chapter the Court's advisory jurisdiction is particularly well suited for this task. The Court by deciding in an impartial manner, with each party given full and fair opportunity to prove their positions, can provide an alternative to violence and freedom from repression. The Court provides the UN and the international community with an avenue to minimize unnecessary violence and protect the international community from violence spilling into neighbouring States. As Judge Ecer writes, far from merely applying international law, the ICJ strengthens the cohesion of the international community.[335]

And that is a very important contribution indeed.

335. Shahabuddeen, *The World Court*, p. 27.

Conclusion

> *We the peoples of the United Nations determined to save succeeding generations from the scourge of war, which twice in our lifetime has brought untold sorrow to mankind ...*[1]

It was stated in the Introduction that the purpose of this monograph was to investigate the extent to which the ICJ should and could assist with the resolution of claims for self-determination, and thus help avoid at least some of the 'scourge of wars of independence,'[2] and perhaps as Weller describes it the 'self-determination trap'.[3] This question was prompted for a number of reasons, not least of which was the observation made by commentators such as Geoffrey Robertson, that a major factor causing these conflicts was the absence of any meaningful opportunity to have a people's claims adjudicated, or even heard.[4] The aim of this monograph has been to argue that violence is not the only way to successfully achieve self-determination nor is it necessarily inevitable.

The answer to whether the ICJ should assist with the resolution of claims for self-determination is a resounding 'yes' for many reasons, but mainly because States need the Court to act as the legal guardian for the international community.[5] States cannot be expected to act in a manner contrary to their self-interest, and there is little that affects their interests more than claims for self-determination. As Otto Kimminich noted, self-determination

1. Preamble to the *UN Charter*.
2. This is paraphrasing the Preamble of the *UN Charter*.
3. Marc Weller, *Escaping the Self-Determination Trap*, Leiden: Martinus Nijhoff, 2008.
4. As cited in the Introduction: Geoffrey Robertson, *Crimes Against Humanity: The Struggle for Global Justice*, London: Penguin Press, 1999, p. 144.
5. *Questions of Interpretation and Application of the 1971 Montreal Convention Arising From the Aerial Incident at Lockerbie (Libyan Arab Jamahiriya v United Kingdom)* [1992] ICJ Rep 3, 26 (Separate Opinion of Judge Lachs).

is a right available to peoples not States[6] and, as a legal right available to peoples against States, it makes no sense to have States determine the appropriateness of individual claims, particularly when the State opposes the claim.[7]

Chapter 1 examined the issue of how a Court could identify which people would be a legitimate claimant through the use of four pre-conditions, namely: (1) the claimants are a distinct people subject to alien and foreign subjugation; (2) they have expressed their free will in an internationally monitored plebiscite to achieve statehood; (3) the people accept and agree to be bound by the terms of the *UN Charter* and the norms of international law; and (4) the people are capable of forming a State that satisfies the Montevideo criteria. In essence, this chapter provided the basis for the argument that the ICJ *could* assist in the resolution of self-determination claims by clearly identifying a legitimate claimant: arguably the first and most important step in the peaceful resolution of claims for self-determination.

Chapter 2 discussed the approaches of States to the recognition of newly emergent States. Political influences have been so overpowering, and have resulted in such obvious unhelpful inconsistencies that commentators like Franck argue that States have eroded their ability to confer legitimacy to the process of recognition.[8] No legal system can be effective, or perhaps even survive, if notions of fairness and justice are replaced with considerations of self-interest and partiality,[9] and where the development of legal norms have been heavily influenced by dominate members seeking to protect their privileged position. Whilst States understandably act in their best interests, the Court acts in the best interests of the entire international community: States, peoples, international organisations, and other non-State actors.[10] Furthermore, placing a question of recognition into a legal framework: that is involving the preparation of the written memorials and the counter-memorials with all the necessary research that requires, and presenting the

6. Otto Kimminich, 'A "Federal" Right of Self-Determination?' in Christian Tomuschat (ed), *Modern Law of Self-Determination*, The Hague: Kluwer Academic Publishers incorporating Martinus Nijhoff Publishers, 1993, p. 83.
7. As noted by Meijknecht, 'can a sovereign State, who itself poses the greatest danger to minorities and indigenous peoples, be entrusted with their protection?': Anna Meijknecht, *Towards International Personality: The Position of Minorities and Indigenous Peoples in International Law*, Antwerpen: Intersentia-Hart, 2001, pp. 20–21.
8. Thomas M Frank, *The Power of Legitimacy Among Nations*, New York: Oxford University Press, 1990, pp. 112, 134.
9. More importantly, States go one step further and manipulate norms of international law.
10. The Court has repeatedly demonstrated this in numerous cases and Advisory Opinions such as: *Military and Paramilitary Activities in and against Nicaragua (Nicaragua v United States of America) (Merits)* [1986] ICJ Rep 14; *Frontier Dispute Case (Burkina Faso v Republic of Mali) (Provisional Measures)* [1986] ICJ Rep 3; *Western Sahara (Advisory Opinion)* [1975] ICJ Rep 12; *East Timor (Portugal v Australia) (Judgment)* [1995] ICJ Rep 90 ('*East Timor*'); *Legality of the Threat or Use of Nuclear Weapons (Advisory Opinion)* [1996] 1 ICJ Rep 226.

case to the Court for judicial consideration, all increase the possibility of an authoritative solution.

For the above reasons the necessity of an impartial independent authoritative body to act as the legal guardian in any community is self-evident,[11] and one that States recognised when planning the UN. As discussed in Chapter 3 guiding the UN political organs in an impartial manner *is* exactly the role envisaged for the Court's advisory jurisdiction. Furthermore, the advisory jurisdiction overcomes the otherwise insurmountable obstacles of the ICJ's contentious jurisdiction. So it is the Court's advisory jurisdiction that is more likely to assist people resolve their claims for self-determination. The role of the Court's advisory jurisdiction is to answer a legal question so that a political solution can be found either by the parties themselves or by the appropriate organ of the UN. The value of such guidance is that it can minimise the chance that a party may feel cheated because they were not treated equally, or the final decision made impartially. Practical issues, such as border disputes can be resolved, removing potential future flashpoints and creating long-term solutions. The *Frontier Dispute* is a clear example and, as shown by the *Western Sahara Opinion* the Court retains the ability to closely examine historical records to determine the authenticity of respective parties' claims. More importantly such guidance ensures that the correct norms of international law are developed.

The *Kosovo Opinion* showed that the question in the Request for an Advisory Opinion must be crafted carefully for the Court to be able to offer helpful evidence on the legal issues involved. To minimise the chance that the Court would consider the Requesting Body to be acting *ultra vires*, it was suggested in Chapter 3 that whilst it would be appropriate if the Decolonisation Committee, part of the UN General Assembly, were to make the Request, to guarantee that the Court did not refuse the Request it would be preferable if the General Assembly was the Requesting Body.

It is the extent of the role played by the Court's advisory jurisdiction that is more contentious. This is because there is no guarantee that an Opinion in favour of independence will directly result in such independence. In fact, there is no guarantee that the Requesting UN organ will even act upon the Court's Opinion, and certainly there is even less of a guarantee of States acting upon it.[12] If the provision of an Advisory Opinion is meaningless, then arguably using the advisory jurisdiction may do more harm than good, it would only increase a people's frustration and further entrench the view that violence is the only way to successfully achieve self-determination. It would

11. JG Merrills, *International Dispute Settlement*, (5th ed) Cambrdge; Cambrdige University Press, 2011, pp. 292–294.
12. Although not a direct example, but Israel's attitude towards the decision of the *Legal Consequences of the Construction of a Wall in the Occupied Palestinian Territory (Advisory Opinion)* [2004] ICJ Rep 136, is fairly indicative.

also certainly damage the Court's reputation, which is important if the Court is to play a meaningful role in the resolution of self-determination claims. It is arguable that damage to the Court's reputation may even be greater where a State ignores a Court's decision in a contentious matter, because this result would indeed pose a more direct, and potentially damaging challenge to the Court's authority.[13] Increased use of the Court's ability to reword the Request could provide a means to avoid its reputation from being compromised or tarnished.

Chapter 4 demonstrated the Court's ability to ride out such difficult challenges to its credibility and, indeed, it actually prospered after the *Nicaragua Case*. Smaller less powerful States became more confident that they too would be provided with an opportunity to be heard, that they could challenge a more powerful State and have their dispute decided in an impartial manner in contrast to the power politics of the UN's General Assembly and in particular the Security Council. In fact despite many opportunities for diminution of the Court's credibility because States refused to comply with its determinations, the Court continues to function, continues to guide the UN in resolving matters and continues to provide parties with an opportunity to resolve their differences in a peaceful manner.[14]

Chapter 4 showed that the Court makes its strongest contribution to resolving highly political matters when it is acting as a guide, as a teacher.[15] The Court's advisory jurisdiction is especially suited to this task. The Court's expertise in clarifying the legal principles and its ability to sift through dubious and biased statements made by national representatives in the guise of evidence can provide crucial assistance to the UN's political organs. But it is the Court's ability to clarify and even develop norms of international law that is the true strength of the advisory jurisdicition's ability to resolve self-determination claims. The role of the Court's advisory jurisdiction is to answer a legal question so that a political solution can be found either by the parties themselves or by the appropriate organ of the UN. This approach is dependent upon close cooperation between the ICJ and the other organs of the UN. Article 94 of the *UN Charter* allows the Security Council to decide what measures to take to give effect to the

13. For example, despite the Order of 9 April 1998 by the ICJ to delay execution until it had decided the merits of the dispute the US proceeded with the execution of a Paraguayan national. See *Case Concerning the Vienna Convention on Consular Relations (Paraguay v USA) (Provisional Measures)* [1998] ICJ Rep 248.
14. Sir Arthur Watts, 'The Importance of International Law' in Michael Byers (ed), *The Role of Law in International Politics: Essays in International Relations and International Law*, Oxford: Oxford University Press, 2000, p. 14.
15. Susan Tiefenbrun, 'The Role of the World Court in Settling International Disputes: A Recent Assessment' (1997) 20 *Loyola of Los Angeles International and Comparative Law Journal*, p. 24.

judgment of the ICJ.[16] Commentators like Jennings believe that political and legal decision-making processes are complementary and if used together can be effective.[17] The argument here is for clever management of judicial proceedings.[18] Turning to the latter part of Geoffrey Robertson's comments where he stated:

> ... while it may be idealistic to hope that both sides will respect an international court decision, at least that reasoned adjudication would provide some guide as to whether and on what side other states or the Security Council should intervene to stop the conflict.[19]

Using the Court's advisory jurisdiction to guide the Requesting Body on the legal issues of claims for self-determination, but to then allow the UN bodies or States themselves to then proceed to resolve the claim is clever use of the Court. The Court's timely provision of an Advisory Opinion of the respective rights of the protagonists may enable them to negotiate in a manner that will ensure that they feel secure that their respective legal rights have been respected and will continue to be protected in the future. Alternatively an Advisory Opinion could resolve or clarify legal norms that could be used as a framework for a subsequent arbitration agreement.[20]

As also mentioned in Chapter 4 it must be emphasised that the ICJ should not be expected to find a *political* solution. Placing the discussion of this chapter in the context of peoples seeking self-determination one point is clear: that one thing the ICJ cannot do is to simply wave a magic wand changing

16. It must be remembered that the Security Council has the problem of the veto powers of the permanent members.
17. Sir Robert Jennings, 'Presentation by Sir Robert Jennings' in Connie Peck and Roy Lee (eds), *Increasing the Effectiveness of the International Court of Justice: Proceedings of the ICJ/UNITAR Colloquium to Celebrate the 50th Anniversary of the Court*, The Hague: Kluwer Law International incorporating Martinus-Nijhoff Publishers, 1997, p. 79.
18. To paraphrase Jennings where he stated: 'In the first place, it has to be recognised that there are even essentially legal disputes where an attempt to settle by resort to a court or tribunal might only exacerbate tensions, rather than resolve them and where what is needed, instead, is clever "management" of the situation': Jennings, *Presentation by Sir Robert Jennings*, p. 78.
19. Robertson, *Crimes Against Humanity*, p. 144.
20. Such as the agreement between Sudan and South Sudan: 'The Government of Sudan/The Sudan People's Liberation Movement/Army (Abyei Arbitration)' available at the Permanent Court of Arbitration's website: www.pca-cpa.org/showpasge.asp?pag_id=1306 (accessed 23 June 2013); Markus Bockenforde, 'The Abyei Award: Fitting a Diplomatic Square Peg into a Legal Round Hole' (2010) 23 *Leiden Journal of International Law*, 555; Elizabeth Ward, 'Abyei: an Examination of the Effectiveness of Arbitration for African Land Disputes' available at moritzlaw.osuedu/epub/mayhew-hite/wp-content/uploads/012/03/student-spotlight-march-2012.pdf (accessed 25 June 2013).

the lives of an oppressed people instantly.[21] Gerry Simpson writing in 1994 regarding the *East Timor Case*, noted (the article was written before the decision was handed down) that even if the decision would be in favour of Portugal, it will not on its own '...transform the lives of the residents of Dili, the capital of East Timor.'[22] In other words a simple decision of the ICJ cannot provide a central government, a national economy: all the elements of national sovereignty.[23] However, this does not mean that the ICJ does not have a role to play. What the Court can do is to guide the UN's political organs and States to assist peoples achieve those elements in a peaceful manner. Surely this will benefit both parties and also the international community.

In the introduction to this monograph it was asked: 'Do States benefit from the involvement of the ICJ?' Perhaps the question could be answered by looking at it from a slightly different perspective: would the international community benefit? Undoubtedly yes. Does the international community benefit from being ruled by law or power by 'Realpolitik'? After all it could be argued that the rule of law has not helped the Saharawi people at all. Perhaps, but has the international community benefited from the rule of power in this instance? There are serious consequences of allowing geopolitics to supersede international law; increased tensions between Algeria and Morocco; recurrent tensions between France and Algeria; friction between Morocco and Spain; increased socio-economic problems caused by Algeria and Morocco's arms race; and increased potential for a regional war.[24] All of which could be averted if there existed the will to comply with the ICJ's opinion, in the words of Zoubir, in this '... straightforward case of decolonization'.[25]

In Gwynne Dyer's book *War*, he refers to a discussion he held with the then Under Secretary-General of the UN Brian Urquhart during the Cold War. The Under Secretary-General noted the following:

> There are two possibilities, ... The first one is that we run into another global disaster, which doubtless, if there's anything left, will finally

21. Herbst makes a very interesting point that sovereignty cannot be simply given, it has to be 'earned': Jeffery Herbst, 'Responding to State Failure in Africa' in Michael Brown et al (eds), *Nationalism and Ethnic Conflict*, Cambridge: MIT Press, 1997, p. 375.
22. Gerry Simpson, 'Judging the East Timor Dispute: Self-Determination at the International Court of Justice' (1994) 17 *Hastings International and Comparative Law Review*, p. 347.
23. Musgrave notes that one of the reasons some newly freed colonies failed was because the UN did not consider completely these issues: Thomas D Musgrave, *Self-determination and National Minorities*, Oxford: Oxford University Press, 1997, p. 31.
24. Yahia H Zoubir, 'Geopolitics and *Realpolitik* as Impediments to the Resolution of Conflict and Violations of International Law: The Case of Western Sahara' in Karin Arts and Pedro Pinto Leite (eds), *International Law and the Question of Western Sahara*, Leiden: International Platform of Jurists for East Timor 'IPJET', 2007, p. 276.
25. Ibid. See also Toby Heeley, *Endgame on the Western Sahara, What Future for Africa's Last Colony?*, London: Zed Books, 2004, pp. 199–206.

> change people's minds about the benefits of unlimited national sovereignty. The second alternative is something much more gradual and slower, which is that we convince governments that, just as they have given up sovereignty in certain specialized fields – for example, radio frequencies or postal systems ... – that they have to do this also in the political field.[26]

I believe that currently we are still faced with these two alternatives. Whilst the Cold War is over, the threat of a future global disaster is not. However, it is not groups claiming self-determination that threaten the international community, it is how they are treated that threatens the international community. Something must be done to avoid Weller's self-determination trap.

Thus the announcement at the end of 2007 by Serbian President Boris Tadić that Serbia would seek an Advisory Opinion regarding the legality of Kosovo's claim for independence arguably marked an important shift in Serbia's attitude and the international community's towards resolving self-determination.[27] *Even if* Serbia's motivation for seeking an Advisory Opinion was merely part of some strategic political policy, this approach is far preferable to their previous policy of violent repression. The series of conflicts that resulted from such a policy caused severe misery and bloodshed on a scale that horrified the international community.[28]

By enabling the issue of the Kosovars' claim for independence to be referred to the ICJ, rather than brutally repressing it, not only Serbia, but the entire international community embarks upon Brian Urquhart's second option above, and continues the journey started by the creation of the UN, and the ICJ: an attempt to ensure the rule of law, and not force, regulates the international community.

This monograph has argued that the ICJ and legal methodology can assist with the determination of claims for self-determination. By doing so the monograph seeks, in the words of Allan Buchanan, to domesticate self-determination.

> The question is not whether to recognise a right to secede but, rather, how to domesticate it. For many political actors in today's world, the issue is not so much, Shall we recognize a right to secede? As it is, assuming that the notion of a right to secede is ... an inescapable item on the

26. Brian Urquhart, Under-Secretary-General UN, as cited in Gwynne Dyer, *War*, London: The Bodley Head, 1983, p. 258.
27. To ask the Security Council to Request an Advisory Opinion on the legality or illegality of the possible independence of Kosovo 'Serbia to Seek UN Court Ruling on Separatists in Kosovo', *Serbianna*: <http://www.serbianna.com/news/2007/03050.shtml> (accessed 13 Dec 2007).
28. *Case Concerning the Application of the Convention on the Prevention and Punishment of the Crime of Genocide (Bosnia-Herzegovina v Serbia and Montenegro)* [2007] ICJ Rep 43.

political agenda, how can we utilize clear moral thinking and wise institutional design to enable us to live with it?[29]

Another way of expressing this is to argue that the ICJ through the judicial process can avoid a repetition of tragedies like Eritrea, or East Timor. In other words, the ICJ can provide a means for the peaceful birth of States. If, through the involvement of the ICJ, a repetition of Eritrea's or East Timor's protracted and bloody campaigns for self-determination can be avoided, even if only once, then that would be a worthy outcome, and the endeavour of this monograph vindicated.

29. Allen Buchanan, 'Toward a Theory of Secession' (1991) 101(2) *Ethics*, p. 339.

Bibliography

Monographs

Alexandrov, Stanmir A, *Reservations in Unilateral Declarations Accepting the Compulsory Jurisdiction of the International Court of Justice* (Maartinus Nijhoff Publishers, Dordrecht [Distributed by Kluwer Academic Publishers, The Hague] 1995).

Altman Andrew & Christopher Heath Wellman, Christopher Heath, *A Liberal Theory of International Justice* (Oxford University Press, Oxford, 2009).

Amr, Mohammed Sameh M., *The Role of the International Court of Justice as the Principal Judicial Organ of the United Nations* (Kluwer Law International, The Hague, 2003).

Anand, Vijay Kumar, *Conflict in Nagaland* (Chanakya Publications, New Delhi, 1980).

Anderson Benedict, *Imagined Communities* (revised edition) (London, Verso, 1983).

Arts, Karin, & Leite Pedro Pinto (eds) *International Law and The Question of Western Sahara* (International Platform of Jurists for East Timor 'IPJET', Leiden, 2007).

Author unknown, *SBS World Guide, the Complete Fact File on Every Country* (13th ed., Hardie Grant Books, Prahran, 2005).

Bayefsky, Anne F, *Self-determination in International Law: Quebec and Lessons Learned* (Kluwer Academic Publishers, The Hague, 2000).

Bekker, Peter HF (ed) *Commentaries on World Court Decisions (1987–1996)* (Martinus Nijhoff [Distributed by Kluwer Academic Publishers, The Hague] 1998).

Ben-Ami, Shlomo, Pled, Yoav & Alberto Spektorowski, Alberto (eds) *Ethnic Challenges to the Modern Nation State* (Macmillan Press Ltd, Basingstoke, 2000).

Bloomfield, Lincoln P (et al), *International Military Forces, the Question of Peacekeeping in an Armed and Disarming World* (Little Brown & Company, US, 1964).

Boahen, A. Adu, *African Perspectives on Colonialism* (Johns Hopkins University Press, Baltimore, 1987).

Bobbitt, Philip, *The Shield of Achilles, War, Peace and the Course of History* (Penguin Books, London, 2002).

Bodin, Jean, (edited and translated by Julian H. Franklin) *On Sovereignty, Four Chapters from the Six Books of the Commonwealth* (Cambridge University Press, Cambridge, 1992).

Brean, Susan, *Humanitarian Intervention: the United Nations and Collective Responsibility* (Cameron May, London, 2005).

Broinowski, Alison, & Wilkinson, James, *The Third Try, can the UN Work?* (Scribe Publications Pty Ltd, 2005).

Brown, Chris, *Understanding International Relations* (2nd ed., Palgrave, New York, 2001).

Brown, Michael, (et al.) (eds) *Nationalism and Ethnic Conflict* (MIT Press, Cambridge, 1997).
Brown, Seyom, *The Causes and Prevention of War* (2nd ed., St. Martin's Press, New York, 1994).
Brown, Sheryl J. & Schraub, Kimber M. (eds) *Resolving Third World Conflict, Challenges for a New Era* (United States Institute for Peace, Washington, 1992).
Brownlie, Ian, *Principles of Public International Law* (5th ed., Oxford University Press, Oxford, 1998).
Brownlie, Ian, *Principles of Public International Law* (6th ed., Oxford University Press, Oxford, 2003).
——, *The Rule of Law in International Affairs, International Law at the Fiftieth Anniversary of the United Nations* (Kluwer Law International, The Hague, 1998).
Buchanan, Allan, *Secession: the Morality of Political Divorce from Fort Sumter to Lithuania and Quebec* (Westview Press, Boulder, 1991).
Burchill, Scott, (et al.) (ed) *Theories of International Relations* (2nd ed., Palgrave, Hampshire 2001).
Burroughs, John, *The Legality of Threat or Use of Nuclear Weapons: A Guide to the Historic Opinion of the International Court of Justice* (LIT, Munster, 1998).
Byers, Michael, (ed) *The Role of International Law in International Politics, Essays in International Relations and International Law* (Oxford University Press, Oxford, 2000).
Calvocoressi, Peter, & Wint, Guy, *Total War Causes and Courses of the Second World War* (Penguin Books, Harmondsworth, 1972).
Cassese, Antonio, *Self-Determination of Peoples* (Cambridge University Press, Cambridge, 1995).
Castellino, Joshua, *International Law and Self-Determination* (Kluwer Law Internationals, The Hague, 2000).
Catholic Institute for International Relations (CIIR) & International Platform of Jurists for East Timor (IJPET), *International Law and the Question of East Timor, (Catholic Institute for International Relations & International Platform for Jurists for East Timor* (Catholic Institute for International Relations & International Platform for Jurists for East Timor, London, 1995).
Chadwick, F. Alger (ed) *The Future of the United Nations System: Potential for the Twenty-First Century* (United Nations University Press, Tokyo, 1998).
Chamberlain, Muriel Evelyn, *Decolonization: The Fall of the European Empires* (2nd ed., Blackwell Publishers, Malden, 1999).
Chirot, Daniel, & Seligman, Martin, *Ethnopolitical Warfare, Causes, Consequences, and Possible Solutions* (American Psychological Association, Washington DC, 2001).
Chomsky, Noam, *Deferring Democracy* (Vintage, London, 1992).
Clark, Donald, & Williamson, Robert (eds) *Self-Determination: International Perspectives* (Macmillan Press, New York, 1996).
Crawford, James, *The Creation of States in International Law* (2nd ed) (Clarendon Press, Oxford, 2006).
——, (ed) *The Rights of Peoples* (Oxford University Press, Oxford, 1988).
Crocker, Chester A., Hampson, Fen Osler & Aall Pamela (eds) *Managing Global Chaos* (United States Institute for Peace, Washington, 1996).
Damrosch, Lori (ed) *The International Court of Justice at a Crossroads* (Transnational Publishers, New York, 1987).

Delupis, Ingrid Detter, *International Law and the Independent State* (Gower Press Limited, Essex, 1974).

——, *The International Legal Order* (Dartmouth, Aldershot, 1994).

De Chazournes, Laurence Boisson, and Sands, Phillipe (eds) *International Law, the International Court of Justice and Nuclear Weapons* (Cambridge University Press, Cambridge, 1999).

De Votta, Neil, *Blowback, Linguistic Nationalism, Institutional Decay, and Ethnic Conflict in Sri Lanka* (Stanford University Press, Stanford, 2004).

Dixon, Martin & McCorquodale, Robert, *Cases & Materials on International Law* (3rd ed., Blackstone Press, London, 1991).

Duffield, Mark, *Global Governance and the New Wars, the Merging of Development and Security* (Zed Books, New York, 2001).

Dugard, John, *Recognition and the United Nations* (Grotius Publications, Cambridge, 1987).

——,(ed) *The South West Africa/Namibia Dispute* (University of California Press, Berkeley, 1973).

Dunn, James, *East Timor a Rough Passage to Independence* (3rd ed., Longueville, Double Bay, 2003).

Duursma, Jorri, *Fragmentation and the International Relations of Micro-States, Self-Determination and Statehood* (Cambridge University Press, Cambridge, 1996).

Dyer, Gwynne, *War* (The Bodley Head, London, 1983).

Ferro, Marc, *Colonization: A Global History* (Routledge, New York, 1997).

Fowkes, Ben (ed) *Russia and Chechnia: The Permanent Crisis, Essays on Russo-Chechen Relations* (St Martin's Press, New York, 1998).

Fox, Gregory, & Roth, Brad (eds) *Democratic Governance and International Law*, (Cambridge University Press, Cambridge, 2000).

Franck, Thomas, M. *The Power of Legitimacy Among Nations* (Oxford University Press, New York, 1990).

——, *Fairness in International Law and Institutions* (Clarendon Press, Oxford, 1995).

Franklin, Julian H. (ed) *On Sovereignty: Four Chapters from the Six Books of the Commonwealth* (Cambridge University Press, Cambridge, 1992).

Fukuyama, Francis, *The End of History and the Last Man* (New York, 1992).

Gill, Terry, *Rosenne's The World Court, What it is and How it Works* (6th ed., revised by Terry Gill Martinus Nijhoff, Leiden, 2003).

Goss, Leo (ed) *The Future of the International Court of Justice* (Oceana Publications, New York, 1976) vol. 1.

Graham, Robert A SJ, *Vatican Diplomacy, a Study of Church and State on the International Plane* (Princeton University Press, Princeton, 1959).

Grant, Thomas D, *The Recognition of States, Law and Practice in Debate and Evolution* (Praeger, Westport, 1999).

Grief, Nicholas, *The World Court Project on Nuclear Weapons and International Law a joint project of the International Association of Lawyers Against Nuclear Weapons and the International Physicians For the Prevention of Nuclear War* (Alethia Press Northampton first published 1992, 2nd ed., 1993).

Gros-Espiell, Hector, *The Right to Self-Determination of United Nations Resolutions* (UN, New York, 1980).

Guibernau, Montserrat, *Nations without States, Political Communities in a Global Age* (Polity Press, Oxford, 1999).

Gunasingam, Murugar, *Sri Lankan Tamil Nationalism: A Study of its Origins* (MV Publications, Sydney, 1999).
Gundevia, Y.D, I.C.S. (Retd.) *War and Peace in Nagaland* (Palit & Palit, New Delhi, 1975).
Gurr, Ted Robert, *Why Men Rebel* (Princeton University Press, Princeton, 1970).
——, *Minorities at Risk, A Global View of Ethnopolitical Conflicts* (United States Institute of Peace Press, Washington DC, 1993).
——, *Peoples Versus States* (United States Institute of Peace Press, Washington DC, 2000).
Gurr, Ted Robert & Harff Barbara, *Ethnic Conflict in World Politics* (Westview Press, Boulder, 1994).
Hampson, Fen Osler & Malone, David M, (eds) *From Reaction to Conflict Prevention, Opportunities for the UN System* (A Project of the International Peace Academy, Lynne Rienner Publishers, Boulder, 2002).
Hannum, Hurst, *Autonomy, Sovereignty, and Self-Determination, the Accommodation of Conflicting Rights* (University of Pennsylvania Press, Philadelphia, 1990).
Harris, David John, *Cases and Materials in International Law* (5th ed) (Sweet & Maxwell, London, 1998).
Heere, Wybo, (ed) *Contemporary International Law Issues: New Forms New Applications (Proceedings of the Fourth Hague Joint Conference held in the Hague, The Netherlands, 2–5 July 1997)* (T.M.C. Asser Instituut, The Hague, 1997).
Heiberg, Marianne, (ed) *Subduing Sovereignty and the Right to Intervene* (Pinter Publishers, London, 1984).
Hewitt, Christopher, & Cheetham, Tom, *Encyclopaedia of Modern Separatist Movements* (ABC-CLIO, Oxford, 2000).
Higgins, Rosalyn, *The Development of International Law through the Political Organs of the United Nations* (Oxford University Press, London, 1963).
——, *Problems and Process, International law and How We Use It* (Clarendon Press, Oxford, 1994).
——, 'The Role of the International Court of Justice at the Turn of the Century', *Presidential Address to the Holdsworth Club of the University of Birmingham* (The Holdsworth Club of the University of Birmingham, Birmingham, 1999).
Hinsley, F.H., *Sovereignty* (2nd ed., Cambridge University Press, Cambridge, 1986).
Holmes, George, (ed) *The Oxford History of Medieval Europe* (Oxford University Press, Oxford, 1992).
Hunczak, Taras, (ed) *Russian Imperialism from Ivan the Great to the Revolution* (Rutgers University Press, New Jersey, 1974).
Hussain, Ijaz, *Dissenting and Separate Opinions at the World Court* (Martinus Nijhoff, Dordrecht, 1984).
Igantieff, Michael, *Blood and Belonging* (Vintage Random House, London, 1994).
Ingram, David, *Law, Key Concepts in Philosophy* (Continuum, London, 2006).
Janis, Mark W, (ed) *International Courts for the Twenty-First Century* (Martinus Nijhoff, Dordrecht [Distributed by Kluwer Academic Publishers The Hague], 1992).
Jasentuliyana, Nandasiri, (ed) *Perspectives on International Law* (Martinus Nijhoff Publishers, Dordrecht [Distributed by Kluwer Academic Publishers, The Hague], 1995).
Kaikobad Kaiyn H, *The International Court of Justice and Judicial Review: A Study of the Court's Powers with Respect to Judgments of the ILO and UN Administrative Tribunals,* (Kluwer International, The Hague, 2000).
Keen, Maurice, *The Penguin History of Medieval Europe* (Penguin Books, London, 1968).

Keith, Kenneth James, *The Extent of the Advisory Jurisdiction of the International Court of Justice* (A.W. Sijthoff, Leydon, 1971).
Keegan, John, *War and Our World, the Reith Lectures 1998* (Pimlico, London, 1999).
Keep, John L.H., *Last of the Empires, a History of the Soviet Union 1945–1991* (Oxford University Press, Oxford, 1995).
Kelsen, Hans, *General Theory of Law and State* (Russell & Russell, New York, 1961).
——, *Principles of International Law* (2nd ed., revised edition by Robert W Tucker, Holt, Rinehart, and Winston, New York, 1966).
Kennedy, John F, *Public Papers of the Presidents of the United States: John F Kennedy, 1961* (Vol. 1, Government Printing Office, Washington DC, 1962).
Kennedy, Paul, *The Rise and Fall of the Great Powers, Economic Change and Military Conflict from 1500–2000* (Fontana Press, London, 1989).
Kennedy, Paul, & Hitchcock, William I, (ed) *From War to Peace, Altered Strategic Landscapes in the Twentieth Century* (Yale University Press, New York, 2000).
Khan, Ali L., *The Extinction of Nation-States: A World Without Borders* (Kluwer Law International, The Hague, 1995).
King, Michael and Thornhill, Chris (eds) *Luhmann on Law and Politics* (Hart Publishing, Oxford, 2006).
King, Peter, *West Papua & Indonesia since Suharto, Independence, Autonomy or Chaos?* (UNSW Press, Sydney, 2004).
Kipling, Rudyard, *Kim* (1901).
Kleveman, Lutz, *The Great New Game, Blood and oil in Central Asia* (Atlantic Books, London, 2004).
Knecht, R.J. *The Rise and Fall of Renaissance France* (Fontana Press, London, 1996).
Knop, Karen, *Diversity and Self-Determination in International Law* (Cambridge University Press, Cambridge, 2002).
Kornbluh, Peter, *Nicaragua, the Price of Intervention: Reagan's Wars against the Sandinistas* (Institute for Policy Studies, Washington DC, 1987).
Kreyenbroek, Philip G. & Sperl, Stefan (eds) *The Kurds, a Contemporary Overview* (Routledge, London, 1992).
Lauterpacht, (Sir) Hersch, *Recognition in International Law* (Cambridge University Press, Cambridge, 1947).
——, *The Development of International Law by the International Court* (reprinted by Grotius Publications, Cambridge, 1982, first published by Stevens & Sons, London, 1958).
Leggett, Jeremy, *Half Gone, Oil, Gas, Hot Air and the Global Energy Crisis* (Portobello Books, London, 2005).
Lissitzyn, Oliver J, *The International Court of Justice: Its Role in the Maintenance of International Peace and Security* (Greenwood Press, Westport, 1978).
Louis, Roger, WM (ed) *Imperialism, The Robinson and Gallagher Controversy* (New Viewpoints, New York, 1976).
Lowe, Vaughan, & Fitzmaurice, Malgosia, (ed) *Fifty Years of the International Court of Justice Essays in Honour of Sir Robert Jennings* (Cambridge University Press, 1996).
Macartney, W.J.A (ed) *Self-determination in the Commonwealth* (Aberdeen University Press, Aberdeen, 1988).
MacMillan, Margaret, *Peacemakers Six Months that Changed the World* (John Murray Publishers, London, 2001).
McCormack, Timothy L.H. & Saunders Cheryl (AO), *Sir Ninian Stephen, a Tribute* (The Miegunyah Press, Carlton, 2007).

McCorquodale, Robert, and Orosz, Nicholas, *Tibet: The Position in International Law* (Report of the Conference of international Lawyers on Issues Relating to Self-Determination and the Independence for Tibet, London 6–10 Jan 1993) (Serinda Publications, London, 1994).
McWhinney, Edward, *Judicial Settlement of International Disputes: Jurisdiction, Justiciability and Judicial Law-Making on the Contemporary International Court* (M. Nijhoff Dordrecht, Kluwer Academic Publishers, 1991).
Margolis, Eric S. *War at the Top of the World* (Routledge, New York, 2001).
Martinkus, John, *Indonesia's Secret War in Aceh* (Random House, Australia, 2004).
Max Planck Institute for Comparative Public Law and International Law, *Judicial Settlement of Disputes: International Court of Justice, Other Courts and Tribunals, Arbitration and Conciliation – An International Symposium* (Springer Verlag, New York, 1974).
Mazuri, Ali A. & Tidy, Michael, *Nationalism and New States in Africa* (Heinemann, London, 1984).
Meier, Andrew, *Chechnya, to the Heart of a Conflict* (W.W. Norton, New York, 2005).
Meijknecht, Anna, *Towards International Personality: The Position of Minorities and Indigenous Peoples in International Law* (Intersentia-Hart, Antwerpen, 2001).
Menon, PK, *The Law of Recognition in International Law, Basic Principles* (The Edwin Mellen Press, Lampter, 1994).
Moore, Margaret, (ed) *Self-National Self-Determination and Secession* (Oxford University Press, New York, 1998).
Morris, Christopher W, *An Essay on the Modern State* (Cambridge University Press, Cambridge, 1998).
Mosler, Hermann, & Bernhardt, Rudolph, (eds) *Judicial Settlement of International Disputes: International Court of Justice, Other Courts and Tribunals, Arbitration and Conciliation; an International Symposium/Max Planck Institute for Comparative Public Law and International Law* (Springer, Berlin, 1974).
Mullen, Christopher A, & Ryan J Atticus (eds) *Unrepresented Nations and Peoples Organisation, Yearbook 1996* (Kluwer Law International, The Hague, 1997).
Muller, AS, Raič D., & Thuránszky J. M., (eds) *The International Court of Justice: Its Future Role after Fifty Years* (Kluwer Law International, The Hague, 1997).
Musgrave, Thomas D, *Self-determination and National Minorities* (Oxford University Press, Oxford, 1997).
Nikolaev Yu. V., (ed) *The Chechen Tragedy Who is to Blame* (Nova Science Publishers, New York, 1996).
Noortmann, Math, *Enforcing International Law, From Self-help to Self-contained Regimes* (Ashgate, Aldershot, 2005).
O'Ballance, Edgar, *The Cyanide War, Tamil Insurgency in Sri Lanka 1973–1988* (Brassey's, London, 1989).
Ofuatey-Kodjoe, Wentworth B, *Self-Determination in International Law: Towards a Definition of the Principle* (University Microfilms International, Ann Arbour, 1985).
Ojo, Bamidele A., *Human Rights and the New World Order: Universality, Acceptability and Human Diversity* (Nova Science Publishers, New York, 1997).
Orford, Anne, *Reading Humanitarian Intervention, Human Rights and the Use of Force in International Law* (Cambridge University Press, Cambridge, 2003).
Pakovic, Aleksandar, & Radan, Peter (eds) *On the Way to Statehood, Secession and Globalisation* (Ashgate, Aldershot, 2008).
Parker, Geoffrey, *The Geopolitics of Domination* (Routledge, New York, 1988).

Pasqualucci, Jo M. *The Practice and Procedure of the Inter-American Court of Human Rights* (Cambridge University Press, Cambridge, 2003).
Patil, Anjiali, *The UN Veto in World Affairs 1946–1990* (UNIFO/Mansell Publishers, United Kingdom, 1992).
Peck, Connie, *The United Nations as a Dispute Settlement System, Improving Mechanisms for the Prevention and Resolution of Conflict* (Kluwer Law International, The Hague, 1996).
Peck, Connie & Lee, Roy S, (eds) *Increasing the Effectiveness of the International Court of Justice, Proceedings of the ICJ/UNITAR Colloquium to Celebrate the 50th Anniversary of the Court* (Kluwer Law International, The Hague, 1997).
Pemberton, Gregory, *All the Way: Australia's Road to Vietnam* (Allen and Unwin, Sydney, 1987).
Peterson, M.J. *Recognition of Governments, Legal Doctrine and State Practice, 1815–1995* (Macmillan Press, London, 1997).
Politkovskaya, Anna, *A Dirty War, a Russian Reporter in Chechnya* (The Harvill Press, 2001).
——, *A Small Corner of Hell, Dispatches form Chechnya* (University of Chicago Press, Chicago, 2003).
Pomerance, Michla, *The Advisory Function of the International Court in the League and UN Eras* (Johns Hopkins University Press, Baltimore, 1973).
Porter, Bruce D., *War and the Rise of the State, the Military Foundations of Modern Politics* (The Free Press, New York, 1994).
Pratap, Dharma *The Advisory Jurisdiction of the International Court* (Oxford University Press, Oxford, 1972).
Radan, Peter, *The Break-up of Yugoslavia* (Routledge, New York, 2002).
Raic, David, *Statehood and the Law of Self-Determination* (Kluwer Law International, The Hague, 2002).
Raymond, Gregory, *Conflict Resolution and the Structure of the State System, An Analysis of Arbitrative Settlements* (Allannheld Osmun, New Jersey, 1980).
Reus-Smit, Christian, (ed) *The Politics of International Law* (Cambridge University Press, Cambridge, 2004).
Rezun, Miron, (ed) *Nationalism and the Break-up of an Empire, Russia and its Periphery* (Prager, US, 1992).
Robertson, Geoffrey, *Crimes Against Humanity, the Struggle for Global Justice* (Penguin Press, London, 1999).
Rosefielde, Steven, *Russia in the 21st Century, the Prodigal Superpower* (Cambridge University Press, Cambridge, 2005).
Rosenne, Shabtai, *The World Court, What it is and How it Works* (5th ed., Kluwer Academic Publishers, 1995).
——, *Provisional Measres in International Law, the International Court of Justice and the International Tribunal for the Law of the Sea* (Oxford University Press, Oxford, 2005).
——, *The Law and Practice of the International Court, 1920–2005, Volume I The Court and the United Nations* (Martinus Nijhoff Publishers, Leiden, 2006).
Rotberg, Robert, (ed) *Creating Peace in Sri Lanka, Civil War and Reconciliation* (The World Peace Foundation and the Belfer Centre for Science and International Affairs, Harvard University Brookings Institution Press, Washington DC, 1999).
Roth, Brad R, *Governmental Illegitimacy in International Law* (Claredon Press, Oxford, 1999).

Schater, Oscar, & Joyner, Christopher C., (eds) *United Nations Legal Order* (vol. 1) (Cambridge University Press, Cambridge, 1995).
Schlesinger, Stephen C, *Act of Creation, the Founding of the United Nations* (Westview Press, 2003).
Schulte, Constanze, *Compliance with Decisions of the International Court of Justice The Project on International Courts and Tribunals* (Oxford University Press, London, 2004).
Schwarz, Adam, *A Nation in Waiting, Indonesia's Search for Stability* (2nd ed., Westview Press, Boulder, 2000).
Seeley, Robert, *Russo-Chechen Conflict 1800–2000, A Deadly Embrace* (Frank Cass, London, 2001).
Shaw, Malcolm N, *International Law* (5th ed., Cambridge University Press, Cambridge, 2003).
Shearer, Ivan Anthony, *Starke's International Law* (11th ed., Butterworths, Sydney, 1994).
Singh, Nagendra, *The Role and Record of the International Court of Justice* (Kluwer Academic Publishers, Dordrecht, 1989).
Smith, Tony, (ed) *The End of the European Empire, Decolonisation after World War II* (DC Heath and Company, Lexington, 1975).
Snider, Don M. & Schwartzstein, Stuart J.D. (eds) *The United Nations at Fifty, Sovereignty, Peacekeeping and Human Rights* (CSIS, Washington, 1995).
Spencer, Jonathon, (ed) *Sri Lanka, History and the Roots of Conflict* (Routledge, London, 1990).
Starke, Joseph Gabriel, *Introduction to International Law* (9th ed., Butterworths, London, 1984).
Steinberger, Helmut, 'The International Court of Justice', in *Judicial Settlement of International Disputes* (Springer Verlag, New York, 1974).
Summers, James, *Peoples and International Law How Nationalism and Self-Determination Shape a Contemporary Law of Nations* (Martinus-Nijhoff, Leiden, 2007).
Sureda, A. Rigo, *The Evolution of the Right of Self-Determination, A Study of United Nations Practice* (A. W. Sijthoff, Leiden, 1973).
Szafraz, Renata, *The Compulsory Jurisdiction of the International Court of Justice* (Kluwer Law International, The Hague, 1993).
Tacsan, Joaquin, *The Dynamics of International Law in Conflict Resolution* (Kluwer Law International, The Hague, 1992).
Tambiah, Stanley Jeyaraja, *Sri Lanka, Ethnic Fratricide and the Dismantling of Democracy* (IB Tauris & Co, London, 1986).
Tamkoc, Metin, *The Turkish Cypriot State, the Embodiment of the Right of Self-Determination* (K Rustem & Brother, London, 1988).
Taylor, John G. *Indonesia's Forgotten War* (Pluto Press, Leichhardt, 1991).
Tiryakian, Edward, & Rogowski, Ronald, (eds) *New Nationalisms of the Developed West* (Allen and Unwin, Boston, 1980).
Tomuschat, Christian, *Modern Law of Self-Determination* (Kluwer Academic Publishers, The Hague, 1993).
Trenhaile, John, *Nocturne for the General* (Grafton, London, 1999).
Turchin, Peter, *War & Peace & War, the Life Cycles of Imperial Nations* (Pi Press, New York, 2006).
Twining, William (ed) *Issues of Self-Determination* (Aberdeen University Press, Abderdeen, 1991).
Umozurike Oji, Umozurike, *Self-Determination in International Law* (Shoe String Press, Connecticut, 1972).

Van Creveld, Martin, *The Rise and Decline of the State* (Cambridge University Press, Cambridge, 1999).

van Horne, Winston, *Global Convulsions, Race, Ethnicity, and Nationalism at the End of the Twentieth Century* (State University of New York Press, Albany, 1997).

Verzijl, JHW, *International Law in Historical Perspective* (Volume 1, AW Sijthoff-Leydon, Leydon, 1968).

Waites, Bernard, *Europe and the Third World, from Colonisation to Decolonisation, c. 1500–1998* (St. Martin's Press, New York, 1999).

Wambaugh Sarah, *Plebiscites Since the World War* (Carnegie Endowment for International Peace, Washington, 1933) Vol. 1 & Vol. 2.

Weller Marc & Metzger Barbara, (eds) *Settling Self-Determination Disputes, Complex Power-Sharing in Theory and Practice* (Martinus Nijhoff Publishers, The Hague, 2008).

——, Weller, *Escaping the Self-Determination Trap* (Martinus Nijhoff Publishers, Leiden, 2008).

Wesseling, H.L. (translated by Diane Webb), *The European Colonial Empires, 1815–1919* (Pearson/Longman, New York, 1994).

Willens, Howard P, & Siemer, Deanne C *National Security and Self-Determination, United States Policy in Micronesia (1961–1972)* (Praeger, London, 2000).

Wilson, Heather A, *International Law and the Use of Force by National Liberation Movements* (Clarendon Press, Oxford, 1988).

Ydit, Meir, *Internationalised territories from the "Free City of Cracow" to the "Free city of Berlin." : A Study in the historical development of a modern notion in international law and international relations (1815–1960)* (A.W. Sythoff, Leyden, 1961).

Articles

Anthony Aust, 'Advisory Opinions', (2010) 1(1) *Journal of International Dispute Settlements* 123.

Barrie, George N, '*Uti Possidetis* Versus Self-determination and Modern International Law: in Africa the Chickens are Coming Home to Roost', (1988) *Journal of South African Law* 456.

Batistich, Marija, 'The Right to Self-Determination and International Law' (1992–1995) 7 *Auckland University Law Review* 1013.

Becker, Tal, 'Self-Determination in Perspective: Palestinian Claims to Statehood and the Relatively of the Right to Self-Determination', (1998) 32 *Israel Law Review* 301.

Bekker, Peter, 'Questions of Interpretation and Application of the 1971 Montreal Convention Arising from the Aerial Incident at Lockerbie' (1998) 92 *American Journal of International Law* 503.

Bercovitch, Jacob, 'Managing Internationalised Ethnic Conflict: Evaluating the Role and Relevance of Mediation' in (2003) 166 *World Affairs* 166.

Blay S. Kwan Nyameke, 'Changing African Perspectives on the Right of Self-Determination in the Wake of the Banjul Charter on Human and Peoples' Rights, (1985) 29(2) *Journal of African Law* 147.

——, 'Self-Determination: A Reassessment in the Post-Communist Era,' (1994) 22 *Denver Journal of International Law and Policy* 275.

——, 'Self-Determination *Versus* Territorial Integrity in Decolonization' (1985–86) 18 *New York Journal of International Law and Politics* 441.

Bleimaier John Kuhn, 'The Future of Sovereignty in the 21st Century', (1993) 6 *Hague International Yearbook of International Law* 17.

Boyle, Francis, 'Determining US Responsibility for Contra Operations Under International Law' (1987) 81 *American Journal of International Law* 86.

Brecht, Greg 'The World's Worst Massacres', (1987), 74 (2) *Whole Earth Review* <http://findarticles.com/p/articles/mi_m1510/is_1987_Fall/ai_5151514> at 7 December 2007.

Brilmayer, Lea 'Secession and Self-Determination: A Territorial Interpretation', (1991) 16 *Yale Journal of International Law* 177.

Buchanan, Allen 'Toward a Theory of Secession', (1991) 101 (2) *Ethics* 322.

——, 'Theories of Secession', 26 (1) *Philosophy and Public Affairs* 30.

Burri Thomas, 'The Kosovo Opinion and Secession: The Sounds of Silence and Missing Links' (2010) 11 *German Law Journal* 881.

Christakis Theodore, 'The ICJ Advisory Opinion on Kosovo: Has International Law Something to Say about Secession?' 24 (1) (2011) *Leiden Journal of International Law* 73.

Condorelli, Lugi, 'Nuclear Weapons: A Weighty Matter for the International Court of Justice' (1997) 316 *International Review of the Red Cross* 9.

Cribb, Robert, 'Not the Next Yugoslavia: Prospects for the Disintegration of Indonesia', (1999) 53 (2) *Australian Journal of International Affairs* 169.

Crook, John R, 'The 2001 Judicial Activity of the International Court of Justice' (2002) 96 *American Journal of International Law* 397.

Currie, John, 'NATO's Humanitarian Intervention in Kosovo: Making or Braking International Law?', 36 (1998) *Canadian Yearbook of International Law* 303.

D'Amato, Anthony, 'Trashing Customary International Law' (1987) 81 *American Journal of International Law* 101.

David, Eric, 'The Opinion of the International Court of Justice on the Legality of the Use of Nuclear Weapons' (1997) 316 *International Review of the Red Cross* 21.

Drew, Catriona, 'The East Timor Story: International Law on Trial' (2001) 12 *European Journal of International Law* 651.

Dugard, John 'Namibia–South Africa's Presence Found to be Illegal–United Nations' Measures Declared Valid' (1972) 5 *New York University Journal of International Law and Politics* 117.

Evans, Malcolm, '*The East Timor Case*' (1996) 45 *International and Comparative Law Quarterly* 712.

Falk, Richard, 'The *Kosovo* Advisory Opinion: Conflict Resolution and Precedent' (2011) 105(1) *American Journal of International Law*, 50.

Fassberg, C Wasserstien, 'Israel and the Palestinian Authority', (1994) 28 *Israel Law Review* 319.

Field, Andrew, 'The Legality of Humanitarian Intervention and the Use of Force in the Absence of United Nations Authority' 26 (2000) *Monash University Law Review* 339.

Fielding, Lois, 'Taking the Next Step in the Development of New Human Rights: The Emerging Right of Humanitarian Assistance to Restore Democracy', (1995) 5 *Duke J. Comp. & Int'l L.* 329.

Foster, Caroline E, 'Articulating Self-Determination in the Draft Declaration o the Rights of Indigenous Peoples', (2001) 12 (1) *European Journal of International Law* 141.

Franck, Thomas M, 'The Emerging Right to Democratic Governance' (1992) 86 *American Journal of International Law* 46.

——, 'Some Observations on the ICJ's Procedural and Substantive Innovations' (1987) 81 *American Journal of International Law* 116.

——, 'Legitimacy in the International System', (1988) 82 *American Journal of International Law* 705.

Glennon, Michael, 'The New Interventionism (Getting Involved in Other Nations' Conflicts and Affairs)' (1999) 78(3) *Foreign Affairs* 1.

Goss, Leo, 'The International Court of Justice: Consideration of Requirements for Enhancing its Role I the International Legal Order', (1971) 65 *The American Journal of International Order* 253.

Gowlland-Debbas, Vera, 'The Relationship Between the International Court of Justice and the Security Council in Light of the *Lockerbie Case*' (1994) 88 *American Journal of International Law* 643.

Green, Fergus, 'Fragmentation in Two Dimensions: the ICJ's Flawed Approach to Non-State Actors and International Legal Personality' (2008) 9 *Melbourne Journal of International Law* 47.

Greenwood, Christopher, 'International Humanitarian Law and the *Tadic* Case' 7 (1996) *European Journal of International Law* 265.

——, 'The Advisory Opinion on Nuclear Weapons and the Contribution of the International Court to International Humanitarian Law' (1997) 316 *International Review of the Red Cross* 65.

Gruda, Zejnullah, 'Some Key Principles for a Lasting Solution of the Status of Kosova: *Uti Possidetis* the Ethnic Principle, and Self-Determination', (2005) 80 *Chicago Kent Law Review* 353.

Halberstam, Malvina, 'Self-Determination in the Arab-Israeli Conflict: Meaning, Myth, and Politics' in (1989) 21 *International Law and Politics* 465.

Hannum, Hurst, 'The Specter of Secession, Responding to Claims for Ethnic Self-determination', (1998) 77 (2) *Foreign Affairs* 17.

Hargrove, John, 'The *Nicaragua* Judgment and the Future of the Law of Force and Self-Defense' (1987) 81 *American Journal of International Law* 135.

Hensley, Thomas, 'National Bias and the International Court of Justice' (1968) 12 *Mid-west Journal of Political Science* 568.

Highet, Keith, 'Between a Rock and a Hard Place – The United States, the International Court, and the *Nicaragua Case*' (1987) 21 *The International Lawyer* 1083.

——, 'The Peace Palace Heats Up: The World Court in Business Again?' (1991) 85 *American Journal of International Law* 646.

Hill, Mitchell, 'What the Principle of Self-Determination Means Today' (1995), 1 *ILSA Journal of International and Comparative Law* 119.

Hillgruber, Christian, 'The Admission of New States to the International Community', (1998), 9 *European Journal of International Law* 491.

Hobe, Stephan, 'The Era of Globalisation as a Challenge to International Law', (2002) 40 *Duquesne Law Review* 655.

Hooper, James R, 'Earned Sovereignty: The Political Dimension', (2002–2003) 31 *Denver Journal of International Law and Policy* 355.

Howse Robert and Teitel Ruti, 'Delphic Dicum: How Has the ICJ Contributed to the Global Rule of Law by its Ruling on Kosovo?' (2010) 11 *German Law Journal* 841.

Janis, Mark, 'Somber Reflections on the Compulsory Jurisdiction of the International Court' (1987) 81 *American Journal of International Law* 144.

Kahn, Paul, 'Speaking Law to Power: Popular Sovereignty, Human Rights, and the New International Order' (2000) 1 *Chicago Journal of International Law* 1.

Kelsen, Hans, 'Recognition in International Law, Theoretical Observations', (1941) 35 *American Journal of International Law* 605.

Kaladhran Nayar MG, 'Self-Determination Beyond the Colonial Context: Biafra in Retrospect', (1975) 10 *Texas International Law Journal* 321.

Kaufmann, Chaim, 'Possible and Impossible Solutions to Ethnic Wars' (1996) 20 (4) *International Security* 136.

Kofman, D 'Secession, Law, and Rights: The Case of Former Yugoslavia', (2000) 1 (2) *Human Rights Review* 13.

Kohen Marcelo G and del Mar Katherine, 'The Kosovo Advisory Opinion and UNSCR 1244 (1999): A Declaration of 'Independence from International Law'? (2011) 24 (1) *Leiden Journal of International Law* 109.

Lauterpacht, Sir Hersch, 'Recognition of Sates in International Law' (1944) 53 (1) *The Yale Law Journal* 385.

Levene, Mark, 'Why Is the Twentieth Century the Century of Genocide?' (2000) 2 (2) *Journal of World History* 305.

Maier, Harold, 'Appraisals of the ICJ's Decision: *Nicaragua v United States (Merits)*' (1987) 81 *American Journal of International Law* 77.

Mason, T. David & Fett, Patrick J, 'How Civil Wars End: a Rational Choice Approach' (1996), 40, (4) *Journal of Conflict Resolution* 546.

McCormack, Timothy L H, 'A *Non Liquet* on Nuclear Weapons – The ICJ avoids the Application of General Principles of International Humanitarian Law' (1997) 316 *International Review of the Red Cross* 76.

McNeill, John, 'The International Court of Justice Advisory Opinion in the *Nuclear Weapons* Cases – A First Appraisal' (1997) 316 *International Review of the Red Cross* 103.

Menon, PK, 'The Subjects of Modern International Law' (1990) 3, *Hague Yearbook of International Law* 30.

Moore, John, 'The *Nicaragua* Case and the Deterioration of World Order' (1987) 81 *American Journal of International Law* 151.

Morrison, Fred, 'Legal Issues in the *Nicaragua Opinion*' (1987) 81 *American Journal of International Law* 160.

Murphy, Sean, 'Democratic Legitimacy and the Recognition of States and Governments', (1999), 48 *International and Comparative Law Quarterly* 545.

Naldi, Gino J, 'The Statehood of the Saharan Arab Democratic Republic', (1985) 25 *Indian Journal of International Law* 448.

Olivier, Marius, 'Aspects of the Establishment of Sovereignty and the Transfer of Government Authority' (1988–1989) 14 *South African Yearbook of International Law* 85.

Peters Anne, 'Does Kosovo Lie in the *Lotus-Land* of Freedom?', (2011) 24 (1) *Leiden Journal of International Law* 95.

Piiparinen, Touko, 'The Lessons of Darfur for the Future on Humanitarian Intervention' (2007) 13 *Global Governance* 365.

Pomerance, Michla, 'The Badinter Commission: the Use and Misuse of the International Court of Justice's Jurisprudence', (1998) 20 (1) *Michigan Journal of International Law* 31.

Quane, Helen, 'The United Nations and the Evolving Right to Self-Determination' (1998) 47 (3) *International and Comparative Law Quarterly* 537.

Radan, Peter 'Post-Secession International Borders: A Critical Analysis of the Opinions of the Badinter Commission', 24 (2000) *Melbourne University Law Review* 50.

Ratner, Steven, 'Drawing a Better Line: *Uti Possidetis* and the Borders of New States', (1996) 90 *American Journal of International Law* 590.

Reichler, Paul, 'Holding America to its Own Best Standards: Abe Chayes and Nicaragua in the World Court' (2001) 42 *Harvard International Law Journal* 15.

Rosenne, Shabtai, 'On the Non-Use of the Advisory Competence of the International Court of Justice' (1963) 39 *British Yearbook of International Law* 1.

Sanborn III, McCleary H, 'Standing Before the International Court of Justice: the Question of Palestinian Statehood Exemplifies the Inconsistencies of the Requirement of Statehood', (1977) 7 *California Western International Law Journal* 454.

Scharf, Michael P. 'Earned Sovereignty: Juridical Underpinnings', (2002–2003) 31 *Denver Journal of International Law and Policy* 373.

Shaw, Malcolm, 'Peoples, Territorialism and Boundaries' (1997) 8 *European Journal of International Law* 478.

Shen, Jianming, 'The Non-Intervention Principle and Humanitarian Interventions Under International Law' 7 (2001) *International Legal Theory* 1.

Simpson, Gerry, 'Judging the East Timor Dispute: Self-Determination at the International Court of Justice' (1994) 17 *Hastings International and Comparative Law Review* 323.

——, 'The Diffusion of Sovereignty: Self-Determination in the Post-Colonial Age', (1996) 32 (2) *Stanford Journal of International Law* 255.

Sofaer, Abraham, 'International Law and Kosovo' (2000) 36 *Stanford Journal of International Law* 1.

Summer, Brian Taylor 'Territorial Disputes at the International Court of Justice' [2004] 53 *Duke Law Journal* 1810.

Thomas, Katherine Reece, 'Non-Recognition, Personality and Capacity: The Palestine Liberation Organisation and the Palestinian Authority in English Law' (2000) 29 *Anglo-American Law Review* 228.

Tiefenbrun, Susan, 'The Role of the World Court in Settling International Disputes: A Recent Assessment' (1997) 20 *Loyola of Los Angeles International and Comparative Law Journal* 1.

Travalio, Gregory, 'Terrorism, International Law, and the Use of Military Force' (2000) *Wisconsin International Law Journal* 145.

Tsairis, Aphrodite, 'International Terrorism: Prevention and Remedies: Lessons of Lockerbie' (1996) 22 *Syracuse Journal of International Law and Commerce* 3.

Turp, Daniel, & van Ert, Ginram, 'International Recognition in the Supreme Court of Canada's *Quebec Reference*' in the *Notes and Comments* 36 (1998) *Canadian Yearbook of International Law* 335.

Vidmar, Jure, 'Remedial Secession in International Law: Theory and (Lack of) Practice' in (2010) 6(1) *St Anthony's International Review* 37.

——, 'The *Kosovo* Opinion Scrutinized' (2011) 24 (2) *Leiden Journal of International Law* 355.

Voon, Tania 'Closing the Gap Between Legitimacy and Legality of Humanitarian Intervention: Lessons from East Timor and Kosovo', (2002–2003) 7 *UCLA Journal of International Law and Foreign Affairs* 31.

Wani, Ibrahim, J 'The Future of Compulsory Jurisdiction: Rethinking the Political Question Doctrine After *Iran* and *Nicaragua*' (1986) *American Society of International Law: Proceedings of the 80th Annual Meeting* 468.

Warbrick, Colin, 'Recognition of Governments', [1953] 56 *Modern Law Review* 92.

Watson, Geoffrey R, 'The "Wall" Decisions in Legal and Political Context' (2005) 99 *American Journal of International Law* 6.

Wellman, Christopher H. 'A Defense of Secession and Political Self-Determination' 24 (2) (1995) *Philosophy and Public Affairs* 142.

Weller, Marc, 'Modesty can be a Virtue: Judicial Economy in the *Kosovo* Opinion?', (2011) 24 (1) *Leiden Journal of International Law* 127.

Williams, Paul R. 'Earned Sovereignty: the Road to Resolving the Conflict Over Kosovo's Final Status', 31 (2002–2003) *Denver Journal of International Law and Policy* 387.

——, Sharf, Michael P, & Hooper, James A 'Resolving Sovereignty-Based Conflicts: the Emerging Approach of Earned Sovereignty' 31 (2002–2003) *Denver Journal of International Law and Policy* 349.

—— & Pecci, Francesca Jannotti 'Earned Sovereignty: Bridging the Gap Between Sovereignty and Self-Determination' 40 (2004) *Stanford Journal of International Law* 347.

Reports

Gurr, Ted Robert, Marshall, Monty G, & Khoola, Deepa, *Peace and Conflict 2001*, Centre for International Development & Conflict Management University of Maryland (2000).

Gurr, Ted Robert, & Marshall, Monty G, *Peace and Conflict 2003, A Global Survey of Armed Conflicts, Self-Determination Movements, and Democracy*, (Centre for International Development & Conflict Management, University of Maryland, February 2003).

King, Peter *Reconciliation and Consolidation Among Papuans: Report on Workshop III*, 2–3 September 2002, Centre for Peace and Conflict Studies, The West Papua Project, Position Paper No. 4, January 2003 at pp. 9, 12, http://www.arts.usyd.edu.au/cpacs.

Kooistra, Mieke, *Indonesia: Regional Conflicts and State Terror*, a report prepared by the Minority Rights Group International, a NGO, (June 2001).

Marshall Monty G, & Gurr, Ted Robert, *Peace and Conflict 2005*, Centre for International Development & Conflict Management, University of Maryland (2005).

McCulloch, Lesley, *Aceh: Then and Now*, a report prepared by the Minority Rights Group International, a NGO, (2005).

Noonan, Michela, King, Peter, & Wing, John, *Position Paper No. 5, November 2004*, 'Peace building and development in West Papua – Dialogue versus Violence: Hearing Other Voices' *Workshop IV, August 16–17, 2004, West Papuan Project*, Centre for Peace and Conflict Studies, the University of Sydney.

Opinion No. 1 of the Arbitration Commission of the Peace Conference on Yugoslavia (Opinion No. 1) (1992) 31 ILM 1494.

Opinion No. 2 of the Arbitration Commission of the Peace Conference on Yugoslavia (Opinion No. 2) 11 January 1992, (1992) 31 ILM 1497.

Opinion No. 3 of the Arbitration Commission of the Peace Conference on Yugoslavia (Opinion No. 3) (1992) 31 ILM 1499, 1500.

Opinion No. 4 on the International Recognition of the Socialist Republic of Bosnia-Herzegovina by the European Community and Its Members (Opinion No. 4) (1992) ILM 1501.

Opinion No. 8 of the Arbitration Commission of the Peace Conference on Yugoslavia (Opinion No. 8) (1992) 31 ILM 1521.

Peart, K, 'A Brief History of West Papua', on the West Papua Association website at <http://www.converge.org.nz/wpapua/history.html>.

Rees, Stuart, Ondawame, John O. & Peter King, *Reconciliation and Consolidation Among Papuans: Report on Workshop III*, 2–3 September 2002, Centre for Peace and Conflict Studies, The West Papua Project, Position Paper No. 4, January 2003.

Report of the International Commission of Jurists (1920) LNOJ Spec. Supp, 3.

Shehadi, K.S., *Ethnic Self-Determination and the Break-Up of States*, (International Institute for Strategic Studies, Adelphi Paper 283, London, 1993).

Suter, Keith, 'East Timor, West Papua/Irian and Indonesia', A Report by Minority Rights Group International, a NGO, (1997).

Williams, Sharon A, *International Legal Effects of Secession by Quebec*, Background Studies of the York University Constitutional Reform Project, Study No. 3, (1992) Ontario.

Wing, John, & King, Peter, *The West Papua Project*, Centre for Peace and Conflict Studies, The University of Sydney, *Genocide in West Papua? The Role of the Indonesian State Apparatus and a Current Needs Assessment of the Papuan People*, (August 2005).

Newspaper articles

Editorial, 'Indonesia: the Next East Timor' in *World Press Review*, (New York) March 2004, 25.

Harris, David, 'Let Aceh Hold an Independence Referendum', *Wall Street Journal*, (New York) 8 January 2000.

'Indonesian Government, Aceh Rebels Sign Peace Deal', *Japan Economic Newswire*, (Tokyo) 15 August 2005, at <http://web.lexis-nexis.com>.

'Key Passages from Aceh Peace Agreement', *Agence France Presse*, (Paris) 15 August 2005, <http://web.lexis-nexis.com>.

O'Callaghan, Mary-Louise, 'Paradise Lost', *The Weekend Australian*, (Melbourne) 5–6 February 2000, 27.

'PNG's Foreign Minister Urges West Papuan Activists to Embrace Autonomy', *Australian Associated Press Pty Ltd*, (Rhodes, NSW, Australia) 19 August 2005, <http://web.lexis-nexis.com>.

'Russia's Next President?', *Time Magazine*, (Melbourne) 6 December 1999, 32.

'Russia's Brass from the Past', *Time Magazine*, (Melbourne) 22 November 1999, 42.

'West Papuans Seek Support from Pacific Islands Forum' in *Australian Associated Press Pty Ltd*, (Rhodes, NSW, Australia) 28 October 2005, <http://web.lexis-nexis.com>.

UN documents

Authored reports

Al-Farsy, Nasrat, Rapporteur of the First Committee of the Fourth Commission of the San Francisco Conference. *Documents of the United Nations Conference on International Organisation* (UNICO) San Francisco, 1945, 13 UNICO 393 (1945) (Doc. 913 IV/1/74 (1), June 12, 1945.

Ghali, Boutros-Boutros, *Agenda for Peace-Preventive Diplomacy, Peace Making, and Peace Keeping*, UN Doc. A/47/277, 1992: S/24111 (17 June 1992).

The Situation in the Middle East, Including the Palestinian Question, UN SC Res 1515, UN SCOR, 4862nd mtg, UN Doc S/Res/1515 (19th November 2003) ('*Roadmap*').

Bantustans and South Africa

Bantustans, UN GAOR 34th sess, 100th plen mtg, [G] UN Doc A/Res/34/93 (12 December 1979).

Note [Condemning Proclamation by South Africa of independence of Ciskei] by President of Security Council, UN SCOR, UN Doc S/14794, (15 December 1981).

Policies of Apartheid of the Government of South Africa, UN GAOR, 42nd mtg, UN Doc A/Res/31/6 (26 October 1976).

Policies of Apartheid of the Government of South Africa, UN GAOR, 37th sess, 97th plen mtg, UN Doc A/Res37/69, (9 December 1982).

Policies of Apartheid of the Government of South Africa, (Bantustans) UN GAOR 32nd sess, 102nd plen mtg, [N] UN Doc A/Res/32/105 (14 December 1977).

Security Council 401 (1976) on South Africa's Closure of Border Posts between Lesotho and South Africa, UN SCOR, 31st sess, 1982nd mtg, UN Doc S/Res/402 (22 December 1976).

Security Council Resolution 407 on Assistance to Lesotho, UN SCOR 2009th mtg, UN Doc S/Res/407 (25 May 1977).

Congo

Admission of the Republic of the Congo … to Membership in the United Nations, UN GAOR, 15th sess, 864th plen mtg, UN Doc A/Res/1480 (XV) (20 September 1960).

Security Council Resolution 142 (1960) [On Admission of the Republic of Congo … to Membership in the United Nations] UN SCOR, 872nd mtg, UN Doc S/Res/142 (7 July 1960).

Security Council Resolution 261 (1961) [On an Arms Embargo against the Congo…] UN SCOR, 982nd mtg, UN Doc S/Res/169, (24 November 1961).

Security Council Resolution 241 (1967) [On the Question Concerning the Democratic Republic of the Congo (Zaire)] UN SCOR, 1378th mtg, UN Doc SC Res/241 (15 November 1967).

Cyprus

Security Council Resolution 514 (1983) [On Declaration by the Turkish Cypriot Community of its Secession from Cyprus] UN SCOR, 2500th mtg, [15] UN Doc S/Res/514, (19 November 1983).

Security Council Resolution 550 (19840 [On Secessionist Actions in Cyprus], [13] UN Doc S/Res/550 (11 May 1984).

East Timor

Question of Timor, UN GAOR, 31st sess, 85th plen mtg, UN Doc, A/Res/31/35 (1 December 1976).

Security Council Resolution 384 (1975) [on the East Timor Question], UN SCOR, 1869th mtg, UN Doc S/Res/384 (22 December 1975).

Security Council Resolution 389 (1976) [on the East Timor Question], UN SCOR, 1914th mtg, UN Doc S/RES/389 (22 April 1976).

General

Admission of New Members to the United Nations, UN SCOR, 28th sess, 1730 mtg, [17] UN Doc S/Res/335, (22 June 1973).

Charter of the United Nations.

Continuation of the Discussion of the Admission of New Members, UN GAOR, 3rd sess (III/1), Ad Hoc Political Comm, 9th mtg, UN Doc A/617, A/597, A/586 and A/618 (23 November 1948).

Convention on the Privileges and Immunities of the United Nations opened for signature 13 February 1946, 1 UNTS 15, art VIII, section 30 (entered into force 17 September 1946).

Convention on the Privileges and Immunities of the Specialized Agencies, opened for signature, 21 November 1947, 33 UNTS 261, (entered into force 2 December 1948).

Credentials Committee Reports Adopted (1987) 24 UN Chronicle 16.

Declaration on Principles of International Law Concerning Friendly Relations and Co-operation Among States in Accordance with the Charter of the United Nations, GA Res 2625, UN GAOR, 25th sess, 1883 plen mtg, item 85, UN Doc A/RES/2625(XXV) (1970).

Declaration on the Granting of Independence to Colonial Countries and People, GA Res 1514, UN GAOR, 15th sess, 947 plen mtg, UN Doc A/Res/1514 (XV), art 2 (14 December 1960).

Declaration on Principles of International Law Concerning Friendly Relations and Co-operation Among States in Accordance with the Charter of the United Nations, GA Res 2625, UN GAOR, 25th sess, 1883 plen mtg, item 85, UN Doc A/RES/2625(XXV) (1970).

Definition of Aggression, GA Res 3314 (XXIV), 29th sess, 2319th plen mtg, Annex, art 7 (14 December 1974).

General and Complete Disarmament, GA Res 49/75, UN GAOR, 49th sess, 90th plen mtg, UN Doc A/RES/49/75.

Importance of the Universal Realization of the Right of Peoples to Self-Determination and of the Speedy Granting of Independence to Colonial Countries and Peoples for the Effective Guarantee and Observance of Human Rights, UN GAOR, 37th sess, 90th plen mtg, UN Doc A/Res/37/43 (3 December 1982).

Letter Dated 8 March 1950 from the Secretary-General to the President of the Security Council Transmitting a Memorandum on the Legal Aspects of the Problem of Representation in the United Nations, UN SCOR 3 sess, UN Doc S/1466 (9 March 1950).

Libyan Arab Jamahiriya, SC Res 731, UN SCOR, 47th sess, 3033rd mtg, art 3, UN Doc S/RES/731 (1992).

Need for Greater Use by the United Nations and its Organs of the International Court of Justice, UN GAOR 2nd sess, 113th plen mtg, UN Doc A/Res/171 (II) (14 November 1947).

Principles Which Should Guide Members in Determining Whether or not an Obligation Exists to Transmit called for in Article 73(e) of the Charter of the United Nations, UN GAOR, 15th sess, Supp No 16, Annex, UN Doc A/4684 (15 December 1960).

Reservations Opinion in Reservations to the Convention on the Prevention and Punishment of the Crime of Genocide: Advisory Opinion of the International Court of Justice, UN GAOR (VI), 6th Comm, 266th mtg, [80] [81] UN Doc A/C.6/SR.266 (1951).

The Situation with Regard to the Implementation of the Declaration on the Granting of Independence to Colonial Countries and Peoples, UN GAOR, 17th sess, 1195th plen mtg, UN Doc A/Res/1810 (VXII) (17 December 1962).

The Situation with Regard to the Implementation of the Declaration on the Granting of Independence to Colonial Countries and Peoples, UN GAOR 16th sess, 1066th plen mtg, UN Doc A/Res/1654 (XVI), (27 November 1961).

Statute of the International Court of Justice.

Universal Declaration of Human Rights, UN GAOR 3rd sess, 183rd plen mtg, UN Doc A/Res/217 (III) (10th December 1948).

United Nations Documents of the Conference on International Organisation (1945–52) vol VI.

Namibia

Consideration of Proposed New Trusteeship Agreements, if Any: Question of South West Africa, GA Res 141 (II), UN GAOR, 105th plen mtg, UN Doc A/Res/141 (II) (1 November 1947).

Establishment of a Good Offices Committee on South West Africa, GA Res 1143 (XII), UN GAOR, 12th sess, Supp No 18, 709th plen mtg, UN Doc A/Res/1143 (XII) (25 October 1957).

Future Status of South West Africa, GA Res 65 (I), UN GAOR, 64th plen mtg, UN Doc A/Res/65(1) (14 December 1946).

Legal Action to Ensure the Fulfilment of the Obligations Assumed by the Union of South Africa in respect of the Territory of South West Africa, GA Res 1142 (XII) (A), UN GAOR, 12th sess, Supp No 18, 709th plen mtg, [A], (25 October 1957).

Legal Actions to Ensure the Fulfilment of the Obligations Assumed by the Union of South Africa in respect of the Territory of South West Africa, GA Res 1565 (XV), 15th sess, Supp No 16, 954th plen mtg, UN Doc A/1565 (XV)(18 December 1960).

Question of South West Africa, GA Res 2372 (XXII), UN GAOR, 22nd sess, supp 16A, 1671st plen mtg, UN Doc A/Res/3314 (21 June 1968).

Question of South West Africa, GA Res 227 (III), UN GAOR, 164th plen mtg, UN Doc A/Res/227 (III) (26 November 1948).

Question of South West Africa: Request for an Advisory Opinion of the International Court of Justice, GA Res 338(IV) UN GAOR, 4th sess, 269th plen mtg, UN Doc A/Res/338(IV) (1949).

Question of South West Africa, GA Res 449(V), UN GAOR, 5th sess, Supp No 20, 322 plen mtg, UN Doc A/Res 449(V) (13 December 1950).

Question of South Africa, GA Res 749(A), UN GAOR, 8th sess, 460th plen mtg, UN Doc A/Res 749 (28 November 1953).

Study of Legal Action to Ensure the Fulfilment of the Obligations Assumed by the Mandatory Power under the Mandate for South West Africa, GA Res 1060 (XI), UN GAOR, 11th sess, Supp No 17, 661st plen mtg, UN Doc A/Res/1060 (XI) (26 February 1957).

Palau

Security Council Resolution 956 (1994) [On Termination of the Status of Palau as a Trust Territory] UN SCOR 3455th mtg, [UN Doc S/Res/956 (1994) (10 November 1994).

Palestine

Illegal Israeli Actions in Occupied East Jerusalem and the Rest of the Occupied Palestinian Territory, UN GAOR, 10th Emergency Special Session, 22nd plen mtg, UN Doc A/Res/ES-10/13 (27 October 2003).

Rhodesia

Security Resolution 216 (1965) [Calling on all States not to Recognize the Minority Regime in Southern Rhodesia] UN SCOR, 1258th mtg, [8] UN Doc S/Res/216 (12 November 1965).

Security Council Resolution 217 (1965) [on the Proclamation of Independence by the Minority Regime in Southern Rhodesia] SC Res 217, [8–9] UN Doc S/Res/217 (20 November 1965).

Security Council Resolution 232 (1966) [Imposing Sanctions on Commodities Against Southern Rhodesia], UN SCOR, 1340th mtg, [7] Un Doc S/Res/232, (16 December 1966).

Security Council Resolution 253 (1968) [Establishing a Committee to Monitor Sanctions Against Southern Rhodesia] UN SCOR, 1428th mtg, [5–6] Un Doc S/Res/253 (29 May 1968).

Security Council Resolution 277(1970) [on Expansion of Sanctions Against the Southern Rhodesia Regime] UN SCOR, 1535th mtg, UN Doc S/Res/277 (18 March 1970).

Security Council Resolution 288 (1970) [Deciding that Sanctions against Southern Rhodesia Shall Remain in Force] UN SCOR, 1557th mtg, [7] UN Doc S/Res/288 (17 November 1970).

The Question of Southern Rhodesia, UN GAOR, 16th sess, 1121st plen mtg, [3] UN Doc A/Res/1747 (XVI), (28 June 1962).

Socialist Federal Republic of Yugoslavia, SC Res 713, UN SCOR, 46th sess, 3009th mtg, art 6, UN Doc S/RES/713 (25 September 1991).

Press releases

'Assembly to be Asked to Upgrade UN Standing of Palestine, to be Footing with Member States, Except for Voting', Press Release GA/PAL/769 (28 November 1997).

'Fourth Committee, Concluding General Debate on Decolonization Issues, Hears Petitioners from Western Sahara and New Caledonia', Press Release GA/SPD/186 (29 September 2000).

'Questions of Gibraltar, Guam, Western Sahara Discussed in Special Political and Decolonization Committee', Press Release GA/SPD/184 (27 September 2000).

'The General Assembly of the United Nations Requests an Advisory Opinion from the Court on the Unilateral Declaration of Independence of Kosovo' (*International Court of Justice Press Release* 10 October 2008, available at www.icj-cij.org last accessed on 11 October 2008).

Treaties and other international materials

African Charter of Human Rights, (adopted by the 18th Assembly of the Heads of State and Government of the Organisation of African Unity in Nairobi, Kenya on 26th of June 1986).

Agreement on Bilateral Relations, opened for signature 2 July 1972, India–Pakistan, 858 UNTS 71 (entered into force 4 August 1972).

Arbitration Agreement Between Great Britain and France, opened for signature 14 October 1903, 194 ConTS 194 (entered into force 14 October 1903).

Arbitration Convention, opened for signature 16 October 1925, 54 LNTS 303 (entered into force 14 September 1926).

Bogota Charter of the Organisation of American States, open for signature 30 April 1948, 119 UNTS 48 (entered into force 13 December 1951) ('Bogota Charter').

Convention for the Suppression of Unlawful Acts against the Safety of Civil Aviation; Opened for signature 23 September 1971, 974 UNTS 178 (entered into force 26 January 1973) ('*Montreal Convention*').

Convention (IV) Relative to the Protection of Civilian Persons in Time of War, opened for signature 12 August 1949, 75 UNTS 287, art 53 (entered into force 21 October 1950).

Final Act of the Conference on Security and Cooperation in Europe (1975) <http://www.osce.org/docs/english/1990-1999/summits/helfa75e.htm> at 23 April 2003 (Conference for Security and Cooperation in Europe).

General Act of Arbitration (Pacific Settlement of International Disputes), League of Nations Doc 2123 (1929).

Hague Convention for the Pacific Settlement of International Disputes, opened for signature 29 July 1899 (entered into force 4 September 1900).

Hague Convention for the Pacific Settlement of International Disputes, opened for signature 18 October 1907 (entered into force 26 January 1910).

Inter-American Treaty of Reciprocal Assistance, opened for signature 2 September 1947, 21 UNTS 77 (entered into force 3 December 1948).

International Covenant on Civil and Political Rights, opened for signature 16 December 1966, 999 UNTS 171, art 6 (entered into force 23 March 1976) ('*ICCPR*').

International Covenant on Economic, Social and Cultural Rights, opened for signature 16 December 1966, 933 UNTS 3 (entered into force 3 January 1976).

Libyan Arab Jamahiriya, SC Res 731, UN SCOR, 47th sess, 3033rd mtg, art 3, UN Doc S/Res/731 (21 January 1992).

Montevideo Convention on the Rights and Duties of Sates, signed 26 December 1993, 135 LNTS 19 (entered into force 26 December 1934).

Protocol Additional to the Geneva Conventions of 12 August 1949, and relating to the Protection of Victims of International Armed Conflicts, opened for signature 8 June 1977, 1125 UNTS 3 (entered into force 7 December 1978).

Treaty between Australia and the Republic of Indonesia on the Zone of Cooperation in an Area between the Indonesian Province of East Timor and Northern Australia, opened for signature 11 December 1989, [1991] ATS 9 (entered into force 9 February 1991) ('*Timor Gap Treaty*'.

Treaty of Amity, Economic Relations and Consular Rights, opened for signature 15 August 1955, United States of America–Iran, 284 UNTS 93 (entered into force 16 June 1957).

Treaty of Friendship, Commerce and Navigation (with Protocol), opened for signature 21 January 1956, United States of America–Nicaragua, 367 UNTS 3 (entered into force 24 May 1958).

Treaty on the Non-Proliferation of Nuclear Weapons, opened for signature 1 July 1968, 729 UNTS 169 (entered into force 5 March 1970).

Treaty of Versailles, protocol to *Treaty Between the Allied and Associated Powers and Germany*, open for signature 29 June 1919, TREATY SERIES (entry into force 10 January 1920).

Universal Declaration on Human Rights of 1948 UN GAOR, 3rd sess 1083rd plen mtg, UN Doc A/Res/217 (III)A (10 December 1948).

Vienna Convention on the Law of Treaties, opened for signature 23 May 1969, 1155 UNTS 331, art 31(1) (entered into force 27 January 1980) ('*VCLT*').

Websites

Centre for Peace and Conflict Studies, Faculty of Arts, University of Sydney: <http://www.arts.usyd.edu.au/cpacs>.

Friends of West Papua/West Papua Association: <http://www.converge.org.nz/wpapua/history.html>.

International Court of Justice: <http://www.icj-cij.org>.

Lexis-Nexis <http://web.lexis-nexis.com>.

Naga International Support Centre: http://www.nagalim.nl/naga/index-2.html.

Nagalim (Homeland of the Nagas) : <http://www.angelfire.com/nm/nagalim>.

Organisasi Papua Merdeka (OPM) (Free Papua Movement): <http://www.converge.org.nz/wpapua/events.html>.

Other sources

Government of Australia, *Declarations Recognizing as Compulsory the Jurisdiction of the Court* (2002) International Court of Justice <http://www.icj-cij.org/icjwww/ibasicdocuments/ibasictext/ibasicdeclarations.htm#dane> at 27 April 2003.

Jane's Intelligence Review, Vol. 7, Issue 6, 1st June 1995.
'Land of the Morning Star' (2003) by *Film Australia, National Interests Group*, Lindfield NSW, written and Directed by Mark Worth, and produced by Janet Bell, with the assistance of the Australian Broadcasting Corporation.

CASES

Permanent Court of International Justice [PCIJ]

Access to, or Anchorage in, the Port of Danzig, of Polish War Vessels (Advisory Opinion) [1931] PCIJ (ser.A/B), No. 43.
Access to German Minority Schools in Polish Upper Silesia (Advisory Opinion) [1931] PCIJ (ser A/B), No.40.
Appeal from a Judgment of the Hungaro-Czechoslovak Mixed Arbitral Tribunal (The Peter Pazmany University v the State of Czechoslovakia) (Judgement of 15 December 1933) [1933] PCIJ, (ser. A/B), No. 61.
Austro-German Customs Regime (Customs Unions Case), (Advisory Opinion) [1931] PCIJ (ser. A/B), No. 41.
Case Concerning Certain German Interests in Polish Upper Silesia (Merits) [1926] PCIJ, (ser. A), No. 7.
Competence of the International Labour Organisation in Regard to the Regulation of the Conditions of the Labour of Persons Employed in Agricultural Production (Advisory Opinion) [1922] PCIJ (ser. B), Nos. 2.
Competence of the International Labour Organisation to Examine Proposal for the Organization and Development of the Methods of Agricultural Production (Advisory Opinion) [1922] PCIJ (ser. B), No. 3.
Competence of the International Labour Organisation to Regulate, Incidentally, the Personal Work of the Employer (Advisory opinion) [1926] PCIJ (ser. B), No. 13.
Consistency of Certain Danzig Legislative Decrees with the Constitution of the Free City [1935] PCIJ (ser A/B), No. 65.
Customs Regime Between Germany and Austria [1931] PCIJ Rep 41.
Danzig and the ILO (Advisory Opinion) [1930] PCIJ (ser B), No. 18.
Delimitation of the Czechoslovak-Polish Frontier (Question of Jaworzina)(Advisory Opinion) [1923] PCIJ (ser. B), No. 8.
Eastern Carelia Case (Advisory Opinion) [1923] PCIJ (ser B) No. 5.
Free Zones of Upper Savoy and the District of Gex, (Judgement of 7 June 1932) [1932] PCIJ (ser A/B), No. 46.
German Settlers in Poland (Advisory Opinion) [1923] PCIJ, (ser. B), No. 6.
Interpretation of the Greco-Turkish Agreement of 1st December 1926(Final Protocol, Article IV) (Advisory Opinion) [1928] PCIJ (ser B), No. 16.
Jurisdiction of the Courts of Danzig (Advisory Opinion) [1928] PCIJ (ser B), No. 15.
Minority Schools in Albania Case (Advisory Opinion) [1935] PCIJ, (ser. A/B) No. 64.
Monastery of Saint-Naoum (Advisory Opinion) [1924] PCIJ (ser B) No. 9.
Nationalities Decrees in Tunis and Morocco (Advisory Opinion) [1923] PCIJ (ser B) No. 4.
Phosphates in Morocco (Italy v France) (Preliminary Objections), [1938] PCIJ, (ser. A/B), No. 74.
Polish Postal Service in Danzig (Advisory Opinion) [1925] PCIJ, (ser. B) No. 11.
S S Lotus Case (France v Turkey) [1927] PCIJ (ser A) No 10 ('*Lotus Case*').
Treatment of Polish Nationals and other Persons of Polish Origin or Polish Speech in Danzig (Advisory Opinion) [1932] PCIJ (ser A/B) No. 4.

International Court of Justice [ICJ]

Accordance with International Law of the Unilateral Declaration of Independence in respect of Kosovo (Advisory Opinion) [2010] ICJ Rep 403.
Admission of a State to the United Nations (Advisory Opinion) [1948] ICJ 57.
Admissibility of Hearings of Petitioners by the Committee on South West Africa Case (1955–1956) (Advisory Opinion), [1956] ICJ Rep 23.
Aerial Incident of 7 November 1974 (US v USSR) (Preliminary Objections) [1959] ICJ Rep 127.
Aerial Incident of 3 July 1988 (Islamic Republic of Iran v United States of America) (Order) [1989] ICJ 132.
Aegean Sea Continental Shelf (Greece v Turkey) (Jurisdiction) [1978] ICJ Rep 3.
Ambatielos Case (Greece v United Kingdom) (Preliminary Objections) [1952] ICJ Rep 28.
Anglo-Iranian Oil Co (United Kingdom v Iran) (Interim Protection) [1951] ICJ Rep 89.
Anglo-Iranian Oil Co. Case (United Kingdom v Iran) (Preliminary Objection), [1952] ICJ Rep 93.
Application for Review of Judgement No. 273 of the United Nations Administrative Tribunal (Advisory Opinion), [1982] ICJ Rep 325.
Application of the Convention on the Prevention and Punishment of the Crime of Genocide (Bosnia-Herzegovina v Yugoslavia) (Provisional Measures) [1993] ICJ Rep 325.
Arbitral Award of 31 July 1989 (Guinea-Bissau v Senegal) (Judgment) [1991] ICJ Rep 53.
Arrest Warrants Case [2002] ICJ Rep 3.
Asylum (Columbia v Peru) (Merits) [1950] ICJ Rep 266.
Barcelona Traction, Light and Power Company Case (Belgium v Spain)(Second Phase) [1970] ICJ Rep 3.
Case Concerning the Application of the Convention on the Prevention and Punishment of the Crime of Genocide (Bosnia Herzegovina v Yugoslavia) (Provisional Measures, Order of 13 Sept. 1993), [1933] ICJ Rep 3.
Case Concerning Application of the Convention on the Prevention and Punishment of the Crime Against Genocide (Bosnia Herzegovina v Yugoslavia, Serbia and Montenegro) (Indication of Provisional Measures) [1993] ICJ Rep 29.
Case Concerning the Application of the Convention on the Prevention and Punishment of the Crime of Genocide (Bosnia-Herzegovina v Serbia and Montenegro) [2007] ICJ Rep 43.
Case Concerning Border and Transborder Armed Actions (Nicaragua v. Honduras) (Judgement and Admissibility of the Application) [1988] ICJ Rep 69.
Case Concerning Certain Norwegian Loans (France v Norway) (Judgement of July 6 1957) [1957] ICJ Rep 9.
Case Concerning East Timor (Portugal v Australia) (Judgment of 30 June 1995) [1995] ICJ Rep 4.
Case Concerning Questions of Interpretation and Application of the 1971 Montreal Convention Arising From the Aerial Incident at Lockerbie (Lybian Arab Jamahiriya v United Kingdom) (Provisional Measures) [1992] ICJ Rep 3.
Case Concerning Right of Passage Over Indian Territory (Portugal v India) (Preliminary Objections) [1957] ICJ Rep 125.
Case Concerning the Northern Cameroons (Cameroons v UK), (Preliminary Objections) [1963] ICJ Rep 15.
Case Concerning Pulp 'Mills' on the River Uruguay (Argentina v Uruguay) [2010] ICJ Rep 14.
Case of Military and Paramilitary Activities in and against Nicaragua (Nicaragua v the United States of America) (Jurisdiction and Admissibility) [1984] ICJ Rep 551.

Certain Expenses of the United Nations (Advisory Opinion) [1962] ICJ Rep 151.
Certain Phosphate Lands in Nauru (Nauru v Australia) (Order) [1989] ICJ Rep 12.
Competence of the General Assembly for the Admission of a State to the United Nations (1949–1950) (Advisory Opinion of 3 March 1950) [1950] ICJ Rep 57.
Conditions of Admission of a State to Membership in the United Nations (Article 4 of the Charter) (Advisory Opinion) [1947–48] ICJ Rep 57.
Constitution of the Maritime Safety Committee of the Inter-Governmental Maritime Consultative Organization, (Advisory Opinion) [1960] ICJ Rep 150.
Corfu Channel Case (UK v Albania) (Merits) [1949] ICJ Rep 35.
Corfu Channel Case (UK v Albania) (Preliminary Objections) [1947–8] ICJ Rep 15.
Effect of Awards of Compensation Made by the United Nations Administrative Tribunal (Advisory Opinion) [1954] ICJ Rep 47.
Fisheries Jurisdiction (Federal Republic of Germany v Iceland) (Interim Protection) [1972] ICJ Rep 30.
Fisheries Jurisdiction (Federal Republic of Germany v Iceland) (Merits) [1974] ICJ Rep 175.
Fisheries Jurisdiction (Federal Republic of Germany v Iceland) (Jurisdiction) [1973] ICJ Rep 49.
Fisheries Jurisdiction (United Kingdom v Iceland) (Interim Protection) [1972] ICJ Rep 12.
Fisheries Jurisdiction (United Kingdom v Iceland) (Jurisdiction) [1973] ICJ Rep 3.
Fisheries Jurisdiction (United Kingdom v Iceland) (Merits) [1974] ICJ Rep 3.
Fisheries Jurisdiction Case (United Kingdom and Federal Republic of Germany v Iceland) (Jurisdiction) [1973] ICJ Rep 3.
Frontier Dispute (Burkina Faso v Republic of Mali) (Merits) [1986] ICJ Rep 554.
Frontier Dispute (Burkina Faso v Republic of Mali) (Provisional Measures) [1986] ICJ Rep 3.
Haya de la Torre (Colombia v Peru) (Merits) [1951] ICJ Rep 71.
International Status of South West Africa (1949–1950) (Advisory Opinion) [1950] ICJ Rep 128.
Interpretation of Peace Treaties with Bulgaria, Hungary and Romania (Advisory Opinion 30 March 1950) (1st Phase) [1950] ICJ Rep 65.
Interpretation of Peace Treaties with Bulgaria, Hungary and Romania (Advisory Opinion 18 July 1950) (2nd Phase) [1950] ICJ Rep 221.
Interpretation of the Agreement of 25 March 1951 Between the WHO and Egypt, Advisory Opinion [1980] ICJ Rep 73.
Judgments of the Administrative Tribunal of the International Labour Organisation upon Complaints Made Against the United Nations Educational, Scientific and Cultural Organization (UNESCO Case) (Advisory Opinion) [1956] ICJ Rep 77.
Judgment No 2867 of the Administrative Tribunal of the International Labour Organization Upon a Complaint Filed Against the International Fund for Agricultural Development (Advisory Opinion) [2012] ICJ Rep 1.
La Grand (Germany v United States of America) (Judgment) [2001] ICJ Rep 466.
Legal Consequences for States of the Continued Presence of South Africa in Namibia (South West Africa) Notwithstanding Security Council Resolution 276 (1970) (Advisory Opinion) [1971] ICJ Rep 16.
Legal Consequences of the Construction of a Wall in the Occupied Palestinian Territory (Advisory Opinion) (2004) ICJ Rep 136.
Legality of the Threat or Use of Nuclear Weapons, (Advisory Opinion) [1996] ICJ Rep 226.
Legality of Use of Force (Yugoslavia v United Kingdom) (Provisional Measures) [1999] ICJ Rep 826, 838.

Maritime Delimitation and Territorial Questions between Qatar and Bahrain (Qatar v Bahrain) (Merits) [2001] ICJ Rep 40.

Maritime Delimitation and Territorial Questions between Qatar and Bahrain (Qatar v Bahrain) (Order) [1991] ICJ Rep 50.

Maritime Delimitation between Guinea-Bissau and Senegal (Guinea-Bissau v Senegal) (Order) [1995] ICJ Rep 423.

Maritime Delimitation in the Area between Greenland and Jan Mayen (Denmark v Norway) (Order) [1988] ICJ Rep 66.

Military and Paramilitary Activities in and Against Nicaragua (Nicaragua v United States of America) (Provisional Measures) [1984] ICJ Rep 392.

Military and Paramilitary Activities in and Against Nicaragua (Nicaragua v USA), (Merits) [1986] ICJ Rep 14.

Monetary Gold Removed from Rome in 1943 (Italy v France, United Kingdom and the United States of America) (Merits) [1954] ICJ Rep 19.

North Sea Continental Shelf (Federal Republic of Germany/Denmark; Federal Republic of Germany/Netherlands) (Merits) [1969] ICJ Rep 3.

Nottebohm (Liechtenstein v Guatemala) (Preliminary Objection) [1953] ICJ Rep 111.

Nottebohm Case (Liechtenstein v Guatemala)(Second Phase) [1955] ICJ Rep 4.

Nuclear Tests (Australia v France) (Judgment) [1974] ICJ Rep 253.

Nuclear Tests (New Zealand v France)(Judgment) [1974] ICJ Rep 457.

Oil Platforms (Iran v United States of America) (Preliminary Objections) [1996] ICJ Rep 803.

Passage through the Great Belt (Finland v Denmark) (Provisional Measures) [1991] ICJ Rep 12.

Questions of Interpretation and Application of the 1971 Montreal Convention Arising from the Aerial Incident at Lockerbie (Libyan Arab Jamahiriya v United Kingdom) (Order) [1992] ICJ Rep 3.

Reparation for Injuries Suffered in the Service of the United Nations (Advisory Opinion) [1949] ICJ Rep 174.

Reservations to the Convention on the Prevention and Punishment of the Crime of Genocide (1950–1951) (Advisory Opinion), [1951] ICJ Rep 15.

Right of Passage over Indian Territory (Portugal v India) (Merits) [1960] ICJ Rep 6.

South-West Africa Cases (Ethiopia v South Africa; Liberia v South Africa), (Second Phase) [1966] ICJ Rep 6.

South-West Africa Cases (Preliminary Objections) [1962] ICJ Rep 319.

Sovereignty over Pedra Branca/Pulau Batu Puteh, Middle Rocks and South Ledge (Malaysia/Singapore) [2008] ICJ Rep 12; and *Certain Questions of Mutual Assistance in Criminal Matters (Djibouti v France)* [2008] ICJ Rep 177.

Sovereignty over Pulau Ligitan and Pulau Sipadan (Indonesia v Malaysia) (Judgment) [2001] ICJ Rep 575.

Territorial Dispute (Libyan Arab Jamahiriya v Chad) (Judgment) [1994] ICJ Rep 6.

Trial of Pakistani Prisoners of War (Pakistan v India) (Interim Protection) [1973] ICJ Rep 328.

United States Diplomatic and Consular Staff in Tehran Case (US v Iran) (Merits) [1980] ICJ Rep 3.

Vienna Convention on Consular Relations (Paraguay v United States of America) (Provisional Measures) [1998] ICJ Rep 248.

Voting Procedures on Questions Relating to Reports and Petitions Concerning the Territory of South West Africa (Advisory Opinion) [1955] ICJ Rep 67.

Western Sahara Case (Advisory Opinion) [1975] ICJ Rep 12.

Other courts/tribunals

A.B. Others v Italy, HRC Communication, No. 413/1990.

Canea Catholic Church v Greece, EctHR, 16 December 1997, Reports of Judgements and Decisions 1997-VIII.

In the Matter of Section 53 of the Supreme Court Act, R.S.C. 1985, and in the Matter of a Reference by the Governor in Council Concerning Certain Questions Relating to the Secession of Quebec from Canada as Set Out in Order in Council P.C. 1996–1997 [1998] 2 SCR 217.

Kitok v Sweden, HRC Communication No. 197/1985; *E.P. and Others v Colombia*, HRC Communication No 318/1988.

Morgan Guaranty Trust Co. v Republic of Palau, 639 F. Supp. 706, 713 (SDNY 1986).

Ominayak and the Lubicon Lake Band v Canada HRC Communication No. 167/1984.

Prosecutor v Tadic (Defence Motion for Interlocutory Appeal on Jurisdiction), Case No IT-94-1-AR72 (2 October 1995) ('*Tadić Case*').

Upright v Mercury Business Machine Co 13 AD 2d 36, 213 NYS 2d 417 (1961).

Index